ROUTLEDGE LIBRARY EDITIONS: FINANCIAL MARKETS

Volume 3

THE STOCK EXCHANGE AND INVESTMENT ANALYSIS

T0358402

THE STOCK EXCHANGE AND INVESTMENT ANALYSIS

R. J. BRISTON

LONDON AND NEW YORK

First published in 1973 by George Allen & Unwin Ltd.

This edition first published in 2018
by Routledge
2 Park Square, Milton Park, Abingdon, Oxon OX14 4RN

and by Routledge
711 Third Avenue, New York, NY 10017

Routledge is an imprint of the Taylor & Francis Group, an informa business

British Library Cataloguing in Publication Data
A catalogue record for this book is available from the British Library

ISBN: 978-1-138-56537-1 (Set)
ISBN: 978-0-203-70248-2 (Set) (ebk)
ISBN: 978-1-138-55410-8 (Volume 3) (hbk)
ISBN: 978-1-138-55477-1 (Volume 3) (pbk)
ISBN: 978-1-315-14918-9 (Volume 3) (ebk)

Publisher's Note
The publisher has gone to great lengths to ensure the quality of this reprint but
points out that some imperfections in the original copies may be apparent.

Disclaimer
The publisher has made every effort to trace copyright holders and would welcome
correspondence from those they have been unable to trace.

The Stock Exchange
and Investment Analysis

BY

R. J. BRISTON
B.Sc.(Econ.), A.C.A.

Revised Edition

London
GEORGE ALLEN & UNWIN LTD
RUSKIN HOUSE   MUSEUM STREET

FIRST PUBLISHED IN 1970

SECOND EDITION 1973

© George Allen & Unwin Ltd., 1973

ISBN: 0 04 332052 x

PRINTED IN GREAT BRITAIN
in 10 point Times New Roman type
BY T. AND A. CONSTABLE LTD
EDINBURGH

TO SHIRLEY AND VICTORIA
in thanks for their patience and consideration

PREFACE

In the subject of investment analysis there is a wide gap between the chatty and often over-simplified approach, which is aimed at those investors naïve enough to expect that it will make their fortune overnight, and the highly academic approach of the latest American books of readings on investment. This void has been filled in the USA by the excellent textbooks of Cohen and Zinbarg; Graham, Dodd, and Cottle; Amling, etc. These books, however, are lengthy and American-orientated. In this country, apart from the texts by Cummings and Rowlett and Davenport, the needs of the serious investor and the professional student have been largely disregarded. Similarly, there has been no single volume which provides the undergraduate with the groundwork necessary for an understanding of the papers collected in the books edited by Frederickson, Wu and Zakon, Archer and d'Ambrosio, Ball, Lerner, etc.

I have attempted to fill this gap with a book which describes the mechanism of the London Stock Exchange and the broad principles and practice of finance, investment, and investment analysis, without however employing advanced mathematical techniques. As such it is hoped that it will prove suitable for:

(a) those studying for professional qualifications as company secretaries, accountants, bankers, actuaries, stockbrokers, and for those in various branches of public administration;

(b) undergraduates and students at business schools who need a basic course in investment and stock market theory;

(c) professional advisers such as bankers and accountants;

(d) members of the general public who appreciate that investment is a serious subject which requires a relatively academic approach.

I may be accused of too much detail, but I have found as teacher and examiner that it is better to explain a point at too great a length than to explain it inadequately. At the same time I have included a great deal of reference material in order to make the book as self-sufficient as possible.

Finally I must thank the authors, publishers, and official bodies, far too numerous to mention separately, who have given permission for the reproduction of copyright material. The source of all such material is clearly stated in the text. Thanks are also due to Mrs M. J. McCarthy, Mrs M. E. Walker, and Mrs Irene Baldwin who typed a difficult manuscript with care and speed.

Bradford
April 1970

PREFACE TO THE SECOND EDITION

In preparing this second edition I have not substantially altered the text. However, it has been necessary to update the statistics and certain parts of the text and to decimalize the practical examples. A new chapter has been written covering the important taxation changes proposed in the 1972 Budget and the work being performed by the Institute of Chartered Accountants to improve the quality of published accounts.

With these changes and additions the book is entirely up to date and I hope that it will serve its readers as successfully as did the first edition.

R.J.B.

University of Strathclyde
May 1972

ACKNOWLEDGMENTS

In the Compounding Tables values of 0·25 per cent and 0·5 per cent are based on *Compound Interest and Annuity Tables* by F. C. and M. E. Kent (1954 edition). They are used by kind permission of the McGraw Hill Book Co. The other values are based on *Inwood's Tables of Interest and Mortality* (33rd edition), and are used by kind permission of the Technical Press Ltd.

The Discounting Tables are based on the tables in *Capital Budgeting and Company Finance* by A. J. Merrett and Allen Sykes, published in 1966. They are reproduced by kind permission of Longmans, Green & Co. Ltd.

CONTENTS

TABLES

PART I: THE STOCK EXCHANGE—
HISTORY, FUNCTIONS, CRITICISM

INTRODUCTION

Opinions expressed on the subject of the Stock Exchange tend to be couched in emotional language and to be coloured by the moral and political views of the critic concerned. Two of its more ardent proponents are Harold Wincott, who states:

'The Stock Exchange is . . . woven into the very texture of our national civilisation and could not be abolished without radically altering our national way of life,'[1]

and F. E. Armstrong who ecstatically writes:

'The Stock Exchange as an institution has been evolved by time and perfected by experience. It exists for the purpose of providing a market wherein to buy and sell the world's capitalised values. Here, interests small or large, in the whole of man's activities can be exchanged. It is the Citadel of Capital, the Temple of Values. It is the axle on which the whole financial structure of the Capitalistic System turns. It is the Bazaar of human effort and endeavour, the Mart where man's courage, ingenuity, and labour are marketed.'[2]

The opposite view was taken by Keynes who severely criticized stock markets in general and the New York Stock Exchange in particular:

'When the capital development of a country becomes a by-product

[1] *Beginners, Please* (London: Eyre & Spottiswoode for the *Investors Chronicle*, 2nd Ed. 1960, p. xi).
[2] *The Book of the Stock Exchange* (London: Pitman, 4th Ed. 1949, p. 26).

13

of the activities of a casino, the job is likely to be ill-done. The measure of success attained by Wall Street, regarded as an institution of which the proper social purpose is to direct new investment into the most profitable channels in terms of future yield, cannot be claimed as one of the outstanding triumphs of *laissez-faire* capitalism .... That the sins of the London Stock Exchange are less than those of Wall Street may be due, not so much to differences in national character, as to the fact that to the average Englishman Throgmorton Street is, compared with Wall Street to the average American, inaccessible and very expensive. The jobber's "turn", the high brokerage charges and the heavy transfer tax payable to the Exchequer, which attend dealings on the London Stock Exchange, sufficiently diminish the liquidity of the market (although the practice of fortnightly accounts operates the other way) to rule out a large proportion of the transactions characteristic of Wall Street.'[1]

An altogether more balanced and moderate judgment is that of W. J. Baumol, who, in analyzing the efficiency of the New York Stock Exchange, draws conclusions which could well be applied to that of London:

'All in all, one cannot escape the impression that, at best, the allocative function (of the stock market) is performed rather imperfectly as measured by the criteria of the welfare economist. The oligopolistic position of those who operate the market, the brokers, the floor traders and the specialists; the random patterns which characterize the behaviour of stock prices; the apparent unresponsiveness of supply to price changes and management's efforts to avoid the market as a source of funds, all raise some questions about the perfection of the regulatory operations of the market. But though its workings are undoubtedly imperfect, it does not follow that they are beyond the pale. Rather, its operation must be judged to be somewhat on a par with that of the bulk of America's business. Far from the competitive ideal, beset by a number of patent shortcomings, it nevertheless performs a creditable job. Bearing in mind that its ramifications were never planned by organized human deliberation, one can only marvel at the quality of its performance.'[2]

---

[1] *The General Theory of Employment Interest and Money* (London: Macmillan, 1936, pp. 159–60).

[2] *The Stock Market and Economic Efficiency* (New York: Fordham University Press, 1965, p. 83).

INTRODUCTION

The objects of the next section are to explain the functions of the London Stock Exchange, to describe the mechanism by which it provides a market for investors and a source of capital for the Government and industry, and to assess the extent to which it performs its functions under modern conditions.

CHAPTER I

The London Stock Exchange—
Its History and Functions

In order to appreciate the functions of the London Stock Exchange it is necessary to understand something of its history, for its functions have grown and become gradually more clearly defined over the period of its development. Similarly an understanding of its history involves knowledge of the legal and economic development of the two major groups of securities that are dealt in, namely Government and industrial. For these reasons this chapter is divided into four parts, dealing with the growth of Government securities, the development of the industrial sector, the history of the Stock Exchange, and, finally, its functions.

1. THE GROWTH OF GOVERNMENT SECURITIES

At March 31, 1971, the National Debt of the United Kingdom in nominal terms stood at £33,420 m. composed of the following Government obligations:

	£m
Redeemable Marketable Securities	18,057
Irredeemable Marketable Securities	3,494
Total Marketable Securities	21,551
Annuities	315
Debts to the Bank of England	11
National Savings Certificates, Stamps and Gift Tokens	1,968
Defence Bonds, National Development Bonds and British Savings Bonds	753
Premium Savings Bonds	807
Save As You Earn	29
Tax Reserve Certificates	326
Treasury Bills	3,291

	£m
Ways and Means Advances	556
Other debt (payable in sterling)	1,664
Other debt (payable in external currencies)	2,149
	33,420

Based on *Financial Statistics*, HMSO May, 1971.

Note: (*a*) The irredeemable or funded[1] securities now comprise only some 10% of the National Debt, whereas up till 1914 they had accounted for between 85% and 99%. Their growing unpopularity has meant that more reliance has been placed by the Government on unfunded debt, the bulk of which is repayable on or before a definite date. The last major issue of irredeemable securities was that of $3\frac{1}{2}$% War Loan in 1932, when £1,920,804,243 of the stock was issued to replace a 5% War Loan stock, which had been effectively redeemable in that it could be tendered in payment of death duties. £1,909·4 m. $3\frac{1}{2}$% War Loan is still outstanding and this particular stock comprises more than half of the total of irredeemable Government securities. For this reason it has borne the brunt of the disillusionment of investors with such securities, which was evidenced by the fall in its price from over £100 in the 'cheap money' period after the last war to £36 during 1969. As a result, investors who held War Loan, many of whom were widows and retired persons who felt that it offered them a good degree of security, not only lost much of their capital in money terms but also found that the remainder had depreciated further in real terms due to the impact of inflation.

(*b*) The figure of Ways and Means advances represents temporary advances made by Government departments to the Exchequer.

(*c*) The amount of other debt payable in external currencies is comprised mainly of amounts due to the US Government and the Canadian Government under agreements made at the end of the Second World War.

(*d*) If sundry items such as Ways and Means advances, other debt, and debts to the Bank of England are excluded, the remainder of the Debt is held primarily by investors. These securities may be either irredeemable, redeemable on or before some definite future date, or repayable on demand. In the case of loans which are repayable on demand, such as National Savings Certificates, Defence Bonds,

[1] The word 'funded' originally referred to loans whose interest was secured against specific revenue of the State. With the passage of time it came to be applied to loans for which the Government was not required to make any provision for redemption.

Premium Savings Bonds and Tax Reserve Certificates there is clearly no scope for a market, for they may be bought from or sold to the Government at specified prices on demand. Of the redeemable securities, Treasury Bills are repayable 91 days after the date of issue, so that there is once again little call for an organized market other than is provided by the normal banking mechanism to enable holders to liquidate their Bills. The actual market in which Bills are purchased from the Government at each date of tender is, of course, highly organized. However, in the case of redeemable securities which are not repayable in the very short term and irredeemable securities there is a definite need for a market in which investors can exchange their holdings for cash. Such a market is provided by the London Stock Exchange and at March 31, 1971, the nominal value of Government securities quoted thereon stood at £22,533 m. This differs from the total of marketable securities included in the above analysis of the National Debt due to differences of definition, such as the practice of the Stock Exchange to include in the total quoted nominal amount of a given security, any amounts which have been tendered in payment of death duties and are now held by the National Debt Commissioners. Such amounts arise, for example, in the case of 4% Funding Loan 1960–90 and 4% Victory Bonds and are excluded by the Treasury in their calculation of the total of the National Debt.

The origins of the National Debt are surrounded by a certain amount of confusion, which is the result of problems of definition rather than lack of information. Certainly most authorities trace the National Debt back to the last half of the seventeenth century, though they are not unanimous as to the actual point of origin.

During the seventeenth century one of the most common methods of short-term borrowing by the Crown was by means of tallies, which were wooden sticks with notched sides indicating the amount due from the Exchequer to the holder of the tally. After the Restoration steps were taken to formalize their use. In 1660 their holders were granted interest and repayment was guaranteed against given classes of Exchequer revenue, while an Act of 1663 provided for their repayment in the order in which they were issued and also made them negotiable by endorsement.

The formalization of the use of tallies was accompanied by the introduction of fiduciary orders or notes issued by the Exchequer in payment of debts. Ultimately these orders were sold by the recipients, usually at a heavy discount, to bankers who at the time were mainly goldsmiths or Jews. On December 18, 1671, Charles II 'stopped' the Exchequer, defaulting on a total of £1,328,526 of fiduciary notes, most of which were held by the goldsmith bankers. He did, however, agree to pay interest at 6% on the amount due and did so for six years, after which he again defaulted. After many years of dispute a compromise was effected in 1705 whereby the Government assumed responsibility for half of the amount due and issued £664,263 6% notes to the original holders of the debt and their descendants.

Up to the Revolution of 1688 the Crown continued to rely on short-term borrowings for its finance. Thereafter the concept of the State grew in importance and lenders came to be regarded as giving credit to the State rather than to the Crown. Though this did not necessarily represent a very material increase in credit-worthiness it did make the issue of long-term loans much easier. In 1693 the first such loan was offered to the public, who were asked to subscribe £1 m. either by way of participation in a tontine or by the purchase of an annuity. The Tontine Loan, by which the seven survivors out of all the lenders would receive the highest returns, received sub-scriptions totalling £108,000, the remainder of the £1 m. consisting of purchases of annuities.

In 1694 the first permanent irredeemable State Debt was accepted on the establishment of the Bank of England. This was formed by a syndicate which agreed to lend £1·2 m. to the Government in per-petuity, receiving in return an annual payment of £100,000 (com-prising interest at 8% totalling £96,000 and management expenses of £4,000) plus the right to do banking business and to issue currency notes up to an amount of £1·2 m. At the same time the Government raised a further £300,000 through the sale of annuities and later in 1694 issued a State Lottery Loan of £1 m.

In 1696 Exchequer Bills were issued for the first time. These were the offshoots of the tallies and the forerunners of the Treasury Bill. They were mainly of denominations of £5 and £10, carried interest of £4 11s% per annum and were repayable in the short term at a specified date. In the same year a financial crisis occurred, the Bank of England suspended payments and Exchequer Bills and Bank of England notes fell to discounts of 60% and 20% respectively. Three sources of finance were now resorted to. The permanent debt was increased by means of a perpetual loan of £2 m. from the East India Company, in return for which it was given a monopoly of trade with India. The long-term debt was increased by a further issue of State Lottery Loan amounting to £1·4 m. and the short-term debt was augmented by another issue of Exchequer Bills bearing interest at £7 12s% per annum. At the same time the capital of the Bank of England was increased by £1 m., much of which was subscribed for by holders of Exchequer Bills, who were given credit for four-fifths

19

of the amount of their bills to set against the amount due to the Bank by way of subscription to the increased capital. The million pounds thus raised was lent to the Government and the Bank of England was, in return, allowed to increase its note issue by the same amount.

Thus by the end of the crisis the foundations of the National Debt had been well and truly laid and it amounted at the end of 1698 to £17·3 m. The actual date at which the Debt can be said to have begun is stated by different authorities to be either 1671, when the Exchequer was stopped, 1693, when the first State Loans were issued, or 1694, when the Bank of England was formed and the first perpetual Government Debt was established. Of these dates 1694 seems preferable, but the problem entirely depends upon the way in which 'National Debt' is defined—whether it should be Crown Debt or Government Debt, and whether it is to be regarded in its inception as perpetual, long-term or short-term debt.

Since 1698 the National Debt has increased from £17·3 m. to over £30,000 m. By far the greatest part of this increase has been due to Government expenditure in times of war. By 1714 at the end of the war against Louis XIV the Debt had more than doubled to £36·2 m. It then rose steadily through the eighteenth century and in 1793 stood at £242·9 m. By 1819, forced upwards by the Napoleonic Wars, it had reached £844·3 m. This proved to be the highest point for nearly a century, for a long period of contraction of the Debt followed and it stood at £568·7 m. in 1900 and at £720·2 m. at the end of 1914. An enormous increase occurred as a result of the First World War and at the end of 1919 it stood at £7,414 m. It was then relatively static and had only increased to £8,149·6 m. at the end of 1938. By the end of the Second World War it had reached £22,500 m., since when it has continued to rise, though more gradually, to its present level.

2. THE DEVELOPMENT OF INDUSTRIAL SECURITIES

The predominant forms of business organization during the medieval period were the sole trader and the partnership, both of which equated the business enterprise with its members. However, the concept of incorporation, whereby an organization is regarded as possessing a corporate personality which makes it entirely distinct from its members and gives it perpetual succession and the right to own property and to sue or be sued in its own name, gradually became dominant. At first incorporation was only conferred upon ecclesiastical and public bodies such as monasteries and boroughs, though in the field of commerce it was often granted to merchant guilds.

The privilege was normally granted by means of a Royal Charter and although there are instances as early as the fourteenth century where such charters were given to trading concerns, it was not until the expansion of overseas trade during the sixteenth century that this practice became common. Even then incorporation was used mainly to secure monopoly rights in the name of the corporation, while the financial organization of the enterprise was still largely based on the partnership system, with each member usually providing a proportion of the cost of each individual voyage and receiving at the end of the voyage his original contribution together with his share of the profit.

These corporations gradually developed into permanent joint-stock companies whose capital was subscribed by their members on a permanent basis. The first such company was the Russia Company, formed in 1553, and the earliest one which still survives was the New River Company which was founded in 1619 and is the oldest company still quoted on the London Stock Exchange. The largest and most famous of the trading corporations was the East India Company, which was incorporated by charter in 1600. Until 1613 this was financed by separate subscriptions for each voyage. Then a semi-permanent capital fund was established and this was made permanent in 1692.

Transactions in the shares held by the members of these companies took place on the basis of private negotiation as early as 1568, and shares of the East India Company were publicly auctioned in the first quarter of the seventeenth century. However, at this stage there was little scope for an organized share market partly because the shares were normally terminable in the relatively short term, partly because the membership of a corporation was often severely restricted by its charter, and partly because the shares, due to the small number of members, were often of a very high denomination.

By the end of the seventeenth century, permanent joint-stock companies were becoming much more common. Moreover, they were increasingly being used not only to finance home industry rather than overseas trade but also to bring together enterprise and capital. This trend continued into the first two decades of the eighteenth century, when a wave of speculation caused a frantic boom in company flotations which culminated in the South Sea Bubble of 1720.

The South Sea Company had been incorporated in 1711 by the compulsory conversion of over £9 m. of floating debt into shares of the company, in return for which the Government provided an annual sum sufficient to pay 6% interest on the capital and conferred a monopoly of South American trade on the company. In 1720 the company put forward a scheme to acquire almost the whole of the non-perpetual part of the National Debt, consisting of annuities which were given a capitalized value of £15 m. and theoretically redeemable stocks totalling £16·5 m.

This integration of the capital of a company into the National Debt was but an extension of the capital loans made by the Bank of England in 1694 and 1697 and by the East India Company in 1698, and also represented on an increased scale the method used in the incorporation of the South Sea Company itself. As a result of acquiring £31·5 m. of the National Debt the company hoped to obtain further trading privileges and anticipated also that ownership of the Debt would provide a sound basis for raising sums to finance the expected expansion of trade.

The company had to outbid the Bank of England for the right to acquire the Debt and ultimately contracted to submit to terms which would have been excessive even had its most optimistic anticipations been realized. Nevertheless the prevailing speculative atmosphere, accompanied by judicious bribery, manipulation of the market to support the price of the stock, and loans by the company on stock, enabled the company to carry out successive issues of stock at 300 and at 400 in April 1720 and at 1,000 in June 1720.

At this stage the Bubble Act was passed, enacting that all companies which had not been incorporated by a charter or under an Act of Parliament, or which were trading under a charter originally granted for a different purpose, should be illegal and all transactions in their shares should be void. At the same time brokers dealing in their shares and persons responsible for the promotion of such companies were to be liable to heavy penalties. The declared object of the Act was to prevent investors from being defrauded by companies which either had not become legally incorporated or had assumed the charter of a defunct company. The more probable object of the Act was to reduce the funds available for competing securities, thus helping to support the price of the South Sea Company stock.

This attempt failed miserably and the price of the stock fell from a high point of £1,050 in June to £200 in September and £125 at the end of 1720. The conversion scheme thus collapsed completely, much of the fraud and manipulation was revealed and investment in companies was dormant for the rest of the century.

The Bubble Act certainly retarded the spread of incorporation for, apart from those companies which already had charters, incorporation could only be obtained by means of Royal Charters or specific Acts of Parliament, and both the Crown and Parliament were much

22

more cautious in granting these privileges. Consequently the partnership once again become the predominant form of enterprise, and many variations were devised to increase their flexibility. Where a large capital was required, investors might subscribe to a deed of settlement which provided for the division of the capital into a given number of shares which were transferable only with the consent of the other members, for the delegation of management to a board of directors and for the property to be vested in the trustee of the settlement.

These unincorporated associations were very unwieldy and had definite legal disadvantages. They were quite unsuitable for financing large-scale industrial expansion and the largest enterprises such as the canals were normally managed by companies formed by a separate Act of Parliament, which became somewhat easier to obtain towards the end of the eighteenth century. Nevertheless, it was still a very complicated procedure to obtain incorporation in this way and some promoters tried to adapt still further the concept of the unincorporated association by making their shares freely transferable and declaring the liability of the members to be limited to the amount of their agreed subscription, both of which privileges were available to companies incorporated through the normal channels.

This led to successful prosecutions under the Bubble Act and the *status quo* was re-established until that Act was repealed in 1825. The repeal did nothing constructive and companies which required sizeable amounts of capital, particularly the railway companies, still had to undertake the promotion of an Act of Parliament.

In order to facilitate incorporation, two Acts were passed, in 1834 and 1837, which empowered the Crown to grant this privilege by means of letters patent rather than by a charter. Limited liability could not, however, be granted in this way. Then, in 1844 came the Joint Stock Companies Act which provided for the formation of companies by means of registration with the Registrar of Companies. All new companies which had more than twenty-five members or whose shares were freely transferable without the consent of all the members were to submit to registration and the registered documents were to be available for public inspection.

The final concession was made in 1855 when under the Limited Liability Act registered companies were permitted to limit the liability of their members to the nominal value of their shares. There was considerable controversy over this but it was clearly necessary, due to the innumerable bankruptcies and enormous legal complications that occurred on the failure of a large unlimited company. From the viewpoint of industrial expansion it was also essential, for the existence of unlimited liability restricted the flow of capital to industry. Obviously a capitalist would hesitate to invest in an industrial undertaking if its failure was likely to lead to his bankruptcy, and he would be still more reluctant to diversify his investments for this would only multiply his risk.

The advent of limited liability had the obvious effect of increasing the number of company registrations, which rose from 339 in 1853 to over 900 in 1865. In 1883 a total of 1,416 companies were registered and in 1897 and 1913 registrations totalled about 4,750 and 6,900 respectively. Although many of these companies traded only for a short time or not at all, and although only a very small proportion of them were important enough to acquire a Stock Exchange quotation, the above figures indicate that the registered company had become the predominant form of business organization in the United Kingdom.

The continuation of this trend is shown in the following table, compiled by F. W. Paish.[1]

	Public Companies			Private Companies		
	1928	*1939*	*1962*	*1928*	*1939*	*1962*
Number of com- panies at year end	16,700	13,900	10,700	89,000	146,700	412,500
Percentage of total	15·8	8·4	2·5	84·2	91·6	97·5
Paid-up capital (£m.)	3,517	4,117	5,024	1,461	1,923	2,833
Percentage of total	70·6	68·3	63·9	29·4	31·7	36·1
Average capital per company (£1,000)	210	296	470	16·5	13·1	6·9

This table indicates that private companies have been steadily increasing their share of the company sector both in terms of absolute numbers and of paid-up capital. But at the same time the average size of public companies has increased considerably, while that of private companies has fallen. This is an indication of the ease with which private companies may be formed, for a company with a nominal capital of £100 can be registered through a firm of registration agents for about £35.

Less than half of the public companies are quoted on the London Stock Exchange, but they account for by far the greatest part of the total paid-up capital of all public companies.

[1] *Business Finance* (London: Pitman, 1965, p. 46).

3. THE DEVELOPMENT OF THE LONDON STOCK EXCHANGE

During the second half of the seventeenth century there existed a considerable volume of securities, both commercial and gilt-edged, and the need for a market to facilitate their transfer was becoming evident. At first, Government securities were predominantly short-term, such as Exchequer Tallies, and liquidation was effected by discounting them with bankers. Similarly many company stocks were still relatively short-term relating to a particular voyage or adventure. Where an investor wished to realize his share before the completion of the voyage, this was normally achieved by private negotiation with potential buyers.

During this period the discount market, which formed part of the banking system, became well developed, but dealings in stock were still sporadic and unorganized. However, during the last decade of the century the continuing trend of companies towards permanent joint-stock capital, and the establishment of the National Debt with long-term and perpetual issues of loan stock, called for an organized market to enable investors in these long-term stocks to liquidate their holdings. Had such a market not existed investors would have been much less willing to invest their capital. The establishment of a stock market was thus necessary to encourage the flow of funds both to the Government and to commerce and industry.

Towards the end of the seventeenth century an organized market existed for the purchase and sale of stocks and shares. Brokers were licensed by the Lord Mayor of the City of London, and carried a silver medal as evidence thereof. These brokers were entitled to trade in any commodity or commodities within the City, so that it is impossible to tell how many of them were actually stockbrokers, and, in addition, there were many unlicensed brokers.

After the financial crisis of 1696 the Government attempted to regulate the market and in 1697 passed an Act 'to Restrain the number and ill Practice of Brokers and Stock jobbers'. This provided that no person was to act as a broker in commodities or stocks and shares unless licensed by the City of London and that the total number of brokers so licensed was to be limited to one hundred. In its definition of a stockbroker the Act contains a list of stocks likely to be dealt in, which gives an interesting picture of the scope of the market at that time. A stockbroker is described as a person under-taking transactions:

'Concerning any Talleys or Orders, Bills of Credit, or Tickets payable at the Receipt of The Exchequer, or at any of the Public offices, or concerning any of the Bills or Notes payable by The

Governor and Company of The Bank of England, or their Successors, or for or concerning any part of the Capital or Joint Stock belonging, or to belong to the said Governor and Company or their Successors, or to any Members of the said Company, or for or concerning any Part of Share of the Capital or Joint Stock, belonging, or to belong to any Company or Society, that is, or shall be Incorporated by Act of Parliament or Letters Patents.'

The Act also declared that brokers were not to deal on their own account and that option dealings for more than three days ahead were to be void. Both this Act and the Barnard Act of 1733, which made it illegal to buy stock without immediate payment or to sell it without immediate delivery, were largely unenforced, and both the number of practising stockbrokers and the volume of speculative transactions increased. One interesting effect of these attempts to regulate the activities of stockbrokers is that they probably induced the separation of jobbers and brokers. As there were no provisions requiring persons dealing as principals to acquire a licence and because brokers were not allowed to deal on their own account, there was a great incentive for the growth of a separate class of unlicensed principals holding shares on their own account who performed the functions carried out today by jobbers.

Up to 1698 the stockbrokers had congregated in the Royal Exchange, which was the centre for all commodity transactions in the City. As their business grew in size they needed a specialized centre purely for dealings in stocks and shares and from 1698 they began to meet in the coffee houses in Change Alley, particularly Garroway's and Jonathan's. In 1762 a group of 150 stockbrokers formed a club and attempted to obtain exclusive rights to the use of Jonathan's. This attempt failed and in 1773 a group of brokers raised a subscription and obtained control of a coffee house in Threadneedle Street, which they called the Stock Exchange. Outsiders were allowed to enter the Exchange on payment of sixpence per day.

The history of this first Stock Exchange building is rather obscure, but the premises do not appear to have been sufficiently large and there seems to have been dissension between its members. In 1801 a further subscription of some £20,000 was raised and a new building was constructed in Capel Court and opened for dealing in 1802. Although the majority of stockbrokers had always congregated together, there were still some outside centres for dealing in particular types of stock. Much of the business in foreign stocks, for example, had remained at the Royal Exchange and continued to be transacted there until 1823, when a Foreign Loan Exchange was set up in a building next to the Stock Exchange, by which it was eventually absorbed. Similarly, when the Rotunda of the Bank of England was constructed in 1764, much of the business in Government stock was transacted there, until 1838, when brokers were expelled from the Rotunda.

With the disappearance of these outside markets, the Stock Exchange had a monopoly of legal business in stocks and shares in London, though there were still dealings of doubtful legality in the shares of unincorporated associations which were transacted outside the Exchange. Unsuccessful attempts had been made in 1810, first to establish a National Fund Exchange, and then to allow the public to have access to the Exchange. Since the failure of these attempts the only real competition to the Stock Exchange has come from the provincial stock exchanges, which are now in the process of being federated with the London Exchange, and, to a much lesser extent, from other exchanges abroad, especially Wall Street, which with the growth of international communications and the activities of overseas brokers in London, are much more accessible to the British investor.

The first rules of the new Stock Exchange were published in 1812 and in many ways the operations of the Exchange under these rules very much resembled those of today. The dealing techniques were very similar, stockbrokers were specialists, and very few of them did any dealing other than stockbroking; the distinction between brokers and jobbers was accepted, though some members still performed both activities and the official list of prices was already in existence. Lists of prices had been published since 1698, but they were not published with the authority of the Stock Exchange Committee until 1803.

During the first half of the nineteenth century the London Stock Exchange thus became an organized market, broadly similar in structure to that of today. Due to the effects of the Bubble Act there were relatively few companies in existence, and the bulk of the dealings on the Exchange were transacted in the stocks which constituted the National Debt. Professor E. Victor Morgan and W. A. Thomas in their authoritative history of the Stock Exchange[1] have compiled some interesting tables of statistics indicating the growth of joint-stock enterprise and of Stock Exchange activity. Their first table, which is reproduced from *A Complete View of the Joint Stock Companies formed during the years 1824 and 1825* written by Henry English and published in 1827, analyzes the joint-stock companies which were established prior to 1824.

[1] *The Stock Exchange: Its History and Functions* (London: Elek Books, 1962, pp. 278–81).

| No. of Companies | Description | Capital | |
		Authorized	Paid-up
63	Coal	12,202,096	12,202,096
7	Docks	6,164,590	6,164,590
25	Insurance	20,488,948	6,548,948
16	Waterworks	2,973,170	2,973,170
4	Bridges	2,452,017	1,952,017
27	Gas	1,630,700	1,215,300
7	Roads	494,964	479,814
7	Miscellaneous	1,530,000	1,530,000
156		£47,936,485	£33,065,935

A further table shows that by 1842 there was a total of 755 companies with a total paid-up capital of £150,121,690 quoted on the London Stock Exchange, with railroads, banks and assurance companies well ahead of canals both in terms of members and amount of paid-up capital, while mining companies were close behind.

The most interesting and useful table is one which shows the nominal value of securities quoted on the Stock Exchange at approximately ten-year intervals between 1853 and 1962. Figures for the earliest years during that period together with those for 1971, in respect of both nominal and market values of quoted securities, are reproduced in the table on pages 30 and 31.

The main drawback to this table is that it is based on the nominal value of quoted securities rather than the market value. The use of nominal values can be misleading in several ways. For instance, an increase in the amount of quoted capital in a particular group might merely indicate a series of capitalization issues which would not of themselves cause any change in the share of that group in the total market. Also, a particular group might seem to have a relatively low share of the market in nominal terms while in reality it has a much larger share because its securities have a high value relative to their nominal value. This is particularly true of the insurance and mining sectors. A further drawback, which is inherent in all Stock Exchange statistics, is the practice of preparing only total figures in respect of the huge commercial, industrial group, which comprises nearly half of the total market value of quoted securities. This makes detailed analysis of the statistics very difficult, and it does seem that the Stock Exchange should break this group down into different industrial categories similar to those used by most newspapers in their listings of daily share prices.

The fact that nominal values are used in the table does not render it useless, for it was not until the 1950s that market values in aggregate became substantially out of line with nominal values. Consequently the information provided for the years up to 1946 is useful on an aggregate basis, while the data for 1971 is shown in both nominal and market terms.

The table shows that the Stock Exchange was dominated by gilt-edged securities in terms of nominal value during the first half of the nineteenth century. Between 1850 and the start of the First World War the National Debt was relatively stable and the increase in the amount of quoted gilt-edged and foreign securities was caused by the flotation of foreign loans on the market. This is an indication of the importance of London as an international capital market during that period, which is also borne out by the increase in quotations of stock in overseas railways. At the same time industry was expanding and the number of joint-stock companies grew enormously due to the passage of the Companies Acts at the middle of the century. Consequently, the financial, commercial and industrial sector gradually grew in importance until by 1913 it had taken a greater share of the market than that of the gilt-edged sector.

With the huge increase in the National Debt as a result of the 1914–18 War the size of the gilt-edged market increased. The depressed economic conditions of the 1930s prevented an expansion of industrial securities in terms either of nominal value or of market value, so that the gilt-edged market was able to maintain its superiority. During the Second World War and the immediate post-war years the amount of the National Debt rose still further, partly to pay for the war, and partly to finance the post-war nationalization schemes. At the same time the industrial sector contracted due to the loss of the nationalized industries. Consequently, the gilt-edged market reassumed much of its earlier dominance.

Since 1945 the number of quoted industrial securities has risen enormously due partly to general economic expansion, and partly to the increased interest of investors in the Stock Exchange and their growing demand for equities. This demand was caused by the realization that gilt-edged securities only gave security as to payment of capital (in the case of redeemable securities) and interest in money terms, so that in times of inflation an investor might receive a negative return in real terms. At the same time the size of the gilt-edged sector was increasing, though at a lower rate. Consequently, the financial, commercial and industrial sector increased its share of the total market in nominal terms from 28·7% in 1946 to 45·5% in 1971, while in terms of market value, due to the rising prices of equities, they accounted for 82·7% of the market.

29

Nominal Value of Securities Quoted on the London Stock Exchange (£m)

	Jan. 1, 1853	Jan. 1, 1883	Dec. 13, 1913	Dec. 31, 1920	Apr. 1, 1946	Nominal Mar. 31, 1971	Market Mar. 31, 1971
British Government, Guaranteed and Nationalization Stocks	853·6	871·6	1,013·0	5,418·2	12,838·2	22,533·0	17,109·5
Northern Ireland Loan Stocks, Trade Facilities and Other Acts Securities	—	—	—	—	89·9	62·0*	51·2
Corporation, County Stocks, Public Boards, etc. Gt Britain and N. Ireland	—	50·0	277·1	335·0	772·7	2,159·2	1,814·5
Corporation Stocks, Indian, Colonial and Foreign	—	13·0	156·5	159·5	141·3	119·3	69·1
Dominion, Provincial and Colonial Government Securities	—	130·6	455·7	540·5	580·4	672·0	518·8
Foreign Stocks, Bonds, etc.	69·7	831·5	3,133·9	2,394·2	2,000·5	2,126·6	1,301·3
Total Gilt-Edged and Foreign Stocks	923·3	1,896·7	5,036·2	8,847·4	16,423·0	27,672·1	20,864·4
Percentage of Total Quoted Securities	*76·0*	*52·1*	*44·7*	*53·4*	*71·3*	*54·5*	*17·3*
Railways: Gt Britain and N. Ireland	193·7	658·1	1,217·3	1,259·5	1,151·7 ⎱	237·9	511·8
Indian (and Native Loan)	Included in Foreign	80·0	151·4	159·9	86·4 ⎰		
Dominion and Colonial		—	313·4	323·3	197·1		
American	—	51·6	1,729·6	2,534·7	215·4	145·4	40·8
Foreign	31·3	307·6	736·1	870·9	585·8	81·4	30·2
Banks and Discount Companies	6·5	378·0	294·4	392·0	211·0	1,502·2	6,501·9
Breweries and Distilleries	—	55·8	103·8	120·8	243·0	1,228·8	2,709·3

Canals and Docks	16·6	33·2	19·9	14·8	44·4	22·2	21·8
Commercial, Industrial etc.	21·9	18·9	438·6	669·2	1,629·5	11,583·2	53,554·7
Electric Lighting and Power	—	—	75·3	105·8	229·9	65·6	258·1
Gas	5·7	21·8	74·2	70·6	162·1	23·0	65·8
Financial Trusts, Land, Investment and Property	—	33·5	248·7	255·8	275·4	1,540·8	3,098·5
Insurance	6·6	12·8	66·4	67·2	42·8	337·0	2,438·8
Investment and Unit Trusts	—	—	—	—	322·3	1,824·7	4,558·6
Iron, Coal, Steel and Copper	—	13·4	329·8	413·1	312·3	383·3	1,353·3
Mines	7·4	20·8	60·2	11·4	330·1	1,116·1	6,866·6
Nitrate	—	—	7·6	6·5	6·3	—	—
Oil	—	—	23·6	79·6	187·7	2,314·6	15,132·1
Rubber	—	1·6 }	24·9	32·3	85·6	78·8	126·3
Tea and Coffee	—		—	—	37·2	50·9	28·7
Shipping	—	10·8	45·3	66·8	76·4	213·5	465·3
Telegraphs and Telephones	—	29·6	141·1	146·0	53·7	168·8	1,732·8
Tramways and Omnibus	—	6·4	117·5	119·7	73·3	16·2	14·0
Waterworks	2·1	10·8	7·2	8·8	38·8	200·4	130·4
Total Financial, Commercial and Industrial	291·8	1,744·7	6,226·3	7,728·7	6,598·2	23,134·8	99,639·8
Percentage of Total Quoted Securities	24·0	47·9	55·3	46·6	28·7	45·5	82·7
	1,215·1	3,641·4	11,262·5	16,576·1	23,021·2	50,806·9	120,504·2

(The values for Rubber and Tea and Coffee in the second column are bracketed together as 1·6.)

* Trade Facilities and Other Acts Securities are included in British Government, Guaranteed and Nationalization Stocks at March 31, 1971.

The basic trend in the market has, therefore, been that gilt-edged securities have been predominant in times of war, due to the pressure on the National Debt, while the industrial sector has grown in relative importance during the two periods of expansion before the First World War and after the Second World War, up to a point where in terms of market value it far exceeds the gilt-edged and foreign market.

While the emphasis of its dealings has been changing there have been relatively few alterations in the structure and mechanism of the market. Due to the rapid expansion of business in the first half of the nineteenth century, the Stock Exchange building soon became overcrowded and it became necessary to rebuild it. The old premises were demolished in 1853 and a new building was erected and opened in 1854. This building, which is now known as the Old House, still forms part of the current Stock Exchange premises. By 1884 still more space was necessary and a further building, known as the New House, was erected. At the present time plans are in hand for the construction of a totally new Stock Exchange building, work on which has already begun and is likely to be completed during 1972.

The mechanism and functions of the Stock Exchange were considered in great detail by the Royal Commission on the Stock Exchange which was appointed in 1877 and reported in 1878. In general the report of the Commission was very favourable. It found that the Exchange provided an efficient market for the transfer of stocks and shares without encouraging an excessive amount of speculation and that neither its monopolistic position nor its unique distinction between brokers and jobbers did anything to detract from its efficiency.

Nevertheless the Commission did make several proposals for reform, the most important of which are listed below:

    (i) It was proposed that pre-allotment bargains should be prohibited. Although such bargains were illegal and not recognized by the Committee of the Stock Exchange they still took place though they seem to have died out almost completely by the end of the nineteenth century.

    (ii) Under the then current management structure of the Exchange, dual control was held by the Trustees and Managers, who represented the proprietors of the Stock Exchange, and the Committee for General Purposes, representing the members of the Stock Exchange. This system was proving very cumbersome and it was recommended that a system of unitary control should be established. This was eventually achieved in 1945 when the Council of the Stock Exchange was constituted and assumed the functions of the previous two bodies.

(iii) In order to prevent any public suspicion regarding the privacy of the Stock Exchange it was suggested that members of the public should be admitted and allowed to watch the members at work. Problems of space made this very difficult but in November 1953 a public gallery was at last opened enabling the general public for the first time to watch the Exchange in action.

(iv) It was felt that the Stock Exchange should be more severe in its requirements for the admission of new members and particularly for the re-admission of defaulting members. This was ultimately achieved by the formation of a sub-committee for the election of new members. The entrance requirements have been reinforced since August 1, 1971 by the provision that all new members must have passed the examination of the Federated Stock Exchange.

(v) It was argued that the fact that a company had a Stock Exchange quotation encouraged the public to accept it too readily as sound and stable and that investigation into companies applying for a quotation should be carried out by some public body. This recommendation is still relevant, for despite protestations to the contrary from the Stock Exchange Council many investors regard the grant of a Stock Exchange quotation as a guarantee of the probity and efficiency of the company concerned.

(vi) It was proposed that the Stock Exchange should become an incorporated or chartered body. Nothing has been done about this, though the current moves towards the formation of a National Stock Exchange may ultimately result in incorporation.

(vii) It was recommended that all deals transacted on the Exchange should be marked and recorded in the *Stock Exchange Official List*. At the moment such marking is still voluntary and the only movement towards the provision of more information about Stock Exchange transactions is the monthly publication of turnover statistics since September 1964.

(viii) Although the Commission approved in general of the distinction between brokers and jobbers it felt that some stocks were dealt in so infrequently that the jobbers ceased to perform their function of providing a competitive market.

B

It was recommended that such stocks should be recorded in a book, so that brokers could enter their requirements with regard to these stocks. A buying and selling broker could thus be brought together without the intermediary function of a jobber. Needless to say, jobbers have opposed both this recommendation and the suggestion that either brokers or jobbers should be given monopolistic specialist rights over particular inactive stocks on the basis that is adopted on the New York Stock Exchange. Their opposition to this recommendation was repeated as recently as January 1966 in a report prepared by a committee of jobbers on the current state of jobbing. The problems with which jobbers are faced are considered in more detail in Chapter 4.

The Report of the Royal Commission did not therefore induce many alterations in the mechanism of the Stock Exchange. This remains broadly similar to that of the nineteenth century, with the exception of the introduction of the New Transfer System in 1963. On the other hand, the Stock Exchange has done much to regulate the activities of brokers and jobbers and to remind companies of their obligations towards investors. Thus, although its structure has not changed a great deal, its supervisory function has become much more evident and its public image has consequently improved.

4. THE FUNCTIONS OF THE STOCK EXCHANGE

The object of this section is to describe the theoretical functions of the Stock Exchange, while a critical assessment of the actual performance of these functions is given in Chapter 4.

It is clear that the Stock Exchange developed in order to meet two demands. First, the increased issue of securities of a long-term or permanent nature required a market for the purchase and sale of these securities, so that their holders could liquidate their investments in the short-term. Also the expansion of industry during the nineteenth century necessitated the discovery of new sources of finance. One of the main such sources was the Stock Exchange which has continued ever since to be an important source of capital for industry. These two functions are, of course, very much connected, for it would be impossible for a company to raise capital from private investors if their securities were not easily marketable.

The two major functions of the Stock Exchange are thus the provision of a market for the purchase and sale of securities and the provision of capital for the purposes of industry and Government, both central and local. In its performance as a securities market the Stock Exchange is often spoken of as perfect, or at least highly competitive. The normal description of the dealing process envisages an almost infinite number of buyers or sellers of securities who make their deals, through the agency of brokers, with a large number of jobbers who are in competition with each other. It is this competition between jobbers which reputedly gives the Stock Exchange its perfect nature. Each jobber specializes in a particular group of securities and the theoretical view of the market envisages a relatively large number of jobbers specializing in each group and acting independently of each other. The floor of the Exchange is divided into different sectors in each of which may be found the jobbers who specialize in that particular group. A broker who wishes to deal in a particular security will thus go to the appropriate section of the market and will bargain with each jobber until he obtains the best price for his client. Each sector may be regarded as an individual market and the prices of securities within that sector will be determined by the normal market forces of supply and demand. Thus, if there is an increase in the demand for a security, jobbers will find that their stocks of that security are falling and that in order to maintain their stocks they will have to raise the price they are prepared to pay for that security. At the same time the price at which they will sell the security will also rise, thus reducing the pressure on their stocks. Conversely a fall in the demand for a particular security will induce a fall in both the buying and selling price, thus discouraging sellers and encouraging buyers until the equilibrium position is regained.

In this way, it is suggested, a degree of perfection is attained, for the prices of securities are fixed through the interaction of the supply and demand schedules for those securities, schedules which reflect the views of a huge number of investors and which are translated into prices on the Stock Exchange by the competing jobbers.

The Stock Exchange, therefore, in theory at least, satisfies the main prerequisite of a perfect market in that it has a large number of independent buyers and sellers. Other characteristics of a perfect market are free entry and perfect knowledge. With regard to free entry it is true that members of the public do not have physical access to the market and can only deal though the agency of a stockbroker. However, their decisions will be passed on to the market by their brokers and will thereby influence the overall levels of supply and demand. Moreover, although investors do not have direct access to the market, they are protected by the Exchange in their dealings with stockbrokers.

THE STOCK EXCHANGE AND INVESTMENT ANALYSIS

In recent years the Stock Exchange has done much to safeguard the interests of investors. In 1950 a compensation fund was established to provide compensation for any investor who might suffer loss due to the negligence or dishonesty of a member of the Exchange. Then in 1962 the membership requirements were strengthened. All firms were in future to have at least two partners and were to maintain capital of at least £5,000 per partner. In the case of jobbing firms the minimum capital requirement was set at £15,000 and that for broking firms was established as £10,000. At the same time all one-man firms were required to amalgamate with other firms and all firms were asked to provide each year an accountant's report in respect of their latest balance sheet. Finally, since 1971 all new members of the Stock Exchange have been required to pass an examination on various financial subjects before being admitted to membership. In these ways the solvency and ability of member firms have been substantially enhanced, so that investors should have more confidence in their agents in the market. In addition to regulating the activities of its member firms the Stock Exchange carefully examines all applications by companies for a quotation enabling their securities to be dealt in on the Exchange. As described in Chapter 3 it makes every effort to ensure that the company is genuine and is financially sound before it will grant a quotation.

As far as perfect knowledge is concerned, this is something that no human agency could hope to achieve. Nevertheless, the Stock Exchange requires quoted companies to provide information for investors which up to the enactment of the Companies Act, 1967 was well in excess of statutory requirements, while the information which it provides through the *Stock Exchange Daily Official List*, the *Stock Exchange Year Book* and the monthly turnover statistics are all extremely valuable to investors. In this way the level of knowledge of investors is increased though it is still very imperfect.

The Stock Exchange therefore appears to have at least some of the characteristics of a perfect market. In addition, its authorities endeavour to prevent any imperfections entering the market. For example, in 1965 Rule 73 (*b*) of the *Rules and Regulations of the Stock Exchange* was approved:

1. No member shall knowingly or without due care deal in such a manner as shall promote or assist in the promotion of a false market.
2. A false market is defined as a market in which a movement of the price of a share is brought about or sought to be brought about by contrived factors, such as the operation of buyers and

36

sellers acting in collaboration with each other, calculated to create a movement of price which is not justified by assets, earnings or prospects.

In cases where it is felt that such a market has been created or where for any other reason it is felt that further information is necessary regarding the affairs of a company or the state of the market in its shares, the Stock Exchange has the power to suspend the quotation of the company concerned. This, however, is an extreme step which often harms the investors whom it is designed to protect, for it not only deprives their securities of marketability but often results in a fall in price when the quotation is resumed.

A further feature of the market is its relative stability, which is brought about in two ways through the operations of the jobbers. In the first place they provide a market for securities in which deals take place only rarely. If jobbers did not exist a broker who had an order to sell such a security might have to accept a very low price, due to the narrowness of the market. However, under present market conditions he can sell the security to a jobber who will hold it in stock until a buyer appears who is prepared to pay a more realistic price. A further function of jobbers is to minimize short-term fluctuations in security prices. If, for example, a quick burst of selling takes place jobbers should act as a buffer by taking the stock on to their books without bringing down the price of the security too sharply. When the trend has been reversed they can gradually unload their stock on to the market until an equilibrium position has been regained. Similarly, if a wave of speculative buying occurs and the jobber, with his specialized knowledge of the security concerned, feels that it represents a short-term movement which will soon be reversed he will sell stock which he does not actually possess, thus preventing too sharp a rise in the price of the security, in the expectation that he would be able to acquire the amount of stock required when the level of demand has reverted to its previous position.

The Stock Exchange thus endeavours to provide a competitive, stable and regulated market for the purchase and sale of securities. In so doing it provides a measure of value which is extremely useful. For many purposes, such as the assessment of capital gains and estate duty where securities are involved, the quoted Stock Exchange price is the legal standard of value. Similarly, the quoted price provides an admirable measurement of value for many comparisons of business efficiency and structure, one example being the assessment of the gearing of a company, where the Stock Exchange values of the securities of the company provide a much more accurate indication of value than that given by other commonly accepted criteria, such as the nominal value of the share capital.

A further function commonly attributed to Stock Exchange prices is that they furnish companies with an estimate of their cost of capital. It should be pointed out that in this context it is not the price itself, but the yield on the security which is important. This is because the price of a security is ultimately determined by its yield, which represents the return that an investor would expect to receive on his investment in that security. Thus a security with a gross yield of $6\frac{1}{2}\%$ would give a return of £6 10s per annum on an investment of £100. This yield indicates the return that a company would have to offer to investors, other things being equal, if it wished to raise further capital.

In providing companies with this information the Stock Exchange is performing its other important basic function as a capital market. It not only provides a source of capital for industry but it also allocates the available capital in the most efficient way by charging different rates of interest to different companies according to the market expectations regarding their profitability. Thus a company which was regarded as speculative and unprofitable would have to pay a higher rate of interest for any new capital which it raised than would a more profitable and more stable company. As a result the most efficient firms will find it most easy to obtain new capital, while the least efficient will have most difficulty in so doing.

In addition to providing a source of capital for industry the Stock Exchange is also a source of finance for the central Government and local authorities. In recent years local authorities have been prolific borrowers from the market while the Government has also issued a vast amount of quoted securities partly as a direct increase of the National Debt and partly to finance nationalization schemes.

Although the Government is in competition with other borrowers in the market it has much greater control over the terms on which it borrows. In the first place it can affect overall market conditions by the traditional techniques of monetary and fiscal policy, while in the second place it has a rather more limited scope for manipulation of the gilt-edged market itself, in that it is in a position to stabilize the gilt-edged market, but is unable, except within narrow limits, to induce price movements without having a similar effect on other sectors of the Stock Exchange. Stabilization of the gilt-edged market is achieved by the activities of the Government broker, who has the full resources of the Government behind him, including the vast holdings of gilt-edged stock held by the Government agencies such as the Post Office Savings Bank and the National Insurance

Funds. By releasing Government-held securities to prevent a rise in gilt-edged prices and by purchasing securities to prevent a fall, the Government broker is able to support the market whenever necessary.

Having explained the theoretical dual role of the Stock Exchange both as a securities market and as a capital market it is now necessary to describe the mechanism of these two markets in more detail. Chapter 2, therefore, describes the procedure for the purchase and sale of securities, while in Chapter 3 the workings of the new issue market are outlined.

The Structure and Dealing Mechanism
of the London Stock Exchange

1. THE STRUCTURE OF THE LONDON STOCK EXCHANGE

a. *The Council of the Stock Exchange*

The Council has absolute power over the administration of the Exchange with regard to both the admission and expulsion of members and the formation of the rules regulating the procedure of the stock market. The Council is composed of not less than thirty and not more than thirty-six members, exclusive of the Government Broker, who is a member *ex officio* (Rule 1 (1)).[1] With the exception of the Government Broker, all of the members must be elected by ballot by the members of the Stock Exchange, must themselves have been members of the Stock Exchange for at least five years and are elected for a three-year term of office (Rules 1 (2) and 2). From its members the Council elects each year a chairman, known as the Chairman of the Stock Exchange, and two deputy chairmen. The Council is required to appoint a Property and Finance Committee and any other Committees which are deemed necessary for the performance of its powers and duties (Rule 7). Among those which have already been formed are Committees dealing with the admission of members and clerks, the Compensation Fund, official lists and publications, public relations, quotations, and rules and disputes.

The day-to-day administration of the Stock Exchange is the responsibility of the Secretary of the Stock Exchange, aided by a staff of some five hundred, divided into departments of which the largest are the Share and Loan Department, the Settlement Department and the Official Lists Department.

[1] All references to rules relate to the *Rules and Regulations of the Stock Exchange*, as published by the Council of the Stock Exchange in 1970.

THE STRUCTURE AND DEALING MECHANISM

b. *The Membership of the Stock Exchange*

Admission to Membership

A candidate for membership must satisfy the following requirements:

- (i) He must be a British-born subject, or, at the discretion of the Council, a naturalized citizen of five years' standing (Rule 21 (3)).
- (ii) Prior to 25 March, 1970 he needed to obtain a nomination from a retiring or deceased member. The cost of these nominations was determined by supply and demand and fluctuated between £1 and £4,000, a peak reached in 1927. As from 25 March, 1970 all new members must either have acquired a nomination before that date or must pay £1,000 to the Trustees of the Nomination Fund, which was set up to redeem the existing nomination rights of members on retirement or death. The £1,000 will not be returnable and may be varied by the Stock Exchange (Rule 25).
- (iii) Neither he nor his wife may be a principal or employee in any business other than that of the Stock Exchange without the consent of the Council (Rule 27).
- (iv) If he has been bankrupt he must only have been bankrupt once and must have been discharged with a payment of 20s in the pound (Rule 30).
- (v) He must be at least twenty-one years of age (Rule 31 (1) (a)).
- (vi) He must have completed three years training, three months of which must be served on the floor of the House. The Council may exempt from training a candidate who has commercial experience or a suitable professional qualification. Since August 1, 1971 candidates have been required to pass the examinations of the Federated Stock Exchange (Rule 31 (1) (b)).
- (vii) He must obtain a Proposer and a Seconder, each of whom is a member of at least four years' standing and has not less than two years personal knowledge of the candidate (Rule 31 (2)).
- (viii) Every applicant for re-election, admission or re-admission shall declare whether he proposes to act as a Broker, Jobber or Clerk, or that he is not engaged in active business (Rule 22).
- (ix) An entrance fee, currently standing at £1,050, must be paid (Rule 21 (4)).
- (x) The election of new members is by ballot and must be carried

by a majority of not less than three-fourths of those members of the Council who are present at a meeting at which not less than twelve members are present (Rule 34).

Strictly speaking, admission to membership is only granted for a term of one year, and all members, both old and new, must offer themselves for re-election each year on March 24th.

Cessation of Membership

The Council has the power to censure, suspend or expel any member who violates any of the rules or regulations, fails to comply with any of the Council's decisions, or is guilty of dishonourable or disgraceful conduct (Rule 16). It also has the right both to require members and their clerks to attend the Council and give information regarding any matter under investigation and to appoint an accountant to report on any matters relating to a firm's finances. As the result of information obtained in this way it may suspend a firm or any of its partners from trading (Rule 15). Any resolution which involves the expulsion or suspension of a member must be passed by a majority of not less than three-fourths of those members of the Council who are present at a meeting of which special notice has been given and at which not less than twelve members are present (Rules 12, 18).

Membership will also cease on the death or resignation of a member, in both of which cases the right of nomination may be surrendered by the member or his estate to the Trustees of the Nomination Redemption Fund for £1,000 (Rules 25, 44). Similarly, membership may be terminated where a member does not apply for re-election before March 24th (Rule 24 (1)).

Finally, membership may cease where a member is unable to meet his obligations. For instance, it is provided that a member who fails to pay any entrance fees, subscriptions or other payments due to the Council, or who is proved to be insolvent, even though he is not a defaulter on the Stock Exchange, shall cease to be a member upon resolution of the Council to that effect (Rule 176). Also, any member who is unable to fulfil his trading commitments on the Stock Exchange is publicly declared a defaulter by direction of the Chairman, a Deputy Chairman, or any two members of the Council, and thereby ceases to be a member (Rule 175 (1)). This involves the procedure known as 'hammering' whereby two waiters make an announcement to the whole House to the effect that a firm of members cannot comply with their bargains. In all cases of default all of the partners of the firm are personally liable in respect of its trading obligations.

Where such default occurs the books of the firm are taken over by the Official Assignee, who will settle the unclosed bargains of the firm at the current market price of the stock concerned and will realize its assets and settle its debts as far as is possible (Rules 170–4, 179). If a member is a creditor of a firm and realizes that that firm is unable to fulfil its engagements he should not come to any compromise, but should inform the Council immediately (Rule 177).

In order to protect the clients of a stockbroker from loss as a result of his default a Compensation Fund was set up in 1950. In March 1971 it stood at £710,442 and it is available at the discretion of the Council and without admission of legal liability to compensate clients who have suffered loss through the default, dishonesty or negligence of their stockbrokers, having regard to any contributory negligence on the part of the client.

Classes of Membership—Their Functions, Numbers and Fees

At July 30, 1971 the following categories of members and non-members had access to the floor of the House:

	Brokers	*Jobbers*
Limited partners	1	1
Partners	1,774	259
Associate members	1,108	275
Authorized clerks	570	124
Unauthorized clerks	528	164
Members not in active business (130)		
External members (e.g. limited companies) (4)		

	Fees (1971–72)	
	Entrance Fee £	*Annual Subscription* £
Members		
Members (other than member clerks)	1,050	262·50
Authorized member clerks	1,050	262·50
Unauthorized member clerks	1,050	262·50
Not active in business etc.	1,050	—
	Admission Fee	
Non-members		
Authorized non-member clerks	63	210
Unauthorized non-member clerks	21	63

The functions of the different classes of members and non-members are as follows:

43

(i) Partners and associate members. These are all partners or employees in firms of brokers or jobbers or, since 1969, members of companies. Until 1962 they were allowed to trade as individuals, but since that date individual brokers and jobbers have been required to amalgamate into firms with at least two partners. Members must state whether they are going to act as brokers or jobbers and cannot act as both. The function of the brokers is to act as agents for the public in the market. They thus undertake the purchase and sale of shares for investors, arrange more speculative transactions such as share options and contango operations, and sponsor the introduction of new shares on behalf of companies coming to the market for capital. Their income consists primarily of commission charged in respect of these services. In addition to these remunerated services they also provide free information and advice for investors. They not only have access to the major sources of information, such as Exchange Telegraph cards, but also in many cases maintain their own investment analysis department and provide regular surveys of particular industries or companies. Finally, they are not allowed to advertise for business.

The function of jobbers is to maintain stocks of securities. Each firm of jobbers specializes in particular groups of securities and all jobbers dealing in a particular group will congregate in the same part of the House so that brokers will know where to go in order to buy or sell shares in that group. The jobbers make their profit partly from the jobber's turn, which is the difference between the price at which they offer to sell a particular share and the price at which they offer to buy it, and partly from the appreciation of their stock of securities at times when the market is rising. Conversely, when prices move downwards their stock will suffer depreciation, and they will for this reason try to reduce their holdings when prices are falling.

(ii) Clerks. All clerks, whether or not they are actually members, are divided by function into authorized, unauthorized and Settling Room clerks. Authorized clerks are the only ones who are allowed to deal on the market, and then only in the name of their firm. Unauthorized clerks, who are known as 'blue buttons' because of the blue badge which they wear in their lapels, are not allowed to deal and merely carry messages for their seniors on the floor of the House. Finally, the Settling Room clerks, who are known as 'red buttons', perform clerical duties in the Settling Room which is underneath the floor of the House, and do not have access to the floor itself. The number of clerks given access to the floor is restricted to two, one of whom may be authorized to deal, for each partner in the firm.

c. *The Volume of Business on the Stock Exchange*

Both the size of the market and the volume of business are revealed by the booklet *Statistics Relating to Securities Quoted on the London Stock Exchange* which is published annually by the Stock Exchange. Between 1939 and 1963 the number of securities officially quoted on the Exchange fell from 10,297 to 9,134 largely due to industrial mergers and takeovers and the nationalization of many companies. There was then a rise to 9,586 in 1967, but by March 31, 1971, the number of quoted securities had fallen to 9,024. This total was composed as follows:

	Number of Securities	Nominal Amount £	Market Valuation £
Gilt-edged and Foreign Stocks	1,251	27,672,113,001	20,864,436,226
Securities of companies in the Commercial Industrial, etc. group	4,452	11,583,207,073	53,554,742,683
Securities of all other companies	3,321	11,551,586,661	46,084,986,248
Securities of all companies	7,773	23,134,793,734	99,639,728,931
All securities	9,024	£50,806,906,735	£120,504,165,157

An analysis of securities within the company sector shows their distribution between different classes of securities and between British and overseas companies:

Analysis of Quoted Company Securities at March 31, 1971

(1) Quoted securities of companies registered and managed within the UK and securities of overseas companies in sterling denominations.

No. of Securities	Classification	Total value (£) Nominal	Total value (£) Market
2,492	Loan capital (incl. convertibles)	5,917,579,857	4,407,352,605
1,677	Preference and preferred capital	1,089,921,813	565,843,769
3,074	Ordinary and deferred capital	10,174,589,727	36,936,172,632
7,243		17,182,091,397	41,909,369,006

(2) Quoted securities of companies not registered and managed within the UK.

| No. of Securities | Classification | Total value (£) | |
		Nominal	Market
58	Loan capital	383,357,963	265,984,113
94	Preference and preferred capital	236,343,462	296,231,416
352	Ordinary and deferred capital	5,333,000,912	52,153,196,397
26	Shares of no par value: Ordinary shares	[315,100,915]	5,014,947,999
530		5,952,702,337	57,730,359,925
7,773	*Overall Totals*	23,134,793,734	99,639,728,931

The above table shows the international character of the London Stock Exchange. Although the number of overseas securities with official quotations is relatively small, their total market value is larger than that of the securities of British companies. This indicates that it is mainly the largest overseas companies which have a London quotation. In two respects the table is rather misleading. In the first place many of the quoted securities of British companies, particularly the preference shares, are dealt in very rarely so that in effect the Stock Exchange does not provide an active market for them. The same argument applies to many of the gilt-edged and foreign securities, so that the number of securities for which an active market exists is considerably less, probably by half, than the figure suggested by the Stock Exchange statistics. To counter-balance this there is the fact that dealings are permitted under Rule 163 in several securities which do not have a formal quotation. The most important of these are:

(a) Treasury Bills and the bills, mortgages and short-term securities of local government authorities and public boards of Great Britain and Northern Ireland.
(b) Securities which have been granted a Primary Listing on the Johannesburg Stock Exchange or have been granted a quotation on any other Stock Exchange or Stockbrokers Association recognized by Rule 217 (1) (i.e. Adelaide, Auckland, Brisbane, Calcutta, Calgary, Canadian Stock Exchange, Christchurch, Delhi, Dunedin, Hobart, Hong Kong, The Johannesburg Stock

Exchange, Karachi, Lagos, Madras, Melbourne, Montreal, Nairobi, Perth, Rhodesia, Sydney, Toronto, Vancouver, Wellington, Winnipeg, Colombo Brokers Association, and Malayan Stock Exchange) or on a Foreign Stock Exchange.

(c) Obligations of or guaranteed by the Governments of the USA, Canada and South Africa or any of their provinces, states or municipalities.

(d) A wide range of Federal agencies, banks, trusts, insurance companies, and public utilities in the USA and Canada.

The other main feature of these tables is the preponderance of equities in terms of market value due to their inherent resistance to inflation. This is because in times of inflation, profits tend to be a stable percentage of rising prices and thus themselves increase, thereby exerting an upward pressure on dividends and share prices. Gilt-edged securities, loan stock and preference shares do not share this characteristic because their return is fixed and therefore remains constant in money terms, while falling in real terms. The popularity of equities has been a comparatively recent feature of the London market, partly because inflation has been most serious in the post-war period and partly because it was only realized during that period how vulnerable gilt-edged securities were to inflation.

As far as the volume of business is concerned the statistics prior to September 1964 relate only to the number of bargains which were marked during each month. However, although it was recommended by the Royal Commission of 1878 that all bargains should be recorded in the Official List, marking has never been made compulsory and it is doubtful whether many more than half the bargains made are actually marked. As a result, statistics based on markings only give an indication of the broad trend of business, and do not enable an accurate estimate of the actual volume of business to be made. However, in September 1964 the Council of the London Stock Exchange began to publish a monthly statement of turnover, showing the number of bargains and total turnover for each class of security during the month. While there is still considerable room for improvement, at least from the point of view of the investor, by, for example, the publication of daily turnover in every quoted stock and the compulsory marking of all bargains, the publication of turnover statistics represents a very welcome step forward. Moreover, the Council of the Stock Exchange intends to publish, in the near future, an analysis of the monthly turnover of different classes of clients.

The volume of business as revealed in the table of marks recorded published in *Statistics Relating to Securities Quoted on the London*

Stock Exchange reached a peak of 4,288,149 bargains in 1959. Since then the number of bargains recorded each year have been:

1960	3,514,166	1965	2,670,390
1961	3,639,983	1966	2,482,009
1962	3,234,440	1967	2,825,201
1963	3,613,592	1968	3,384,857
1964	3,552,817	1969	2,862,612
1970	2,394,201	1971	2,894,450

Even allowing for variations in the size of each bargain and in the proportion of bargains actually marked each year, it seems clear that the volume of business has declined in recent years, though there was a substantial recovery during 1968.

Although the full statistics of turnover have not yet been available long enough for trends in the volume of business to become noticeable, the table on p. 49 which contains the statistics published between January 1965 and December 1971 provides interesting information relating to the composition of turnover.

In terms of the number of bargains the market is dominated by ordinary shares, which are responsible for over 75% of all transactions. At the same time, British Government short-dated securities account for between 2·0 and 3·5% of all bargains. However, in terms of value of turnover Government securities are predominant, accounting for approximately 60% of total turnover. Ordinary shares, by contrast, only constitute about one-fifth of the market. Obviously, as the table shows, these features are attributable to the much higher average size of dealings in gilt-edged securities relative to those in company securities. However, the average size of transactions in ordinary shares is gradually increasing, possibly due to the greater share of this market now taken by the institutional investors.

2. THE PROCEDURE FOR THE PURCHASE AND SALE OF SECURITIES ON THE LONDON STOCK EXCHANGE

The Stockbroker and his Client

A member of the general public who wishes to acquire or dispose of securities on the London Stock Exchange must do so through the agency of a stockbroker. The investor may either be a direct client of the stockbroker, or he may give instructions to his bank to undertake a transaction on his behalf, in which case the bank will pass on the

	British Government Securities					Local Authority Securities	%	Overseas Government, Provincial and Municipal Securities	%	Fixed Interest Preference and Preferred Ordinary Shares	%	Ordinary Shares	%
	Total	Up to 5 Years to Maturity	%	Over 5 years and Undated	%								
Value of Turnover (£m)													
1965	20,487	10,594	51·7	5,402	26·4	331	1·6	201	1·0	480	2·3	3,479	17·0
1966	21,590	10,581	49·1	6,026	27·9	694	3·2	138	0·6	585	2·7	3,566	16·5
1967	35,956	16,524	46·0	11,448	31·8	1,202	3·4	190	0·5	787	2·2	5,804	16·1
1968	31,976	14,502	45·3	6,532	20·4	732	2·3	150	0·5	942	3·0	9,117	28·5
1969	30,391	11,621	38·2	7,839	25·8	839	2·8	141	0·5	1,238	4·1	8,713	28·6
1970	38,767	12,940	33·4	14,409	37·2	1,310	3·4	136	0·3	1,159	3·0	8,813	22·7
1971	64,262	22,062	**34·3**	25,394	**39·5**	1,521	**2·5**	218	**0·3**	1,679	**2·6**	13,377	**20·8**
Number of transactions (thousands)													
1965	4,361	98	2·2	265	6·1	96	2·2	54	1·2	431	9·9	3,417	78·4
1966	4,145	118	2·8	255	6·2	98	2·3	51	1·2	504	12·2	3,119	75·3
1967	5,006	161	3·2	289	5·8	116	2·3	48	0·9	501	10·0	3,891	77·8
1968	6,523	142	2·2	251	3·8	98	1·5	45	0·7	674	10·3	5,313	81·5
1969	5,787	160	2·8	280	4·8	98	1·7	35	0·6	675	11·7	4,539	78·4
1970	5,312	150	2·8	326	6·1	103	1·9	31	0·6	604	11·4	4,098	77·2
1971	6,623	144	**2·2**	386	**5·8**	93	**1·4**	38	**0·6**	704	**10·6**	5,258	**79·4**
Average size of deal (£ thousands)													
1965		108·0		20·4		3·4		3·7		1·1		1·0	
1966		89·7		23·6		7·1		2·7		1·2		1·1	
1967		102·6		39·6		10·4		4·0		1·6		1·5	
1968		102·1		26·0		7·0		3·3		1·4		1·7	
1969		72·6		28·0		8·6		4·0		1·8		1·9	
1970		86·3		44·2		12·7		4·4		1·9		2·1	
1971		153·3		65·8		1·63		5·7		2·4		2·6	

instructions to its own stockbroker and will be given a share of up to a quarter of the broker's commission.

In general, investors who deal in small quantities of securities tend to deal through their banks, while large-scale investors normally deal direct with a stockbroker. This is because many stockbrokers are reluctant to undertake deals involving less than £200, claiming that their commission on such deals is insufficient to cover the costs of the transaction. This may well be an indictment of the general small scale of stockbroking on the London market, for the larger American brokers, most of whom are incorporated, claim that even the smallest bargains can be profitable.

A comparison of the services provided for investors by banks and stockbrokers suggests the superiority of the latter for all but the smallest investors. The main advantage offered by banks is that they will willingly undertake the most minute transactions, which a stockbroker would refuse or at least be extremely reluctant to undertake. On the other hand, the information and advice provided by banks normally originates from their stockbroker, so that an investor could have access to the same information by becoming the direct client of a broker. In this way he would not only have the most up-to-date information regarding shares but would also have the benefit of advice regarding the suitability of particular shares in relation to his portfolio of investments and his overall financial position. Moreover, he would have the further advantage of receiving the periodical circulars, reviewing particular shares or industries, which are prepared by the investment research departments of the larger firms of stockbrokers.

As stockbrokers are not allowed to advertise, an investor is normally introduced to a broker on the basis of the recommendation of a friend. Alternatively, he may write to the Secretary of the Stock Exchange who will forward a short list of brokers. This list is changed monthly and contains a selection from a register of brokers who are prepared to accept new clients and to undertake small or medium-sized transactions.

In recent years the rules of the Stock Exchange relating to advertising and publicity have been relaxed very slightly. In 1962 stockbrokers were permitted for the first time, under Rule 57 (e), to establish overseas branch offices on obtaining the consent of the Council in respect of each office opened. The offices, which must be outside the UK and the Republic of Ireland, must be wholly under the control of the London firm and must be used solely for the conduct of Stock Exchange business. It is necessary for the branch office to comply with Stock Exchange rules (including Rule 78 which prohibits advertising) and with the laws of the country in which the branch office is situated. Finally, it is provided that the business of the office may be conducted by a company incorporated with limited or unlimited liability in the country in which it is situated.

Then in September 1965 the Council announced that Rule 78 would not be considered to have been contravened in the following circumstances:

(i) Where the name of a member firm is mentioned in the editorial columns of the Press.

(ii) Where the name of a broker firm appears in the report and accounts or other documents issued by a pension, charitable or similar fund.

(iii) Where in a prospectus or other similar document a member who is also a director of the company issuing the prospectus, is described as a partner in a named firm who are members of the Stock Exchange.

(iv) Where in his local directory in normal type a member is described as a member of the Stock Exchange, London.

In October 1965 under Rule 59 (1) firms of stockbrokers were permitted for the first time to open branch offices in Great Britain or Ireland. Any such office must receive the consent of the Council, be controlled by the firm and operated in its name, and be used solely for the conduct of Stock Exchange business. The introduction of this rule seems likely to encourage amalgamations of London and provincial brokers, thus increasing the scale of stockbroking.

In November 1965 the Council made a further slight relaxation of Rule 78 when it announced that this rule would not be considered to have been contravened where the name of an individual is mentioned in the editorial columns of the Press either as a member of the London Stock Exchange or as a partner in a member firm. However, members registered as regular contributors to the Press were to continue to be required to remain anonymous. Furthermore, members were to be permitted to encourage mention by the Press, by submitting investment surveys for review provided they were marked 'For Private Circulation Only'. At the same time the Council stated that member firms must seek its approval when they wish to issue a Press release relating to a special event, such as the introduction of a new investment service.

More recently it has been stated that Rule 78 would not be deemed to have been contravened either where a member occasionally taking part in a radio or television interview is introduced as 'Mr . . . of Messrs . . ., Members of the Stock Exchange, London', or where a member contributing an occasional Press article describes himself by name and as a Member of the Stock Exchange, London or publishes his picture and the name of his firm.

Although most brokers appear to oppose such relaxation of Rule 78 they are facing fierce competition from the large firms of stockbrokers on the New York Exchange who have established branch offices in Great Britain and are allowed to advertise freely for business for the New York Exchange. In the face of this competition they may well be forced to relax still further their restrictions on advertising.

In describing the procedure for the purchase and sale of shares it will be assumed that an investor wishes to purchase 500 shares in XYZ Ltd and that he is the client of a stockbroker. The procedure for the sale of shares is very similar to that for a purchase, and any points of difference will be explained.

The investor will contact his broker, who will have access to the latest Exchange Telegraph cards relating to the company in which he is interested. These cards give a mass of information including a ten-year summary of profits and capital employed, the salient points from the latest chairman's statements and share price statistics for the past ten years. In the light of this information and having regard to the existing portfolio commitments and the financial circumstances of his client, he will make an appropriate recommendation.

If a purchase is recommended he will telephone his authorized clerk or one of his partners on the floor of the House to ascertain the approximate current price of shares in XYZ Ltd. This price may turn out to be between 100p and 102½p. The investor may then instruct his broker to buy 500 shares 'at best', which means at the best obtainable price, or he may set a limit, say at 100p, in which case he will buy 500 at the best price with a maximum of 100p.

The Dealing Process

In this example it is assumed that the investor instructs his broker to purchase 500 shares in XYZ Ltd 'at best'. These instructions will be telephoned to the broker's authorized clerk who will then go to that part of the floor of the House in which may be found jobbers specializing in shares of the sector to which XYZ Ltd belongs. He may find that there are five jobbers dealing in this group and he will approach each in turn asking 'What are XYZs ?' He will not indicate whether he wishes to buy or sell and will not state the quantity of shares involved, though it is assumed that the amount is both reasonable in size and marketable. Thus if the amount of shares involved was, say, 100,000, an amount which might be expected to affect substantially the market, or if it was a small amount such as 10 shares with which the jobber might have difficulty in dealing, then the jobber must be informed so that he may have the opportunity of quoting a special price.

The jobber will reply with a quotation of two prices, the lower of which is the one at which he offers to buy the shares, and the higher being the price at which he will sell them. The difference between the two prices is known as the 'jobber's turn' and is commonly, though incorrectly, regarded as his profit. If there is a very restricted market in a particular share the difference between the quoted prices may be relatively wide to compensate the jobber for the risk that he may not be able to replace the shares which he is selling from his stock or may not be able to sell the shares which he is adding to his stock. If the market is extremely restricted or 'thin' the jobber may make a 'one-way price'. Thus a quotation of '35p bid, not offered' would indicate that he is prepared to buy the shares at 35p but has none for sale. Conversely, a quotation of '35p offered, not bid' would signify that he is only interested in selling the shares.

The five jobbers approached in connection with the shares of XYZ Ltd might give the following quotations:

First jobber	99 –101
Second jobber	98 –100
Third jobber	98½–100½
Fourth jobber	99½–101½
Fifth jobber	100 –102

Out of this range of prices the best buying price is the 100p offered by the second jobber, and the authorized clerk will say to him 'Buy 500 XYZs at 100p'. The jobber will repeat this and both of them will record the deal in their notebooks. There is no formal contract for the purchase and sale of the shares and there is no legal liability in respect of the deal. However, in this respect the Stock Exchange motto '*Dictum meum pactum*' (My word is my bond) has generally been strictly observed by its members, though there have from time to time been accusations of rather convenient cases of amnesia.

In some ways the above description is misleading. For example, in the vast majority of stocks there would be considerably less than five jobbers who were prepared to offer a double quotation with a fairly narrow range. In fact only about 300 industrial stocks are dealt in by five or more jobbers. Also the broker, or his clerk, would know the general state of the market and might concentrate on haggling with one of the jobbers rather than obtaining formal quotations from each jobber.

The above range of prices would appear in the *Official List* as 98–102, thus giving the impression that the jobber's turn in this share was fourpence, which would give him a profit of £20 on a deal involving 500 shares. However, it should be clear that the amount of the turn is far less. In fact, on the basis of the prices given above there is no scope for a profit at all, for brokers would buy from the second jobber at 100p and execute selling orders with the fifth jobber also at 100p. However, each jobber's prices would fluctuate according to the state of their books, and the second jobber, as his stock of shares in XYZ Ltd became depleted, would increase his quotation, perhaps to 99–101. At this price he would become a buyer at 99p replacing shares which he had sold at 100p, representing a turn of 1p per share and a profit on 500 shares of £5. Similarly, the fifth jobber, who had been buying shares in XYZ Ltd at 100p would find that his books were becoming unbalanced, and, in order to attract buyers of those shares, he would decrease his quoted price, perhaps to $98\frac{1}{2}$–$100\frac{1}{4}$. In this way, prices are constantly fluctuating in reaction to the forces of supply and demand and the effect of those forces on the books of the jobbers. Because of these fluctuations in prices the jobbers very rarely receive what is regarded as their normal turn and it is claimed by them that the average turn or profit on a share in which there is a busy market is unlikely to be more than one penny and might even be less than one halfpenny. In fact, the actual turn made by the jobber is probably a less important constituent of his profits than the appreciation or depreciation of his stock due to movements in the general level of Stock Exchange prices.

If the broker wishes he may 'mark' the bargain on a 'marking slip', giving details of the shares and the price. The slip will be placed in a box where it provides the basis for the list of bargains in the *Stock Exchange Daily Official List*.

The Contract Note

From the moment that the verbal deal between the broker and jobber has been made the client is responsible for any liabilities and is entitled to all rights arising therefrom. The next morning the clerks of the brokers and jobber meet in the Settling Room and compare the entries made in their seniors' notebooks, any differences normally being settled amicably. Once the verbal bargain has been made, its details will be telephoned through to the stockbroker's office, where a contract note will be prepared and sent to the client to inform him of the deal which has been made on his behalf.

The Structure and Dealing Mechanism

<table>
<tr><td>*Name of firm*</td><td>*Address*</td></tr>
<tr><td>*List of partners*</td><td>*Date of contract*</td></tr>
<tr><td>*Telephone and telex numbers*</td><td>*(August 25, 1971)*</td></tr>
</table>

We beg to advise having bought for your account, for settlement September 14, 1971.

		£
500 XYZ Ltd		
Ordinary Shares of 50p each @ 100p		500·00
	£	
Brokerage	6·25	
Contract Stamp	10	
Stamp Duty	5·00	
Registration Fee	12½	
	——	11·47½
		£511·47½

Subject to the rules and regulations   *Members of the London*
of the London Stock Exchange   *Stock Exchange*

The contract note states the company whose shares were bought or sold, the class of share or stock and the price at which the bargain was made. To the cost or proceeds of the deal are added or deducted the various expenses, which are calculated as follows:

(i) *Brokerage*

The scales of brokers' commission are laid down in Appendix 39 to the rules of the Stock Exchange which states the minimum rates chargeable.

The rates for the major categories of securities are:

		Consideration £	*Rate* %
(1.) *Gilt-edged and other securities*			
(*a*) Securities having no final redemption date within 10 years			
(i) Bargains up to £50,000 consideration	First	2,000	0·5
	Next	12,000	0·2
	Next	36,000	0·1
(ii) Bargains over £50,000 consideration	First	4 million	0·14
	Excess		0·07

(b) Securities having 10 years or less
to final redemption
  (i) Bargains up to £50,000

consideration	First	2,000	0·5
	Next	2,000	0·1
	Next	46,000	0·05

  (ii) Bargains over £50,000

consideration	First	4 million	0·07
	Excess		0·035

(c) Securities having five years or
less to final redemption   At discretion

(2) *Debentures, bonds, etc.*

First	5,000	0·75
Next	15,000	0·375
Next	5,000	Nil
Next	475,000	0·375
Excess		0·3

(3) *Stocks and shares*

First	5,000	1·25
Next	15,000	0·625
Next	5,000	Nil
Next	50,000	0·625
Excess		0·5

(4) *American and Canadian shares*
(with the exception of shares
which are deliverable by
transfer)

First	5,000	0·75
Next	15,000	0·375
Next	5,000	Nil
Excess		0·375

(5) 'Givers' of option money are charged on the same scale as laid down above for bargains.

(6) 'Takers' of option money are charged at half the above scales.

(7) In the case of short-dated securities (i.e. having less than five years to run) and unquoted units of unit trusts commission may be charged at the discretion of the broker.

(8) No lower commission than £4 may be charged except in the case of:

(a) Transactions on which the commission may be at discretion.

(b) Transactions amounting to not less than £100 in value on which a commission of not less than £2 must be charged.

(c) Transactions amounting to less than £10 in value on which the commission may be at discretion.

(d) Gilt-edged securities. These carry a minimum commission of £2, which is reduced to £1 on deals less than £100 in value.

There are certain circumstances under which a broker may, by concession, charge reduced rates of commission:

(1) Closing Transactions (Rule 206 (1), (2)). Where a bargain done for the Account is closed by a corresponding bargain in the same security made for the same principal and for the same Account, a broker may at his discretion waive commission on either the original bargain or the closing bargain. A similar provision applies in respect of bargains done for cash.

(2) Aggregation under Rule 207 (1). Where a broker carries out deals in one security for the same principal he is permitted to aggregate for a period of three calendar months from the date of the first bargain the considerations of the first and any subsequent bargains and may then charge commission at such lower rates as apply in accordance with the above scales of minimum commission.

(ii) *Contract Stamp*

This is a Government Stamp Duty which is levied on all contract notes, whether in respect of a bought or a sold transaction. The current scale is as follows:

Amount of Consideration			Amount of Stamp
	£	£	p
From	5 and not exceeding	100	5
above	100 and not exceeding	500	10
above	500 and not exceeding	1,000	20
above	1,000 and not exceeding	1,500	30
above	1,500 and not exceeding	2,500	40
above	2,500 and not exceeding	5,000	60
above	5,000 and not exceeding	7,500	80
above	7,500 and not exceeding	10,000	100
above	10,000 and not exceeding	12,500	120
above	12,500 and not exceeding	15,000	140
above	15,000 and not exceeding	17,500	160
above	17,500 and not exceeding	20,000	180
above 20,000			200

(iii) *Stamp Duty*

The Government charges an *ad valorem* stamp duty on the transfer of all securities, with the exceptions listed below. The duty is paid by the purchaser of the securities, though in some cases, where, for example, he is acquiring a small or odd amount of shares at the request of the seller, he may recover the duty from the seller. The current rate of duty is 1% on the consideration. Where the consideration does not exceed £5 the duty is 5p, where the consideration exceeds £5 but does not exceed £100 the duty is 10p for every £10 or part of £10 of the commission. Where the consideration is between £100 and £300 it is 20p for every £20 or part thereof. If the consideration is above £300 the duty is 50p for every £50 or part thereof.

Under certain circumstances the 1% rate does not apply:

(*a*) In the case of securities which are exempt from stamp duty:

(1) British Government, corporation, public board and Commonwealth securities.

(2) American or Canadian securities passing by endorsement. The certificates for American and Canadian securities state the name of the registered holder on the face and have a form of transfer on the reverse. If this form is signed or endorsed by the registered holder, duly witnessed, and the remainder of the form left blank, entitlement to the certificate may pass by delivery in the same way as with bearer securities. So long as the buyer does not have the securities registered out of the name of the registered holder and into his own name, no transfer duty is payable on the transfer of these securities.

(3) Bearer securities are exempt from stamp duty on transfer, though they are charged with a bulk rate of duty when they are originally issued.

(4) All new issues of securities are free from transfer duty so long as they are still in the form of allotment letters or provisional certificates. Once the date for the issue of definitive certificates has passed any transfers will attract stamp duty.

(*b*) If a transaction in a registered security to which stamp duty is normally applicable is opened and closed within the same Account then no transfer duty is payable.

(*c*) In some cases the transfer is subject to a fixed stamp duty of 50p instead of the *ad valorem* charge. This occurs most commonly in transfers of shares representing a distribution under the terms of a will or liquidation and in cases where no beneficial interest in the shares passes (e.g. a transfer from one nominee of the transferer to another).

(iv) *Registration Fee*

This is a fee, normally 12½p, which many firms still charge to defray the cost of registering the purchaser in the register of members of the company. The Stock Exchange has recommended that existing companies should cease charging this fee, and currently only about half of the companies quoted on the Exchange still maintain the charge. Moreover, the general undertaking to which all companies seeking a quotation for their securities must adhere now requires them to register holders of these securities without charge. Thus in time the fee will disappear altogether, for as existing companies seek quotations for new securities they must adhere to the new requirements of the undertaking in respect of all of their securities.

(v) *Settlement Date*

The Stock Exchange year is divided for dealing purposes into twenty-four Accounts. Twenty of these last for a fortnight each, the remaining four, which cover the main public holidays of Easter, Whitsuntide, August Bank Holiday and Christmas, being of three weeks' duration. Each Account begins on a Monday, except where that day is a public holiday, and finishes on a Friday. All transactions performed within an Account must be settled by means of delivery of the stock and payment therefor on the following Settlement Day, which falls on a Tuesday, eleven days after the end of the Account.

In the example of a contract note reproduced above, the Account in which the purchase was made ran from Monday, August 23rd to Friday, September 3rd. Settlement Day was eleven days from the end of the Account, on Tuesday, September 14th, and the contract note specifies that the client must pay for the shares on that day, while the seller is bound to deliver them on that day.

Under certain circumstances settlement does not occur on Settlement Day:

(*a*) *'New Time' bargains* (Rule 96 (4) (a)). Bargains may be made on the last two days of an Account for completion on the Settlement Day of the following Account. In return for delaying delivery and payment in this way a jobber will normally charge a slightly higher selling price.

(*b*) *Delayed Delivery* (Rule 96 (4) (b) (i), (ii)). Delivery in completion of a bargain may be postponed by agreement when the bargain is made if and to the extent that additional time is required for the execution and transit of the necessary documents. Similarly, completion may be postponed at the request of a jobber by agreement when the bargain is made if he reasonably anticipates difficulty in obtaining the security which is the subject of the bargain.

(*c*) *Dealings for cash* (Rules 96 (4) (c), 97). Unless otherwise arranged, bargains in new issues passing by delivery in scrip form or by letters of renunciation are for cash. Dealings in British Government, corporation, public board and Commonwealth stocks are normally for settlement on the business day following the day of the bargain.

(*d*) *'Contangos'*. If a purchaser of shares wishes to defer payment until a Settlement Day subsequent to that on which payment is due, he may do so if his broker can find a seller of the shares who is prepared to delay receipt of the payment. Operations of this sort are arranged on the last day of an Account, known as Preliminary Contango Day and are confirmed on the first day of the next account, known as Contango Day. All contango operations must be effected at the 'Making-up' Price of the security which is fixed by the Share and Loan Department of the Stock Exchange on the basis of prices ruling at the close of business on the last day of the Account. Where no making-up price is fixed contangos must be effected at the existing market price.

The investor who wishes to delay payment, known as the 'giver', will pay contango interest to the seller who is deferring delivery, known as the 'taker'. A contango arrangement represents a bargain and requires a duly stamped contract note. No formal commission is charged, but the broker compensates himself by charging the 'giver' a rather higher rate of interest than that actually paid over to the 'taker'.

If, for example, the purchaser of shares in XYZ Ltd had carried over his purchase on September 3rd (Preliminary Contango Day) into the next account at a making-up price of 110p, and had taken up the shares at the end of the next account, namely September 17th for settlement on September 28th, he would receive the following statement of account from his broker:

For settlement September 14, 1971

Dr		£	Cr		£
Cost of shares in XYZ Ltd	(1)	511·47½	500 shares in XYZ Ltd carried over @ 110p	(2)	550·00
Contract Stamp	(3)	20	Stamp and fee	(4)	5·12½
Cheque	(5)	43·45			
		£555·12½			£555·12½

Dr   *For settlement September 28, 1971*

			£
500 shares in			
XYZ Ltd			
carried over			
@ 110p	(6)	550·00	
Interest 14 days			
@ 10%	(7)	2·11	
Stamp and Fee	(8)	5·62½	

£557·73½ (Amount due from client)

Notes: (1) Cost of shares plus expenses as per contract note.
      (2) Cost of shares carried over at making-up price of 110p.
      (3) Contract stamp on the contango contract note, based on the making-up price.
      (4) Credit in respect of transfer stamp and registration fee, which are not charged until the shares are taken up.
      (5) Cheque from the broker in respect of the difference due to the client on September 14th.
      (6) Cost of shares at making-up price brought forward.
      (7) Interest at 10% on £550 for fourteen days.
      (8) Charge in respect of registration fee and transfer stamp based on the price of 110p at which the shares are taken up.

(*e*) '*Backwardation*'. This is the exact opposite of a contango, and occurs in a bear market where there is a preponderance of sellers, who are prepared to pay a 'backwardation' charge to buyers to induce them to permit delayed delivery of the shares. The charge is normally expressed as an amount per share, rather than as a rate of interest.

From the contract note it will be seen that the total cost of the 500 shares in XYZ Ltd is £511·47½, representing an average cost per share of approximately 102½p. If the investor is to show a profit on these shares, he must sell them at a price which would, after deducting all expenses of the sale, exceed 102½p per share. If, in fact, the shares were sold at a price of 104p, the sale proceeds would be:

XYZ Ltd

		£
Sale of 500 Ordinary Shares of 50p		
each at 104p		520·00
	£	
Brokerage @ 1¼%	6·50	
Contract stamp	20	
	——	6·70
	Net proceeds	£513·30

Note: (1) No transfer stamp is charged in respect of a sale of shares.

(2) If the shares were bought and sold within the same Account no transfer stamp or registration fee would be charged in respect of the purchase, and the broker may, at his discretion, waive his commission on either the bought or the sold transaction.

In order that the shares may be sold at a profit they must rise in price by fourpence, which represents an increase of 4% on the original purchase price. This, however, ignores the effect of the jobber's turn. Although this is relatively small in the more competitive stocks, it must be taken into account, and it seems reasonable to suggest that shares in which there is a competitive market must rise in price by between 5% and 10% before they may be sold at a profit, unless they are bought and sold within the same Account. In the case of shares for which there is only a very thin market the jobber's turn is much more substantial and a rise in price of nearer 20% might be necessary if a profit is to be shown.

The Settlement Procedure between the Buying and Selling Broker

Under Rule 96 (2) the Settlement Period is defined as the seven business days ending on an Account Day and consists of

Contango Day	(Monday)
Making-up Day	(Tuesday)
Ticket Day	(Wednesday)
First Intermediate Day	(Thursday)
Second Intermediate Day	(Friday)
Third Intermediate Day	(Monday)
Account Day (or Settlement Day)	(Tuesday)

During this period the brokers representing the purchaser and seller in a particular transaction will be brought into contact with each other through the agency of the jobber who has handled the transaction. The selling broker will then deliver the shares and a signed transfer form to the buying broker, who will in return render payment for them. This process of identification is performed with the use of name tickets. The buying broker fills in a ticket with his name and details of the stock purchased and places it in the box of the jobber from whom he bought the stock. The jobber will then pass the ticket on to the broker from whom he bought the stock and the two brokers will complete the transaction on Settlement Day. The selling broker will credit the jobber with the surplus of the buying price over the selling price or will debit him if the selling price exceeds the buying price. In the case of stocks in which there are a large number of dealings, the Settlement Department will collect all the tickets and link them mechanically with selling brokers. There is currently a list, which is revised periodically, of about 200 of these Clearing House stocks.

The actual process of delivery and payment is performed by a computer in the Central Stock Payment Department. This system, which came into full operation on May 31, 1966, requires each firm to deliver its full commitments of stock each day to the Central Stock Payment Department. In return the firm will receive a single cheque in respect of the total value of the stock delivered. The Department will in turn be reimbursed by a single cheque from each firm which takes receipt of the stock. In this way the number of cheques passing hands in an Account is likely to be reduced to about 7,000, compared with a maximum of some 200,000 under the old system whereby firms made out a separate cheque in respect of each delivery of stock that was received. The cost of operating the Department is met by a quarterly *pro rata* charge levied on each firm in proportion to the total value of its deliveries.

The Registration of the New Member

On Settlement Day the stage has been reached where the buying broker is normally in possession of a share certificate relating to the shares which have been bought, together with a transfer form to effect the change of ownership of the shares, while the selling broker has received payment. It now merely remains for the selling broker to pay to his client the proceeds of the sale, less commission and contract stamp, and for the buying broker to effect the transfer of the shares into the name of his client.

Section 26 (2) of the Companies Act 1948 provides that every person who agrees to become a member, and whose name is entered in its register of members, shall be a member of the company. Thus a purchaser of shares in a company, although he is the legal owner of the shares from the date of purchase, is not regarded as a member of the company and is therefore not entitled to the rights of membership, until the shares are registered in his name in the register of members.

The procedure for effecting this transfer has been greatly simplified by the introduction of the New Transfer System. This was given legal effect by the Stock Transfer Act 1963, which applies to all fully paid-up registered securities.

The system is based on the use of a white Stock Transfer Form and, where necessary, an appropriate number of blue Brokers Transfer Forms. The Stock Transfer Form contains the instruction of the seller to the registrar of the company concerned to transfer the shares out of his holding as stated in the register of members of the company. Where the seller is present with his stockbroker when he gives selling instructions the broker will normally ask his client there and then to sign the Stock Transfer Form, and to hand over the share certificate or certificates relating to the shares to be sold. If this is not possible the broker will send the form, together with the contract note relating to the sale, as soon as the sale has been made, requesting his client to sign the form and return it immediately. The form at this stage will contain only the details of the shares to be transferred. Once it has been returned by the client the procedure will depend upon whether the whole of the shares represented by the certificates are being sold and whether they are being transferred to one purchaser or to several:

(i) *Where the Full Amount of the Shares are Transferred to One Buyer*

The selling broker will enter the amount of the consideration for the sale in the form, have it stamped by the Inland Revenue in respect of transfer duty and will pass it together with the share certificate to the buying broker, through the agency of the Central Stock Payment Department. This will be done immediately in the case of transactions for cash, or before the Settlement Day in the case of transactions done for the Account, and will constitute valid delivery of the stock which has been sold.

The buying broker having taken delivery of the form and the share certificate will insert the particulars of the buyer in the form and will send them with the registration fee where required to the registrar of the company concerned. The registrar checks the transfer form to see that its details are correct, cancels the old share certificate, and then reduces the holding of the transferor as recorded in the register of members or, where the whole of his shares are sold, erases him altogether from the register of members. Then he enters the transferee as a member in the register, or, where he is already a member, increases the amount of his registered share-holding. Finally, a new share certificate in respect of the appropriate number of shares is prepared, authorized by the directors, sealed, and sent to the purchaser. The registration procedure, which prior to the introduction of the new system often took three months or more, is now completed by many companies within a fortnight of the receipt of the transfer instrument.

Once the purchaser is the registered holder of the shares he is entitled in the eyes of the company to all the rights appertaining to those shares. He will thus be entitled to vote in respect of his shares, where such a right is given, and will receive dividends, and, where relevant, capitalization issues and any rights arising under rights issues. In order to facilitate the payment of dividends, most companies send a dividend mandate form to the purchaser, enabling him to authorize the company to pay his dividend direct to his bank. The company can then, when dividends are paid, bulk together all those shareholders who use the same bank and pay a single cheque to the bank, together with a list of the shareholders, dividend amounts and branches concerned.

(ii) *When Part of the Shares Represented by the Certificate are Sold to One Buyer*

On receipt of the signed form from his client the selling broker will enter the amount of the consideration and will have the form stamped by the Inland Revenue. In this case the broker will be unwilling to hand over the share certificate to the buying broker because it represents an amount of shares in excess of those which have been sold. In order to enable him to make a valid delivery it is necessary that the Stock Transfer Form should be certified, either by the Secretary of the Stock Exchange or by the registrar of the company concerned, to the effect that the transferor has a *prima facie* title to the shares which are to be transferred. In most cases the Secretary of the Stock Exchange will undertake the certification, stamping the top right-hand corner of the Stock Transfer Form with the words 'Certificate Lodged', whereupon the handing over of the form alone will constitute valid delivery. At the same time the Secretary will remit the share certificate to the registrar of the company so that it may be cancelled and a new certificate for the remaining balance of the shares eventually sent to the seller.

In certain circumstances the Secretary is unable to perform the certification process. This happens where there is no certificate against which the Stock Exchange can certify (e.g. where the certificate has been lost or where the seller, having himself purchased the shares recently, has not yet received a certificate), or where the title of the transfer to deal with the shares is not evident from the certificate (e.g. where the shareholder's name has been changed and the certificate still bears the old name). In these cases the certification must be carried out by the registrar of the company, who will mark

C

the Stock Transfer Form with the words 'Certificate Lodged' and return it to the selling broker, cancelling and retaining the share certificate. The selling broker on Settlement Day will deliver the form to the buying broker, who will insert the details of the buyer and submit the form to the registrar of the company. New share certificates will then eventually be prepared and sent to the purchaser and to the seller (in respect of the unsold portion of his certificate).

(iii) *Where All or Part of the Shares Represented by the Certificate are Sold to More than One Buyer*

In these circumstances there are special difficulties, for the selling broker is clearly unable to deliver his client's single share certificate to the several buyers. To surmount this problem Brokers Transfer Forms are used. The selling broker, on receipt of the signed Stock Transfer Form from his client, will cancel the lower part of the form, which relates to a sole purchaser, and fill in the details of the various sales in the space provided on the reverse of the form. He will then prepare a Brokers Transfer Form in respect of each sale, inserting details of the shares sold, the consideration therefor, and the particulars of the seller. Each form will be stamped by the Inland Revenue with the appropriate amount of transfer duty. The broker will then send all of the Brokers Transfer Forms, the Stock Transfer Form and the share certificate to the Secretary of the Stock Exchange, who will certify each of the Brokers Transfer Forms and return them to the selling broker. At the same time the Secretary will forward the Stock Transfer Form and the share certificate to the registrar of the company. The selling broker will be able to use the Brokers Transfer Forms to undertake valid delivery on Settlement Day to the appropriate buying brokers, receiving due payment in return. Each buying broker will then insert the details of his client on the relevant Brokers Transfer Form and will submit it to the registrar of the company concerned so that his client may receive a new share certificate. Where there is no certificate or the seller's title is not evident from the certificate, the certification procedure must be performed by the registrar of the company.

Under certain circumstances the New Transfer System is inappropriate:

(*a*) Where by law the old system must still apply. This occurs most often where partly paid shares or Government stock on the Post Office register are being transferred. On the sale, for instance, of a holding of partly paid shares, the selling broker will prepare a transfer deed, inserting particulars of the seller and the class and number of shares sold. The deed will be sent to his client who will sign it before two witnesses, whose signatures must be appended, and return it to his broker. If the holding is disposed of by way of several sales, then a separate transfer deed must be prepared in respect of each sale, and must be similarly signed and witnessed. Each separate deed should then be certified by the Secretary of the Stock Exchange or the registrar of the company.

The selling broker will then deliver the deed or the certified deeds to the buying broker or brokers in return for the due payment, after inserting details of the purchaser from the Name Ticket. The buying broker will send the transfer deed to his client for his signature, which must again be witnessed by two people. Once the deed has been returned by his client it will be submitted to the registrar of the company so that he may be registered as a member.

It is clear that this procedure is much more cumbersome than that of the new system, the main disadvantages being that the signature of the purchaser is required, that two witnesses are required both for the signature of the seller and for that of the purchaser, and that a separate transfer deed, involving the signatures of the seller, the purchaser, and up to four witnesses, is required for each component sale out of a particular block of shares.

(b) Where the shares being transferred are not registered securities. Transfer procedures which have so far been described are those relating to registered securities, the rights appertaining to which can only be secured by entry of the owner's name in the register of members of the company or, in the case of British Government securities, by entry in the Bank of England register or the Post Office register. Evidence of such ownership is provided by a share certificate or a stock certificate. There are, however, two other types of securities, namely inscribed securities and bearer securities. Holders of inscribed securities have no certificate of ownership, the only evidence of ownership being the entry in the register of owners maintained by the registration authority. If the holder wishes to transfer all or part of his holding it is necessary that he, or his representative appointed by power of attorney, should attend the offices of the registration authority and sign the register in the presence of a clerk of the authority. The selling broker will have received details of the purchaser from the buying broker. These details will be inserted in the register and the seller will then be required to sign a receipt for the purchase money. This receipt states that the seller has received a certain sum of money by way of consideration for the transfer to the purchaser of a particular amount of stock. The receipt is then handed over to the buying broker, thereby effecting delivery of the stock, and it is then passed on to the buyer who will already have paid for the stock on the appropriate settlement date. Before 1939 the bulk of British Government stocks were transferable in this way, but the enactment of the Government and Other Stocks (Emergency Provisions) Act in that year provided that all British Government stocks entered in the Bank of England register should be transferred in the same way as registered stocks. At the present time there are only a few inscribed Government stocks entered in the registers of some Commonwealth and foreign banks which are transferable in the manner described above. Holders of bearer securities, on the other hand, possess a share certificate which constitutes the only legal proof of entitlement, while the body which issued the certificate has no record at all of its owner. Consequently no registration is necessary and the title to the security can pass merely by physical delivery of the certificate concerned. However, under the Exchange Control Act, 1947, all bearer securities and shares passing by endorsement must be lodged with an 'Authorized Depositary', which title includes banks, members of the London and provincial stock exchanges, and solicitors. As a result, these securities must be transferred by means of a formal deed of transfer, which will be prepared on the Stock Exchange in the normal way and will effect the transfer of the security from the authorized depositary of the seller to that of the buyer. As the body responsible for issuing bearer securities is unaware of the names of its stockholders it is unable to pay interest or dividends to them, but must instead instruct the stockholders to claim the due payment from the issuing body or its agent. This is normally achieved by means of coupons, or talons, which are attached to the stock certificate and which entitle the person presenting the appropriate coupon to the dividend or interest payment to which it relates. The authorized depositary will normally undertake the responsibility of presenting the coupons on the due date on behalf of their client. The Exchange Control Act, 1947, also provides that 'except with the permission of the Treasury, no person shall, in the United Kingdom, and no person resident in the United Kingdom shall, outside the United Kingdom, issue any bearer certificate or coupon or so alter any document that it becomes a bearer certificate or coupon'. As the coupons for interest on existing bearer securities became exhausted after 1947, Treasury approval was required before new coupon sheets could be issued. As a result the bulk of bearer securities held in the United Kingdom are those issued by Commonwealth and foreign governments or companies.

Proposals for the Reform of the Settlement Procedure

In July 1970, the City Working Party on Securities Handling, under the chairmanship of Mr R. E. Heasman, published a report on settlement and transfer procedures. Its main recommendation was that the present fixed Account system should be replaced by a rolling ten-day settlement cycle. As a result bargains would be settled ten days after they were transacted thus providing an even flow of work for brokers and registrars.

In August 1971, an interim report on settlement procedure prepared for the Stock Exchange Council by the Directorate of Information Systems concluded that a new transfer system based on the proposals of the Heasman Committee was both practical and desirable. A fundamental feature of the proposed new system would be a centrally managed stock pool to simplify the settlement process. On completion of a bargain both the broker and the jobber would send details to a new centre where a computer would take over many of the subsequent steps necessary for the transfer of securities from one investor to another.

Such a system would involve radical changes from the current system. For instance, all market accounting would be with the centre, so that no tickets would need to be passed, all bought and sold documentation would be segregated and submitted to registrars by the centre, and all jobbers' accounting and stock dispositions would be carried out by the centre. The proposed system would be capable of operation under a daily, weekly or fortnightly Account, though the report of the Directorate decisively rejects a daily Account cycle. Instead it is proposed that dealers should be allowed to specify for settlement any day which falls within the rules of the Stock Exchange, though there should be a bias towards the standard Account cycle which is eventually selected.

It is predicted that the new system would reduce settlement costs, which are at present estimated at £21 m. per annum, and should facilitate the prompt delivery of stock, which is at present being delayed due to the sharp peaks of work for each fixed Account which must be dealt with in a short period of time and the huge volume of paperwork during prolonged periods of intense market activity.

Miscellaneous Matters

(i) '*Ex Div.*' and '*Cum Div.*'

Because there is a time lag between the purchase of shares on the Stock Exchange and the recognition of membership on the part of the company through registration in the register of members, it often happens that the company pays a dividend to a person who has already sold his shares. The normal procedure is for the company to close the register of members for some fourteen days before the date on which the dividend is paid. Thus share transfers received during that fortnight will not be entered in the register until after the dividend has been paid, and the dividend will only be paid to those shareholders entered in the register at the date of closure. Consequently, investors who have purchased shares in the company before the date of closure, but have not been registered before that date, and those who have acquired shares between the date of closure and the date of dividend payment, will be contractually entitled to the dividend. The dividend, however, will be paid to the seller and the purchaser will be faced with the problem of claiming the dividend from him.

In order to minimize this problem the Council of the Stock Exchange has provided that, for some time before the date of the dividend payment, securities should be transferred on an 'ex dividend' basis, whereby the vendor, not the purchaser, is entitled to the immediately forthcoming dividend. Rule 111 lays down that most shares will be quoted 'ex div.' on the first day of the Account whose Settlement Day is on or is the first following the date of closure of the register of members. As a result all purchases during that Account will be 'ex div.' for the purchasers could not possibly be registered in time to receive the dividend.

If a security is not quoted as 'ex div.' it is automatically sold 'cum div.', so that the purchaser acquires the right to receive the next dividend payment. When a security changes from a 'cum div.' quotation to an 'ex div.' quotation the effect will be to reduce the price of the share by the net amount of the imminent dividend, which by that date will have been declared. If a transfer which is made 'cum div.' is not registered before the date of closure and the seller receives the dividend to which the buyer is entitled, then the buyer will inform his broker who will request the selling broker to claim the dividend from the seller on behalf of his client. Similar provisions apply where a share is quoted 'ex cap.' and 'ex rights'. Shares which are sold 'ex cap.' do not entitle the purchaser to receive the forthcoming issue of bonus or capitalization shares, while a purchase on an 'ex rights' basis will not entitle the purchaser to any benefits emanating from a forthcoming rights issue.

(ii) 'Buying-in' and 'Selling-out'

If the selling broker is unable to deliver the securities which he has contracted to sell, then the purchasing broker may request the

Buying-in and Selling-out Department of the Stock Exchange to purchase the required block of securities on his behalf, charging the selling broker with any difference between the buying-in price and the original contract price. Under Rule 149 securities bought for the Account and undelivered may be bought-in as follows:

(a) Securities deliverable by transfer on or after the tenth day after the Account Day.

(b) Securities passing by delivery on or after the third business day after the Account Day.

Securities bought for cash or for a specified day and not delivered on the following day (in the case of purchases for cash) or on the specified day may be bought-in on the next or any subsequent day.

Normally buying brokers will hesitate before enforcing the buying-in rules, for the delay will often be due to factors outside the control of the selling broker, such as the death of his client or the loss of the transfer documents. The rules would thus only be invoked where it is clear that the seller is deliberately delaying delivery. This might occur where a speculative seller has taken a bear position and has sold securities which he does not possess in the expectation that their price will shortly fall, thus enabling him to acquire the securities required for delivery at a price lower than that which he receives. However, he may find that the price of the security rises, so that he has insufficient resources to meet his obligations, or there may not be a sufficient amount of the security forthcoming in the market to enable him to purchase enough to complete delivery. Under either of these circumstances the Buying-in and Selling-out Department would probably be requested by the buying broker to acquire the required securities at the best available price, charging the excess over the contract price to the selling broker, who will pass the cost on to his client.

Selling-out is a completely different operation, which is undertaken by a selling broker against a buying broker who has omitted to pass on a name ticket in respect of the shares purchased. Until he receives this ticket the selling broker cannot make delivery of the stock sold and receive payment for it. He is, therefore, entitled to request the Buying-in and Selling-out Department to require the buying broker to identify himself.

CHAPTER 3

The New Issue Market

The second major function of the London Stock Exchange is the provision of a capital market, where borrowers and lenders are brought together. Any would-be borrower, whether a government, a local authority, or a commercial company, may apply to the Stock Exchange for permission to offer securities to the public and to have those securities dealt in on the Exchange. Investors will be more prepared to acquire such securities than those which are not quoted on the market, because a quotation indicates first that the Council of the Stock Exchange have carefully examined the affairs of the borrower and secondly that the securities will have the advantage of marketability.

The Stock Exchange will not consider any application from a company for a quotation unless the expected market value of the company is at least £250,000 and the expected market value of any one security for which quotation is sought is £100,000.

THE MAIN CATEGORIES OF NEW ISSUES

(i) *Issue by Prospectus*

This constitutes an offer of securities by or on behalf of a company or any other authority to the general public at a fixed price. A condition of the offer is that the securities will be quoted on the Stock Exchange, and the objects of the issue will depend upon the nature of the issuing body. If it is a government or a public authority the object will be to raise funds, either for public expenditure or for the redemption of an existing commitment of the authority concerned. If the issue is made by a company then it will normally be prompted by one or more of the following motives:

(*a*) To raise funds to finance an expansion scheme.

(*b*) To raise funds to redeem existing securities of the company which have fallen due for redemption, or to reduce its overdraft commitments.

(*c*) In many cases a company has expanded under the management of a director who owns a majority shareholding in the company. As the managing director approaches retirement he may wish to sell all or part of his shareholding, partly to raise money for the future payment of estate duty and partly to obtain a stock market value for the remainder of his shares to facilitate their future liquidation and the calculation of the liability to estate duty. In these circumstances it is more usual for the issue to take the form of an offer for sale rather than an issue by prospectus.

Of the motives described above, only the first results in an increase in the physical investment in real assets by the company, and even in these cases there may be no increase in the national stock of real assets—as, for instance, where an investment trust expands by means of a new issue and uses the funds thus raised only to purchase existing securities. An issue of the latter sort and those motivated by the other two objectives need have no effect on the level of physical investment, for the proceeds are not used to acquire real assets but merely represent a transfer of money from the buyer either to the vendor or to the persons whose securities are to be redeemed. In fact, less than half of the money raised on the Stock Exchange as a result of new issues makes any contribution to the national rate of capital formation.

The normal procedure for an issue by prospectus is for the company or authority to employ an issuing house to advise on and organize the issue. The major issuing houses are represented by the Issuing Houses Association, which was formed in 1945 and which is composed of old merchant banks, such as Rothschilds and Lazards, the more recent acceptance houses, investment banks and financial trusts, such as the Charterhouse Investment Trust and the London and Yorkshire Trust, and some of the larger firms of stockbrokers.

In connection with the issue the issuing house will normally perform the following work:

(a) *Preliminary Investigation*

Because the issuing house is lending its name to the borrower or vendor and is thus giving the issue the stamp of respectability, it must investigate the affairs of the issuing body to ensure that it warrants such backing. If the issue is made on behalf of a government or a local authority the main object of the investigation is to ensure that the anticipated net revenue of the authority is more than adequate to cover the annual interest due on the stock which is to be issued.

In the case of new issues made on behalf of companies, the investigation into the affairs of the company must be far more comprehensive. The issuing house must satisfy itself that the company is strongly-based, has good prospects, is well-managed and is worthy of a Stock Exchange quotation. It will initially request full details of the financial history of the company, supported by audited copies of past profit and loss accounts and balance sheets. It would also require details of the management of the company, the current level of capital commitments, the scope for expansion and the specific uses to which the funds raised by the issue are to be put. If favourably impressed, it will send a representative to the company to obtain a first-hand impression of its management, reputation and prospects. His opinion will be reinforced by reports from financial contacts both in the City and in the vicinity in which the company operates. In this way an impression of the past performance, current reputation and future prospects of the company is created. If the result of these preliminary enquiries is favourable, then a more formal and intensive investigation is begun. A firm of accountants will be appointed to examine the accounts of the company for the past ten years, ascertaining that these have been prepared on a consistent basis, and that, in particular, stock and work-in-progress have been valued consistently. They will ensure that any non-recurrent profits or losses have been clearly indicated in the accounts and will report on the adequacy of the accounting and costing systems and the efficiency of the system of internal control. They will also make a realistic examination of the prospects of the company as forecast by its management.

An investigation of this sort will always be necessary if the company has not been known to the issuing house prior to the proposed issue. If, however, the company already has a Stock Exchange quotation and merely wishes to issue a further class of securities, the issuing house will already be familiar with the company and the investigation will be concentrated more on its present position and future outlook rather than on its past history.

If, as a result of its inquiries, the issuing house decides that the issue is worthy of its sponsorship then the formal organization of the issue will begin.

(b) *The Determination of the Class of Security to be Issued and the Price of the Issue*

The issuing house has a great deal of influence over the decision

74

regarding the class of security to be issued in order to raise the required amount of cash. It may well happen that a company is controlled by its managing director, who does not wish to relinquish any of his share in its equity and prefers to raise funds by means of an issue of fixed-interest securities. The issuing house, on the other hand, may feel that the state of the market is such that only an issue of equities would be successful and would probably insist that the issue take that form.

An interesting example of this factor was seen in August 1966 when the Ross Group offered £2 m. 8% Cumulative Preference Shares to its existing shareholders and debenture-holders at par. The object of the issue was to reduce its bank debts and finance its capital expenditure programme. Because of the non-deductibility of preference dividends in the determination of the company's corporation tax liability a gross amount of 13·3% would have to be earned on the capital to meet the dividend. An issue of 8% debentures, on the other hand, due to the deductibility of debenture interest for tax purposes, would only have required earnings of 8%. However, the merchant bank which organized the issue felt that the level of the existing borrowings of the group prevented an issue of debentures or loan stock, though it might have been argued that preference dividends, like debenture interest, are effectively fixed-interest commitments which should be taken into account in measuring the capital gearing of a company. Probably a more relevant factor was that preference dividends rank as franked investment income for tax purposes and are thus more acceptable to some classes of institutional investors. As a result the company issued preference shares rather than debenture stock.

Having decided the class of security which is most appropriate having regard to the circumstances of the company or issuing authority and the amount to be raised, the issuing house will determine the price at which the security is to be issued and the most suitable method of issue. For the purpose of this section it is assumed that an issue by prospectus is chosen. This type of issue is most appropriate for large capital-raising operations in view of the high level of expenses which is involved. The offer of securities is made nominally by the issuing company or authority on the advice of an issuing house, which receives a commission for its services. The distinguishing features of the other main methods of issue are described in the later sections of this chapter.

The determination of the price at which the securities are to be offered is probably the most controversial part of the whole operation. If the issue is of gilt-edged securities the terms can be determined relatively easily, for the size of the gilt-edged market is so great that there will invariably be an existing stock issued by a similar authority and with similar redemption terms. It will already have been decided whether the authority should issue a long-dated security, thus committing itself to the payment of current interest rates for a long period, or whether it would be better advised to borrow for the short-term in the hope that interest rates will fall so that further borrowing may be made at a lower rate of interest. If the issuing house ascertains that the gross redemption yield on a comparable stock is 9%, it might decide to offer a 9% stock at a price of £99 per £100 par value, thus offering a gross redemption yield of slightly more than 9%. It is necessary to offer a return which is rather higher than that available elsewhere in the market in order to encourage investors to apply for the stock, thus enabling the market to absorb the relatively large amount of stock which will be offered to the market in one day. A further inducement to the market to take up the stock is the use of instalment terms, as a result of which the purchase is spread over a period of some months. For instance an issue at a price of £99 might require a payment of £10 per £100 unit of stock on application, with a first call of £40 being made after three months and a second call of £49 after six months.

The major difficulty in determining the issue price of a gilt-edged security lies in the fact that the market is so volatile, and the issue terms so finely judged, that a relatively small change in the level of gilt-edged prices might occur between the date at which the issue price is determined and the date for which applications for stock are invited, thus rendering unrealistic the terms of the issue. This may lead to a heavy over-subscription if gilt-edged prices rise during the interim period, while a fall might cause the issue to be substantially under-subscribed.

The same problems apply to the determination of the price of fixed-interest securities issued by companies. The price will be largely determined by reference to the current yields on similarly dated existing stocks, issued on similar terms regarding security and by companies of comparable standing. In the same way, the issue price will be established at a level which provides a yield which is attractive in comparison with current yields and payment will normally be spread over a period of some months.

An issue of ordinary shares presents considerably more problems, largely because there are not usually many comparable companies so that it is difficult to establish an appropriate yield to determine the issue price. Moreover, as the market is smaller the shares will have a greater impact and will have to be made extremely attractive in order to induce their absorption.

It is, of course, extremely important both to the company and to the issuing house that an issue should be successful. If the issue is a failure this might affect the reputation of the issuing house, making it more difficult for it to place and to arrange underwriting for future issues. At the same time the failure would be bad publicity for the company whose shares are being offered. The success of the issue is thus essential and is sought by offering the shares at an attractive price, which is rather lower than that at which they are expected to settle once the issue has been absorbed by the market.

In addition to this bonus element which is consciously offered to applicants, there is often an unintended bonus where the issuing house underestimates the demand for the shares. This happens most often in cases where the company coming to the market cannot be satisfactorily compared with a company which is already quoted, either because it is in a small industry or because it is a household name, so that the likely response to the issue is difficult to estimate. When faced with this situation many issuing houses appear to have erred on the side of caution and have established issue prices which, while ensuring the success of the issue and maintaining the reputation of the issuing house, have been far below the price which investors were prepared to pay, with the result that the issuing company receives much smaller proceeds than would have been obtained had the issue price been more realistic.

This over-caution on the part of issuing houses has been in evidence since the boom in equity prices which gained impetus in 1958 and consistently during the period since that date there have been numerous examples of the under-estimation of the issue price and very few instances of its over-estimation. Peak periods of under-estimation appeared in 1961, 1963 and 1967. On May 12, 1961, for example, the list of market prices of recent issues in *The Times* included the following shares:

Issue price		*Market price on May 11, 1961*
23s 9d	Barro Investment	37s 0d
14s 0d	Centrovincial Estates	29s 6d
22s 0d	Empire Stores	42s 0d
11s 0d	W. D. Evans	14s 3d
20s 3d	Hammond (L.)	36s 3d
5s 0d	Hume Holdings	9s 7½d
13s 0d	Jaeger Holdings	20s 3d
6s 9d	Kennedy Leigh Properties	12s 6d
12s 0d	Penguin Books	16s 1½d
2s 10½d	Steel and Glover	4s 6d
9s 0d	Tonibell	24s 0d

Most of the above issues were made direct to the public and it soon became obvious that riskless and tax-free profits could easily be made by applying for shares in new issues and selling them when dealings started at a higher price. Such applicants, who are known as stags, had no intention of holding the shares as an investment, but merely wanted to make a quick profit. As a result many issues were vastly over-subscribed, causing more work for the issuing house. Moreover, most long-term investors had to buy shares when dealings commenced and had to pay far more than the original issue price for their shares, while the issuing company received much less than investors were prepared to pay for its shares.

Between November 1960 and April 1961 the following over-subscriptions occurred:

M. Samuel	over-subscribed	65 times
Jaeger Holdings	over-subscribed	47 times
Tonibell	over-subscribed	138 times
Keith Prowse	over-subscribed	77 times
Kennedy Leigh Properties	over-subscribed	58 times
Centrovincial Estates	over-subscribed	50 times
Penguin Books	over-subscribed	150 times

Even higher levels of over-subscription occurred during 1963 with the offer of shares in Headquarters and General Supplies Ltd being over-subscribed 177 times. At the time it was commented by *The Times* that heavy over-subscription is not a measure of success, but an indication that the issue has been made too cheaply.

The original economic argument in favour of stags was that they enable the market to absorb large issues of shares by holding them for the short-term until sufficient investors have come forward to take them off their hands. It was argued that the profit which they made remunerated them for the performance of this function. This argument is now largely obsolete partly because of the relatively small size of most equity issues and partly because there are more than sufficient funds available for applications under all but the most depressed conditions.

In recent years, then, there has been considerable criticism of stags on the following grounds:

(1) By causing heavy over-subscription they increase the administrative work involved in an issue.

(2) The applications of genuine investors may be turned down and they will have to buy shares when dealings start at a price which gives a gratuitous profit to stags.

(3) The company whose shares are being sold will receive an amount lower than that at which the market values them.

(4) Members of the general public have become aware of the profits to be made from stagging operations. Consequently, whenever an issue appears to have been under-priced, individual applicants, knowing that in the event of an over-subscription they are unlikely to receive all the shares for which they apply, send in a vast number of applications, each accompanied by a cheque, in the expectation that they would receive only as many shares as they could afford. The greater the level of over-subscription expected by the public, the greater the number of multiple applications—with the result that the issue becomes still more heavily over-subscribed.

Because of the abuse of the new issue system by stags certain steps have been taken to discourage their activities:

(1) Many issuing houses state in the prospectus advertising the issue that multiple applications will be totally rejected. It was discovered in one new issue that an individual had made over 300 separate applications for shares, while at the height of the craze there were reports of schoolmasters directing classes of children to fill in application forms and of students being employed on a paid basis to complete applications. This remedy merely tested the ingenuity of the stags and resulted in a proliferation of pseudonyms and new bank accounts.

(2) In a few cases the issuing house has warned applicants that all cheques accompanying applications may be presented to the bank for payment. This, however, adds further time to the procedure for the allotment of shares and also leads to the criticism that the issuing house will have the use of applicants' money for a short period during which time it might well earn a material amount of interest for itself. In any case, in the few issues where the cheques of all applicants were cashed it was found that the vast majority of them were genuine—an indication of the extent of money available for stagging operations.

(3) In April 1962, the short-term Capital Gains Tax was introduced primarily as a result of public criticism of the tax-free profits made by stags and property speculators. This measure seems to have had little effect upon the extent of stagging operations, partly because a profit that is subject to tax is better than none at all, and partly because as the level of revenue arising out of the short-term Capital Gains Tax would suggest, the Inland Revenue has no means of enforcing the disclosure of stagging profits.

(4) The most successful method of discouraging stags has been

the use of issues of shares by tender, which are described in a later section. The main object of such issues is to attempt to secure for the issuing company at least a part of the excess of the eventual market price over the issue price.

(c) *The Procedure for Obtaining a Stock Exchange Quotation*

If the issue is to be successful it is obvious that a Stock Exchange quotation must be obtained to enable the shares to be dealt in on the market, thus giving them the advantage of marketability. Application for a quotation must be made to the Share and Loan Department of the London Stock Exchange, whose Committee on Quotations will fully investigate the issue and decide whether it is worthy of a quotation.

The quotation requirements for a company, none of whose securities are already quoted, are reproduced in full in the appendix to this chapter. Applications must be submitted at least fourteen days before the date on which the issue is to be announced and must be accompanied by copies of the prospectus, which invites applications from the public for the securities, and various other documents, such as the Memorandum and Articles of Association of the company. The Share and Loan Department, on the basis of the information provided by the company, will investigate the issue having regard to the standing of the company, the genuineness of its profits, the safeguards provided for the interests of shareholders and the reputation of all connected with the offer. If the issue is approved, whether outright or subject to certain alterations in the terms of issue, it may proceed and the prospectus will be published in at least two daily newspapers.

Once the prospectus has been published at least two days must elapse before a formal application for a quotation is made to the Committee on Quotations. The delay is deemed necessary to allow any member of the public who wishes to give evidence to contact the Share and Loan Department after reading the prospectus. If the application is granted the issuing company must sign a general undertaking to provide certain information for its shareholders and the Stock Exchange, and must, on the completion of the issue, give full details of the way in which the shares have been allocated between the applicants therefor.

The procedure for issues by companies, some or all of whose securities are already quoted, and by authorities other than companies is broadly similar.

The fees payable in respect of a quotation are laid down in

Schedule X to Appendix 34 of the *Rules and Regulations of the Stock Exchange*. At the time of writing they range from nil (for quotations granted below £5,000 money value) to 5,000 guineas (for quotations granted above £75 m. money value). There is also an annual quotation charge of 100 guineas per company.

(d) *Prospectus*

A prospectus is defined by section 455 of the Companies Act 1948 as 'any prospectus, notice, circular, advertisement or other invitation offering to the public for subscription or purchase any shares or debentures of a company'. Under the rules laid down by the same Act all prospectuses must be registered with the Registrar of Companies and must adhere to the statutory requirements as to disclosure as set out in the Fourth Schedule of the Act.

The quotation requirements of the London Stock Exchange contain additional provisions relating to disclosure in a prospectus. In the case of an issue by prospectus, the prospectus must be approved by the Share and Loan Department, published in two leading London daily newspapers, and drawn up in accordance with the Stock Exchange rules as to the contents of a prospectus, which are reproduced in Appendix II. These rules are in many ways more rigorous than those of the Companies Act and are more positive in that they are aimed more at the provision of material for investment analysis than at the mere protection of the investor from fraudulent promotions.

The preparation of the prospectus by the issuing house will be a relatively straightforward operation, for most of the information required will have been obtained first by the accountants who investigated the company and secondly by the issuing house itself in the course of its initial inquiries. All that is now required is to ensure that the prospectus, when drawn up and advertised, conforms with the requirements of both the Companies Act and the Stock Exchange.

In general a prospectus will contain the following relevant information for an investor:

(1) The names, addresses and qualifications of the directors, secretary, bankers, solicitors, auditors, brokers and registrar of the company.

(2) Details of the history, business and management of the company.

(3) Its prospects, expected profits and dividends.

(4) An accountants' report containing a table of the profits for the previous ten years, a statement of the net assets at the date of the

81

most recent balance sheet, and details of such matters as commitments for capital expenditure.

(5) Statutory and general information relating to the detailed organization of the issue, any contracts made by the company during the previous two years outside its normal course of business, and relevant extracts from its articles of association.

(6) The prospectus may also contain an application form on which an investor may apply for the shares which are to be sold.

On the basis of the information contained in the prospectus an investor can decide whether the shares are being offered at a generous price. Particular regard must be had to the quality of the management, whether the existing directors have contracted to stay in office, the purpose of the issue, the trend of past profits, the capital and asset structure, the proportion of the total equity being retained by the vendors and the probable prospects of the company. In addition to forming his own opinion an investor should also take note of the assessment of the issue made by the financial Press. These assessments are not normally very detailed, but they do stress the most important factors and are extremely influential. A major influence is their forecast of the likely price at which dealings in the security will commence. These forecasts tend to be self-inducing, for a prediction of an opening dealing price which stands at a considerable premium above the issue price tends to encourage stagging, which causes oversubscription and thus encourages the predicted premium when dealings commence.

Where securities are issued by a government, municipality, local authority, or a statutory body other than a registered company, the contents of the prospectus, as required by the Stock Exchange, are considerably less detailed. The main feature of the required contents is the information relating to the rights of the security-holders and the revenue and capital against which the security is charged.

(e) *Underwriting*

Under the Companies Act a prospectus issued by a company must state the minimum subscription which is necessary to enable the company to carry out the project in respect of which the issue is being made. Furthermore Section 47 of the Act provides that where any *share capital* of a company is *first* offered to the public for subscription, no allotment shall be made unless the amount stated in the prospectus as the minimum subscription has been subscribed, and the sum payable on application for the amount so stated has been paid to and received by the company. If the minimum subscription has not been subscribed within forty days after the first issue of the prospectus, all money received from applicants for shares must be forthwith repaid to them without interest.

The minimum subscription is now relatively unimportant, for it only applies where the share capital of a company is being offered both for the first time and direct to the public by means of an issue by prospectus. Such issues are extremely rare, for companies making such issues normally use the offer for sale method of issue.

Although the minimum subscription is largely a legalistic irrelevance, the risk of the failure of an issue is still very considerable. If a failure were to occur the company would find itself committed to pay the heavy issue expenses without receiving the expected proceeds from the issue. To avoid this the issuing house will arrange for the issue to be underwritten. Various financial institutions will contract to take a specified proportion of any part of the offer which is not subscribed by the public. In return for this service they will receive an underwriting commission, normally amounting to between 0·25% and 3% of the cost of the shares underwritten. Consequently, if the issue is under-subscribed, the underwriters will purchase the securities for which applications have not been received and the issuing house thus ensures that all of the available securities are sold.

It has already been argued that it is important for an issuing house to have a reputation for successful issues so that it will be easier for it to find institutions which are prepared to underwrite its issues. In recent years, however, it has been most uncommon for issues of ordinary shares to fail, largely because the issuing houses have ensured their success by generous estimation of the issue price, and, as a result, the underwriters have done little to earn their commission. On the other hand, issues of fixed-interest securities, because their price is so finely calculated, have often been unsuccessful, with a large proportion of many issues under-subscribed and left with the underwriters. Nevertheless the rates of underwriting commission charged in respect of equity issues are normally rather higher than those for the issues of fixed-interest securities. It might be argued that this is justified by the greater risk inherent in equities, in that the opening price of a new issue might be substantially lower than the issue price at which the underwriters are committed to buy in the event of an under-subscription. The market in fixed-interest securities, however, is much less volatile, and though there is more risk of the failure of an issue, there is not likely to be a very great difference between the market price and the price at which the underwriter may be required to take up the security.

Despite these arguments, it is still suggested that in the case of equity issues the underwriters provide little service at a relatively high expense, having regard to the fact that the issue price is normally set at a very generous level. In these circumstances the underwriters run a minimal risk and it might be argued that their commission might similarly be of a minimal amount.

(f) *The Allotment of Securities*

The prospectus gives full details of the procedure for applications, including the amount to be paid on application, the minimum amount of securities for which applications will be considered, and the closing date for applications. Normally equity issues are made on a cash basis and a cheque for the full cost of the number of shares required must accompany the application. Issues of fixed-interest securities, however, are normally issued on an instalment basis, partly because they tend to be larger than equity issues so that the market needs a greater inducement to absorb them and partly because the basic unit of the issue is much larger, usually £100.

The application lists will open and close on a day stated in the prospectus, usually a few days after the date of its publication. If the issue is a popular one more than sufficient applications will have been received by the date of the opening of the lists, and they will be closed immediately with the issue over-subscribed. When an over-subscription occurs the issuing house has the problem of allotting the available securities between the applicants. In doing this it must ensure that a sufficiently large number of applicants receive securities for a ready market to exist when dealings commence and that the allotments are made in marketable quantities. With these objects in mind the normal basis of allotment in the event of an over-subscription is for large applications to be scaled down (usually to the nearest hundred), while a certain number of small applications, selected by ballot, are accepted in full. Thus, in the case of an equity issue, there will be a large number of shareholders and, if the minimum number of shares which may be applied for is one hundred, all of them will have a marketable holding of shares of a hundred or a multiple thereof.

The successful applicants will receive renounceable allotment letters stating the number of shares which have been allotted to them, together with a cheque in respect of any part of their application which was unsuccessful, while those who were totally unsuccessful will have their cheque returned to them together with a letter of regret. The allotment procedure must be completed very quickly—normally within a couple of days—so that the successful applicants receive their letters of allotment before dealings in the shares commence. The start of dealings will be about a week after the closing date for applications. The allotment letter must be surrendered for a definitive share certificate on a date specified, normally about two months after the start of dealings. During the interim period the holder of an allotment letter may sell his shares by renouncing his entitlement in favour of the buyer or split them by renouncing part and retaining part. Any dealings that take place will be free of stamp duty and registration fee. At the end of the specified period the persons who ultimately hold the allotment letters will surrender them to the registrar of the company, who will compile the register of members from the letters and issue share certificates to the members.

(ii) *Offer for Sale*

The only substantial difference between an issue by prospectus and an offer for sale lies in the manner in which the issuing house is remunerated for its services. In the former case, a direct fee is charged against the issuing company based upon the size of the issue and the complications involved in its supervision. In an offer for sale, however, the issuing house purchases from the company the shares which are to be offered to the public and itself invites applications for those shares at a slightly higher price. The difference between the offer price and the price at which they are acquired from the company represents the remuneration of the issuing house. Out of this remuneration the issuing house will meet some or all of the subsidiary expenses connected with the issue, such as underwriting commission and the cost of advertising the prospectus.

(iii) *Placing*

A placing is defined by the Stock Exchange[1] as 'the sale by an Issuing House or Broker to their own clients of securities which have previously been purchased or subscribed'. Each issuing house has a list of large private and institutional investors who are prepared to subscribe for any securities which are issued in this manner. As with other methods of issue the subscription price is fixed at a level somewhat below the anticipated market price, so that there is usually considerable competition for places on these placing lists. At the same time, the issuing houses appreciate the advantages of being able to place shares smoothly in this way and will endeavour to

[1] *Admission of Securities to Quotation* (Committee of the Federation of Stock Exchanges in Great Britain and Ireland, 1966), p. 4.

ensure the success of the issue by carefully vetting the company concerned and offering generous subscription terms.

The main advantage of this method of issue lies in its relative cheapness, ignoring the cost implicit in the difference between the market value and the issue price. Many of the main items of expense which are necessary for an issue by prospectus or an offer for sale are avoided. For example, neither underwriting commission nor the expenses of administering the applications and allotment procedure need to be incurred, for the issuing house will itself allocate the shares to the investors of its choice. A further economy lies in the fact that the Stock Exchange requirements relating to the contents of the prospectus and its advertisement are less onerous in the case of placings. The basic requirements in this respect are as follows:

(a) In the case of placings or introductions (see below) of United Kingdom securities it shall be sufficient for the prospectus to be published in one leading London daily newspaper only, provided abridged particulars appear in a second such newspaper.

(b) In the case of placings or introductions of fixed interest securities (other than those having equity conversion rights) denominated solely in a foreign currency, it shall be sufficient for abridged particulars to be published in one leading London daily newspaper only, provided that the advertisement indicates that further particulars are contained in the new issue cards circulated by the Exchange Telegraph Company Ltd and Moodies Services Ltd.

Moreover, the above requirements may be modified where UK securities are concerned if the Stock Exchange feels that the publication of abridged particulars alone will provide sufficient protection for investors.

Section 39 of the Companies Act, 1948 provides a similar relaxation of the prospectus requirements of the Fourth Schedule:

(1) Where:

(a) It is proposed to offer any shares in or debentures of a company to the public by a prospectus issued generally (that is to say, issued to persons who are not existing members or debenture holders of the company); and

(b) Application is made to a prescribed stock exchange for permission for those shares or debentures to be dealt in or quoted on that stock exchange;

There may, on the request of the applicant, be given by or on behalf of that stock exchange a certificate of exemption, that is to say, a certificate that having regard to the proposals (as stated in the request) as to the size and other circumstances of the issue of shares or debentures and as to any limitations on the number and class of persons to whom the offer is to be made, compliance with the requirements of the Fourth Schedule would be unduly burdensome.

(2) If a certificate of exemption is given, and if the proposals aforesaid are adhered to and the particulars and information required to be published in connection with the application for permission made to the Stock Exchange are so published, then a prospectus giving the particulars and information aforesaid in the form in which they are so required to be published is to be deemed to comply with the requirements of the Fourth Schedule.

Although the placing method is normally regarded as advantageous for the issuing company it has not been favourably received by the investing public. This is primarily due to the fact that the securities available are only offered to a select group of investors, who alone will reap the benefit of the differential between the anticipated market price and the issue price. As a result the Stock Exchange will only allow the placing method to be used where it is felt either that the issue is too small to justify the expenses entailed in a public issue or that it is unlikely to arouse much interest among the general public.

When a placing of securities is permitted the quotation requirements of the Stock Exchange are designed to ensure that an adequate market exists in those securities when dealings commence. In the first place it is laid down that at least 35% of the issued amount of equity capital or securities convertible into equity capital and at least 30% of the issued amount of fixed income securities should be placed. Furthermore it is required that of the amount placed not less than 25% of equity capital or securities convertible into equity capital and 20% of other securities should be made directly available to the market. In the case of fixed-interest securities, where the amount placed lies between £1 m. and £5 m., 10% of the amount placed should be initially offered to the market, and the balance (though not more than £250,000) should be at the call of the market until noon on the next business day after the advertised particulars appear in the Press.

A further safeguard is that a quotation will not be granted until the securities have actually been placed. The issuing house will prepare a marketing statement which specifies the manner in which the securities have been allocated to its clients and to the market. Only if the Stock Exchange is satisfied that this allocation has led to the creation of a satisfactory market will a quotation be granted.

(iv) *Issue by Tender*

This method of issue was used extensively by water boards for the issue of fixed interest capital, but it was not until June 1961, when Kleinwort, Benson Ltd, adopted it for an issue of ordinary shares in Parway Land and Investments Ltd, that it was used for an equity issue. The main feature of this method is that the public are invited to apply for the available securities at or above a certain minimum price. In this way it is hoped that investors will offer to buy the securities at or just below the anticipated market price, with the result that the differential between the ultimate market price and the issue price is minimized to the benefit of the issuing company. This method is particularly appropriate in the cases explained earlier where the differential is likely to be high.

An example, which is very much over-simplified, particularly with reference to the factors which determine the issue price, will illustrate the basic features of the issue by tender. It is assumed that a large private company wishes to be floated on the London Stock Exchange. The issuing house ascertains that the company is likely to have £60,000 available for dividends each year and estimates that the current dividend yield on a comparable share is 6%. This would place a total market value of £1 m. upon the company. The issued capital of the company is 800,000 ordinary shares of £1 nominal value and all of these shares are to be offered to the public. The market value of each share would therefore be

$$\frac{£1,000,000}{800,000} = 125\text{p}$$

In order to ensure the success of the issue this price might be reduced to 120p, thus securing for the vendors an amount of

$$800,000 \times 120\text{p} = £960,000.$$

However, the issuing house might feel that their estimate of the appropriate market yield is very uncertain and that an issue by tender might be more suitable for the flotation. Thus a prospectus would be issued inviting applications for shares at or above a minimum price of, say, 120p. Applicants would then have to make their own assessment of the ultimate market price of the shares and would submit applications at a somewhat lower price. When all of the applications have been received they are tabulated in order to ascertain the number of shares which have been applied for at different prices. For the hypothetical issue described above the table of applications might appear as follows:

THE NEW ISSUE MARKET

Table of Applications

Price p	Total shares applied for	Number of applicants
250	10,000	10
237½	20,000	10
225	20,000	15
212½	30,000	20
200	40,000	25
187½	60,000	30
175	80,000	35
162½	90,000	45
157½	100,000	45
155	110,000	50
152½	120,000	55
150	120,000	60
	800,000	400
145	130,000	70
140	130,000	100
137½	140,000	130
	1,200,000	700
135	200,000	140
132½	240,000	150
130	300,000	150
127½	200,000	100
125	150,000	80
122½	100,000	70
120	10,000	10
	2,400,000	1,400

From the table it can be seen that 1,400 applications were received for a total of 2·4 m. shares, so that the issue was subscribed three times. On the basis of this table the issuing house must decide the price at which allotment will be made to all applicants for shares at or above that price. It should be noted that all allottees will receive shares at the same price, regardless of the fact that they may have offered considerably more than that price. The issuing house could choose to allot the shares at 150p, so that the 400 applicants at or above that price would receive in full the shares for which they had applied. However, the Stock Exchange rules require that the Share and Loan Department must be satisfied as to the procedure for determining the price and basis of allotment in the case of offers by tender, and it might be felt that an initial body of only 400 shareholders would not provide a sufficiently broad market for the commencement of dealings in the shares. Consequently, the allotment price might be established at $137\frac{1}{2}$p, at which level there would be 700 shareholders, each of whose applications had been scaled down by one-third.

With an allotment price of $137\frac{1}{2}$p the vendors would receive $800,000 \times 137\frac{1}{2}$p = £1·1 m., representing an increase of £140,000 over the anticipated proceeds of an offer for sale at 120p per share. It may well be that the market will value the shares on the basis of a 5% dividend yield when dealings start. This would place a value of £1·2 m.

$$\left(\text{i.e. } \frac{60,000}{5} \times 100 \right)$$

on the company and would induce a market price of 150p

$$\left(\text{i.e. } \frac{£1,200,000}{800,000} \right)$$

per share. Thus the original allottees would receive a premium of $12\frac{1}{2}$p. However, the potential differential between the dealing price of 150p and the proposed issue price of 120p was as much as 30p and the adoption of the method of offer by tender has secured $17\frac{1}{2}$p of that differential per share for the vendor company.

Despite its relative cheapness, the offer by tender has been ignored by many issuing houses. One argument which has been propounded against this method is that it is derogatory to the dignity of the City. Other adversaries claim that the determination of the application price is left to the uninformed public rather than to the City experts. However, this only suggests that more information should be made available to the investing public. Moreover, there is no evidence that prices established by this method prove in the long run to have been any more unrealistic than prices determined by other methods of issue.

Probably the most potent argument of its opponents is that this method does not create the same interest and public response as the offer for sale. Certainly many stags are deterred by the difficulty of assessing an appropriate price at which to tender, for there is the constant fear that if too many investors tender at an extremely high level in order to ensure the success of their applications, this might lead to an artificially high allotment price and a consequent loss for the allottees on the commencement of dealings.

However, the deterrence of stags does not represent a very great loss to the market for their undignified scramble for shares in many issues has been a most unpleasant feature of dealings in recent years.

At the same time the opportunity of large risk-free gains given to the most ephemeral investors due to the under-pricing of many issues has led to a philosophy of investment far removed from that which the Stock Exchange should aim to encourage.

(v) *Introductions*

An introduction is different from other new issues in that it does not have as its primary object the sale of shares in the company. The major function of an introduction is to enable a company whose shares are already fairly widely held to obtain a Stock Exchange quotation. The prospectus requirements of the Stock Exchange for such an issue are similar to those for a placing and similarly the company must convince the Committee of Quotations that provision has been made for the establishment of a free market in its shares. For this to be achieved not only must there be a relatively large number of existing shareholders, but also sufficient shares must be made available to jobbers for the creation of an adequate market. The normal procedure will be to give jobbers an option on a certain number of shares at a stated price, with a further option on an additional number of shares at a rather higher price. In this way any immediate surge of demand in the shares can be satisfied.

The main advantage of an introduction is that it confers the benefit of marketability upon the shares of a company. As a result they have an easily ascertainable market value which can be used as the basis of a sale or for the determination of estate duty. Moreover, this market value would tend to be higher than that which would obtain if the company were unquoted, because its shares would be more easily realizable by a purchaser.

Probably the bulk of introductions on the London Stock Exchange consist of companies which are already quoted on a provincial or overseas exchange and in whose shares a market already exists. Many private companies first become public through admission to quotation on the provincial exchange which is nearest to their centre of operations. This is because interest in their shares is limited and their shareholders predominantly originate from the immediate vicinity. As the company expands and public interest increases, so the range of shareholders will broaden and a London quotation will be sought to provide a wider market in order to serve their interests.

Like a placing, an introduction is much less expensive than other types of issue if the differential between the dealing price and the option price given to the jobbers is ignored. The expenses of underwriting and supervising the application and allotment procedure are

91

avoided, while advertising costs are kept to a minimum. Moreover, even the price differential is likely to be relatively narrow if the company is already quoted on a provincial exchange, for the existing market price on that exchange will give an indication of the price to be expected when dealings begin on the London Exchange.

(vi) *Rights Issues*

A rights issue is an issue of securities for cash, applications for which are invited only from the existing shareholders of a company. It is thus only appropriate for a company whose shares are already both quoted and widely held. Such an issue is relatively inexpensive, for the only advertising expenses are those of sending to each share-holder a letter of rights indicating the number of shares for which he is entitled to apply and informing him of the procedure for payment. The entitlement of each shareholder is determined on a proportionate basis by the number of existing shares which he holds. Moreover, the management of applications and allotments is a much less cumbersome operation, because the number of applications will be limited. Other expenses, such as underwriting and the commission of the issuing house, will, however, still be incurred.

One major expense which is avoided is the differential between the dealing price and the issue price. Where any of the other methods of issue are used this differential will represent a loss either, in the case of a company which is newly admitted to quotation, to the initial vendors of the shares, or, in the case of a company which is already quoted and is offering new shares to the public, to the existing share-holders who are being required to admit new shareholders on beneficial terms.

Strangely enough, it is in the case of a rights issue, where a price differential or bonus is most commonly thought to exist, that its effect is most illusory. This illusion stems from the fact that shares are normally made available in a rights issue at a price materially lower than the current market price of the shares of the company. Consequently, the shareholders are able to sell on the market their 'rights', or their entitlement to the new shares, without disturbing their existing holding of shares. It is thus often thought that the existence of these saleable 'rights' represents a bonus for the shareholders.

However, it is clear that no bonus, in the true sense of the word, can exist. For example, a company which has a share capital of 2,000,000 shares of £1 nominal value and a market value of 150p each, may decide to raise £500,000 by means of a rights issue, whereby each shareholder in respect of every four shares which he holds is entitled to apply for one new share at par. Thus 500,000 shares will be made available at £1 each. A shareholder who owns 20,000 shares will be entitled to apply for 5,000 of the new shares and will have four alternatives open to him:

(a) He may decide to sell his entitlement to the new shares on the market. This may be done by renouncing in favour of the purchaser the letter of rights which he has received from the company. The purchaser is thus given the right to subscribe for 5,000 shares at par. Other things being equal, the price which he will be prepared to pay for the rights will be determined as follows:

Market value of company before issue: 2,000,000 @ 150p	£3,000,000
Cash raised by the issue: 500,000 @ £1	500,000
New total market value of the company	£3,500,000
Divide by the new number of shares	2,500,000

New market price $= £1 \cdot 4 = 140p$

For the right to acquire 5,000 shares at £1 each the purchaser would thus be ready to pay 40p per share, which would give a total payment of £2,000. It is normal to calculate the market value of the rights on the basis of the old shares. Each of the old shares would entitle the holder to one-quarter of a new share, so that the market value of the rights would be quoted as 10p per share. The total value of the rights would still be the same at $20,000 \times 10p = £2,000$.

The shareholder has thus made a gain of £2,000, without disturbing his existing holding. However, his failure to take up his rights will have two effects. In the first place, his percentage stake in the company will have fallen from 1% (20,000 shares out of 2,000,000) to 0·8% (20,000 shares out of 2,500,000). If he had wished to maintain his proportionate interest he would have had to apply for the full amount of shares available to him. Secondly, the market value of his old shares would have fallen from £30,000 (20,000 @ 150p) to £28,000 (20,000 @ 140p), representing a loss of £2,000. This loss would exactly balance his gain from the sale of the rights, so that he would effectively have sold £2,000 worth of his original holding.

(b) He may decide to take up the full amount of new shares to which he is entitled. His new holding would be as follows:

Number of Shares	Original Value	New Value	Gain or Loss
20,000	£30,000	£28,000	−£2,000
5,000	5,000 (cost)	7,000	+£2,000
25,000	£35,000	£35,000	—

As a result of taking up the new shares the shareholder would have effectively invested a further £5,000 in the company. The bonus that is commonly supposed to exist in the pricing of the new shares is balanced by the fall in value of the old shares, so that in reality there is no bonus whatsoever.

(c) In the two alternatives described so far the shareholder has either effectively decreased or increased his investment in the company. However, if he does not wish to realize part of his investment or to add to it he may sell such a proportion of his rights as will give him enough cash to take up the remainder.

Thus, he might sell his right to subscribe to 3,572 shares at a price of 40p per share, giving a total of £1,428·80. This money could then be used to take up the remaining 1,428 shares (5,000−3,572) to which he is still entitled. After this operation he will own 21,428 shares, each of which has a market value of 140p, giving a total value for the holding of £29,999·20p. As a result he has maintained the market value of his holding (ignoring the realization of 80p), though not his percentage share in the company. Instead of undertaking such a precisely calculated operation, the investor could, of course, sell any proportion of his rights that he wishes, while retaining the right to take up the remainder.

(d) The final alternative would be to allow the rights to lapse, thus neither selling them nor taking up any of the shares to which he is entitled. In the example above this would, of course, be foolish, for it would result in a fall in value of the original holding without any compensating gain from the sale of the rights. However, it may happen that the price of the new shares was fixed rather closely to the original market price and that, by the time payment is due for the new shares, the original price has fallen below the offer price. Very few shareholders would take up their rights in this case, and there would be no market for the sale of the rights. Consequently, the issue would be a failure, and it is to avoid this that the underwriting of rights becomes necessary. However, companies can avoid this risk and thus the need for underwriting by setting the issue price substantially lower than the current share price.

The effect of a rights issue on the market price of the shares of a company has so far been considered in a purely theoretical fashion. There are, however, many important market factors which might prevent the attainment of the theoretical equilibrium. In the first place, many shareholders will sell their rights, and the consequent flow of shares on to the market will have a depressive effect upon the share price. Moreover, the response of the market to the factors which have motivated the issue must be taken into account. If it is anticipated that the injection of new capital into the company will not only enable highly profitable projects to be undertaken, but will also enhance the profitability of the existing capital, then the share price may well exceed the theoretical equilibrium. On the other hand, the market may regard the issue as indicative of financial difficulty for the company and may take an extremely pessimistic view of the probable effect of the new capital upon profits. In this latter case the share price would tend to fall still further. Two other important factors are the size of the issue and the expected course of future dividends. If the issue is small in relation to the market value of the existing capital, it is unlikely that there will be a substantial rise in the number of shares sold in the market, and the share price might not be materially depressed. Moreover, if it is expected that the existing dividend rate will be maintained on the increased capital, the current share price might be unaffected by the issue.

Other things being equal, a rights issue is normally expected to depress the share price below the theoretical equilibrium point in the short term. For this reason, a rights issue is often regarded as providing a cheap way of buying the shares of a company. A further advantage of buying at this time is that buying expenses are minimized. The letter of rights will be saleable by the shareholder up to the time (usually some weeks later) that it must be presented to the company with due payment for the new shares. During this period it may be purchased without payment of stamp duty. Furthermore, the brokers' commission is calculated only upon the amount for which the rights are acquired, and not upon the total amount which must ultimately be paid for the shares.

(vii) *Capitalization Issues*

This type of issue is also known as a bonus issue or a scrip issue. It does not result in the acquisition of any new funds by the company, and merely represents the rearrangement of the existing capital structure.

For example, a company commenced trading with a paid-up capital of £200,000 divided into 200,000 ordinary shares of £1. Over a period of years, the company followed a policy of expansion financed by means of retained profits. Retained profits are that part of a company's annual profits which is held back by the company to finance its growth, the remainder of the profit having been paid out as dividends. At the present time the company has retained a total of £1·6 m. in this way, so that the total amount invested in the company by its shareholders is £1·8 m. The current profit is £200,000 per annum, of which £120,000 is used for the payment of dividends.

The dividend yield that the market requires from the shares of such a company, having regard to such factors as its profit potential and risk, is 6%. A total dividend of £120,000 would thus place an aggregate market value of £2 m. upon the company, which would result in a market price of £10 for each of its 200,000 shares.

This state of affairs is rather unsatisfactory for the company. One drawback is that the price of its shares is somewhat heavy. This would deter many investors, who feel illogically that a share costing £10 is more expensive than one which costs, say, £2, and that it is better to invest £200 in 100 shares at a price of £2 rather than in 20 shares at a price of £10 each, regardless of the fact that the total dividend on the £200 invested may be the same in both cases.

A further disadvantage lies in the fact that the share capital is out of line with the amount which has actually been invested in the company, for the share capital is only £200,000 compared with the total of £1·8 m. invested by the shareholders. As a result a comparison of the profit and dividend with the nominal share capital would produce a profit percentage of 100% (£200,000 : £200,000) and a dividend percentage of 60% (£120,000 : £200,000). Inflated percentages of this sort have been used in the past by trade unions to support charges of profiteering and of excessive dividends paid by the company concerned. Such charges are often believed by the layman, although they are entirely without foundation. The true profit percentage should be based on the market value of capital invested in the company, not on the nominal value of that capital, thus giving a profit percentage of 10% (£200,000 : £2,000,000). Similarly the correct dividend yield should be based on what investors are required to pay in order to receive that dividend, namely £10 per share. The company has a total market value of £2 m. and pays out dividends of £120,000 representing a dividend yield of 6%.

The above situation may be overcome to some extent by means of a capitalization issue, whereby all or part of the reserves of the company are used as the basis of an issue of free fully paid shares to the shareholders. In the example above, the company may decide to capitalize £1·4 m. of its retained profits in this way, by means of an issue of seven new shares for every one held. This would increase the share capital to £1·6 m., while the reserves would fall to £200,000.

Such an issue would not of itself have any effect either upon the assets of the company or upon its profits or dividends paid. Thus, unless the capitalization issue was accompanied by an increase in the total dividends to be paid by the company, the total market value of the shares would be expected to remain at £2 m. This total market value would now be represented by 1,600,000 shares, which would place a value of 125p upon each share. Thus an investor who previously held 100 shares in the company with a total market value of £1,000 would now hold 800 shares, each priced at 125p, giving the same market value, and would receive the same total dividend.

Under certain circumstances the share price might not fall in direct proportion to the rate of increase of the share capital. This might occur where the enhanced marketability of the new share capital is regarded as especially beneficial. In other cases, the mere announcement of the issue might provide publicity for the company which would be regarded as a bull point by market speculators. In each of these cases, however, the short-term influx of the new shares on the market might act as a counter-balancing depressive influence.

In many instances the capitalization issue might be accompanied by an effective dividend increase, which would tend to pull the share price above the theoretical equilibrium point. Such a dividend increase would occur where a company makes an issue of bonus shares and maintains the previous dividend rate on the increased capital. For example, a company may pay a dividend of 10% based on the nominal value of its shares, which is £1. If the market required a dividend yield of 5% from shares of this standing the market value of each share would then be £2 $\left(\frac{10}{5} \times £1\right)$. The company then decides to make a 1 for 10 capitalization issue and to maintain the dividend percentage at 10%. A shareholder who initially held 1,000 shares with a market value of £2,000 and received dividends of £100, would now own 1,100 shares and would receive dividends of £110. Assuming that the market capitalization rate remains unchanged at 5% the value of each share would remain at £2, giving a market value of £2,200 for the whole holding. The shareholder is thus in a better position after the capitalization issue but it must be appreciated that the improvement is due entirely to the effective increase in the dividend, and not to the issue itself.

Similarly, a company may round up the dividend rate after it has been adjusted to take account of a capitalization issue, thus increasing the total dividend payout. For instance, another company which is also valued by the market on the basis of a required yield of 5% may pay a dividend of 25% on its £1 shares, thus placing a value of £5 on each share. If a 2 for 1 capitalization issue were made the dividend percentage necessary to maintain the previous level of dividends would be $8\frac{1}{3}$% $\left(\frac{25}{1+2}\right)$. However, it might be felt that this percentage is too unwieldy and it might be raised to 9%. If this were done a shareholder who initially owned 1,000 shares with a market value of £5,000 and received a dividend of £250 would now hold 3,000 shares, which would entitle him to a dividend of £270. With a constant market capitalization rate of 5% the value of the holding would rise to £5,400, the increase being entirely attributable to the effective dividend increase rather than to the capitalization issue.

Two procedural matters which are relevant in a discussion of capitalization issues are the treatment of fractions and the use of renounceable certificates:

Fractions

In any issue smaller than a 1 for 1 issue the problem of fractions is likely to arise. In the case of a 1 for 3 issue, for instance, the owner of 100 shares would become entitled to $33\frac{1}{3}$ new shares. It is not possible to issue a certificate for one-third of a share, so the company may decide to ignore fractions altogether, thus unfairly penalizing the shareholders concerned. Alternatively, the shareholders concerned might acquire fractions from each other on the market until they all have either whole shares or cash for their fractions. The normal method of dealing with fractions is for the company to allot them to trustees, who will sell them as whole shares in the market and split the proceeds among the shareholders who were entitled to them.

Renounceable Certificates

Until comparatively recently, the usual method of administering a capitalization issue was to send a scrip certificate to each shareholder representing the number of new shares to which he was entitled. For a few weeks dealings would take place in these certificates, after which they had to be surrendered to the company for conversion into definitive certificates. Many companies have now adopted the practice of issuing renounceable certificates on the occasion of a capitalization issue, which either may be renounced by the shareholder and dealt with on the market or may be retained by the shareholder as a permanent certificate. In this way only those which have been renounced need to be replaced with new certificates.

Before leaving the subject of capitalization issues it is necessary to describe the operations of splitting and consolidating the shares of a company. Splitting shares is a procedure for reducing the market value of the shares, which is often resorted to when it has become heavy. Thus a company which has shares of a nominal value of £1, which are quoted at £20 on the market, may decide to split the shares, giving them a nominal value of 10p. Every shareholder would then have ten shares of 10p, each with a market value of £2, for each £1 share which he had previously held. In this way a company can reduce the market value of its shares without capitalizing its reserves. For this reason this practice is often resorted to by banking and insurance companies, who are not required by law to disclose their reserves and who do not wish to make a capitalization issue which would result in the permanent disclosure and freezing of at least part of those reserves.

The consolidation of shares is the reverse procedure, where the shares of a company have a very low price and they are consolidated to give them a higher and more respectable market value. In the same illogical way that shares with a high market value are regarded as expensive, so extremely low-priced shares are looked upon, though with perhaps more justification, as too cheap, and indicative of a small, struggling company. For this reason a company which has shares of a nominal value of 5p and a market value of 7½p may decide to consolidate the shares, making them 50p shares, with a market value of 75p. Thus, for every ten 5p shares which he previously held, a shareholder would have one 75p share with the same total market value.

APPENDIX I

QUOTATIONS FOR SECURITIES OF COMPANIES NO PART OF WHOSE CAPITAL IS ALREADY QUOTED.

I. Application, which should be made at the earliest possible date in the form set out in Schedule 1, can only be made in respect of a Company if that Company has a minimum market value of £250,000 and in respect of any security only if that security has a minimum market value of £100,000. If a Placing or Introduction is intended the application must be accompanied or preceded by a request to use such method, together with a statement as to whether or not any application or approach of any kind has been made to any other Stock Exchange and any result thereof, supported by such other information as the Committee may from time to time require.

II. (A) Applicants must submit for initial approval, at least fourteen days prior to publication or posting:

(i) four proof prints of the Prospectus which, in the case of a Placing or Introduction and, in such other cases as the Committee may require, must, unless the Committee otherwise agree, take the form of an Advertisement for circulation by the Exchange Tele-graph Company Limited and Moodies Services Limited in their statistical services, which must be published in two leading London[1] daily newspapers, save that

   (a) in the case of Placings or Introductions of United Kingdom securities it shall be sufficient for the Prospectus to be pub-lished in one leading London[1] daily newspaper only provided abridged particulars appear in a second leading London[1] daily newspaper;

   (b) in the case of Placings or Introductions of fixed interest securities (other than those having equity conversion rights) denominated solely in a foreign currency, it shall be sufficient for abridged particulars to be published in one leading London[1] daily newspaper only provided that the advertisement indicates that further particulars are contained in the new issue cards circulated by the Exchange Telegraph Company Limited and Moodies Services Limited;

four proof prints of such abridged particulars must also be sub-mitted.

  (ii) four proof prints of the Temporary Document of Title proposed to be issued, which must comply with Schedule III;

  (iii) two proof prints of the Definitive Certificate or other definitive documents of title proposed to be issued, which must comply with Schedule IV; as indicated in that Schedule, it is advisable for proofs to be submitted as early as possible.

  (iv) two proof prints or copies of the Memorandum and Articles of Association or other corresponding document, which must comply with Part A of Schedule VII.

  (v) in the case of Loan Capital two proof prints or copies of the Trust Deed or other document securing or constituting the Loan Capital. These must comply with Part B of Schedule VII.

(B) The Prospectus must comply with Part A of Schedule II.

(C) Where it is desired to advertise abridged particulars or a Preliminary Announcement of a Public Offer in the Press, Applicants must submit four copies of the drafts of such documents (which must not contain any material information not included in the Prospectus), for approval at least four days prior to insertion in the Press.

(D) Where, following submission pursuant to this paragraph II, any amendment is made in any document, a like number of further copies must be submitted for approval. Such copies must be marked in red to indicate amendments made to conform with points raised by the Depart-ment and in blue or black to indicate other amendments.

III. The following documents must be lodged at least two days prior to the hearing of the Application by the Committee:—

(A) A formal application in the form issued by the Department, signed

[1] Where no application is made to The Stock Exchange, London, but application is being made to another Federated Stock Exchange, the newspapers may be those circulating in such centres as the Committee may determine.

by the Broker appointed by the Company and supported, in the case of The Stock Exchange, London, by at least two firms of Jobbers in the Market concerned who are prepared to deal, together with payment of the appropriate charge for quotation.

(B) (i) Four copies of the Prospectus one of which must be dated and signed by every person who is named therein as a Director or proposed Director of the Company or by his agent authorised in writing.

(ii) Where any document referred to in (i) is signed by an Agent a certified copy of the authorisation for such signature.

(C) A copy of the Exchange Telegraph and Moodies Services cards (if any) and of each newspaper (if any) in which the Prospectus or any Abridged Particulars or Preliminary Announcement appeared.

(D) A certified or photostat copy of the Certificate of Incorporation.

(E) A certified or photostat copy of the Certificate (if any) entitling the Company to commence business.

[1](F) A specimen of the Memorandum and Articles of Association or other corresponding document.

[1](G) A specimen of the Trust Deed or other document securing or constituting the Loan Capital.

(H) (i) The general undertaking in the form set out in Part A of Schedule VIII.

(ii) Where required by the Committee, a certified copy of a resolution of the Board of Directors in the following terms:

"In compliance with the requirements of the Council of The Stock Exchange, London [or, as the case may be, other Federated Stock Exchanges] it was resolved that the Company shall not act as Stock or Share Brokers or Dealers in Securities and shall exercise all voting and other rights or powers of control exercisable by the Company in relation to its subsidiary companies for the time being so as to secure (so far as by such exercise the Company can secure) that no such subsidiary shall act in manner aforesaid."

(I) A certified copy of—

(i) the Resolution(s) of the Board authorising the issue of all securities for which quotation is sought and subsequently allotting the same; and

[1] In the event of any of these documents not complying with the requirements of the Committee and if it is impracticable for the Company to alter them before making the application for quotation, the Committee may accept an undertaking to amend these documents at the earliest possible opportunity. Where Loan Capital is to be secured by a Trust Deed and such Trust Deed will not have been entered into by the time of the hearing, a copy of the latest draft should be lodged for approval by the Department and in that event a copy of the Trust Deed must be lodged with the Department as soon as possible after execution together with a letter from the Trustees' solicitors certifying that it complies in all respects with the draft as finally approved by the Department except (if such be the case) as otherwise subsequently agreed with the Department, particulars of the agreed variation(s) being given in the letter.

(ii) the Resolution(s) of the Board approving and authorising the issue of the Prospectus.

(J) In the case of a Placing, a copy of the Placing Letter and a Marketing Statement by the Broker in the form set out in Schedule IX or as near thereto as circumstances admit.

(K) A certified copy of every Letter, Report, Balance Sheet, Valuation, Contract, Resolution or other document any part of which is extracted or referred to in the Prospectus.

(L) A certified copy of the written consent by any expert to the inclusion in the Prospectus of
> (i) a statement purporting to be a copy of or extract from or summary of or reference to a Report or Valuation or other statement by such expert;
> (ii) any recommendation by such expert in relation to acceptance or rejection of an offer or proposal.

(M) Three specimens of the Notice(s) of Meeting referred to in the Prospectus and Temporary Document of Title.

(N) A specimen of the Definitive Certificate or other definitive document of title.

(O) A statement in the form set out in Schedule V, which includes an undertaking to submit the Declaration set out in Schedule VI.

(P) Where any scrip is to be issued by any person other than the Company whose scrip it is, a certified copy of the Resolution or other document, evidencing the authority to issue the scrip.

(Q) Where the vendor of a security offered for sale has not paid in full for that security at the date of the offer:—
> (i) a certified copy of an irrevocable authority given by the vendor to the Bankers to the offer authorising the Bankers to earmark the proceeds of the offer to discharge the obligation of the vendor to make payment for the security on the date or dates for payment as laid down in the Contract for the acquisition of the security by the Vendor, and
> (ii) a certified copy of the Bankers' acknowledgment of this authority and an agreement to act on it.

(R) A letter from the issuing house, or, in the absence of an issuing house, from the sponsoring brokers, stating that they have satisfied themselves that the statement in the Prospectus as to the sufficiency of working capital has been made by the Directors after due and careful enquiry. Such letter will normally be required to state that there is written confirmation from persons or institutions on whom reliance is placed for the provision of finance that such facilities exist.

IV. The following documents may be required:—

(A) Where the promoter or other interested party is a limited company or a firm a Statutory Declaration as to the identity of those who control it or are interested in its profits or assets.

(B) A declaration by each Director in conformity with the Rules and Regulations of the Stock Exchange.

SCHEDULE II.

PART A.

CONTENTS OF PROSPECTUS

In the case where quotation is sought for securities of a Company *no part* of whose capital is already quoted.

1. The full name of the Company.

2. In the case of an Advertisement required to be circulated by the Exchange Telegraph Company Limited and Moodies Services Limited in their statistical services, a statement as follows:

"This Advertisement is issued in compliance with the Regulations of the Council of The Stock Exchange, London [or, as the case may be, other Federated Stock Exchange] for the purpose of giving information to the Public with regard to the Company. The Directors collectively and individually accept full responsibility for the accuracy of the information given and confirm, having made all reasonable enquiries, that to the best of their knowledge and belief there are no other facts the omission of which would make any statement in the Advertisement misleading."

3. A statement that application has been made to the Council of The Stock Exchange, London [or, as the case may be, other Federated Stock Exchange] for permission to deal in and for quotation for the securities.

4. The authorised share capital, the amount issued or agreed to be issued, the amount paid up and the description and nominal value of the shares. In cases where 25% or more of the voting capital (unclassified shares being counted as voting capital) is unissued, a statement that no issue will knowingly be made which could effectively alter the control of the Company without prior approval of the shareholders in general meeting.

5. (i) The authorised loan capital of the Company and any of its subsidiaries, the amount issued and outstanding or agreed to be issued, or, if no loan capital is outstanding, a statement to that effect.

(ii) Particulars of any bank overdrafts or other similar indebtedness of the Company and any of its subsidiaries as at the latest convenient date or, if there are no bank overdrafts or other similar indebtedness, a statement to that effect.

(iii) Particulars of any mortgages, charges, hire purchase commitments or guarantees or other material contingent liabilities of the Company and any of its subsidiaries, or, if there are no such liabilities, a statement to that effect.

6. The full name, address and description of every Director and, if required by the Committee, particulars of (A) any former Christian names and surname, (B) his nationality, if not British, and (C) his nationality of origin if his present nationality is not the nationality of origin.

7. The full name and professional qualification of the Secretary and situation of Registered Office and Transfer Office (if different).

8. The names and addresses of the Bankers, Brokers, Solicitors, Registrars and Trustees (if any).

9. The name, address and professional qualification of the Auditors.

10. The date and country of incorporation and the authority under which the Company was incorporated.
In the case of a Company not incorporated in the United Kingdom, the address of the head office and of the principal place of business (if any) in the United Kingdom.

11. If the application is in respect of shares:—
    (i) The voting rights of shareholders.
    (ii) If there is more than one class of share, the rights of each class of share as regards dividend, capital, redemption, and the creation or issue of further shares ranking in priority to or *pari passu* with each class other than the lowest ranking equity.
    (iii) A summary of the consents necessary for the variation of such rights.

12. The provisions or a sufficient summary of the provisions of the Articles of Association, By-Laws or other corresponding document with regard to:—
    (i) Any power enabling the Directors, in the absence of an independent quorum, to vote remuneration (including pension or other benefits) to themselves or any members of their body.
    (ii) Borrowing powers exercisable by the Directors and how such borrowing powers can be varied.
    (iii) Retirement or non-retirement of Directors under an age limit.

13. Where quotation is sought for loan capital, the rights conferred upon the holders thereof, and particulars of the security (if any) therefor.

14. A statement of:—
    (i) any alterations in the share capital of the Company within the two years preceding the publication of the Prospectus; and
    (ii) the persons holding or beneficially interested in any substantial part of the share capital of the Company and the amounts of the holdings in question together with particulars of the interests of each director (and also, so far as he is aware of or can by reasonable inquiry ascertain the same, of his family interests) in the share capital of the company and, otherwise than through the company, any of its subsidiaries, distinguishing between beneficial and other interests; the expression "family interests" includes, in relation to a director, spouse, children under 21 years of age, trusts of which the director or spouse is a settlor or trustee and in which the director or spouse or any of such children are beneficiaries or discretionary objects and companies known to him to be controlled by him and/or spouse and/or such children and/or the trustees of any such trusts as aforesaid in their capacity as such trustees.
Subject to the necessity to distinguish between beneficial and other interests, between the Company and each subsidiary and between each class of capital each director's interests may be aggregated with those of his family interests.

15. The general nature of the business of the Company or Group and, in cases where the Company or Group carried on two or more activities which are material, having regard to profits or losses, assets employed or any other factor, information as to the relative importance of each such activity. If the Company or Group trades outside the United Kingdom a statement showing a geographical analysis of its trading operations.

16.   (i) In regard to every company the whole of, or a substantial proportion of whose capital (either directly or indirectly is held or is about to be held, or whose profits or assets make or will make a material contribution to the figures in the Auditors' Report or next published accounts, particulars of: The name, date, country of incorporation, whether public or private, general nature of business, issued capital and the proportion thereof held or about to be held.

    (ii) In regard to the company and every subsidiary or company about to become a subsidiary, particulars of: The situation, area and tenure (including in the case of leaseholds the rent and unexpired term) of the factories and main buildings, the principal products and approximate number of employees.

17. Wherever possible a statement showing the sales turnover figures or gross trading income during the preceding three financial years which should contain a reasonable breakdown between the more important trading activities. In the case of a group, internal sales should be excluded.

18.   (i) A statement as to the financial and trading prospects of the Company or Group, together with any material information which may be relevant thereto, including, where known to the directors, special trade factors or risks (if any) which are not mentioned elsewhere in the prospectus and which are unlikely to be known or anticipated by the general public, which could materially affect the profits, and details of any waiver of future dividends.

    (ii) Where quotation is sought for fixed income securities, particulars of the profits cover for dividend/interest and of the net tangible assets available for capital cover.

19. A statement by the Directors that in their opinion the working capital available is sufficient, or, if not, how it is proposed to provide the additional working capital thought by the Directors to be necessary.

20. Where the securities for which quotation is sought were issued for cash within the two years preceding the publication of the Prospectus, or will be issued for cash, a statement or an estimate of the net proceeds of the issue and a statement as to how such proceeds were or are to be applied.

21. A report by the Auditors of the Company:—

    (i) with respect to the profits or losses of the Company in respect of each of the ten completed financial years immediately preceding the publication of the Prospectus, or in respect of each of the years since the incorporation of the Company, if this occurred less than ten years prior to such publication; and, if in respect of a period ending on a date earlier than three months before such publication no accounts have been made up, a statement of that fact;

(ii) in the case of an issue by a holding company, in lieu of the report in (i), a like report with respect to the profits or losses of the Company and of its subsidiary companies, so far as such profits or losses can properly be regarded as attributable to the interests of the holding company;

(iii) as to the rate of dividend for each class of shares during each of the five financial years preceding the issue of the prospectus with details of any waiver of dividends in such years;

(iv) with respect to the assets and liabilities of the Company and in the case of an issue by a holding company, a like report with respect to the assets and liabilities of the Company and of its subsidiary companies so far as such assets can properly be regarded as attributable to the interests of the Company, including an explanation of the bases used for the valuations of fixed assets and a reasonably detailed indication of the nature of the tangible assets;

(v) with respect to the aggregate emoluments paid to the Directors by the Company during the last period for which the accounts have been made up and the amount (if any) by which such emoluments would differ from the amounts payable under the arrangements in force at the date of the Prospectus;

(vi) with respect to any other matters which appear to the auditors to be relevant having regard to the purpose of the report.

In making such report the auditors shall make such adjustments (if any) as are in their opinion appropriate for the purposes of the Prospectus.

22. If after the latest date to which the accounts of the Company have been made up and audited the Company or any of its subsidiaries has acquired or agreed to acquire or is proposing to acquire a business or shares in a company which will by reason of such acquisition become a subsidiary of the Company or any of its subsidiaries and no part of the securities of that subsidiary is already quoted, a report made by qualified accountants who shall be named in the Prospectus:—

(i) with respect to the profits or losses of the business or to the profits or losses attributable to the interests acquired or being acquired in respect of each of the ten completed financial years immediately preceding the publication of the Prospectus, or in respect of each of the years since the commencement of the business or the incorporation of such subsidiary company if this occurred less than ten years prior to such publication; and if in respect of a period ending on a date earlier than three months before such publication no accounts have been made up, a statement of that fact:

Provided that where any such subsidiary is itself a holding company the report shall be extended to the profits or losses of that company, and its subsidiary companies which shall be ascertained in the manner laid down in sub-paragraph (ii) of paragraph 21;

(ii) with respect to the assets and liabilities of the business or of the subsidiary and where such subsidiary is itself a holding company, the report shall be extended to the assets and liabilities of that company and of its subsidiary companies in the manner laid down in sub-paragraph (iv) of paragraph 21;

(iii) with respect to any other matters which appear to the accountants to be relevant having regard to the purpose of the report.

In making such report the accountants shall make such adjustments (if any) as are in their opinion appropriate for the purposes of the Prospectus.

23. Particulars of any capital of the Company or of any of its subsidiaries which has within two years immediately preceding the publication of the Prospectus been issued or is proposed to be issued fully or partly paid up otherwise than in cash and the consideration for which the same has been or is to be issued.

24. Particulars of any capital of the Company or of any of its subsidiaries, which has within two years immediately preceding the publication of the Prospectus been issued or is proposed to be issued for cash, the price and terms upon which the same has been or is to be issued and (if not already fully paid) the dates when any instalments are payable with the amount of all calls or instalments in arrear.

25. Particulars of any capital of the Company, or of any of its subsidiaries which is under option, or agreed conditionally or unconditionally to be put under option, with the price and duration of the option and consideration for which the option was or will be granted, and the name and address of the grantee.

Provided that where an option has been granted or agreed to be granted to all the members or debenture holders or to any class thereof, it shall be sufficient, so far as the names are concerned, to record that fact without giving the names and addresses of the grantees.

26. (i) Particulars of any preliminary expenses incurred or proposed to be incurred and by whom the same are payable.

(ii) The amount or estimated amount of the expenses of the issue and of the application for quotation so far as the same are not included in the statement of preliminary expenses and by whom the same are payable.

27. Particulars of any commissions, discounts, brokerages or other special terms granted within two years immediately preceding the publication of the Prospectus in connection with the issue or sale of any capital of the Company or of any of its subsidiaries.

28. Details of Directors' existing or proposed service contracts including those (if any) with any subsidiary.

29. Full particulars of the nature and extent of the interest direct or indirect, if any, of every Director in the promotion of, or in any assets which have been, within the two years preceding the publication of the Prospectus, acquired or disposed of by or leased to, the Company or any of its subsidiaries, or are proposed to be acquired, disposed of by or leased to the Company or any of its subsidiaries, including

(A) the consideration passing to or from the Company or any of its subsidiaries; and

107

(B) short particulars of all transactions relating to any such assets which have taken place within two years immediately preceding the publication of the Prospectus.

30. A statement that the Company has or has not (as the case may be) any litigation or claims of material importance pending or threatened against it.

31. (i) The name of any promoter; and (if a company) the Committee may require a statement of the issued share capital; the amount paid up thereon; the date of its incorporation; the names of its Directors, Bankers and Auditors; and such other particulars as the Committee think necessary in connection therewith.

    (ii) The amount of any cash or securities paid or benefit given within the two years immediately preceding the publication of the Prospectus, or proposed to be paid or given to any promoter and the consideration for such payment or benefit.

32. Where the Prospectus includes a statement purporting to be made by an expert, a statement that the expert has given and has not withdrawn his written consent to the issue of the Prospectus with the statement included in the form and context in which it is included.

33. When relevant, in the absence of a statement that income tax and sur-tax clearances have been obtained, a statement that appropriate indemnities have been given. (The Committee may require such indemnities to be supported by continuing guarantees.)

34. When relevant, in the absence of a statement that estate duty indemnities have been given, a statement that the Directors had been advised that no material liability for estate duty would be likely to fall upon the Company or any subsidiary. (The Committee may require any indemnities to be supported by continuing guarantees.)

35. The dates of and parties to all material contracts (not being contracts entered into in the ordinary course of business) entered into within two years immediately preceding the publication of the Prospectus, together with a description of the general nature of such contracts, and particulars of any consideration passing to or from the Company.

36. A reasonable time (being not less than fourteen days) during which and a place in the City of London [or such other centre as the Committee of a Federated Stock Exchange, other than London, may determine] at which the following documents (or copies thereof) where applicable may be inspected: The Memorandum and Articles of Association; Trust Deed; each contract disclosed pursuant to paragraph 35 or, in the case of a contract not reduced into writing, a memorandum giving full particulars thereof; all reports, letters, or other documents, balance sheets, valuations and statements by any expert any part of which is extracted or referred to in the Prospectus; a written statement signed by the auditors or accountants setting out the adjustments made by them in arriving at the figures shown in their report and giving the reasons therefor; and the audited accounts of the Company and its subsidiaries for each of the two financial years preceding the publication of the Prospectus together with all notes, certificates or information required by the Companies Act.

CHAPTER 4

Recent Criticisms of the
London Stock Exchange

In theory, a stock exchange performs two major functions. In the first place it provides a perfect market in which securities may be bought or sold at prices which reflect the prevailing state of supply and demand. At the same time, these prices act as an allocatory mechanism in that they indicate the yield that investors require from particular companies and thereby the cost of capital to a company which seeks to raise funds from the market.

This analysis is rather over-simplified for, as Baumol has shown,[1] it may be seriously criticized on theoretical grounds. Nevertheless, it represents the view which is commonly expressed by the more elementary textbooks and by stock markets themselves. However, it has become evident in recent years that the London Stock Exchange in particular does not perform completely the responsibilities which are attributed to it. This would appear to be due partly to the maintenance of outdated practices and partly to circumstances entirely outside its control. In each of its two major functions there are serious deficiencies in its performance.

1. THE LONDON STOCK EXCHANGE AS A PERFECT MARKET

The normal view is that prices on the London Stock Exchange are established by the interaction of the forces of supply and demand. The buying and selling orders of a multitude of investors are passed to the market through the agency of stockbrokers and are there translated into prices by jobbers. The jobbers not only establish prices in response to the existing state of supply and demand, but also

[1] William J. Baumol, *The Stock Market and Economic Efficiency* (New York: Fordham University Press, 1965).

smooth out short-run fluctuations by purchasing and selling on their own account. The entire market is supervised by the Stock Exchange Council, which supervises the activities of brokers and jobbers and attempts to ensure the maintenance of a free market.

There are four major prerequisites for a perfectly competitive market which are commonly identified by textbooks on economics. These are the existence of a large number of firms, none of whose scale of production is sufficiently large to influence prices in the market; homogeneity of the product in which it deals; freedom of entry into the market; and perfect knowledge concerning conditions therein.

It is clear that the mechanism described above does not satisfy these theoretical requirements. The securities of each class in which it deals are admittedly homogeneous but are in all cases in limited supply, and in many cases very seriously so. The number of buyers and sellers is limited and has tended to become dominated by institutional investors. Moreover, the market does not permit of free entry and exit, for dealing costs are relatively expensive and are likely to become more so with the decline of competition among jobbers. Finally the extent of knowledge regarding market conditions is far from perfect.

Moreover, the imperfections of the London market have become much more evident in recent years due to three major factors:

(a) *The Decline of the Jobbing System*

The major function of jobbers is the provision of a free and competitive market. Brokers who wish to buy or sell a security on behalf of a client should be able to approach several competing jobbers in the knowledge that each of them will be prepared to meet the order either against outstanding orders which he holds or by undertaking the transaction on his own account. In order to ensure that jobbers have sufficient capital to maintain a satisfactory level of holdings in the shares in which they deal, the rules of the Stock Exchange provide that each firm of jobbers must contain at least two partners and should have an excess of assets over liabilities amounting to £5,000 for each partner, with a minimum total capital of £15,000.

The essence of the system is that jobbers should provide a competitive market for the more popular shares, with competition forcing down considerably the jobber's turn which can be one of the most expensive costs of dealing, while they also provide a continuous market for securities in which deals occur less frequently. This latter function is extremely important, for if the holder of a security in which there is a thin market wishes to sell it at a time when demand for that security is extremely slack, he might be forced to sell it at an abnormally low price. Similarly, a few weeks later an eager buyer might appear when there are no sellers in the market, so that he might be forced to pay an extremely high price for the security. As a result the prices of such securities would tend to be extremely unstable and the market in that stock would be unsatisfactory for both investors and the companies concerned, though not, of course, for speculators. However, the jobbers provide an essential service in that they are prepared to buy the security on their own account, holding it until a seller appears, or to sell the security out of their own holding or to sell it short until such time as a seller appears and they are able to deliver the stock. In this way the time span which separates a buyer and seller is bridged and a continuous market is created. At the same time the jobber is accepting a considerable degree of risk by dealing on his own account and he is quite justified in requiring a rather higher than usual turn for undertaking the transaction.

In addition, it is often claimed that jobbers perform an essential service by counter-balancing speculative price movements and thus stabilizing the market. In this respect it is argued that they smooth out short-run price fluctuations by taking securities into their own stock when there is a short-run excess of sellers, thus reducing the consequent fall in price, and by selling short when there is a short-term excess of buyers. However, the jobber does not perform this service gratuitously. If the price of a security falls and he predicts that the fall is only temporary it would obviously be in full accordance with his profit motive to take up any shares which are on offer, thus automatically reversing the fall in price, in the expectation that he would be able to sell them at a profit when the price reverts to its former level. Similarly, it would be profitable for him to sell short on the occasion of a temporary rise in the price of a security. In this way he would not only check the price rise but would also make a profit when he ultimately delivers stock by buying it when it reverts to its previous lower level.

Long-run fluctuations, on the other hand, cannot be smoothed out by jobbers, nor should they be, for they indicate the changing attitudes of investors to a particular stock. Whether or not those attitudes are based on the correct criteria is, of course, another matter. If a jobber were to combat such trends he would invite bankruptcy unless his resources were unlimited, for he would be selling short during a relatively long upward price movement and buying for stock when prices were falling.

Although it is common to separate short-run and long-run

fluctuations in theory[1] such classification is wellnigh impossible in practice, when the jobber has not got the advantage of hindsight. For instance, if a jobber is faced with a series of selling orders for a particular stock, which would suggest that the stockholders were taking a pessimistic view of that stock, he must attempt to predict whether the selling trend will continue, in which case it would be a long-run movement, or whether it is likely to be reversed, thus suggesting a short-run fluctuation. If he predicts a long-run trend he will not take any action to reverse it, but will lower the price of the stock until a new equilibrium point is reached. If, however, the selling is regarded as temporary, then he will at the same time satisfy his profit motive and stabilize the market by purchasing the excess supply on his own account. Similar considerations would apply if there was an excess demand for a stock. If it was regarded as long-run the jobber would push up prices and would perform no stabilization function, while he would sell short if he thought that the excess was only temporary.

There are several interesting conclusions which may be drawn from the above argument. Firstly, it is clear that jobbers only provide stabilization for the market if this is profitable for them. Their stabilization function is neither automatic nor gratuitous. Moreover, such stability as they do provide by dealing on their own account or selling short is extremely risky, for in doing so they are taking a view which is opposite to that currently expressed by the market. Often, despite the experience of the jobbers, the market view is correct. This is particularly true in the case of insider dealings, where the buyer or seller has greater immediate knowledge than the jobber and can use this to his own advantage. Finally, it should be appreciated that jobbers are endeavouring to predict the attitudes that will be taken towards a particular stock by investors in the near future. They are not concerned with any notions of investment value, fundamental value, or intrinsic value, except insofar as these factors might influence the impending views of investors.

It is thus argued that the major duty of jobbers is the provision of a competitive market and that their stabilization function is merely an adjunct of dealings made on their own account with a view to the maximization of profit. In order to operate satisfactorily a jobber must have adequate capital to enable him to service thin markets and to offset short-term fluctuations. There must also be a relatively high level of business to provide, by means of the jobber's turn, a satisfactory rate of regular income which is much less hazardous than that earned by personal dealings.

[1] Cf. Baumol, *op. cit.*, pp. 25-6.

Unfortunately, during recent years these two prerequisites have been met less adequately. As a result of the vast appreciation in the price of quoted securities since the war, jobbers have required an ever-increasing amount of capital in order to finance their operations. At the same time, the amount of capital available to them has decreased as a result of Surtax, Estate Duty and Capital Gains Taxation. Moreover, much of the capital is in the hands of older members who are near to retirement and may consequently wish to withdraw it.

In order to help to overcome the shortage of finance, the Stock Exchange Council provided in 1966 that a new class of member, an external member, should be created, and that such members should be allowed to become limited partners in member firms. The object of this step was to enable financial institutions to invest up to 35% of the capital of a consortium company, the remainder being subscribed by the existing partners, the company then becoming a limited partner in the jobbing firm. The provision of finance was further facilitated by the Companies Act 1967, which removed the restriction which had previously limited to twenty the number of members of a Stock Exchange firm. This change, however, seems more likely to encourage further amalgamations rather than an increase in the size of existing partnerships.

In June 1969 members were permitted for the first time to trade as limited liability companies, though only under very restricted conditions:

(i) The Articles of Association of the Company must restrict the right of transfer of the Company's shares without both the approval of the Directors and the consent of the Council and must prohibit any general invitation to the public to subscribe for shares or debentures of the Company. It would thus be impossible for any such company to obtain a Stock Exchange quotation.

(ii) Only members may be appointed as directors.

(iii) Directors will be held personally liable for the debts of the Company in the same way that partners are so held in a trading firm.

(iv) Other members in the Company may voluntarily assume personal liability for the debts of the Company.

(v) Each Director must have an interest in the Company of £10,000 consisting either of shares, loans or a mixture of each.

(vi) Shareholders of the Company who are members of the Stock Exchange must hold not less than 51% of the voting rights in the Company.

(vii) Not more than 10% of the voting rights nor of the share capital may be held by any one non-member shareholder, whether an institution or an individual.

At the same time, however, the level of profitable dealings passing through jobbers' books has declined during the past few years. This is due partly to the introduction of the Capital Gains Tax which initially held back turnover in equities and partly to periodic slumps in equity prices. A further factor has been the increase in put-through business. This occurs where a broker is able to match buying and selling orders without having recourse to the jobbing system. Under Stock Exchange rules such business must be offered to a jobber but at a much lower turn, normally about $\frac{3}{4}$%. In addition, it is suspected, though without direct evidence, that some institutions occasionally transfer securities between themselves without any recourse to the Stock Exchange. The decline in dealings has been further aggravated by the serious shortage of equity stock, which has been caused by the practice of some institutions and private investors of holding on to equities for the long-term, partly due to the difficulty of buying them back if they are sold and partly due to the Capital Gains Tax. The stocks thus withdrawn from the market have not been replaced by new issues, for debentures rather than equities have been the most favoured form of new issue during the same period.

The scarcity of capital and the reduced profitability of jobbing have caused a sharp fall in the number of jobbing firms. This decline has been brought about by both amalgamations and outright withdrawals. In 1930 there were as many as 324 jobbing firms. By 1951 the number of firms had fallen to 179 and by 1955 to 139. The decline continued steadily thereafter until 1962, at which time only 86 firms had survived. Since then trading conditions have been considerably more difficult and the number of firms fell to 26 during 1971.

Furthermore, those jobbers who remain in the market have endeavoured to reduce the competition between themselves which would otherwise have resulted in severe pressure on their turns and thus on their profitability. This has been achieved by the system of joint books, whereby two or more jobbers who maintain books in the same security agree to operate their holdings of that security as if they were one firm. As a result the resources of more than one firm are available to maintain the necessary stock level and to cover any market operations which would previously have been the responsibility of each individual firm. On the other hand, the number of firms operating competitively in that market will have been reduced, for the firms which operate the joint book will quote similar prices to all brokers seeking to deal in that stock.

The joint books system together with the oligopolistic position of the small number of firms, predominantly large and strong though they are, which have survived, has led to a decrease in the number of jobbers who are prepared to deal in a particular stock and an increase in the spread of prices quoted by those who remain to provide the market. Due to the lack of available statistics in this connection and the traditional secrecy of jobbers it is difficult to furnish complete proof of the existence and extent of these phenomena. However, the following table indicates to some extent the degree of competition which exists within the jobbing system.

Number of Jobbers Dealing in Industrial Equities
(extracted from the Industrial Jobbers Index 1963–64)

No. of Jobbers	No. of Stocks	No. of Jobbers	No. of Stocks
1	942	10	7
2	1,107	11	2
3	990	12	5
4	457	13	1
5	166	14	6
6	80	15	2
7	28	16	4
8	15	17	—
9	16	18	1

The above figures overstate the degree of competition between jobbers, for they ignore joint books and the considerable number of amalgamations which have taken place since their publication.

A further criticism of the extent of perfection of the market is that jobbers' turns have tended to widen with the decrease in competition. This has made dealings much more expensive than on the New York Stock Exchange and has been a contributory factor to the rather lower level of activity on the London market in recent years, for the higher turns make switching operations considerably more expensive.[1]

The fact that the London Stock Exchange is the only major market which has persisted in a rigid distinction between brokers and jobbers poses the question whether the continuation of the system is an example of archaic traditionalism. This question can be answered by a description of the system used on the New York Stock Exchange and by a comparison of the two.

[1] See for example an article in *The Times* Business News Section, Thursday August 3, 1967, by Robert Jones entitled 'The Threat of the Third Market'.

Trading on the New York Stock Exchange is conducted primarily by commission brokers and specialists, who numbered 993 and 373 respectively during 1971. At that time the specialists were organized into 73 firms, each consisting of between one and nine specialists. The Board of Governors of the Stock Exchange allocate quoted stocks to the firms of specialists, each of which is responsible for between six and fifteen stocks. The degree of competition between specialists has declined enormously in recent years. Whereas in 1957 fifty firms competed in 228 stocks, there were only two firms competing in twelve stocks in 1964.

The trading floor of the Exchange contains a number of trading posts to each of which are assigned a number of stocks. When a broker receives an order from a client he goes to the post at which the stock in question is traded. At this post will be other brokers who have current orders in that stock and specialists who have outstanding orders for or personal holdings of the stock. If the order which the broker has is a market order, which is to be transacted at market price, an auction will take place and the broker will fulfil the order on the best terms. Where the order is a limited order and the price limits set by the client cannot be satisfied immediately the broker will pass it on to the specialist who will enter it in his book and will execute it at the first possible opportunity. In return for his services the specialist receives a brokerage commission.

The main responsibility of the specialist is to maintain an orderly market in the stocks which have been assigned to him. To do this he must undertake dealing transactions on his own account when the market is thin or subject to temporary disturbances. This clearly requires considerable personal capital and the market regulations provide that each specialist must as a minimum capital have sufficient to finance a holding of 1,200 shares of each stock in which he deals.

The *Special Study of Securities Markets*[1] showed that in 1960 55% of the gross income of all specialists came from brokerage commissions, the remainder being attributable to trading activities on their own account. Fourteen of the 110 firms earned the whole of their income from brokerage commissions, having suffered a loss on their trading account. Of the remainder, 56 earned more than half their gross income from commissions, 18 earned half therefrom and 22 earned less than half.[2]

The specialist serves many diverse functions. He may act as the

[1] *Report of Special Study of Securities Markets of the Securities and Exchange Commission*, Part II, 88th Congress, First Session, House Document No. 95, Part 2, July 17, 1963 (Washington: US Government Printing Office, 1963, p. 68).
[2] *Ibid.*, p. 371.

agent of a broker, as the agent of his own client or as a principal, entirely on his own behalf. An action taken in one of these guises might well impede transactions arranged in another role, or might run counter to his overall responsibility for ensuring the smoothness of the market. Oddly enough, at a time when it has been argued that the London Exchange should adopt the system of the New York Exchange, thus removing the rigid distinction between broker and jobber, there is a school in New York which argues conversely that the trading and commission activities of the specialist should be separated in order to prevent any conflict of interest. However, the surveillance of the Securities and Exchange Commission and the severe sanctions which it is able to impose have led to a continued preference for the present system.

The major defect in the jobbing system as compared with the use of specialists lies in the field of active and popular stocks. The relatively inactive stocks are served equally well and at a similar cost by both jobbers and specialists. Moreover, in those stocks for which there is real competition between jobbers and a consequent minimization of their turn, there can be little criticism of the jobbing system. However, there is a wide range of active stocks for which jobbers do not provide competitive quotations with the result that the spread of prices remains artificially wide. This would not occur in New York where the specialist in an active stock faces competition from brokers in the auctioneering procedure.

Any criticism of the jobbing system must, however, have regard to the difficult trading conditions of recent years and the degree of risk that they must take in dealing on their own account, which in a slack market must form a higher proportion of their total activities. Nevertheless, although the jobbers deserve a certain amount of sympathy, this fact must not discourage the quest for an improved system. All in all, the use of specialists seems to have distinct advantages, and could well be incorporated into the structure of the UK Stock Exchange, when it ultimately appears. Since many of the provincial exchanges already allow brokers to perform the duties of jobbers there is a case for requiring London to conform to the provinces, rather than the provinces to London in this respect when amalgamation ultimately occurs. Should this eventualize, the supervisory functions and sanctions of the Stock Exchange Council would need to be greatly increased to guard against any conflict of duty on the part of brokers.

Finally, it has been argued in the USA that some of the functions of specialists could be satisfactorily performed by the use of computers. In particular, their responsibility for limited orders would be very amenable to computerization.[1] Such an innovation is unlikely in the immediate future either in the New York or the London Stock Exchange due partly to vested interests and partly to the extreme complexities of the two markets. Nevertheless, computers have already made their mark, particularly in clearing house activities, and they may well ultimately take over other market procedures.

(b) *The Control Function of the Stock Exchange Council*

The Stock Exchange Council has absolute power over the members of the Stock Exchange and can reprimand, suspend or expel any member who:

  (i) violates any of the rules or regulations of the Exchange,
  (ii) fails to comply with any of the decisions of the Council,
  (iii) is guilty of dishonourable or disgraceful conduct,
  (iv) acts in a manner detrimental to the interests of the Stock Exchange or unbecoming the character of a member, or
  (v) conducts himself in an improper or disorderly manner or wilfully obstructs the business of the House.

The disciplinary powers of the Stock Exchange in relation to quoted companies are considerably less cogent. Prior to the grant of a quotation, applicant companies are carefully vetted and fairly comprehensive undertakings are required to be given regarding their future behaviour and the information to be provided for investors. Unfortunately, the only remedy which is available to the Council should a quoted company fail to honour any of its undertakings or act in any way detrimental to an orderly market is to suspend the quotation. Such an action not only does far more damage to the shareholder than to the company but may also result in the creation of an unofficial market in the shares.

The primary aim of the Council is the establishment of an efficient and orderly market in the securities for which a quotation has been granted. To this end the disciplinary powers described above may be wielded. On paper the strength of the remedies available to the Council in its control of the market appears to be quite considerable. Unfortunately, the events of recent years indicate that many quoted companies, some of them very large and respectable, pay little regard to the spirit of the Council's rules and regulations. This has been evident in the field of takeover bids, which are supposedly regulated by unofficial rules of conduct which were drawn up by the merchant banks in 1959 and later endorsed by the Stock Exchange

[1] Viz. Roland I. Robinson and H. Roberts Bartell Jr, 'Uneasy Partnership: SEC/NYSE', *Harvard Business Review*, January, February, 1965, p. 87.

Council. A series of bids and battles in 1966 and 1967, including the bid by Philips Lamps for Pye and the battles between Courtaulds and Macanie for Wilkinson Riddell and between Thorn Electrical and Aberdare Holdings for control over Metal Industries, were conducted in a manner which flagrantly violated the spirit of the so-called 'Queensberry Rules'. Despite the call by the financial Press for the suspension of some of the companies concerned in this series of bids, the only action taken by the Council was the creation of a body, on which City institutions were represented, to inquire into the need for a more rigid code of procedure for takeover bids. The report of this committee, which was published in March 1968, laid down a more stringent set of rules to be observed by companies in a takeover bid and established a permanent advisory panel. These rules were incorporated by the Stock Exchange into the general undertaking, but were soon abused in spirit if not in letter in a further series of bids. After a fierce battle between American Tobacco and Philip Morris for control of Gallaher, the bankers (Morgan Grenfell) and the stockbrokers (Cazenove) acting on behalf of American Tobacco were declared by the Takeover Panel to have breached the Takeover Code. Their defence was that the rules were ambiguous and the Stock Exchange Council cleared Cazenove of any blame for its actions, though it did criticize the firm for a minor technical infringement of its rules on put-through prices.

It was clear that the Takeover Panel, because it lacked sanctions, was powerless to enforce the Takeover Code and a further revision of both the Panel and the Code took place. These revisions were completed in April 1969 and a permanent Takeover Panel was established and empowered to make recommendations to the Stock Exchange Council, the Issuing Houses Association and the Board of Trade regarding action that should be taken against offending companies, brokers, jobbers and bankers. At the same time, the rules in the Code relating to market deals during bids were tightened. The success of the new Panel will clearly depend upon its readiness to use the sanctions which have been placed at its disposal.

The Council has demonstrated similar timidity in its disciplinary dealings with its members. Expulsion is very rare, being accorded normally only to brokers who have been 'hammered'. Even the much less severe punishment of suspension has been imposed infrequently and then often only after the actions of those suspended have been revealed by the Government or by the financial Press. However, it must in fairness be added that the Council has in recent years become much more willing to act quickly to deal with abuses of the market by its members and to pass regulations to prevent their recurrence.

For example, in December 1964 the Council suspended nine members for periods of up to three months for permitting 'dealings to take place without due care in such a way as to assist in the promotion of a false market in the shares of H. W. Phillips and Co. between June 7, 1963 and October 9, 1964'. It is regrettable that during a period of some eighteen months the shares concerned should have risen from 1s 7½d to 31s 3¾d without any inquiry being made at the behest either of brokers, jobbers or the Council. However, within a few days of the suspensions the Council warned that it would maintain a continuous review of small or semi-moribund companies and that the quotation of their shares would be temporarily suspended in the event of any suspicious circumstances, thus entailing a new application for quotation. This was followed by the introduction of three new regulations to be observed by members, including one which forbade members to assist in the promotion of a false market, which was defined as:

'. . . a market in which a movement of the price of a share is brought about or sought to be brought about by contrived factors, such as the operations of buyers and sellers acting in collaboration with each other, calculated to create a movement of price which is not justified by assets, earnings or prospects.'

Then in January 1966 eight members were suspended for periods varying from three to twelve months in connection with actions which involved bond-washing, with a consequent loss of tax to the Inland Revenue. Again the rules of the Stock Exchange were altered and the Inland Revenue took upon itself additional powers to prevent a recurrence of such activities. Similarly, in May 1967, just prior to the vesting date for the nationalization of the steel industry, steel shares had the characteristics of gilt-edged securities and bond-washing was again possible. In this case the Council acted in time to prevent a recurrence of the bond-washing scandal by giving the executive chairman and his two deputies the duty of approving any cum dividend deals in steel stocks after the date on which they went ex-dividend.

Despite these actions, the fact remains that the remedies available to the Council are weak and too rigid. The suspension of a member is admittedly a serious step, but the member can normally continue to supervise business within his firm, so long as the firm itself has not been suspended. Similarly, the suspension of the quotation of a company is an extremely serious matter but it is very infrequently resorted to, and then, with rare exceptions, only against small companies.

For these reasons it is often argued in the financial Press that the Council should either regulate the market much more strongly, with matching powers, in terms of both severity and flexibility, to enforce such regulation, or that it should submit to the control of a government agency established on the lines of the Securities and Exchange Commission in the USA.

The Securities and Exchange Commission was established by the Federal Securities Act of 1933 and its powers were extended by the Securities Exchange Act of 1934. This latter Act was largely the result of the recommendations of a US Senate Committee on Stock Exchange Practices, which revealed the vast extent of manipulation in American securities markets during the 1920s, a period which ended with the Great Crash of 1929 and the ensuing years of depression. The Commission has control over the national securities exchanges and there are serious restrictions placed upon the activities of brokers, dealers and exchanges that are not registered with the Commission or have not been exempted therefrom. All exchanges which are registered with the Commission must agree to enforce all regulations which the Commission requires and to inform it of any changes which it makes in its rules.

As a result the S.E.C. has absolute power over the activities of all registered exchanges. All new issues must be registered with the Commission at least twenty days before the date of offer. The S.E.C. will then check the accuracy of the information being made available to the public and will ensure that it satisfies the stringent disclosure provisions which it has laid down. All corporations any of whose securities are listed on a registered exchange must provide a degree of information in many respects in excess of that required by the London Stock Exchange, particularly in the requirement of quarterly reports.

There is also considerable day-to-day control over market operations. A constant watch is maintained over price movements and an explanation is sought for any sharp fluctuations which may occur. Furthermore, corporations are required to provide details on a monthly basis of all transactions carried out by holders of more than 10% of their listed stock or by directors or officers of the corporation. If it is suspected that the market for a security has become artificial or is subject to manipulation the listing of that security may be temporarily suspended in order that the situation may be clarified. If manipulation is found to have occurred action may be taken against the members concerned, resulting possibly in suspension, expulsion or a lawsuit for damages. Moreover, the S.E.C. has the absolute sanction of being able, with the approval of the US President, to suspend all trading on any national stock exchange for up to ninety days.

In 1964, following a further Senate report on securities markets, the Securities Acts were amended. In particular it was enacted that all companies with assets of at least $1 m. and 500 or more stockholders must report earnings and other financial information and report insider dealings in the same way as companies listed on the New York Stock Exchange. As a result a large part of the informal over-the-counter market which had previously largely been conducted outside S.E.C. regulation was brought within its ambit.

All in all, the continuous surveillance of the S.E.C., its independence of the exchanges and the flexibility of its remedies compare very favourably with the work performed by the London Stock Exchange. A further definite advantage is that the ordinary investor feels that he is getting more unbiased treatment due to the regulation of the exchanges by an outside body. It seems probable that the London Stock Exchange will ultimately have to provide such a watchdog for itself or have one imposed upon it by the Government, despite the fact that there is not at present any Government department which appears to have the necessary experience.

(c) *The Secrecy and Conservatism of the Market*

The London Stock Exchange has always prided itself upon the secrecy with which its operations are conducted and the long traditions of its market. The value which it places on secrecy is shown by the following extracts from a description of the Exchange written by one of its members:

'Inter-jobber competition places a premium on secrecy, and the facilities provided by nominee accounts in Britain enable purchasers to conceal their identity at every stage of the transaction. However, the Stock Exchange on Government insistence will soon be publishing turnover figures covering six main classes of securities.'[1]

'The jobbing system effectively precludes the publication of accurate and meaningful statistics on the daily volume and value of transactions. . . . The advantages claimed for the jobbing system are generally considered to outweigh the non-availability of turnover statistics. Moreover, there is a good case for saying that this non-

---

[1] John M. Weiner 'The London Stock Exchange and Other Stock Markets in Great Britain'. This forms Chapter 8 of *The Principal Stock Exchanges of the World—Their Operation, Structure and Development*, ed. David E. Spray (Washington, D.C.: International Economic Publishers, 1964, p. 176).

availability contributes to the steadiness of the market, whilst their availability in other markets may well lead to greater price swings.'[1]

These extracts amply demonstrate the extent of the cult of secrecy and the degree of reluctance with which turnover statistics were eventually published in 1964. However, one of the prerequisites of a perfectly competitive market is the availability of full information for all participants, and clearly the London Exchange is seriously deficient in this respect. Moreover, the lack of information encourages the perpetuation of the view that the Stock Exchange is a club which considers the interests of its members over and above those of the investing public.

Although the Stock Exchange Council has in recent years greatly increased the degree of disclosure which it requires from companies as a condition of the granting of a quotation, it has done little to provide more information about the market and its members. This is particularly true in the case of jobbers, whose activities are masked from the public, and who are continuously bemoaning their lot without providing any tangible evidence to enable the profitability of their activities to be assessed. For example, a report was commissioned by a committee of jobbers from a firm of accountants on the subject of declining profitability and other financial problems faced by jobbers. The report was completed within nine months and was presented to the Council of the Stock Exchange at the end of September 1966. Nevertheless, despite the supposed urgency of the situation, its contents were still a closely guarded secret two years later.

This may have been due to the fact that jobbing turned out to be very profitable after all. The 1969 annual report of Smith Brothers, a leading firm of jobbers, showed pre-tax profits of £1,020,000 and the chairman described the two previous years as "exceptionally prosperous". The decline in competition is shown by the fact that this one company had a turnover in shares of £700 m.—nearly 10% of all London deals in equities during 1969. Moreover, at the end of May 1969 the company held shares to the value of £2,773,000 and had sold short to the extent of £1,545,000.

Second only to its insistence upon secrecy is the regard of the Stock Exchange for tradition. It might have been expected that the construction of a new and modernized Stock Exchange building would have led to the removal of some of the outmoded ideas and practices which were the feature of the old trading floor. Even in 1967 the members refused to accept an amendment to their rules which would have permitted the election of women members, though still refusing

---

[1] *Ibid.*, pp. 203–4.

them admission to the trading floor. Ironically enough, this decision coincided with a decision of the Jockey Club to allow women to be licensed as trainers—an interesting indication of the relative extent of conservatism in the Stock Exchange. It was not until 1972 that women were finally admitted to membership of the Stock Exchange.

Although many advantages are claimed by members for the maintenance of the traditions, especially those relating to secrecy, these are not especially potent. The main argument seems to be that the jobbing system is responsible for the steadiness of the market and that the jobbers can only operate satisfactorily under conditions of secrecy. However, because of this secrecy it is impossible to measure the contribution of jobbers to market stability. In fact, intuitive judgment would suggest that stability results from the conservative characteristics of British investors just as much as from the activities of jobbers. Against the rather ephemeral advantages of the maintenance of secrecy there must be balanced the suspicion with which the Stock Exchange is held by the general public, whose only knowledge of the Exchange is based on the rather smug advertisements, films and brochures published by the Council. Moreover, there is a strong economic argument for requiring an investigation into the functions and operations of the Stock Exchange, so that their value and efficiency may be tested and more information may be made available to analysts and theorists who seek to discover the forces which determine share values. It is not suggested that such an investigation need be critical of the Stock Exchange. In fact the last Government investigation in 1877 and 1878 vindicated the Stock Exchange and the jobbing system in particular, and did much to create public faith in the market and the conduct of its members.

Probably the most encouraging development on the London Stock Exchange has been its support for the creation of a federation of United Kingdom stock exchanges. There are three major organizations outside London which provide markets for the purchase and sale of securities:

(i) *The Associated Stock Exchange*

These are provincial stock exchanges which were formerly independent, but have now, with the exception of the Irish exchanges (Belfast, Dublin and Cork) been amalgamated into three regional exchanges, the Scottish Stock Exchange (consisting of the Aberdeen, Dundee, Edinburgh and Glasgow Exchanges as well as four members of the Provincial Brokers' Stock Exchange in Scotland), the Northern Stock Exchange (comprising the Bradford, Halifax, Huddersfield, Leeds, Liverpool, Manchester, Newcastle-upon-Tyne, Oldham and

Sheffield Exchanges plus the Northern Country Brokers' Association), and the Midlands and Western Stock Exchange (Birmingham, Bristol, Cardiff, Nottingham and Swansea). These exchanges which now form part of the Federation of Stock Exchanges in Great Britain and Ireland had a total of 889 members in 1971.

(ii) *The Provincial Brokers' Stock Exchange*

This is an association of brokers who deal in various provincial towns in the British Isles. Their headquarters is at York and they do not possess a trading floor. In 1964 the association had a membership of 264, carrying on business in over 100 towns. By 1971 their membership had fallen to 188, due largely to the transfer of some brokers to the regional stock exchanges. In 1966 the association put forward proposals that would enable its members to obtain admission to the London Stock Exchange but these were put first before one sub-committee, then another. In August 1967, a leading firm of London stockbrokers announced plans to merge with four provincial stock-brokers. This has effectively by-passed any verdict which the sub-committee on amalgamations may in the fullness of time agree upon, and has also signalled a trend which will result in further inroads into the membership of the Provincial Brokers' Stock Exchange. This, however, is in the long run a very beneficial course of events, for the transference of provincial brokers to the regional stock exchanges and to London will facilitate the ultimate formation of a National Stock Exchange. It is a reflection upon the London Exchange that this movement towards amalgamation has been precipitated first by the provincial brokers themselves and then by a single firm of London stockbrokers.

(iii) *The Association of Stock and Share Dealers*

This association consists of some fifty firms, including limited companies, who are authorized by statute to deal in securities and who are permitted to advertise.

All Stock Exchange transactions throughout the United Kingdom are performed under the same general rules. In April 1962 a committee was set up by the London Stock Exchange, the Associated Stock Exchanges and the Provincial Brokers' Stock Exchange to determine what further degree of co-ordination was desirable and how it might be achieved. Its first report, which was published in 1963, argued in favour of the establishment of a federation of the three bodies concerned, in preference to a National Stock Exchange. It was recommended that a Federal Committee should be appointed and given authority to enforce a common policy in certain matters. The Committee should have twenty-four members, fourteen nominated by the Council of the London Stock Exchange, eight by the Council of the Associated Stock Exchanges and two by the Council of the Provincial Brokers' Stock Exchange. A 75% majority would be necessary for a resolution to become effective, and once adopted, any such resolution would be binding on the governing bodies of all exchanges which belonged to the Federation.

Two further reports were issued in 1964 which provided for the adoption by the Federation of the rules of the London Stock Exchange in respect of quotation requirements and, to a large extent, compensation fund contributions. On the other hand, it was recommended that a system should be established to provide for the written examination of prospective future members, a practice previously enforced only by the Provincial Brokers' Stock Exchange. However, it was not until late in 1966 that the scheme for implementing the examinations was passed to the constituent exchanges for their comment. Finally, the controversial question of dual capacity members who exist outside the London Stock Exchange was resolved in favour of London, for it was provided that all such members must select a single capacity in which to deal, though only at the end of a time period which was originally established at ten years and later extended for an indefinite period. The Federation, based on the above recommendations, formally came into existence on July 1, 1965.

It now seems certain that the Federation will ultimately form the basis of a National Stock Exchange and it is difficult to understand why this was not resolved upon by the original co-ordination committee. It is still more difficult to comprehend why the London Stock Exchange, whose members have continually complained of unfair competition from the provinces due to lower overhead expenses outside London and the free availability of London prices as a basis for provincial deals, should not be positively urging the formation of such an exchange where all members may compete freely and on equal terms.

2. THE ALLOCATORY FUNCTION OF THE LONDON STOCK EXCHANGE

The argument that the Stock Exchange is an important source of capital for British industry and that it acts as an efficient allocatory mechanism in the distribution of available funds is now patently outdated, as may be evidenced by several factors:

(a) *The Reliance of Industry Upon Sources of Finance External to the Stock Exchange*

British industry has, in recent years, utilized many sources of finance, including retained profits, bank loans, trade credit, and new capital. As is shown below retained profits represent by far the most important source.

Finance of quoted companies **1961–68**[1] (*£m.*)

Accounts for 'Year'[2]	*1963*	*1964*[4]	*1964*[3,4]	*1965*[4]	*1966*[4]	*1967*[4]	*1968*[4]
No. of companies	2,004	1,916	2,283	2,198	2,109	1,993	1,829
Receipts from issues of:							
Long-term loans	165	209	220	377	565	662	541
Ordinary shares	208	262	295	265	269	425	1,343
Preference, etc., shares	20	23	30	9	−77	−13	−50
Total loan and share capital issued	**392**	**493**	**546**	**651**	**756**	**1,073**	**1,834**
Increase in amount owing to:							
Banks	120	170	187	339	210	65	225
Trade creditors	357	528	559	498	271	486	644
Other creditors	17	4	4	4	4	4	4
Addition to accruals:							
Tax	9	75	85	−57	171	54	905
Dividends and interest	41	20	22	−34	−27	20	14
Total increase in credit received	**544**	**793**	**852**	**746**	**626**	**626**	**1,789**
Balance retained in reserves	503	613	640	880	430	357	497
Provisions out of income for depreciation, etc.	716	752	770	861	927	942	1,050
Additions to future tax reserves	72	158	164	−34	60	82	−658
Total addition to reserves and provisions	**1,290**	**1,522**	**1,574**	**1,707**	**1,416**	**1,381**	**889**
Increase in liability to minority shareholders	16	4	4	4	4	4	4
Surplus on disposal of fixed assets	60	4	4	4	4	4	4
Other receipts on capital account	7	48	48	50	39	317	292
Total of other sources	**83**	**48**	**48**	**50**	**39**	**317**	**292**
Total source of funds	**2,310**	**2,856**	**3,020**	**3,154**	**2,836**	**3,397**	**4,803**

[See overleaf for Notes

¹ The figures are derived from the accounts of quoted companies engaged mainly in the United Kingdom in manufacturing, distribution, construction and certain miscellaneous services. They exclude companies whose main interests are in agriculture, shipping, insurance, banking, finance and property and those operating wholly or mainly overseas.

² The 'year' is, for each company included, its accounting year which ended between April 6 of the year shown and April 5 of the following year.

³ These figures for 1964, with comparable figures for later years, are confined to quoted companies with net assets of £500,000 or more or income of £50,000 or more in 1964.

⁴ The figures for 1964–1968 take account of a revised system of analysis which results in certain figures being absorbed in other headings than those in which they appear in 1963.

The above table, extracted from the *Annual Abstract of Statistics 1970* indicates that retained profits, depreciation provisions and future tax reserves accounted for over 48% of the sources of finance utilized by quoted companies in every year. New issues of share and loan capital accounted for not more than 20% of such finance in each year except 1967 and 1968. However, the level of capital issues greatly overstates the extent to which they are used as a source of new funds, for many of the issues were made in connection with takeover bids. This was particularly true in 1967 and 1968, when the expenditure on subsidiaries was £739 m. and £1,694 m. respectively.

A more realistic assessment of their importance is provided by Malcolm Crawford,¹ who compiled the following table:

Main Sources of Capital of Industrial and Commercial Companies
(£m.)

	1960	1961	1962	1963	Average %	%
Retained profits (net)	1,798	1,492	1,297	1,619	67	73·1
Increase in bank borrowing	380	255	282	486	15	16·6
Other non-market borrowings (net)	115	100	23	39	3	3·3
Capital issues for cash by quoted companies	320	430	325	328	15	—
Less: Quoted companies, other securities, transactions (cash, net)	200	200	200	200	—	—
Net capital market finance	120	230	125	128	—	7·1

¹ Malcolm Crawford, 'The 1965 Reforms in the British Tax System', *Moorgate and Wall Street* (Winter 1965, p. 40).

Notes: Figures for retained profits are obtained from those given in *Financial Statistics* for gross savings of industrial and commercial companies, less estimates of capital consumption derived from those given in *National Income and Expenditure.*

Figures for external finance are from the *Bank of England Quarterly Bulletin,* September 1963, June 1964, and June 1965. Those for capital issues do not include issues by unquoted companies; but, apart from inter-company issues, these are believed to be comparatively small. The estimates for 'other transactions' are described in one issue of the *Bulletin* as 'precarious', but the sign of the error items suggests that they are probably under-estimated. In the main, they indicate net purchases by quoted companies of shares for cash, by way of takeover bids and trade investments.

This table differs from that extracted from the *Annual Abstract* in that it is based upon all companies as opposed to quoted companies alone. As a result the importance of new capital issues is lessened, for unquoted companies very rarely have recourse to this method of finance. However, the figure of 7·1% for the contribution of net capital market finance to company funds indicates the relative un-importance of the stock market to companies as a whole and casts serious doubts upon its ability to act as an allocatory mechanism. The table is also different in that it shows net retained profits, after a charge for capital consumption, rather than gross retentions.

Still further statistics prepared by the Bank of England[1] suggest that retained profits, as a proportion of funds from all sources, have fallen from 93% in 1952–58 to 85% in 1959–65. The major problems in the use of official statistics relating to companies are the extent to which they are forced to rely upon estimates and the serious differences of definition between various sets of data. All in all, however, it seems likely that net capital issues do not constitute much more than 10% of the total sources of company funds, while retained profits account for considerably more than 50% of those funds.

The reliance of British companies upon retained earnings may be attributed to several factors:

(i) *Conservatism.* Profits may be retained by management without the provision for shareholders of more than the barest details of the use to which the funds thus withheld are to be put. Normally a brief reference to expansion or the need to provide against future contingencies will suffice in this respect. By contrast, the disclosure provisions which must be adhered to in the event of a new issue require the preparation and publication of far more information.

[1] 'Company Finance: 1952–65', *Bank of England Quarterly Bulletin,* Vol. 7, March 1967, pp. 29–42.

(ii) *Cheapness.* Company directors often regard retained profits as free of cost, with regard to both the original retention and its annual servicing. This is, of course, incorrect, for regard must be had to the opportunity cost of such funds, representing the external income that the company foregoes by investing those funds internally. There is some force in the argument that such funds are cheaper in that there are no issue costs. Furthermore, shareholders do not have to bear the Income Tax which would be payable if the profits were distributed, their tax being limited to any Capital Gains Tax payable on the disposal of the shares. This, however, is advantageous to the shareholders only if the company reinvests its profits efficiently with the result that the value of the company's shares will tend to increase. Unfortunately, however, the noted study by I. M. D. Little[1] on this subject revealed no correlation between the rate of ploughback of British companies in the period 1951–59 and the rate of growth of earnings per share. This suggests that the growth of earnings of firms which retained a large proportion of their earnings was not noticeably different from that of firms which tended to distribute their profits, and suggests that retained profits have been invested inefficiently. However cheap retained profits may appear to be in the eyes of management, any benefits to shareholders seem to have been largely illusory.

(iii) *Fear of Disclosure.* Successive amendments to the requirements of the general undertaking to which all companies must subscribe upon the grant of a quotation have been made applicable only to companies requiring a quotation for any of its securities after the date on which the amendment is to take effect. Consequently, companies with an existing quotation are affected only if they seek a quotation for a subsequent issue of securities. Such an issue would therefore increase the disclosure provisions to which the company is required to adhere.

As a result of the above factors companies have become increasingly dependent upon retained earnings, most companies retaining a certain proportion of profits each year almost as a matter of course, and coming to the market only when an unusually large amount of capital is required. Due to the importance of retained profits, companies are therefore only infrequently subjected to market discipline and the strength of that discipline has been considerably reduced.

[1] I. M. D. Little, 'Higgledy Piggledy Growth', *Bulletin of the Oxford Institute of Statistics*, **24** (November 1962).

(b) *The Failure of the Stock Exchange to Predict the Profitability of Companies*

The random walk theory, as explained in Chapter 14, suggests that any prediction of the future price of a share based on its past performance will not provide a better result than a random forecast. It would follow from this that future profitability cannot be assessed on the basis of past profitability. Moreover, surveys have shown that shares which the market has favoured in the past have not performed noticeably better than those which have been unpopular.[1] As a result it is seriously doubted whether the market has in the past satisfactorily predicted the relative profitability of quoted companies, and it is unlikely that its capacity can be substantially improved.

Because of the difficulty of anticipating the relative efficiency of companies, which is not an indictment of the Stock Exchange but of the vast uncertainty of the economic system in which it operates, most new issues are assessed not on profitability but on such factors as the size of a company and the reputation of its management. Consequently, a large firm with a stable profit record could obtain funds from the market much more cheaply than a smaller, more speculative concern, whatever the merits of the projects into which the funds were to be invested.

In any case, writers on the theory of resource allocation often ignore two important factors. In the first place companies, when making investment decisions, ignore non-monetary factors such as social benefits and costs so that national interests cannot possibly be optimized by the market mechanism. Consequently it is impossible from the start to ensure perfect allocation at the national level through the medium of the Stock Exchange.

A second weak point of the theory of allocation is the argument that the current or past yield on the equity of a company can in some way be used as the basis for calculating the cost of equity capital of the company.[2] However, the equity yield is based on predicted future profits and share values. Thus a company whose shares offer a dividend yield of 1% would need a substantially higher yield both on

---

[1] Viz. Terence E. Adderley and Douglas A. Hayes, 'The Investment Performance of Selected Growth Stock Portfolios: 1939–1955' and G. Howard Conklin, 'Growth Stocks—A Critical View'. Both of these articles first appeared in the *Financial Analysts Journal* and were subsequently reprinted in *Readings in Financial Analysis and Investment Management*, ed. Eugene M. Lerner (Homewood, Ill.: Irwin, 1964). Also see Peter L. Bernstein, 'Growth in Companies *vs.* Growth Stocks', *Harvard Business Review*, Vol. 34, No. 5 (September-October, 1956) pp. 87–98.

[2] Cf. W. J. Baumol, *op. cit.*, p. 3.

a new issue and on its existing shares, for the market is clearly already anticipating increased dividends. Thus it is the anticipated yield on a share which should indicate the cost of capital, not the current dividend yield. There is, however, no way in which this anticipated yield can be measured with any accuracy.

Whatever the defects of current theory, it is clear that the market does not possess the information to act as an allocator of resources, especially at the national level. Moreover, any chance that it might have of serving such a function has been lost due to the failure of companies to approach the capital market for more than a fraction of their financial requirements.

(c) *The Costs of New Issues*

The cost of entrance to the capital market has already been mentioned as one of the factors which has caused companies to avoid it and seek finance elsewhere. The extent of these costs is illustrated in a paper by A. J. Merrett and G. D. Newbould,[1] which calculated the costs of issue of new issues during 1963, having regard to the fact that the discount at which the shares are issued below their intrinsic market value should be regarded as an issue expense. The authors show that the mean market discount based on the market price of the shares the second day after the commencement of dealings was 18·9% of the issue proceeds in the case of offers for sale and 23·2% for placings. When the direct issue expenses of between 7% and 8% are added to these figures the full cost of new issues, ignoring indirect costs in connection with managerial and administrative time spent on the issue by the company, appears quite enormous. By contrast the cost of issues by tender, where the market discount was estimated at 3·5%, appears relatively low.

On the whole there seems to be every justification for regarding the market discount as an issue cost, for it represents part of the value of the shares being issued which is forgone by the issuing company, often to the advantage of stags, in order to ensure the success of the issue. If this is accepted then the method of issue by tender has obvious advantages and it is difficult to understand why it is not more often favoured. Clearly it is not necessary in the case of an equity issued by a company whose shares are already quoted, for the appropriate issue price can be determined with substantial accuracy by reference to the existing price. However, in the case of issues of equities by companies which are new to the market, particularly

[1] A. J. Merrett and G. D. Newbould, 'The Comparative Efficiency of Methods of Issue', *The Manchester School*, January 1966, pp. 1–14.

those for whom there is no comparable stock already quoted (a group which has seen some of the more spectacular miscalculations on the part of issuing houses), the tender seems very appropriate.

Nevertheless the market and, surprisingly, much of the financial press seems adamantly opposed to tenders. Much of the opposition appears to be ill-founded and suggests that members of the Stock Exchange are more concerned with the success of an issue notwithstanding the expensive insurance provided by underwriting, than with maximizing the proceeds received by the issuing company.

The normal criticisms of this method are very well expressed in the City section of the *Sunday Telegraph*,[1] where a staff journalist writes as follows:

'I can see one very strong objection to the use of tenders, which is that the public has an acute dislike of a method of issuing shares which it just does not understand. On the whole, issues by tender evoke a much poorer response than do conventional offers for sale. Investors find them complicated and much prefer the chance of getting shares at a fixed price to the chance of hitting on the right price to put on their tender forms. I believe consumer preference counts.

'Nor can I altogether accept the idea that if an issue goes to a large premium, this represents a loss to the vendor. After all, part of the purpose of the sale is to put a value on the major part of the equity which the vendor usually retains. If the result of giving the public a "stagging" profit is that dealings start at a higher price than they would have, had the issue been barely subscribed, then on balance the vendor must be better off.'

This represents a rather credulous view of the virtues of the conventional offer for sale, which is so often attended by a herd of stags baying for a risk-free profit on a minimum of capital resources. Under present conditions of equity shortage, such so-called investors do nothing to aid the market in the new security, for they only buy in order to sell out quickly at a profit to a more genuine investor. If the ranks of applicants are limited to those seriously interested in obtaining and maintaining a holding of the new shares this will represent no loss to the issuing company for, whatever the activities of stags, the price that is ultimately established must be based upon the investment merits of the issue.

The second argument is still more flimsy. There is no apparent reason why dealings in an issue which has been stagged should start at a higher level than in an issue which has been made by tender. In

[1] *Sunday Telegraph*, August 20, 1967, p. 17.

fact, there are cases in evidence of issues which have been well over-subscribed yet which have opened at a discount due to a high level of stag selling. Similarly, it is generally found that, due to stag selling, the opening price of an over-subscribed issue is lower than the price at which the share eventually settles. It is difficult, in fact, to see how the allotment of shares to a substantial body of impatient sellers is likely to exercise a beneficial effect upon their market price. In fact, whatever the type of issue, the shares will ultimately be held by genuine investors who are prepared to judge the shares on their investment merits and bid up the price to an equilibrium value.

The drawbacks of the offer for sale were, ironically, shown in a new issue advertised the very next day of which the Financial Editor of *The Times* had the following to say:[1]

'These seem generous terms, sufficiently generous to suggest the shares deserve to go to a premium of 1s 6d or 2s when market dealings begin. Even at a 2s premium the indicated yield would still be 5 per cent. which is more than the returns presently obtainable on most other comparable . . . shares. Thus the offer is likely to be over-subscribed and in current circumstances could be well over-subscribed.'

In fact the issue was about twenty-five times over-subscribed and when dealings commenced those applicants who were successful in the ballot for shares were able to make a profit of 3s 6d per share when dealings commenced. If the offer price had been increased by 2s 6d there seems little reason to doubt that the shares would still have been taken up, and the clients of the issuing house would have been richer by nearly £200,000.

Surely the function of the issuing house is to obtain a market price based on investment merits and to secure most of that price for its client, rather than to stir up a temporary speculative market which increases turnover and brokers' commissions without endeavouring to maximize the return to the issuing company. If this is not the case one is tempted to ask what service is provided by issuing houses in return for the generous fees which they charge, in view of the fact that underwriting of equity issues is so often a free distribution of commission and the pricing seems to be based on maintaining the reputation of the issuing house rather than optimizing the proceeds for the client.

Probably the weakest argument against tenders was that adopted by a representative of an issuing house which has been responsible for several 'successful' issues which have attained a dealing price far

[1] *The Times*, August 21, 1967, p. 18.

in excess of the offer price: 'Offer by tender is not only derogatory to the dignity of the City but is analogous to a barker at a market stall inviting all and sundry to make a bid for his wares.'

If the Stock Exchange is not to be regarded as a market place, it becomes difficult to justify its very existence!

PART II: STOCK EXCHANGE SECURITIES AND OTHER INVESTMENTS

CHAPTER 5

Fixed Interest Securities and their Characteristics

Stock Exchange securities[1] are commonly classified in one of two ways—either by reference to the nature of the organization responsible for their issue or by reference to the nature of the return which they give. The first method in very broad terms distinguishes between gilt-edged, foreign government and company securities, while the second recognizes the distinction between fixed-interest and variable interest securities. This chapter describes the main characteristics of fixed-interest securities and they are then analyzed according to the source of issue. For the sake of convenience preference shares are discussed in this chapter though their return is in the nature of dividend rather than interest.

1. CHARACTERISTICS OF FIXED-INTEREST SECURITIES

It is relatively easy for an investor to calculate precisely his return on a fixed-interest security, for he knows with certainty the fixed rate of return that he will receive each year. Nevertheless, there are still three unknown factors which can have a very serious effect on calculations of the return. In the first place there is the possibility that the organization undertaking the issue might default on its obligations, whether in respect of interest payments or repayments of capital. This risk is much greater in the case of securities issued by some foreign governments and many companies, than in the case of those

---

[1] The word 'securities' is intended to cover all types of stocks and shares dealt in on the London Stock Exchange. The formal distinction between stocks and shares is explained in the appendix to this chapter.

issued by the British Government. Secondly, there is the distinct probability that the value in real terms of the interest and capital payments received will be very different from their monetary value. Thus a person lending a sum of money for a fixed period of, say, twenty years must take into account the fact that, although the money value of the capital when repaid will be as agreed, its real value will almost certainly have deteriorated considerably. As a result any estimation of the rate of return should attempt to take into account the expected rate of inflation. The final element of uncertainty depends on the date, if any, on which the security is due for redemption. The more distant the date of redemption the greater the likelihood that the holder of the security will sell it on the market rather than hold it to redemption. If this happens the rate of return must incorporate the anticipated sale proceeds rather than the maturity receipts. These sale proceeds will depend on the future price of the security, which will in turn be affected by the economic situation at the time and the resultant structure of interest rates.

The date of redemption is thus extremely important and fixed-interest securities are normally classified on the basis of that date:

(i) *Short-dated Securities*

These are securities whose date of redemption is within the next five years. In many cases the redemption date is not specified exactly, the terms of the issue being that the security must be redeemed between two stated dates, depending upon the wishes of the issuing body. An example of such a security is Treasury $5\frac{1}{2}\%$ 2008/12, which must be redeemed between September 2008 and September 2012, though the exact date of redemption will be decided by the Government of the time. The decision will depend upon the level of interest rates between 2008 and 2012, for the cost of redemption will have to be met out of funds raised by a further issue of securities at the appropriate interest rate then in force. If that rate is well in excess of $5\frac{1}{2}\%$ the Government would allow the security to survive until the last possible date for redemption, while if it is below $5\frac{1}{2}\%$ it would redeem it as soon as possible out of the proceeds of an issue at a lower rate of interest.

It follows that where a security must be redeemed within two dates, one of which is less than five years hence and the other is more than five years hence, the classification of the security will depend upon the current levels of interest rates. Thus Electricity $4\frac{1}{4}\%$ 1974/79 may be redeemed by the Government at any time between 1974 and 1979. So long as interest rates are above $4\frac{1}{4}\%$ the Government will not exercise its option to redeem this security. Consequently, in 1971 it

E*   137

could not be regarded as a short-dated security because it was unlikely to be redeemed before 1979.

Because of the close proximity of the redemption date and the relatively small influence of rises in the price level in the very short run the return on short-dated securities can be calculated with reasonable certainty. Moreover the risk element is lessened still further by the price stability of this group, for the approaching redemption ensures that the share price does not move away too far from the redemption price.

The inherent certainty of these securities makes them most attractive to institutional investors such as banks and insurance companies, who are glad to invest money on terms involving a competitive yield, a certain repayment of the nominal capital at a fixed date within five years, and the probability of a fairly stable market price.

One peculiar feature of 'shorts' is that where the security is quoted on a 'cum div.' basis the buyer has to pay in addition to the market price the gross amount of the interest accrued to the date of purchase. Similarly if he buys the security 'ex div.' he will receive the gross amount of interest accruing from the purchase date to the date of the next interest payment.

(ii) *Medium-dated Securities*

These are stocks which have a potential life of between five and fifteen years. Because the redemption date is rather more distant than is the case with short-dated securities and thus exercises less of a magnetic effect, the price of such stocks is more liable to fluctuate with short-term movements in interest rates. It is thus more difficult for an investor to estimate his probable return, partly because he is more likely to sell the stock before redemption at an unknown future price, and partly because rising prices will cause a greater erosion in the real value of the proceeds. Because of the greater risk attached to such securities it is usual for them to offer a slightly higher return than short-dated securities. However, if interest rates are abnormally high and it is felt that they will probably fall in the short-term, medium-dated securities may offer a lower yield than 'shorts' because their abnormally high return will be maintained over a longer period. Alternatively, a fall in interest rates would cause a rise in the market price of the security and the investor could realize a capital gain.

(iii) *Long-dated Securities*

These are redeemable stocks which have a potential life of above fifteen years. Although the fact that they are redeemable will always eventually pull their price up towards par, short-term fluctuations in the market rate of interest will tend to exert rather more influence. Consequently this group is rather more risky and would tend to offer a rather higher yield than other redeemable securities.

(iv) *One-way Option Securities and Irredeemable Securities*

One-way option stocks are redeemable only at the option of the issuing body. The two most famous of these stocks are $3\frac{1}{2}\%$ War Loan, 1952 or after and $2\frac{1}{2}\%$ Treasury Stock, 1975 or after. The first of these stocks has been redeemable at the option of the Government since December 1952, but redemption is unlikely to take place until an equivalent amount of stock could be issued at a lower rate of interest to provide the funds for the redemption. At the present, redemption is inconceivable. In the same way $2\frac{1}{2}\%$ Treasury Stock, 1975 or after, can be regarded as irredeemable. The technically irredeemable stocks are those which are entirely undated.

Irredeemable securities are the most speculative of the fixed-interest group. There is no ultimate redemption date to act as a price stabilizer and their price is determined entirely by the market rate of interest and expectations as to its future movements. As a result the market price is subject to fluctuations within a relatively wide range.

If, for example, the market rate of interest was 7% the price of £100 nominal value of $3\frac{1}{2}\%$ War Loan would be £50, for with an investment of £100 an investor could then buy £200 nominal value of the stock, which would provide interest of £7.

If the rate of interest fell to 6% the price would be £58, for an investor could now buy nearly £171 nominal value of stock for £100 which would yield interest of £6.

Because of the volatile nature of their market price, securities within this group have a definite appeal for speculators who anticipate a fall in the rate of interest. They also appeal to investors who wish to ensure the perpetual receipt of income at the current level of interest rates. Thus an investor who acquired £100 nominal value at $3\frac{1}{2}\%$ War Loan at a price of £50 would be certain of receiving £3·50 per annum in perpetuity, representing a return of 7%. However, although the income is guaranteed, neither the money value nor the real value of the capital is assured, and the market price would be subject to wide fluctuations.

Because of their greater risk, irredeemable securities must offer a higher yield than redeemable securities in order to attract investors. However, when interest rates are regarded as abnormally high,

139

investors might accept a rather lower yield in order to guarantee its receipt for perpetuity.

The pattern of yields on securities with different lives is illustrated in the following table, based on British Government securities and extracted from *Financial Statistics:*

	Short-dated	Medium-dated	Long-dated	2½% Consols
	Gross Redemption Yield	Gross Redemption Yield	Gross Redemption Yield	Gross Flat Yield
1962	5·31	5·76	5·90	5·98
1963	4·83	5·17	5·43	5·58
1964	5·54	5·70	5·98	6·03
1965	6·57	6·55	6·56	6·42
1966	6·77	6·87	6·94	6·80
1967	6·66	6·70	6·80	6·69
1968	7·59	7·51	7·55	7·39
1969	8·81	8·83	9·05	8·88
1970	7·89	8·64	9·25	9·16
1971	6·83	7·84	8·75	9·05

Between 1962 and 1964 the yield structure followed a normal pattern, with irredeemable stocks offering the highest yield and short-dated the lowest. As the level of interest rates increased in 1965, the yield on dated stocks rose to above that on Consols. During 1966 and 1967 the high interest rates continued and a more normal structure of rates was established with 'shorts' offering the lowest yield, but with Consols giving a better return than the other dated stocks. The precipitate rise in rates during 1968 caused the rate on 'shorts' to rise above that on other stocks, while Consols offered a lower return than any dated stocks. When investors became accustomed to high interest rates in 1969 and 1970 the normal structure of rates was restored, but with Consols slightly out of line until 1971.

The relative volatility of securities with different lives is indicated in the following list of prices as at December 31, 1968, from *The Financial Times.*

1968

	High	Low
Conversion 3½% 1969	99$\frac{15}{32}$	95$\frac{11}{16}$
Funding 3% 1959/69	99	95$\frac{7}{8}$
Electricity 4½% 1967/69	98$\frac{7}{16}$	95$\frac{15}{32}$

FIXED INTEREST SECURITIES

	High	*Low*
Exchequer $6\frac{1}{2}\%$ 1969	$99\frac{15}{16}$	$98\frac{1}{16}$
Exchequer 6% 1970	$98\frac{17}{32}$	$96\frac{1}{2}$
Savings 3% 1960/70	$92\frac{13}{16}$	$85\frac{5}{8}$
Treasury $6\frac{1}{2}\%$ 1971	$98\frac{1}{32}$	$96\frac{1}{2}$
Conversion 5% 1971	$94\frac{3}{16}$	92
Gas $3\frac{1}{2}\%$ 1969/71	$90\frac{7}{8}$	$87\frac{5}{16}$
Exchequer $6\frac{3}{4}\%$ 1971	$98\frac{5}{16}$	$96\frac{9}{16}$
Conversion 6% 1972	$95\frac{7}{8}$	$93\frac{3}{4}$
Gas 4% 1969/72	89	$86\frac{5}{16}$
Exchequer $6\frac{1}{4}\%$ 1972	$95\frac{29}{32}$	$93\frac{3}{4}$
Exchequer $6\frac{3}{4}\%$ 1973	$97\frac{11}{16}$	$96\frac{3}{16}$
Electricity 3% 1968/73	$83\frac{9}{16}$	$80\frac{3}{4}$
Transport 3% 1968/73	$89\frac{3}{8}$	85
Unweighted averages	95	$92\frac{7}{32}$

Percentage fluctuation in price
(difference between high and
low prices expressed as percentage of the low price)

$$\frac{2\frac{25}{32}}{92\frac{7}{32}} \times 100 = 3 \cdot 02\%$$

1968

Medium-dated	*High*	*Low*
Victory 4% 1976	$98\frac{3}{8}$	95
Conversion $5\frac{1}{4}\%$ 1974	$92\frac{1}{4}$	$87\frac{5}{8}$
Funding 4% 1960/90	$98\frac{1}{4}$	$94\frac{1}{4}$
Savings 3% 1965/75	$76\frac{1}{2}$	$73\frac{3}{4}$
Treasury $6\frac{1}{2}\%$ 1976	$98\frac{3}{8}$	93
Electricity 3% 1974/77	$72\frac{3}{4}$	$70\frac{1}{8}$
Transport 4% 1972/77	$79\frac{1}{8}$	$73\frac{7}{8}$
Exchequer 5% 1976/78	$85\frac{7}{16}$	80
Electricity $4\frac{1}{4}\%$ 1974/79	$78\frac{1}{4}$	$73\frac{1}{8}$
Electricity $3\frac{1}{2}\%$ 1976/79	$72\frac{1}{2}$	$67\frac{1}{8}$
Treasury $3\frac{1}{2}\%$ 1977/80	$75\frac{13}{16}$	$67\frac{3}{4}$
Funding $5\frac{1}{4}\%$ 1978/80	$85\frac{5}{8}$	$78\frac{1}{2}$
Treasury $3\frac{1}{2}\%$ 1979/81	$72\frac{3}{4}$	$66\frac{1}{2}$
Unweighted averages	$83\frac{17}{32}$	$78\frac{1}{2}$

Percentage fluctuation in price $\quad \dfrac{5\frac{1}{32}}{78\frac{1}{2}} \times 100 \quad = \quad 6 \cdot 41\%$

1968

Long-dated	High	Low
Funding $5\frac{1}{2}\%$ 1982/84	$85\frac{3}{16}$	$76\frac{3}{8}$
Funding $6\frac{1}{2}\%$ 1985/87	$93\frac{7}{8}$	$83\frac{7}{8}$
Transport 3% 1978/88	$57\frac{1}{4}$	$50\frac{5}{8}$
Treasury 5% 1986/89	$77\frac{15}{16}$	$68\frac{7}{8}$
Funding $5\frac{3}{4}\%$ 1987/91	$85\frac{1}{4}$	$75\frac{7}{8}$
Funding 6% 1993	$87\frac{5}{8}$	$77\frac{7}{8}$
Gas 3% 1990/95	53	$46\frac{1}{8}$
Redemption 3% 1986/96	$53\frac{1}{4}$	$46\frac{1}{4}$
Treasury $6\frac{3}{4}\%$ 1995/98	$95\frac{1}{2}$	84
Funding $3\frac{1}{2}\%$ 1999/2004	$55\frac{1}{4}$	$48\frac{1}{8}$
Treasury $5\frac{1}{2}\%$ 2008/12	$79\frac{15}{16}$	70
Unweighted averages	$74\frac{29}{32}$	$66\frac{3}{16}$

Percentage fluctuation in price $\quad \dfrac{8\frac{23}{32}}{66\frac{3}{16}} \times 100 = 13 \cdot 17\%$

1968

Undated	High	Low
Consols 4%	$56\frac{1}{4}$	$49\frac{1}{4}$
War Loan $3\frac{1}{2}\%$ 1952 or after	$50\frac{3}{8}$	43
Conversion $3\frac{1}{2}\%$ 1961 or after	$50\frac{3}{8}$	$43\frac{7}{8}$
Treasury 3% 1966 or after	$42\frac{7}{8}$	$36\frac{5}{8}$
Consols $2\frac{1}{2}\%$	$35\frac{5}{8}$	$30\frac{1}{2}$
Treasury $2\frac{1}{2}\%$	36	31
Unweighted averages	$45\frac{1}{4}$	$39\frac{1}{32}$

Percentage fluctuation in price $\quad \dfrac{6\frac{7}{32}}{39\frac{1}{32}} \times 100 = 15 \cdot 93\ \%$

This table is not totally accurate in that it is not based on weighted averages, but it does demonstrate that long-dated and irredeemable stocks are much more prone to fluctuation than are other stocks. Although these conclusions are based on an analysis of Government

FIXED INTEREST SECURITIES

securities they apply to all fixed-interest stocks, though they may be affected by differences in the status of the borrower.

2. CHARACTERISTICS OF DIFFERENT CLASSES OF BORROWER

As a general rule, the higher the investment standing of the borrower, the lower the yield necessary to attract funds. British Government securities, for instance, would tend to yield a lower return than industrial debentures due to the smaller risk of default on the part of the Government. The various bodies likely to issue fixed interest securities may be described under three heads:

(1) *Gilt-edged Securities*

These are securities which are regarded as absolutely free from risk with respect to both payment of interest and the ultimate repayment of the capital in the case of redeemable stocks. At March 31, 1971 the gilt-edged market consisted of the following securities:

	Nominal value (£m.)	*Market value* (£m.)
British Funds, Guaranteed Stocks etc.	22,595	17,161
UK Corporations, Counties, Public Boards	2,159	1,814
Commonwealth and Provincial Securities	732	561
	25,486	19,536

All of the above stocks, with the possible exception of some of the Colonial issues, are absolutely secure. The British Government and Nationalization stocks are guaranteed by the British Government, and the corporation and county stocks and those issued by public boards are well backed by assets, while the interest payments are a charge against rates. Those Commonwealth and Colonial loans which have not got the backing of the British Government are rather more vulnerable and their security depends upon the stability and wealth of the country concerned.

An illustration of the yields offered by a group of comparable gilt-edged securities is provided by the following table showing yields as at August 6, 1971.

143

	Gross Redemption Yield
	£
Treasury 3½% 1977/80	6·99
Funding 5¼% 1978/80	7·36
Treasury 3½% 1979/81	7·07
Herts 5¼% 1978/80	8·49
London County Council 5½% 1977/81	8·47
Middlesex 5¼% 1980	8·51
Australia 5½% 1977/80	8·53
Northern Rhodesia 6% 1978/81	11·47
Nyasaland 6% 1978/81	11·64
Southern Rhodesia 6% 1978/81	—

Having regard to the date of redemption these securities are almost identical, yet they offer widely different yields. The normal pattern is that, within a range of gilt-edged securities with a similar life, those guaranteed by the British Government will offer the lowest yield, followed by corporation stocks. Commonwealth stocks with a good risk status would offer a similar yield to corporation stocks, while securities issued by the former Colonial Governments would vary depending upon the standing of the Government concerned due partly to their lower risk, but mainly to their virtual exemption from Capital Gains Tax.

This pattern is borne out in the table above, the only points of comment being the lower yields on the Government stocks, due to their exemption from Capital Gains Tax, and the absence of a yield on Southern Rhodesia 6% 1978/81, on account of the suspension of interest payments.

One characteristic which distinguishes certain gilt-edged securities is the fact that interest on them is paid gross. In other words tax is not deducted at source and the holder receives the gross amount of the interest. The most important example of this is interest on 3½% War Loan which is automatically paid gross, both to resident and non-resident holders, unless the holder requests otherwise. Moreover, there are about twenty-five stocks which are exempt from tax in the hands of non-resident holders, who may apply to have the interest paid gross. Among these stocks are 3% Savings Bonds 1965/75, 5% Exchequer Stock 1976/78, 5¼% Funding Loan 1978/80, 5½% Funding Loan 1982/84, 4% Funding Loan 1960/90, 5¾% Funding Loan 1987/91, 5½% Treasury Stock 2008/12, 4% Victory Bonds, 3½% War Loan, Treasury 6½% 1976, 8½% Treasury 1980/82 and 6¾% Treasury 1995/98.

The advantage of receiving interest gross is that, although tax has to be paid ultimately on the interest, the investor, rather than the Inland Revenue, has the use of the amount of the tax for a measurable time and can invest it to increase his income still further. The greater the amount of tax involved, the greater the benefit to the investor of receiving interest gross.

There are two circumstances under which a resident investor can ensure the receipt of gross interest other than by buying $3\frac{1}{2}\%$ War Loan. The most common method is by the acquisition of stocks through the Post Office Savings Department or the Trustee Savings Banks Government Stocks Departments. The majority of British Government stocks may be bought or sold in this way and these transactions are entered in the Post Office Register as opposed to the Bank of England Register, which records all other dealings in these securities.

The purchase of stocks by this method has two advantages. Firstly, the interest is paid gross, thus giving the investor the use of the tax thereon and freeing him from the burden of making a tax repayment claim where he is subject to tax at less than the standard rate. Secondly, the cost of such a purchase is less than one made through a stockbroker. The basic rate charged by the Post Office or a Trustee Savings Bank is 10p per £100 nominal value compared with 50p per £100 consideration charged by a stockbroker. The practice of basing commission on the nominal rather than the actual value of a security means that the purchase or sale of a security whose price is high relative to its nominal value, is cheaper than a deal in a security with a relatively low price.

The disadvantages of this method of purchase are that no arrangements can be made to buy or sell at a specified price, all transactions being carried out at the price ruling on the date of the deal. Moreover, the size of a purchase is limited to £1,000 nominal amount of a particular stock, though there are no restrictions on the number of separate acquisitions that can be made. There is, however, no limit on the size of any sale. An investor who already holds relevant British Government securities registered on the Bank of England Register can apply to have them transferred to the Post Office Register subject to the £1,000 limit on individual transfers.

Interest is also receivable gross where the interest is paid through the Bank of England and its half-yearly amount is not in excess of £2·50. This provision is clearly designed to relieve small investors of the necessity of making repayment claims.

Although the market value of gilt-edged securities accounts for less than a quarter of the market value of all stocks and shares

145

quoted on the London Stock Exchange, they wield a greater influence than this proportion would suggest. Since the Stock Exchange began the publication of statistics relating to dealings in September 1964 the dominance of transactions in gilt-edged securities in terms of total value has become clear, as explained in Chapter 4.

This is largely accounted for by the activities of institutional investors. *Financial Statistics* records the following institutional holdings at December 31, 1970 of securities guaranteed by the British Government:

	Total (£m.)	Short-dated (£m.)	Other (£m.)	Basis of Valuation
UK Banking sector[1]	2,171	1,543	628	Book value (31.3.1971)
Building Societies	573	435	138	Book value (31.12.1969)
Unit Trusts	26	9	17	Market value
Investment Trusts	56	7	49	Market value
Insurance Companies	3,263	79	3,184	Nominal value
Superannuation Funds:				
Public Sector	134	11	123	Market value (31.12.1969)
Local Authorities	243	6	237	Market value (31.3.1970)
Private Sector	544	49	495	Market value (31.12.1969)
Trustee Savings Banks[2]	320	85	235	Market value
National Savings Bank[2]	153	25	128	Market value
	7,483	2,249	5,234	

[1] The Banking sector comprises the domestic banks, accepting houses, overseas banks, the discount market and the Bank of England Banking Department.
[2] Investment Accounts only.

A conservative estimate of the total market value of the above securities would be £6,000 m. At December 31, 1970 the market value of all British Government securities was £15,415 m.[1] so that the institutions probably held over one-third of these securities. At the same time the institutions are extremely active in their dealings with these stocks. In the first quarter of 1971, for instance, insurance companies increased their holdings of Government securities by £196·2 m. This increase, however, was composed of purchases of £810·0 m. less sales of £613·7 m. In short, it would appear that the market in short-dated Government securities is dominated by the banks while dealings in other Government securities are most greatly influenced by insurance companies.

(2) *Securities Issued by Foreign Governments*

At March 31, 1971 the nominal value of securities issued by foreign governments or corporations and quoted on the London Stock

[1] 'Interests and Dividends upon Securities quoted on the Stock Exchange', 1970.

Exchange totalled £2,186 m., while their market value was only £1,328 m. This indicates the extreme riskiness of many of the securities within this group. The extent of the risk varies enormously from one stock to another, depending upon the terms of the issue and the standing of the country concerned:

(i) *Absolutely speculative: e.g. Russian 5% Loan 1906*

This issue comprised bonds with a nominal value of £89,325,000 all of which are outstanding. The original terms provided for redemption at par by May 1, 1956, by annual drawings (commencing in 1917). The interest payment due on May 1, 1918, was not made and all interest due since that date is in arrears. An investor who acquires these bonds, which have a current market value of about £1 per £100 nominal value, clearly cannot expect any income from his investment and the only conceivable objects in acquiring bonds of this sort are the decorative nature of many of them, the esoteric thrill of owning them, or the extremely remote possibility that the present Russian Government might be prepared to pay some compensation to the current holders.

(ii) *Very speculative: e.g. Greek 5% Loan 1914*

Bonds with a total nominal value of £13,302,438 were issued and £11,578,505 is still outstanding. The terms of the issue provided for redemption by March 1964, by means of purchase under par or by half-yearly drawings. No redemptions have taken place since 1932. Regular payment of the interest ceased in 1932 and no interest at all has been paid since 1941. Although there is no certainty that an investor will receive any income from such bonds there is at least a possibility of some repayment of capital and arrears of interest. A settlement might result from the desire of the Greek Government to regain its credit-worthiness, thus making it possible to borrow money at a later date. Also a settlement might be made a condition upon which further American or British aid might depend. The price of this particular bond stood at about £32 during 1971, indicating its very speculative nature.

(iii) *Risky: e.g. Peru Assented 3% Bonds*

In 1931 the Peruvian Government suspended payment of its obligations on the entire public debt and this moratorium was extended indefinitely during 1932 in respect of its external debt. In 1947 an offer was made for conversion into new bonds of 1947, for the cancellation of all arrears of interest, for the payment of interest at the rate of 1% for 1947 and 1948, 1½% for 1949 and 1950, 2% for 1951 and 1952 and 2½% for 1953 and thereafter, and for a cumulative sinking fund of ½% per annum. Both the Foreign Bondholders Protective Council Inc., New York and the Council of Foreign Bondholders in London recommended the refusal of the offer.

In January 1953 a revised offer was made to holders of the dollar loans, which was extended in December 1953 to the sterling bondholders:

(1) The contractual dollar options in respect of principal, future interest and sinking fund instalments will be honoured by payment of £1·74 sterling for each £1 sterling nominal amount, and the expression 'new par value' means the sterling amount so calculated. The contractual dollar option refers to the right of the holder to receive his interest in either pounds or dollars at a fixed rate of exchange. In 1931, when the Peruvian Government defaulted, the exchange rate between US dollars and pounds sterling was about $4·87 to the pound. At the date of the settlement the rate had dropped to about $2·80. If the dollar option is taken into account each £100 bond becomes worth

$$£100 \times \frac{4·87}{2·80} = £174$$

(2) Funding certificates will be issued in respect of unpaid interest up to December 31, 1946 for an amount in sterling equal to 10% of the original sterling value thereof.

(3) A cash payment of £11 5s 0d per bond of £100 original sterling face value will be made against coupons due April 1, 1947 to October 1, 1953 inclusive representing interest at 1% per annum for 1947 and 1948, 1½% for 1949 and 1950, 2% for 1951 and 1952 and 3% for nine months of 1953.

(4) Interest at the reduced rate of 3% per annum payable in sterling on the new par value will be paid in full satisfaction of coupons due April 1, 1954 and thereafter until final redemption.

(5) The final date for redemption of assented bonds will be postponed until October 1, 2007 on which date any assented bonds not previously redeemed will be repaid in sterling at the new par value.

(6) A half-yearly cumulative sterling sinking fund of ½% per annum of the new par value of all bonds now outstanding

(namely £3,189,246, the original value being £1,832,900) will be applied to the redemption of assented bonds by purchase at or below the new par value or drawings at the new par value.

Bondholders wishing to assent to this offer were notified on February 28, 1955 to present their bonds to the bankers representing the Peruvian Government for enfacement of their bonds, the issue of funding certificates, cash payments in respect of coupons to October 1, 1953 and payment at the new rate of coupons due April 1, and October 1, 1954. At the end of July 1971 the price of the assented bonds was about £60. At the same time unassented bonds were quoted, though their price was much higher because their holders had not assented to the settlement and the bonds therefore still contained the coupons in respect of all interest payments due since 1947. The details of this particular issue were extracted from the *Stock Exchange Year Book* and provide an illustration of the negotiation of a settlement in respect of defaulted bonds.

(iv) *Gilt-edged: German 3% Funding Bonds 1953*

These bonds were issued under the London Agreement of 1953 for funding of arrears of interest up to October 15, 1964 on assented bonds of the sterling issues of the German External Loan 1924. They are redeemable at par on October 15, 1972 and a cumulative sinking fund of 2% per annum was established on April 15, 1958. This operates by purchase below par or by drawings for repayment at par. The price of these bonds during 1971 was about £99.

Another distinguishing feature of foreign securities is that the majority of them are issued in the form of bearer bonds, as contrasted with British Government securities which are registered on the Bank of England or the Post Office Register, interest being paid to the registered holder. The main feature of bearer bonds is that they can be transferred by mere physical transfer from one person to another, thus avoiding the preparation of a transfer form and the registration procedure. Because of this the original borrower has no record of their ultimate holders. Thus when interest payments fall due it is necessary for the holder to apply for payment. This is done by cutting off a coupon or talon which is attached to the bond and sending it to the borrower. Each bond contains coupons in respect of the interest payments due for a certain number of years and on expiry of the coupons the bond is submitted to the borrower who will replace it with a further one containing a further supply of coupons.

All bearer bonds, whether issued by governments or companies, are free from government stamp duty when transferred. In return for this exemption borrowers who issue bearer bonds must pay a once-for-all amount of duty based on the nominal value of the bond. The advantages to the holder of easy transfer and freedom from stamp duty are balanced by the possibility that the bond will be destroyed or lost, whether due to carelessness, theft, or some natural disaster. In this case it would be very difficult to prove ownership. From the point of view of the issuing organization the expenses of maintaining a register of members are avoided. On the other hand, it is almost impossible to make contact with the bondholders and, because the onus of claiming interest is on the bondholders, there are likely to be far more cases of unclaimed interest.

In the past the existence of bearer securities has facilitated the anonymous holding and transfer of wealth. In order to control the movement of these bonds all UK holders are required under the Exchange Control Act 1947 to deposit their bonds with an authorized depositary, such as banks, solicitors or stockbrokers. As a result transfer is controlled and there is no fear of physical loss, so that many of the advantages and disadvantages referred to above are largely illusory.

(3) *Securities Issued by Public Companies*

A public company may issue either fixed or variable interest securities in order to obtain funds. The latter consist primarily of various types of ordinary shares, which are discussed in Chapter 6. The fixed-interest securities are also of many varieties, distinguished primarily by the extent of security given by the borrower. This must be measured both by the legal security provided by the terms of the issue and the economic security indicated by the profitability and economic status of the company. For example, legally unsecured loan stock issued by I.C.I. might be issued on a lower yield basis than heavily secured stock in a much less prosperous company. Thus, although the legal security is important in defining the rights of the stockholders the underlying economic state of the company is normally more important, for the legal rights will normally only be invoked when the trading situation of the company causes a default. The different types of fixed-interest securities that a company might issue and the legal rights of each can be described under two heads:

(i) *Funds Provided by Creditors of the Company*

This class of finance includes bank overdrafts, private loans, trade credit, etc. but the only loans with a Stock Exchange quotation in this group are debentures and loan stocks. These stocks are invariably given the first charge against profits in respect of the annual interest payment, while their priority and security as to repayment of capital will depend upon the terms of the trust deed in accordance with which the stock is issued. Although the different varieties of debentures and loan stocks may be formally described in a vast number of ways, the main factors determining the yield of a particular stock are the redemption provisions, the security offered and the overall economic situation:

(a) *Redemption provisions.* Where the terms of the issue provide for redemption on or before a particular date, the factors affecting the price of the stock will be the same as those determining the market value of redeemable gilt-edged securities. Often, however, provision is made for the establishment of a sinking fund out of which stock is redeemed annually by purchases in the market or by annual drawings for redemption at a given price. Where the latter alternative is adopted the price at which the drawn stocks are to be redeemed acts as a magnet and prevents violent fluctuations in the market price.

(b) *Security.* The legal security offered by a company in connection with long-term borrowings may consist of either a mortgage charge on a specific asset or a floating charge on the present and future assets of the company. Both types of charge must be registered with the Registrar of Companies. A fixed or specific charge involves the mortgage of a particular asset to the trustees representing the debenture holders. These trustees are appointed under the trust deed setting out the terms of the issue and they would be authorized to prevent any dealings by the company in the mortgaged property which might be to the detriment of the debenture-holders. They would also be empowered to secure the liquidation of the mortgaged asset should the company default under the terms of the deed.

A floating charge gives priority over unsecured creditors in the event of a liquidation, but the borrowing company is empowered to continue to deal with its assets as it wishes, even to the extent of subsequently creating a fixed charge on any of them.

In addition to secured debentures there are those which are naked or unsecured. Although these create no charge on the assets of the company they may still provide adequate effective security. This is due to the fact that the types of legal security described above are only relevant in the event of the failure of the company. Therefore, so long as the company maintains and is likely to continue to maintain a high and stable level of profits relative to its fixed interest commitments, legal security is relatively unimportant.

151

A debenture-holder, in assessing the value of his stock, must therefore have regard first to the probability of the maintenance of the due interest payments and then to the underlying security of his capital. Obviously, the greater the security in these two instances, the lower the yield he would be prepared to accept on his investment. Therefore, a company will be able to issue debentures offering a lower rate of return the greater and more stable its profits and the more reliable the value of its fixed assets available for security.

Another important factor is the adaptability of the properties available for security. Generally speaking, the less specific a particular property the more likely it is to maintain or increase its market value in the event of a liquidation, because there will be a larger number of potential buyers.

The required yield is also influenced by the amount of debentures already issued by the company, for the greater the quantity of debentures already in issue the smaller the proportion of profits and the smaller the amount of property available for securing the interest and capital commitments on a subsequent issue.

(c) *The overall economic situation.* As with fixed-interest securities the yield on debentures will be affected by general economic factors, particularly expectations as to the direction and timing of future movements in interest rates and the extent of inflation. Both of these factors can be influenced by the borrower. Future movements in interest rates may be combated in various ways. For instance, a loan may be made for a very short term, thus giving both the borrower and the lender the opportunity of liquidating after a short period and re-negotiating the loan at a new level of interest rates. An investor in short-dated securities is constantly investing at new levels of interest in this way. On the other hand an investor in a perpetual debenture is committed to the current rate of interest until such time as he sells his stock on the market at a price which will have been determined by the new level of interest. Thus, although he always receives the fixed nominal rate of interest, the underlying value of his capital will fluctuate.

Another method of combating changing interest rates is by means of variable interest rates, which may be adjusted according to movements in the market rate. This is the normal procedure with loans to and from building societies and banks, but it is most uncommon in the case of quoted securities.

The impact of inflation is on the purchasing power of the income and capital payments received by the debenture-holder. The greater the rate of inflation the lower the real value of income receipts and the greater the real loss of capital on redemption or on a market sale, unless this ultimate liquidation takes place at a price sufficiently above the acquisition price to cover the loss of purchasing power and any capital gains tax payable on the realization profit.

The effects of inflation may be countered in at least two ways. One method is to tie the rate of interest payable on the debenture to the cost-of-living index, so that as the cost of living rises the interest rises. This to a great extent maintains the real value of the income provided by the debenture, though if the stock is eventually redeemable at par some loss of capital in real terms will occur.

The most common method of dealing with the effects of inflation is by the issue of convertible debentures which give the debenture-holders the right to convert their stock into ordinary stock at some future date on given terms. Where the company has been profitable and the value of the ordinary shares has risen this will enable the debenture-holders to share in the growth of the company and thus guard against inflation.

(ii) *Funds Provided by Members of the Company*

The normal form of fixed-interest finance involving membership of the company is the issue of preference shares. The rights of such shares are determined first by the Memorandum of Association, then by the Articles of Association, then by the resolution authorizing the issue and the stated terms of the offer. As is the case with issues of debentures the rights of the shareholders will differ from one issue to another in respect of dividend rights, redemption rights and membership rights:

(a) *Dividend rights.* Preference shareholders normally have priority over the ordinary shareholders for dividend payments, in return for which they agree to accept a dividend of a fixed percentage. However, the company cannot normally be required to declare a preference dividend whatever the level of profits in a particular year. The main protection given to the preference shareholders lies in the fact that no ordinary dividend may be declared unless the preference dividend has been paid. Moreover, unless the provisions relating to the issue state otherwise, the shares will be deemed to be cumulative, with the result that dividends not declared in any year must be made good out of the profits of subsequent years before other shareholders can receive any dividend. In the relatively few cases where the shares are non-cumulative a dividend not declared in a particular year cannot be recovered in this way.

153

In addition to the distinction between cumulative and non-cumulative preference shares, there is the problem of determining whether participating rights have been given, enabling the preference shareholders to participate in the profits remaining after the payment of their basic dividend. For instance, the terms of the issue may provide for the payment of a preference dividend of 6% with the right to share equally with the ordinary shareholders in any distribution after 20% has been paid on the ordinary shares up to a maximum preference dividend of 15%. Thus if the ordinary dividend was 25% the preference dividend would be 11%. In view of the fact that preference shareholders are deemed to have foregone any right to participate in surplus profits in return for their priority of payment of the fixed dividend, it is presumed that their shares are non-participating unless the terms of the issue expressly provide such a right.

(b) *Redemption rights.* Unless redemption is provided for by the terms of the issue it will only take place at the instigation of the company or on winding-up. Where the company is faced with a deficiency of capital on winding-up, the preference shareholders will only be entitled to priority as to return of capital if there is some provision to this effect. Otherwise they rank on equal terms with the ordinary shareholders and will share equally in any loss of capital after all the creditors and liquidation expenses have been paid off.

Where there is a surplus of assets they have no right to share in it unless express provision has been made for this. Even where such a right is given they cannot claim to participate in any part of the surplus which is attributable to profits which were available for distribution to the ordinary shareholders but were ploughed back.

The strict enforcement of these rules can involve considerable hardship for preference shareholders. There have, for example, been cases where a company has redeemed at par preference shares which had a considerably higher market value due to the fact that the market rate of interest was much lower than the nominal rate of interest on the preference shares.[1] Such redemption might be made either to maximize the return to the ordinary shareholders on winding-up, or to replace the preference shares with capital bearing interest at a lower current rate. Some companies have overcome the hardship to preference shareholders by providing that the redemption value of their shares, other than those which are specifically stated to be redeemable, should be based upon the Stock Exchange price just prior to redemption.

[1] E.g. Scottish Insurance Corporation Ltd. *v.* Wilsons and Clyde Coal Co. Ltd (1949), A C.462.

(c) *Membership rights.* Although preference shareholders are regarded as members of a company, rather than its creditors, they are not usually given the right to vote at meetings of the company except where their dividend is in arrear or where a proposal is made which affects their rights. Even this right was eroded by the decision in Coulson *v.* Austin Motor Co. (1927; 43 T.L.R.493) when it was held that where preference dividends were non-cumulative and had not been paid for some years due to trading losses incurred by the company they should not be regarded as in arrear and the preference shareholders were thus not entitled to attend and vote at meetings of the company.

The rights pertaining to a particular issue of preference shares should be carefully examined by reference to the *Stock Exchange Year Book.* For example, the Shell Transport and Trading Co. Ltd has £12 m. preference stock outstanding, which is described as follows: Issued capital—£2 m. 1st Preference Stock and £10 m. 2nd Preference Stock. First and 2nd Preference Stocks are entitled, in that order, to a cumulative $5\frac{1}{2}\%$ and 7% and, also in that order, to priority for capital and arrears of dividend, plus in a winding-up or reduction of capital, a premium equal to the amount by which the average of the means of the daily quotations on the Stock Exchange, London (after deducting unpaid arrears of dividend) during the preceding six months exceeds the paid-up amount of the shares, but not to further participation. The creation or issue of further capital ranking in priority to or *pari passu* with the 1st or 2nd Preference Capital shall be deemed to be a modification of the rights of that class (except an issue of the unissued balance of 1st Preference Stock, i.e. £1 m.).

In view of their restricted legal rights as to income and return of capital, preference shares have been unpopular with investors for several years. Moreover, the introduction of the Corporation Tax has brought about a similar unpopularity from the viewpoint of companies raising funds. This is because debenture interest is deductible from profits in determining the liability to Corporation Tax, while preference dividends are not. This extremely artificial distinction arises from the fact that debenture-holders are legally regarded as creditors of a company so that their interest is considered to be a charge against profits. Preference shareholders, by contrast, are legally members of the company and their dividend represents a distribution of profits. This distinction has resulted in a substantial fall in new issues of preference shares, except on the part of companies with extensive overseas interests which are not liable to tax in this country due to the high level of overseas taxation borne by them.

155

Nevertheless preference shares often offer a far greater effective security than the provisions governing their issue might indicate. Such shares in a highly profitable and reputable company might give higher real security than legally secured debentures in a more speculative concern. Because very few preference shares have any material rights as far as return of capital is concerned, except in the case of winding-up, their valuation depends entirely upon expectations as to the future movements of interest rates and the level of and extent of fluctuation in the profits of the company concerned. In the last resort they are broadly comparable with irredeemable fixed-interest securities, but with a greater risk of default.

Although they are legally more risky than debentures they tend to offer a lower yield than debentures, mainly because preference dividends are franked investment income for tax purposes. Companies which receive these dividends can pass them on to their own shareholders without suffering Corporation Tax and without the deduction of Income Tax. Consequently preference shares are more popular than debentures with most institutional investors.

APPENDIX TO CHAPTER 5

THE DISTINCTION BETWEEN STOCKS AND SHARES

Until the enactment of the Companies Act 1948 there were two main distinctions between stocks and shares. In the first place shares were regarded as indivisible units and transfers could only take place in units of one share, while stock could be transferred in any amount. Thus, if a person held a hundred shares with a nominal value of £1 each he could only make a transfer in units of £1. If these shares were converted into stock, as is possible where they are fully paid, then the shareholder would hold stock to the value of £100 and transfers might be made in units of one penny, so that he could, for instance, sell stock with a nominal value of £56·19, retaining a holding of £43·81.

The second distinction lay in the fact that all shares were required to have distinguishing numbers. This meant that all transfers had to state the number of each share concerned and the register of members and the share certificate had to state the number of each share held by a member. When the shares had been in issue for many years the numbers were less often consecutive and the process of recording them became very arduous. There was thus a definite incentive for companies to convert their shares into stock.

Neither of the two distinctions described above is particularly relevant today. Although stock is theoretically transferable in any unit the conversion terms normally provide that it can only be transferred in units identical to the nominal value of the previous issue of shares. Thus a shareholder owning one hundred shares, each with a nominal value of £1, might have his holding converted to £100 stock transferable only in units of £1.

With regard to distinguishing numbers the Companies Act 1948 provides that, where all the issued shares of a class are fully paid, none of these shares need have a distinguishing number so long as it remains fully paid and ranks *pari passu* with all other shares of the same class. There is thus in most cases no practical difference between stock and shares and the two terms are now used interchangeably. The only relevance of the distinction obtains in the case of those companies, examples of which can be found in the insurance sector, which have partly-paid shares which cannot be converted into stock and have to be numbered separately.

CHAPTER 6

Variable Interest Securities

Variable interest securities are those whose nominal rate of return may vary from one period to another in an unpredictable fashion. Ordinary stocks and shares are the most common example, though their return is strictly speaking in the form of dividends rather than interest. While certain preference shares and debentures, such as participating preference shares and debentures whose interest rate is tied to the cost of living, provide a return which may vary over time, the rate is calculated according to a predetermined formula. They cannot therefore be regarded as variable interest securities in the same way as ordinary shares, whose return is determined entirely by the directors of the company concerned.

1. THE LEGAL POSITION OF ORDINARY SHAREHOLDERS

The legal rights of ordinary shareholders are laid down in the articles of association of a company. These govern the internal organization of the company, dealing with such matters as the election of directors, the procedure for general meetings and the rights of members. The founders are responsible for drafting the articles, which will normally be based on the model regulations contained in Table A of the Companies Act 1948. Even where the articles are not so based, section 8 of the Act declares that, insofar as the articles do not exclude or modify the regulations contained in Table A, those regulations, so far as applicable, are the regulations of the company in the same manner and to the same extent as if they were contained in duly registered articles.

The articles must be registered with the Registrar of Companies,

158

whereupon they will become available for public inspection. Thereafter they may be altered by special resolution of the members, which must be passed by a majority of at least three-quarters of those members who legitimately vote.

In order to ascertain his rights, therefore, a member of a company must examine the articles. Although these will differ from one company to another, the regulations of Table A will normally be included either in full or in a modified form. Some of the more relevant regulations (from the viewpoint of the investor) of Table A are the following:

(a) If at any time the share capital is divided into different classes of shares, the rights attached to any class (unless otherwise provided by the terms of issue of that class) may be varied with the consent in writing of the holders of three-fourths of the issued shares of that class, or with the sanction of an extraordinary resolution passed at a separate general meeting of the holders of the shares of the class.

(b) Subject to certain conditions, any member may transfer all or any of his shares by an instrument in writing in any form which the directors may approve.

(c) The company may from time to time by ordinary resolution increase the share capital by such sum, to be divided into shares of such amount, as the resolution shall prescribe.

(d) An annual general meeting and a meeting called for the passing of a special resolution shall be called by twenty-one days' notice in writing at the least, and any other meeting of the company shall be called by fourteen days' writing at the least.

(e) At any general meeting a resolution put to the vote of the meeting shall be decided by a show of hands unless a poll is demanded:

(i) by the chairman, or
(ii) by at least three members present in person or by proxy, or
(iii) by any member or members present in person or by proxy and representing not less than one-tenth of the total voting rights of all the members having the right to vote at the meeting.

(f) Subject to any rights or restrictions for the time being attached to any class or classes of shares, on a show of hands every member present in person shall have one vote, and on a poll every member shall have one vote for each share of which he is the holder.

(g) On a poll, votes may be given either personally or by proxy.

(h) The business of the company shall be managed by the directors, who may pay all expenses incurred in promoting and registering the company, and may exercise all such powers of the company as are not, by the Act or by the articles, required to be exercised by the company in general meeting.

(*i*) The company may, by ordinary resolution, of which special notice has been given, remove any director before the expiration of his period of office notwithstanding anything in the articles or in any agreement between the company and such director. Such removal shall be without prejudice to any claims such director may have for damages for breach of any contract of service between him and the company.

(*j*) The company in general meeting may declare dividends, but no dividends shall exceed the amount recommended by the directors.

(*k*) The directors may, before recommending any dividend, set aside out of the profits of the company such sums as they think proper as a reserve or reserves, which shall, at the discretion of the directors, be applicable for any purpose to which the profits of the company may be properly applied, and pending such application may, at the like discretion, either be employed in the business of that company or be invested in such investments (other than shares of the company) as the directors may from time to time think fit. The directors may also without placing the same to reserve carry forward any profits which they may think prudent not to divide.

Under the standard regulations of Table A the shareholders in general meeting are regarded as the ultimate arbiters of the company. They appoint directors to undertake the general management of the company and have the right to remove any or all of these directors if dissatisfied. However, this control is largely illusory. The directors control the day-to-day administration of the company and have complete discretion over the retention and distribution of profits. A discontented shareholder has to choose between selling his shares or removing the directors, or at least securing an alteration of their policies. In practice, the first of these alternatives is generally adopted, for it is wellnigh impossible for an individual shareholder to force the resignation of a director.

There are several factors which produce the security of tenure which directors enjoy. They may, for instance, have entrenched themselves by means of service contracts, so that their removal might be inordinately expensive. Furthermore, many shareholders are unable to attend general meetings because they are held at an inconvenient time or place, while still more are too apathetic concerning the affairs of their company. As a result of this non-intervention any shares or proxies held by the directors assume a greater significance.

Another factor is the issue by many companies of non-voting

shares, which like the issue of preference shares or debentures, allow further capital to be raised without any relaxation of the control of the directors. Such shares have been used in connection with takeover bids whereby other companies have been acquired without any increase in the voting capital of the bidder. Although they are now regarded with disfavour by the Stock Exchange, institutional investors and the financial press, there is still nothing tangible to prevent their issue.

Finally, in the case of many companies which have a Stock Exchange quotation the directors themselves own or are in a position to control the votes of more than half of the voting shares, so that their command is complete. In such companies the minority shareholders are wholly at their mercy, subject to the provision of section 210 of the Companies Act 1948, which enables the Court to take such action as it thinks fit where it is shown that the affairs of a company are being conducted in a manner oppressive to some part of the members. However, actions under this section are expensive, difficult to prove and consequently very rare. Most shareholders who feel that they have been treated unfairly would adopt the more facile remedy of selling their shares.

All in all, everything is in favour of the maintenance of control by the existing directors, and their position is enhanced by the influence which they are sometimes able to exert over the investment policies of their company's pension funds, which may be used to buy shares in their company. The votes attributable to these shares might then be cast in favour of the directors where necessary. Moreover, the directors often have links with institutional investors by means of cross-directorships, thus securing the backing of those institutions in respect of any shares which they hold in the company. In any event, the institutional investors have in the past been unwilling to play an overtly active part in disputes between management and shareholders.

Despite the strength of the directors' position, they must maintain a certain standard of performance, for if trading results are excessively depressed they face danger from two sides. In the first place, the shareholders, who have seen their capital and income eroded, will be more inclined to join in an active revolt against the management. Secondly, the inefficient use of the company's assets may tempt other companies to make a takeover bid in order to acquire those assets at a deflated price, with the chance of making much higher profits by employing them more efficiently within their own organization. The success of the bid would be encouraged by the dissatisfaction felt by the shareholders with existing management.

In the USA it is quite common for the existing directors to be replaced by another group, who secure a majority of the proxies of the voting shareholders. In this way, the shareholders can retain their membership of the company, instead of relinquishing it to a bidding company. These proxy battles are uncommon on the London Stock Exchange, partly because the directors are so well entrenched and partly because there is a shortage of dynamic managerial talent with the funds necessary to meet the heavy expenses of such a battle.

The impotence of the ordinary shareholder has been widely publicized in recent years,[1] and now seems to be accepted. Nevertheless the Stock Exchange has done little to remedy the situation. Their regulations lay down certain provisions with which the articles of quoted companies must conform. Most of these provisions confirm those already stated in Table A rather than adding to them, the only relevant additions being as follows:

(*a*) Transfers and other documents relating to or affecting the title to any shares shall be registered without payment of any fee.

(*b*) Fully-paid shares shall be free from any restriction on the right of transfer and shall also be free from all lien.

(*c*) Where power is taken to forfeit unclaimed dividends, that power shall not be exercised until twelve years or more after the date of declaration of the dividend.

(*d*) The structure of the share capital of the company shall be stated, and where the capital consists of more than one class of security it must also be stated how the various classes shall rank for any distribution by way of dividend or otherwise.

(*e*) Where the capital of the company includes shares which do not carry voting rights, the words non-voting must appear in the designation of such shares.

(*f*) Where the equity capital includes shares with different voting rights, the designation of each class of shares, other than those with the most favourable voting rights, must include the words 'restricted voting' or 'limited voting'.

(*g*) Where provision is made in the articles as to the form of proxy this must be so worded as not to preclude the use of the two-way form. This is associated with the rule in the General Undertaking which requires quoted companies 'to send out with the notice convening a meeting to all shareholders and debenture holders entitled to vote thereat proxy forms with provision for two-way voting on all resolutions intended to be proposed (other than resolutions relating to the procedure of the meeting or to the remuneration of the auditors)'.

[1] Viz. Alex Rubner, *The Ensnared Shareholder* (London: Macmillan, 1965).

These requirements are intended to ensure that shareholders may transfer their shares without hindrance, that they are warned of any restriction on their voting or dividend rights, and that they may vote by proxy either for or against any important resolution. However, they do little to redress the balance of power as between the directors and the shareholders.

In many ways it is arguable that the directors are entitled to their position of supremacy. Certainly, their personal prosperity is much more closely identified with the progress of the company than is that of the shareholder, for whom the shares may represent only a small part of a large, diversified portfolio. Moreover, the shareholders can move from one company to another much more easily and more frequently than can directors. Finally, it should be pointed out that the remedy is in the hands of the shareholders, for they have the legal power in most cases to oppose the directors, and are only prevented from doing so by their own apathy.

Although the Stock Exchange requires any restriction on voting or dividend rights to be made clear in the designation of the shares, the full extent of the restriction can only be found by examining the articles of the company which are filed at Companies House. Alternatively the *Stock Exchange Year Book* provides the appropriate information. For example, the entry for Hoveringham Gravels Ltd in 1968 shows the following capital structure:

	Authorized £	Issued £
7% Redeemable preference shares	2,000,000	1,750,000
Ordinary shares of 5s	1,171,875	1,171,875
Restricted voting ordinary shares	1,500,000	1,168,593
Deferred ordinary shares	546,875	546,875
	£5,218,750	£4,637,343

The following information was given in respect of the rights of the different classes of ordinary shares:

(*a*) Ordinary, restricted voting ordinary and deferred ordinary shares rank *pari passu* except as regards voting, and in the case of the deferred ordinary also as regards dividend and a right of conversion.

(*b*) Deferred ordinary shares shall (i) not participate in any dividends in respect of any period ending prior to January 1, 1974 payable out of revenue profits and (ii) be converted into ordinary shares of 5s on January 1, 1974.

163

(c) In any distribution of share capital by way of capitalization of profits or reserves, the ordinary, restricted ordinary and deferred ordinary shares shall entitle holders to receive rateable allotments in shares of the class held by them.

(d) Voting: 5 votes per 5s ordinary capital and 1 vote per 5s restricted ordinary. Deferred ordinary shares as such confer no voting rights prior to January 1, 1974.

It is extremely difficult to provide watertight classifications of the different types of ordinary shares which are available on the Stock Exchange, due both to the different degrees of restriction of rights which exist from one company to another and to the different terminology which is encountered. The following broad categories, however, can be distinguished:

(i) *Non-voting or Restricted Voting*

The object of such shares is to enable the management more easily to maintain its control over the company on the occasion of a new issue of shares either to the public or to the owners of a company which is being taken over. It is important for an investor to ascertain the exact extent of any restriction, for under certain circumstances there may be a considerable differential between the relative prices of voting and non-voting shares, depending upon the importance which is placed upon the vote.

If there are relatively few voting shares in issue, not only will each provide the owner with a voice (however small) in the management of the business, but also it will be far more valuable than the non-voting in the event of a takeover bid. Thus, they will tend to be worth materially more if a bid is anticipated, either because the company is in a depressed state or for other reasons. Thus at April 12, 1967 the relative prices of voting and non-voting shares in some companies which had either produced disappointing results or were tipped as targets for possible takeover bids were as follows:

	Voting	Restricted Voting
Hoveringham Gravels Ltd	19s 6d	12s 1½d
Rootes Motors Ltd	11s 6d	5s 0d
Mecca Ltd	29s 0d	18s 4½d
Three years earlier (on April 13, 1964) the relative prices had been:		
Hoveringham Gravels Ltd	36s 0d	33s 3d
Rootes Motors Ltd	9s 6d	6s 11¼d
Mecca Ltd	50s 0d	29s 9d

It is thus clear that the depressed trading results of Hoveringham Gravels and Rootes had substantially increased the differential between the voting and restricted voting shares. In the case of Rootes the position was exaggerated by the takeover by Chryslers and the consequent shortage of stock. The differential between the different classes of ordinary shares issued by Mecca seems rather more permanent and is attributable partly to the fact that the number of voting shares in issue is less than one-tenth of the number of non-voting, and partly to persistent takeover rumours.

On the other hand, there were many cases where no such differential existed. These were mainly companies whose voting shares were widely held and which were unlikely to fall prey to a takeover bid. An example is provided by the following share prices at April 12, 1967:

	Voting	Restricted Voting
Decca	85s 0d	84s 6d
Rank Organization	30s 0d	30s 0d
Hoover	40s 3d	39s 9d
Great Universal Stores	45s 6d	44s 0d

Nevertheless by the end of 1968 a gap had been created between the prices of the two classes of shares in the cases of Decca, due to disappointing results and Great Universal Stores, due probably to the thinness of the market in the voting shares.

It should be pointed out that while 'A' shares and 'B' shares are often non-voting, these designations do not of themselves indicate a restriction of voting. Where there are two such designations, the lower of the two will normally suffer some restriction. For example, the capital of Brooke Bond & Co. Ltd as stated in the 1968 *Stock Exchange Year Book* included £787,500 'A' ordinary and £18·9 m 'B' ordinary, all in shares of 5s. One vote was given for each 'A' ordinary share and one vote for every 24 'B' ordinary shares.

Finally, it should be mentioned that there are some companies whose voting shares are not often dealt in because they are tightly held by the management, so that only non-voting shares are generally available to the public. This, of course, represents the ultimate in director control.

(ii) *Deferred Shares*

These are shares which are sometimes issued to the founders or promoters of a company, partly to demonstrate their faith in the company and partly to reduce the pressure on profits during its early years. Dividends are normally only paid after a given number of years or after the ordinary shareholders have received a certain level of dividend. The ordinary shareholders must take account of these shares for they could have a substantial effect on the available profits when they rank for dividend. They are often unquoted and invariably tightly held. Nevertheless, there are a few companies in which the deferred share capital represents the major portion of the shares available to the public. In such cases the term 'deferred' is normally only used to distinguish that class of shares from a preferred class. Here the preferred class will tend to provide the minority of the capital, and the deferred the majority. For example, the whole of the share capital of P. and O. Steam Navigation Co., other than the preference shares, consists of deferred shares.

Similarly the issued ordinary share capital of the City of London Brewery and Investment Trust Ltd at June 30, 1966 was divided into £589,672 preferred ordinary shares and £2,987,863 deferred ordinary. By far the greater proportion of Stock Exchange dealings in the company were in respect of the deferred shares.

(iii) *Preferred Ordinary Shares*

These are ordinary shares which normally carry full voting rights and which rank after the preference shares but before the other ordinary shares with respect to dividend. Often the level of the dividend is restricted to a maximum figure.

(iv) *Unrestricted Ordinary Shares*

These normally represent the major proportion of the share capital and have the attributes which have been described earlier in this chapter.

An interesting capital structure by way of illustration is that of the British Electric Traction Co. Ltd which at March 31, 1967 stood as follows:

	(*Authorized and issued*)
	£
Participating preference shares	712,745
Preferred ordinary shares	1,326,264
Deferred ordinary shares	790,752
'A' Deferred ordinary shares	6,680,016
	£9,509,777

The dividend and voting rights of each class were as follows:

Dividend

Preference stock is entitled to a cumulative 6% and, after paying a non-cumulative 8% on preferred ordinary stock to a further dividend (not exceeding 2%) at a rate of 1% for every sum equal to 1% on preferred ordinary stock which may be paid as dividend on deferred ordinary stocks. Deferred and 'A' deferred ordinary stocks rank *pari passu* as to dividend.

Voting

One vote per £1 preference, preferred ordinary or deferred ordinary capital. 'A' deferred ordinary capital confers no voting rights.

2. THE INVESTMENT CHARACTERISTICS OF ORDINARY SHARES

In view of the fact that the return on debentures and preference shares is a prior charge against profits before any ordinary dividend can be declared, the ordinary shareholders are the ultimate risk-bearers. Consequently, the greater the fluctuations in profit and the higher the proportion of debentures and preference shares in the capital of the company, the greater will be the fluctuations in the ordinary dividend and the price of the ordinary shares. The return on such shares is therefore far more risky than that on fixed-interest securities, for neither future dividends nor future market values can be predicted with any certainty. Thus an investor who depends upon the income from his securities or who may have to realize part of his capital at a given date regardless of market conditions should not invest in ordinary shares unless he has a sufficiently large capital to diversify his portfolio, thus reducing the overall level of risk.

Although dividends tend to vary over time with the level of profits, the determination of the amount to be distributed is entirely at the discretion of the directors. Shareholders are normally empowered under the articles to vote to reduce the dividend, but not to increase it. If they desire higher dividends, this can only be achieved by voting to replace the directors with others who are prepared to adopt a more liberal policy.

There are many factors which the directors should take into account in the determination of the dividend. In the first place they must ensure that the profits for the year are sufficient to justify legally the proposed payment. For this purpose the legal definition of profits is very different from that advocated by the accountant or the economist, being based upon a series of rules established by case law:

(*a*) A company may distribute the amount by which current income exceeds current expenses after providing for the depreciation of current assets and the payment of current liabilities. It is not always necessary to provide for the depreciation of fixed assets.

(*b*) Capital profits are distributable provided that they are realized and that there is still a surplus after a valuation of all of the assets of the company has been made. It is also necessary that the articles should permit such a distribution.

(*c*) Revenue losses of the year must be met before revenue profits may be distributed and, as stated above, capital losses must be made good before capital profits can be distributed. However, dividends may normally be paid out of current profits without making good either accumulated revenue losses brought forward or capital deficiencies of the current year or earlier years.

Having determined the amount of legally distributable profits, the directors must decide what proportion is to be paid as a dividend. In this connection they should have regard to the liquid position of the company, ascertaining the anticipated sources and dispositions of cash during the coming months in order to decide what amount of cash could be paid out without overstraining liquidity. It is important to appreciate that the existence of distributable profits does not mean that there is necessarily sufficient cash to pay a dividend. Often a company will automatically retain profits during the year by increasing stocks, giving extended credit to debtors, or replacing machinery.

They must then balance the advantages of retaining a large proportion of profits against the disadvantages of causing a possible fall in the price of the company's shares by a miserly dividend policy. The advantages of retained profits are that they enable the company, and thus the status of its directors, to grow by means of a source of finance which is obtainable without a prospectus, without risk and without any binding terms as to the rate of return payable thereon. On the other hand, if, as many experts argue, share prices are determined by dividend expectations, a niggardly dividend policy might depress the shares to the point at which they are sufficiently undervalued to provoke a takeover bid. Consequently directors tend to pay out at least enough to maintain the share price at a level which will discourage a takeover. This is evidenced by the speed with which companies announce an intended dividend increase, where possible, as a defence against a takeover bid.

Another important factor is dividend stability. Directors hesitate to reduce a dividend below the level of the previous year or to increase it to a level which might prove difficult to maintain. Research[1] has shown that dividends tend to be more stable than profits—an indication that directors can and do control the stability of dividends. One major reason is that a dividend cut is regarded as a stigma, which depresses both the market status of the company and the value of its shares. Admittedly a share might rise after a dividend cut, but only where the market had anticipated a still higher cut and is readjusting the price in the light of the actual dividend.

Finally, the amount of the dividend paid by some companies is affected by legal considerations. Investment trusts and close companies, for example, may be required by the Inland Revenue to pay out a stated proportion of their accounting profits or to pay tax as if such a proportion had been distributed. Similarly the Government may at times follow a policy of dividend restraint, requesting companies not to increase their dividends.

Although ordinary dividends may be varied at the discretion of the directors and although ordinary shares are relatively risky due to their residual position, they are nowadays regarded as more secure than fixed-interest securities. This is because dividends and share prices tend to vary upwards, for as the cost of living rises so do prices and company profits. Equities thus provide protection against the erosion of capital and income by inflation. Fixed-interest securities do not offer such protection and this accounts for the 'reverse yield gap' in recent years, when the average dividend yield on equities has been substantially lower than that on the supposedly more secure gilt-edged stocks. These dividend yields, however, are based on the last stated dividend and thus do not necessarily represent the anticipated yield. In fact, after taking into account expectations in respect of future dividends and changes in the cost of living, equities should yield sufficiently more than gilt-edged stocks to compensate for their greater risk.

In two extremely influential articles, Merrett and Sykes[2] analyzed the historical real returns obtained from equities and gilt-edged

[1] E.g. John Lintner, 'Distribution of Incomes of Corporations Among Dividends, Retained Earnings and Taxes', *American Economic Review*, vol. 46, no. 2 (May 1956), pp. 97–113. Also R. J. Briston and C. R. Tomkins 'The Impact of the Introduction of Corporation Tax on the Dividend Policies of U.K. Companies' *Economic Journal*, vol. LXXX, no. 319 (September 1970), pp. 617–37.

[2] A. J. Merrett and Allen Sykes, 'Return on Equities and Fixed Interest Securities: 1919–1966', *District Bank Review*, June 1966. This article brought up to date and extended the analysis of a similar article which appeared in the *District Bank Review*, December 1963.

securities between 1919 and 1966. Basing their analysis on the indices of ordinary shares and fixed-interest stocks prepared by De Zoete and Gorton, they found that the following average net real returns, measured by taxed dividends and capital appreciation (taxed where necessary) were received:

(i) *Annual investment of a constant real sum over a ten-year period*

	Equities	Fixed Interest Securities
Periods 1919–29 to 1929–39 Average return %	11·1	8·4
Periods 1930–40 to 1945–55 Average return %	0·4	−3·3
Periods 1946–56 to 1956–66 Average return %	8·0	−4·7
Whole period 1919–66　　　Return %	5·8	−0·3

(ii) *Investment of a single sum for a ten-year period*

	Equities	Fixed Interest Securities
Periods 1919–29 to 1929–39 Average return %	11·4	8·3
Periods 1930–40 to 1945–55 Average return %	1·3	−1·8
Periods 1946–56 to 1956–66 Average return %	6·2	−5·7
Whole period 1919–66　　　Return %	8·0	0

It should be stressed that this analysis is based on the medium- and long-term performance of a representative group of shares. An investor who acquires only a small number of shares or who maintains an unbalanced portfolio will have a much more volatile performance and a greater risk of failing to counteract inflation. Similarly an investment for a short period such as one or two years is less likely to beat inflation than the above averages might suggest. However, it seems clear that equities provide a better hedge against inflation in the long run than fixed-interest securities.

3. THE VALUATION OF ORDINARY SHARES

The problem of deriving a basis for the valuation of ordinary shares has been at the forefront of investment analysis throughout its development as a science. Ultimately share prices are determined by the interaction of supply and demand subject to the imperfections of the stock market. The major problem is the measurement of the different factors which influence supply and demand. These factors can be isolated quite easily in a qualitative fashion, but a quantitative analysis is fraught with difficulties.

In particular there has been considerable dissension over the relative impact of dividends and earnings on share prices. In the first edition of *Security Analysis*, Graham and Dodd[1] argued that a dollar paid out as dividend had a much higher impact than a dollar of retained earnings. Statistical surveys by Gordon[2] and Durand[3] confirmed this assertion, though subsequent research by Friend and Puckett[4] has suggested that retained earnings might be valued more highly than dividends in a growth company and rather lower than dividends in a static company.

At the theoretical level Gordon[5] has argued that share prices are influenced by the expected rate of growth of dividends. In direct contrast Modigliani and Miller[6] have claimed that there is no distinction between dividends and retained earnings in the valuation of shares. Their argument, however, is based upon the assumption of a perfect market with no transaction costs and ignores the effects of taxation. Moreover, their empirical evidence is largely based upon companies which are not truly representative of the industrial market.

In practice it seems clear that there are a host of variable factors, some quantifiable, some subjective, which determine share prices, and the current direction of research is the attempted isolation and measurement of these variables. Attempts are made to analyze and measure the effect of such factors as the anticipated future earnings and dividends of a company relative to others in its industry, the stability of sales, the dispersion of shareholdings, the level of gearing, the quality of management and the response of the company to overall economic stimuli. The development of the computer has made it possible for vast quantities of historical data to be analyzed in order to establish correlationships between the variable factors. This data can be used to assess the impact on price of predicted future developments. Research of this kind is being performed by leading firms of American stockbrokers and some of the results to date have produced

[1] Benjamin Graham and David L. Dodd, *Security Analysis* (New York: McGraw Hill, 1st ed., 1934).

[2] Myron J. Gordon, 'Dividends, Earnings and Stock Prices', *Review of Economic Statistics*, vol. 41, May 1959, pp. 99–105.

[3] David Durand, 'Bank Stocks and the Analysis of Covariance', *Econometrics*, January 1955, vol. XXIII, pp. 30–45.

[4] Irwin Friend and Marshall Puckett, 'Dividends and Stock Prices', *American Economic Review*, vol. LIV, September 1964, pp. 656–82.

[5] Myron J. Gordon, 'Corporate Saving, Investment and Share Prices', *Review of Economics and Statistics*, vol. XLIV, February 1962, pp. 37–51.

[6] 'Dividend Policy, Growth, and the Valuation of Shares', *Journal of Business*, vol. XXXIV, October 1961, pp. 411–33.

investment portfolios which have significantly out-performed the market averages.[1]

A similar statistical approach has been adopted by the *Value Line Investment Survey*, which provides in respect of over a thousand stocks, quantitative ratings which measure such factors as anticipated share price performance, predicted dividends, quality of the company and suitability for stated investment objects. Here again the results seem to have out-performed the market, though with any generally available advisory service it is impossible to determine the extent to which the predictions have been self-inducing. Although no service with this degree of sophistication is available in London due to the paucity of corporate information there is no doubt that it would, if available, cause jobbers to adjust their prices at once, thus securing the benefit of at least the immediate change for themselves.

A detailed analysis of these methods is outside the scope of this book. There is little doubt that they constitute an important development in the theory of investment analysis, but they still require many subjective assessments of current information and predictions regarding the future. The method adopted in this book is a simple modification of the present value approach expounded by Williams,[2] into which is incorporated a realization price. Consequently the current value of a share to an investor is based upon the present value of the anticipated dividends and of the realization proceeds. The predicted selling price will depend upon the assessment by an investor of relevant future developments and their impact. These arguments are amplified in Chapter 8 and it is suggested that, in view of the poor quality of information available to the market, they still represent a simple and useful framework for investment decisions.

4. CONVERTIBLE DEBENTURES

Strictly speaking, convertible debentures are fixed-interest securities which may be converted into ordinary shares at the option of the holder in accordance with specified terms. Also included in this category, however, are ordinary debentures which give their holders the right to apply for ordinary shares at a stated price and during a stated period, while maintaining their entitlement to the debentures.

---

[1] Fuller details of the work being performed in this direction by practitioners are provided in the papers of the 4th Congress of the European Society of Investment Analysts 1966, obtainable from the Society of Investment Analysts, London E.C.4.

[2] John B. Williams, *The Theory of Investment Value* (Cambridge, Mass.: Harvard University Press, 1938).

Initially, convertibles were issued by companies with a relatively low credit rating, where it was felt that due to the degree of risk it was unrealistic to expect debenture holders to supply funds with only a fixed share in the speculative proceeds. The provision of convertible rights encouraged investors to subscribe to the issue, knowing that they would possess a fixed prior charge should the venture fail and an increasing return should it succeed.

Another situation in which an issue of convertibles would seem appropriate occurs where a company intends to use the proceeds of the issue to finance a project which is not expected to produce profits for one or two years. In these circumstances a large issue of equities would probably have to be made at a price lower than the present market value. The existing level of earnings would be spread over a larger share capital, thus reducing the earnings yield and probably reducing the share price still further, though this downward movement should be counteracted by favourable market expectations regarding future higher earnings. An issue of convertible debentures, on the other hand, would not dilute equity earnings to the same extent and should enable the value of the equity to be maintained. The terms of the issue might provide for conversion at a price rather higher than the present equity value, so that when redemption does occur less equities would be issued than would be required for an immediate equity offer in order to obtain the funds for the project. There is, however, the danger that the establishment of too high a conversion price might make the issue unsuccessful or, should the equity price not reach that level when the date for conversion arrives, result in a failure to convert so that the debentures remain part of the capital structure of the company.

A major advantage of convertibles to the issuing company is that, so long as they remain in the form of debentures, the interest is deductible from profits in the computation of corporation tax. In this way, the company may achieve the tax advantages of a debenture issue until conversion occurs, while the debenture holder has the benefit of an effective equity stake in the company.

A final advantage is that these stocks are regarded as narrow range investments for trustees governed by the Trustee Investment Act 1961 and thus enables them to increase the equity content of their portfolios beyond that indicated by the Act. Should the stocks be converted, however, they must be transferred into the wider range section of the portfolio.

From the point of view of the investor, convertible debentures combine many of the advantages of both fixed-interest stocks and equities. They offer both the fixed prior charge income and capital

173

security of the debenture and the potential growth and protection against inflation of the equity. Moreover, the investor is given a further safety factor in that the price is bolstered by virtue of its two minimum levels. It cannot fall below its market value as a pure debenture, nor should it fall far below its equity value, based upon the market value of the number of shares into which it could be converted at the earliest conversion date.

The growth potential of most British convertibles is somewhat limited by the fact that they are normally only convertible during a period of two or three years, say the third, fourth and fifth years after their issue. Sometimes the conversion price will increase during that period and the stocks will be reduced to basic debentures if they are not converted during the specified years. In the USA, by contrast, conversion rights are often granted over the entire life of the stock, thus giving the holder much more discretion over the timing of conversion and allowing him to retain the debenture rights without forfeiting any equity entitlement.

Because of their dual nature, the market value of convertibles is determined by the separate factors which affect the prices of debentures and equities. Thus the redemption date, the rate of interest, and the quality of the company will influence the debenture element of the stock, while a vast complex of factors such as the future prospects of the company will determine the expected share price at the conversion dates, and thus the value of the conversion option.

For instance, a company might issue at par a 9% Debenture Stock which is convertible in three years' time into 200 ordinary shares for every £100 stock held. Assuming that the market value of the pure debenture rights remained at £100 the market value of the stock would depend upon the value of the right to convert, which would itself depend upon the price of the ordinary shares. If the market price were 25p it is doubtful whether the conversion right would have a great deal of value, for it would enable the holder only to convert a debenture worth £100 into equities at present worth £50. The current share price would have to more than double to justify conversion. There is thus little growth potential and the stock would only warrant a very small premium in respect of the remote possibility of growth.

If the market price were 37½p a rise of one-third would be necessary to warrant conversion. Over a three-year-period this is not improbable and the value of the conversion right would be rather higher than in the previous example. In effect the investor would be prepared to pay rather more than £100 for the chance to benefit from any growth in the share price above 50p, while remaining secure in the knowledge that the value of the stock is unlikely to fall far below £100.

By the same reasoning a market price of 50p would induce a still higher premium, while at prices higher than 50p the value of the stock would be determined primarily by reference to the market value of the ordinary shares. If the market value were 62½p this alone would warrant a price of £125 for the convertible. To this an amount should be added in respect of the debenture rights which will act as a barrier to prevent the price falling much below £100. Such an investment is more secure than a straightforward investment in equities and warrants a rather higher price.

A share price of 75p would suggest a value of £150 for the convertible. In this case protection is given only against a loss greater than one-third, which is worth only a relatively small premium, while at higher prices the premium would disappear altogether.

Another relevant factor in the appraisal of these stocks is the difference in yield between the convertible and the ordinary shares. This difference might be in favour of either, but should not of itself cause price differentials of a substantial amount due to the short period to conversion of most stocks.

CHAPTER 7

Investment Opportunities Outside the Stock Exchange

Although the London Stock Exchange steals the limelight there are many other classes of investment that are available, some of which may be far more appropriate for particular types of savers. In each case, however, the questions which must be asked are identical to those applicable to the assessment of a Stock Exchange security. Thus the investor should have regard to such factors as yield, degree of risk, capital security and marketability. He must also consider how suitable the investment is to his financial circumstances and his present portfolio.

Moreover, although these investments are not so glamorous as Stock Exchange securities, in terms of the number of investors and the amounts invested they are just as important. For example, at March 31, 1971 the total amount invested in national savings and commercial bank deposit accounts amounted to over one-third of the market value of ordinary shares in UK companies quoted on the London Stock Exchange. Furthermore, many of these investments have a direct influence upon the Stock Exchange for they accumulate funds from small investors, who would be unlikely to invest directly in shares, for investment on the Stock Exchange.

The major categories of investments external to the Stock Exchange are as follows:

1. DEPOSIT ACCOUNTS

The main feature of such accounts is that cash is deposited with an organization on stated terms and may normally be withdrawn either in part or in full when requisite notice is given. It is customary for interest to be made variable according to movements in the general level of interest rates. Because of this, deposit accounts are preferable to gilt-edged stocks when interest rates are rising, for the money value of the capital will remain constant. When rates are falling gilts are better because their capital value will rise as compared with deposits, whose interest rates will fall while the capital investment is unchanged.

Of the many different types of organization which solicit deposits, the following are the most important:

(i) *National Savings Bank*

This has been in existence since May 1861, and offers several services to investors:

(a) *Ordinary accounts.* These may be opened by anyone over the age of seven with a minimum deposit of 25p. The total amount held by any person in these accounts must not exceed £10,000 and the deposits and interest payments are guaranteed by the Government. The rate of interest is $3\frac{1}{2}\%$ per annum. This is credited monthly, accumulating from the first day of the month following the deposit and ceasing from the first day of the month in which withdrawal takes place. Sums not in excess of £20 may be withdrawn on demand at any of nearly 21,000 post offices throughout the country. Another advantage is that the first £21 of interest each year is free from income tax. This concession is available for both husband and wife so that each is entitled to £21 interest free of tax where they have a joint account or separate accounts. For a standard rate taxpayer who does not have an excess of charges over unearned income this is the equivalent of a gross return of $5\cdot71\%$. However, for an individual who pays no tax the equivalent return is only $3\frac{1}{2}\%$. Consequently, these accounts appeal mainly to standard rate taxpayers, and even then there are much more remunerative investments available. In fact, their main advantage lies in their encouragement of saving and the ease of withdrawal. Where a depositor has regular outward payments of a fixed amount the bank will pay them direct at a charge of 5p per transaction, payable in advance.

At June 30, 1971, the amount held in these accounts totalled £1,456·9 m, compared with over £1,800 m. five years earlier. This decrease was mainly due to deposits transferred into investment accounts.

(b) *Investment accounts.* Any investor may open such an account so long as he maintains a balance of at least £50 in an ordinary account. Not more than £10,000 in total may be held by an individual investor and the interest rate at August, 1971 was $7\frac{1}{2}\%$. The gross amount of interest is credited at the end of each year and the entire amount is subject to both income tax and surtax. One month's notice must be given for the withdrawal of deposits. These accounts were introduced on June 20, 1966, and by June 30, 1971, there were some 300,000 accounts with balances totalling £337·2 m.

(c) *Stock purchase facilities*. The Post Office Savings Bank offers facilities for the purchase and sale of National Savings Certificates, Premium Savings Bonds, National Development Bonds and a wide range of quoted Government securities. Dealing in Government securities in this way is usually cheaper than doing so through a broker and has the advantage that interest will be paid without deduction of tax, though not without liability thereto.

(d) *Giro system*. This system was introduced towards the end of 1968. It provides a cheap form of settlement of bills which competes directly with the cheque system operated by the commercial banks and, to a lesser extent, with the Post Office's own postal order system. Anyone wishing to settle an outstanding bill will fill in a Giro form and send it to the Giro centre, where the transaction will be effected and the payee informed of the payments. The cost of the service is extremely competitive, being 4p for payments settled by persons who do not maintain a Giro account and $2\frac{1}{2}$p for transfers to an account held at another bank. Transfer between Giro accounts is free and there are no postage costs. On the other hand, no interest is paid on balances held in Giro accounts, nor are overdraft facilities granted.

(ii) *Trustee Savings Banks*

These offer much the same range of services as those provided by the Post Office Savings Bank. They were introduced in Scotland at the start of the eighteenth century and have since been made subject to Government supervision, in return for which deposits are guaranteed by the State. There are now some eighty banks in existence with about 1,400 branches, and due to extensive inter-bank facilities a nation-wide service is provided. The main facilities offered are as follows:

(a) *Ordinary department*. These are similar to ordinary accounts with the Post Office Savings Bank. The rate of interest is $3\frac{1}{2}\%$ and the first £21 of interest is exempt from income tax, this exemption being available for both husband and wife. However, for the purpose of exemption this interest must be aggregated with any interest received

178

on an ordinary account with the Post Office Savings Bank. The total invested in such an account may not exceed £10,000. Normally up to £50 may be withdrawn on demand, while for larger amounts most banks require a short period of notice. These accounts are useful for small savers and have the advantage that the monetary amount of the capital and interest is guaranteed. However, the return which they provide is not very competitive, despite the £21 tax concession.

At June 30, 1971, there was a total of £1,123·1 m. held in these accounts.

(b) *Special investment department.* Persons wishing to open investment accounts must maintain a balance of at least £50 in an ordinary account. The total balance on the account must not exceed £10,000. The rate of interest varies from time to time and from one bank to another. At the time of writing the rate payable is between 7 and $7\frac{1}{2}\%$. The interest is credited gross at the end of each year and is liable in full to both income tax and surtax. The notice required for withdrawal varies between banks and will normally be between one and six months. Earlier repayments may be obtained, but will normally result in the loss of interest for a period.

At June 30, 1971 the balances on special investment accounts amounted to £1,541·7 m.

(c) *Government stock department.* This provides for the purchase and sale of certain Government securities on the same terms and with the same advantages as those offered by the Post Office Savings Bank.

(d) *Cheque accounts.* These were first provided in May 1965 and are now offered by the vast majority of branches. The charges are $2\frac{1}{2}$p per cheque, but for every £50 which is maintained as a balance on the account for a half year the handling charges will be reduced by 50p. This represents a return of only 2% and should not motivate the maintenance of excess cash in such an account. Apart from this concession, no interest is paid and no overdraft facilities are offered. At June 30, 1971 the balances on cheque accounts amounted to £19·7 m.

In addition to the above facilities Trustee Savings Banks offer the normal auxiliary services provided by the commercial banks, such as the custody of valuables and the issue of travellers' cheques.

(iii) *Commercial Banks*

The commercial banks have a long history and, although they are not specifically guaranteed by the Government, it is unthinkable that any of the major banks will default on its obligations. However, an investor must be careful when dealing with a bank to ensure that it is one of the clearing banks, for the term 'bank' is used very loosely by many foreign companies, and their true status and operations may be far removed from those usually attributed to British banks. The main classes of account which are available are:

(a) *Current accounts.* The main advantage of current accounts is that one can receive and pay amounts by cheque without running the risk of handling cash. No interest is paid but the bank will normally fix its charges in relation to the volume of transactions compared with the average balance on the account. Unfortunately the actual basis on which charges are calculated is not usually disclosed, a policy for which banks have been criticized by the Prices and Incomes Board. Thus it is very difficult to establish how much one saves by maintaining a given balance on a current account. However, it is extremely doubtful whether the amount saved by holding an excessive balance is at all comparable with what could be obtained at the same degree of risk in other types of investment. In fact, it is recommended that as soon as an investor's current account exceeds his immediate requirements, he should transfer the excess into a deposit account where it will earn a moderate rate of interest until a more permanent investment can be found. Payments may also be made by standing order or by credit transfer. The first of these authorizes the bank to make payments of a fixed amount at regular intervals until the order is countermanded. Under the credit transfer system, slips may be filled in giving details of the payee and the amount to be paid. These are totalled and passed to the bank with a cheque for the total amount. The bank will then transfer the payments accordingly. This is cheaper than the use of cheques, both with respect to handling charges and postage costs, but it can only be used where one's payees have a bank account.

Amounts may be withdrawn on demand at the branch at which the account is held up to the full balance on the account. Elsewhere, withdrawal facilities may be arranged in advance or a credit card may be obtained which enables amounts of up to £30 to be withdrawn virtually anywhere in the United Kingdom and the Irish Republic. Overdraft facilities are generally available depending upon the creditworthiness of the applicant and the extent of credit restrictions within the economy. Such overdrafts may also be granted in the form of a personal loan, though this is less flexible and more expensive, for it must be repaid by fixed instalments and the interest charged is based on the full amount of the loan regardless of the amount which

180

has been repaid. On the other hand, an overdraft may be called in at the discretion of the bank manager, while the period of a personal loan is established in advance.

(b) *Deposit accounts.* These accounts earn interest at a rate which is usually 2% below Bank Rate. Amounts may be withdrawn after giving the requisite notice, normally seven days, or earlier subject to the forfeiture of interest. The interest is credited gross half-yearly and is calculated on a daily basis on the outstanding balance. The full amount of interest is subject to income tax and surtax and where the total interest in any one year exceeds £15, its amount will be notified to the Inland Revenue. Although the rate of interest is not particularly competitive, a deposit account is useful for accumulating excess funds for other purposes such as Stock Exchange investment.

(c) *Savings accounts.* Many banks operate schemes to encourage small savings. The procedure and the rate of interest vary from one bank to another, but the return, due to the relatively small amounts involved, is usually rather lower than that obtainable on a deposit account.

(iv) *Building Societies*

These date back to the late eighteenth century and their object is to enable the savings of their members to finance the purchase or construction of houses by members who borrow from the society. Largely due to amalgamations, the number of societies has fallen to about 500, compared with three times that figure at the start of the century. At the same time the volume of business has increased enormously—total assets, for instance, having multiplied seven-fold since 1945—and this has led to the growth of much larger and much more secure societies.

However, despite the increasing size and status of building societies they are not an entirely risk-free method of investment, as was shown by the collapse of the State Building Society in 1959. Since then, however, more severe standards of conduct have been required as a result of legislation consolidated in the Building Societies Act 1962, and depositors can have far more confidence in the societies in which they invest.

Nevertheless, a depositor still has a wide variety of societies competing for his funds and he must be careful in his choice. In particular he should ensure that share accounts and deposits with the society qualify as a trustee investment under the Trustee Investments Act 1961. In order to achieve this it must:

181

(*a*) have total assets of at least £500,000;
(*b*) have liquid funds, in the form of cash or investments, whose market value is at least $7\frac{1}{2}\%$ of its total assets;
(*c*) have net reserves equal to at least $2\frac{1}{2}\%$ of its total assets; and
(*d*) conform to accepted practices in its mortgage and investment policies.

The fact that a society has not achieved trustee status does not mean that it is insecure or inefficient. It may, for example be debarred purely by reasons of size and may be a member of the Building Societies Association, which itself enforces the other three conditions. However, as a general rule, investors should confine themselves to societies which have trustee status, and should invest in another society only if they have a personal interest in it and then after careful study of its latest accounts. In particular they should beware of societies which offer a return substantially higher than those of other societies. For, in order to pay high interest rates the society must be charging a proportionately higher rate of mortgage interest and is thus attracting borrowers who have not been able to obtain cheaper mortgages elsewhere. Its business is therefore more risky and the same degree of risk attaches to the interest which it pays to its depositors. However it must be borne in mind that many provincial societies, whose overhead expenses tend to be lower, may offer a higher return in order to compete against the larger societies.

In addition to the problem of the choice of a building society, an investor is faced with the many different types of investment which societies offer:

(a) *Deposits.* These carry a first call on profits and assets and, due to this extra security, usually offer a rather lower interest rate than that payable on shares. However, shares in the major societies are now so secure that there seems little point in foregoing a quarter or a half per cent increase in yield in order to acquire a nominal increase in security. The interest rate may be varied and withdrawal terms will depend upon the society concerned. Normally a month's notice is required, but most societies would repay moderate amounts on demand.

(b) *Term deposits.* A few societies will accept deposits which may only be withdrawn after a given period of time, and will offer a higher and fixed rate of interest in return for this restriction. If it is absolutely necessary the money may be withdrawn before the end of the stated period, but only by forfeiting part of the interest due. In terms of security these deposits are similar to ordinary deposits.

(c) *Shares*. A share account is similar to a savings bank account and is the major source of capital for building societies. The rate of interest varies, the current rate being between 5 and 5½% and it is normally calculated from the exact day of deposit to the day of withdrawal, though there may be a penalty if amounts are withdrawn without giving one month's notice.

(d) *Subscription shares*. These are designed to encourage small, regular savings. The investor agrees to deposit a regular amount each month for a given number of years. During this period the rate of interest is normally the same as that on ordinary share accounts, but a bonus is paid on completion of the scheme. These accounts are rather inflexible for there is often a penalty if they are not completed so that the return might fall below that on ordinary share accounts if withdrawals take place. On the other hand, they provide an excellent method for saving the deposit for the purchase of a house, for existing depositors normally receive favourable consideration on an application for a mortgage.

At March 31, 1971, the total value of share and deposit accounts stood at £10,508 m.

The major feature of building society deposits is that interest is paid on a tax-paid basis. The Inland Revenue each year takes a sample of depositors and ascertains the rate of income tax which each would pay if assessed direct. The average rate of tax that would have been payable by all depositors is computed and the building society pays tax on all interest paid at this 'composite rate'. This rate, which is currently 31p in the pound, has been rising in recent years, due largely to the realization by investors paying a low rate of tax that a building society investment is not very remunerative. However, the reduction of standard rate in 1971 has caused a fall in the 'composite rate'.

Because interest is paid in a tax-paid form, investors have no further income tax liability in respect thereof. On the other hand, there is no provision for repayment of tax if the investor does not pay tax at standard rate. The effective return therefore depends upon the rate of tax payable by the investor:

Net rate of interest (%)	Gross yield at given rates of tax		
	Nil £	30% [1] £	38·75% £
4	4·00	5·71	6·53
4¼	4·25	6·07	6·94

[1] The 30% represents approximately standard rate less earned income relief.

Net rate of interest (%)	Gross yield per cent at given rates of tax		
	Nil £	30%[1] £	38·75% £
4¼	4·50	6·43	7·35
4¾	4·75	6·79	7·75
5	5·00	7·14	8·16
5¼	5·25	7·50	8·57
5½	5·50	7·86	8·98
5¾	5·75	8·22	9·38
6	6·00	8·57	9·80

[1] The 30% represents approximately standard rate less earned income relief.

It is thus clear that standard rate taxpayers obtain the highest return and that they are still substantially subsidized by lower rate taxpayers. Interest is not exempt from surtax and must be grossed up at standard rate to obtain the figure on which surtax will be payable.

Finally, the total which an individual has invested in a particular building society, regardless of the type of account or accounts which he maintains, must not exceed £10,000. However, this limit is not especially important, for a husband and wife may each have up to £10,000 invested in each of any number of building societies.

(v) *Local Authorities*

Local authorities may obtain loans either by an issue of fixed-interest securities on the Stock Exchange or by advertising for private loans through the Press. Interest is usually paid net of tax and the entire amount is subject to both income tax and surtax. These loans vary from one council to another, but the following are the major variants:

(a) *Mortgage loans.* The terms depend upon the amount invested and the period of the loan. At the time of writing the average rate of interest for loans for a period of at least two years is 7% for amounts between £100 and £500, 7¼% between £500 and £2,000 and 7½% for amounts in excess of £2,000. Very occasionally, loans will be accepted at a discount, so that a capital bonus is received at the end of the agreed period. Local authority loans differ from most other deposit investments in that the rate of interest is fixed over the period of the loan. They are thus virtually identical to dated Government stock, except in marketability, for they may only be repaid before the agreed date under exceptional circumstances. They offer the advantage of a good yield and do not entail any dealing expenses. On the other hand they are not very flexible, for the terms once agreed cannot usually be varied.

(b) *Escalator mortgage loans.* This is a type of loan which has been introduced in recent years and which provides the investor with the option to withdraw the loan on seven days' notice once the loan is six months old. The local authority, on the other hand, may give notice to repay at any time after the expiry of two years. The main feature of the loans is that the interest rate is variable. For example, interest at the rate of $5\frac{1}{2}\%$ per annum might be payable for the first six months, 6% for the second, $6\frac{1}{2}\%$ for the third and 7% for the fourth. Thereafter, a fixed rate of 7% might be payable. Such a loan clearly has the advantage of security and flexibility, but the authority may opt to repay the loan if interest rates fall, so that the stated return cannot be counted on. If an investor expects interest rates to fall he would be better advised to purchase long-dated or irredeemable Government stock.

(c) *Short-term deposits.* Many local authorities are prepared to accept loans for periods of up to a year at a rate of interest just below or equal to Bank Rate. Normally these may be terminated by either side on seven days' notice and the minimum amount accepted is £5,000. Most such loans are obtained through the discount market, but deposits are accepted from private individuals.

(d) *Bonds.* Another recent variant has been the yearling bond. This is a short-dated corporation stock of a minimum amount of £100. They are equivalent to a Government security and offer a return similar to that on a Government stock redeemable in one year.

At March 31, 1971, the total temporary debt (up to 12 months) of local authorities stood at £1,919 m., while the longer-term borrowing amounted to over £14,253 m.

(vi) *Finance Houses, Investment Banks, etc.*

These organizations operate in widely different ways and with varying degrees of risk. They include hire purchase companies, finance houses, industrial banks and even companies purporting to be finance houses who are merely financing their own manufacturing activities by means of deposits and short-term loans. Because of the high effective rates of interest which they charge, they can afford to pay interest on loans at a rate well above Bank Rate. However, experience has shown that they can suffer severely from bad debts, and consequently the quality of the return is generally lower than that on building society deposits.

An investor must exercise care when depositing money with any of these companies, as was shown by the collapse of Davies Investments and the Pinnock Group, which caused substantial loss to many thousands of investors. He should ascertain whether it is a member of the Finance Houses Association or the Industrial Bankers Association. Then he should make absolutely certain what type of business the company carries out. This may be done by examining the latest report and accounts, which any company soliciting loans should be prepared to provide. If the nature of the business is not evident on the face of the accounts, then it is an essential precaution to contact the city editor of one of the leading newspapers for information. The accounts should then be examined to see the extent to which the company is relying on depositors to finance its operations. Depending on the nature of the business, external loans should not total more than five times the amount of issued capital and reserves. However, their amount should be substantially less in the case of a company which is merely financing its own industrial operations by means of deposits. The asset structure should be analyzed and the investor must see that interest and rentals received in advance have been apportioned on a recognized basis and that adequate provision has been made for bad debts. Also, where possible, the nature of the investments held by the company should be ascertained. This is important, for where these investments are unquoted they may prove to be worth far below their book value in the event of a forced realization. The extent of asset cover for the deposit should be calculated, having regard to the fact that there may be other loans which rank higher in the event of a liquidation. The trend of profits should be determined from the profit and loss account and the cover for payment of deposit interest calculated.

In fact, it would be advisable for an investor with little financial experience to seek the opinion of a qualified accountant on the accounts. As far as the terms of the loan are concerned, these will vary enormously from one company to another, and the investor should make sure that he fully understands the conditions to which he is committing himself. In particular, he must make absolutely certain of the conditions for withdrawal. It will normally be found that interest will be paid net of tax, unless the period of the loan is less than one year, and the entire amount is subject to both income tax and surtax.

2. NATIONAL SAVINGS

These are designed, together with the Post Office Savings Bank, to enable the Government to raise funds from small savers, though, as will be seen, some types of National Savings offer far more advantages to surtax payers than to low rate taxpayers. For this reason, plus the expense of maintaining the national savings movement, it is often asked whether it should be dismantled or made more remunerative for small savers alone. At the present time the main types of investment concerned are as follows:

(i) *National Savings Certificates*

These were first issued in 1916 at a price of 15s 6d and were distinguished from other savings media by the fact that interest was not paid in cash, but was added to the value of the certificate so that they became worth 26s at the end of ten years. The interest was free from income tax and surtax. Moreover, certificates could be cashed at any time, but in order to encourage investors to hold them until maturity the interest additions were relatively small in the earlier years.

The investment characteristics of these certificates can be illustrated by a description of the terms of the current issue. This is the 'Decimal' issue, which was introduced in July 1970. The certificates cost £1 and the stated interest accretions are:

> 3p at end of first year. 1½p for each completed 4 months during second year. 2½p for each completed 4 months during third year. 3p for the first completed 4 months during fourth year and 4p for the final 4 months of the fourth year.

At the end of four years the certificate matures with a value of £1·25. The value of the certificate at the end of each year of its life, and the simple interest which the annual accretion represents, is shown in the following table:

Years held	Value (p)	Net yield %	Compound annual rate (%)
1	103	3·0	3·0
2	107½	4·4	3·6
3	115	7·0	4·6
4	125	8·0	5·74

This represents a net compound annual yield of £5·74% over the four-year period, which grossed up at standard rate provides a gross return of £9·37%. For surtax payers the gross equivalent return is much higher, rising substantially with the rate of surtax payable. Because these certificates offer such marked tax advantages for surtax payers, there is a limit on the number of each issue which may be held. Although the certificates are relatively illiquid because the maximum yield is only achieved if they are held to maturity, there are schemes which provide a relatively high cash yield for each of the four years. For example, an investor who holds the maximum amount of 1,000 could cash some certificates each year to provide an annual income, retaining sufficient to repay his initial capital at the end of four years.

End of year	No. of certs. to cash	Proceeds
		£
1	54	55·62
2	52	55·90
3	49	56·35
4	45	56·25
	200	

The remaining 800 certificates will have a maturity value of £1,000, and will represent the return of the initial capital invested. This will provide an average annual net yield of 5·60%, which is the equivalent to 9·14% for a standard rate taxpayer whose charges do not exceed his unearned income from other sources. However, if he has a material excess of charges over earned income the equivalent gross yield falls to about 8%.

National Savings Certificates provide high yields for surtax payers and seem ideally suited for them. For other savers, the equivalent return is barely competitive with other Government securities, for the certificates, being entirely exempt from tax, cannot give rise to a tax repayment claim. Thus for an individual who has no tax liability the equivalent gross return is only 5·74%, which is definitely uncompetitive. Nevertheless, most Government advertising is aimed at the small saver, who benefits least from the certificates.

Many investors still hold certificates from earlier issues, most of which may still be held. Each of these issues earns a different rate of return, depending upon the rules relating to the issue and the dates on which the certificates were acquired. In most cases the annual return diminishes each year, for a fixed amount, for example 5p in the case of the first issue, is added each year to the value of the certificates. This constant increment will necessarily represent a declining percentage of the increasing value of the certificate.

In order to explain the investment merits of these earlier issues the table on pp. 190–191 overleaf indicates the terms of previous issues of National Savings Certificates and the current increment that each offers.

At June 30, 1971, the total value outstanding of National Savings Certificates was £2,523·8 m., comprised of a principal value of 1,973·8 m. and accrued interest of £555·0 m.

(ii) *National Development Bonds and British Savings Bonds*

National Development Bonds were introduced on May 15, 1964 to replace Defence Bonds. The first two issues carried interest of 5% and were redeemable after five years at the rate of £102 for every £100 bonds held. The redemption premium is entirely free from income tax, surtax and capital gains tax, and any individual may hold up to £2,500 bonds of each issue. If it is wished to cash the bonds before maturity, one month's notice is required, though if they have been held for less than six months any interest already paid will be deducted from the face value when repaid.

Subsequent issues pay interest at 5¼% half-yearly on January 15th and July 15th. The interest is paid gross, but is subject to tax. The bonds are redeemable at 102% on the next interest date after they have been held for five years, and the redemption premium is tax-free. The gross yield over the entire life of the bonds is 5·85% and the grossed-up redemption yield is 6·10%.

There are, it is true, materially better yields to be obtained from short-dated Government securities, but these bonds offer many advantages to small savers. They are free of all dealing expenses; the capital is secure and may be withdrawn at one month's notice; interest is paid gross; and bonds may be bought in multiples of only £5. While Government securities on the Post Office register offer many similar advantages, the money value of the capital invested can only be obtained with certainty on redemption.

For standard rate taxpayers and surtax payers building society deposits are preferable with regard to both yield and liquidity, while Government securities offer a yield advantage together with the chance of a capital gain should interest rates fall.

From April 1, 1968 National Development Bonds were replaced by British Savings Bonds. These initially offered interest of 6% plus a tax-free bonus of £2%, tax-free if held for the full five years. They are sold in units of £5 and may be cashed at one month's notice. They may be bought at post offices and banks and the maximum holding is £10,000. From April 28, 1969 their interest was increased to 7%, which is paid half-yearly on May 1st and November 1st. In 1971 the capital bonus on redemption was increased to £3% on the new issue which was first on sale on May 3, 1971. This issue provides a gross redemption yield of 7·6% and a grossed-up redemption yield of nearly 8%.

Details of all Issues of National Savings Certificates

Issue	Dates of Issue	Period for which Certificates may be held	Purchase Price per Unit
First	Feb. 21, 1916, to Mar. 31, 1922	Indefinitely, unless notice to the contrary is given by the Treasury	15s 6d
Second	April 1, 1922, to Sept. 29, 1923	Indefinitely, unless notice to the contrary is given by the Treasury	16s 0d
Third	Oct. 1, 1923, to June 30, 1932	Indefinitely, unless notice to the contrary is given by the Treasury	16s 0d
Conversion	Jan., 1932, to May, 1932	Indefinitely, unless notice to the contrary is given by the Treasury	16s 0d
Fourth	Aug. 2, 1932, to May 31, 1933	Indefinitely, unless notice to the contrary is given by the Treasury	16s 0d
Fifth	June 1, 1933, to Feb. 28, 1935	Indefinitely, unless notice to the contrary is given by the Treasury	16s 0d
Sixth	Mar 1, 1935, to Nov. 21, 1939	Indefinitely, unless notice to the contrary is given by the Treasury	15s 0d
Seventh	Nov. 22, 1939, to Mar. 31, 1947	29 years from date of purchase	15s 0d
£1	Jan. 11, 1943, to Mar. 31, 1947	29 years from date of purchase	20s 0d
Eighth	April 1, 1947, to Jan. 31, 1951	25 years from date of purchase	10s 0d
Ninth	Feb. 1, 1951, to July 31, 1956	22 years from date of purchase	15s 0d
Tenth	Aug. 1, 1956, to Mar 12, 1963	15 years from date of purchase	15s 0d
Eleventh	May 13, 1963, to Mar. 26, 1966	6 years from date of purchase	20s 0d
Twelfth	Mar. 28, 1966	5 years from date of purchase	20s 0d
Decimal	Oct. 5, 1970	4 years from date of purchase	100p.

INVESTMENT OPPORTUNITIES OUTSIDE STOCK EXCHANGE

How each Unit Increases in Value	*Maximum Holding*
Value at end of 10th year £1 6s 0d. Then 1d for each complete month	
Value at end of 10th year £1 6s 0d. Then 1d for each complete month	
Value at end of 22nd year £1 13s 0d. Then 1d for each complete month	
Value at end of 22nd year £1 13s 0d. Then 1d for each complete month	A total of 500 in any combination of these issues
Value at end of 20th year £1 9s 0d. Then 2½d for each complete 3 months	
Value at end of 21st year £1 9s 0d. Then 2½d for each complete 3 months	
Value at end of 10th year £1 0s 0d. Then 3½d for each complete 6 months till £1 7s 0d. Then 3d for each complete 3 months	
Value at end of 10th year £1 0s 6d. Then 3½d for each complete 6 months till £1 7s 0d. Then 3d for each complete 3 months till end of 29th year when 6d bonus added making value £1 15s 0d. 5d for each complete 4 months during the 30th year, 6d for each complete 4 months thereafter until the end of the 35th year, when a bonus of 3d is added.	
Value at end of 10th year £1 3s 0d. Then 1d for each complete 3 months till £1 7s 6d. Then 3d for each complete 4 months till end of 29th year when 1s 0d bonus added making value £1 13s 3d. 2½p for each complete 4 months during the 30th year. 2½p for each complete 4 months thereafter until the end of the 33rd year when a bonus of 4½p is added.	250
Value at end of 10th year 13s 0d. Then 1½d for each complete 3 months till 18s 0d. Then 2d for each complete 4 months till 19s 0d. Then 3d for each complete 4 months till £1 0s 6d. Then 4d for each complete 4 months till end of 25th year when value £1 1s 6d. 1½p for each complete 4 months thereafter until the end of the 29th year when a bonus of 4½p is added.	1,000
3d at end of 1st year. ½d for each complete 2 months during 2nd year. 1d for each complete 2 months during 3rd to 7th years. Then 1½d for each complete 2 months till £1 0s 3d at end of 10th year. Then 3d for each complete 4 months till end of 17th year when 6d bonus added making value £1 6s 0d. Then by 4d each complete 4 months up to the end of the 22nd year when 6d bonus is added making value £1 11s 6d	1,400
4d at end of 1st year. 1d for each complete 3 months during 2nd year. 1½d for each complete 3 months during 3rd year. 2d for each complete 3 months during 4th and 5th years. 3d for each complete 3 months during 6th and 7th years with an extra 6d at end of 7th year making value £1 0s 0d. Then 3d for each complete 4 months till the end of 15th year when 6d bonus added making value £1 6s 6d. 4d for each complete 4 months during the 16th year, 2p for each complete 4 months thereafter until the end of the 19th year, when a bonus of 4½p is added.	1,200
5d at end of 1st year. 2d for each complete 4 months during 2nd year. 3d for each complete 4 months during 3rd year. 4d for each complete 4 months during 4th, 5th and 6th years with a bonus of 4d at end of 6th year. 4d for each complete 4 months thereafter until the end of the 12th year when a bonus of 5p is added.	600
6d at end of 1st year. 3d for each complete 4 months during 2nd year. 5d for each complete 4 months during 3rd, 4th and 5th years. 1½p for each complete 4 months thereafter until the end of the 9th year, when a bonus of 7p is added. 3p at end of 1st year, 1½p for each complete 4 months during 2nd year. 2½p for each complete 4 months during 3rd year. 3p for each complete 4 months during 4th year and 1p at the end of the 4th year.	

Note: A month is reckoned from the day of the month in which the certificate is purchased to the corresponding day in the following month, e.g. a certificate purchased on June 15th has been held a complete month on July 15th.

At June 30, 1971 the total amount remaining invested in British Savings, Defence and National Development Bonds was £751·3 m.

(iii) *Premium Savings Bonds*

These were introduced in November 1956 and bonds to the value of £845·2 m. were outstanding at June 30, 1971. They may be bought in units of £1, with a maximum individual holding of 2,000. Once they have been held for three clear months they become eligible for inclusion in the monthly draw for prizes. The prize fund is built up by a monthly Government contribution amounting to an annual rate of interest of 4¾% and the prizes paid from the fund are entirely free of all taxes. One prize of £25,000 is drawn from the prize fund each week. The remainder of the fund is distributed in monthly prizes of which the highest is a single prize of £50,000. Each remaining complete £100,000 in the prize fund is then divided into the following prizes:

	£
1 prize of £5,000	5,000
10 prizes of £1,000	10,000
10 prizes of £500	5,000
10 prizes of £250	2,500
25 prizes of £100	2,500
500 prizes of £50	25,000
2,000 prizes of £25	50,000
	100,000

Each remaining complete £10,000 is split into one prize of £1,000, one of £500, two of £250, five of £100, fifty of £50 and 200 of £25. Any balance then remaining is divided into prizes of £25.

The exact odds against a single bond winning a prize in a particular monthly draw depends upon the composition of the prize fund, for the division of the £100,000 units in the fund is on a rather less favourable basis than that of the remaining balance. However, the odds for a single bond will vary roughly between 9,600 to 1 against and 9,700 to 1 against, and for the sake of clearer exposition will be assumed to be one win in every 10,000 draws. Thus, for an individual who owns the maximum permitted holding of 1,250 bonds, a prize would be won on average once in every eight months. Assuming that the prizes won are of the £25 category, which comprise approximately 90% of all prizes, this would represent an average return of £37·50 per year. This would provide a tax-free yield of £3·00%, which grossed up at a standard rate would be the equivalent of £5·11%.

For high rate surtax payers the grossed-up equivalent would be substantially higher.

The above figures are theoretical averages, based on the retention of the bonds for an infinitely long period. In fact, even a maximum holding may not produce a prize for a period of many years. On the other hand the return calculated above is rather understated, because prizes higher than £25 may be won.

If these bonds are bought as an investment, then sufficient must be held to provide a reasonable chance of a prize in the short term. For this purpose the maximum holding seems most appropriate. The minimum holding should be 400 which gives a chance of winning once in every 25 draws, so that on average a prize should be won once in every two years. A much smaller holding becomes a considerably greater gamble, and should be regarded as a pure speculation. For instance, a holder of 100 bonds can expect to win on average once in every eight years. For a holder of 10 bonds a win can be expected once in eighty-three years, while a holder of a single bond can expect to win once in every 833 years.

It must be remembered that all holdings are speculative in that no level of prizes can be guaranteed. Moreover, a single bond has just as much chance of winning a prize of £25,000 as a given unit of a block of a thousand bonds, though, of course, the entire block has a thousand times better chance of getting a prize. For this reason, the bonds satisfy the gambling motive of savers who balance the chance of obtaining a large prize against the much greater probability of getting none at all.

An investor in Premium Savings Bonds must have regard to their opportunity cost, which represents the interest which is forgone by holding them. For instance, an investor who holds 2,000 will forgo the interest which he could have earned on £2,000 in order to accept the gamble of a lower return or a higher one. Even at this level, the bonds are very speculative and appeal as investments only to the high rate surtax payer, for whom their opportunity cost is relatively low, while the value of tax-free income is extremely high.

Finally, the speculative element of the bonds is somewhat reduced by the fact that their nominal value is guaranteed by the Government, who will cash them in full on written demand. Consequently the money value of the capital invested is secure, the only loss being the interest forgone plus any inflationary capital erosion.

(iv) The 'Save as you Earn' Scheme

This scheme was introduced in 1969 and is intended to encourage regular saving on a contractual basis. Any person may invest a fixed monthly sum not exceeding £20 in total, with the SAYE Office, a Trustee Savings Bank, or an approved Building Society. Payments may be made by cash, standing order or deduction from salary. At the end of a five-year period the saver will receive a tax-free bonus of £12 for every £60 paid, which represents a net return of about 7% and a grossed-up yield of 11·42%. Alternatively he may leave the accumulated sum for a further two years without making any further monthly payments, in which case the bonus will be doubled, giving a net yield of 7·4% and a grossed-up yield of 12·10%.

Six payments may be missed during the contract period without losing the bonus, the bonus date simply being deferred by the number of months missed to give the saver the opportunity to complete the payment of the sixty instalments due under the contract. If the contributions are withdrawn during the first year no interest will be paid, while subsequent withdrawals before the end of the five-year period will earn only $2\frac{1}{2}$% tax-free. Alternatively the amount saved may be left in the scheme until the end of the five years when interest will be paid at the rate of $4\frac{1}{2}$% tax-free.

The SAYE scheme thus offers the advantages of regular contractual saving and a generous rate of interest, but only at the expense of liquidity.

At June 30, 1971, the number of contracts and amounts saved stood as follows:

	No. of Contracts	Amount Paid (£m.)	
		Principal	Interest
National Savings Bank	251,000	23·5	0·4
Trustee Savings Bank	139,000	13·4	0·2
Building Societies	266,400	25·1	not disclosed

3. INSURANCE POLICIES

There are three major groups of insurance policies which may be classed as investments:

(i) *Whole Life and Endowment Policies*

The distinction between these is that a whole life policy provides for payment of the sum assured on death, while under an endowment policy the sum assured is paid at the end of a stated number of years or at death, if it occurs earlier. Either type of policy may be written on either a 'with profits' or a 'without profits' basis. In the latter case the insured person or his estate receives only the sum assured when the policy falls due for payment. On a 'with profits' policy, however, the policy-holder is entitled to share in the income which the insurance company earns on its investments and the basic sum assured is increased by periodic bonus declarations. Naturally the policy-holder has to pay rather higher premiums in order to secure a share in the profits.

As the sum assured under whole life policies is only payable on death, they are primarily designed to provide protection for the dependants of the policy-holder in the event of his early demise. Endowment policies, which are normally expected to mature during the lifetime of the policy-holder, are more in the nature of an investment, for they provide for the regular saving of a fixed amount which is expected to accumulate to an unknown sum receivable at the end of a given number of years. In addition protection is provided for the dependants of the person insured during the term of the policy.

As an investment, endowment policies have many advantages. In the first place they provide a method of compulsory saving. For example a monthly premium of £2·50 might offer immediate life assurance of £500 and at the end of twenty years might accumulate to a maturity value of over £1,000. In this way a regular small payment would result in the accumulation of a relatively large sum of money. Another advantage is that insurance premiums rank for tax relief in the following amounts:

Total annual premiums	Amount deducted from taxable income
Below £10	Full amount of annual premium
Between £10 and £25	£10
Above £25	Two-fifths of the annual premium

In the computation of this tax relief the total allowable premiums are restricted to one-sixth of the income of the claimant and the allowable premium on each policy is restricted to 7% of the sum assured. Tax relief is given in respect of all policies which provide a capital sum on death. The value of this relief to a standard rate taxpayer whose annual premiums exceed £25 is two-fifths of 38·75p in the £, which is equivalent to 15·5%.

Under the Finance Act, 1968, policies must conform to rather stringent rules in order to qualify for tax relief. The main requirements are that the policy should not be for a term shorter than ten years, that premiums should be paid at yearly or shorter intervals, and that the total premiums payable in any twelve-month period should not exceed twice the amount of premiums paid in any other such period.

The insurance company itself pays tax on its income at 37·5%, which gives it a definite advantage for surtax payers and a rather marginal advantage for standard rate taxpayers. Capital gains tax is payable by the insurance company at 30%, which is considerably higher than the rate paid by a standard rate taxpayer, but it is only paid on realizations, which tend to be relatively few as most companies can meet their commitments out of current income instead of disposing of their investments. The policy-holder does not have to pay income tax, surtax or capital gains tax in respect of any capital sums which are derived from the policy.

By virtue of their tax advantages insurance policies offer important advantages in connection with house purchase. A person who wishes to buy a house will normally repay the loan from the building society by an agreed number of payments which are partly interest and partly repayment of capital. However, if the building society agrees, he may defer repayment until the end of the period of the loan, paying interest on the full amount of the loan throughout its term. At the same time he takes out and assigns to the building society a 'with profits' assurance policy, the sum assured on which is sufficient to cover the amount of the loan and which matures on or before the due date for its repayment. When the policy matures the loan is repaid out of the proceeds, and the excess, representing the accumulated bonuses, will belong to the policy-holder. This is more expensive than a straightforward mortgage repayment but it has tax advantages in that both the interest paid on the mortgage and the life assurance premiums give rise to tax relief while only the interest element of the monthly repayments are available for relief under the normal method. Moreover, the purchaser obtains free life protection during the period of the loan and receives a substantial capital sum when it is repaid. It should be stressed, however, that this method is only worth while where the purchaser is, or expects shortly to be, in receipt of a salary which is sufficiently high to allow him to derive full benefit from the available tax reliefs.

Insurance policies suffer from a serious disadvantage in that they are an extremely illiquid form of investment. Very few companies offer a worth-while guaranteed surrender value in the event of the policy being allowed to lapse before it reaches maturity. On the other hand most companies will pay a surrender value if requested, often much higher than the level of any guaranteed values, and many will offer a loan of 90% of the surrender value.

All in all, the level of surrender values is poor and a policy-holder should not surrender his policy unless it is absolutely necessary. Normally if the policy has been running for a few years it will prove better either to accept a paid-up policy for a lower sum assured, in which case the bonuses accrued to the date of lapse of premiums will not be lost and further bonuses will accrue on the new sum assured, or to borrow from the insurance company.

In the assessment of insurance policies as an investment, the investor must balance their advantages of compulsory saving and tax relief against their inherent illiquidity. Also he should endeavour to measure the return which he expects to achieve from the policy. This is extremely difficult, for companies change their bonus rates at regular intervals, usually triennially, and it is almost impossible to predict future rates. Moreover, companies differ in their premium rates and their methods of bonus declaration. Some declare a simple bonus, others a compound bonus, compounded annually or triennially, and others a bonus which is part simple and part compound.

As a general rule a higher level of simple bonus is better than a rather lower compound rate for a short-term policy. However, over the longer term the compound rate tends to be more beneficial. This may be illustrated by calculating the bonus accretions to two policies with a sum assured of £1,000 with bonus rates of £3·50p annual simple and £2·50p triennial compound respectively. For the first policy the increment to the sum assured will be £35 each year throughout the life of the policy. The second policy will be increased by $7\frac{1}{2}\%$ of its accumulated value every three years.

The comparative value of the policies at three-year intervals will be as follows:

	£3·50 Simple £	£2·50 Triennial Compound £
At the end of 3 years	1,105	1,075
At the end of 6 years	1,210	1,156
At the end of 9 years	1,315	1,242
At the end of 12 years	1,420	1,335
At the end of 15 years	1,525	1,436
At the end of 18 years	1,630	1,543
At the end of 21 years	1,735	1,659
At the end of 24 years	1,840	1,783
At the end of 27 years	1,945	1,917
At the end of 30 years	2,050	2,061

A survey carried out by *Which* in 1967, covering over 100 insurance companies, revealed that for a monthly premium of £5, payable until death, a man aged 25 could purchase a 'without profits' whole life policy with a sum assured ranging between £3,500 and £6,676, depending upon the company chosen. This would represent a net compound yield of between $1\frac{1}{2}$ and 4% after taking into account the full tax relief attributable to the premiums. If he required a 'with profits' whole life policy for the same premium the estimated maturity value of the policy on death, assuming that he lived for the normal life span, would range between £5,478 and £12,373, representing a net compound return of between 3 and 6%.

With regard to endowment policies it was shown that, for a man aged 25 a monthly premium of £5 would purchase a 'without profits' 20-year-term policy with a sum assured between £1,250 and £1,591, depending upon the company selected. The net compound return could thus vary between $2\frac{1}{2}$ and $4\frac{1}{2}$%. For the same premium the available 'with profits' endowment policies over a 20-year term offered estimated maturity values between £1,446 and £2,073, representing net compound returns of between $3\frac{1}{2}$ and $7\frac{1}{4}$%.

In view of the tremendous range of insurance companies and their varying degrees of efficiency and profitability, it is clear that several quotations should be obtained before buying a policy, and a reputable insurance broker should be consulted. Far too often, however, policies are taken out to placate persistent salesmen rather than as a positive and considered act of investment.

(ii) *Annuities*

In return for the payment of a single amount an insurance company may contract to pay a stated annual sum until the death of the annuitant. It must be stressed, however, that the initial capital payment is irrevocably lost on death. Each annual payment is regarded partly as interest and partly as repayment of the cost of the annuity. Theoretically the interest element decreases with each annual payment but the Inland Revenue, for the sake of simplicity, have adopted a formula whereby the capital and interest proportions of an annuity are constant, the capital proportion, which is free from tax, being based upon the number of years which it would take, given average expectation of life, to repay the initial cost of the annuity. Thus for a man of 70, whose average expectation of life is about ten years, the capital element of an annuity costing £10,000 would be roughly £1,000 per annum, the remainder being taxable income.

The main advantages of an annuity are that it guarantees a fixed income for life and enables the annuitant to consume his capital without any fear as to his future income. On the other hand there is the possibility that he might live much longer than expected, with the result that in his final years, due to inflationary erosion, the annuity is insufficient to maintain his standard of living. Another disadvantage is that the consumption of his capital will reduce the amount which may be left to his dependants.

Some of these drawbacks are overcome by annuity schemes, which are tied to the cost of living or to equities. Others provide for the payment of an annuity over the joint lives of two persons, such as a husband and wife, which takes account of the most important dependant.

In view of these characteristics annuities are most suitable for those above retirement age, and even then a proportion of capital should be held in equities to combat inflation, to retain a pool of free capital and to provide for one's dependants.

(iii) *Pensions*

Pensions are rather outside the scope of this book, though they have the characteristics of an investment in that they involve the payment of present amounts in order to secure an annuity on retirement. However, they are rarely judged on their investment merits, for they are normally provided by employers to attract and retain scarce labour. For self-employed persons and employed persons who are not members of a pension scheme, substantial tax relief is available should they purchase a retirement annuity on their own behalf.

Although insurance has been described in this chapter primarily as an investment, pure insurance is also extremely important to an investor. He should, for example, insure against any insurable contingency which might erode his invested capital, such as fire, theft, accident, disability, etc. Also, if his capital would provide insufficient income to support his family in the event of death, a life policy, whether whole life, term or endowment should be purchased. In this connection it is often sensible to take out a convertible term policy which provides life cover for a stated term, with no payment should he survive that term, and which gives him the right to convert the policy into an endowment policy at a future date when he can afford the higher premiums.

In this connection it must be repeated that a reputable insurance broker should be consulted on all matters involving insurance, whether general or life. A good broker has contacts with a wide range of insurance companies and will direct his client to the one which best satisfies his requirements.

4. UNIT TRUSTS

There are normally three parties which contribute to a unit trust—the management company, the trustees and the unit-holders. The management company is responsible for the formation, organization and investment policy of the trust. In addition it establishes and maintains the market in the units of the trust. The trustees, on the other hand, are normally only responsible for supervizing the legal administration of the fund, and to ensure that it adheres to the terms of the trust deed which establishes the rules for the organization of the trust by the management company on behalf of the unit-holders. They are also generally charged with the duty of safeguarding the shares held by the trust. Normally, they will be a bank or an insurance company.

The primary object of a unit trust is to acquire a portfolio of securities, the value of which is subdivided into units of a small denomination which are available for public subscription. For instance, a portfolio with a value of £1 m., comprised of holdings of 200 different securities, might be split into four million units of 25p each, which are made available for public subscription with a minimum holding of £25. In this way an investor could invest £25 and acquire an interest in a portfolio of 200 securities, thus attaining a high degree of diversification for a small outlay.

The first unit trust was the Foreign and Colonial Government Trust, established in London in 1868. Due to legal complications it was found that a corporate structure was more suitable than a trust deed for the organization of such trusts. Consequently most of them were converted into limited liability companies and became the first investment trusts. The unit trust movement was moribund in the United Kingdom until 1928, when American mutual funds offered their units here. Then in 1931 the First British Fixed Trust was introduced by Municipal and General Securities Co. Ltd. By 1935 54 trusts had been formed and the number rose to 98 in 1939.

The early unit trusts were fixed trusts, in that the trust deed stated which securities were to be bought. The managers were allowed to sell a security only under certain conditions, such as a dividend cut, and the proceeds could only be used to buy other securities stated in the trust deed. Normally the deed provided for the termination of the trust at the end of a given period.

The trust deeds of successive trusts were made more flexible by giving the managers greater discretion over the sale and purchase of securities and by allowing the managers and unit-holders to choose whether to wind up or continue the trust at the end of its contractual life. Eventually the present-day flexible trust was evolved, with managers given complete discretion over the purchase and sale of securities within a long list of securities, with a limit on the proportion of the fund to be invested in one security. Such trusts are normally extended by a supplementary deed at the end of their life. Alternatively, the units may be converted into units of another trust managed by the same management company.

The market in the units is maintained by the management company, who quote an 'offer price' at which they will sell units and a 'bid price' at which they will repurchase them. An investor may buy or sell units through a stockbroker, who will receive commission of $1\frac{1}{4}\%$ from the management company in the case of a purchase, but will charge normal brokerage on the unit-holder in respect of a sale. It is thus much cheaper to sell direct to the managers, which probably explains why unit trusts do not generally bother to secure a Stock Exchange quotation.

The bid and offer prices are determined in accordance with paragraph 1 of the first schedule to the Prevention of Fraud (Investments) Act 1958. The offer price is calculated each day on the basis of the closing prices at the end of the previous day's trading of the securities held by the trust. The total value of the securities of the trust is increased by the Government stamp duties, broker's commission and registration fees that would be payable at those prices, thus making up the total buying cost of the securities if bought on that day. To this amount is added the $\frac{1}{4}\%$ unit trust instrument duty which is payable on the creation of units, the amount of the initial management charge, and any net income which has accumulated to the date of the calculation. The total value of the trust so determined is divided by the number of units in issue to compute the value of a single unit. The managers may round up this figure by 1·25p or 1%, whichever is the lower.

The bid price is determined by reference to the selling prices at the end of the previous day's trading of the trust's securities, less dealing expenses. The total notional sales proceeds are divided by the number of units and the resultant figure may be adjusted downwards by the lower of 1·25p or 1%.

The effect of these rules is to secure both broker's commission and the jobber's turn for the management company, which could result in a margin between the bid and offer prices of over 10%. Consequently, many management companies increase their bid prices above the statutory minimum to reduce the margin to about 5%.

In addition to its gains derived from maintaining a market in the units the management company imposes service charges upon the unit-holders to cover the initial cost and running expenses of the trust. This is normally done by means of an initial charge based on the cost of the units and a half-yearly charge based on the half-yearly value of the trust. The total percentage of these charges is restricted by the Board of Trade to $13\frac{1}{4}\%$ over the life of the trust.

For a trust with the usual life of twenty years the charges might consist of an initial service charge of $3\frac{1}{4}\%$ and a half-yearly charge of $\frac{1}{4}\%$. Alternatively the initial charge might be $5\frac{1}{4}\%$ with a half-yearly charge of $\frac{1}{8}\%$. These costs are relatively high compared with those of investment trusts, but are considerably smaller than those of the American mutual funds.

In addition to the permanent market which they maintain in their units the managers from time to time make a block offer of units to the public. This is usually done at the formation of the trust, but an offer may be made after it has been in operation for some years. This involves the publication of a prospectus and expensive Press advertisements and if it fails to encourage a reasonable level of subscriptions the management company could bear a heavy loss. The applicants do not gain anything, for they could buy the units through the normal market maintained by the managers at a similar price. However, it is argued that the block offer results in the sale of more units than a perpetual publicity campaign advertising the availability of units from the managers.

Each half-year the net dividends received by the fund during the previous six months are totalled and divided by the number of units to determine the half-yearly distribution per unit. Each unit-holder will receive a cheque representing the net distribution attributable to his holding. The gross amount of the distribution should be included in his tax return and a tax credit will be given in respect of the tax borne by the unit trust by deduction from its own dividend and interest receipts. Some trusts provide for the accumulation of all dividends for reinvestment in the fund. Where this is done the dividends, though undistributed to the unit-holders are still regarded as part of their income and the trust must prepare warrants in respect of each unit-holder's dividend entitlement so that he may declare it to the Inland Revenue.

In order to avoid the double taxation of capital gains on both the unit trust, when it sells securities at a profit, and the unit-holder, when he sells units at a profit, unit trusts pay capital gains tax at the reduced rate of 15% on their accrued gains. Moreover the capital gains tax payable by the unit holder on the disposal of his units is reduced by the smaller of

(a) the amount of that tax.

(b) 15% of the chargeable gains arising on the disposal of the units;

(c) 15% of all chargeable gains arising in the year of assessment. This system has applied from April 6, 1972, and replaces the system of apportionment by which relief was previously given.

The main advantage of unit trusts is that they enable an investor with small resources to obtain the advantages of diversification. If an investor had available capital totalling £50 he would be unwise to invest this directly in equities, partly because of the disproportionate level of brokers' minimum charges and partly because of the risk of loss of capital should the company of his choice fail. With an investment in a unit trust he can achieve a diversified portfolio for a small outlay. It should be stressed, however, that some unit trusts are more diversified than others. In recent years, in order to promote sales of units, more specialized trusts have appeared, whose portfolio consists of shares in one industry or with a special characteristic, such as commodity shares, bank and insurance shares, capital goods industries, shares concerned with the development of North Sea gas, etc. Careful attention must be paid to the investments held by each trust if a share in a diversified portfolio is required.

Another advantage of unit trusts is that they encourage regular saving. Not only do they channel into equities the savings of small investors, who would otherwise avoid the Stock Exchange, but they also offer facilities for the regular purchase of small amounts of units. For instance, an investor may pay a small monthly amount to the managers for the purchase of units. Furthermore, the half-yearly distributions may be automatically reinvested in units at the request of the unit-holder.

Against these advantages there is the argument that unit trusts force prices against themselves in the market, for their regular flow of investment funds exacerbates periods of stock shortage. In the same way it is feared that, if repurchases of units substantially exceeded sales of units, the managers would be forced to liquidate some of the securities owned by the trust, thus pushing share prices down, lowering the value of the remaining units and encouraging further sales by unit-holders. This vicious circle could have the effect of inducing a market break.

The importance of these fears cannot be accurately assessed, for, since unit trusts have been large enough to influence market prices, annual sales of units have substantially exceeded repurchases. In fact, between 1961 and 1968 the annual excess rose from £7·36 m. to £258·48 m., and even during the low market of 1969 and 1970 the annual excess was £186·2 m. and £97·8 m. respectively and there was no single month in which re-purchases exceeded sales of units. However, it seems reasonable to suggest that the specialized trusts could be more easily affected by adverse market movements. This applies particularly to some of the commodity trusts which are forced to invest in relatively small companies or in companies whose shares have a thin market, if they are to achieve a satisfactory degree of diversification. If they are required to liquidate any of their securities due to an excess of repurchases over sales their choice is very limited, for the sale of the less marketable shares could force their price down very sharply. For this reason they may be forced to sell a high quality, marketable holding which they might otherwise prefer to keep.

At March 31, 1971 there were over 250 unit trusts authorized by the Board of Trade. Clearly the investor is faced with a considerable problem of selection. Ideally he would expect a performance which is sufficiently better than that of the share price index which is appropriate to the portfolio of the trust to cover the management expenses. There is no reason to assume that such a performance will be automatically achieved. In America the Wharton School study of mutual funds[1] argued that the performance of mutual trusts did not materially outstrip that of the market as a whole during the period of the survey, while Cohen and Zinbarg[2] drew interesting conclusions concerning the investment performance of investment companies:

(a) Investment company performance in respect of their return and its volatility has approximated to that which would have been expected under unmanaged conditions.

(b) A disproportionately large number of investment companies have been consistently poor performers.

Little work has been done in the United Kingdom on the performance of unit trusts apart from the information provided by the monthly journal *Unitholder*, but a *Which* survey in 1963 concluded that 'taken as a whole, unit trusts have probably done about as well as ordinary shares'. Nor is past performance necessarily a guide to the future. Cohen and Zinbarg found that less than 20% of the companies studied out-performed their own group's average performance for more than 60% of the years studied. Moreover, the trust which showed the best performance between 1957 and 1963 according to the *Which* survey suffered a capital loss over the next five years.

The selection of a unit trust is thus very difficult. First the investor must decide whether he wants a specialized trust, in which case he loses the defensive qualities of diversification, or a general trust in

---

[1] Irwin Friend *et al.*, *A Study of Mutual Funds*, prepared for the S.E.C. by the Wharton School of Finance and Commerce. Published U.S. Government Printing Office, 1962.

[2] Jerome B. Cohen and Edward D. Zinbarg, *Investment Analysis and Portfolio Management*, Homewood, Ill.: Richard D. Irwin, 1967, Ch. 17.

which event he cannot expect a performance materially better than the ordinary share index. Having decided upon the type of trust which he requires, he should isolate the trusts of that class and examine their management record. If a managing company has consistently beaten the average for its group and if its record for the other trusts which it manages is similarly good, then this is an indication, though no more, that the company is more efficient than its competitors.

5. INVESTMENT TRUSTS

Investment trusts are limited liability companies whose function is the management of a portfolio of investments. Their market value, in the case of quoted trusts, is determined by the forces of supply and demand which are affected by such considerations as the dividend policy of the trust, the value of its portfolio, the quality of its management, the marketability of its shares and its capital structure. Because their market value is based upon market forces rather than the value of the underlying portfolio, the aggregate market value of the equity of a trust will generally stand at a discount or a premium compared to the value of its portfolio. The size of this discount or premium measures the assessment of the market of the investment and dividend policy of the management and the financial structure of the company.

Investment trusts have many advantages over unit trusts. In the first place they are able to raise funds on a fixed-interest basis, thereby introducing gearing into their capital structure. These funds can be invested in equities which should over time provide increasing income and an increasing capital value. In this way the return to the ordinary shareholders of the trust can be increased without any further investment on their part. On the other hand should equity prices fall the shareholders might suffer a loss when the fixed-interest funds fall due for repayment. However, debentures issued by investment trusts are normally for such a long term that a short-run fall in the value of equities is not crucial. Nevertheless a high level of gearing does increase the risk attached to a company and might seriously affect its performance in the short run. The extent of gearing can be diminished by the acquisition of fixed-interest securities in the portfolio of the trust and these should be cancelled out against those issued by it in the measurement of its gearing.

Another advantage is that the management expenses of investment trusts tend to be smaller than those of unit trusts. Their average amount is $\frac{1}{5}$% of the value of the assets of the trust per annum, while for the larger trusts, which have the benefit of economies of scale, the proportion is rather less. This contrasts with average management expenses for unit trusts amounting to about $\frac{1}{2}\%$, which are largely attributable to their greater advertising expenditure.

Investment trusts are also preferable in that they can invest in a wider range of assets. While unit trusts are largely restricted to quoted securities and cash, investment trusts often have the power to invest in unquoted securities, mortgages and property. This gives them more flexibility and the opportunity of attaining a greater degree of diversification than unit trusts.

A further advantage is that investment trusts have a certain amount of discretion in the determination of the dividend paid to their shareholders. Since the Finance Act of 1965 they have been required to distribute at least 85% of their earnings after deduction of expenses. The remainder may be ploughed back into the company to provide for growth or for dividend stabilization.

The major disadvantage of investment trusts is that the market in their shares tends to be relatively narrow. In part this is due to the fact that they are 'closed end' organizations, in that the nominal value of their share capital tends to remain constant, as opposed to 'open end' unit trusts, which may expand by issuing further units in response to demand. Moreover the shares which are in issue tend to be fairly tightly held by institutional investors. Because the market is so thin the jobbers' turn tends to be relatively high and this, together with other dealing expenses, causes the initial cost of purchase to be rather expensive.

Partly for this reason investment trusts are not particularly attractive for the small investor. There are no such things as monthly share purchase schemes or provision for the reinvestment of dividends. Furthermore, an investor with less than £100 to invest would find that dealing expenses are rather high.

Finally, it should be mentioned that the provisions for avoiding double taxation of capital gains which apply to unit trusts have been adopted by the Inland Revenue for investment trusts.

The appraisal of investment trusts is very difficult in view of the many factors which affect their price. The investor should have regard to the level of management expenses, the extent of diversification of its portfolio, the past performance of the management compared with the appropriate share index, the net level of gearing of the company, the extent to which there is a free market in the shares and the premium or discount at which the shares stand compared with the market value of the underlying securities held by the company. With regard to the latter point it must be realized that the premium

206

or discount is calculated by reference to the market value of the securities of the company as disclosed at the end of the previous month. However, the value of these securities, and thus the premium or discount, will change from day to day. An indication of the current differential may be obtained by multiplying the different groups which comprised the portfolio of the company at the start of the month by the appropriate group indices, thereby estimating the total current value of the portfolio. The loan capital of the company should then be deducted and the remaining net value may be compared with the market value of the equity of the company.

An interesting recent development has been the formation of split capital trusts in which the share capital is divided into income shares and assets shares. The income shares entitle their owners to the dividends arising from the portfolio and they thus have the characteristics of debentures with income rising to match the cost of living but with eventual redemption at par. Such redemption is generally provided for by the articles of the company, usually after twenty years, to enable the assets shareholders to realize their capital profits. The assets shareholders are entitled to all appreciation in the capital value of the portfolio. The appraisal of these two classes of shares is especially difficult because so much depends upon managerial policy. If a high-yielding portfolio is held the income shares will benefit at the expense of the assets shares, while the reverse will apply if a growth portfolio is acquired.

6. UNIT TRUSTS AND LIFE ASSURANCE

For many years the main advantages of endowment policies over unit trusts were the life cover provided in the event of death and the tax relief on premiums. In recent years, however, the growth of unit trust-linked insurance policies has eroded this advantage. At the present time there are about one hundred unit trusts which are linked to life insurance schemes. Under these the investor pays a regular premium in respect of an insurance policy. Part of this is used to pay for life insurance over the term of the policy, the remainder being invested in units of the trust concerned. In this way the unit-holder receives life cover, tax relief on premiums, and a return on his policy which is directly linked to equities. There is normally no guarantee that the units will have a stated value on the maturity of the policy, but this can be obtained on payment of a higher premium and renders the policies acceptable for use in house purchase schemes.

The main advantage which pure endowment policies now have is the greater flexibility of the investment policies available to insurance companies. There is a vast range of assets in which they may invest, while unit trusts are normally restricted to quoted securities. Moreover, insurance companies may establish reserves in order to maintain their bonus rates in future years. This is not necessarily an advantage for it may mean that policy-holders in prosperous years have to accept moderate bonuses in order to subsidize the bonuses of later policy-holders. On the other hand, unit trusts are unable to operate equalization policies so that their accumulating dividends and prices may fluctuate considerably. Finally, bonuses once credited to a policy cannot be withdrawn by the company. The policy-holder is thus assured of receiving at least the sum assured and the bonuses credited to date when the policy matures. With a linked scheme, unless a maturity guarantee is written into the policy, the value of the units on maturity will depend entirely upon the state of the market at that time.

The choice between linked schemes and straightforward endowment assurance depends upon the risk attitude of the investor and his view of the future of the economy. If he insists on security or if he is dubious about the long-term prospects of equities, he would be best advised to select endowment assurance. If he is prepared to accept a fluctuating value for his policy or if he is optimistic about the long-term outlook for equities, a linked scheme would be preferable. The selection of the trusts with which he wished to link his insurance would depend upon the premium rates and his choice of management and degree of diversification of the portfolio.

A final factor which must be taken into account is the relative illiquidity of endowment policies. Linked schemes normally offer much higher surrender values, but do not provide loan facilities similar to those made available by insurance companies.

7. INVESTMENT CLUBS

Investment clubs mushroomed in Great Britain during the equities boom of the late 1950s. The normal procedure is that a group of individuals agree to pay a regular monthly sum into a fund for the purchase of shares. In effect, the club members run a small unit trust and select the securities for its portfolio. Regular meetings are held to determine investment policy and individual members are often given the task of analyzing particular shares.

From a purely financial viewpoint these clubs do not offer any advantages over unit trusts. They are difficult to administer and club members are faced with the burdensome task of maintaining investment records, registering securities, apportioning dividends, writing minutes, etc. Also the taxation problems and the repayment of contributions to members who leave the club present considerable difficulties. Finally, there is no reason to assume that clubs will perform better than unit trusts in their selection of securities.

On the other hand they provide an interesting hobby for investors who are enabled to meet other investors socially and to air their views on investment. Also they provide a means of regular saving with a reasonable degree of diversification in a manner which is more interesting and less impersonal than other methods. Although subscriptions to an investment club should not dominate the portfolio of an investor there is no reason why they should not supplement it in an interesting and educational fashion.

PART III: THE ANALYSIS OF INVESTMENTS

CHAPTER 8

The Principles of Investment Analysis

1. THE OBJECTS OF INVESTMENT ANALYSIS

The basic object of investment analysis is to compute the present value of a security in accordance with the principles laid down in Chapter 12, in order to determine whether this value is higher or lower than the current market price. The process of computation involves estimates of future dividends, market values, tax rates and inflationary levels. The net real cash flows thus derived are then discounted at a rate of interest which compensates for the degree of risk.

For example, an investor with £400 to invest may wish to compare ordinary shares in ABC Ltd with those in XYZ Ltd. Shares in ABC Ltd are currently priced at 100p to yield 5%. It is anticipated that the dividend will be increased by one-fifth during the second year and will be maintained at that level for the third year after purchase. It is further predicted that it will be possible to sell the shares at 150p cum div. towards the end of the fourth year. The shares of XYZ Ltd now stand at 200p and give a gross dividend yield of 8%. The investor feels that this dividend level will be maintained and that it will be possible to sell the shares at 250p cum div. at the end of the fourth year. Although the shares of ABC Ltd provide a lower yield than those of XYZ Ltd, it is felt that they are rather more risky because it is a company in a new industry which could suffer badly if the industry runs into difficulties. XYZ Ltd operates in a cyclical industry which is currently suffering a downturn, but the company has adequate reserves and has in the past maintained its dividend despite falling profits. The long-term prospects for the company are quite satisfactory.

Because of the difference in the risk element between the two companies, the investor requires a yield of 5% net of inflation and taxes from ABC Ltd and 4% from XYZ Ltd. It is anticipated that over the next four years the standard rate of income tax will be 40%, while the capital gains tax rate will be 30%. The rate of inflation is expected to be 3% compound per annum.

Computation of net present value on an investment of £400 in

(a) *ABC Ltd*	*Year 1*	*Year 2*	*Year 3*	*Year 4*	*Total*
	£	£	£	£	£
Dividends anticipated	20	24	24	—	—
Expected sale proceeds	—	—	—	600	—
Less: Income tax (40%)	8	10	10	—	—
Capital gains tax (30%)	—	—	—	60	—
Net cash flows	12	14	14	540	—
3% Present value factor (to adjust for inflation)	0·97087	0·94260	0·91514	0·88849	—
Real value of net cash flows	12	13	13	480	—
5% Present value factor	0·952381	0·907029	0·863838	0·822702	
Present value of net real cash flows	11	12	22	395	440
Cost of investment	—	—	—	—	400
Net present value of investment in real terms					£40

(b) *XYZ Ltd*	*Year 1*	*Year 2*	*Year 3*	*Year 4*	*Total*
	£	£	£	£	£
Dividends anticipated	32	32	32	—	—
Expected sale proceeds	—	—	—	500	—
Less: Income tax (40%)	13	13	13	—	—
Capital gains tax (30%)	—	—	—	30	—
Net cash flows	19	19	19	470	—
3% Present value factor (to adjust for inflation)	0·97087	0·94260	0·91514	0·88849	—
Real value of net cash flows	18	18	17	418	—
4% Present value factor	0·961538	0·924556	0·88896	0·854804	—
Present value of net real cash flows	17	17	15	357	406
Cost of investment	—	—	—	—	400
Net present value of investment in real terms					£6

On the basis of this calculation the investor should select the shares in ABC Ltd assuming that he is not aware of an investment which gives a higher net present value and that the share is compatible with his overall portfolio requirements. An institutional investor would be able to examine a far greater number of securities in this way, ranking them in order of size of net present value. Securities could then be selected on the basis of profitability and portfolio requirements. It is essential that securities already held should be constantly reappraised to ensure that changes in expectations, taxation and the rate of interest have been taken into account. If, on this reassessment, another share seems more suitable it should be acquired and the previous holding sold.

2. THE METHODS OF INVESTMENT ANALYSIS

While the major object of investment analysis is to predict the future performance of a share both in terms of dividends and share price, there are three competing theories regarding the method of analysis:

(i) *Traditional or Fundamental Analysis*

Proponents of traditional analysis assert that future trends in share prices and dividends can be predicted by examining all factors which are likely to affect the performance of the company and its shares and attempting to quantify these influences to provide estimates of future cash flows accruing to the shareholder. During this and the ensuing four chapters the principles and methods of traditional analysis will be considered in detail. At the present time such analysis is being subjected to considerable criticism, primarily based upon the inaccuracy of its past predictions. However, the faults lie not in the theory itself but in the lack of information made available to investors and in the extreme difficulties encountered in making predictions in an uncertain world. In fact, traditional analysis is merely an extension of the discounted cash flow techniques which are so fashionable in the world of industry and the theoretical arguments behind the two methods are identical.

(ii) *Technical or Chart Analysis*

This theory of analysis, which is described in more detail in Chapter 13, relates primarily to the prediction of future share prices rather than future dividends. The basic assumption is that past price movements both of particular shares and of share prices generally reveal prophetic patterns on the basis of which future trends may be predicted. The more fanatical advocates of charts argue that technical analysis alone is sufficient for predictive purposes on the grounds that the current price pattern of a share reflects all of the information available and the attitudes and expectations of the market regarding that share. Therefore, an analysis based on price movements alone would automatically recognize all of the factors which a fundamentalist would incorporate, though much more laboriously, into his analysis. Other chartists, however, accept that the conclusions indicated by technical analysis should be confirmed by reference to fundamental factors.

Traditional analysts, on the other hand, tend to regard charts merely as a diagrammatic representation of only one of the many groups of information which they must examine—a representation which has the advantage of clarity but which has no predictive powers except to the extent that the considerable number of investors whose policy is determined by charts may sometimes induce the predicted result.

(iii) *The Random Walk Theory*

This theory, which is explained in Chapter 14, accepts the premise of the chartist that a share price at a particular time reflects all the knowledge and expectations of the market regarding that share. Thus, assuming that the stock market is relatively perfect, the price of a share will reflect its intrinsic value subject to minor day-to-day fluctuations. It is then argued that the emergence of new information and of new expectations is entirely a matter of chance, with the result that future price movements are of an entirely random character and are not influenced by past movements. It follows that past price patterns have no predictive value and that the claims of purist technicians cannot be supported. It follows, too, that traditional analysis can only be defended so long as it consistently produces results which are sufficiently superior to those produced by a random selection of securities to compensate for the cost of the analysis. In theory traditional analysis is more efficient in the identification and satisfaction of subjective portfolio objectives, but in practice it is often reduced to a near-random process due to the infrequency and poor quality of available information.

3. TECHNIQUES OF FUNDAMENTAL ANALYSIS

It has already been shown that the object of investment analysis is to estimate future dividends or interest and future share prices and to determine the appropriate rate of interest at which these amounts are to be discounted to the present for comparison with the current share price. In order to predict these figures it is necessary to analyze in depth the future prospects of both the company and the stock market:

(i) *Prediction of Future Dividends*

As dividends represent the proportion of profits which the directors decide are available for distribution it is essential to estimate future profits and likely dividend policies. In the prediction of profits it is necessary to examine three different groups of information:

(a) *The National Economy*

The profits of a company will normally be dependent upon the state of the economy within which it operates. Consequently an investor must assess the future course of the national economy or economies in which the company trades. For all of the major industrial countries such forecasts are available, emanating either from the government in the form of national plans or official forecasts or from independent research teams. In the UK for instance, there is a wide range of publications. The first National Plan, it is true, proved very inaccurate in its forecasts, but subsequent plans should profit from its experience. Short-term forecasts are contained in White Papers prepared by the Treasury. In addition to, though often contradicting, official publications there are the predictions of independent groups such as the National Institute of Economic and Social Research. For the investor who wishes to make his own predictions there is still more material available in the *Annual Abstract of Statistics* and *National Income and Expenditure* (*Blue Book*), which are supplemented during the year by the *Monthly Digest of Statistics, Financial Statistics, Economic Trends*, and the *Board of Trade Journal*, all of which are Government publications. Among the most important national statistics for the investment analysts are those relating to the gross national product. The logic which underlies the concept of national income can best be illustrated by the table relating to the gross national product which appears in the *Annual Abstract of Statistics* for 1970, and which is reproduced overleaf.

It is clear from this table that the gross national product can be computed in two ways:

(*a*) By computing the money spent on the goods and services generated by the economic activity of the nation during the year. This is ascertained by estimating the total domestic expenditure for the year at market prices, and adjusting this figure to the overall national product (by adding exports and income received from abroad and deducting imports and income paid abroad) valued at factor cost (by deducting indirect taxation from the market value of expenditure).

(b) By computing the total incomes received by the factors of production including corporate profits, which must by definition equal the market value of, and thus the amount expended on, the goods and services provided by those factors. It may be argued that this equality does not occur because personal savings are not expended on goods and services. However, the computation of expenditure includes investment by firms in capital equipment and increased holdings of stock. This figure automatically equals the total of savings because payments of income by firms are equal to both the income of factors of production and the value of output at factor cost. The income of factors of production consists of consumption expenditure plus savings, while the value of output consists of the amount sold for consumption plus the amount held as physical investment. As the amount sold for consumption must equal the sum of consumption expenditure, savings by factors of production and investment by firms must be identical. Consequently, as the calculations of national income on the basis of expenditure includes gross capital formation or investment it is not necessary to separate savings from total incomes received.

Whichever method of computation is used the figure of gross national product will be the same, subject, of course, to a residual error due to the complex character of the data. This error is adjusted against the computation based on factor incomes so that it is made to agree with that based on expenditure.

In estimating the trend of national income it is essential to eliminate movements which are caused merely by changes in the price level. For this reason the *Blue Book* provides tables which show the national income valued at constant prices, so that analysis in real terms may be undertaken.

The value of aggregative national income statistics for the investment analyst is somewhat debatable. Certainly they give an indication of the level of overall economic activity and can be used as a starting point for predictions of the future course of the economy. However, there are several conceptual and practical problems involved in their use. Among the conceptual difficulties are the valuation

215

TABLE I

Gross national product

£ million

	1959	1960	1961	1962	1963	1964	1965	1966	1967	1968	1969
Expenditure											
Consumers' expenditure	16,117	16,933	17,830	18,910	20,087	21,459	22,885	24,232	25,362	27,113	28,618
Public authorities' current expenditure on goods and services	4,001	4,248	4,589	4,920	5,184	5,512	6,043	6,572	7,276	7,705	8,118
Gross domestic fixed capital formation	3,736	4,120	4,619	4,731	4,907	5,857	6,304	6,704	7,239	7,889	7,927
Value of physical increase in stocks and work in progress	174	594	323	58	198	649	401	267	215	210	294
Total domestic expenditure at market prices	24,028	25,895	27,361	28,619	30,376	33,477	35,633	37,775	40,092	42,917	44,957
Exports and property income from abroad	6,016	6,309	6,587	6,840	7,225	7,677	8,289	8,709	8,845	10,669	11,986
less Imports and property income paid abroad	− 5,791	− 6,483	− 6,480	− 6,607	− 6,964	− 7,886	− 8,157	− 8,437	− 8,911	− 10,713	− 11,318
less Taxes on expenditure	− 3,200	− 3,391	− 3,643	− 3,896	− 4,047	− 4,458	− 4,986	− 5,611	− 5,996	− 6,944	− 7,868
Subsidies	369	487	586	600	560	509	563	555	787	890	844
Gross national product at factor cost	21,422	22,817	24,411	25,556	27,150	29,319	31,342	32,991	34,817	36,819	38,601

Factor incomes

Income from employment	14,107	15,174	16,407	17,306	18,190	19,702	21,261	22,746	23,626	25,334	27,174
Income from self-employment[1]	1,890	2,014	2,116	2,156	2,217	2,346	2,536	2,677	2,812	2,919	3,009
Gross trading profits of companies[1][2]	3,317	3,736	3,643	3,595	4,108	4,591	4,758	4,442	4,620	5,024	4,948
Gross trading surplus of public corporations[1]	391	539	645	751	846	931	996	1,051	1,142	1,372	1,461
Gross trading surplus of other public enterprises[1]	164	179	96	71	78	91	96	87	88	108	114
Rent[3]	1,153	1,244	1,338	1,454	1,567	1,698	1,865	2,028	2,192	2,379	2,601
Total domestic income[1]	21,022	22,886	24,245	25,333	27,006	29,359	31,512	33,031	34,480	37,136	39,307
less Stock appreciation	− 90	− 135	− 173	− 147	− 202	− 301	− 333	− 318	− 187	− 634	− 815
Residual error	230	− 165	87	37	− 46	− 134	− 279	− 102	156	−	− 342
Gross domestic product at factor cost	21,162	22,586	24,159	25,223	26,758	28,924	30,900	32,611	34,449	36,502	38,150
Net property income from abroad	260	231	252	333	392	395	442	380	368	317	451
Gross national product	21,422	22,817	24,411	25,556	27,150	29,319	31,342	32,991	34,817	36,819	38,601
less Capital consumption	− 1,844	− 1,933	− 2,065	− 2,197	− 2,318	− 2,492	− 2,697	− 2,937	− 3,149	− 3,378	− 3,694
National income	19,578	20,884	22,346	23,359	24,832	26,827	28,645	30,054	31,668	33,441	34,907

[1] Before providing for depreciation and stock appreciation. [2] From 1966 selective employment tax is included on a cash basis and refunds or premiums are allowed for when they are received. [3] Before providing for depreciation.

Source: Central Statistical Office

of Government services and the omission of non-monetary services such as the work of housewives. Other problems are the valuation of benefits derived from occupation of one's own house and the computation of depreciation, which is used to reduce gross national product to net national product.

Furthermore the statistics are susceptible to serious computational errors, as explained by Oskar Morgenstern,[1] which can cause a drastic distortion of any forecasts for which they have been used as a basis. Finally, international comparisons are extremely prone to error due to differences in techniques of compilation and to different patterns of distribution and composition of the national income.

In addition to the national income statistics there are several important aggregative statistics which act as indicators of the state of the economy:

Unemployment. Figures of unemployed persons are prepared by the Ministry of Labour on the basis of numbers registered with employment exchanges. These statistics are published in the *Ministry of Labour Gazette* (monthly) and *Statistics on Incomes, Prices, Employment and Production* (quarterly) and are also summarized in the *Monthly Digest of Statistics*. In addition to the basic figures of unemployed persons, seasonally corrected figures are also published. These provide a more realistic indication of the underlying trend of unemployment.

Production. The major source of information relating to industrial production are the reports of the Census of Production. These are published only after a considerable delay and are more relevant to the study of particular industries. More useful is the Index of Industrial Production which attempts to measure in real terms changes in the level of industrial production. The overall index and the separate indices for each manufacturing industry are published in the *Monthly Digest of Statistics* in both an unadjusted and a seasonally adjusted form. The indices are normally published within six weeks of the month to which they relate, though they are subject to revision thereafter.

Hire Purchase Credit. Statistics relating to new credit extended, repayments and amount of hire purchase debt outstanding at the end of each quarter are published in the *Board of Trade Journal*. Indices and other statistics based on this information are published in *Financial Statistics* and the *Monthly Digest of Statistics*. These

---

[1] Oskar Morgenstern, *On the Accuracy of Economic Observations* (Princeton: University Press, 1963).

figures are extremely important, for a net increase in hire purchase debt is normally regarded as inflationary and will often give rise to Government action. Moreover, deflationary or reflationary Government policies will normally be implemented by imposing or relieving hire purchase restrictions either totally or in respect of particular commodities.

Balance of Payments. Detailed figures of the UK balance of payments with the rest of the world are published annually in the *United Kingdom Balance of Payments* (*Pink Book*) and also, in summary form. in the *Annual Abstract of Statistics.* Quarterly estimates of the balance of payments figures and monthly statements of the level of the gold and currency reserves are available in *Economic Trends*, the *Monthly Digest of Statistics* and *Financial Statistics.* Despite their inherent inaccuracies as explained by Oskar Morgenstern[1] and F. M. M. Lewes,[2] these statistics receive considerable publicity and wield great influence over Government policy and the Stock Exchange.

Index of Retail Prices. This is the most commonly used indicator of the inflationary trend of the economy and shows the change in price of the average budgets of representative households. The basic data is published in the *Ministry of Labour Gazette* and reproduced in *Statistics on Incomes, Prices, Employment and Production* and the *Monthly Digest of Statistics.*

(b) *The Industry within which the Company Operates*

For the analysis of a particular industry the supplementary tables in the national income statistics are extremely helpful. Tables II and III overleaf are particularly important.

Although their analysis is insufficiently detailed for the calculation of the size of the home market of a particular industry, it does provide a basis for its estimation, and if taken in conjunction with the tables which show production and exports by product and industry gives a rough indication of the market of each industry.

Tables IV and V provide an analysis of gross fixed capital formation classified by the type of capital asset acquired and, in very broad groups, by the industry which has undertaken the investment. Although the statistics are not sufficiently detailed for research into a particular industry, they are broadly indicative of the size and nature of investment, which is a useful pointer to the future level of production.

[1] *Op. cit.*, Chapter IX.
[2] F. M. M. Lewes, *Statistics of the British Economy* (London: George Allen & Unwin, 1967).

TABLE II

Consumers' expenditure at current prices

£ million

	1959	1960	1961	1962	1963	1964	1965	1966	1967	1968	1969
Household expenditure on food:											
Total	4,158	4,228	4,370	4,565	4,695	4,895	5,065	5,321	5,481	5,663	5,977
Bread and cereals	548	558	576	610	630	653	674	695	719	749	775
Meat and bacon	1,086	1,140	1,176	1,221	1,247	1,334	1,387	1,476	1,515	1,586	1,673
Fish	155	153	151	157	159	180	190	193	197	197	204
Oils and fats	240	220	208	227	238	247	250	249	243	237	245
Sugar, preserves and confectionery	402	413	416	450	467	476	492	500	519	537	574
Dairy products	616	640	660	661	702	712	748	763	787	831	873
Fruit	260	260	282	291	280	299	306	331	339	355	373
Potatoes and vegetables	449	437	482	528	533	533	551	625	653	643	705
Beverages	271	270	277	281	292	308	309	323	338	346	361
Other manufactured food	131	137	142	139	147	153	158	166	171	182	194
Alcoholic drink:											
Total	920	957	1,060	1,121	1,185	1,328	1,432	1,529	1,613	1,714	1,824
Beer	554	566	624	671	704	772	854	904	959	981	1,073
Wines, spirits, cider, etc.	366	391	436	450	481	556	578	625	654	733	751
Tobacco	1,061	1,140	1,217	1,242	1,286	1,343	1,428	1,504	1,512	1,578	1,694
Housing:											
Total	1,569	1,660	1,775	1,955	2,161	2,343	2,586	2,835	3,056	3,293	3,590
Rent, rates and water charges	1,297	1,367	1,455	1,602	1,770	1,931	2,129	2,338	2,502	2,686	2,926
Maintenance, repairs and improvements by occupiers	272	293	320	353	391	412	457	497	554	607	664
Fuel and light:											
Total	686	751	796	911	1,010	1,000	1,087	1,161	1,208	1,340	1,421
Coal and coke	288	323	325	359	379	348	357	370	361	355	351
Electricity	212	236	269	328	384	402	456	490	521	607	636
Gas	134	136	145	159	173	183	206	233	258	301	353
Other	52	56	57	65	74	67	68	68	68	77	81
Clothing:											
Total	1,525	1,664	1,729	1,771	1,873	1,971	2,099	2,154	2,188	2,320	2,417
Footwear	263	293	304	310	327	341	359	368	374	391	410
Other clothing	1,262	1,371	1,425	1,461	1,546	1,630	1,740	1,786	1,814	1,929	2,007
Durable goods:											
Total	1,364	1,400	1,351	1,419	1,581	1,745	1,775	1,770	1,889	2,061	1,957
Motor cars and motor cycles, new and second-hand	506	568	500	538	633	723	697	693	784	867	782
Furniture and floor coverings	411	410	430	447	473	530	574	578	571	608	588
Radio, electrical and other durable goods	447	422	421	434	475	492	504	499	534	586	587

Other household goods	518	536	571	592	616	659	701	733	753	812	839
Books, newspapers and magazines:											
Total	225	243	262	271	279	297	327	350	362	408	420
Books	48	53	54	53	57	61	64	74	79	84	84
Newspapers	131	134	150	157	161	173	196	204	209	242	244
Magazines	46	56	58	61	61	63	67	72	74	82	92
Chemists' goods	232	247	266	279	294	320	339	359	370	403	422
Miscellaneous recreational goods	309	342	364	382	404	446	476	505	541	601	637
Other miscellaneous goods	216	233	249	249	256	281	297	309	320	356	359
Running costs of motor vehicles	405	454	526	614	682	778	914	1,045	1,178	1,368	1,518
Travel:											
Total	545	572	604	633	663	705	741	792	819	861	924
Rail	134	145	152	156	159	165	170	179	181	183	205
Bus, coach and tram	302	312	326	337	346	361	370	387	387	394	398
Other	109	115	126	140	158	179	201	226	251	284	321
Communication services	132	140	147	157	169	183	208	221	244	262	284
Entertainment and recreational services	264	285	304	324	332	348	375	403	419	434	472
Domestic service	102	103	105	110	112	116	122	130	136	143	149
Catering (meals and accommodation)	874	906	958	1,029	1,093	1,162	1,228	1,284	1,310	1,387	1,477
Wages, salaries, etc. paid by private non-profit-making bodies	123	137	148	173	197	217	237	268	303	336	367
Insurance	162	166	179	206	220	238	258	278	301	338	368
Other services	642	689	760	807	849	923	999	1,098	1,233	1,371	1,470
Income in kind not included elsewhere	50	46	44	44	46	47	50	52	51	49	49
Less Expenditure by foreign tourists in the United Kingdom	−199	−225	−231	−236	−242	−245	−249	−279	−303	−355	−429
Consumers' expenditure in the United Kingdom	15,883	16,674	17,554	18,618	19,761	21,100	22,495	23,822	24,984	26,743	28,206
Consumers' expenditure abroad	234	259	276	292	326	359	390	410	378	370	412
Total	16,117	16,933	17,830	18,910	20,087	21,459	22,885	24,232	25,362	27,113	28,618

Source: Central Statistical Office

TABLE III

Consumers' expenditure at 1963 prices

£ million

	1959	1960	1961	1962	1963	1964	1965	1966	1967	1968	1969
Household expenditure on food:											
Total	4,423	4,518	4,600	4,646	4,695	4,769	4,770	4,854	4,901	4,916	4,921
Bread and cereals	610	615	610	620	630	623	620	612	611	604	599
Meat and bacon	1,114	1,161	1,198	1,233	1,247	1,237	1,233	1,263	1,276	1,280	1,280
Fish	169	159	155	161	159	170	171	168	170	167	163
Oils and fats	235	230	234	242	238	242	240	245	244	244	247
Sugar, preserves and confectionery	457	471	474	478	467	458	468	474	478	470	461
Dairy products	650	668	683	694	702	721	721	722	734	742	747
Fruit	275	273	277	278	280	298	296	308	293	306	310
Potatoes and vegetables	492	515	531	517	533	563	570	592	612	612	611
Beverages	277	279	288	283	292	305	300	313	324	328	335
Other manufactured food	144	147	150	140	147	152	151	157	159	163	168
Alcoholic drink:											
Total	1,023	1,074	1,146	1,146	1,185	1,264	1,246	1,280	1,315	1,358	1,368
Beer	635	661	698	696	704	736	742	758	780	787	824
Wines, spirits, cider, etc.	388	413	448	450	481	528	504	522	535	571	544
Tobacco	1,231	1,275	1,294	1,246	1,286	1,270	1,224	1,264	1,271	1,265	1,250
Housing:											
Total	1,924	1,977	2,018	2,089	2,161	2,196	2,274	2,343	2,440	2,533	2,608
Rent, rates and water charges	1,622	1,657	1,685	1,733	1,770	1,798	1,846	1,895	1,948	2,016	2,066
Maintenance, repairs and improvements by occupiers	302	320	333	356	391	398	428	448	492	517	542
Fuel and light:											
Total	775	843	856	940	1,010	973	1,035	1,068	1,097	1,151	1,224
Coal and coke	358	386	366	379	379	341	337	321	297	281	265
Electricity	215	248	281	336	384	384	420	438	464	487	527
Gas	143	145	146	158	173	182	211	242	271	314	358
Other	59	64	63	67	74	66	67	67	65	69	74
Clothing:											
Total	1,641	1,767	1,806	1,798	1,873	1,943	2,026	2,025	2,027	2,117	2,123
Footwear	294	317	325	317	327	339	350	345	343	352	359
Other clothing	1,347	1,450	1,481	1,481	1,546	1,604	1,676	1,680	1,684	1,765	1,764
Durable goods:											
Total	1,314	1,351	1,300	1,363	1,581	1,725	1,724	1,699	1,779	1,851	1,696
Motor cars and motor cycles, new and second-hand	430	494	436	487	633	731	706	703	774	812	719
Furniture and floorcoverings	462	453	461	455	473	512	532	521	503	514	474
Radio, electrical and other durable goods	422	404	403	421	475	482	486	475	502	525	503

Other household goods	554	573	594	599	616	646	663	676	692	723	709
Books, newspapers and magazines:											
Total	272	288	285	279	279	278	277	287	288	278	273
Books	54	57	56	51	57	58	58	64	65	64	60
Newspapers	158	163	162	164	161	161	161	161	161	156	151
Magazines	60	68	67	64	61	59	58	62	62	58	62
Chemists' goods	247	261	269	274	294	311	323	333	335	338	333
Miscellaneous recreational goods	330	368	381	388	404	431	454	461	485	514	505
Other miscellaneous goods	234	250	260	249	256	269	278	280	282	277	264
Running costs of motor vehicles	438	488	550	620	682	770	837	922	1,008	1,092	1,134
Travel:											
Total	664	657	653	653	663	681	684	704	705	697	723
Rail	188	178	170	162	159	162	155	153	153	146	154
Bus, coach and tram	364	360	356	348	346	341	335	331	324	320	316
Other	112	119	127	143	158	178	194	220	228	231	253
Communication services	146	155	161	161	169	179	196	201	214	223	227
Entertainment and recreational services	277	291	306	319	332	349	359	363	367	368	369
Domestic service	119	117	114	113	112	110	110	108	105	105	106
Catering, insurance and other services[1]	2,047	2,106	2,179	2,280	2,359	2,463	2,521	2,575	2,640	2,717	2,771
Income in kind not included elsewhere	54	48	46	44	46	46	47	47	45	42	40
Less Expenditure by foreign tourists in the United Kingdom	-225	-245	-242	-241	-242	-235	-225	-239	-248	-279	-318
Consumers' expenditure in the United Kingdom	17,488	18,162	18,576	18,966	19,761	20,438	20,823	21,251	21,748	22,286	22,326
Consumers' expenditure abroad	259	283	295	303	326	345	360	368	326	284	303
Total	17,747	18,445	18,871	19,269	20,087	20,783	21,183	21,619	22,074	22,570	22,629

[1] Including wages, salaries, etc. paid by private non-profit-making bodies.

Source: Central Statistical Office

TABLE IV

Gross domestic fixed capital formation

At current prices

£ million

	1959	1960	1961	1962	1963	1964	1965	1966	1967	1968	1969
By type of asset											
Buses and coaches	20	22	23	27	29	29	29	29	28	29	29
Other road vehicles	258	306	324	292	325	390	408	419	430	476	532
Railway rolling stock	96	92	81	66	48	41	48	34	25	30	17
Ships	175	178	144	116	92	130	105	105	146	251	220
Aircraft	25	43	33	21	28	41	40	18	36	86	43
Plant and machinery	1,390	1,503	1,764	1,767	1,880	2,164	2,421	2,703	2,835	2,957	2,942
Dwellings	661	750	829	891	944	1,211	1,271	1,327	1,458	1,580	1,495
Other new buildings and works	1,061	1,171	1,364	1,494	1,504	1,792	1,924	2,011	2,219	2,414	2,582
By industry group											
Agriculture, forestry and fishing	151	157	168	163	177	178	182	181	195	222	225
Mining and quarrying	116	95	106	99	90	102	107	121	140	125	119
Manufacturing	877	1,035	1,253	1,183	1,070	1,236	1,420	1,521	1,485	1,615	1,748
Construction	61	70	86	74	99	130	145	131	151	163	152
Gas, electricity and water	429	426	455	523	647	757	823	979	1,055	900	795
Transport and communication[1]	500	541	507	447	433	518	549	567	685	903	818
Distributive trades	241	257	287	284	313	363	355	329	344	398	430
Other service industries[2]	284	347	401	436	459	552	596	621	637	734	848
Dwellings	661	750	829	891	944	1,211	1,271	1,327	1,458	1,580	1,495
Social services	191	196	234	290	313	373	392	427	501	573	561
Other public services	175	191	236	284	305	378	406	442	526	610	669
Transfer costs of land and buildings	50	55	57	57	57	59	58	58	62	66	67
Total	3,736	4,120	4,619	4,731	4,907	5,857	6,304	6,704	7,239	7,889	7,927

Revalued at 1963 prices

£ million

	1959	1960	1961	1962	1963	1964	1965	1966	1967	1968	1969
By type of asset											
Buses and coaches	21	22	24	27	29	29	29	28	27	27	26
Other road vehicles	243	299	310	279	325	389	399	403	410	432	466
Railway rolling stock, ships and aircraft	296	309	251	198	168	210	185	147	192	332	246
Plant and machinery	1,505	1,613	1,833	1,802	1,880	2,117	2,265	2,432	2,536	2,543	2,449
Dwellings	742	834	895	924	944	1,175	1,198	1,206	1,300	1,368	1,229
Other new buildings and works	1,164	1,283	1,477	1,544	1,504	1,741	1,815	1,826	1,979	2,090	2,120
By industry group											
Agriculture, forestry and fishing	157	163	172	165	177	175	173	167	177	193	189
Mining and quarrying	127	103	111	101	90	101	102	113	129	111	101
Manufacturing	957	1,118	1,315	1,210	1,070	1,212	1,327	1,366	1,328	1,390	1,447
Construction	65	74	87	74	99	129	138	122	139	143	129
Gas, electricity and water	456	454	473	531	647	738	774	876	933	767	649
Transport and communication[1]	517	556	517	451	433	503	514	512	614	779	675
Distributive trades	252	270	296	287	313	357	341	308	318	356	370
Other service industries[2]	300	368	420	441	459	541	570	579	586	655	728
Dwellings	742	834	895	924	944	1,175	1,198	1,206	1,300	1,368	1,229
Social services	208	212	250	297	313	363	371	390	451	500	467
Other public services	190	208	254	293	305	367	383	403	469	530	552
Transfer costs of land and buildings	54	58	57	55	57	59	58	58	61	65	66
Total	4,025	4,418	4,847	4,829	4,907	5,720	5,949	6,100	6,505	6,857	6,602

[1] Excluding road haulage and, before 1960, taxi and private-hire car businesses. [2] Including road haulage and, before 1960, taxi and private-hire car businesses.

Source: Central Statistical Office

Company gross trading profits[1]
Analysis by industry

TABLE V

£ million

	1959	1960	1961	1962	1963	1964	1965	1966	1967	1968
Forestry and fishing	5	5	7	7	7	10	10	9	9	9
Mining and quarrying	22	25	26	27	32	41	44	39	42	42
Manufacturing:										
Food, drink and tobacco	358	380	405	425	474	457	488	477	496	524
Coal and petroleum products	61	69	66	63	69	74	78	73	69	83
Chemicals and allied industries	221	250	234	242	262	325	343	323	350	393
Metal manufacture	265	315	269	224	241	261	303	285	253	205
Mechanical engineering	257	273	299	289	291	352	352	346	338	397
Instrument engineering	30	31	29	29	36	44	41	41	63	46
Electrical engineering	164	174	158	178	211	264	237	233	248	322
Shipbuilding and marine engineering	30	22	21	12	10	11	11	11	12	22
Vehicles	203	204	148	169	227	239	247	221	234	298
Metal goods not elsewhere specified	105	130	126	119	125	158	172	162	157	163
Textiles	167	185	170	170	218	182	192	173	173	247
Leather, leather goods and fur	11	11	9	9	10	12	13	11	11	16
Clothing and footwear	53	63	56	50	59	59	65	58	55	68
Bricks, pottery, glass, cement, etc.	90	106	105	101	108	147	131	119	129	147
Timber, furniture, etc.	24	28	24	25	29	37	37	32	32	50
Paper, printing and publishing	153	182	161	170	183	216	225	209	216	255
Other manufacturing	53	65	63	62	75	95	91	88	88	94
Total manufacturing	2,245	2,488	2,343	2,337	2,628	2,933	3,026	2,862	2,924	3,330

Construction	116	133	138	152	181	233	230	213	197	206
Gas, electricity and water	18	27	27	18	19	25	26	28	23	22
Transport and communication	195	232	219	241	266	272	300	273	259	341
Distributive trades	571	637	646	680	771	855	870	861	846	941
Insurance, banking and finance[2]	482	566	636	662	699	784	910	984	1,060	1,204
Other services	185	206	211	184	263	268	279	261	288	311
Adjustments	−522	−583	−610	−713	−758	−830	−937	−1,088	−1,028	−1,382
Total gross trading profits	3,317	3,736	3,643	3,595	4,108	4,591	4,758	4,442	4,620	5,024

[1] Before providing for depreciation and stock appreciation. [2] Profits of insurance, banking and finance companies include net receipts of interest.

Source: Central Statistical Office

TABLE VI

Gross national product by industry [1]

£ million

	1959	1960	1961	1962	1963	1964	1965	1966	1967	1968	1969
Agriculture, forestry and fishing	877	912	951	988	984	1,029	1,063	1,083	1,131	1,151	1,197
Mining and quarrying	689	687	709	745	750	755	731	725	730	713	678
Manufacturing	7,509	8,239	8,498	8,615	9,117	10,084	10,920	11,247	11,633	12,631	13,346
Construction	1,236	1,363	1,497	1,623	1,727	2,015	2,179	2,291	2,365	2,500	2,559
Gas, electricity and water	571	617	674	739	835	917	1,029	1,073	1,140	1,284	1,364
Transport	1,293	1,532	1,575	1,636	1,766	1,861	2,005	2,066	2,072	2,285	2,348
Communication	393	421	448	479	522	580	646	702	751	803	930
Distributive trades	2,570	2,756	2,872	3,012	3,174	3,400	3,573	3,752	3,763	4,028	4,193
Insurance, banking and finance (including real estate)	625	686	780	861	927	964	989	1,025	1,107	1,197	1,250
Ownership of dwellings	835	901	964	1,052	1,149	1,262	1,395	1,520	1,654	1,802	1,991
Public administration and defence	1,262	1,323	1,383	1,458	1,551	1,672	1,801	1,965	2,103	2,257	2,391
Public health and educational services	822	906	976	1,082	1,184	1,271	1,420	1,558	1,682	1,828	1,987
Other services	2,340	2,543	2,918	3,043	3,320	3,549	3,761	4,024	4,349	4,657	5,073
less Stock appreciation	− 90	− 135	− 173	− 147	− 202	− 301	− 333	− 318	− 187	− 634	− 815
Residual error	230	− 165	87	37	− 46	− 134	− 279	− 102	156	—	− 342
Gross domestic product at factor cost	21,162	22,586	24,159	25,223	26,758	28,924	30,900	32,611	34,449	36,502	38,150
Net property income from abroad	260	231	252	333	392	395	442	380	368	317	451
Gross national product at factor cost	21,422	22,817	24,411	25,556	27,150	29,319	31,342	32,991	34,817	36,819	38,601

[1] The contribution of each industry to the gross national product before providing for depreciation and stock appreciation.
Source: **Central Statistical Office**

TABLE VII

Index numbers of output at constant factor cost [1]
1963 = 100

	1959	1960	1961	1962	1963	1964	1965	1966	1967	1968	1969
Agriculture, forestry and fishing	87	93	93	96	100	104	107	107	111	111	111
Industrial production:											
Mining and quarrying	102.5	98.8	97.5	100.1	100.0	99.8	95.8	90.1	89.1	84.8	80.2
Manufacturing[2]	88.3	95.5	95.7	96.1	100.0	108.7	112.4	114.2	114.2	121.4	125.6
Construction	87.3	92.1	98.8	99.8	100.0	111.3	114.3	115.3	119.4	121.8	118.9
Gas, electricity and water	77.1	83.1	86.9	93.8	100.0	105.1	112.3	116.9	121.2	128.2	136.2
Total industrial production	88.3	94.5	95.7	96.7	100.0	108.3	111.7	113.2	113.9	119.8	122.9
Transport and communication[3]	89	94	96	97	100	106	108	110	112	115	119
Distributive trades	90	94	96	97	100	103	106	107	108	111	112
Insurance, banking, finance and business services	86	91	94	95	100	105	108	112	118	127	133
Ownership of dwellings	93	95	96	98	100	102	104	107	110	114	117
Professional and scientific services	89	91	94	98	100	103	107	111	114	119	123
Miscellaneous services	88	92	95	96	100	105	106	107	107	108	108
Public administration and defence	99	97	97	98	100	100	101	104	107	106	105
Gross domestic product[1]	89.0	93.8	95.5	96.8	100.0	105.8	108.6	110.5	112.2	116.6	119.3

[1] This table provides a measure of changes in the volume of goods and services produced. For further details of the index, see *The index of industrial production and other output measures*. Studies in Official Statistics, No. 17 (HMSO November 1970). Alternative estimates of the gross domestic product obtained from statistics of expenditure are given in Tables 303 and 306. [2] Figures for individual manufacturing industries are given in Table 156. [3] Covers all road goods vehicles including those owned by other industries.

Source: Central Statistical Office

Table VI is extremely useful in that it helps an analyst to estimate the trend of absolute profits of particular industries. The profit trend of a particular company can then be compared with that of its industry to see whether its performance is above or below average. Such information, however, must be used very cautiously for the results may be distorted, partly due to the broad categories of industry used in the statistics and partly because many companies have diversified to such an extent that it is unrealistic to allot them to any single industry. Moreover, even within an individual industry some operations may be extremely profitable while others are in a state of serious decline.

Yet again the statistics suffer from lack of detail, but they are useful in that they show the contribution that the major industrial groups have made to the gross national income. Changes in the proportionate contribution of each group can serve as a guide to their likely future share.

The indices in Table VII provide a measurement of the direction and extent of changes in the volume of goods and services produced by each productive sector, based on the 1963 production. As such they indicate changes in the relative contribution of each sector to the gross domestic product valued at constant prices.

In addition to the national income statistics, there is a wide range of Government publications which relate to particular industries:

Census of Production Reports. Since 1945 there have been full censuses of production in 1948, 1951, 1954, 1958, 1963 and 1968, supplemented by a smaller census, on a sample basis, in the intermediate years. It is anticipated that in future a full census will be taken every five years. The information is obtained by post and the statistics for each industry are published separately. In the 1958 census there were 131 separate industrial classifications. With regard to firms which employed fewer than twenty-five persons on average the only information sought was the average numbers of male and female employees and the nature of the work done. Larger firms were required to provide a far wider range of information, relating to:

Working proprietors of unincorporated businesses
Analysis of number of employees
Analysis of wages and salaries
Purchases of materials and fuel
Value of work given out to other firms
Transport costs of materials, fuel and finished goods

Analysis of stocks between materials and fuel, work in progress
and finished goods
Analysis of capital expenditure
Value of total production and sales.

This information permits the comparison of the performance of a
company with that of its industry in the above respects for, under
the Companies Act 1967, all companies must now provide details of
employees, wages, sales and capital expenditure, though the composition of stock and the figures of production costs are not yet
required. Considerable caution must be exercised in undertaking any
comparison between a company and its industry. In particular, most
large companies are diversified and operate within more than one
industry. Moreover, there are serious difficulties both in the definition of production (many activities, such as bakehouses attached to
retail shops, were excluded from 1958 onwards) and in the allocation
of employees and costs between activities where one establishment
manufactures for two industries. Furthermore the analysis of trends
on the basis of these statistics is hindered by changes in procedure
from one census to another. In 1958, for instance, a wide range of
fringe activities, accounting for about 5% of total manufacturing
employment, were excluded and the exemption limit below which a
full census was not required was raised from eleven to twenty-five
employees. However, comparable figures for the previous census are
normally provided with each census. Finally it should be realized
that the industrial censuses are often not published until three years
after the year to which they relate, so that much of their information
is primarily of historical interest.

The National Economic Development Council. The N.E.D.C. was
proposed in 1961 and established in 1962. Its terms of reference are:

(a) To examine the economic performance of the nation with
particular concern for plans for the future in both the private
and the public sectors of industry.
(b) To consider together what are the obstacles to quicker growth,
what can be done to improve efficiency and whether the best
use is being made of our resources.
(c) To seek agreement upon ways of improving economic performance, competitive power and efficiency.

In 1963 the N.E.D.C. decided to establish Economic Development
Committees for individual industries which would have the same
functions with regard to the industry concerned as those performed
by the N.E.D.C. for the national economy. By the end of 1965 the

following E.D.C.s had been established: Building; Chemicals; Chocolate and Sugar Confectionery; Civil Engineering; Distributive Trades; Electrical Engineering; Electronics; Food Processing; Machine Tools; Mechanical Engineering; Movement of Exports; Newspapers, Printing and Publishing; Paper and Board; Post Office; Rubber; Wool Textiles.

At the same time agreement had been formally reached for the formation of Committees in respect of Agriculture; Clothing, Hosiery and Knitwear; and Hotels and Catering. Since then further Committees have been established, including one for the motor industry. From time to time these Committees produce reports on their industry which are available to the investor. These provide information concerning the problems and prospects of that industry and can be used in connection with the census of production data to analyze the development and future trends of the industry.

The Reports of the Monopolies Commission. The reports of the Monopolies Commission and the published proceedings of the Restrictive Practices Court have provided investors with considerable information regarding the trading conditions of different firms and industries. By January 1964, the Monopolies Commission, which was originally established under the Monopolies and Restrictive Practices Act 1948, had published twenty-six reports covering such diverse products as tea, cigarettes, wallpaper, chemical fertilizers and cast-iron rainwater goods.

Finally, information relating to a particular industry may be obtained from trade organizations, trade journals and the financial press, though some industries are better served than others in this respect. One trade organization which provides regular up-to-date information is the Society of Motor Manufacturers and Traders, which produces monthly details of vehicle production. The statistics made available from such sources are especially valuable because they are often published far more frequently and promptly than those provided by Government agencies.

When all of the available information has been collected the investor is in a position to examine the past performance of the industry and to assess its present position. In particular it is important to examine the relationship of the industry to the national economy or particular sectors thereof. For example, the sales and profits of some industries might be found to remain relatively constant during booms and slumps while other industries fluctuate with the level of the national economy.

By far the most hazardous task is the prediction of future prospects.

232

To achieve this it is necessary to forecast the future growth of the economy and the likely contribution of each industry to that growth. Such forecasts may be distorted by unpredictable factors such as the discovery of substitutes, political decisions (e.g. a cutback in building and arms expenditure), strikes, cancer scares, breathalyser tests, etc. That the preparation of such forecasts is wellnigh impossible was demonstrated by the fate of the National Plan. It might have been thought that the Government would be in a more favourable position than individual industries or companies to encourage the achievement of its forecasts, but the end result was a dismal failure.

The investor must have particular regard to overseas conditions in the analysis of an industry. Relevant information is very difficult to obtain but it is essential to assess, for example, the likely weight of foreign competition in the home and foreign markets, the possible effects of devaluation, the anticipated growth of foreign markets and the expected foreign government policies with regard to imports in those markets.

As an example of industrial analysis some of the better stockbrokers' research studies should be examined. Many firms specialize in particular industries and regularly publish surveys of those industries. These are normally reviewed in the financial press and many firms are prepared to make them available to investors other than their own clients.

(c) *The Assessment of the Company*

This involves a detailed examination of the past performance of the company, an assessment of its current situation and an estimate of its future prospects.

The analysis of past performance will largely be based upon information from accounts of previous years, and will depend upon the extent of disclosure in those accounts. Where no figures of sales are provided past performance can only be assessed by comparing the trend of profits of the company with that of the profits of the entire industry. Such analysis can give extremely misleading results due to such problems as diversification, the definition of industries, and changes in capital employed.

Where figures of sales are made available, changes in the company's share of the market and in its sales margins can be estimated and used to predict future sales and profits. In the case of multi-product firms such predictions should be made especially cautiously, for it is not normally possible in such cases to identify either the company's market share for a particular product or the profitability of individual products.

H*   233

It is also useful to examine past reports to find information on such matters as the extent to which it is prone to, and suffers financially from, strikes, the quality of previous forecasts, its vulnerability in overseas markets to devaluation and nationalization, the extent of diversification and the proportion of income which is devoted to research.

The next step is to analyze the current situation of the company. This analysis will be based partly upon its accounts as explained in Chapter 10 and partly upon qualitative factors. For example, it is necessary to assess its standing within the industry in which it operates. This will involve an estimation of the market share and competitive position of the company. Its competitive strength will depend upon such factors as the quality of its management, the amount and quality of expenditure on research, investment and advertising, and the firmness of its existing goodwill. While little quantitative information is available on these matters, they are usually referred to in the chairman's report. These tend, of course, to be somewhat over-confident, but past experience will generally indicate their reliability.

The future prospects of the company will depend upon the outlook for its industry and the extent to which the company is likely to benefit from the future progress of the industry. Again the chairman's report will be useful, and will normally indicate at least the direction, if not the extent, of future profit movements.

On the basis of this information, an estimate should be prepared of the anticipated future profits of the company over the next few years, This, of course, is an extremely difficult task, for even the management, which has possession of far more data, will often make forecasts which prove to be wildly inaccurate. However, insofar as there are so many uncertain variables which depend to a large extent upon guesswork, the predictions of the investor may often prove as accurate as those of the management.

In connection with the prediction of future dividends the absolute level of earnings need not be forecast with complete accuracy. It is only necessary to predict whether the change will be sufficiently great to justify an alteration in the dividend rate. An examination of past dividend policies of the company will indicate the proportionate change in profits which is likely to induce a dividend alteration.

One method commonly advocated for forecasting dividends and earnings is the use of averages weighted on the basis of probability. Instead of merely selecting the most likely profit and dividend of a company for a particular year, the investor examines a range of possible results and assesses the probability of occurrence of each of these results. The probability factors are expressed as a fraction of

1 and, as there is only one eventual outcome, their total will be 1. Each possible outcome is then multiplied by its probability factor and the resultant figures are totalled to give the weighted average expected result.

For example, the following estimates may be made of the profits for the next year of a company which has current profits of £50,000 and pays a dividend of £30,000:

Profit £	Probability of occurrence	Weighted value £
100,000	0·25	25,000
80,000	0·40	32,000
50,000	0·25	12,500
20,000	0·10	2,000
	Average anticipated profits	£71,500

Thus, the average anticipated profits of £71,500 are considerably different from the most likely estimate of profits, which is £80,000. In order to estimate the dividend for the next year it is necessary to examine the likely dividend policies of the company at each possible level of profit. Again the probability of the adoption of each policy must be determined and an average anticipated dividend will be calculated for each level of profit. These will then be averaged as above in order to determine the overall anticipated dividend.

Adopting the figures from the previous example, the possible dividend policies may be analyzed as follows:

Profit Level £	Total Dividend £	Probability of Occurrence of Dividend	Weighted Value £	Probability of Occurrence of Profit	Overall Weighted Value £
100,000	50,000	0·20	10,000		
	40,000	0·70	28,000		
	30,000	0·10	3,000		
			41,000	0·25	10,250
80,000	40,000	0·25	10,000		
	35,000	0·45	15,750		
	30,000	0·30	9,000		
			34,750	0·40	13,900

Profit Level £	Total Dividend £	Probability of Occurrence of Dividend	Weighted Value £	Probability of Occurrence of Profit	Overall Weighted Value £
50,000	35,000	0·20	7,000		
	30,000	0·80	24,000		
			31,000	0·25	7,750
20,000	30,000	0·20	6,000		
	25,000	0·70	17,500		
	20,000	0·10	2,000		
			25,500	0·10	2,550
		Average anticipated dividend			£34,450

However, this method has many drawbacks. In the first place, it does not overcome the problem of uncertainty, for a subjective estimate has still to be made of the various probability factors. This involves just as much uncertainty as the estimation of a unique figure of profit. Moreover, there are a vast number of possible profit figures and several different dividend policies which may be applied to each. For each figure of profit and dividend there will be a chain of an infinite number of possible figures for future years. Thus the longer the calculation is extended the more impossible it becomes.

Finally, this method ignores the problem of risk. For example a company which has an equally probable profit of either £1 m. or nil is shown as having the same average anticipated profit as a company with equally probable profits of £500,001 and £499,999, although the first company is obviously much more risky. However, risk may be taken into account by adjusting the rate of interest used to discount future dividends.

Because of the prevalence of uncertainty, most predictions of future profits and dividends are based on a projection of past trends, adjusted to take account of anticipated economic developments. Where a trend cannot be established due to the volatile nature or the youth of the company, the forecaster will begin with the profits of the preceding year and will adjust this figure in the light of his predictions of future developments in the economy, the industry, and the company. Fortunately, due to the relative stability of company dividend policies, the prediction of dividends is much less difficult, the normal procedure being to commence with the current dividend and to adjust this in response to major changes in profit.

Finally, the importance of estimating future dividends will depend upon the length of the period for which the investment is likely to be held. The longer the period of tenure, the more important is the dividend prediction in the evaluation process. Where, however, the intention is to hold the investment for the short term only the prediction of the realization price is more crucial.

(ii) *Prediction of Future Security Prices*

This involves a detailed analysis of all of the factors which are likely to affect security prices. Of prime importance in this connection will be the information which the analyst himself has accumulated concerning the economy and particular industries and companies. All of this information will be available to the Stock Exchange and its members, who will use it as the basis of their own predictions. Share prices will be based on these predictions and will be adjusted from time to time in response to unforeseen circumstances. Thus, while a predictable event, such as a change in Bank Rate, may have already been discounted in the establishment of current security prices, so that the actual announcement of the change has no effect on prices, an unforeseen event, such as the sudden outbreak of war or a change of Government, would cause an immediate readjustment of prices to incorporate the likely effect of the new situation.

As a result an investor must not only analyze all available information but must also endeavour to assess the likely reaction of the stock market to that information. For example, he may feel that a Labour Government will be in power for the next five years and that this would be beneficial to the economy. If, however, he guesses that other investors take, and will continue to take, a pessimistic view of the effects of a Labour Government, then this must be taken into account in estimating future security prices. Much of the work involved in predicting security prices is thus a matter of guesswork, with investors guessing at the reaction of other investors to the events which they have predicted.

General economic and political information will have an effect on the state of confidence in the market. Thus a vast improvement in the balance of payments figures might be regarded as indicative of a booming economy and increased profits and would improve confidence and cause an increase in share prices. A deflationary budget, on the other hand, might suggest falling company profits, thus reducing confidence and depressing share prices. Usually, however, the market has made its own predictions concerning these and most other events, and the effect of the actual occurrence will depend upon the extent to which it coincides with market expectations. Thus the Government might reduce the standard rate of income tax by threepence yet security prices might fall because the market had anticipated a much larger reduction and had valued securities accordingly.

In addition to the general state of confidence, information relating to a particular security will be important in the determination of its price. In this connection the investor needs to make more use of the estimates of future earnings which were prepared in the computation of future dividends, for although the dividend yield is still very important in the determination of share prices, earnings have become much more significant since the price-earnings ratio has been used as a tool of appraisal. However, the investor is again faced with the task of guessing how other investors have appraised the security in question, for it is the sum total of investment opinion which determines security prices. Fortunately, the flow of information tends to be sufficiently frequent to allow for at least annual reassessment of securities, so that an investor whose predictions have challenged market opinion will find that prices will ultimately be changed in his favour if he is proved right.

Despite this, there are still some factors which may never be adjusted. For instance, an investor may feel that a particular company is extremely risky. However, if he guesses that the market irrationally regards the company as very safe and that it will continue to overvalue its shares, he may choose to invest in the company even though he personally regards the company as inferior. Conversely, he may refuse to invest in a company which he regards as extremely safe because he suspects that other investors will not share his view.

The dominance of market psychology and its encouragement of speculation have been admirably stressed by Keynes[1]:

'As a result of the gradual increase in the proportion of the equity in the community's aggregate capital investment which is owned by persons who do not manage and have no special knowledge of the circumstances, either actual or prospective, of the business in question, the element of real knowledge in the valuation of investments by those who own them or contemplate purchasing them has seriously declined. . . .

'It might have been supposed that competition between expert

1 John Maynard Keynes, *The General Theory of Employment, Interest and Money* (London: Macmillan & Co., 1936, Ch. 12).

professionals, possessing judgment and knowledge beyond that of the average private investor, would correct the vagaries of the ignorant individual left to himself. It happens, however, that the energies and skill of the professional investor and speculator are mainly occupied otherwise. For most of these persons are, in fact, largely concerned, not with making superior long-term forecasts of the probable yield of an investment over its whole life, but with foreseeing changes in the conventional basis of valuation a short time ahead of the general public. They are concerned, not with what an investment is really worth to a man who buys it "for keeps", but with what the market will value it at, under the influence of mass psychology, three months or a year hence. Moreover, this behaviour is not the outcome of a wrong-headed propensity. It is an inevitable result of an investment market organized along the lines described. For it is not sensible to pay 25 for an investment of which you believe the prospective yield to justify a value of 30, if you also believe that the market will value it at 20 three months hence.

'Thus the professional investor is forced to concern himself with the anticipation of impending changes, in the news or in the atmosphere, of the kind by which experience shows that the mass psychology of the market is most influenced. . . . The social object of skilled investment should be to defeat the dark forces of time and ignorance which envelop our future. The actual private object of the most skilled investment today is "to beat the gun", as the Americans so well express it, to outwit the crowd, and to pass the bad, or depreciating, half-crown to the other fellow. . . .

'. . . professional investment may be likened to those newspaper competitions in which the competitors have to pick out the six prettiest faces from a hundred photographs, the prize being awarded to the competitor whose choice most nearly corresponds to the average preferences of the competitors as a whole; so that each competitor has to pick, not those faces which he himself finds prettiest, but those which he thinks likeliest to catch the fancy of the other competitors, all of whom are looking at the same problem from the same point of view. It is not a case of choosing those which, to the best of one's judgment, are really the prettiest, not even those which average opinion genuinely thinks the prettiest. We have reached the third degree where we devote our intelligences to anticipating what average opinion expects the average opinion to be. And there are some, I believe, who practise the fourth, fifth and higher degrees.'

Despite the improvement in the extent and quality of available information since the date at which he wrote and despite the greater

239

prominence of institutional investors, whose research departments might be expected to show more efficiency than individual investors, the bulk of Keynes' criticism is still relevant. Thus, the investor must form some opinion concerning the movement of future prices, however rough, and his estimates must, of necessity, be based largely upon his assessment of market psychology, though the importance of this assessment will tend to be lower, the longer the period for which the investment is to be held.

An investor who holds securities for the long-term will not maximize his return, for he will not take advantage of short-term price fluctuations. Moreover, he will need considerable financial resources to guard against the possibility that he might be forced to sell his securities at a disadvantageous time. As a further drawback he might miss profitable switching opportunities due to his too inflexible investment policy. On the other hand, the appraisal of competing investments will not present so many problems, for the calculation of future prices will be much less important as the realization date is far in the future. Consequently the present value of the realization proceeds will be much less significant.

In addition to the general factors which affect confidence and expectations there are certain short-term influences which may be very important:

Technical Factors. A wide range of topics may be discussed under this head, but because they all relate to the very short-term and are thus only relevant for the professional investor, only two examples will be given, both of which relate to the momentary misvaluation of a share. For instance a share may receive favourable Press comment, thus immediately increasing the demand to a level where there are not sufficient shares forthcoming from sellers to meet the demand. This temporary shortage of stock may be countered by jobbers by widening their quotations and raising the price to discourage buyers. Although this becomes the quoted price of the stock no dealings take place until shares become available and the price is reduced to bring buyers back to the market. Similarly a group of bears may take a pessimistic view concerning a particular share, and sell stock which they do not hold in the hope of being able to deliver by means of purchases at a lower price. However, the price of the share may in fact rise. When they are called upon to make delivery, they will have to buy the shares on the market thus increasing demand and pushing the share price up to an artificially high level. Once they have made delivery, the share price will be allowed to revert to its previous level.

240

Special Situations. Very often the market will appear to have miscalculated the prospects of a company or to have mistakenly valued it on a different basis from other companies. This will often give rise to Press comment (in itself an important source of information for the market) which will normally be self-inducing in that jobbers will anticipate the response to the comment and will adjust prices accordingly. Other special situations may occur where the company should not be valued by the market purely in terms of expected earnings and dividends. Where, for instance, it is predicted that a company is to be liquidated and that this will provide a surplus over the current market price this factor will replace the expected earnings as the price determinant, even though the liquidation may not occur. Similarly, if it is anticipated that a company will be taken over by another company at a price higher than the current level this, too, will outweigh the influence of predicted earnings. Thus rumours of takeover bids may, in the short-run, exert as much influence as the bids themselves.

(iii) *Determination of the Rate of Discount*

The investor is faced with many serious difficulties in the selection of the appropriate rate of discount for calculating the present value of the cash flows which are expected to emanate from his investment. The major problem lies in the method to be adopted for incorporating the risk attached to an investment into the calculation of its net present value. The methods commonly advocated argue that an appropriate adjustment should be made either to the cash flows themselves or to the rate at which they are discounted.

An adjustment to cash flows in respect of risk has been advocated by many writers including Hicks[1] and Bierman and Smidt.[2] The latter authors advocate the use of utility analysis on the lines expounded by Friedman and Savage.[3] Where this method is adopted the investor must determine a utility function which describes his attitude towards risk. Within this function the investor measures the satisfaction which he would gain from possible outcomes of an investment and assigns an index number to each which measures his relative satisfaction therefrom. Each conceivable net present value of

[1] J. R. Hicks, *Value and Capital* (Oxford: Oxford University Press, 2nd ed. 1946, pp. 126 and 225).

[2] Harold Bierman Jr. and Seymour Smidt, *The Capital Budgeting Decision* (New York: Macmillan & Co., 2nd ed. 1966, Ch. 15 and 16).

[3] Milton Friedman and Leonard J. Savage, 'The Utility Analysis of Choices Involving Risk', *The Journal of Political Economy*, vol. LVI, no. 4, August 1948, pp. 279–304.

an investment is then multiplied by its probability of occurrence and by the appropriate index of utility. The investment which provides the highest expected utility should then be accepted.

For example, an investor may be faced with two investments, one of which offers a certain net present value of £200, the other offering possible returns of £40, £100, and £1,000. The expected utility of each investment would be derived as follows:

	Net Present Value £		Probability		Utility	Expected Utility
Investment 1	200	×	1·0	×	200	200
Investment 2	40	×	0·2	×	100	8
	100	×	0·6	×	150	90
	1000	×	0·2	×	400	80
						178

Thus, although the second investment has a higher mean return of £380 and a higher average return weighted by probability of £268, the risk attitude of the investor, as measured by his utility function, leads him to prefer the first investment.

Where this method is used it is essential to ensure that a pure riskless rate of interest is used for discounting. If this is not done there may well be a double adjustment in respect of risk. For example a company might raise funds from its shareholders for a risky project on which they require a return of 12%. If the company adjusts the cash flows for risk and discounts them by 12%, risk would be taken into account twice. Either the cash flows must be adjusted for risk and discounted at a pure rate of interest which values time preference alone, or the unadjusted cash flows should be discounted at a rate of interest which includes a risk premium.

This second method of adjustment for risk, namely the selection of a rate of discount, which includes a risk premium to measure the investor's estimate of the degree of risk attached to the investment, is described by Hicks[1] and advocated by Fisher.[2] Hirshleifer[3] has progressed further to show that, given rather rigid conditions, the market rate of interest for that class of security (which itself includes

[1] Op. cit., pp. 143–4.
[2] Irving Fisher, The Nature of Capital and Income, p. 277.
[3] Jack Hirshleifer, 'Risk, The Discount Rate and Investment Decisions', American Economic Review, vol. LI, no. 2, May 1961, pp. 112–20.

a risk premium) should be adopted by the individual investor for this purpose.

Although there are many theoretical arguments in favour of adjusting the cash flows for risk, it is felt that the selection by the investor of an appropriate discount rate is the simpler method. In particular, it avoids the assessment of a pure rate of interest, which in an imperfect market and an uncertain world is almost impossible to define. Should it be measured by Bank Rate, the yield on gilt-edged securities, deposit account rates, short-term loan rates, or long-term loan rates, each of which is based upon indefinable expectations concerning future interest rates and price levels? As the pure rate of interest cannot be determined objectively, the appraisal of risk-adjusted cash flows involves two subjective factors, namely the estimation first of the utility function and then of the pure rate of interest.

Hirshleifer's argument is also less acceptable in an imperfect market, for he assumes that the market rates of discount for given classes of security are ascertainable. Here again the different rates are affected by expectations. For example, the fact that the stated dividend yield on equities has in recent years been lower than that on gilt-edged securities does not mean that they are regarded as less risky. It merely indicates that the immeasurable predictions of the market as to the future level of dividends, share prices and inflation are leading investors to anticipate a higher actual return on ordinary shares. How high a return is expected or how high it will actually be cannot be determined. Recourse might be had to the past rates of return which were actually received on different classes of securities, but this would not indicate how well they corresponded to the returns which had previously been predicted and on the basis of which past investment decisions had been made.

All in all, in an imperfect and uncertain market the simplest method of accounting for risk is the selection by the investor of the rate of discount which is sufficiently high to compensate for the degree of risk which he feels is attached to the investment having regard to his own preparedness to accept risk.

CHAPTER 9

The Information Available to an Investor

In order to undertake the analysis of an investment a potential investor must have the relevant information available so that he may come to a rational decision. The information which is currently available emanates from three major sources, namely individual companies, the Stock Exchange, and the financial press.

1. THE INFORMATION PROVIDED BY
INDIVIDUAL COMPANIES

All companies which are resident in the United Kingdom must be registered with the Registrar of Companies, and are required by the Companies Acts of 1948 and 1967 to provide certain information which will be available to the general public, either at Companies House in London or at the registered office of the company.

At Companies House a separate file is kept in respect of every registered company. This may be inspected by any member of the public on payment of 1s, and contains the following documents of interest to an investor:

(i) *Memorandum of Association*

This contains the name of the company, its domicile, its objects, the amount of its share capital and the types of shares into which the capital is divided, together with a statement of the extent of the liability of the members for the debts of the company.

(ii) *Articles of Association*

These are the regulations which govern the internal organization of the company and embrace such matters as board meetings, meetings of shareholders, and the rights of particular classes of shareholders.

(iii) *Prospectus*

When a company makes an offer of shares to the public it is required to publish a prospectus which must include, among other things, a report by a firm of accountants of the profits or losses, the dividends paid and the assets and liabilities of the company for each of the five years immediately preceding the report. In the case of quoted companies the prospectus requirements of the Stock Exchange, as outlined in Chapter 3, are more onerous than those of the Companies Act.

(iv) *Mortgages and Charges*

Where a company has created a charge on any of its assets it must be registered with the Registrar of Companies within twenty-one days of its creation. The file of a particular company will therefore contain details of all of its assets which are the subject of a charge.

(v) *Annual Return and Annual Report and Accounts*

The annual return must provide details of the company's share capital, its directors, its secretary, and its indebtedness in respect of mortgages and charges. It must also report all changes in its membership during the year, and every three years a full list of the members and the number of shares which they hold must be included. Finally, it is provided that a copy of any annual report and accounts which has been published during the period to which the return relates must be appended.

The annual report and accounts will normally contain the following information:

(*a*) The date, venue and agenda of the next annual general meeting of the company. All companies must hold an annual general meeting each year in addition to any other meetings which may have been held, and it must be held not more than fifteen months after the previous annual general meeting. All members of the company are entitled to attend and they must receive at least twenty-one days' notice of the meeting.

(*b*) A list of the directors of the company and details of its secretary, auditors, solicitors, bankers and the registered office.

(*c*) The directors' report, which will normally deal as a minimum with the following matters:

(1) A statement of the balance of profit or loss in the accounts indicating the proportion to be distributed as dividends and the proportion which is to be retained to finance the growth of the company.

(2) Details of any directors who have been appointed since the previous annual general meeting and the names of any directors who may be required by the articles of association to retire. The retiring directors will normally offer themselves for re-election.

(3) Where relevant, a statement that the auditors will be re-appointed in accordance with section 159(2) of the Companies Act 1948.

(4) Additional information in accordance with the requirements of the Companies Act 1967, as stated in the Appendix to this chapter.

(d) The chairman's report. This generally consists of a review of the activities and trading performance of the company during the previous financial year together with an assessment of the future prospects of the company.

(e) The accounts relating to the preceding financial year. These accounts must by statute include a profit and loss account and a balance sheet. The profit and loss account indicates the profit or loss for the year and the manner in which it is to be divided between distributions and retentions. The balance sheet states the assets and liabilities of the company at the end of the financial year. Where a company owns subsidiary companies it must prepare group accounts which will give information similar to that described above in respect of the group.

The full requirements of the Companies Acts relating to the annual report and accounts are reproduced in the Appendix to this chapter.

In addition to the information which is available for public inspection at Companies House a company must also maintain at its registered office certain registers which may be inspected by the general public on payment of 1s for each register inspected and by the members of the company without any payment.

(a) *Register of Charges*

This will contain information relating to all mortgages and charges which are secured on the assets of the company, whether specifically or otherwise.

246

(b) *Register of Directors and Secretaries*

This must state the names, addresses, nationalities, business occupations and other directorships of the directors and secretary of the company.

(c) *Register of Directors' Shareholdings*

Under section 195 of the Companies Act 1948 every company is required to maintain a register which shows in respect of each director of the company (unless the director is its holding company) the number, description and amount of any shares in or debentures of the company or the company's subsidiary or holding company, or a subsidiary of the company's holding company, which are held by or in trust for him or of which he has any right to become the holder (whether on payment or not). It must also include the dates and prices of any dealings in the said shares or debentures.

(d) *Register of Members*

This must contain the name and address of each member of the company, the number of shares held, the date of attaining membership and the date of cessation of membership.

(e) *Register of Debenture Holders*

A company is not required by statute to keep this register, though its maintenance is normally required by the terms of an issue of debentures.

Any changes in these registers are also available to the public at Companies House because they will have been included in the annual return. The main information provided by them relates to current alterations which have occurred since the submission of the latest annual return. Thus an investor who is investigating recent changes of ownership of the shares of a company would need to inspect the register of members at the registered office, for the company's file at Companies House would not contain a sufficiently up-to-date record.

Under the provisions of the Companies Act 1967, companies are required to make available still more information at their registered office. In particular, many directors' service contracts and registers stating interests of directors in the shares of the company and interests of any party which total more than one-tenth of the issued capital must be open to inspection.

So far, in the discussion of information provided by companies, only the statutory requirements have been covered. These requirements should be regarded as a bare minimum, sufficient only for companies whose shares are not available to the general public, in which case only the creditors of the company are likely to make use of the statutory information, which is, in fact, largely aimed at their protection.

In cases where the public at large are able to acquire the shares of a company it is felt that a greater degree of disclosure is required and, as a result, the Stock Exchange compels all companies which seek a quotation for their shares or debentures to give an undertaking to provide certain information for shareholders and potential investors over and above the statutory requirements.

At the current time the additional requirements of the Stock Exchange are that a company applying for a Stock Exchange quotation must undertake:

(i) To circularize to the holders of securities, not later than six months from the date of the notice calling the annual general meeting of the company, a half-yearly interim report containing the following information:

- (a) (Group) profit or loss after all charges including taxation.
- (b) United Kingdom and, where material, overseas taxation charged in arriving at (a).
- (c) (Amount of (a) attributable to members of holding company, i.e. after deduction of outside interests.)
- (d) If material, extent to which (a) has been affected by special credits, including transfers from reserves, and/or debits.
- (e) Rates of dividend or dividends (of holding company) paid and proposed and amount absorbed thereby.
- (f) Comparative figures of (a) to (e) inclusive for the corresponding previous period.
- (g) Any supplementary information which in the opinion of the directors is necessary for a reasonable appreciation of the results or of other material changes in the aggregate of the balance on profit and loss account and other reserves of the group.

The words in brackets refer to companies which are holding companies within the meaning of the Companies Act 1948.

(ii) To include in or circulate with each annual directors' report and audited accounts or chairman's statement:

(*a*) (1) A description of the operations carried on by the company or, if the company has subsidiaries, the group.

(2) If the company or, as the case may be, the group carries on widely differing operations, a statement showing the contributions of such respective differing operations to its trading results.

(3) If the company, or, as the case may be, the group trades outside the United Kingdom, a statement showing a geographical analysis of its trading operations.

(*b*) If the company has subsidiaries, a list giving for each:

(1) Its name and country of operations;

(2) The percentage of its equity capital attributable to the company's interest (direct and/or indirect).

(*c*) If the company or, as the case may be, the group has interests in associated companies, a list giving for each:

(1) its name and country of operations;

(2) particulars of its issued share and loan capital and the total amount of its reserves;

(3) the percentage of each class of share and loan capital attributable to the company's interest (direct and/or indirect).

(*d*) A statement of persons holding or beneficially interested in any substantial part of the share capital of the company and the amounts of the holdings in question together with particulars of the interests of each director (and also, so far as he is aware of, or can by reasonable inquiry ascertain the same, of his family interests) in the share capital of the company and, otherwise than through the company, any of its subsidiaries, distinguishing between beneficial and other interests. The expression 'family interests' includes, in relation to a director, spouse, children under 21 years of age, trusts of which the director or spouse is a settler or trustee and in which the director or spouse or any of such children are beneficiaries or discretionary objects and companies known to him to be controlled by him and/or spouse and/or such children and/or the trustees of any such trusts as aforesaid in their capacity as such trustees. Subject to the necessity to distinguish between beneficial and other interests, between the company and each subsidiary and between each class of capital each director's interests may be aggregated with those of his family interests.

(iii) (*a*) To prepare and make available for inspection at the registered office or transfer office during the usual business hours on any weekday (Saturdays and public holidays excluded) from the date of the notice convening the annual general meeting until the date of the meeting and to make available for inspection at the place of meeting for at least fifteen minutes prior to the meeting and during the meeting:

(1) a statement, made up to a date not more than one month prior to the date on which it is made available for inspection, for the period from the end of that covered by the last previous statement (or, in the case of the first such statement, for not less than twelve months) of all transactions (including put or call options, whether or not exercised) of each director (and also, so far as he is aware of or can by reasonable inquiry ascertain the same, of his family interests) in each class of the equity share capital of the company and any of its subsidiaries during the period concerned. The expression 'family interests' is defined in the same way as in section (ii)(*d*) above. The word 'director' includes a person who was a director at any time during the relevant period but the information required shall not extend to transactions at a time when he was not a director.

(2) copies of all contracts of service unless expiring, or determinable by the employing company without payment of compensation, within one year, of any director of the company with the company or any of its subsidiaries and, where any such contract is not reduced to writing, a memorandum of the terms thereof.

(*b*) To state in or by way of note to the notice convening the annual general meeting or any accompanying circular letter, that the said statement or summary of transactions and copies or, as the case may be, memoranda of the said contracts of service will be available for inspection as aforesaid.

(iv) In the absence of circumstances which have been agreed by the Committee of the Stock Exchange to be exceptional to obtain the consent of equity shareholders in general meeting prior to issuing for cash to other than the equity shareholders of the company:

(*a*) equity capital or capital having an equity element,
(*b*) securities convertible into equity capital, and
(*c*) warrants or options to subscribe for equity capital.

The above extracts from the General Undertaking relate to the provision of information for shareholders and potential investors. The remaining sections relate partly to the information to be submitted by the company to the Share and Loan Department of the Stock Exchange and partly to the provision of an efficient share transfer service for shareholders of the company.

Before August 1964 the whole of the Undertaking covered only the latter two matters, and ignored completely the needs of investors for fuller and more up-to-date information. In that month sections (i) and (ii) as described above were first proposed as requirements for quotations after March 26, 1965. At the same time recommendations, which were not compulsory, as to fuller disclosure in company accounts were made by the Committee of the Stock Exchange.

The initiative taken by the Stock Exchange in requiring more information was followed by the Government in the Companies Act 1967. This not only enforced the disclosure required by the Stock Exchange, with the exception of half-yearly reports, but also enacted many of the recommendations which the Committee had made. Among these recommendations were the disclosure of turnover and its analysis by activity, a statement of the number of employees, the analysis of land and buildings between freeholds and leaseholds, and information regarding any controlling shareholdings.

These requirements represent a bare minimum, especially by comparison with those of the New York Stock Exchange which specify, for example, the publication of quarterly reports. Their main achievement is to ensure that shareholders know more about the activities of their company and that they receive more frequent reports. However, these reports are in many cases published some months after the period to which they relate, so that there is still a considerable period during which directors, senior executives and other persons with an intimate knowledge of the state of the company are in a position to use their personal knowledge to their own advantage and to the possible detriment of the shareholders.

This 'insider dealing' has been countered to some extent by the provision that all companies seeking a quotation after September 1, 1966, would have to agree to comply with section (iii) of the Undertaking as described above. These provisions, too, are minimal compared with those of New York Stock Exchange, laid down by the Securities Exchange Act of 1934. Section 16(a) of this Act requires 'insiders' (defined as officers, directors and those owning directly or indirectly more than 10% of the voting securities of the company) to report to the Securities Exchange Commission on a monthly basis any changes in their holdings or equity securities, including convertible bonds. These figures are then published by the S.E.C. In order to guard against any unfair use of inside information, section 16(*b*) of the Act declares that any profits realized by an insider from deals completed within a six-month period are to be forfeitable to the company itself.

As well as its attempt to control insider dealings section (iii) above requires that service agreements between the directors and the company should be made available to the shareholders. This possibly resulted from the publicity surrounding the dispute between the directors of the British Printing Corporation when it was revealed that the chairman, Mr Wilfred Harvey, was entitled to remuneration of £270,000 for the year 1964 under the terms of a service agreement, the existence of which was unbeknown to some of his fellow directors.

Finally, section (iv) above has the result that no share in the equity of the company may be issued without the consent of the existing shareholders, so that no shareholder may suffer a fall in his proportionate interest in the company without having at least the opportunity to vote on the matter.

2. INFORMATION PROVIDED BY THE STOCK EXCHANGE

The information which the Stock Exchange provides for investors falls into three groups. There are first the publications relating to manner in which the Stock Exchange functions. These include *Rules and Regulations of the Stock Exchange, The New Transfer System, Admission of Securities to Quotation* and *The Stock Exchange*. In addition a number of pamphlets and films on the subject are available. These are, of course, of a very limited interest to investment analysts, though it is important to understand the way in which the Stock Exchange works before attempting to analyze the investments in which it deals. Also under this heading falls *How does Britain Save*, a booklet which describes the results of a survey which attempted to enumerate and define investors in Great Britain.

Of more interest to investors are the publications detailing the prices of securities on the Stock Exchange. By far the most important is *The Stock Exchange Daily Official List*. This shows the official quoted price for the day in question for all quoted securities. The importance of these prices is that they are generally accepted for the purposes of determining capital gains tax, estate duty, etc. The *Official List* also gives details of the marks received in respect of each security for the day, or, where no marks were recorded, the price and date of the last recorded mark.

The Information Available to an Investor

The information provided in respect of a particular security might appear as follows:

Dividends/Interest

When last ex div.	Pay Date	Rate % Actual	Total for year %	Name	Unit of Quotation	Quotation June 30th	Business done
31.5	30.6	5	20	*Anonymous* Ltd Ord. Stock	£1	340·360	340φ, 5, 8‡, 52, 57, 44φ, 60, 55, 3.

The figures of business show the prices at which deals took place during the day. The sign φ indicates bargains which were done on the previous day and took place after 2.15 p.m., the time at which the list of bargains is compiled, or which were inadvertently omitted. The sign ‡ indicates bargains which were made at special prices, possibly because an especially large number of shares was involved.

The marks relating to the bargains are normally recorded by either brokers or jobbers after a deal has taken place. However, this information is extremely defective for several reasons. In the first place, it is not compulsory for brokers or jobbers to mark the deals which they make. In fact it has been estimated that only half the deals actually made are marked and a comparison of deals marked with the total deals shown by the Stock Exchange turnover statistics indicates that this estimate is broadly accurate. For instance, the total number of bargains done during the twelve months to March 31, 1970 was 4,807,540, of which 2,213,812 were marked, a percentage of 46%. Moreover, such marks as are recorded are not necessarily in the sequence in which the bargains were done, so that it is not possible to determine the course of the day's trading from the list of marks. Further drawbacks are that the size of the bargains are not revealed, only one mark in any one security is recorded at any one price, and it is not stated whether a mark represents the sale or purchase price of a particular security. All in all, the details of business done are very defective and their most useful function for investors is to indicate broadly the trend of activity in the shares of a company. If only two marks per day have been recorded on average in respect of a particular security and the number of marks suddenly jumps to ten or twenty in one day this would indicate an increase of interest in the security and would lead an investor to investigate its cause.

Two other Stock Exchange publications which deal with security

253

prices are *Statistics Relating to Securities Quoted on the London Stock Exchange* and *Interest and Dividends upon Securities Quoted on the Stock Exchange, London,* both of which are published annually. The first of these booklets is extremely useful and contains the following information annually in respect of the year ended March 31st.

(*a*) Nominal and market values of all quoted securities both in total and analyzed under market sections for the current and the two preceding years.

(*b*) Classification of quoted securities of United Kingdom companies and of overseas companies, distinguishing between loan, preference and ordinary capital. This classification is made in respect of all commercial sections of the market and in total.

(*c*) Total nominal and market value of all quoted securities for each year since 1939.

(*d*) Details of all companies which were granted a quotation for the first time during the previous year.

(*e*) An analysis of all applications for quotation granted during the previous year.

(*f*) An analysis over market sections of all marks received during the previous year.

(*g*) Figures of turnover, calculated on the aggregate of all purchases and sales, on the London Stock Exchange, according to category of security.

While the above information is only relevant for an analysis of the market as a whole or of particular sectors of the market, it can be used for calculating ratios for particular market sectors with which individual companies within the sector may be compared. Moreover, the turnover statistics are very useful as a guide to the level of activity in the Stock Exchange.

The second booklet, *Interest and Dividends upon Securities Quoted on the Stock Exchange, London,* is also published annually, though it relates to the year ended December 31st, and provides the following information in respect of all United Kingdom quoted securities:

(*a*) The combined totals of interest and dividends with percentage changes on the preceding year.

(*b*) Figures of nominal capital, interest and dividends.

(*c*) Nominal loan capital and interest, nominal preference capital and dividends and nominal ordinary capital and dividends in respect of the current and the two preceding years both in total and for each market section.

(*d*) Market values, half-yearly, by groups and as a percentage of

254

the corresponding nominal capital for the current year and the three years immediately preceding.

This information is not especially useful for analytical purposes because the figures of total market value of securities are given only as at June 30th and December 31st. These dates might well be un-representative of the year as a whole and consequently it is impossible to relate the figures of dividends to the market value of securities in order to obtain an exact estimate of the yield on each group of securities.

The remaining class of information provided by the Stock Exchange is that related to individual companies. By far the most important source is the *Stock Exchange Official Year Book*, which is published annually in two parts by Thomas Skinner Ltd. The first part gives full particulars of all gilt-edged and foreign securities and of all company securities with the exception of those comprising the commercial and industrial group. The latter group are dealt with in the second volume.

In respect of gilt-edged and foreign securities the *Year Book* gives details of the amount of stock issued, the date and price of issue, the amount currently outstanding, the date of and the provisions for re-demption of the stock, dates of payment of interest, price range of the stock in the *Official List* during the previous year, and the procedure for transfer.

In respect of companies it gives the following information:

(*a*) The name of the holding company, where the company is a subsidiary.

(*b*) The names of the directors, secretary, auditors, solicitors and bankers of the company.

(*c*) Date of incorporation and a brief history of the commercial activities of the company.

(*d*) Details of the capital structure of the company, stating both the authorized and issued amounts of each class of shares.

(*e*) A history of the capital structure, giving details of all changes in the capital.

(*f*) A brief outline of the rights of the various shareholders with regard to voting, return of capital, etc.

(*g*) Details of any limitation by the articles of association on the borrowing powers of the company together with details of any loan capital which has so far been issued.

(*h*) A summary of the latest balance sheet.

(*i*) The amounts of ordinary dividends declared since 1947.

(*j*) Rules relating to the transfer of shares of the company.

The above information is easily accessible, as copies of the *Year Book* are available in the reference section of most public libraries, and it is also extremely valuable, for it provides in a nutshell the bulk of the information contained in the company's file at Companies House, with the exception of the list of members and the annual reports and accounts.

Also under the heading of Stock Exchange information might be mentioned the advice provided by brokers. Many firms of brokers maintain specialized investment analysis departments which produce monthly circulars which are sent to their larger clients. These circulars range in quality from a general survey of the economic situation with a few tips thrown in for good measure to a highly sophisticated survey of a particular company or industry. The fact that these circulars may now be commented upon by the financial press with the mention of the names of the brokers concerned has led to a general increase in their quality. In addition, many firms of brokers send to their clients monthly investment booklets which give details in respect of most quoted companies of issued capital, the two latest dividend payments, the dates on which dividends are due, the latest market price, and the high and low prices for the current year and sometimes some previous years.

As well as the information which brokers provide themselves for their clients, they are normally able to obtain on their behalf information from other sources, such as *Exchange Telegraph* cards, which are described below.

3. INFORMATION PROVIDED BY FINANCIAL, GENERAL AND GOVERNMENT PUBLICATIONS

(i) *Financial Publications*

For the investor who does not wish to collect for himself the available information relating to a company in which he is interested there is a wide range of specialist organizations and publications to which he may refer:

(a) *Exchange Telegraph Co. Ltd*

This company provides daily statistical information in respect of practically all companies quoted on the London and Provincial Stock Exchanges and for leading European and Australian companies. These statistics are available in the form of cards and subscribers may take all or part of the services provided, even to the extent of subscribing to the card for just one company. The following information is provided by the cards:

(1) Information similar to that provided by the *Stock Exchange Year Book* in respect of the trading and capital history of the company, its past dividends, its directors, etc.

(2) Detailed extracts from the profit and loss account for as many years as possible, together with figures of sales, where given.

(3) A priority percentages table for the past three years.

(4) Figures of the high and low share prices for the past ten years.

(5) A summary of the balance sheets of the past three years.

(6) Extracts from the latest chairman's statements, together with all recent statements regarding acquisitions, trading prospects, interim dividends, capital issues, etc.

In addition to the service provided by the main card which mainly summarizes the available accounting information and other information emanating from the company, there is an auxiliary service provided on a supplementary card which may be obtained at an additional cost and which gives the following information:

(1) Figures of capital employed for the past ten years, analyzed between bank overdrafts, loans, share capital, minority interest (where relevant), and net reserves.

(2) Figures of employment of capital for the past ten years, showing the way in which the company has invested its available capital in property, machinery, trade investments, stock, debtors and cash.

(3) Income statistics for ten years, indicating the profitability of sales (where given), the percentage of before tax and after tax profit on capital employed and the division of profits between dividends and retentions.

(4) Priority percentages tables for the past ten years.

(5) A record of the ordinary share price over the past ten years, stating for each year-end the net asset value, the cash flow, the earnings percentage and the dividend percentage per share, the times covered, the date on which the share became ex dividend and that on which the dividend was payable, and the net UK rate (where relevant).

(6) A comparison of the earnings and dividend yields of the company with those of the group to which the company belongs, as calculated by *The Financial Times-Actuaries* Shares Indices.

(7) A logarithmic chart showing the adjusted earnings and dividend yields and share prices for the last ten years.

(b) *Moodies Services Ltd*

This company maintains a card service similar to that of the Exchange Telegraph Co. in respect of about 5,000 British, 140 Canadian, 410 American, 200 Australian and New Zealand and 200 South African companies. Here again, cards may be subscribed to either singly or in groups. In addition to its statistical cards the company supplies the following services for investors:

(1) *Industries and commodities service.* This provides detailed analyses and forecasts for seventy leading industries and commodities. Each of the forecasts is brought up to date each month and is backed by charts and statistical series.

(2) *Moodies Review.* This is published weekly and comments upon the current state of the stock market together with a weekly analysis of the prospects for a particular industry and the shares of its principal companies. There is also a supplement which describes the latest events on the major European and American markets as well as a monthly supplement giving the latest recommendations of shares to buy.

(3) *Moodies Investment Handbook.* This is published in two parts each quarter and covers some 950 companies. The main information provided is:

> (*a*) A ten-year summary of sales (where stated); total profits; amount earned for the ordinary shareholders expressed both in absolute terms and as a percentage of the latest year's ordinary capital; dividend percentage, net assets per share and average price, all based on the latest year's ordinary capital; yield ratio, which shows the relationship between the dividend yield of the company and the average yield on the Moodies Equity Index; the amount of ordinary share capital; and the amount of capital employed and the pre-tax profits expressed as a percentage thereof.
>
> (*b*) A priority percentages table showing the proportion of earnings taken by debenture interest, preference dividends and ordinary dividends respectively.
>
> (*c*) The latest dividends expressed as a percentage and as an amount per share; the date of declaration, the date of payment and the date on which the share became ex. div.; and where relevant, the net UK rate.

(*d*) Details of capital employed and an analysis of assets held at the end of the latest and previous financial year.

(*e*) A chart showing the movement of the share price over the last six years with a note of the price on April 6, 1965, which is necessary in many cases for the computation of capital gains tax.

(*f*) Information relating to the background of the company and recent developments, such as chairman's statements.

The information above is extremely comprehensive and is invaluable for the serious investor who has not got the time to compile his own data. Moreover, although a private investor could probably gather much more information relating to one or a few companies, he could not hope to maintain his own records in such detail over such a large number of companies.

(4) *Moodies Investment Digest.* This is an annual publication which contains in respect of 600 companies a condensed version of the information provided by the *Investment Handbook*. It is a very useful reference book, and is surprisingly cheap considering the breadth of its coverage. However, for analytical purposes, the information contained in the *Investment Handbook* is much more comprehensive.

(c) *The Investors Chronicle*

This is a weekly publication which describes and comments upon recent events affecting the Stock Exchange generally. The bulk of the journal is devoted to extracts from chairman's statements and from recently published company accounts. The analysis of the company accounts is very useful, giving for each of the past five years figures of trading profit, gross profit, net profit, the percentage amounts earned and paid on the ordinary capital, and the earnings expressed as a percentage of total assets, less current liabilities and goodwill. In addition, in respect of the current year only, details are given of the issued capital, the priority percentages table, cash flow, net borrowings, total commitments, share price (with the high and low prices for the year), net assets per share, dividend yield, earnings yield and price-earnings ratio. Finally, there are articles of general interest to investors, features on particular companies with recommendations, where relevant, for the purchase of their shares and occasional supplementary surveys of particular industries or regions.

A further service provided by the publishers of the *Investors Chronicle* is the *I.C. News Letter*, which contains an outline of the current investment situation together with detailed surveys of two or three companies. This is available weekly on special subscription terms.

The *Investors Chronicle* is extremely useful for an investor, for not only does it provide up-to-date information relating to a wide range of companies, but it may also be filed, thus comprising a permanent reference system using the indices provided by the publishers. Also the journal is prepared to answer readers' queries relating to their investment problems generally or to a particular security.

(d) *The Financial Times*

The Financial Times is probably the most famous and respected financial journal in England. Published daily it provides a comprehensive news service relating to such matters as current economic developments, both home and overseas, the trading prospects for different industries and companies and the previous day's trading on the principal stock exchanges in the world. In short, it contains all information likely to be of interest to anybody concerned with finance, investment or economics. For investors, in particular, it provides a list of the previous day's stock market quotations which is second only to the *Official List* in the number of companies quoted. Also, the high and low prices for the year, the dividend percentage or amount, the times covered, the percentage gross yield and the price-earnings ratio are all stated in respect of the companies listed. Moreover, for an even larger number of companies, details are given of the previous day's trading, based on the marking lists which are reproduced in the *Official List*. Finally, a comprehensive series of price indices are published covering the whole market and its various sectors.

(e) *Academic Journals*

Two publications in this field which are very important for the practising investment analyst are the *Investment Analyst* which is published three times each year by the Society of Investment Analysts and the quarterly *Journal of Business Finance*, which contain papers written by investment experts, both practising and academic. The *Journal of Business Finance* is the more theoretical, but both are essential to any student of investment who desires to keep abreast of the latest ideas and methods in the field of investment analysis.

Also of high quality are the bank reviews published quarterly by the major banks. These are available, generally free of charge, from the bank concerned and contain articles on general economic and financial subjects.

(f) *Books*

There are a vast number of books on the subject of investment ranging from the chatty and extremely elementary approach to the highly sophisticated exposition. A bibliography listing the most recommendable books is included at the end of this book.

(ii) *General Publications*

(a) *Daily Newspapers*

Most daily newspapers now provide at least a column of news and comment of interest to investors. Obviously the quality and the scope of the coverage varies considerably, depending largely on each editor's views as to the powers of assimilation of his readers. For the specialist investor the best City pages are those of *The Times*, the *Guardian* and the *Daily Telegraph*. The city columns of the more popular Press tend to be written in a more journalistic style, though they nevertheless serve the useful function of presenting investment data in an interesting light, thus arousing the curiosity of a reader who might otherwise completely ignore the subject. Most papers give daily lists of Stock Exchange prices of the leading securities.

(b) *Weekly Newspapers*

The Sunday newspapers appear to exercise a considerable influence over investors' decisions. Together with the *Investors Chronicle* they are digested by investors over the weekend and probably help to account for the fact that Monday is traditionally the busiest day on the Stock Exchange. The *Sunday Times* leads the field with its 'Business News' section which is devoted to events in the world of business and finance, together with articles on various aspects of taxation and investment policy. The *Observer*, the *Sunday Telegraph*, and the *Sunday Express* (in a rather more lively style) all have pages devoted to investment.

On the subject of the Press, it should be mentioned that financial journalists both in daily and Sunday newspapers have recently shown a healthy tendency to criticize company managements where justified. Previously the only comments on company directors were largely favourable and the only recommendations in respect of particular shares were for purchase. Nowadays, in contrast, journalists are assuming the function of watchdogs, criticizing such matters as secret activities of directors for their own benefit, the late publication of accounts, and pressure by directors to obstruct takeover bids which are clearly in the interest of the shareholders.

(c) *Weekly Journals*

The most important journal in this field is *The Economist* which provides a commentary on events in the fields of economics, business, finance and investment, both home and overseas. It should be regarded as essential reading in that it provides full information regarding the economic background within which the investor operates.

(d) *Monthly Journals*

The two journals in this field which are most relevant to investors are the *Times Review of Industry* and *Management Today*, both of which contain articles on business and investment together with detailed comment on individual companies. The emphasis is on business and industry rather than investment, but the information provided is still extremely useful to an investor who is attempting, for example, to assess the prospects of a particular industry. A recent journal, *Planned Savings*, specializes in the analysis of unit trusts, insurance schemes and investment trusts.

(e) *Trade Journals*

An investor who is interested in the prospects facing a particular industry will find much relevant information in the weekly or monthly trade journals relating to the industry.

(f) *Government Publications*

The most important Government publication as far as investors are concerned is *Financial Statistics*. This is a monthly publication containing statistical tables prepared by the Central Statistical Office and published by Her Majesty's Stationery Office. Each issue is divided into fourteen sections;

(1) Financial accounts; showing financial transactions and net acquisitions of financial assets analyzed by sectors.

(2) Public sector accounts.

(3) Exchequer and central government; this section comprises central government accounts and includes tables relating to Inland Revenue and Customs and Excise duties, National Savings, Treasury Bill tenders, and issues and redemptions of Government marketable securities.

(4) Local authorities; receipts and expenditure accounts and tables of local authorities' borrowing.

(5) Public corporation accounts.

(6) Banking; consisting of a number of tables relating to such matters as bank advances, special deposits with the Bank of England, activities of the discount market, the clearing banks, accepting houses and overseas banks in the United Kingdom, money supply, currency circulation and bank clearings.

(7) Money supply and domestic credit expansion.

(8) Other financial institutions; including building societies, hire purchase finance activities, unit trusts, investment trusts, insurance companies, superannuation funds. The tables show primarily the sources and uses of the funds of these institutions.

(9) Companies. This group of tables consists of an appropriation account of companies, sources and use of capital funds of industrial and commercial companies, and income and finance of quoted companies.

(10) Personal sector.

(11) Overseas sector.

(12) Capital issues and Stock Exchange transactions.

(13) Interest rates, security prices and exchange rates, including British Government securities, company activity, prices and yields, and short-term money rates.

(14) Supplementary tables, including such data as composition of the national debt, transactions in securities by financial institutions, etc.

Much of the above information is extremely useful for an investor, though naturally it only relates to overall trends rather than to individual securities. In particular it provides details of changes in the size and type of security holdings of the major institutional investors; of changes in the sources, use and profitability of the capital funds of companies; of capital issues and redemptions made by United Kingdom companies; of the number and size of Stock Exchange transactions on a monthly basis; and of movements in different types of interest rates. An investor thus gets a good picture of the level of activity on the Stock Exchange, of the type of security that is most active, of the influence of the financial institutions on this activity, and of the overall financial situation within which this activity is taking place.

In addition to *Financial Statistics* there is a vast range of Government publications relating to either the economy as a whole or any of its various sectors. Clearly, these cannot be described in detail, but those which are likely to be of most use to an investor are *The Board of Trade Journal*, the *Monthly Digest of Statistics, Economic Trends* (monthly), the *Annual Abstract of Statistics*, the *National Income and Expenditure Blue Book*, and separate digests of Scottish, Welsh and Northern Ireland statistics.

4. THE DEMAND FOR FURTHER INFORMATION

The sources of information which have been described above permit of analysis at three levels, namely the overall economy, the particular industry, and the individual company within the industry. At all levels the available statistics are faulty and often too outdated to permit of worth-while analysis. The problems involved in analyzing Government statistics are immense, for these statistics are so prone to errors that it is wellnigh impossible to use them as the basis of a worth-while forecast.

It might be expected that the information relating to particular companies would be less variable in its accuracy. Companies are required under the Companies Act 1948 to maintain adequate accounting records in respect of all their transactions. The accounts which are prepared from these records and audited by an independent firm of accountants should therefore provide an illuminating picture of the trading activities of the company during the year and of its assets and liabilities at the end of the year.

Unfortunately, however, company accounts are an inadequate tool of analysis for three reasons. In the first place, it often happens that accounts are not presented to the members until several months after the end of the year to which they relate. A delay of six months in this respect is by no means uncommon. Furthermore, certain accounting conventions, particularly those relating to the valuation of assets, have the result that the accounts present a very misleading view of the profit or loss for the year. These conventions and their effects are described in detail in Chapter 10. Finally, the average set of company accounts published by companies prior to 1968 was prepared in accordance with the minimum requirements of the Companies Act 1948. While the provisions of this Act definitely represent a vast advance compared with the previous Companies Act of 1929 and at the same time put Britain far ahead of most European countries in the field of corporate reporting, there is no doubt that a considerable amount of invaluable information is withheld from investors by company managements. The normal grounds for this lack of disclosure are either that it protects companies from their competitors or that the provision of further information would be too costly when compared with the benefit that investors would receive from the information. This latter argument overlooks that point that the further information which shareholders require to undertake the analysis of a company must already be available to the company itself if it has any concept of good management, so that the provision of that information for shareholders should not be unduly expensive.

In recent years the growth of public interest in investment, the emergence of investment analysts as a distinct professional class, and the realization that companies have an obligation to the state to operate efficiently, has increased the call for greater disclosure. The first step in this direction was the appointment on December 10, 1959 of the Jenkins Committee to consider in the light of modern conditions and practices, including the growth of takeover bids, what should be the duties of directors and the rights of shareholders, and generally to recommend what changes in the law were desirable.

The Committee reported in June 1962 and made several recommendations as to the information that companies should disclose in their accounts. Their main drawback lies in the fact that they perpetuate the legalistic doctrine of protection of a company's creditors and investors which motivated earlier Acts, rather than seeking to increase the efficiency of a company by the threat of revealing stagnant and uncompetitive performance for all to see.

The Jenkins Report was criticized and its deficiencies expounded in October 1963 by Harold Rose,[1] who later became Professor of Finance at the London Business School. In his extremely influential paper he made certain proposals many of which went far beyond the recommendations of the Jenkins Committee. Probably the most far-reaching of his suggestions is that companies should be required to provide full profit and loss accounts which 'show separately, in addition to sales or operating revenue, the following items: The cost of goods sold, as normally computed by the company; administrative, sales and general expenses; and other outlays, such as research costs and advertising expenditure, that would normally fall within the trading account'. Similar information is required of listed companies by the Securities and Exchange Commission of the United States, and it is clearly of the utmost importance to investment analysts.

Before the Companies Act of 1967 it was left to the Stock Exchange to take steps to improve the standard of corporate reporting. At the end of August, 1964 the Chairman of the Stock Exchange sent a letter to the chairmen of all quoted companies stating that all

[1] *Disclosure in Company Accounts* (Institute of Economic Affairs, Eaton Paper no. 1, 1963, second edition 1965).

companies applying for a quotation in future would have to meet certain requirements:

(a) The provision of information as to the composition of a group of companies and as to any major interests in associated companies;

(b) Where a company or group of companies carries on widely differing operations the provision of an analysis of trading results;

(c) The issue of quarterly or half-yearly reports.

These requirements were eventually enforced in respect of all companies seeking a quotation after March 26, 1965, and now apply not only to companies applying for a quotation for the first time, but also to companies with an existing quotation which are seeking quotations for new securities arising from rights issues, new acquisitions, debenture issues, scrip issues and share splits.

The letter of August, 1964 also contained certain recommendations made by the Council of the Stock Exchange regarding the information which a company should provide for its shareholders, though it was not compelled to do so. Although these recommendations were not particularly far-reaching and were not in any case compulsory, they represented a welcome advance. Moreover, they covered most of the points made by the Jenkins Committee and in many ways went further. However, two of the most important recommendations made by Harold Rose were still ignored, namely that companies should publish detailed profit and loss accounts and should insert in the balance sheet realistic valuations of fixed assets.

For the next few years the Stock Exchange was far ahead of parliamentary legislation with regard to the provision of information. However, on February 2, 1966 the Companies Bill was presented to Parliament. Although it included most of the recommendations of the Stock Exchange their impact was considerably stronger in view of the fact that they became compulsory and applied to all limited companies, whether or not they possessed a Stock Exchange quotation, and whether or not they were public or private companies.

The Companies Act was eventually passed in July 1967 and its accounting requirements apply to all accounts for financial years ending after January 27, 1968, with the exception of the requirement of a detailed analysis of turnover under section 18, which came into operation for accounts for financial years ending after July 27, 1968. Although the Act is relatively unimaginative in that its disclosure provisions are not materially more demanding than the requirements of the Jenkins Report, it must be firmly welcomed by investors. In particular, the activities of directors are made subject to far more supervision and regulation than ever before. For instance, option dealings by directors in shares of any company in the group are banned, while their interests in shares of the company, broad details of their salaries, and interests in contracts entered into by companies in the group must all be revealed.

It is, however, very disappointing that clauses providing for the disclosure of rents paid in respect of land and the provision of a five-year summary of capital and reserves, profit, dividends and turnover should have been deleted from the Bill before it became law. A similar fate was met by a clause providing for the division of turnover between business done by the company with other members of the group and business done by it with companies outside the group.

The main developments since 1967 have been the accounting recommendations published by the Institute of Chartered Accountants which are described in Chapter 17 and the statement by the Council of the Stock Exchange in August, 1971 that from January 1, 1972 all new company prospectuses and directors' reports of existing companies shall disclose details of significant contracts in which their directors have a material personal interest. Such contracts will include those which in aggregate represent in sum or in value more than 1% of the company's total purchases, sales, payments, receipts, or, in the case of capital transactions, net assets.

APPENDIX

(a) THE PRODUCTION OF ACCOUNTS UNDER THE COMPANIES ACT 1948

Under the Companies Act 1948 the following provisions apply with respect to the accounts to be provided by a company:

s. 147
Every company must keep proper books of account with respect to:

(i) all sums of money received and expended by the company, and the matters in respect of which the receipt and expenditure takes place;

(ii) all sales and purchases of goods by the company;

(iii) the assets and liabilities of the company.

A company will not be deemed to have kept proper books of account unless it has kept such books as are necessary to give a true and fair view of the state of the company's affairs and to explain its transactions.

The books of account are to be kept at such office as the directors think fit, and are to be always open for their inspection.

s. 148

The directors of every company shall at some date not later than eighteen months after the incorporation of the company, and subsequently once at least in every calendar year, lay before the company in general meeting:

(i) a profit and loss account or, in the case of a company not trading for profit, an income and expenditure account; and

(ii) a balance sheet as at the date to which the profit and loss account or the income and expenditure account, as the case may be, is made up.

This date must be not more than nine months, or in the case of a company carrying on business or having interests abroad, not more than twelve months earlier than the date of the meeting.

s. 149

Every balance sheet of a company must give a true and fair view of the state of affairs of the company as at the end of its financial year, and every profit and loss account must give a true and fair view of the profit and loss for the financial year.

The contents of the balance sheet and profit and loss account must be such as will comply with the requirements of the *Eighth Schedule of the Act* (reproduced below).

s. 150

Where at the end of its financial year a company has subsidiaries, accounts or statements (referred to as 'group accounts') dealing with the state of affairs and profit and loss of the company and the subsidiaries must be laid before the company in general meeting when the company's own balance sheet and profit and loss account are so laid, except that:

(i) group accounts are not required where the company is at the end of its financial year the wholly owned subsidiary of another body corporate incorporated in Great Britain. A wholly owned subsidiary is one which has no members other than its holding company and that holding company's subsidiaries and its or their nominees; and

(ii) group accounts need not deal with a subsidiary of the company if the company's directors are of opinion that:

(*a*) it is impracticable, or would be of no real value to the members of the company, in view of the insignificant amounts involved, or would involve expense or delay out of proportion to the value to members of the company; or (*b*) the results would be misleading, or harmful to the business of the company or any of its subsidiaries; or

(*c*) the business of the holding company and that of the subsidiary are so different that they cannot reasonably be treated as a single undertaking;

and, if the directors are of such an opinion about each of the company's subsidiaries, group accounts shall not be required.

It is provided, however, that the approval of the Board of Trade shall be required for not dealing in group accounts with a subsidiary on the ground that the results would be harmful, or on the ground of the difference between the business of the holding company and that of the subsidiary.

s. 151

The group accounts laid before a holding company must be consolidated accounts comprising:

(i) a consolidated balance sheet dealing with the state of affairs of the company and all the subsidiaries to be dealt with in group accounts;

(ii) a consolidated profit and loss account dealing with the profit or loss of the company and those subsidiaries.

If, however, the company's directors are of opinion that it is better for the purpose of presenting the same or equivalent information about the state of affairs and profit or loss of the company and those subsidiaries, so that it may be readily appreciated by the company's members, the group accounts may be prepared in some other form.

s. 156

The profit and loss account and, so far as not incorporated in the balance sheet or profit and loss account, any group accounts laid before the company in general meeting, must be annexed to the balance sheet, and the auditors' reports must be attached thereto.

Any accounts so annexed must be approved by the Board of Directors before the balance sheet is signed on their behalf.

s. 157

There must be attached to every balance sheet laid before a company in general meeting, a report by the directors with respect to the company's affairs, the amount, if any, which they recommend should be paid by way of dividend, and the amount, if any, which they propose to carry to reserves within the meaning of the *Eighth Schedule to the Act*.

The report must deal, so far as is material for the appreciation of the state of the company's affairs by its members and will not in the directors' opinion be harmful to the business of the company or of its subsidiaries, with any change during the financial year in the nature of the company's business, or in the company's subsidiaries, or in the classes of business in which the company has an interest, whether as a member of another company or otherwise.

s. 158

A copy of every balance sheet, including every document required by law to be annexed thereto, which is to be laid before a company in general meeting, together with a copy of the auditors' report, must, not less than twenty-one days before the date of the meeting, be sent to every member of the company (whether he is or is not entitled to receive notices of general meetings of the company), every holder of debentures of the company (whether he is or is not so entitled) and all persons other than members or holders of debentures of the company, being persons so entitled.

s. 196

In any accounts laid before a general meeting, or in a statement annexed thereto, there must be shown, so far as the information is contained in the company's books and papers or the company has the right to obtain it from the persons concerned:

(i) the aggregate amount of the directors' emoluments;

(ii) the aggregate amount of directors' and past directors' pensions; and

(iii) the aggregate amount of directors' or past directors' compensation for loss of office.

s. 197

The accounts which are required by the Act to be laid before the company in general meeting must also contain particulars showing:

(i) the amount of any loans made during the company's financial year to:

(a) any officer of the company; or

(b) any person who, after the making of the loan, became during that year an officer of the company;

by the company or a subsidiary thereof or by any other person under a guarantee from or on a security provided by the company or a subsidiary thereof; and

(ii) The amount of any loans made in manner aforesaid to any such officer or person as aforesaid at any time before the company's financial year and outstanding at the expiration thereof.

s. 124

Except in the case of exempt private companies, and of assurance companies which have complied with the provisions of section 8 of the Assurance Companies Act 1958, a copy of every balance sheet laid before the company in general meeting during the period to which the return relates, together with a copy of the auditor's report, and including every document required by law to be annexed to the balance sheet (e.g. profit and loss account, directors' report etc.), must be annexed to the annual return.

(b) THE DISCLOSURE REQUIREMENTS OF THE COMPANIES ACT 1967

(1) Subject to certain exceptions, where, at the end of its financial year, a company has subsidiaries, there shall, in the case of each subsidiary, be stated in, or in a note on, or statement annexed to, the company's accounts laid before it in general meeting:

(a) the subsidiary's name:

(b) the country (if other than Great Britain) in which it is incorporated; and

(c) in relation to shares of each class of the subsidiary held by the company, the identity of the class and the proportion of the nominal value of the issued shares of that class represented by the shares held. (s. 3)

(2) Subject to certain exceptions, if, at the end of its financial year, a company holds shares of any class in another company (not being its subsidiary) exceeding in nominal value one-tenth of the nominal value of the issued shares of the class, there shall be noted in the accounts of the first-mentioned company laid before it in general meeting the name of that other company and the country (if other than Great Britain) in which it is incorporated, and:

(a) the identity of the class and the proportion of the nominal value of the issued shares of that class represented by the shares held; and

(b) if the company also holds shares in that other company of another class or classes, the like particulars in respect thereof. (s. 4(1))

(3) If, at the end of its financial year, a company holds shares in another company (not being its subsidiary) and the amount of all the shares therein which it holds (as stated or included in the accounts of the first-mentioned company laid before it in general meeting) exceeds one-tenth of the amount of the assets of the first-mentioned company (as so stated), there shall be noted in those accounts:

271

(*a*) the name of that other company and the country (if other than Great Britain), in which it is incorporated; and

(*b*) in relation to shares in that other company of each class held, the identity of the class and the proportion of the nominal value of the issued shares of that class represented by the shares held. (s. 4(2))

(4) Subject to certain exceptions in the case of companies operating outside the UK, where, at the end of its financial year, a company is the subsidiary of another body corporate, there shall be noted in the company's accounts laid before it in general meeting the name of the body corporate regarded by the directors as being the company's ultimate holding company and, if known to them, the country in which it is incorporated. (s. 5)

(5) In any accounts of a company laid before it in general meeting there shall be shown, so far as the information is contained in the company's books and papers or the company has the right to obtain it from the persons concerned:

(*a*) the emoluments of the chairman, or if during the financial year, more persons than one have been chairman, the emoluments of each of them.

(*b*) the number (if any) of directors who had no emoluments or whose several emoluments amounted to not more than £2,500 and, by reference to each pair of adjacent points on a scale whereon the lowest point is £2,500 and the succeeding ones are successive integral multiples of £2,500, the number (if any) of directors whose several emoluments exceeded the lower point but did not exceed the higher.

(*c*) the number of directors who have waived rights to receive emoluments which, but for the waiver, would have fallen to be included in the amount shown in those accounts under s. 196 of the principal Act, together with the aggregate amount of the said emoluments.

(*d*) the number of persons in the company's employment whose several emoluments exceeded the lower point but did not exceed the higher of pairs of adjacent points on a scale whereon the lowest point is £10,000 and the succeeding ones are successive integral multiples of £2,500 beginning with that in the case of which the multiple is five. (ss. 6, 7, 8)

(6) The power is to be given to the Board of Trade to revoke in part or in whole the existing exemption of banking and discount companies from the requirements of Schedule 8 of the principal Act. (s. 12)

(7) The directors' report shall state the names of the persons who,

at the end of the financial year, were directors of the company and the principal activities of the company and of its subsidiaries during that year, and any significant change in those activities during that year, and shall also:

(a) if significant changes in the fixed assets of the company or of any of its subsidiaries have occurred during that year, contain particulars of the changes, and, if, in the case of those assets, the market value thereof (as at the end of the financial year) differs substantially from the amount thereof as shown in the balance sheet and the difference is, in the opinion of the directors, of such significance as to require that the attention of members of the company or of holders of debentures thereof should be drawn thereto, indicate the difference with such degree of precision as is practicable:

(b) if, during the financial year, the company has issued any shares, stock or debentures, state the reason for making the issue, the classes of shares, stock or debentures issued, the number of shares of each class, and the amount of stock or debentures of each class, and the consideration received by the company in respect of the shares, stock and debentures of each class;

(c) if, at the end of that year, there subsists a contract with the company in which a director of the company has, or at any time in that year had, in any way, whether directly or indirectly, an interest, or there has, at any time in that year, subsisted a contract with the company in which a director of the company had, at any time in that year, in any way, whether directly or indirectly, an interest (being, in either case, in the opinion of the directors, a contract of significance in relation to the company's business and in which the director's interest is or was material), contain:

(i) a statement of the fact of the contract's subsisting or, as the case may be, having subsisted;

(ii) the names of the parties to the contract (other than the company);

(iii) the name of the director (if not a party to the contract);

(iv) an indication of the nature of the contract; and

(v) an indication of the nature of the director's interest in the contract.

(d) if, at the end of the year, there subsist arrangements to which the company is a party, which enable directors of the company to acquire benefits by means of the acquisition of shares in, or debentures of, the company or any other bodies corporate, or

273

there have, at any time in that year, subsisted such arrangements and giving the names of the persons who at any time in that year were directors of the company and held, or whose nominees held, shares or debentures acquired in pursuance of the arrangements;

(e) as respects each person who, at the end of that year, was a director of the company, state whether or not, according to the register kept by the company for this purpose, he was, at the end of that year interested in shares in, or debentures of, the company or of any other company in the group, and, if he was, the number and amount of shares in, and debentures of, each body (specifying it) in which, according to the register, he was then interested and whether or not, according to the register, he was, at the beginning of that year (or, if he was not then a director, when he became a director), interested in shares in, or debentures of, the company or of any other company in the group, and, if he was, the number and amount of shares in, and debentures of, each body (specifying it) in which, according to the register, he was interested at the beginning of that year or, as the case may be, when he became a director;

(f) contain particulars of any matters other than those required to be dealt with by the foregoing paragraphs in the circumstances therein mentioned so far as they are material for the appreciation of the state of the company's affairs by its members, being matters the disclosure of which will not, in the opinion of the directors, be harmful to the business of the company or of any of its subsidiaries. (s. 16)

(8) If, during a financial year, a company or a group of companies carries on business of two or more classes that differ substantially from each other, there shall be contained in the directors' report relating to that year a statement of:

(a) the proportions in which the turnover for that year is divided amongst those classes; and

(b) as regards business of each class, the extent or approximate extent (expressed in either case, in monetary terms) to which, in the opinion of the directors, the carrying on of business of that class contributed to or restricted, the profit or loss of the company or the group for that year before taxation. (s. 17)

(9) If, at the end of a financial year, a company does not have subsidiaries, there shall be contained in the directors' report relating to that year a statement of:

(a) the average number of persons employed by it in each week in that year; and (*b*) the aggregate remuneration paid or payable in respect of that year to the persons by reference to whom the number stated under the foregoing paragraph is ascertained.

If, at the end of a financial year, a company has subsidiaries the directors' report shall state:

(*a*) the average number of persons employed between them in each week in that year by the company and the subsidiaries; and

(*b*) the aggregate remuneration paid or payable in respect of that year to the persons by reference to whom the number stated under the foregoing paragraph is ascertained. (s. 18)

(10) If a company (not being the wholly owned subsidiary of a company incorporated in Great Britain) has, during a financial year, given money for political purposes exceeding £50 in amount, there shall be contained in the directors' report relating to that year a statement of the identities of the political parties and names of the persons to whom money exceeding £50 in amount has, during that year, been given by the company for those purposes and the amount of money which, during that year, has been so given to each of them for those purposes. (s. 19)

(11) Where the business of a company or a group of companies consists in, or includes, the supplying of goods then, unless the turn-over for that year does not exceed £50,000, there shall be contained in the directors' report relating to that year:

(*a*) if, during that year, goods have been exported by the company from the United Kingdom, a statement of the value of the goods that have been so exported by the company, and, where relevant, each of its subsidiaries;

(*b*) if, in the case of the company and, where relevant, of each of its subsidiaries, no goods have been exported by it during that year from the United Kingdom, a statement to that fact. (s. 20)

(12) A director of a company who buys:

(*a*) a right to call for delivery at a specified price and within a specified time of a specified number or amount of quoted shares or quoted debentures of any company in the group (i.e. a call option); or

(*b*) a right to make delivery at a specified price and within a specified time of a specified number or amount of such shares or debentures (i.e. a put option); or

(*c*) a right (as he may elect) to call for delivery at a specified price and within a specified time or to make delivery at a specified price and within a specified time of a specified number or amount of such shares or debentures (i.e. a put and call option); shall be guilty of an offence and liable:

275

(i) on summary conviction, to imprisonment for a term not exceeding three months or to a fine not exceeding £200, or to both;

(ii) on conviction on indictment, to imprisonment for a term not exceeding two years or to a fine, or to both (s. 25)

(13) Every company shall keep at its registered office, or the place where its register of members is kept, or at its principal place of business:

(a) in the case of each director whose contract of service with the company is in writing, a copy of that contract;

(b) in the case of each director whose contract of service with the company is not in writing, a written memorandum setting out the terms of that contract.

This requirement does not apply to:

(i) a contract which requires the director to work either wholly or mainly outside the United Kingdom;

(ii) a contract of which the unexpired portion is less than twelve months or which can, during the ensuing twelve months, be terminated by the company without payment of compensation. (s. 26)

(14) Each director of a company is obliged to notify it of his interest in, and of any changes of his interest in shares or debentures of the company or of any companies in the group. This information must be recorded in a register which must be open to public inspection. (ss. 27–31 inc.)

(15) Any person who is, or becomes interested in one-tenth of the issued share capital of a class carrying unrestricted voting rights in a quoted company must inform the company of this fact and of any changes in their interest. This information must be recorded in a register which must be available for public inspection. (ss. 33, 34)

(c) THE EIGHTH SCHEDULE OF THE COMPANIES ACT 1948
AS AMENDED BY THE COMPANIES ACT 1967

PART I

*General Provisions as to Balance Sheet and
Profit and Loss Account*

Balance Sheet

1. (This merely contains preliminary comments.)

2. The authorized share capital, issued share capital, liabilities and assets shall be summarized, with such particulars as are necessary to disclose the general nature of the assets and liabilities, and there shall be specified:

(*a*) any part of the issued capital that consists of redeemable preference shares, the earliest and latest dates on which the company has power to redeem those shares, whether those shares must be redeemed in any event or are liable to be redeemed at the option of the company and whether any (and, if so, what) premium is payable on redemption;

(*b*) so far as the information is not given in the profit and loss account, any share capital on which interest has been paid out of capital during the financial year, and the rate at which interest has been so paid;

(*c*) the amount of the share premium account;

(*d*) particulars of any redeemed debentures which the company has power to reissue.

3. There shall be stated under separate headings, so far as they are not written off:

(*a*) the preliminary expenses;

(*b*) any expenses incurred in connection with any issue of share capital or debentures;

(*c*) any sums paid by way of commission in respect of any shares or debentures;

(*d*) any sums allowed by way of discount in respect of any debentures; and

(*e*) the amount of the discount allowed on any issue of shares at a discount.

4. (1) The reserves, provisions, liabilities and assets shall be classified under headings appropriate to the company's business:

Provided that—

(*a*) where the amount of any class is not material, it may be included under the same heading as some other class; and

(*b*) where any assets of one class are not separable from assets of another class, those assets may be included under the same heading.

(2) Fixed assets, current assets and assets that are neither fixed nor current shall be separately identified.

(3) The method or methods used to arrive at the amount of the fixed assets under each heading shall be stated.

5. (1) The method of arriving at the amount of any fixed asset shall, subject to the next following sub-paragraph, be to take the difference between:

(*a*) its cost or, if it stands in the company's books at a valuation, the amount of the valuation; and

(b) the aggregate amount provided or written off since the date of acquisition or valuation, as the case may be, for depreciation or diminution in value; and for the purposes of this paragraph the net amount at which any assets stand in the company's books at the commencement of this Act (after deduction of the amounts previously provided or written off for depreciation or diminution in value) shall, if the figures relating to the period before the commencement of this Act cannot be obtained without unreasonable expense or delay, be treated as if it were the amount of a valuation of those assets made at the commencement of this Act and, where any of those assets are sold, the said net amount less the amount of the sales shall be treated as if it were the amount of a valuation so made of the remaining assets.

(2) The foregoing sub-paragraph shall not apply:

(a) to assets for which the figures relating to the period beginning with the commencement of this Act cannot be obtained without unreasonable expense or delay; or

(b) to assets the replacement of which is provided for wholly or partly—

    (i) by making provision for renewals and charging the cost of replacement against the provision so made, or

    (ii) by charging the cost of replacement direct to revenue; or

(c) to any quoted investments or to any unquoted investments of which the value as estimated by the directors is shown either as the amount of the investments or by way of note; or

(d) to goodwill, patents or trade marks.

(3) For the assets under each heading whose amount is arrived at in accordance with sub-paragraph (1) of this paragraph, there shall be shown:

(a) the aggregate of the amounts referred to in paragraph (a) of that sub-paragraph; and

(b) the aggregate of the amounts referred to in paragraph (b) thereof.

(4) As respects the assets under each heading whose amount is not arrived at in accordance with the said sub-paragraph (2)(b) of this paragraph, there shall be stated:

(a) the means by which their replacement is provided for; and

(b) the aggregate amount of the provision (if any) made for renewals and not used.

5A. In the case of unquoted investments consisting in equity share capital (as defined by subsection (5) of s. 154 of this Act) of other bodies corporate (other than any whose values as estimated by the directors are separately shown, either individually or collectively or as to some individually and as to the rest collectively, and are so shown either as to the amount thereof, or by way of note), the matters referred to in the following heads shall, if not otherwise shown, be stated by way of note or in a statement or report annexed:

    (*a*) the aggregate amount of the company's income for the financial year that is ascribable to the investments;

    (*b*) the amount of the company's share before taxation, and the amount of that share after taxation, of the net aggregate amount of the profits of the bodies in which the investments are held, being profits for the several periods to which accounts sent to them during the financial year to the company related, after deducting those bodies' losses for those periods (or vice versa);

    (*c*) the amount of the company's share of the net aggregate amount of the undistributed profits accumulated by the bodies in which the investments are held since the time when the investments were acquired, after deducting the losses accumulated by them since that time (or vice versa);

    (*d*) the manner in which any losses incurred by the said bodies have been dealt with in the company's accounts.

6. The aggregate amounts respectively of reserves and provisions (other than provisions for depreciation, renewals or diminution in value of assets) shall be stated under separate headings:

Provided that—

    (*a*) this paragraph shall not require a separate statement of either of the said amounts which is not material; and

    (*b*) The Board of Trade may direct that it shall not require a separate statement of the amount of provisions where they are satisfied that that is not required in the public interest and would prejudice the company, but subject to the condition that any heading stating an amount arrived at after taking into account a provision (other than as aforesaid) shall be so framed or marked as to indicate that fact.

7. (1) There shall also be shown (unless it is shown in the profit and loss account or a statement or report annexed thereto, or the amount involved is not material):

    (*a*) where the amount of the reserves or of the provisions (other than provisions for depreciation, renewals or diminution in value of assets) shows an increase as compared with the amount at the end of the immediately preceding financial year, the source from which the amount of the increase has been derived; and

(b) where—
    (i) the amount of the reserves shows a decrease as compared with the amount at the end of the immediately preceding financial year; or

    (ii) the amount at the end of the immediately preceding financial year of the provisions (other than provisions for depreciation, renewals or diminution in value of assets) exceeded the aggregate of the sums since applied and amount still retained for the purposes thereof;

the application of the amounts derived from the difference.

(2) Where the heading showing the reserves or any of the provisions aforesaid is divided into sub-headings, this paragraph shall apply to each of the separate amounts shown in the sub-headings instead of applying to the aggregate amount thereof.

7A. If an amount is set aside for the purpose of its being used to prevent undue fluctuations in charges for taxation, it shall be stated.

8. (1) There shall be shown under separate headings:
    (a) the aggregate amounts respectively of the company's quoted investments and unquoted investments;

    (b) if the amount of the goodwill and of any patents and trade marks or part of that amount is shown as a separate item in or is otherwise ascertainable from the books of the company, or from any contract for the sale or purchase of any property to be acquired by the company, or from any documents in the possession of the company relating to the stamp duty payable in respect of any such contract or the conveyance of any such property, the said amount so shown or ascertained so far as not written off or, as the case may be, the said amount so far as it is so shown or ascertainable and as so shown or ascertained, as the case may be;

    (c) the aggregate amount of any outstanding loans made under the authority of provisos (b) and (c) of subsection (1) of s. 54 of the Act;

    (d) the aggregate amount of bank loans and overdrafts and the aggregate amount of loans made to the company which—
        (i) are repayable otherwise than by instalments and fall due for repayment after the expiration of the period of five years beginning with the day next following the expiration of the financial year; or

> (ii) are repayable by instalments any of which fall due for
> payment after the expiration of that period:
>
> not being, in either case, bank loans or overdrafts.

(*e*) the aggregate amount (before deduction of income tax) which is recommended for distribution by way of dividend.

(2) Nothing in head (*b*) of the foregoing sub-paragraph shall be taken as requiring the amount of the goodwill, patents and trade marks to be stated otherwise than as a single item.

(3) The heading showing the amount of the quoted investments shall be subdivided, where necessary, to distinguish the investments as respects which there has, and those as respects which there has not, been granted a quotation or permission to deal on a recognized stock exchange.

(4) In relation to each loan falling within head (*d*) of sub-paragraph (1) of this paragraph (other than a bank loan or overdraft), there shall be stated by way of note (if not otherwise stated) the terms on which it is repayable and the rate at which interest is payable thereon:

Provided that if the number of loans is such that, in the opinion of the directors, compliance with the foregoing requirement would result in a statement of excessive length, it shall be sufficient to give a general indication of the terms on which the loans are repayable and the rates at which interest is payable thereon.

9. Where any liability of the company is secured otherwise than by operation of law on any assets of the company, the fact that that liability is so secured shall be stated, but it shall not be necessary to specify the assets on which the liability is secured.

10. Where any of the company's debentures are held by a nominee of or trustee for the company, the nominal amount of the debentures and the amount at which they are stated in the books of the company shall be stated.

11. (1) The matters referred to in the following sub-paragraphs shall be stated by way of note, or in a statement or report annexed, if not otherwise shown.

(2) The number, description and amount of any shares in the company which any person has an option to subscribe for, together with the following particulars of the option, that is to say:

(*a*) the period during which it is exercisable;

(*b*) the price to be paid for shares subscribed for under it.

(3) The amount of any arrears of fixed cumulative dividends on the company's shares and the period for which the dividends or, if

there is more than one class, each class of them are in arrear, the amount to be stated before deduction of income tax, except that, in the case of tax-free dividends, the amount shall be shown free of tax and the fact that it is so shown shall also be stated.

(4) Particulars of any charge on the assets of the company to secure the liabilities of any other person, including where practicable, the amount secured.

(5) The general nature of any other contingent liabilities not provided for and, where practicable, the aggregate amount or estimated amount of those liabilities, if it is material.

(6) Where practicable the aggregate amount or estimated amount, if it is material, of contracts for capital expenditure, so far as not provided for and, where practicable, the aggregate amount, if it is material, of capital expenditure authorized by the directors which has not been contracted for.

(6A) In the case of fixed assets under any heading whose amount is required to be arrived at in accordance with paragraph 5(1) of this Schedule (other than unquoted investments) and is so arrived at by reference to a valuation, the years (so far as they are known to the directors) in which the assets were severally valued and the year, the names of the persons who valued them or particulars of their qualifications for doing so and (whichever is stated) the bases of valuation used by them.

(6B) If there are included amongst fixed assets under any heading (other than investments) assets that have been acquired during the financial year, the aggregate amount of the assets acquired as determined for the purpose of making up the balance sheet, and if during that year any fixed assets included under a heading in the balance sheet made up with respect to the immediately preceding financial year (other than investments) have been disposed of or destroyed, the aggregate amount thereof as determined for the purpose of making up that balance sheet.

(6C) Of the amount of fixed assets consisting of land, how much is ascribable to land of freehold tenure and how much to land of leasehold tenure, and, of the latter, how much is ascribable to land held on long lease and how much to land held on short lease.

(7) If in the opinion of the directors any of the current assets have not a value, on realization in the ordinary course of the company's business, at least equal to the amount at which they are stated, the fact that the directors are of that opinion.

(8) The aggregate market value of the company's quoted investments where it differs from the amount of the investments as stated, and the Stock Exchange value of any investments of which the

market value is shown (whether separately or not) and is taken as being higher than their Stock Exchange value.

(8A) If a sum set aside for the purpose of its being used to prevent undue fluctuations in charges for taxation has been used during the financial year for another purpose, the amount thereof and the fact that it has been so used.

(8B) If the amount carried forward for stock in trade or work in progress is material for the appreciation by its members of the company's state of affairs or of its profit or loss for the financial year, the manner in which that amount has been computed.

(9) The basis on which foreign currencies have been converted into sterling, where the amount of the assets or liabilities affected is material.

(10) The basis on which the amount, if any, set aside for United Kingdom corporation tax is computed.

(11) Except in the case of the first balance sheet laid before the company after the commencement of this Act, the corresponding amounts at the end of the immediately preceding financial year for all items shown in the balance sheet.

Profit and Loss Account

12. (1) There shall be shown:
   (a) the amount charged to revenue by way of provision for depreciation, renewals or diminution in value of fixed assets;
   (b) the amount of the interest on loans of the following kinds made to the company (whether on the security of debenture or not), namely, bank loans, overdrafts and loans which, not being bank loans or overdrafts—
      (i) are repayable otherwise than by instalments and fall due for repayment before the expiration of the period of five years beginning with the day next following the expiration of the financial year; or
      (ii) are repayable by instalments the last of which falls due for payment before the expiration of that period;
      and the amount of the interest on loans of other kinds so made (whether on the security of debentures or not);
   (c) the amount of the charge to revenue for United Kingdom corporation tax and, if that amount would have been greater but for relief from double taxation, the amount which it would have been but for such relief, the amount of the charge for United Kingdom income tax and the amount of the charge

for taxation imposed outside the United Kingdom on profits, income and (so far as charged to revenue) capital gains;

(d) the amounts respectively provided for redemption of share capital and for redemption of loans;

(e) the amount, if material, set aside or proposed to be set aside to, or withdrawn from, reserves;

(f) subject to sub-paragraph (2) of this paragraph, the amount, if material, set aside to provisions other than provisions for depreciation, renewals or diminution in value of assets or, as the case may be, the amount, if material, withdrawn from such provisions and not applied for the purposes thereof;

(g) the amounts respectively of income from quoted investments and income from unquoted investments;

(ga) if a substantial part of the company's revenue for the financial year consists in rents from land, the amount thereof (after deduction of ground-rents, rates and other outgoings);

(gb) the amount, if material, charged to revenue in respect of sums payable in respect of the hire of plant and machinery;

(h) the aggregate amount (before deduction of income tax) of the dividends paid and proposed.

(2) The Board of Trade may direct that a company shall not be obliged to show an amount set aside to provisions in accordance with sub-paragraph (1)(f) of this paragraph, if the Board is satisfied that that is not required in the public interest and would prejudice the company, but subject to the condition that any heading stating an amount arrived at after taking into account the amount set aside as aforesaid shall be so framed or marked as to indicate that fact.

(3) If, in the case of any assets in whose case an amount is charged to revenue by way of provision for depreciation or diminution in value, an amount is also so charged by way of provision for renewal thereof, the last-mentioned amount shall be shown separately.

(4) If the amount charged to revenue by way of provision for depreciation or diminution in value of any fixed assets (other than investments) has been determined otherwise than by reference to the amount of those assets as determined for the purpose of making up the balance sheet, the fact shall be stated.

12A. The amount of any charge arising in consequence of the occurrence of an event in a preceding financial year and of any credit so arising shall, if not included in a heading relating to other matters, be stated under a separate heading.

13. The amount of the remuneration of the auditors shall be shown under a separate heading, and for the purposes of this paragraph,

any sums paid by the company in respect of the auditors' expenses shall be deemed to be included in the expression 'remuneration'.

13A. (1) The matters referred to in sub-paragraphs (2) to (4) below shall be stated by way of note, if not otherwise shown.

(2) The turnover for the financial year, except in so far as it is attributable to the business of banking or discounting or to business of such other class as may be prescribed for the purposes of this sub-paragraph.

(3) If some or all of the turnover is omitted by reason of its being attributable as aforesaid, the fact that it is so omitted.

(4) The method by which turnover stated is arrived at.

(5) A company shall not be subject to the requirements of this paragraph if it is neither a holding company nor a subsidiary of another body corporate and the turnover which, apart from this sub-paragraph, would be required to be stated does not exceed £50,000.

14. (1) The matters referred to in the following sub-paragraphs shall be stated by way of note, if not otherwise shown.

(2) If depreciation or replacement of fixed assets is provided for by some method other than a depreciation charge or provision for renewals, or is not provided for, the method with which it is provided for or the fact that it is not provided for, as the case may be.

(3) The basis on which the charge for United Kingdom corporation tax and United Kingdom income tax is computed.

(3A) Any special circumstances which affect liability in respect of taxation of profits, income or capital gains for succeeding financial years.

(5) Except in the case of the first profit and loss account laid before the company after the commencement of this Act the corresponding amounts for the immediately preceding financial year for all items shown in the profit and loss account.

(6) Any material respects in which any items shown in the profit and loss account are affected:
- (a) by transactions of a sort not usually undertaken by the company or otherwise by circumstances of an exceptional or non-recurrent nature; or
- (b) by any change in the basis of accounting.

CHAPTER 10

The Analysis of Company Accounts

Probably the most important regular source of information concerning the activities of a public company is the annual report and accounts, which indicates the trading performance of the past year, states the assets of the company and its sources of finance as at the end of the year, and provides an assessment of its future prospects.

Of this information the accounts themselves are of prime importance, for they supply the main quantitative facts regarding the performance of a company. Unfortunately they are subject to three important defects. In the first place the information provided is far from comprehensive, and excludes much that is of prime importance for an investment analyst. Secondly, there is usually a considerable lapse of time between the end of the trading year of a company and the publication of the accounts relating to that year. P. A. Bird,[1] in a sample survey, found that the average delay between the year-end and the announcement of the preliminary profit figures was about three months, while a further delay of nearly a month ensued before the publication of the full annual report.

Moreover, many companies only publish accounts once a year, so that a whole year passes before shareholders receive any quantitative information regarding the progress of their company. Even then the information is often out of date and this facilitates 'insider trading'. However, it is becoming much more common for companies to prepare half-yearly and even, in a few cases, quarterly reports, so that the information provided is becoming less discontinuous.

Because of the recent improvement in company accounts it is proposed in this chapter to discuss their analysis at two levels:

[1] 'Waiting for the Accounts', *The Accountant*, Jan. 9, 1965, pp. 34-6.

THE ANALYSIS OF COMPANY ACCOUNTS

(1) Where accounts are prepared in accordance with the requirements of the Companies Act 1948, which cover all accounts
for financial years ended before January 27, 1968.

(2) Where the accounts have been prepared in accordance with
the requirements of the Companies Act 1967.

Finally, the deficiencies inherent even in the most informative
accounts will be described and their effects explained.

1. THE ANALYSIS OF ACCOUNTS PREPARED IN ACCORDANCE WITH THE REQUIREMENTS OF THE COMPANIES ACT 1948

The full disclosure requirements of the Companies Act 1948 are
detailed in Chapter 9. A set of accounts prepared in accordance with
these rules is reproduced below:

HYPOTHETICAL PRODUCTS LTD

PROFIT AND LOSS ACCOUNT FOR THE YEAR ENDED DECEMBER 31, 1971

1970		1971
£		£
2,200,000	Trading profit for the year (Note 1)	3,000,000
570,000	Taxation (Note 2)	870,000
1,630,000	Profit for the year after taxation	2,130,000
1,030,000	Dividends (Note 3)	1,130,000
600,000	Retained Profit for the year	1,000,000

NOTES ON THE PROFIT AND LOSS ACCOUNT

	1970	1971
(1) *Trading profit for the year* is after adding:	£	£
Dividends and interest from investments:		
Trade investments	175,000	200,000
Other investments	60,000	75,000
	235,000	275,000
and after charging:		
Depreciation	1,200,000	1,800,000
Auditors' remuneration	15,000	15,000
Directors' remuneration:		
Fees	5,000	5,000
Other emoluments	80,000	100,000
Pensions	10,000	15,000
	95,000	120,000
Interest on debentures	105,000	337,500

	£	£
(2) *Taxation* based on the profit of the year		
Corporation Tax at 40%	550,000	830,000
Overseas taxation	20,000	40,000
	570,000	870,000

	£	£
(3) *Dividends*		
6% Preference Shares Gross	30,000	30,000
Ordinary: Interim 10% (1970 10%) Gross	500,000	500,000
Proposed Final 12% (1970 10%) Gross	500,000	600,000
	1,030,000	1,130,000

BALANCE SHEET AS AT DECEMBER 31, 1971

ASSETS

December 31, 1970			December 31, 1971	
£	£	*Fixed Assets* (Note 1)	£	£
5,000,000		Freehold and leasehold property		8,000,000
4,000,000		Plant, machinery and equipment		5,000,000
1,000,000		Goodwill, patents, trademarks, etc.		1,200,000
10,000,000		*Total Fixed Assets*		14,200,000
2,000,000		*Investments* (Note 2)		2,500,000
		Current Assets		
		Stocks and work in progress		
	5,000,000	(Note 3)	7,000,000	
	4,000,000	Debtors	5,000,000	
		Cash and short-term invest-		
	1,000,000	ments (Note 4)	400,000	
	10,000,000		12,400,000	
		Less: *Current Liabilities*		
	4,870,000	Trade and other creditors	7,160,000	
		Provision for Corporation Tax		
	830,000	(Note 5)	1,340,000	
	500,000	Proposed final dividend gross	600,000	
	6,200,000		9,100,000	
3,800,000		*Net Current Assets*		3,300,000
15,800,000				20,000,000

288

£		£
	FINANCED BY:	
	Share Capital (Note 6)	
500,000	6% Cumulative Preference Stock	500,000
5,000,000	Ordinary stock	5,000,000
5,500,000		5,500,000
	Reserves	
5,000,000	Capital Reserves (Note 7)	6,000,000
3,800,000	Revenue Reserve (Note 8)	4,000,000
	Total Shareholders' Capital and	
14,300,000	Reserves	15,500,000

	Loan Capital		
1,500,000	7% Loan Stock 1975/80 (Unsecured)	1,500,000	
—	7¼% Loan Stock 1986/91 (Unsecured)	3,000,000	4,500,000
15,800,000			20,000,000

Notes on the Balance Sheet

(1) *Fixed Assets*

	Cost or Valuation £	1971 Accumulated Depreciation £	Balance Sheet £
Freehold properties	6,000,000	—	6,000,000
Leasehold properties	2,500,000	500,000	2,000,000
Plant, machinery and equipment	19,000,000	14,000,000	5,000,000
Goodwill, patents, trademarks, etc.	1,200,000	—	1,200,000
	28,700,000	14,500,000	14,200,000

		1970	
Freehold properties	3,500,000	—	3,500,000
Leasehold properties	1,800,000	300,000	1,500,000
Plant, machinery and equipment	16,800,000	12,800,000	4,000,000
Goodwill, patents, trademarks etc.	1,000,000	—	1,000,000
	23,100,000	13,100,000	10,000,000

Freehold and leasehold properties were valued independently on December 31, 1962 and are included in the accounts at that amount. No provision has been made for the depreciation of freehold property. Investment grants received or receivable have been credited to the cost of the assets concerned. Goodwill, patents, trademarks, etc. are included at the directors' valuation as at December 31, 1971.

K

(2) *Investments*

	1970	1971	Market value 1970	1971
	£	£	£	£
Quoted trade investments	1,500,000	2,000,000	2,800,000	3,700,000
Unquoted trade investments	500,000	500,000	—	—
	2,000,000	2,500,000		

(3) *Stock and work in progress* is stated at cost (including a proportion of overhead expenditure in the case of work in progress) in accordance with the regular practice of the company less allowances where appropriate to reduce to net realisable value.

(4) *Cash and short-term investments*

	1970 £	1971 £
British Government Securities (Market value £175,000; 1970 £380,000)	400,000	150,000
Short-term deposits	200,000	—
Bank balances and cash	400,000	250,000
	1,000,000	400,000

(5) *Taxation*

	1970 £	1971 £
U.K. and Overseas taxes:		
Due within one year	250,000	490,000
Due after one year	580,000	850,000
	830,000	1,340,000

(6) *Share Capital* (in units of £1)

	Authorized £	Issued £	Market Price April 6, 1965 for Capital Gains Tax Purposes
6% Cumulative Preference Stock	1,000,000	500,000	18s.
Ordinary Stock	9,000,000	5,000,000	80s.

(7) *Capital Reserves*

	1970 £	1971 £
Fixed Asset Replacement Reserve	1,500,000	1,500,000
Surplus on Revaluation of Freehold and Leasehold Property	1,400,000	1,400,000
Capital Reserve	2,100,000	3,100,000
	5,000,000	6,000,000

The increase in the Capital Reserve was due to profits, less losses, on sales of fixed assets (£200,000) and a transfer from the Revenue Reserve (£800,000).

(8) *Revenue Reserve*	£
Balance at January 1, 1971	3,800,000
Less: Transfer to Capital Reserve	800,000
	3,000,000
Add: Balance of retained profit for the year	1,000,000
Balance at December 31, 1971	4,000,000

(9) *Capital Commitments*
At December 31, 1971 commitments for future capital expenditure amounted to £1,250,000 (1970 £3,000,000) after taking account of Investment Grants receivable amounting to £100,000 (1970 £325,000)

(10) *Contingent Liabilities*
There are contingent liabilities in respect of:
(a) Guarantees to bank of £500,000
(b) Bills of exchange discounted of £12,500
(c) Uncalled capital on certain shares included under trade investments of £55,000

(11) *Rates of Exchange*
The rates of exchange in force at December 31, 1971 have been utilized for the conversion into sterling of all foreign currencies.

(a) EXPLANATION OF THE ACCOUNTS

The accounts are divided into two sections:

(i) *The Profit and Loss Account*

This indicates the trading performance for the period in question. If the result is a profit, it also shows what tax is payable and how the remainder is to be allocated between distributions to the shareholders and retentions by the company. Unfortunately, very little information concerning the composition of the trading profit was required by the Companies Act 1948, the provisions of which only compelled the disclosure of depreciation, interest paid and received, directors' remuneration, the audit fee and any non-recurring factors which contributed to the profit or loss. The Stock Exchange as explained in Chapter 9 requires all companies seeking a quotation to give additional information concerning the contribution of each of its main activities to its trading results, and the geographical spread of its trading operations.

The published profit and loss account normally contains three sections. The first of these shows the amount of net profit before taxation, after adjustment for the various items whose disclosure is compulsory. The second section indicates how the taxation charge has been calculated and concludes with the figure of net profit after taxation. The final section, which is often called the appropriation account, shows how the balance of profit after taxation is allocated between distributions and retentions.

The first section calls for little comment, largely because it contains so little information. The only item which the average investor might have difficulty in comprehending is the charge for depreciation. Accountants and economists are divided as to the purpose of this charge. Some regard it as an attempt to measure the use that a parti-cular trading period has had of the limited life of the fixed asset in question. Each period is thus charged with an appropriate part of the cost of the asset until, by the end of its effective life, it has been totally written off. Others regard depreciation as a method of computing the decline in value of a fixed asset during a particular time period. Theoretically, value is defined for this purpose as the present value of the discounted net income streams which, it is anticipated, will emanate from the future use of the asset.

Finally, depreciation is often conceived as a method of retaining sufficient funds out of the profits of the company to provide for the replacement of fixed assets when they are worn out or obsolete. Where this is intended a company should retain more than the ori-ginal cost of the asset, for, due to inflation, it is almost certain that the replacement asset will cost considerably more than the original. That part of the retention which is based on original cost is regarded by accountants as the provision for depreciation, and will be charged in the first section of the profit and loss account. The re-mainder, which consists of the excess of the replacement price over original cost, is regarded as a reserve, and will be recorded as a retention in the appropriation section of the profit and loss account.

Whichever depreciation concept is adhered to, an annual charge must be made in respect of fixed assets which decline in value through use, though the method of calculation is normally extremely arbit-rary. The most common is the reducing balance method, whereby a constant percentage is chosen for each class of fixed asset and used as the basis for calculating depreciation each year. Thus if 20% were selected as the appropriate rate for a machine which cost £2,000, the depreciation in the first year would be £400 (20% of £2,000), and in the second year £320 (20% of £2,000 − £400), and so on until the machine is scrapped or sold. When this occurs, the scrap value of the sale proceeds will be compared with the written down value of the machine, and the resultant profit or loss will be recorded in the profit and loss account.

The selection of the percentage rate will depend largely upon the speed with which the asset is likely to deteriorate. Thus fixed assets such as land and buildings which are likely to appreciate in value are not normally depreciated. On the other hand, motor vehicles, which tend to deteriorate quickly, are generally depreciated at a rate of 25%. Although the reducing balance method has an advantage in that it charges the earlier years of the life of an asset (which tend to get the most efficient use) with a higher amount of depreciation, as an economic measurement it is arbitrary and unscientific.

The second section of the profit and loss account which shows the composition of the taxation charge and the determination of the net profit after taxation is self-explanatory. The third section, which indicates the manner in which the net profit after taxation is to be appropriated, requires rather more explanation.

The directors of a company may appropriate the balance of net profit in one of three ways:

(a) They may use it to justify the payment of dividends to the members of the company. At the same time they must have regard to the cash resources of the company to ensure that they are sufficient to meet both the dividend and the day-to-day requirements of the company.

(b) They may retain some of the profits to provide a cushion against future unprofitable trading periods. Profits retained in this way are known as revenue reserves and can be used to justify the payment of a dividend in subsequent periods, even though those periods may show a trading loss. Because the reduction of dividends is detrimental to the standing of the company, many companies retain part of their profits to provide stabilization of dividends.

(c) They may permanently retain part of the profits to finance expansion.

Profits which have been retained by a company may be regarded either as revenue reserves or capital reserves. The Eighth Schedule of the Companies Act 1948 defined these two types of reserves as follows:

'The expression "capital reserve" shall not include any amount regarded as free for distribution through the profit or loss account and the expression "revenue reserve" shall mean any reserve other than a capital reserve.'

Basically, then, a revenue reserve is one which is free for distribution in any future year, while a capital reserve indicates profits which have

293

been reinvested permanently in the business. However, with a few statutory exceptions, the directors may convert a capital reserve, or part thereof, into a revenue reserve, and vice versa, so that the distinction is in many ways illusory. Thus, although logic would suggest that profits retained to support future dividends should be designated revenue reserves and that profits retained to finance growth should be categorized as capital reserves, such exact differentiation is very rarely found in practice.

Under the Companies Act 1967 companies are no longer required to distinguish between these two types of reserves. However many companies are likely to retain the distinction in their accounts.

The economic and moral arguments for and against the retention of profits by companies have been examined in considerable detail by A. Rubner,[1] who advocates that companies should be legally compelled to distribute at least three-quarters of their net profits. Although his conclusion is rather utopian he does provide convincing evidence for requiring companies to give detailed justification for any profits which they may retain. The need for this is also made obvious by I. M. D. Little, who, in his famous article 'Higgledy Piggledy Growth',[2] concludes that those companies which retain a relatively high proportion of profits do not grow significantly faster than companies with a high payout ratio. The conclusions of this article are largely confirmed by a more comprehensive study carried out by Little and A. C. Rayner.[3]

Despite the evidence against the indiscriminate retention of profits and the arguments for requiring companies to pass the tests of a capital market when raising new funds, the Government has declared itself to be in favour of the retention of profits. It seems probable that this is an attack on dividend levels rather than a measure to increase the economic efficiency of the corporate sector.

(ii) *The Balance Sheet*

The balance sheet depicts the net assets of the company (after deduction of current liabilities), and the sources of finance which have been used for their acquisition. The different categories of assets are usually shown in descending order of liquidity, so that those which are held on a permanent or long-term basis are shown first and those which are in the form of cash or near-cash come last. The main categories are as follows:

---

[1] *The Ensnared Shareholder* (London: Macmillan, 1965).
[2] *Bulletin of the Oxford University Institute of Statistics* (November, 1962).
[3] *Higgledy Piggledy Growth Again* (Oxford: Basil Blackwell, 1966).

Fixed Assets

These are assets which are held permanently by the business with a view of earning income. Under normal circumstances they will not be sold in the course of trading. Their classification will depend more upon the nature of the company than upon the physical characteristics of the asset. Thus while motor vehicles would be fixed assets in the case of a transport company, they would be regarded as stock, which is a current asset, in the accounts of a motor distributor. Similarly, trade investments held by an industrial company have many of the characteristics of fixed assets, while the same investments held by a financial trust would be regarded as current assets.

The most common categories of fixed assets are land and buildings and plant and machinery.

Land and buildings. The accounting procedures in respect of leasehold land and buildings are very different from those used to record freehold property. Where a premium is paid for the lease, it will be recorded at original cost and depreciated over its life-span. There are two major drawbacks to this procedure. In the first place the premium payable on renewal might be far in excess of the original payment so that the annual depreciation charge may be too small to allow a sufficient replacement provision to be built up. Secondly, the cost of the lease will be well below the market value of the land and buildings which are occupied under its terms. Consequently, investment analysts are unable to determine the market value of the assets utilized by a company and inter-firm profitability comparisons are rendered extremely difficult.

The same difficulty presents itself in a more extreme form where no initial payment is made for the lease. In this case the accounts will give no indication whatsoever of the extent to which the company uses land and buildings in the course of its operations. To enable more accurate inter-firm comparisons to be made, the market value of leasehold land and buildings should be used in computations of capital employed, while the annual rental, suitably adjusted to provide for anticipated future replacement costs of the lease, should be regarded as a fixed-interest commitment. This solution, however, is impracticable in view of the paucity of available information.

In the case of freehold property inflation works in favour of the company, which is the owner of the asset, while with leasehold property, the company benefits during the tenure of the lease, but on its re-negotiation must pay a rental based upon the inflated price level. In terms of theoretical economics there is no distinction between the two types of ownership because the opportunity cost, or current rental value foregone by using the asset oneself, should be regarded as the cost of occupation in either case. In practice, however, freehold property is normally stated at original cost so that any inflation in value is not reflected in the accounts. Thus, as with leasehold property, the value of capital employed is understated and profitability comparisons become meaningless.

The possible understatement of freehold property is the more serious in that this asset is often easily realizable. For instance, a company may have acquired freehold property fifty years ago at £100,000. Under normal accounting procedures this property would still be recorded at £100,000 in the accounts, though it may now be worth several times that amount because of its advantageous location. Admittedly the Companies Act 1967 requires that the attention of members should be drawn to the difference in value, but the section concerned is phrased very loosely and is far from mandatory.

As a result current practice not only encourages the continuance of inefficient management in that the understatement of true capital employed results in an overstatement of the level of profitability, but also has the result that the removal of that management may well benefit, not the shareholders, but a better informed bidder.

In order to overcome these deficiencies many companies have begun to revalue their property at regular intervals. In such cases the balance sheet will state the market value of this asset, while the difference between current value and original cost is entered as a capital reserve among the sources of finance. Such revaluation is relatively expensive, though the valuation once made can be easily adjusted by reference to a price index, and many companies have used the expense to justify the retention of values based on original cost. Unfortunately there is every incentive to inefficient firms to retain these figures for they mask their poor return on capital employed.

Plant and machinery. Plant and machinery is normally stated in the balance sheet at original cost. From this figure the accumulated depreciation which has been written off is shown as a separate deduction. The balance, which purports to indicate the net value of the asset, is a totally meaningless figure for the purposes of analysis.

To illustrate this point the example is taken of a company which uses the following three machines:

	Date of purchase	Cost
First machine	January 1, 1935	£8,000
Second machine	January 1, 1955	£20,000
Third machine	January 1, 1965	£40,000

It is argued, rather improbably, that the three machines are identical and that each has a life of forty years with no scrap value at the date of retirement. For ease of exposition the straight-line method of depreciation is used. Under this method the net cost of the asset (i.e. original cost less expected scrap value) is spread equally over its anticipated life. Thus for the first machine the annual depreciation charge would be

$$\frac{\pounds8,000 - \pounds0}{40} = \pounds200.$$

Similarly, the annual charge on the second and third machines would be £500 and £1,000 respectively.

At December 31, 1969 the accumulated depreciation provision shown as a deduction from original cost will be made up as follows:

First machine	35 years @ £200	= £7,000
Second machine	15 years @ £500	= £7,500
Third machine	5 years @ £1,000	= £5,000
		£19,500

The balance sheet at that date would give the following information:

Plant and Machinery (at cost)	£68,000
Less: Provision for Depreciation	19,500
	£48,500

This method of presentation suffers from three serious deficiencies:

(i) The cost figure of £68,000 is composed of a mixture of three different units of value, namely 1935 pounds, 1955 pounds and 1965 pounds. Due to rises in the price level the 1955 pound is in real terms an entirely different unit of value to a 1935 pound, and, similarly, neither is comparable to a 1965 pound. It is thus clearly misleading to aggregate amounts which are measured in such dissimilar units. The only valid method of measurement is the use of values expressed in current pounds throughout the balance sheet.

(ii) The depreciation charge is invariably based on original cost. Thus a company which acquired a particular machine at an earlier date and at a lower cost than another company would have a lower depreciation charge, even though the machines

297

were identical and the same basis of depreciation was used. Consequently, their profits net of depreciation could not be compared in a meaningful way.

(iii) The most important deficiency of conventional practice is that the calculation of depreciation on the basis of original cost will not result in the establishment of an adequate reserve for replacement in times of inflation. For instance, when the first machine falls due for replacement at the end of 1974 the amounts set aside from profits in the form of depreciation will only total £8,000. By that date, however, the cost of a replacement machine might well have risen to £50,000. Thus, if the company has distributed the full amount of its profits during the intervening years it will not have sufficient funds to replace the machine. As a result it must either raise more capital or reduce the scale of its activities. In effect the company has not maintained its capital intact and has paid some of its dividends out of capital.

In order to overcome this problem some companies retain profits through the establishment of a fixed asset replacement reserve, whose function is to provide for the anticipated excess of replacement cost. Even where this is done the reserve is usually regarded as an appropriation of profit rather than a charge, so that profits will still be overstated.

However, the above example is somewhat unrealistic in that it presupposes an exceptionally steep rate of inflation and ignores technological change. In fact most firms replace machinery with superior equipment and finance replacement out of assets withheld from distribution either in the form of the depreciation charge or as retained profits, without the establishment of a separate replacement reserve. Nevertheless, even under these conditions, the overstatement and over-taxation of profits persists.

In order to overcome the problems inherent in the treatment of plant and machinery, some companies periodically revalue these assets and adjust the balance sheet accordingly. However, in most cases the basis of the revised figure is stated to be 'as revalued by the directors' and this revaluation may range from a genuine assessment of current replacement cost to a false valuation intended merely to enable the company to avoid the accounting complications imposed by the requirement of the Companies Act 1948 to show original cost and accumulated depreciation as separate figures where revaluation has not occurred.

THE ANALYSIS OF COMPANY ACCOUNTS

Investments

The investments held by a company fall into three main categories:

(i) *Investments in subsidiaries.* These will normally be shown in the accounts of the holding company at original cost. Where they are quoted their market value at the balance sheet date must be disclosed. If unquoted, any permanent diminution in value should be provided for, while appreciation is normally ignored. The value of investments in subsidiaries is not of prime importance, for the group accounts will delete the book value of these investments and will state instead the book values of the assets which are controlled thereby. If the cost of control exceeds the book value of the assets taken over the difference is attributed to goodwill, while if the reverse applies a capital reserve is established.

(ii) *Trade investments.* These are made primarily to further or to protect the business of the company rather than to earn income or capital appreciation. A company may, for example, buy large shareholdings in some of its suppliers and customers in order to protect both the source of supply of its raw materials and the market for its finished goods. Companies whose shares are held in this way are often described as associated companies.

(iii) *Other investments.* These are held primarily to obtain a short-run return, whether in the form of income or capital. Normally, they represent the short or medium-term investment of funds which are surplus to immediate needs.

In the case of all three categories the market value of quoted investments at the balance sheet date must be stated in the balance sheet, while unquoted investments should be depreciated where it is felt that a permanent loss of value has been suffered.

At one time it was customary for investments to be shown in the balance sheet as a separate category. However, the current recommendations of the Institute of Chartered Accountants suggest that the following procedures should be adopted in the case of trading companies whose normal business does not involve either dealing in investments or the holding of investments other than in subsidiaries:

'*Classification*

'*Fixed assets.* Investments which it is intended to hold continuously, for example trade investments and interests in subsidiaries, should be classified as fixed assets. Such investments may be distinguished from other fixed assets by showing them under a separate heading. Where interests in associated companies are material they should be stated separately under the general heading of 'Trade investments' or under a heading of their own.

'*Current assets*. Quoted and other readily realizable investments (other than investments which are regarded as fixed assets, even though they may happen to be quoted or readily realizable) should be classified as current assets.

'*Valuation*

'*Diminution in value*. Provision should be made for the diminution in the value of investments:

 (*a*) where the market value at the date of the balance sheet of investments which are current assets is lower than cost
 (*b*) where the value to the business of investments which are fixed assets appears to have decreased permanently below cost.

'*Appreciation in value*. Exceptional circumstances may arise in which an undertaking, wherein an important trade investment is held, has retained and accumulated profits on such a scale that the income which reaches the investor company and the amount at which the investment is carried in the accounts are a wholly inadequate reflection of the value of the investment, although this fact is not apparent from the trade investments item in the balance sheet or from the accounts as a whole. In such circumstances consideration should be given to the question whether the relative importance of the matter is such that without some explanation in the accounts they would fail to show a fair view.'[1]

The treatment of appreciation in value of unquoted investments has since been improved by the requirement of the Companies Act 1967 that their share of undistributed profits should be revealed, though this of course is not the only determinant of the value of an investment.

Current Assets

There are three major categories of current assets:

(i) *Stock*. Stock-in-trade includes raw materials, work-in-progress and finished goods. Normally only the total figure is shown, with no

[1] It is understood that these rules are likely to be revised to take account of the provision of the Companies Act 1967 for the separate disclosure of assets which are neither fixed nor current.

indication of its composition. The correct valuation of stock is extremely important, for the quantity held by many companies is very high compared with the profit figure, so that a relatively small change in the stock figure would have a disproportionately large effect on profits. The two major problems met in calculating the stock figure are the identification and the valuation of items of stock.

The problem of identification arises where quantities of identical items have been acquired at different prices. For example, a garage may have purchased 500 tyres of a particular size during the year at prices ranging from £5 to £7. If at the end of the year 100 are held in stock, the management must decide from which consignment each came in order to determine its cost. The normal procedure is to use the 'first in, first out' method, which assumes that those items which are sold or used in production are those which have been in stock the longest, while those remaining in stock represent the latest acquisitions or batches of production. It is argued that this overstates profits in times of severe inflation,[1] but at least it accords with common sense and gives a realistic balance sheet value. As such it is not on balance inferior to the other methods of identification which are often advocated, such as the 'base stock' and 'last in, first out' methods.

Some firms overcome the problems of identification by applying the same value to all identical stock items regardless of actual cost. This occurs where the 'average cost', 'standard cost', or 'adjusted selling price' methods of valuation are used.

The Institute of Chartered Accountants recommends that stock should be valued at the lower of cost or net realizable value, with replacement cost being substituted for net realizable value where the latter cannot be accurately determined. Thus where net realizable value is lower than cost, the stock will be written down to that figure. However, any excess of net realizable value over cost will be ignored. Thus accountants follow the conservative policy of taking account of unrealized losses, while disregarding unrealized profits, This may result in the understatement of profits, thus to some extent counteracting the overstatement of profits which may occur where the 'first in, first out' method is used.

Although these valuation principles appear to be quite precise, this precision is in most cases quite illusory. As has already been shown, the value of stock may depend upon the method of identification which is adopted. Moreover, in the valuation of work-in-progress and finished goods, many companies include in the cost an oncharge in respect of overheads. The allocation of overheads is an entirely

[1] E.g. Harold S. Bierman Jr., *Financial Accounting Theory* (New York: Macmillan, 1965), Chapter 8.

arbitrary matter and the method used will differ from one company to another. All that the accountant can hope to achieve is the consistent use of a particular method. Finally, the assessment of net realizable value will often depend upon the subjective view that the directors take regarding the future course of trading. This gives them a material discretion over the value of stock and thereby over the level of declared profits.

All in all, the figure of stock can be very misleading for many reasons. In the first place the investor has no information as to the relative importance of raw materials, work-in-progress and finished goods. This is a serious deficiency, for a preponderance of finished goods, taken together with other factors, might indicate difficulty in selling them, while a relatively high level of raw materials and work-in-progress might suggest that the firm is working at full capacity. Furthermore, different methods of valuation may be used by different companies so that their accounts cease to be comparable. This lack of comparability is heightened by the discretion which directors may exercise over the writing-down of stock to take account of a fall in net realizable value below the cost price.

(ii) *Debtors*. The valuation of debtors is a relatively straightforward process so long as the accounting records of the company are adequately maintained. The only serious problem arises in the estimation of bad debts. Here again the management of the company will have considerable influence in the determination of the amount to be provided. The amount by which the bad debts provision as calculated on the year-end debtors exceeds the provision brought forward at the start of the year will be charged to the profit and loss account and will not be shown separately. As a result the profit figure, as was the case with stock valuation, may be influenced by the subjective judgment of the management. Although this is not normally a crucial point there have been many cases, particularly concerning those companies which customarily give a great deal of credit (such as hire purchase companies), where the bad debts provision has proved to be substantially inadequate, with the consequent overstatement of profits in the years concerned.

(iii) *Cash and short-term investments*. The valuation of these assets presents few problems. So long as it is clear that their ownership is vested in the company their face value plus any accumulated interest may be used in the balance sheet provided, of course, that the borrower is of impeccable status. There is, however, a problem in connection with cash and debtors where these are held in foreign currencies. The normal procedure is to convert foreign currencies on the basis of the rates of exchange in force at the balance sheet date, though it is customary to provide for possible losses resulting from a future expected devaluation.

Goodwill, Patents and Trademarks

Although these are regarded by most companies as intangible fixed assets and are grouped with fixed assets in the balance sheet, they are often shown as a distinct category, entirely separate from current or fixed assets. This practice stems back to the days when it was regarded as financial prudence to write them off as quickly as possible. Any balance not written off was not to be thought of as a true asset, but was to be shown separately almost as a fictitious asset. This attitude still prevails and most companies write these items down wherever possible. An examination of their nature will show that this attitude is quite incorrect and has the result, as do so many other accounting conventions, of understating capital employed and overstating profitability.

Goodwill is commonly regarded as the enhancement of the value of a company due to its high reputation, its advantageous siting or its special market connections, and such goodwill is a saleable commodity. Where a company has paid cash for it this represents the employment of capital and, despite its intangible nature, it should be shown in the balance sheet.

However, the figure of goodwill is usually of an entirely different nature and arises where a company acquires shares in a subsidiary at a price higher than the book value of the assets which have been taken over. In these circumstances an asset called goodwill is created in order to bring the value of the assets up to the takeover price. As the takeover price might reasonably be supposed to approximate to the market value of the assets which have been acquired, the establishment of the goodwill account brings the book value of the assets closer to their market value and thus to the amount of capital employed. Nevertheless, this figure is normally written off, with the predictable result that capital employed is understated. Even where it remains in the accounts many financial analysts ignore it in their computation of capital employed.

It is, however, correct to write down the figure of goodwill where a genuine revaluation of assets has been made, for such a valuation will reduce the difference between the cost and the book value of assets acquired.

Patents and trademarks are rather more tangible in nature in that

303

they confer an enforceable legal right upon their holders, and these rights have a definite market value. Nevertheless the practice of writing them down persists. For example, a company may state in its balance sheet that goodwill, patents and trade marks have a value of £1, despite the receipt of substantial amounts in respect of patent royalties and the sale of 'know-how'. Such practice is very common and renders effective inter-company comparisons almost impossible.

Fictitious Assets

Some companies include in the assets side of the balance sheet debit balances which are valueless. The most obvious example is a debit balance on the profit and loss account, which represents accumulated losses, and has no value.[1] This indicates a loss of the shareholders' capital and should be shown as a deduction from that capital. Other debit balances such as research and development expenses carried forward, advertising expenses carried forward, and repairs equalization accounts are more in the nature of intangible assets, and, so long as they are estimated on a genuine and realistic basis, represent capital employed. However, the normal practice is for these items to be written off in the year in which they are incurred in order to endeavour to reduce the tax burden, so that companies which carry them forward in any substantial amount are often viewed with suspicion. This statement does not apply to research and development costs, which confer tax relief whether or not these costs are capitalized.

The remainder of the balance sheet states the sources of finance which have been used to finance the different assets described above. Three main categories of finance are commonly used:

(A) *Shareholders' Capital and Reserves*

As far as the company is concerned finance provided by members' capital and retained profits is almost free of risk, for there is no legal compulsion to pay dividends to the members. However, there are two factors which encourage companies to distribute at least part of their profits. In the first place the standing of a company and, to some extent, that of its directors undoubtedly suffer if dividends are cut. For this reason directors endeavour to maintain dividends wherever possible and will not increase distributions unless it is

[1] This statement is over-simplified in that if these losses were available for tax purposes, they might induce a profit-making company to purchase the firm merely to acquire the accumulated losses.

expected that the new level is maintainable. Furthermore, directors are motivated to pay reasonable dividends by the fear that the shares of their company will be undervalued if dividends are too low with the result that takeover bids might be made for the company. They are thus torn between ploughing back profits up to the hilt, thus expanding their company on the basis of relatively riskless finance, and paying out large dividends in order to boost the market value of the company, thus discouraging takeover bids.

It is commonly argued that a company should regard ordinary share capital and reserves as having a cost equal to the return that investors expect to obtain from shares in the company. This statement is an over-simplification in that it ignores the tax advantages of retained profits, but its acceptance implies a cost of capital for the company far in excess of the fixed return paid on debentures, for the equity holders normally anticipate increased dividends in the medium and long run. Nevertheless, companies continue to satisfy their financial needs from these sources, largely because experience has shown that shareholders will not remove directors save in very extreme circumstances, so that poor distributions do not normally result in their removal. By contrast the failure to meet the cheaper interest commitments on debentures could lead to the liquidation of the company.

The only drawbacks of equity issues are their expense and the fact that they might take control out of the hands of the directors. Retained profits have none of these drawbacks, and this, together with their freedom from legal cost, has encouraged their use. Between 1955 and 1965 non-voting shares were also often used to prevent the extension and dispersion of the voting power of the equity. In recent years, however, both the Stock Exchange and institutional investors have expressed dissatisfaction with non-voting shares, arguing that they are undemocratic in that they give the shareholders no say in the management of a company, despite the fact that they are its legal owners. As a result their issue has virtually ceased, though there are many previous issues which are still in existence.

(B) Loan Capital

The main advantage of such finance is that the interest payment on loans is fixed. Thus, if the company can earn more on the investment of funds in its business than it has to pay in loan interest, profits will rise without any further investment by the shareholders. At the same time inflation works in favour of the company, for profits will tend to rise while the return to loan creditors in respect of both interest and capital is fixed. Moreover, loan interest is deductible for tax purposes so that the gross rate should be reduced by 45% in order to determine the effective cost. Finally the issue of loan capital does not involve any loss of control, for creditors can normally only exercise control when the company fails to meet its obligations.

The major disadvantage of loan capital is that it increases the risk attached to the company. The greater the dependence upon such capital, the greater the possibility that profits might fall to such an extent that a company cannot meet its commitments, with the result that the creditors are empowered to appoint a receiver to take over the entire company or certain specified assets. Thus it is essential for an analyst to obtain full details of the terms of all of the loans of a company with particular regard to the dates specified for repayment and the rights of the creditors in the event of default.

(C) *Medium- and Short-term Loans and Trade Credit*

Medium- and short-term loans have more of the features of loan capital including a similar cost of capital. Medium-term loans are normally resorted to where the level of interest rates is abnormally high and the company does not wish to commit itself to the payment of current rates for too long a period. They may also be used for projects which have a relatively short life or which are expected to return their initial capital fairly quickly. Short-term loans are predominantly used to tide a company over periods in which its liquidity is under strain. The most common type is a bank overdraft, which has the advantage of an interest charge based upon the amount outstanding from one day to another rather than upon the full overdraft limit. On the other hand, overdraft facilities may be withdrawn almost at a moment's notice, so that they should only be utilized to overcome a temporary shortage of funds.

The other common types of short-term finance are trade credit, current taxation and proposed dividends. These have no monetary cost in that no interest charge is made for their use. However, there may be an opportunity cost suffered in the case of trade credit in that a cash discount may be lost if prompt payment is not made. In this event the cost of trade credit is found by relating the discount foregone to the extra period of credit which the firm takes before payment of the full amount of the debt. Regard should always be had to the deleterious effect of over-extended credit upon the status and goodwill of the company.

A further opportunity cost exists in that the company must seek to earn more on these funds within the business than would be obtained from a short-term investment such as Treasury Bills. Finally, although the taxation liability is often shown as a current liability, thus suggesting that it will fall due in the near future, part of the liability is not due for over a year. The tax charge on a company is not normally payable until, on average, eighteen months after the year end, so that all companies with continuing tax liabilities are effectively in receipt of a permanent loan from the Inland Revenue.

(b) THE ANALYSIS OF ACCOUNTS

The most common method of analysis is ratio analysis, which involves the direct comparison of various figures from the accounts of a company in order to provide a series of yardsticks against which its performance and asset structure may be assessed. While such analysis may provide useful material for comparing the efficiency and structure of a particular company from one year to another, its value in the field of inter-company comparison is almost minimal. In fact, due to the inadequate information provided in company accounts, it is almost impossible to undertake a worth-while comparison of different companies. This is due partly to differences in accounting practices in the valuation of assets and the definition of income and partly to the difficulty, in this age of large, diversified groups, of finding companies which are really comparable.

The emphasis of the analysis will depend upon the standpoint of the analyst, shareholders being more concerned with the prospects and worth of their company as a going concern, while creditors are more interested in the cover provided for their fixed interest payments and repayments of capital.

Analysis by Shareholders

The shareholders will analyse two separate aspects of the activities of their company:

(i) Profitability

In the assessment of profitability it is essential to ensure that any unusual and non-recurring profits or losses are excluded, otherwise the trend of profits is obscured. Thus an exceptionally large loss attributable to a trade investment or a non-recurring profit arising from the sale of goodwill ought to be excluded or spread over a period of years. Unfortunately it is impossible to ensure that the profits of different companies have been computed on a comparable

307

basis. For instance one company might write off an exceptionally large advertising campaign in the year in which it takes place, despite the fact that it is expected to give rise to additional sales over several years, while another company might write the expenditure off over the years concerned. Similar differences of treatment might occur in respect of expenditure on research and development, renovations and redundancy payments.

In view of the paucity of information in the profit and loss account there is little that can be done apart from comparing each expense with the profit figure. Thus depreciation and directors' remuneration might be compared with the figure of profit before charging those items while taxation could be related to the net trading profit before tax. This latter ratio is important for it indicates the proportion of profits paid out in taxation, the trend of which may be attributable either to changes in rates or to switching between geographical areas.

The most common measure of profitability is the ratio of profit to capital employed. There are four separate ratios which are commonly used in this connection:

(A) $$\frac{\text{Profit before deduction of tax and debenture interest}}{\frac{1}{2} \text{ (Value of share capital, reserves and loan capital at the start of the year plus value of share capital, reserves and loan capital at the end of the year)}}$$

This shows the pre-tax return on the average permanent capital used by the company during the year.

(B) $$\frac{\text{Pre-tax profit after deduction of debenture interest and grossed-up preference dividend}}{\frac{1}{2} \text{ (Value of equity at the start of the year plus value of equity at the end of the year)}}$$

This indicates the return before tax earned on the average value of the equity. The equity represents the finance provided by the ordinary shareholders and consists of the ordinary share capital and the reserves of the company. The preference dividend must be grossed-up at the current rate of corporation tax because it is not deductible from profits in the computation of that tax.

(C) $$\frac{\text{Net profit after tax plus debenture interest net of corporation tax}}{\frac{1}{2} \text{ (Value of share capital, reserves and loan capital at the start of the year plus value of share capital, reserves and loan capital at the end of the year)}}$$

(D) $\qquad$ Net profit after tax less gross preference dividend $\qquad$

$\frac{1}{2}$ (Value of equity at the start of the year plus value of equity at the end of the year)

The above two ratios show respectively the after-tax return on the average overall capital employed during the year and the average equity employed.

In order to illustrate the calculation and interpretation of these ratios, those for Hypothetical Products Ltd are computed below for 1966 and 1967 on the assumption that the share capital, reserves and loan capital at the start of 1966 stood as follows:

	£
6% Cumulative Preference Stock	500,000
Ordinary Stock	5,000,000
Capital Reserves	5,000,000
Revenue Reserves	3,500,000
	14,000,000
7% Loan Stock 1975/80	1,500,000
	£15,500,000

For ease of computation corporation tax is taken at the rate of 40% throughout.

(A) *1970* $\quad \dfrac{2,200,000 + 105,000}{\frac{1}{2}(15,500,000 + 15,800,000)} = \dfrac{2,305,000}{15,650,000} = 14\cdot7\%$

1971 $\quad \dfrac{3,000,000 + 337,500}{\frac{1}{2}(18,800,000 + 20,000,000)} = \dfrac{3,337,500}{19,400,000} = 17\cdot2\%$

The average permanent capital employed by the company during 1970 was £15,650,000, assuming, of course, that the increased capital became available at a constant rate throughout the year. The pretax return to this capital was £2,305,000. This figure includes £105,000 debenture interest which, although an expense for accounting purposes, represents a return on the debenture capital, £1·5 m. of which is included in the denominator of the ratio. On this basis the rate of return for 1970 was 14·7%.

At the beginning of 1971 a further £3 m. of debenture finance was raised, evidenced by the fact that a full year's interest was paid during 1971. The funds were thus utilized by the firm throughout the year and should be added to the figure of loan capital at the start of the year. The gross return on average capital employed rose to 17·2%. An investor must enquire whether this is due to exceptional trading conditions or whether it represents a lasting upward trend in efficiency. Moreover, he must have regard to the trend of profitability over a much longer period than two years.

$$\text{(B)} \quad 1970 \qquad \frac{2,200,000 - \left(30,000 \times \dfrac{100}{100-40}\right)}{\frac{1}{2}(13,500,000 + 13,800,000)} = \frac{2,150,000}{13,650,000} = 15\cdot75\%$$

$$1971 \qquad \frac{3,000,000 - \left(30,000 \times \dfrac{100}{100-40}\right)}{\frac{1}{2}(13,800,000 + 15,000,000)} = \frac{2,950,000}{14,400,000} = 20\cdot5\%$$

These figures reveal that the average equity rose from £13,650,000 in 1970 to £14,400,000 in 1971. Profits attributable to the ordinary shareholders increased from £2,150,000 to £2,950,000 representing a rise in profitability from 15·75% to 20·5%. This is the return after payment of prior charges, which are those charges, such as debenture interest and preference dividends, which must be met before a dividend may be paid on the ordinary shares. It is higher than that on the overall capital employed because the prior charges are limited to a fixed amount. Any surplus of earnings on the fixed-interest capital over these rates accrues to the ordinary shareholders and increases the return on the equity. It thus benefits the ordinary shareholders if a company expands by means of fixed-interest finance for, so long as it earns more from the investment of those funds than it has to pay as interest, the equity earnings will increase. At the same time, however, the security of the equity will be reduced for if profits are insufficient to cover the prior charges the dividend may be cut or the company may be forced into liquidation.

$$\text{(C)} \quad 1970 \qquad \frac{1,630,000 + \left(105,000 \times \dfrac{60}{100}\right)}{\frac{1}{2}(15,500,000 + 15,800,000)} = \frac{1,693,000}{15,650,000} = 10\cdot8\%$$

$$1971 \qquad \frac{2,130,000 + \left(337,500 \times \dfrac{60}{100}\right)}{\frac{1}{2}(18,800,000 + 20,000,000)} = \frac{2,332,500}{19,400,000} = 12\cdot0\%$$

$$\text{(D)} \quad 1970 \qquad \frac{1,630,000 - 30,000}{\frac{1}{2}(13,500,000 + 13,800,000)} = \frac{1,600,000}{13,650,000} = 11\cdot7\%$$

$$1971 \qquad \frac{2,130,000 - 30,000}{\frac{1}{2}(13,800,000 + 15,000,000)} = \frac{2,100,000}{14,400,000} = 14\cdot6\%$$

These percentages reveal the net return on the overall capital employed as 10·8% in 1970 and 12·0% in 1971 and that on the average equity as 11·7% and 14·6% in 1970 and 1971 respectively. Again the equity earnings are at a higher rate than the overall earnings for the reasons stated above. For the purpose of efficiency comparisons it is often argued that the gross of tax return should be used, because the trend of profitability might be altered due to a change in tax rates which is entirely outside the control of the firm. On the other hand, where the Government is using discriminatory taxation to encourage investment in different areas and in different types of machinery the net of tax return will show how well a company has taken advantage of the various methods available to reduce its tax burden.

Certainly, as far as the return on the equity is concerned, it is the after-tax profits which are most important for it is this profit which is available for distribution, the gross dividend being payable out of the net profits.

Whatever view is taken concerning the choice between pre-tax and after-tax profits there are several other major problems which are commonly encountered in the computation of the return on capital employed:

(1) It is important to ensure that the figure of average capital employed is computed on a comparable basis. For instance, a new issue of shares or debentures at the end of the financial year should be excluded for those funds were not used during the year. Similarly any large-scale capital expenditure during the year which will not produce profits until future years ought to be excluded or, at least, taken into account when analyzing the trend of profitability. Finally, changes in reserves due to accounting adjustments such as the revaluation of fixed assets will cause a break in the profitability trend and should be spread over the years to which they relate.

(2) There is a considerable conflict of opinion over the components of capital employed. Some analysts advocate that the figure of total assets should be used, while others argue that current liabilities should be deducted. Probably the best compromise is the deduction of trade creditors, current taxation and proposed dividend, for these tend to be free of interest and fluctuate from day to day in the same way as the current assets. A relatively permanent bank overdraft, which appears to be part of the long-run financing structure of the business, ought to be included in capital employed. Very often, in fact, companies issue debentures in order to replace or reduce their bank overdraft and the trend of profitability thereafter would not otherwise be comparable with the previous trend.

311

Another component of capital employed which has occasioned much dissension is goodwill. It is generally argued that intangible assets should be excluded because their value is dependent entirely upon the profitability of the business. However, as explained above, the figure of goodwill in company accounts normally represents the excess of the cost of subsidiary companies over the book value of their assets. This cost is an employment of capital and the exclusion of goodwill would lead to the understatement of capital employed. The writing down of patents and research and development costs without regard to their earning capacity, although this practice is accepted as commercially prudent, will result in a similar understatement.

(3) The most difficult problem is the lack of comparability between companies. It is extremely hard in this age of diversification to find companies whose activities are exactly comparable. For instance two companies might make the same group of products, but in different proportions; or they might be in the same industry, but catering for different classes of consumer within that industry. More probably, however, only some of their products are similar, the remainder being quite uncomparable.

Even if two exactly comparable companies were found there remains the problem that their figures of profit and capital employed may be distorted by differences in accounting practice. One company may have recently revalued its fixed assets, thus increasing the capital employed, while the other has retained those assets at original cost and has also written down goodwill so that capital employed is substantially understated.

Similarly one company may own its fixed assets, while another leases them with the result that no indication of the existence, let alone the value of those assets is given in the balance sheet. Although this factor is not detrimental to the calculation of the return to the equity it does prevent an adequate assessment of operating efficiency on the basis of overall capital employed. In this connection the rent should be regarded as a prior charge and the market value of the asset added to capital employed. Even then allowance must be made for anticipated increases in rents or premiums to be paid on impending renewals of leases.

A further confusing factor is the profusion of methods of accounting for investment grants. Some companies take credit for these immediately, while others spread them over the anticipated life of the asset concerned.

It may thus be doubted whether adequate comparisons of efficiency can be made between different companies on the basis of ratio

312

analysis, and shareholders tend to pay less attention to the return on overall capital employed and more to the return on the equity, based not upon the book value of the equity, but its stock market value. This gives the earnings yield, as described in Chapter 12, which has the advantage of incorporating at least an approximation to the market value of the assets employed into the calculation of the yield.

However, although a direct comparison of the return to overall capital employed in different companies cannot be made, ratio analysis is not useless. It is still possible to ascertain long-run trends in the profitability of single companies even though the absolute rate of return cannot be determined with any accuracy. Moreover, a comparison of the direction and rate of growth of the profitability trend of different companies may be made, so long as the results are used with the utmost caution.

(ii) *Asset Structure*

The predominant facet of the asset structure of a company is the extent of its working capital, which is defined as the excess of current assets over current liabilities. This may be measured by two ratios:

Working capital ratio. This is calculated by dividing current liabilities into current assets. If the ratio is higher than unity the current assets exceed the current liabilities which implies that the firm can meet its liabilities as they fall due for payment. In the accounts under consideration the ratios for 1970 and 1971 would be computed as follows:

$$1970 \quad \frac{10,000,000}{6,200,000} = 1 \cdot 6$$

$$1971 \quad \frac{12,400,000}{9,100,000} = 1 \cdot 4$$

Too much reliance should not be placed upon the absolute value of these figures for their amount, though not their direction from unity, may be affected by paying off liabilities or allowing them to accumulate towards the end of the accounting period. For instance a firm with £80,000 current assets and £40,000 current liabilities just before the year end might pay off £20,000 of its creditors thus reducing its liquid assets to £60,000 and its current liabilities to £20,000 and increasing the working capital ratio from 2 to 3. Furthermore it is necessary to ensure that current assets and liabilities are correctly stated in the balance sheet. Some companies, for example, show taxation payable more than one year hence as a current liability and it may be argued that this should not be included in the working capital ratio. In the computation above, taxation due after one year amounting to £580,000 and £850,000 in 1970 and 1971 respectively (see Note 5 to the accounts) is contained under current liabilities. If these amounts are deleted the ratios for 1970 and 1971 become 1·8 and 1·5.

A further adjustment should be made where quoted investments are shown under current assets at book value. Where this occurs market value should be substituted for book value in the computation of the ratios.

Acid test or quick assets ratio. The major drawback to the working capital ratio as a test of liquidity is that stock is included among the current assets, despite the fact that it may not be realizable. The value of stock is primarily dependent upon future sales. If these sales are not forthcoming and stock is sold under pressure in order to meet current liabilities, it is unlikely to realize its book value.

The acid test recognizes the relative illiquidity of stock and measures liquidity by comparing current assets less stock with current liabilities. If this more stringent test provides a result greater than unity the immediate state of the company's liquidity is sound. The ratios of the company under consideration are:

$$1970 \quad \frac{10,000,000 - 5,000,000}{6,200,000 - 580,000} = 0·9$$

$$1971 \quad \frac{12,400,000 - 7,000,000}{9,100,000 - 850,000} = 0·7$$

The quick assets are thus insufficient to meet current liabilities, with the result that the company is dependent upon future sales to maintain its liquidity. This is not serious so long as the level of sales at present prices is maintained. If, on the other hand, a slump in sales is predicted the company may well require further finance.

The major drawback to the liquidity ratios is that they are purely static and do not explain what has occasioned a change in working capital. In order to analyze the factors which have caused the change in the liquidity position a *statement of sources and dispositions of working capital or of cash* should be prepared.

Such a statement can easily be prepared from the accounts of Hypothetical Products Ltd. The sources of working capital were as follows:

314

	£
Profit for the year	2,130,000
Depreciation	1,800,000
	3,930,000
New issue of debentures	3,000,000
	£6,930,000

Depreciation has to be added back to the profit of the year, for its deduction is purely a book entry between the profit and loss account and the fixed asset accounts, and has no effect upon working capital.

The uses to which these funds were put during the year were:

	£
Acquisitions of fixed assets (net)	5,800,000
Acquisitions of trade investments	500,000
Dividends for the year	1,130,000
	£7,430,000

The figure of acquisitions of fixed assets represents the net surplus of purchases over sales. Due to the lack of information given in accounts it is often impossible to determine the cost of purchases and receipts from sales. It is thus impossible to estimate either the current level of capital expenditure or the extent to which it is being financed by disposals of fixed assets.

In the example above the surplus of the cost of fixed assets purchased over the original cost of fixed assets sold is shown in Note 1 to the balance sheet as £5,600,000 (i.e. £28,700,000 − £23,100,000). In order to compute the cash effect of these acquisitions this figure must be increased by £200,000 due to the fact that the cash receipts from sales were £200,000 less than their original cost, so that the cash value of acquisitions was understated by that amount. This sum of £200,000 is comprised of two elements. In the first place the addition of the depreciation charge for the year (£1,800,000) to the accumulated provision at the start of the year (£13,100,000) gives a total £400,000 in excess of the accumulated provision at the end of the year (£14,500,000). The excess represents depreciation on assets sold during the year and must be deducted from the original cost in order to determine their written down value at the date of sale. Then Note 7 states that profits of £200,000 which arose on the sale of fixed assets were transferred to capital reserves. Thus the

315

cash received from the sale of fixed assets was £200,000 more than their written down value and consequently £200,000 (£400,000 – £200,000) less than their original cost.

Although the Companies Act 1967 provides for the disclosure of separate figures for profits and sales, only the original cost of assets sold will normally be shown. In the absence of information relating to the accumulated depreciation on those assets and the profits or losses arising from their sale it will still be difficult to determine exactly the impact on liquidity of transactions in fixed assets.

In the example above the excess of dispositions of working capital over the sources amounts to £500,000 and explains the fall in working capital from £3,800,000 to £3,300,000.

The importance of this statement is that it enables an investor to analyze the funds which became available to a company during a particular trading period and the manner in which they were invested. Taken in conjunction with details of capital commitments from the notes to the balance sheet and with the forecast of future profits which is usually given in the chairman's statement any potential strain on the liquidity of the company may be foreseen.

A statement of sources and dispositions of cash is still more helpful in the analysis of liquidity. This gives the same information as the statement described above, but also reveals the effect upon cash of changes in the assets and liabilities of which working capital is comprised. Such a statement for Hypothetical Products Ltd would appear as below:

Sources of Cash	£
Profit for the year	2,130,000
Depreciation	1,800,000
Issue of debentures	3,000,000
Increase of trade creditors	2,290,000
Increase in taxation provision	510,000
Increase in outstanding amount of final dividend	100,000
	9,830,000
Disposition of Cash	
Acquisitions of fixed assets	5,800,000
Acquisitions of trade investments	500,000
Dividends for the year	1,130,000
Increase in holdings of stocks	2,000,000
Increase in credit given to debtors	1,000,000
	10,430,000

THE ANALYSIS OF COMPANY ACCOUNTS

The excess of dispositions over sources totals £600,000 and explains the fall in cash and short-term investments from £1,000,000 to £400,000. Although these figures must be taken with some caution, especially where the year-end asset structure is not typical of that maintained by the company during the year, they do indicate the possible areas of liquidity strain. The analyst must ask many questions. Is the expansion of fixed assets likely to continue at the present level? If so, will profits rise sufficiently to provide the requisite funds or will recourse be had to further debenture issues? In this connection the fact that no charge appears to exist against the property of the company augurs well for the use of mortgage finance. Are stocks likely to expand at the present rate and, if so, will further credit be available from trade creditors to finance both stocks and any future increase in the credit given to customers? Is the stock figure representative of the entire year, or are higher or lower stocks held for most of the year?

In addition to those ratios which are used in the assessment of liquidity there are several other ratios which are commonly advocated by investment analysts in the examination of other aspects of the asset structure of a company:

Ratio of stock to net current assets. This measures the extent to which working capital is comprised of stock. A relatively high ratio would suggest that the quantity of stock is too high having regard to the financial resources of the company, while a low ratio might indicate that the company is over-liquid and is not making the best use of its cash. The figure must be viewed in relation to that of other firms in the same industry having regard to seasonal factors and to any capital commitments which might account for a build-up of cash resources.

In the accounts under consideration the ratio is:

$$1970 \quad \frac{5,000,000}{3,800,000+580,000} = 1 \cdot 1$$

$$1971 \quad \frac{7,000,000}{3,300,000+850,000} = 1 \cdot 7$$

These figures suggest that the level of stock is becoming high relative to working capital with possibly serious implications for liquidity. If sales figures were available the stock figure could be compared with sales to ensure that stock was not growing disproportionately. Also sales could be related to total assets to discover whether the company might be overtrading.

317

Ratio of fixed assets to net worth. Net worth represents the stake of shareholders in the company and consists of preference and ordinary share capital plus reserves. Alternatively it may be regarded as total assets less external liabilities, both current and long-term. The ratio indicates the extent to which fixed assets are financed by members of the company. A high ratio suggests that fixed assets are financed at least in part by creditors with consequent pressure on liquidity when repayment is demanded. A low ratio is much safer for both members and creditors, though if it is too low this might indicate that the assets representing the net worth are too liquid and have not been sufficiently invested in productive resources.

This ratio, however, can be very misleading when comparisons are made between different companies for some will own their fixed assets, including them in the ratio, while others rent them, thus excluding them. In the same way differences in the treatment of depreciation and investment grants and dissimilar revaluation policies can lead to distorted comparisons. Finally, even a very high ratio may be justified if the excess of fixed assets over net worth is financed by a long-term creditor stock whose income is adequately covered.

The calculations for Hypothetical Products Ltd, regarding trade investments as fixed assets, appear as below:

$$1970 \qquad \frac{10,000,000+2,000,000}{14,300,000} = 0.8$$

$$1971 \qquad \frac{14,200,000+2,500,000}{15,500,000} = 1.1$$

In 1970 the net worth more than covered fixed assets, but this was reversed in 1971. However, the surplus of fixed assets was financed by a long-term issue of loan stock, while some of the trade investments might be easily realized in the event of a liquidity crisis.

Ratio of fixed assets to total assets. Too high a figure for this ratio might suggest that the company is expanding too rapidly with consequent pressure upon liquidity, while a low figure could indicate the under-utilization of funds in productive resources. Inter-firm comparisons on the basis of this ratio are subject to distortion on account of differences in the balance sheet presentation of fixed assets. Moreover, extremely misleading results can be given due to the omission of current liabilities. One company may have a high figure of current assets, but a still higher level of current liabilities.

Despite this the ratio might suggest that current assets were being under-employed. By contrast a second company might have relatively few current assets, but no current liabilities. Nevertheless, the indiscriminate use of the ratio would suggest that the latter company had over-expanded and was facing liquidity problems.

The relevant figures for Hypothetical Products Ltd are:

$$1970 \quad \frac{10,000,000 + 2,000,000}{12,000,000 + 10,000,000} = 0 \cdot 54$$

$$1971 \quad \frac{14,200,000 + 2,500,000}{16,700,000 + 12,400,000} = 0 \cdot 57$$

Although these figures reveal that fixed assets have remained a constant proportion of total assets, their contribution to net assets has increased considerably due to the disproportionate increase in current liabilities.

Ratio of liabilities to net worth. This reveals the relative contribution of creditors and members to the assets of the company. If it gives a value greater than unity, creditors have supplied most of the funds with potentially serious consequences should the company default. If the value is relatively low the financing policies of the company may be too conservative and recourse could be had to cheaper, but more risky, creditor sources of finance. In the analysis of this ratio regard should always be had to the proportion of long-term and current liabilities in total liabilities. A high level of current liabilities would have serious implications for liquidity, while a predominance of long-term liabilities might suggest a risky capital structure. The ratio may understate total liabilities due to the omission of rented assets, which are effectively financed on the basis of a perpetual loan, and net worth due to the undervaluation of fixed assets.

The ratios for the company under consideration are:

$$1970 \quad \frac{6,200,000 + 1,500,000}{14,300,000} = 0 \cdot 54$$

$$1971 \quad \frac{9,100,000 + 4,500,000}{15,500,000} = 0 \cdot 88$$

The proportion of creditor financing has clearly increased during 1971. The contribution of long-term creditors to this increase is not critical, for the interest on these loans is well covered by annual profits. The increase in current liabilities, however, may have more serious implications. It should be appreciated that this ratio tends to understate the contribution of members due to the persistent undervaluation of assets. There is, for instance, a good case for increasing fixed assets and net worth in this and the other ratios by the excess of market value of quoted trade investments over their book value.

One further exercise which is frequently performed by analysts is the *computation of net assets per ordinary share*. At the end of 1970 the book value of the equity was £13·8 m. The ordinary share capital was comprised of five million shares, indicating a book value of assets per share of about 275p. However, the market value of quoted trade investments at that date exceeded the book value by £1·3 m. thus suggesting a value of £15·1 m. for the equity and a figure of 300p for assets per share. By the end of 1971 the value of the equity had risen to £16·7 m., including £1·7 m. in respect of the excess of the market value of quoted trade investments over their book value. This would indicate assets per share of nearly 335p. Comparisons between the figure of assets per share and the market value of a share can be very misleading, for the assets per share are based upon book values, while the market value is primarily determined by the earning capacity of the assets. If the market value substantially exceeds the assets per share this may indicate either that the book value of the assets is considerably lower than their current value or that the earning power of the company is so great that the assets have a going-concern value far in excess of their replacement cost. Where, on the other hand, the value of assets per share is well in excess of the market value of the share, this is a signal either that the assets have been under-depreciated or that their earning capacity is poor. In these circumstances the fact that assets per share exceed the market value is only relevant to a shareholder if the assets are capable of being adapted to more profitable uses either under the existing management or a takeover bidder.

Analysis by Creditors

Although creditors are, like shareholders, interested in the profitability of a company they are more concerned with the extent to which profit covers the prior charges than with the absolute level of profit. Each class of creditor would compare the profit with the amount of interest payable to that class having regard to the fact that other groups of creditors may have priority.

The accounts of Hypothetical Ltd show that only two groups of creditors are entitled to interest—the holders of the 7% Loan Stock 1975/80 and the 7¾% Loan Stock 1986/91. If the terms of the loan gave priority of payments of interest to the holders of the first stock the interest cover for the two issues would be:

7% Loan Stock 1975/80

$$\frac{\text{Gross trading profit}}{\text{Gross interest}} = \frac{3,000,000}{105,000} = 28 \cdot 6 \text{ times}$$

7¾% Loan Stock 1986/91

$$\frac{\text{Gross trading profit}}{\text{Gross interest}} = \frac{3,000,000}{337,500} = 8 \cdot 9 \text{ times}$$

The second stock has lower cover because the interest on the first stock has priority. If both have equal priority, £337,500 must be paid out before either stock receives the due interest in full and the cover for each is 8·9 times. This indicates that gross profits could fall to nearly one-ninth of their present level without causing the company to default. If this is unlikely to occur, then the cover for the interest is adequate.

A creditor is also concerned with the asset cover for his loan. If it is secured upon a specific asset then the market value of that asset should be estimated and compared with the amount of the loan. If not, the assets which have not been specifically charged should be valued and compared with the total of creditors, having regard to their order of priority and to the fact that the security given to secured creditors may not realize sufficient to repay their loan, in which case they may have a claim against the remaining assets.

Clearly it is impossible to assess the break-up value of the assets of a company on the basis of information given in accounts, for some assets such as land and buildings may realize more than their book value, while stock and plant and machinery would be unlikely to achieve more than a fraction of book value. For this reason the calculation of asset cover is normally made on the basis of book value and should be interpreted with considerable caution.

At December 31, 1971 the assets of Hypothetical Products Ltd had a total book value of £29·1 m., which should be increased by £1·7 m. in respect of quoted trade investments. In the event of liquidation certain debts, such as corporation tax, wages, national insurance stamps, etc., would have absolute priority. If these pre-ferred creditors are assumed to amount to £1·6 m. and if the first

L

loan stock issue has been given priority over the second in the event of liquidation the asset cover for each issue would be:

7% *Loan Stock 1975/80*

$$\frac{29,100,000 + 1,700,000}{1,600,000 + 1,500,000} = 9 \cdot 9 \text{ times}$$

7¾% *Loan Stock 1986/91*

$$\frac{29,100,000 + 1,700,000}{3,100,000 + 3,000,000} = 5 \cdot 0 \text{ times}$$

If the assets realized up to one-fifth of their book value the company would be able to pay in full all of its preferred creditors and the holders of the two issues of loan stock. The relatively high proportion of freehold property, quoted investments and debtors suggests that the company would have little difficulty in obtaining at least one-fifth of the book value of its assets in a liquidation. The loan stock holders thus have little to fear, though there is always the possibility that the directors of the company might, in the event of trading difficulties, mortgage the property, sell off the trade investments and run down the liquid assets. Although such actions would normally become quickly apparent, the only remedy open to the debenture holders before default actually occurred would be to sell their stocks on the market.

It is the trade creditors who normally bear the greatest risk of loss in the event of a liquidation. Their vulnerability may be measured by the ratio of total assets to creditors. At December 31, 1971 this ratio was:

$$\frac{30,800,000}{13,000,000} = 2 \cdot 4 \text{ times}$$

The above figure of creditors excludes the amount of the proposed final dividend, for this is a debt due to the members and would not be paid in the event of an immediate liquidation. In this instance the creditors seem to be secure. However trade creditors are clearly in a more vulnerable position and, apart from the members, are most likely to suffer in the event of the failure of a company. For this reason they are concerned with the maintenance of the company as a going concern, for only then will they receive the full amount due to them. Thus they have an incentive to give further credit to a company which is in difficulties in the hope that it will recover and pay its debts in full.

THE ANALYSIS OF COMPANY ACCOUNTS

2. THE ANALYSIS OF ACCOUNTS PREPARED IN ACCORDANCE WITH THE COMPANIES ACT 1967

Probably the most important information from the viewpoint of the investment analyst required by the Companies Act 1967 is:

(a) Turnover, with details of exports.

(b) Split of turnover and profits between different classes of business.

(c) Average number of employees and amount of wages.

(d) Details of directors' salaries.

(e) Details of subsidiaries.

(f) Assets and profits attributable to unquoted investments.

(g) Date of revaluation of any revalued fixed assets.

(h) Cost of hire of plant and machinery.

(i) Details of directors' interests in shares and changes therein.

(j) Details of persons with interest in more than 10% of share capital.

(k) Identity of ultimate parent company, if any and if known.

Items (a) to (d) above provide more information regarding the operating performance of the company, while (e) to (h) enable a better picture of the assets employed to be constructed and (i) to (k) provide for the disclosure of more information concerning the membership of the company.

(a) Turnover is the most important single piece of information and permits the use of a series of important ratios:

$$\text{(i)} \quad \frac{\text{Gross trading profit}}{\text{Sales}} \times 100$$

This reveals the percentage profit margin earned on the sales of the company. Normally a high margin is preferable, for an upward movement of direct costs would have a more detrimental effect on a firm with a low margin. On the other hand, a cut in direct costs would have a more beneficial effect for such a firm. In fact, a company with a low profit margin is in a very similar position to a company with a highly geared financial structure. A greater percentage of its income is taken up with operating charges and any change in those charges would have an inflated impact on profit. For instance, one company may have a gross profit of £250,000 composed of sales of £1,000,000 less operating expenses of £750,000. A second company might have the same gross profit comprised of sales of £2,500,000 less expenses of £2,250,000. The gross profit margin of the first company is 25% while that of the second is 10%. If operating costs

323

rose by 10% the costs of the first company would become £825,000 and profit would fall to £175,000, a percentage fall of 33%

$$\text{(i.e.} \frac{250,000 - 175,000}{250,000} \times 100\text{).}$$

If the costs of the second company rose by the same percentage they would total £2,475,000 and profits would fall to £25,000 representing a percentage fall of 90%

$$\text{(i.e. } \frac{250,000 - 25,000}{250,000} \times 100\text{).}$$

On the other hand a reduction in costs would have a similarly inflated effect on a company with a low margin, so if increased efficiency and cost reductions were expected such a company may be more attractive.

Although a higher profit margin might seem preferable, other factors must be taken into account. For instance a company with a lower margin may have a dynamic sales policy and may earn a large profit because the turnover is more than sufficient to counteract its low profitability. Alternatively, a company with a high margin might be a vertically integrated firm, in which case the entire profit of all of the individual processes is attained against the selling price of the finished product. A firm which only undertook the last stage of the production process would have a much smaller margin for it would not earn the profit engendered by the earlier stages.

$$\text{(ii)} \quad \frac{\text{Sales}}{\text{Net assets employed}}$$

This ratio shows the extent to which a firm is using its assets to generate sales. If it gives a low figure it suggests that the assets are under-employed, while too high a figure indicates that the firm is over-trading and that the volume of turnover is not supported by a sufficiently broad asset base. 'Net assets employed' in this ratio is defined as the average during the year of fixed assets plus current assets minus current liabilities. This ratio and the previous one can be used for the derivation of the ratio of gross profit to overall capital employed

$$\frac{\text{Sales}}{\text{Net assets employed}} \times \frac{\text{Gross profit}}{\text{Sales}} \times 100 = \frac{\text{Gross profit}}{\text{Net assets employed}} \times 100$$

This equation is important for it shows the relative contributions of turnover and profit margins to the overall return on capital.

If sales are high and the profit margin low, the best scope for increasing profitability is by reducing costs, for an increase in sales might result in over-trading, while an increase in selling price might lead to a fall in sales. Over-trading must be avoided for as sales increase relative to net assets, so stock and debtors increase together with trade creditors and bank overdrafts. If a slump ensues, with stock becoming more difficult to sell and debtors less prompt to pay, there could be a liquidity crisis for the company.

If the return on capital is comprised of low sales and a high profit percentage there is scope for increasing sales either with or without a price reduction. On the other hand operating efficiency, though clearly beneficial, may not have so marked an effect. All in all, the analyst should examine the constituent factors in the return to capital and should estimate in the light of other information concerning the elasticity of demand for the products, the prospects for the market involved and the scope for greater efficiency, what are the prospects for profitability. In particular he should have regard to current trends in the ratio of sales to net assets and in the profitability of sales. Although due to differences in circumstances and definitions between companies, direct inter-firm comparison in these areas is very difficult, at least the direction and strength of trends may be compared.

(iii) $$\frac{\text{Sales}}{\frac{1}{2}(\text{Stock at start of year} + \text{stock at end of year})} = \text{Number of times that stock is turned over during the year.}$$

(iv) $$\frac{\frac{1}{2}(\text{Stock at start of year} + \text{stock at end of year})}{\text{Sales}} \times 12 = \text{Number of months for which stock is held on average.}$$

These two ratios are used to analyze the size of stock in relation to sales and the trend of stock turnover. The level of stock held by a company is very important, for certain costs, such as storage and finance costs, tend to vary directly with the stock level, as does the risk of deterioration and obsolescence.

It should be appreciated that the results given by these ratios are not exact. To achieve this the average stock which is normally valued at cost should be related to cost of goods sold, thus removing the distorting influence of profit. Moreover, regard should be had to seasonal factors which cause the year-end stock to be unrepresentative of the stock levels held during the year. Finally, inter-firm analysis is made difficult by variances in the relative contribution of raw materials, work-in-progress and finished goods in the stocks

325

of different companies and by differences in methods of stock valuation. One company, for example, might include an overhead allocation in the valuation of work-in-progress, while another includes only direct costs.

Nevertheless, these figures indicate the volatility of stock. If it is being turned over less frequently this would suggest that the firm is holding too much stock or is experiencing greater difficulty in selling it. Where this is diagnosed, particular attention should be paid to the liquidity ratios to ensure that the deceleration of turnover is not having too serious an effect. On the other hand too great an increase in stock turnover, though financially desirable, may lead to delivery problems, due to the small size of stock relative to sales, with a consequent diminution of goodwill.

(v)
$$\frac{\frac{1}{2}(\text{Debtors at start of year} + \text{debtors at end of year})}{\text{Credit Sales}} \times 12 = \begin{array}{l}\text{Average number of} \\ \text{months credit given} \\ \text{to debtors.}\end{array}$$

This ratio can only be used where the bulk of sales are made on a credit basis and it measures the efficiency of a company in the collection of its debts. The period of credit given should be kept as low as possible for not only may the sources of funds used to finance credit facilities have a real monetary cost but they will also have an opportunity cost in that the cash due from debtors could have been invested either inside or outside the business to earn a monetary return. If the period of credit is increasing this might suggest that the company is increasing its sales either by giving more favourable terms for payment or by selling to customers of doubtful standing. In the first case the extension of credit facilities may lead to a strain on liquidity. Admittedly it is possible to release the funds tied up in debts or in stock by means of factoring arrangements, but such schemes tend to be relatively expensive. If it is thought that the quality of debtors might have fallen the accounts should be examined to see if they mention any special provision for doubtful debts. Unfortunately an increase in the provision is normally only stated when it is exceptionally large relative to that of previous years.

Finally, in connection with turnover, the disclosure of exports is useful as a guide to the dependence of the company upon the home market. This information is especially relevant in measuring the worth of a share as a hedge against devaluation.

(b) The information relating to the composition of turnover and trading profit will indicate the relative importance of different activities. Unfortunately more detailed analysis might be misleading due to the differing definitions of separate activities, and the diversity of methods which have been adopted for the allocation to different products of joint production costs and overheads. It will thus be virtually impossible to achieve comparability between companies in this field.

(c) The disclosure of data relating to manpower and wages will permit the calculation of a group of important ratios:

(i) *Ratio of sales to total wages*. This ratio reveals the amount of income earned by the company for every pound spent on wages. If the figure is rising this suggests either that the labour force is being deployed more efficiently or that more capital equipment has been purchased. The latter alternative may, of course, be confirmed by reference to the balance sheet. A downward trend in the ratio may indicate a falling-off in sales effort, inefficient labour deployment, or the use of inferior capital equipment. Alternatively it could be attributable to an increase in the level of production necessitating the payment of overtime or an incentive bonus or to an increase in the proportion of skilled, highly-paid workers in the total labour force. Again, reference to other information in the annual report will suggest the most likely causal factor.

(ii) *Ratio of fixed assets to average number of employees*. This measures the capital intensity of a company. While it is more desirable that a rising trend should be established it should be matched by an increase in sales per employee. For this purpose the trend may be compared either with that of the ratio of sales to wages or with that of sales to average number of employees. Inter-firm comparisons on the basis of these ratios, though extremely useful, are made hazardous by the widely differing depreciation and valuation policies adopted by companies. It is necessary, too, in calculating the ratio for an individual firm to eliminate distortions arising from the revaluation of fixed assets.

(iii) *Ratio of total wages to average number of employees*. This ratio provides a broad indication of the average wage paid by the company. A steadily increasing average wage is acceptable so long as the ratio of sales to total wage is at least constant unless there has been an increase in fixed assets per man, in which case it should have risen. A fall in average wages is most unusual and would suggest that the company is employing labour of a poorer quality than before.

(d) The disclosure of the range of salaries paid to directors,

327

though probably politically motivated, is very fair, for the directors are in theory appointed by the shareholders and are responsible to them. It thus seems reasonable that the members should be given more details of the terms of appointment. The total directors' salaries might be related to profits to ensure that any increases are justified by a proportionate increase in profits. If this is not the case the only remedy is to express criticism at the annual general meeting.

(e) to (h) The extension of information relevant for the more realistic valuation of the assets controlled by a company, while removing some of the shortcomings of the Companies Act 1948, still leaves serious deficiencies which still forbid adequate inter-firm comparison. For example, details of assets and profits attributable to unquoted investments enable an investor to make more accurate guesses regarding their worth. Unfortunately, however, the value of those assets will be stated in terms of book value. Similarly, the disclosure of the date of revaluation of any fixed assets permits an estimate of their present value, but a statement of present value by the company would clearly be much more useful. Finally, the disclosure of hiring charges paid in respect of plant and machinery gives more information about the physical capital employed but does not permit of the determination of its replacement cost except by an artificial method such as the capitalization of the annual charge at a chosen rate of interest.

(i) to (k) This information is very useful in that it enables members to examine transactions in shares in which the directors are interested to ensure that they do not take advantage of inside information. The disclosure of the identity of persons interested in more than one-tenth of the issued voting shares of a company enables members to identify any large shareholdings and to investigate any changes in those holdings. Information of this sort might point to an eventual takeover. On the other hand, it could suggest the accumulation of enough shares to give control without a formal takeover, in which case the remaining members would become minority shareholders.

Although the Companies Act 1967 implemented most of the recommendations of the Jenkins Committee concerning disclosure, it was widely recognized by that time that those recommendations omitted many items of information which are vital to an investment analyst. In particular the following data is essential:

(1) An analysis in the profit and loss account of the cost of goods sold and the different classes of overhead expenses particularly the rent paid in respect of land and buildings.

(2) Details in the balance sheet of the composition and valuation of stock, the amount of bad debts and details of accrued liabilities and prepayments.

(3) There should be more standardization in the information made available to investors. For instance sales should be classified according to the categories used for Government statistics.

(4) Full details of sales of fixed assets should be given, including the proceeds, book value, depreciation and profit or loss on sale.

The information described above could already be provided quite easily by most companies. Future developments might be the provision of estimates of the replacement cost of fixed assets, a cash flow forecast for the coming year, details of the capital expenditure programme for the next five years and a management audit, which examines the efficiency of the management as well as the accuracy of the financial records.

CHAPTER 11

Capital Gearing—Its Effects and Measurement

The capital gearing of a company indicates the relative proportions of fixed-interest and variable-interest securities which comprise its capital. The greater the proportion of fixed-interest securities the more highly geared is the company. The nature of the capital structure is extremely important because of the effect that different structures will have upon the market value of the ordinary shares and it follows that an investment analyst should appreciate these effects and should attempt to measure gearing.

1. THE EFFECTS OF CAPITAL GEARING

As far as ordinary shareholders are concerned there are considerable advantages in financing projects by an issue of fixed-interest securities rather than by increasing the equity, whether forcibly through retained earnings or voluntarily by a new issue of ordinary shares. In the first place, so long as the return from the new projects exceeds the rate of interest payable on the fixed-interest securities the ordinary shareholders will benefit from the excess earnings without any further investment on their part. This tendency will be reinforced in times of inflation when a company's trading profits will normally increase while its fixed-interest commitments remain constant. A further advantage is that the ordinary shareholders do not forfeit any part of their control over the company so long as the fixed-interest payments are made on the due dates. Moreover, an issue of debentures as opposed to preference shares has the additional advantage that the interest payable is deductible from profits in the computation of corporation tax. On the other hand an issue of fixed-interest securities renders the ordinary shares more risky, for

330

the fixed-interest payments will rank as a prior charge and must be met before an ordinary dividend is paid.

The effect of an issue of fixed-interest securities on the return to the ordinary shareholders can be illustrated by the following example. It is assumed that a company has an ordinary share capital of £800,000, on which it earns 15%. If it were able to raise further capital by means of an issue of debenture stock at a rate of interest of 6% and could continue to employ those funds within the business at a profit rate of 15% this would clearly benefit the ordinary shareholders, to whom would accrue the excess of the earnings over the fixed-interest rate payable in respect of the new funds. The company might therefore issue £400,000 6% debenture stock, the earnings from which would be £60,000 of which £24,000 would be payable in respect of debenture interest, the remaining £36,000 accruing to the ordinary shareholders. It might then issue a further £1,200,000 6% debenture stock which would increase profits by £180,000, £72,000 of which would be required to service the debenture interest while the remaining £108,000 would boost the return to the ordinary shareholders.

If the profits of the company were to differ from the forecast 15%, the effect of such changes under the three stages of capitalization described above can be demonstrated by the following table:

TABLE 1

	Method of Finance		
	£	£	£
Ordinary shares	800,000	800,000	800,000
6% Debentures	—	400,000	1,600,000
	800,000	1,200,000	2,400,000
Profit (15% return on capital)	120,000	180,000	360,000
Less: Debenture interest	—	24,000	96,000
Available for retention and ordinary dividend	120,000	156,000	264,000
Percentage earnings on ordinary capital employed	15%	19·5%	33%
Effect of a 50% rise in profitability			
	£	£	£
Profit (22½% return on capital)	180,000	270,000	540,000
Less: Debenture interest	—	24,000	96,000
Available for retention and ordinary dividend	180,000	246,000	444,000

331

Percentage earnings on ordinary capital			
employed	22·5%	30·75%	55·5%
Percentage increase over original earnings	50%	57·7%	68·2%

Effect of a 50% fall in profitability

	£	£	£
Profit (7½% return on capital)	60,000	90,000	180,000
Less: Debenture interest	—	24,000	96,000
Available for retention and ordinary dividend	60,000	66,000	84,000

Percentage earnings on ordinary capital			
employed	7·5%	8·25%	10·5%
Percentage decrease from original earnings	50%	57·7%	68·2%

This example is very unrealistic in that it ignores taxation and assumes that additional funds can be both raised at a constant rate of interest and invested within the business at a constant rate of return. Moreover, the effect that the increased risk inherent in an issue of fixed-interest securities might have on the market basis of valuation of the ordinary shares has been ignored. However, the omission of taxation from the example does not affect the principles described therein, while the other points will be considered at a later stage.

The example demonstrates that, although the rate of profit is only 15%, the earnings of the ordinary shareholders can be increased to a considerably higher figure through the use of fixed-interest finance. By using debenture finance amounting to £1·6 m. the company has raised the earnings on the ordinary capital employed to 33%, an increase of 120%. Moreover, a rise in profitability is still more beneficial to the ordinary shareholders for the whole of the increase will be theirs, so long as the previous level of profits was sufficient to cover the amount of the fixed-interest payments. Thus in the example an increase of 50% in profitability caused the return on ordinary capital employed to rise by 57·7% in the case where debentures totalled £400,000 and by 68·2% where they amounted to £1·6 m.

In the same way the return to the ordinary shareholders will fall disproportionately as profits decrease, for the holders of the fixed-interest securities have a guaranteed rate of return regardless of the level of profits, so that the ordinary shareholders must bear the brunt of any fall in profits. There is thus always a risk if profits fall that the market value of the equity will drop or that the holders of the fixed-interest securities might be empowered to force the company into liquidation.

It is thus clear that the main characteristic of a highly geared capital structure is that fluctuations in equity earnings are increased. If a company has relatively stable profits these fluctuations are less crucial, but where profits are unstable the profit movements will be magnified in their effect on the equity earnings and the return to the ordinary shareholders will fluctuate sharply. Moreover, the greater the instability of profits the greater the possibility that they might fall below the minimum point necessary to cover prior charges.

As a result, a high geared company should have stable or steadily increasing profits, and an asset structure which provides adequate security for an issue of loan capital. The type of asset which provides the best security is one which can be specifically identified and which is unlikely to fall in value over time. Land and buildings are ideal for this purpose and it is for this reason that high-geared companies are to be found in the brewing and property sectors.

The type of company for which high gearing is least appropriate is one which operates in a cyclical industry, with profits that fluctuate from year to year causing equity earnings and share prices to fluctuate still more sharply. Nevertheless, even such a company could operate with a highly geared capital structure so long as the directors follow a cautious policy of dividend distribution, whether formally by means of a dividend equalization account, or otherwise. The success of such a policy requires a long-term forecast of approximate profit levels and the ascertainment of the level of dividend that could be maintained in the long-term. Then in good years profits would be set aside to maintain the ordinary dividend when profits slump.

However, there are limits to the extent to which a company may increase its gearing. In the first place it cannot assume either that it will receive constant returns on additional investment projects or that it will be possible to raise additional funds at a constant rate of interest. In practice, as far as the investment of funds are concerned, it would accept the most profitable projects first, leaving the best alternatives to be financed by further fund-raising operations or ignored entirely. At the same time, as it raises more funds on a fixed-interest basis, it must offer a higher rate of interest for, not only will there be less security as to capital available for later issues but also the interest will rank after that on the earlier issues.

According to elementary economic theory a firm would continue to raise funds on fixed interest terms up to the point where the rate of return from the marginal investment project is equal to the rate of interest payable on the marginal issue of fixed-interest securities.

However, it is improbable that a company would attain the theoretical optimum point because a project might give a lower return than that forecast and might show a loss after the payment of debenture interest. Consequently, there will be a tendency to establish an equilibrium position at which there is still a gap between the return on the marginal investment opportunity and the rate of interest payable on the marginal issue of fixed-interest securities. This margin serves to cushion the impact of uncertainty as to the actual return of the projects undertaken.

In practice the margin required by companies to compensate for uncertainty appears to be relatively high. It is often argued that the minimum rate of return normally required by British firms on new investments is 15%,[1] while the current yield on high-class debenture stocks is 10%. This suggests a marked degree of conservatism which is confirmed by the fact that new projects are financed predominantly by retained earnings and new issues of ordinary shares, despite the fact that both of these have a higher cost than debentures, due partly to tax factors and partly to the concept of opportunity cost. It seems clear that companies are attracted by equity finance because of the lower degree of risk involved, in that there is no legal compulsion to pay dividends.

However, there has been a tendency in recent years for more funds to be raised by debenture issues, and this has accelerated dramatically since the introduction of the Corporation Tax in November 1964. This trend is shown by the following table, reproduced from the *Midland Bank Review*, of February 1971.

Table 1

*Types of Company Security**

	Debt				Capital			
			Total £m.	*% of total*	*Pref-erence £m.*	*% of total*	*Ordinary £m.*	*% of total*	*Total £m.*
1951	—	—	49·1	*37·8*	19·7	*15·1*	61·1	*47·1*	129·9
1952	—	—	36·7	*28·6*	4·1	*3·1*	87·8	*68·3*	128·6
1953	—	—	53·1	*50·4*	7·9	*7·5*	44·3	*42·1*	105·4
1954	—	—	101·0	*49·9*	28·3	*14·0*	73·0	*36·1*	202·3
1955	—	—	65·1	*27·2*	18·9	*7·9*	154·9	*64·9*	238·9
1956	—	—	76·0	*33·8*	3·1	*1·4*	145·7	*64·8*	224·7
1957	—	—	183·3	*54·0*	1·7	*0·5*	155·2	*45·5*	340·2
1958	—	—	95·2	*50·4*	1·0	*0·5*	92·6	*49·1*	188·8
1959	—	—	119·5	*29·6*	10·7	*2·6*	274·0	*67·8*	404·2
1960	—	—	121·8	*25·5*	10·4	*2·2*	345·5	*72·3*	477·7

* Excluding railways, gas and water undertakings before 1961.

[1] *Investment Appraisal* (HMSO, 1965), p. 12.

| | Debt | | | | Capital | | | | |
	Convert-ible £m.	Other £m.	Total £m.	% of total	Pref-erence £m.	% of total	Ordinary £m.	% of total	Total £m.
1961	28·1	120·0	148·1	26·5	2·8	0·5	408·9	73·0	559·8
1962	41·0	132·8	173·8	42·1	5·3	1·3	233·9	56·6	413·0
1963	35·3	236·2	271·5	60·3	14·7	3·3	163·9	36·4	450·1
1964	60·2	173·8	234·0	56·6	10·7	2·6	168·9	40·8	413·6
1965	28·1	426·5	454·6	90·3	3·2	0·6	45·5	9·0	503·4
1966	38·4	441·0	479·5	75·1	16·4	2·6	142·5	22·3	638·4
1967	29·7	313·8	343·5	81·5	5·7	1·4	72·6	17·2	421·9
1968	128·3	181·3	309·5	45·8	3·1	0·5	363·7	53·8	676·4
1969	231·7	165·7	397·4	67·1	—	—	195·0	32·9	592·4
1970	101·3	211·6	312·9	82·0	17·2	4·5	51·9	13·6	382·0
1971	96·7	273·4	370·1	53·4	12·8	1·8	310·4	44·8	693·3

Notes

1. This table shows the amount of new money raised by companies in the United Kingdom through the issue of marketable securities. It excludes all issues which do not add to the resources of the company, such as capitalization issues, conversion issues, shares issued to the vendor of a business, issues designed to redeem existing securities, issues representing the liquidation by the proprietors of all or part of their interest in a company, etc.

2. The table ignores any redemptions and does not reveal, for example, that during 1965 the redemptions of preference shares substantially exceeded the amount issued.

The revival of equity issues in 1968 and 1971 was attributable to the high level of share prices during those years, while the rates payable on debenture issues rose to 10%. Equity issues, particularly rights issues, were thus relatively more attractive. It might appear from the table that there were many years prior to 1963 during which new issues of debentures were predominant (e.g. 1954, 1957, and 1958). However, companies were required to limit their dividends up to 1958 and ordinary shares were thus less attractive to investors.

In recent years the Government has attempted by means of the introduction of the Corporation Tax and the imposition of dividend limitation to encourage companies to increase their retained profits, though the growing separation of objectives between the management of a company and its shareholders may well defeat this purpose. Whatever the impact of Corporation Tax there is little doubt that retained profits will continue to be the major source of funds for British companies. F. W. Paish[1] has shown that retained profits alone were greater than new capital issues of all types for every year from 1949 to 1960 inclusive. Moreover, if the funds retained

[1] *Business Finance* (London; Pitman, 1965), pp. 132–3.

by firms in respect of depreciation provisions are added to the retained profits the total retentions constitute more than half of the
total funds obtained by companies from all sources in every year
between 1949 and 1962 inclusive.

It thus seems that, although British managements are more
prepared to issue debentures, they are still extremely conservative
in their overall financing policy. For this reason it seems likely
that they will continue to seek a relatively wide margin between the
yield on the marginal investment project and the rate of return
payable on the marginal source of finance.

In discussing the effects of an increase in gearing no mention has
been made of the effect on the market value of the ordinary shares
of the company. The obvious result is that prior charges will rise
thus making the ordinary shares more risky and causing an increase
in the rate of discount used by the market to value them. The
traditional analysis of the influence of gearing suggests that up to an
optimum point the increased earnings derived by the ordinary
shareholders will be more than sufficient to maintain the market
value of their shares when priced on a higher yield basis on account
of the increased risk element. Once this optimum level has been
passed an increase in gearing will not provide sufficient additional
profits to outweigh the effect of the higher market discount and the
market price of the shares will fall.

This result is regarded as anomalous by many theoreticians in
the field of company finance, and a particularly strong attack was
made on the traditional theory by Modigliani and Miller,[1] who
argue that the aggregate market value of a company is entirely
independent of its capital structure. Therefore, two companies
with identical assets and earnings of identical size and quality will
always have the same total market value, regardless of their methods
of finance.

Their argument in support of this thesis rests upon the use of a
system of arbitrage and while it is extremely ingenious and unassailable at a theoretical level, it is based on several unrealistic assumptions and is less tenable under real world conditions. The traditional
view, though not empirically tested, must be regarded as providing
the most acceptable analysis of the effects of gearing. The normal
reaction of the market to successive injections of loan capital might
thus be:

(a) To increase the market value of the ordinary shares when a
company first begins to issue loan capital, partly because of

[1] F. Modigliani and M. H. Miller, 'The Cost of Capital, Corporation Finance,
and the Theory of Investment', *American Economic Review*, June 1958.

336

the expectation of increased earnings without a material increase in risk, and partly because the publicity given to the issue is a bull factor.

(b) Subsequent issues over a fairly broad range would probably have little effect on the ordinary shares, because the impact on earnings would be rather less than before and would be balanced by the risk element, which would be rather higher than previously.

(c) Where a firm is felt by the market to have become over-geared an increase in gearing would result in a fall in the market price of the shares because the hope of higher equity earnings would be more than balanced by the greater risk involved.

2. THE MEASUREMENT OF GEARING

It has been shown that, so long as a company does not increase its gearing to a point beyond that considered safe by the market, the use of fixed-interest funds will not be detrimental to the ordinary shareholders, and will often be beneficial. The determination of this optimum point will depend upon such factors as the gearing level of similar firms, the expected rate and stability of the return on investment within the firm, and the acceptability of the assets of the firm as security to lenders.

Therefore, as far as the company itself or external analysts are concerned it is important to discover at what level a company can be regarded as over-geared. The techniques of measurement of gearing will depend upon the way in which gearing is defined. In the first place, it can be regarded as the relationship which exists between the fixed-interest capital and the ordinary share capital of a company. Alternatively, it may be defined as the relationship between the profits available for the equity holders and the total profit of a company.

(a) Measurement of Gearing on the Basis of Capital Structure

The most elementary method of measuring gearing in this way, and one which is still propounded in the simpler textbooks, is that which relates the nominal value of a company's fixed-interest capital to the nominal value of its equity capital. A typical illustration of this is:

	A Ltd £	B Ltd £	C Ltd £
Ordinary capital	100,000	150,000	200,000
Preference capital	100,000	75,000	50,000
Debenture stock	100,000	75,000	50,000
	300,000	300,000	300,000

$$\frac{\text{Fixed-interest capital}}{\text{Ordinary capital}} \qquad \frac{200,000}{100,000} = 2 \qquad \frac{150,000}{150,000} = 1 \qquad \frac{100,000}{200,000} = \tfrac{1}{2}$$

A Ltd is defined as high-geared, B Ltd as neutral-geared, and C Ltd as low-geared. It is, of course unrealistic to describe as low-geared a capital structure that contains fixed-interest securities amounting to one-half of the ordinary shares because such a structure would be extremely high-geared by British standards. In any case, this method is quite misleading for it ignores the reserves of the company, which represent additional investment in the company on the part of the ordinary shareholders.

A more accurate method would take reserves into account by adding them to the nominal value of the equity in the calculation of the ratio. For instance, it may be ascertained that the three companies above have reserves of £300,000, £150,000 and nil respectively. The gearing ratios would then appear as below:

	A Ltd £	B Ltd £	C Ltd £
Ordinary capital	100,000	150,000	200,000
Reserves	300,000	150,000	—
Total equity	400,000	300,000	200,000
Preference capital	100,000	75,000	50,000
Debenture stock	100,000	75,000	50,000
	600,000	450,000	300,000

$$\frac{\text{Fixed-interest capital}}{\substack{\text{Ordinary capital and}\\ \text{reserves}}} \qquad \frac{200,000}{400,000} = \tfrac{1}{2} \qquad \frac{150,000}{300,000} = \tfrac{1}{2} \qquad \frac{100,000}{200,000} = \tfrac{1}{2}$$

This gives an entirely different, though more accurate result than that provided by the previous method. Nevertheless, it is still unrealistic in that it assumes that the book value of the ordinary capital and reserves provides an adequate measurement of the real investment of the ordinary shareholders.

It thus ignores the fact that book values of assets are often highly inaccurate, and that it is not normally possible to measure the value of the equity of a company on the basis of its published accounts. Therefore, unless the analyst has intimate knowledge of the company concerned he cannot rely on its accounts for measuring its gearing on the financial structure basis. Fortunately, however, an adequate measurement of the equity interest is easily obtainable. It is suggested that the value of the equity of a company should be regarded, not as the book value or the market value of the assets which represent the ordinary share capital and accumulated reserves, but as the aggregate market value of the ordinary shares. This not only represents an independent assessment of the value of the equity, but it also indicates the opportunity cost to each shareholder of his investment, and the fact that he maintains his investment suggests that the market value of his shares correctly represents the figure at which he values his holding. If he valued his holding at less than its market value then he would sell it, while if he regarded it as worth more he would buy more shares, thus forcing up their price.

A more accurate measurement of gearing is thus given by the ratio,

$$\frac{\text{Nominal value of fixed-interest securities}}{\text{Market value of ordinary share capital}}$$

This ratio is recommended by M. S. Rix[1] and a similar measurement is suggested by R. Marris,[2] who advocates the ratio

$$\frac{\text{Gross liabilities}}{\text{Gross assets}}$$

The distinguishing feature of the second ratio is that it relates the whole of the liabilities of the company to the whole of its assets. As such it is not substantially different from the previous ratio, and, in any case, both are incorrect in that they ignore the rate of interest payable on the fixed-interest stocks.

This may be incorporated into the ratio by using as its numerator the market value of the fixed-interest securities, for this figure automatically reflects the rate of interest offered on the securities, being higher, the greater the amount of interest payable by the company.

Therefore, still greater accuracy is provided by the ratio:

$$\frac{\text{Market value of fixed-interest securities}}{\text{Market value of ordinary share capital}}$$

[1] *Investment Arithmetic* (London: Pitman, 1964).
[2] *The Economic Theory of Managerial Capitalism* (London: Macmillan & Co., 1964).

A variation of this method is given by the ratio:

$$\frac{\text{Market value of fixed-interest securities}}{\text{Market value of ordinary share capital and market value}}$$
$$\text{of fixed-interest securities}$$

Both of the above ratios are advocated by Ezra Solomon,[1] though the second seems the more satisfactory. If the company has no fixed-interest securities then its gearing will be nil, while if it is effectively financed wholly by such securities then the ratio will be one. The ratio can thus range only between nil and one, and the closer that it approaches unity, the higher will be the gearing of the company.

Despite the obvious advantages of this method there are still two drawbacks to its use that have been suggested. In the first place, the ratio will fluctuate with every movement in the market value of the shares or securities of a company. Although this means that no stable measurement of gearing can be obtained, this is not necessarily a bad thing, for gearing ultimately depends upon the relationship between the prior charges and profits and these are reflected in the market valuation of company securities.

A more serious drawback is that it only takes into account fixed-interest securities, thus ignoring other types of interest-bearing finance such as bank overdrafts, mortgages and loans. Also fixed charges payable in respect of leased property and equipment should be incorporated. This could be achieved by capitalizing the charges in respect of all the liabilities described above at the market rate of interest for fixed-interest stocks and including the resultant figure in the total of fixed-interest securities. However, this would be a very cumbersome operation and in any case the requisite information is not often available.

(b) *The Measurement of Gearing on the basis of the Division of Profits*

Many of the methods of assessing gearing ignore capital structure and concentrate instead on the measurement of the relationship between the fixed-interest commitments, known as prior charges, and the profits available for the ordinary shareholder. Three types of measurement which have been advocated for this purpose are described below.

---

[1] *The Theory of Financial Management* (New York: Columbia University Press, 1963), p. 81.

Capital Gearing—Its Effects and Measurement

1. *Estimation of Times Covered and Priority Percentage Tables*

The most elementary method of measuring the relationship between prior charges and equity profits is by the calculation of the cover of the interest and dividends attributable to the various classes of finance of the company. This is done by measuring the payment to each class in order of priority against the profit.

An example of this method might show the following results:

Net profit	£200,000		
Net debenture interest	20,000	Times covered	10·00
	180,000		
Gross preference dividend	80,000	Times covered	2·25
	100,000		
Gross ordinary dividend	25,000	Times covered	4·00
Retained profits	£75,000		

This method, although often advocated, is very misleading, because the cover supposedly available for the ordinary shareholders has already been utilized in the calculation of the cover for the debenture interest and the preference dividend, and it produces the anomalous result that the cover for the ordinary dividend is higher than that for the preference dividend, despite the fact that the latter constitutes a prior charge.

In order to avoid this anomaly successive interest and dividend liabilities should be measured on a cumulative basis. If this method were applied to the first example the results would be:

Cover for debenture interest $\dfrac{200,000}{20,000}$ = 10·0 times covered

Cover for preference dividend $\dfrac{200,000}{20,000+80,000}$ = 2·0 times covered

Cover for ordinary dividend $\dfrac{200,000}{20,000+80,000+25,000}$ = 1·6 times covered

This is much more logical in that it recognizes that senior or prior charges must necessarily be better covered than junior charges. It should be stressed, incidentally, that debenture interest should always be compared with net profits on a net basis, because it is an allowable deduction from profits in the calculation of corporation tax, while preference and ordinary dividends must be incorporated on a gross basis, because they are not so deductible.

Probably the most common method of depicting the relationship between prior charges and equity earnings is the priority percentages table. This shows the percentage of the profits of a company that is taken by prior charges, in order of priority, by ordinary dividends and by retentions. Using the figures from the previous example a priority percentages table can be constructed as follows:

Profit	£200,000	Cumulative %	
Debenture interest	£20,000	0%	–10%
Preference dividend	80,000	10%	–50%
Ordinary dividend	25,000	50%	–62·5%
Retentions	75,000	62·5%	–100%

This table shows that a fall in profits of 50% would cause the equity earnings to disappear completely, while a greater fall would cause the preference dividend to become uncovered. Similarly, a fall in profits of more than 90% would leave the debenture interest uncovered. On the other hand, any rise in profits would accrue entirely to the ordinary shareholders because the prior charges have already been met.

An investor, faced with such a table, would need to consider, first what percentage fall in profits would be necessary to leave the prior charges uncovered, and second what is the likelihood that such a fall might occur. If the company has declared rising profits in the past and there is every chance that this trend will continue, then a high proportion of prior charges need cause no concern either to an investor or to the company. If, on the other hand, profits have shown wide fluctuations in the past, a high proportion of prior charges might well be a sign of weakness. However, if the firm has built up large revenue reserves the existence of heavy prior charges need not be particularly damaging.

One major drawback, in fact, of the use of priority percentages tables is that they do not take into account the amount of reserves. For instance, two companies may each have a profit of £50,000 and prior charges of £45,000. However, on investigation it is ascertained that one has free reserves of £350,000 while the other has none. The priority percentages tables for the two companies would suggest that each provides identical cover for the fixed-interest charges, although the company with the reserves clearly has much more effective cover, so long as it has sufficient liquid funds. This factor would automatically have been taken into account by the measurement method based on capital structure, for the company with reserves would have been regarded as less risky, its ordinary shares would have been valued on a lower yield basis, thus giving a higher market value, and the level of gearing would consequently have been lower. Priority percentages tables cannot therefore be used in isolation and only provide a yardstick against which must be measured the forecast level of future profits and the state of the reserves of a company.

Another factor which is commonly ignored when priority percentages tables are utilized is the existence of fixed-interest commitments such as mortgage interest and rent which are not always regarded as prior charges. The number and size of such commitments have increased enormously in recent years as more and more expenses which were previously regarded as variable or semi-variable in nature are taking on the nature of fixed commitments. Many firms, for example, now regard previously variable expenses, such as wages, as overheads due to the difficulty of divesting themselves of surplus labour in the short-term. In theory the full amount of the overheads of a firm should be regarded as fixed charges and should be brought into the calculation of priority percentages.

2. Assessment of the Effect of a Change in Profits on Equity Earnings

A simple measurement of this effect is provided by a formula suggested by M. S. Rix:[1]

$$\frac{\text{Gross Profit}}{\text{Gross Profit—(Gross interest plus grossed-up Preference Dividends)}} : 1$$

This formula indicates the movement in the equity earnings resulting from a given change in profit. The greater the movement in these earnings, the higher the gearing. Where there are no prior charges the ratio will be 1:1 and equity earnings will be the same as the profit. If, on the other hand, prior charges take half of the profits then the ratio will be 2:1 and an increase in profits of a given percentage will cause equity earnings to rise by double that percentage.

This formula and one which incorporates its reciprocal are advocated by Pearson Hunt[2] for the measurement of the responsiveness of equity earnings to changes in profit. Both are extremely useful, for the higher the value of the ratio, the greater the volatility of equity earnings.

[1] *Investment Arithmetic* (London: Pitmans, 1964), p. 143.
[2] 'A Proposal for Precise Definitions of Trading on the Equity and Leverage', *Journal of Finance*, September 1961.

3. *Other Measurements*

In addition to the methods for the measurement of gearing by reference to the relative share in profits of the holders of fixed-interest securities and the shareholders of a company, certain other formulae have been advocated.

F. W. Paish,[1] for instance, measures gearing as 'The ratio of the annual amount payable on preference shares and other prior charges, if any, to the expected annual distributable profit (with expectations usually based on recent experience)'.

A similar ratio is used by B. Tew and R. F. Henderson[2] whose gearing indicator 'measures the ratio of net fixed-interest distributions in our five-year period to total net income during the same period'. During the period in question, 1949–53, the net fixed-interest distributions of their 'average' company were at the rate of £14,000 per annum while the net income was at the rate of £166,000 per annum, giving a gearing ratio of about 8·5%.

A sample of 2,549 companies for the same period showed the following capital structures:

Level of gearing	Gearing ratio	Number of companies
Very low	0–10%	1,536
Low	11–20%	456
High	21–40%	312
Very high	Over 40%	151
Total companies with positive net income		2,455
Companies with negative net income		94
Total		2,549

This conclusion that British companies are relatively low-geared is borne out by a survey of European capital markets carried out by the Joint Economic Committee of the US Congress which showed the following figures of company bonds and stocks outstanding in the markets surveyed:

	Bonds ($m.)	Stocks ($m.)	Ratio (Bonds : Stocks)
United States	104,500	484,100	1 : 4·6
United Kingdom	4,100	62,000	1 : 15·2
France	7,000	23,100	1 : 3·3
Germany	10,000	9,300	1 : 0·9
Italy	8,400	23,200	1 : 2·8
Holland	800	8,000	1 : 10·0
Belgium	4,000	4,000	1 : 1·0

[1] *Business Finance* (London: Pitmans, 1965), p. 25.
[2] *Studies in Company Finance* (Cambridge University Press, 1959), pp. 20–1.

These figures are somewhat misleading because the total of stocks includes preference stocks, which ought to be added to bonds in the assessment of gearing. Nevertheless, they do seem to bear out the conclusion that British companies have a tendency towards low gearing. One reason for this may be the fact that the British tax system has not, except between 1947 and 1958 with the Differential Profits Tax and since 1965 with the introduction of the Corporation Tax, differentiated very sharply between debenture interest and ordinary dividends. Other possible reasons are managerial conservatism and a reluctance to accept the risks implicit in the use of debenture finance.

CHAPTER 12

The Analysis of Stock Exchange Data:
The Determination of Yield and Cover

(a) *The Concept of Yield*

The yield represents the financial return on an investment which after adjustment for anticipated changes in the value of money and for the degree of risk is the major criterion in the selection of investments.

First it is necessary to distinguish between simple and compound interest. Simple interest is calculated purely on the basis of the original sum invested, so that no interest is given in respect of increments of interest which have already been added. Thus if an amount of £100 were invested at 7% simple interest for a period of five years, the interest would be computed each year only on £100 despite the fact that £7 interest was being added each year to the investment, and at the end of five years it would have accumulated to £135.

Where compound interest is paid it is calculated on the original capital plus any interest credited and retained by the borrower. If in the example above, compound interest was paid the interest after one year would be £7. At the end of the second year it would be 7% of £107, giving £7·49 and after five years the investment would have accumulated to £140·25p, a material increase over the sum provided with simple interest. Simple interest is now relatively uncommon and is ignored in the remainder of this chapter.

These two examples have assumed that the interest is retained by the borrower. If it was paid out each year then this would be equivalent to compound interest for the lender could reinvest each year's interest to earn further interest, though, of course, there is no guarantee that such reinvestment will yield a rate equal to that which is being paid on the capital.

346

Four main sets of formulae are essential for an understanding of yield:

(i) *Accumulation formulae.* A general formula for determining the amount to which a given sum will accumulate at a given rate of compound interest may be derived as follows:

A sum P, invested at a rate of interest of i per period will accumulate to $P+Pi$ after one year. This is equal to $P(1+i)$ and indicates that the principal must be multiplied by $(1+i)$ in order to obtain the accumulated sum at the end of the period. At the start of the second period the principal has risen to $P(1+i)$. At the end of the second period this must be multiplied by $(1+i)$ to obtain the new principal sum of $P(1+i)^2$. At the end of the third period the new principal must again be multiplied by $(1+i)$, giving $P(1+i)^3$. It follows that the sum (S) to which a given principal (P) will accumulate at a given compound rate of interest (i) over a period of n years is given by the formula

$$S = P(1+i)^n$$

A table giving the value of S for a series of representative values of i and n where $P = 1$ is provided at the end of the book. For instance, it can be seen at a glance that the sum to which a principal of £1 will accumulate at 5% over ten years is £1·6289. If it is desired to compute this value for a principal of £1,000, it is merely necessary to multiply £1·6289 by 1,000, giving £1628·90. This table is usually denoted by $(1+i)^n$.

This formula may be adapted to determine the sum to which an annuity will accumulate. If, for example, a constant amount A is invested at the end of each year for a period of n years at a rate of interest per annum of i, at the end of n years the first payment of A would have accumulated to $A(1+i)^{n-1}$, the second to $A(1+i)^{n-2}$, while the final payment, being made on the last day of the life of the investment, will earn no interest.

At the end of n years the accumulated value of the annuity is shown by the formula:

$$S = A(1+i)^{n-1}+A(1+i)^{n-2}+A(1+i)^{n-3}...A(1+i)+A$$

If both sides of this formula are multiplied by $(1+i)$ it becomes

$$S(1+i) = A(1+i)^n+A(1+i)^{n-1}+A(1+i)^{n-2}...A(1+i)^2+A(1+i)$$

If the first equation is subtracted from the second all of the terms are cancelled out except S, $S(1+i)$, $A(1+i)^n$ and A, leaving the equation

347

$$S(1+i)-S = A(1+i)^n-A$$
$$\therefore \quad Si = A[(1+i)^n-1]$$
$$\therefore \quad S = \frac{A[(1+i)^n-1]}{i}$$

A series of values for the formula $\dfrac{(1+i)^n-1}{i}$ for given values of i and n is given in a table at the end of the book, headed by $S_{n\,i}$, which is the conventional symbol for the cumulative value of an annuity of 1. To obtain a value for other sums the value for one should be multiplied by the amount required.

(ii) *Present value formulae.* It is essential that the meaning of present value should be correctly understood, for it is crucial to any investment comparisons where the return is received in different future periods. The essence of present value is that, quite apart from considerations of liquidity preference, a given amount receivable immediately is more valuable than the same amount receivable one year hence because it could be invested during the intervening period to earn interest. For the same reason an amount receivable one year hence is to be preferred to the same amount receivable two years hence. It is thus meaningless to aggregate sums receivable at future dates for they are not similar units of measurement, in that they do not have the same value for the recipient.

For a true comparison between investments, all anticipated receipts must be reduced to a common denomination before they can be aggregated. The denominator generally used is present value, which represents the principal which would have to be invested now in order to accumulate to the amount of the receipt at the time when it becomes receivable. In this way all future receipts may be discounted at the rate of interest which the investor desires to earn, aggregated in terms of a common present value, and compared with the cost of the investment to determine whether it is worth undertaking.

The basic formula for calculating the present value of a future sum receivable may be derived from the accumulation formula:

$$S = P(1+i)^n$$

From this it follows that

$$P = \frac{S}{(1+i)^n} = S(1+i)^{-n}$$

A table of values for P, where $A = 1$ and i and n are given is included at the end of the book and it may be adapted for other values of S in the usual way. This table is usually represented by the symbol v_{n_i}.

From this equation may be derived a formula for computing the present value of an annuity. If a constant amount A is receivable at the end of each year for a period of n years and it is wished to discount this flow of receipts at a rate of discount i, the present value P may be ascertained from the following formula:

$$P = \frac{A}{1+i} + \frac{A}{(1+i)^2} + \frac{A}{(1+i)^3} \ldots + \frac{A}{(1+i)^{n-1}} + \frac{A}{(1+i)^n}$$

If both sides of this equation are multiplied by $(1+i)$ it becomes

$$P(1+i) = A + \frac{A}{1+i} + \frac{A}{(1+i)^2} \ldots \frac{A}{(1+i)^{n-2}} + \frac{A}{(1+i)^{n-1}}$$

If the first equation is subtracted from the second every term is cancelled out with the exception of P, $P(1+i)$, A and $\frac{A}{(1+i)^n}$, leaving

$$P(1+i) - P = A - \frac{A}{(1+i)^n}$$

$$\therefore \quad Pi = A - A(1+i)^{-n}$$

$$\therefore \quad P = A\left(\frac{1-(1+i)^{-n}}{i}\right)$$

A table showing the value of P for given values of i and n where $P = 1$ is given at the end of the book. The symbol generally used for this table is a_{n_i} and it can be used as before to determine the present value of annuities of any amount.

(iii) *The determination of yield.* The above formulae are designed to determine the accumulated value of an investment or the present value of a future receipt. More often, however, an investor will need to compute the yield which is provided by a given flow of receipts (e.g. dividends) arising from a given principal sum invested (e.g. the cost of a share). In calculating the yield of an investment P is replaced by C, representing the cost of the investment. Thus the yield given by an investment costing £C which accumulates to £S at the end of n years is shown by the solution of i for the equation

$$C = \frac{S}{(1+i)^n}$$

This can be achieved either by interpolation from the figures provided by the S_{n_i} table or, more accurately, by the use of logarithms. For instance an investment of £100 might increase to £200 at the end of ten years without any intermediate payments by the borrower.

If the interpolation method is used the yield may be determined by ascertaining from the $(1+i)^n$ table rates of interest at which £100 would increase to nearly £200 after ten years.

It will be seen that at a rate of interest of 7% £100 would accumulate to £196·715, while at a rate of 8% it would increase to £215·892. The yield of the investment thus lies between 7% and 8%, and it may be computed more exactly by linear interpolation, adding to 7% that proportion of 1% which represents the ratio of the amount by which the value at 7% falls short of the required sum to the difference between the values at 7 and 8%:

Required value	200·000
Value at 7%	196·715
Difference	3·285
Value at 8%	215·892
Value at 7%	196·715
Difference	19·177

$$\text{Yield} = 7\% + 1\% \left(\frac{3\cdot285}{19\cdot177} \right) = 7\cdot17\%$$

The same procedure may be used for determining the yield of a series of cash receipts whether they are constant in amount, in which case the annuity formula is used, or different from one year to another, in which case each separate receipt must be discounted to the present using the v_{n_t} table at selected yields in order to find the yield which equates the present value of the investment with its cost. It should be noted that in the use of these formulae the rate of interest should always be expressed as a decimal, so that 3% becomes 0·03 and 15% becomes 0·15.

(iv) *The treatment of receipts which are not annual.* The accumulation and discounting formulae described above relate to unspecified periods of time rather than years. They may thus be used to provide solutions where interest is paid or credited other than annually. Where, for example, interest is credited half-yearly at a nominal rate of compound interest of 6% this represents two periodic

payments at a rate of interest of 3%, as a result of which an investment of £100 would have increased after one year to

$$£100 \ (1 \cdot 03)^2 = £106 \cdot 09.$$

The tables may be adapted for problems of this sort by multiplying
n and dividing i by the frequency of payments per year. Thus to
determine the amount to which £100 would accumulate after ten
years at a rate of interest of 6% compounded quarterly the $(1+i)^n$
table should be consulted to find the value of £1 after forty periods
at a rate of interest of $1\frac{1}{2}\%$. The appropriate value is $1 \cdot 81402$,
indicating the accumulation of £100 to £181·40, compared with a
value of £179·08 if annual compounding at the rate of 6% had been
used.

Where interest is paid more than once a year the effective rate of
interest is higher than the nominal, because the interest paid during
the year is invested to earn still more interest during the remainder
of the year. As a consequence, where investments provide the same
nominal annual yield those which pay interest most frequently
should be preferred.

Using the basic accumulation formula $S = P(1+i)^n$ it is possible
to obtain a formula for calculating the effective rate of interest
where the quoted nominal rate is paid other than yearly. If f is
regarded as the frequency per annum with which interest is paid or
credited the formula becomes $S = P\left(1+\dfrac{i}{f}\right)^{fn}$. In order to find the
effective rate of interest r, it is necessary to determine the value
of r for which

$$P(1+r)^n = P\left(1+\frac{i}{f}\right)^{fn}$$

This may be reduced to

$$1+r = \left(1+\frac{i}{f}\right)^{f}$$

$$\therefore \quad r = \left(1+\frac{i}{f}\right)^{f} - 1$$

Therefore if the nominal rate of interest is 12% payable monthly
this represents an effective rate of

$$\left[\left(1+\frac{0\cdot 12}{12}\right)^{12} - 1\right] \text{ per cent}$$

$$= 12 \cdot 68\%$$

351

Such rates of interest are by no means uncommon for individuals who borrow money and care should be taken to determine what effective rate of interest is being paid on a loan.

(b) *The Yield on Fixed-interest Securities*

(i) *Redeemable Securities*

The yield on a redeemable security is composed of two elements:

(A) *The flat yield.* The flat or running yield indicates the return that an investor receives during the life of the security and is determined from the following formula:

$$100 \times \frac{\text{Coupon rate}}{\text{Market price}}$$

The coupon rate is the nominal rate of interest payable on the security while the market price is the cost of £100 nominal value of the stock.

For example, 3% Savings 1965/75 was priced at $89\frac{9}{16}$ on August 4, 1971. The flat yield would thus be

$$100 \times \frac{3}{89 \cdot 5625} = 3 \cdot 35\%$$

This represents the annual return that the investor would receive up to the redemption date, which in the case of this security will probably be August 15, 1975.

(B) *Profit on redemption.* In addition to the flat yield on the security under consideration there will be a profit on redemption of £10·4375 for each £100 nominal value of stock held. This represents a percentage profit on cost of

$$\frac{10 \cdot 4375}{89 \cdot 5625} = 11 \cdot 65\%$$

This profit will have been earned over a period of nearly 4 years and by dividing 11·65% by 4 it might be estimated very roughly as 2·9% per annum. If this is added to the flat yield of 3·35% it would indicate a yield to redemption of about 6·25%. This method is incorrect, for the yield of the profit on redemption should be determined on a compound interest basis by ascertaining the rate of interest at which £89·5625 would accumulate to £100 after 4 years. However, it does provide an approximation to the correct

352

yield and is helpful in the selection of rates to be used in the trial and error method of calculating the true yield.

An accurate calculation of the *yield to redemption* may be obtained by determining the rate of discount at which the half-yearly interest receipts and the ultimate capital repayment will be equated to the present market value of the security. This must be done on a trial and error basis with the use of appropriate discount tables. However, the naive calculation made above gave an answer of 6·25% and an attempt to find a more exact solution to the problem might be made on the basis of a 5½% yield and a 6% yield. It is certain that the true yield will be well below 6·25% for the effect of compounding the profit on redemption will be to reduce the yield below that obtained above. The yield to redemption will thus be found by aggregating its two components:

(A) the present value of £100 receivable at the end of eight periods of a half-year calculated first at 2¾% (effectively 5½% per annum), then at 3% (effectively 6% per annum). The capital redemption is discounted on a half-yearly basis because the interest payments are made twice a year, in the case of 3% Savings 1965/75 on February 15th and August 1st. The present value of the capital redemption is given by the formula

$$P = \frac{S}{(1+i)^n}$$

where P = the present value

S = the capital redemption

i = the rate of discount

n = the number of periods after which redemption takes place.

For the evaluation of 3% Savings 1965/75 $S = 100$, $n = 8$ and i is taken first as 2¾%, then 3%:

Where $i = 2\frac{3}{4}\%$ $\quad P = \dfrac{100}{(1\cdot0275)^8} = 80\cdot49$

Where $i = 3\%$ $\quad P = \dfrac{100}{(1\cdot03)^8} = 78\cdot94$

(B) The present value of the stream of interest receipts over the remainder of the life of the security. In the case of 3% Savings 1965/75 at August 4, 1971, there were a further eight interest receipts of £1·50 due at each half-year up to the redemption date. The formula for obtaining the present value of an annuity is

$$a_{n_i} = A\left(\frac{1-(1+i)^{-n}}{i}\right)$$

where a_{n_i} = the present value of the annuity

A = the amount of the annuity

i = the rate of discount

n = the number of periods for which the annuity is receivable.

For calculating the yield on 3% Savings 1965/75 $A = 1\cdot5$, $n = 8$, and i is again taken first as $2\frac{3}{4}\%$, then as 3%.

$$\text{Where } i = 2\tfrac{3}{4}\% \quad a_{n_i} = 1\cdot5 \left(\frac{1-(1\cdot0275)^{-8}}{0\cdot0275} \right) = 10\cdot64$$

$$\text{Where } i = 3\% \quad a_{n_i} = 1\cdot5 \left(\frac{1-(1\cdot03)^{-8}}{0\cdot03} \right) = 10\cdot53$$

The aggregate present value of the security is thus:

	$5\frac{1}{2}\%$	6%
Present value of the capital repayment	80·49	78·94
Present value of the interest receipts	10·64	10·53
	91·13	89·47

As the market value of the security is 89·5625 this would indicate a yield to redemption of about 6%.

The above calculation is still somewhat approximate in that the security has not got exactly 4 years to run. In fact, the exact yield on the day in question was 5·953%. Furthermore for an exact assessment of the return an investor should include in the cost of the security the various expenses of purchase and, in the case of securities other than short-dated, should adjust for the net interest accrued in the price.

The two formulae above may be added together to produce the formula

$$P = \frac{A}{i} + \left(S - \frac{A}{i} \right) (1+i)^{-n}$$

where P = the market price of the security

A = the amount of interest received on the security each half year.

i = the redemption yield

S = the redemption value

n = the number of periods up to redemption

Here again the redemption yield can be found by solving the equation for possible values of i. If, for instance, 0·03 is substituted for i the equation produces the following results, remembering that the life of the security and the yield are expressed in terms of a half year,

$$P = \frac{1\cdot5}{0\cdot03} + \left(100 - \frac{1\cdot5}{0\cdot03}\right)(1\cdot03)^{-8}$$
$$= 50 + (50)(0\cdot7894) = 89\cdot47$$

The formula therefore indicates a yield to redemption of approximately 6%.

In addition to the above methods the investor might obtain tables of redemption yields which give a still more precise computation. These, however, still require a certain amount of interpolation. Moreover, they present problems where the redemption takes place at a premium or at a discount, whereas the two methods above automatically incorporate the redemption price into the calculation, whether redemption takes place at par, at a premium, or at a discount. Fortunately *The Financial Times* states the gross flat and redemption yields of the major quoted gilt-edged securities, so that the average investor is not concerned with the calculation of these yields for himself.

The *gross flat yield* and the *gross yield to redemption* both ignore taxation. However, in the case of most securities the interest is paid after deduction of tax at standard rate and unless the investor pays tax at a rate other than standard rate this net amount will represent the net return to the investor.

It is thus necessary to take tax into account using the *net flat yield* and the *net yield to redemption*. The net flat yield is given by the formula:

$$\frac{\text{Nominal interest rate less tax at standard rate}}{\text{Market value of the security}} \times 100$$

With the standard rate of tax at 38·75% the net flat yield on 3% Savings 1965/75 would be

$$\frac{3(1-0\cdot3875)}{89\cdot5625} = 2\cdot05\%$$

The net yield to redemption presents rather more problems, as the flat yield is taxed initially at standard rate, while the profit to redemption is subject to capital gains tax at the rate of 30% only if the stock is sold within twelve months of purchase. The calculation of the yield must again be performed on a trial or error basis and $4\frac{1}{2}\%$ and 5% are chosen as the trial rates.

The present value of a capital repayment of £100 assumed to be free of capital gains tax eight periods hence is calculated at $2\frac{1}{4}\%$ and at $2\frac{1}{2}\%$.

355

$$\text{Where } i = 2\tfrac{1}{4}\% \quad P = \frac{100}{(1\cdot0225)^8} = 83\cdot69$$

$$\text{Where } i = 2\tfrac{1}{2}\% \quad P = \frac{100}{(1\cdot025)^8} = 82\cdot07$$

The present value of an annuity of £1·5 (1−0·3875) per period for eight periods is calculated at $2\tfrac{1}{4}\%$ and at $2\tfrac{1}{2}\%$.

$$\text{Where } i = 2\tfrac{1}{4}\% \quad a_{n_t} = 1\cdot5(1-0\cdot3875)\left(\frac{1-1\cdot0225^{-8}}{0\cdot0225}\right) = 6\cdot66$$

$$\text{Where } i = 2\tfrac{1}{2}\% \quad a_{n_t} = 1\cdot5(1-0\cdot3875)\left(\frac{1-1\cdot025^{-8}}{0\cdot025}\right) = 6\cdot58$$

The aggregate present values yielded by this method are:

	$4\tfrac{1}{2}\%$	5%
Present value of net capital repayment	83·69	82·07
Present value of the net interest receipts	6·66	6·58
	90·35	88·65

The exact yield may now be found by interpolation:
Difference between the interest rates applied $\quad = 0\cdot5$
Difference between the notional market values $= 1\cdot70$
Difference between the higher notional market
value and the actual market value
$(90\cdot35-89\cdot5625) \qquad\qquad\qquad\qquad = 0\cdot7875$
The exact yield is thus

$$4\cdot5+0\cdot5\left(\frac{0\cdot7875}{1\cdot70}\right) = 4\cdot73\%$$

Although the normal practice in the calculation of net redemption yield on stocks with less than one year to redemption is to deduct capital gains tax at 30% there is a case for suggesting that a rate of 19·375% should be used. Under the Capital Gains Tax rules a taxpayer has the option of paying tax at 30% on the whole gain, or of paying no capital gains tax, but including half the gain in his normal income for income tax and surtax purposes. Thus a standard rate taxpayer could opt to pay tax at standard rate on half the gain, giving an average charge of 19·375% on the whole gain.

The net redemption yield indicates the net return to an investor who pays income tax at standard rate. Other investors must calculate their individual net redemption yields for themselves. For instance, for an investor who pays no tax the net redemption yield will be the same as the gross redemption yield, which in the case of 3% Savings 1965/75, was 6% as shown above. At the other extreme an investor who pays surtax at the top rate of 50p in the pound will have a much lower net redemption yield:

Gross redemption yield on 3% Savings 1965/75 at August 4, 1971   6%

Income element (i.e. flat yield)		3·35	
Less: Income tax at 38·75%	1·30		
Surtax at 50%	1·68		
	——	2·98	
		——	0·37
Capital element		2·65	
		——	2·65
Net redemption yield for a top-rate surtax payer			3·02

The net redemption yield for an individual investor will thus fall within the range 3·02–7% for this particular stock, depending upon his tax rate.

It will be seen that the different components of the yield bear tax at different rates, the capital gain being free of tax or, if realized within year of acquisition, taxed at a lower rate than the income element. Consequently a gross redemption yield with a relatively high capital element represents a better return to a person paying high rates of tax than a yield with a high income element. The normal gross redemption yield is not very helpful in that it does not distinguish between these two components. To produce a gross yield which is relevant for a particular investor it is necessary to calculate the *effective gross yield to redemption* or the *grossed-up redemption* yield. This is found by calculating the personal net redemption yield for the investor and grossing this up by the personal tax rate payable by him. This indicates the equivalent amount of income which he would have to receive to produce the same net yield.

In this case the investor who has to pay no tax provides the lower limit of the range, his return still being 6% in the case of 3% Savings 1965/75. The top-rate surtax payer has a much higher return. His personal net redemption yield was 3·02%. When this is grossed up at 88·75% it gives a yield of

$$3\cdot02 \times \frac{100}{100-88\cdot75} = 26\cdot9\%$$

357

Thus, in this case, the grossed-up redemption yield will fall in the range 6%–26·9% depending upon the tax position of the investor. Had the gross redemption yield of 6% been entirely capital the net yield to a top-rate surtax payer would have been 6%, assuming that the stock was held for at least twelve months.

This would represent a grossed-up redemption yield of

$$6 \times \frac{100}{100 - 88 \cdot 75} = 53 \cdot 3\%$$

It is therefore very clear that, even after the introduction of the capital gains tax, the receipt of a capital gain rather than income confers a considerable benefit to investors at the higher levels of surtax.

Up to this point, it has been assumed that the investor will hold the security to redemption. However, it is very possible that he will liquidate his holding before that date. In this event the anticipated realization proceeds should be substituted for redemption price and the number of periods to sale substituted for the number to redemption in the calculation of yields described above. This of necessity introduces a further element of uncertainty and the yields thus calculated are much less likely to be accurately realized than those based on the redemption price.

Also, the investor must have regard to the expected fall in the value of money over the period for which he intends to hold the security and should reduce any estimated yields by the anticipated rise in the cost of living.

It should be noted that although the profit to sale or redemption on any stocks held for more than twelve months is entirely free of Government capital gains tax, other fixed interest stocks are still subject to capital gains tax and this must be taken into account in computing the net redemption yield and the grossed-up redemption yield.

(ii) *Irredeemable Securities*

The financial press only provides details of the flat yield on such stocks, for there is no provision for their redemption. However, an investor who anticipates a material fall in the rate of interest might buy them in the hope of a capital gain. He can therefore regard the anticipated sale proceeds as the redemption value and compute the yield to realization in the normal way, bearing in mind the greater uncertainty of realization proceeds compared with the redemption price.

(iii) *Risk and Cover for Fixed-interest Securities*

Risk and cover are important considerations for investors in fixed-interest securities which are not Government-guaranteed. Such investors will clearly require a higher yield than that available on Government securities to compensate for the greater risk. Normally a top-ranking industrial debenture will yield a $\frac{1}{2}$ to $1\frac{1}{2}\%$ higher than a comparable Government security, while a quoted debenture of lower quality might yield a further 2 or 3%. The yields on preference shares, however, tend to be rather lower than those on debentures of similar quality, for, being regarded as franked investment income, they give a tax advantage to institutional investors.

The extent of the risk attached to a particular industrial fixed-interest security is normally calculated by reference to the cover provided by the profits of the company for the payment of the annual interest or dividend and by the assets of the company for the repayment of the capital where appropriate.

(c) *The Analysis of Data relating to Ordinary Shares*

(i) *Calculation of Yield.* The calculation of the *gross dividend yield* of a share will depend upon the form in which the company declares its dividends. The normal method is to declare it as a percentage of the nominal value of the share. Thus, if a dividend of 20% were paid on shares with a nominal value of £1, each shareholder would receive a gross dividend of 20p for every share held.

The formula for computing the gross dividend yield under these circumstances is

Gross dividend yield $=$

$$\frac{\text{Gross dividend percentage} \times \text{Nominal value of shares}}{100 \times \text{Price of share}} \times 100$$

For example, on August 6, 1971 the 5p ordinary shares of Associated British Foods Ltd had a market value of $57\frac{1}{2}$p. The dividend percentage was 36% and the gross dividend yield, using pence as the unit of computation, was

$$\frac{36 \times 5}{100 \times 57 \cdot 5} \times 100 = 3 \cdot 13\%$$

Some companies, mainly in the insurance sector, declare a dividend of a given amount per share, in which case the nominal value does not enter into the calculation. In these circumstances the formula would be

$$\text{Gross dividend yield} = \frac{\text{Gross dividend amount}}{\text{Market value of share}} \times 100$$

For instance, on August 6, 1971 the 5p ordinary shares of the Legal and General Assurance Society Ltd. had a market value of 314p. The dividend was 5p per share per annum and the gross dividend yield, using pence as the unit of computation, was

$$\frac{7 \cdot 2}{314} \times 100 = 2 \cdot 3\%$$

A few companies declare a 'tax-free' dividend. This does not mean that the dividend is not liable to tax. It merely indicates that the dividend amount or percentage is stated by reference to the net dividend rather than the gross dividend. Thus a tax-free dividend of 6·125% is the same thing as a gross dividend of 10% which has suffered deduction of tax at source of 3·875%. In the shareholder's personal tax computation the gross amount of the dividend must always be entered. The gross yield can be computed by the following formula:

Gross dividend yield =

$$\frac{\text{Tax free dividend amount}}{\text{Market value of share}} \times 100 \times \frac{1}{1 - 0 \cdot 3875}$$

On August 6, 1971 the 5p ordinary shares of the Prudential Assurance Co. Ltd had a market value of 154p. The dividend was 3·2p tax-free per share. The gross dividend yield, computed in terms of pence, was

$$\frac{3 \cdot 2}{1 \cdot 54} \times 100 \times \frac{1}{1 - 0 \cdot 3875} = 3 \cdot 4\%$$

Gross dividend yields for the shares of leading companies quoted on the London Stock Exchange are published each day in *The Financial Times* and are based upon the total dividend paid during the preceding year. If there is any reason to suspect that the dividend and thus the dividend yield for the current year will be changed, as would be the case where the interim dividend had been increased, reduced or passed altogether, the relevant facts are mentioned.

To calculate the dividend yield with greater accuracy the acquisition cost should be added to the market value of the shares, for this represents the true cost of acquiring entitlement to the dividends. Furthermore, it is often argued that the net amount of accrued dividend contained in the purchase price should be deducted from the cost. Thus, if shares are bought on December 31st, and the dividend is paid annually on June 30th, one-half of the anticipated net dividend should be regarded as having accrued at the date of purchase and should be deducted from the purchase price in the determination of the yield. While such an adjustment is justifiable in the case of fixed-interest securities it seems to provide spurious accuracy for calculations involving ordinary shares where uncertainties abound and where the relevance of the dividend yield to investment decisions is by no means certain.

The net dividend yield on an investment may be calculated by determining the marginal amount of tax payable in respect of the dividend and reducing the gross yield accordingly. Where the net yield is published in the financial press it will be calculated purely on the basis of the deduction of tax at standard rate from the gross dividend.

(ii) *Earnings Yield and Price-Earnings Ratio.* Prior to the introduction of the Corporation Tax, earnings yield was a common tool of investment analysis. At that time a company could pay a net dividend out of its earnings, so that, in order to get a meaningful comparison with the gross dividend yield, the net earnings were grossed up at the standard rate of tax in order to compute the gross earnings yield. Under the present system, however, the gross dividend is paid out of net earnings, so that the net earnings yield is compared with the gross dividend yield to establish the cover for the dividend.

Under present circumstances, therefore, the earnings yield of a share is obtained from the formula

$$\text{Earnings yield} = \frac{\text{Net earnings per share}}{\text{Market price per share}} \times 100$$

Although this formula appears straightforward there are many serious problems of definition, such as the treatment of unusual or non-recurring items and matters relating to previous years, concerning which there are no established rules.[1] The normal practice is to remove all such items so that the amount of maintainable profit is obtained, thus providing a more realistic figure of earnings yield for comparative purposes.

[1] Cf. T. A. Hamilton Baynes, *Share Valuations* (London: Heinemann, 1966), pp. 85–8.

The computation of earnings yield may be illustrated by reference to the accounts of Monsanto Chemicals Ltd and its subsidiaries for the year ended December 31, 1966. The following information has been extracted from the consolidated profit and loss account for the year:

	£
Net operating profit	2,564,120
Add: Dividends and interest receivable	315,116
	2,879,236
Deduct: Interest payable	451,324
Profit for the year before taxation	2,427,912
Taxation	954,872
Profit for the year after taxation	1,473,040
Adjustments in respect of outside shareholders	3,284
Net profit attributable to Monsanto Chemicals Ltd	£1,476,324

Appropriations	£
Gross dividends of Monsanto Chemicals Ltd	
Preference	127,500
Ordinary first interim 5%	270,000
Ordinary second interim 10%	540,000
	937,500
Increase of retained surplus by parent company	564,581
	1,502,081
Decrease of retained surplus by subsidiary	25,757
	£1,476,324

Note: Taxation of £954,872 is comprised as follows:	
Based on the profit of the year:	£
Corporation tax at 40%	1,053,200
Less: Relief attributable to investment allowance	1,200
	1,052,000
Income tax	23,137
Overseas tax	8,735
	1,083,872
Prior year adjustment	26,000
	1,109,872
Less: Deferred taxes provisions from prior years now applied	155,000
	£954,872

The Determination of Yield and Cover

The earnings yield indicates on a comparable basis from one year to another the rate of profit earned by the company for its ordinary shareholders, and is often described as the rate 'earned for ordinary'. In the computation of net profit for this purpose the preference dividend must be deducted because it is not available for the ordinary shareholders, while the adjustments to the taxation charge made in respect of prior years should be removed in order to isolate the profitability of the year in question.

The net profit earned for the ordinary shareholders would thus be:

	£
Net profit attributable to Monsanto Chemicals Ltd	1,476,324
Deduct: Gross preference dividend	127,500
	1,348,824
Deduct: Deferred taxes provisions from previous years now applied	155,000
	1,193,824
Add: Prior year adjustment	26,000
Net profit earned for ordinary	£1,219,824

At the date of the accounts the issued ordinary capital of the company was 21,600,000 fully paid shares of 25p each. The earnings per share thus amounted to

$$\frac{£1,219,824}{21,600,000} = £0.0565 = 1.13s.$$

At September 29, 1967 the shares had a market value of $86\frac{1}{4}$p. This indicates an earnings yield of

$$\frac{5.65}{86.25} \times 100 = 6.55\%$$

Due to the introduction of the Corporation Tax in 1964 there is a break in the comparability of earnings yields, those before that date being computed on the basis of gross earnings, while those after are calculated on the net earnings. Most financial journals took this opportunity of discontinuing the use of the earnings yield as an earnings indicator and began to publish instead the price-earnings ratio. This ratio is extremely popular in America and its use in this country provides easier comparison between British and American shares. The price-earnings ratio is calculated from the formula

$$\frac{\text{Market price of share}}{\text{Earnings per share}}$$

In the example of Monsanto Chemicals Ltd the price-earnings ratio at the end of September 1967 would be

$$\frac{17 \cdot 25}{1 \cdot 13} = 15 \cdot 27$$

The ratio indicates the number of years which it would take for the share to earn the amount of its cost and its use is similar in concept to the 'number of years purchase of goodwill' method of business valuation which is often adopted by professional accountants. Clearly, however, it does not represent an enormous departure from previous practice for it is merely the reciprocal of the earnings yield.

Moreover, the reliability of the price-earning ratio is reduced due to the problem of defining earnings, as explained earlier, in Chapter 10, and to the fact that the ratio is based on a historical figure of earnings which relates to a different period for each company, whereas the market evaluates a share by reference to predicted future earnings.

(iii) *Dividend cover.* The dividend cover indicates the extent to which the profits earned for the ordinary were sufficient to cover the dividend payment. As the dividend must be paid gross out of net profits the number of times that it is covered is found by dividing the net earnings for the ordinary by the amount of the gross dividend. This, however, is exactly the same as dividing the earnings yield by the dividend yield:

$$\frac{\text{Earnings yield}}{\text{Gross dividend yield}} = \frac{\text{Earnings per share}}{\text{Market value of share}}$$

$$\times \frac{\text{Market value of share}}{\text{Gross dividend per share}} = \frac{\text{Earnings per share}}{\text{Gross dividend per share}}$$

In the example of Monsanto Chemicals Ltd the dividend cover may be calculated as follows:

$$\textit{Gross dividend yield} = \frac{15 \times 5}{17 \cdot 25} \times 100 = 4 \cdot 35\%$$

$$\textit{Times covered} = \frac{6 \cdot 55}{4 \cdot 35} = 1 \cdot 5 \text{ times}$$

From this information it is clear that the company earned net profits for the ordinary shareholders amounting to one and a half times the gross dividend actually paid. However, the extent of cover for the dividend is not of itself an indicator of the safety of the dividend, for, as normally calculated by the financial press, it ignores prior charges.

An examination of the profit and loss account of Monsanto Chemicals reveals the existence of material prior charges in the form of interest payable, and the preference dividend. Interest payable should be brought into the computation net of corporation tax for it is an allowable deduction against tax, while the preference dividend should be treated as a gross payment for it is non-deductible for tax purposes. The dividend cover on this basis would be:

	£	£
Earned for ordinary		1,219,824
Preference dividend		127,500
Deductible prior charges	451,324	
Less: Tax relief @ 40%	180,530	
		270,794
Profits available for charges and dividends		1,618,118
Total charges and dividends payable:		
Deductible prior charges (net)	270,794	
Preference dividend (gross)	127,500	
Ordinary dividend (gross)	810,000	
		1,208,294

$$\text{Times covered} = \frac{1,618,118}{1,208,294} = 1 \cdot 34 \text{ times}$$

Although the difference between the true and the published figures of times covered is not substantial in this instance, the difference for other companies may be more material and will be greater the higher the level of prior charges and the higher the stated figure of cover. Even when prior charges are taken into account there are still further factors which are relevant, such as the extent to which the manufacturing and trading expenses are fixed rather than variable, for a firm which has a high level of fixed or overhead expenses is clearly more vulnerable in depressed trading conditions than one whose costs are predominantly variable in nature.

(iv) *The importance of dividend, earnings and cover.* It is normally argued that a high dividend yield indicates risk while a low dividend yield suggests growth. In other words a high yield is unlikely to be maintained, while a low one will probably be increased. Similarly a high earnings yield (or a low price-earnings ratio) implies an expected decline in profits or extreme volatility of earnings, and a low yield suggests that increased profits are anticipated. A high dividend cover signifies a safe dividend, while a low cover implies the possibility of a cut in the dividend rate.

However, none of these factors can be taken in isolation. For instance, a low dividend cover may not be serious if the company concerned has a record of steadily increasing profits and has always followed a policy of paying out a high proportion of its earnings. Similarly the price-earnings ratio can often be misleading. For example, in the USA at the height of the Great Depression the average price-earnings ratio based on the Standard and Poor's 500 Composite Index was 138·9 which indicated not that investors were supremely confident about the future, but that earnings had fallen to such an extent that if shares were to have a positive price at all there must be a ridiculously high price-earnings ratio. For this reason the price-earnings ratio must be interpreted with caution during depressions and periods of deflation.

A further drawback to the price-earnings ratio is that it is based on reported earnings. These earnings figures are only available at annual intervals and then several months after the period to which they relate. Consequently the ratios as published in the financial press are historical and should be used very carefully in comparative analysis. The true price-earnings ratio should incorporate current and anticipated future profits, but these are extremely uncertain and subjective.

The relative importance of dividends and earnings is difficult to determine. It is argued in *Security Analysis* that 'for the vast majority of common stocks the dividend record and prospects have always been the most important factor controlling investment quality and value. The success of the typical concern has been measured by its ability to pay liberal and steadily increasing dividends on its capital. In the majority of cases the price of common stocks has been influenced more markedly by the dividend rate than by the reported earnings. In other words, distributed earnings have had a greater weight in determining market prices than have retained and re-invested earnings. The 'outside', or non-controlling, stockholders of any company can reap benefits from their investment in only two ways—through dividends and through an increase in the market value of their shares. Since the market value in most cases has depended primarily upon the dividend rate, the latter could be held responsible for nearly all the gains ultimately realized by investors.'[1]

[1] B. Graham, D. L. Dodd and S. Cottle, *Security Analysis* (New York: McGraw Hill, 4th ed., 1962), p. 480.

This extract from a very influential book on investment indicates the primacy normally accorded to dividends. This largely depends upon the assumption that retained earnings are not adequately incorporated into the market value of a company, despite their tax advantages under the corporation tax. As a result companies with high retention rates tend to become undervalued and prey to take-over bids. This is supported by the fact that the classical response to a bid is to raise the dividend level. Naturally an exception to the undervaluation of retentions is provided by companies whose retained profits appear to be invested so profitably that the market is prepared to accept low dividends until the exceptionally profitable reinvestment opportunities have been exhausted.

At the theoretical level the superior influence of dividends has been disputed, especially by Miller and Modigliani.[1] However, the analysis of the price determinants of share prices is fraught with both conceptual and practical difficulties and no complete proof of either viewpoint has yet been presented. Whichever theory is adopted it seems reasonable to suggest that any change in the market value of a share, whether attributable to earnings or to dividends, is far more important to a short or medium-term investor than the income received from dividends.

It has already been argued in Chapter 8 that shares should be valued on the basis of the present values of the predicted dividend flow and the anticipated capital gain or loss on sale. As such the valuation process is identical with, though far less precise than, the computation of the redemption yield on a redeemable security, except that the investor is determining not the yield on his share, but a personal value to compare with the actual market value. In times of rising share prices the yield on the potential capital gain is usually far in excess of that provided by the dividends.

For example during 1968 *The Financial Times* Industrial Ordinary Index had a low point of 385·0 on January 2nd and a high of 521·9 during September. Thus an investor who purchased the shares comprising the index in equal proportion to the weight given to them in its compilation would have made a profit of over 35% between January 2nd and September 19th. This ignores dealing expenses, but, by way of compensation, also excludes dividend receipts. Such capital profit clearly dwarfs any anticipated dividend yield, and casts doubts upon the relevance of dividends to any but a long-term investor.

[1] M. H. Miller and F. Modigliani, 'Dividend Policy, Growth, and the Valuation of Shares', *Journal of Business of the University of Chicago*, vol. 34, no. 4, October 1961.

It might be argued that *The Financial Times* Industrial Ordinary Index is unrepresentative, being based upon only thirty shares. However, the F.T.-Actuaries 500 Share Index provided an even better result, rising from 127·46 to 186·44 during 1968. Although such a dramatic upward swing is unpredictable and might in any case be followed by a similarly unexpected fall, there is no doubt that the extent of the price movement of all but the most stagnant shares, whether it is up or down, will in any particular year outweigh the dividend yield.

For this reason many investors disregard immediate dividends and choose shares which seem to offer the greatest prospects of growth. Thus a market favourite such as Tesco Ltd, whose shares had already doubled in value during the year were valued on the basis of a dividend yield of only 0·9% at the end of 1968. This clearly anticipated a further considerable increase in the market value of the company, for if it represented hopes of an increased dividend alone, investors would do better to invest in gilt-edged securities and invest in the shares when the dividend increased. The same argument might be applied to all equities which yield less than gilt-edged securities.

The greater emphasis on growth and capital appreciation on the London stock market is shown by the increased acceptance of lower earnings yields. The earnings yield of the shares comprising *The Financial Times* Ordinary Index fell from 8·82% at the end of September 1966 to 4·69% at the end of 1968, while the price-earnings ratio rose during the same period from about 11·25 to 21·33. Over the same period the dividend yield on the Index also fell from 6·38 to 3·66%.

The fact that English investors are more prepared to take a long-term view in respect of earnings and dividends indicates an acceptance of the fact that in the long run inflation and the ploughback of profits tend to bring about growth which is reflected in capital gains. These gains, both in size and taxation advantages, are superior to immediate income. However, a blind adherence to growth prospects can have disastrous results as purchasers of such glamour stocks as Rolls Razor, Elliott-Automation, and I.C.T. found to their cost during the early 1960s.

In fact it may be argued that an investor should look for stocks which are undervalued rather than acquiring stocks which are currently favoured by the market.[1] This is because the market tends to overadjust in respect of new information, with the result that

[1] Cf. Peter L. Berstein, 'Growth Companies *vs.* Growth Stocks', *Harvard Business Review* (Sept.–Oct. 1956), vol. 34, no. 5, pp. 87–98.

both optimistic and pessimistic views are overemphasized in share prices. As a result an investor stands more chance of success if he acquires stocks which are out of favour and thus possibly undervalued than if he purchases those which are highly popular and probably overvalued. This, however, is flimsy ground upon which to build an investment theory and there is no evidence to suggest that stock prices do anything other than represent the overall view of the market concerning the value of a share. If the investor is to make a profit he must predict the future performance of a company and the market reaction thereto. In undertaking such an analysis the dividend yield, earnings yield and cover are merely indicators of the current market opinion of a share and the degree of risk attached to a share, and must be considered simultaneously with all other available information.

CHAPTER 13

The Analysis of Stock Exchange Data:
Technical Analysis and Investment Theories

1. THE LOGIC BEHIND TECHNICAL ANALYSIS

Technical analysts argue that the price movements of a stock reflect the collective opinion of all investors in the light of all information currently available. As a result fundamental or traditional analysis, which is aimed at the assessment of the intrinsic value of a stock, is irrelevant, for it only analyzes information which the market has already taken into account in the determination of the price of the stock. The analysis of charts, however, is much more worthwhile, for the prices recorded therein indicate not only the market opinion regarding the earnings prospects of the stock but also the more intangible market sentiment concerning its quality.

Although only the most purist of chartists would claim that fundamental analysis should be entirely disregarded, most chartists feel that such analysis is only a subservient tool which may be used to confirm or reject the decisions suggested by technical analysis. The main basis of chart analysis is the examination of charts of past price movements in order to find patterns which tend to repeat themselves. When such patterns have been isolated they may be discerned when they reappear and appropriate action taken before the pattern is completed.

Apart from the analysis of individual charts an examination of movements of a series of charts might suggest that some of the price lines exert an influence upon others, so that, for instance, a particular movement in two graphs might suggest that another graph would move in a given fashion. Most analysis of this sort is carried out at the overall market level with a study of the inter-relationship of such indicators as *The Financial Times* Ordinary Index, *The Financial Times* Activity Index and the price of 2½% Consols.

2. THE MAJOR TYPES OF PREDICTIVE PATTERNS

(a) Trends

In the analysis of trends the time period involved is extremely important:

Primary trend. This indicates the general direction in which share prices are moving over a period of a year or more.

Secondary trend. The primary trend is composed of a series of secondary trends, which may last for a few weeks or for several months and which need not necessarily be in the same direction as the primary trend. In fact, they will frequently be in the opposite direction, for in the course of an upward primary trend there will be periodic bouts of selling as investors indulge in profit-taking, while during a bear market there will be reactions as investors take advantage of the opportunity of buying shares at lower prices.

Tertiary trend. This depicts the fluctuations in share prices over a period of days or weeks. As the graph of the tertiary trend covers such a short period the fluctuations are relatively wide and it is normally very difficult to determine the direction of the trend.

The charts below, which represent the price movement of a fictitious share, illustrate the importance of the time period in trend analysis. The scale of the graphs is logarithmic rather than arithmetic in that price movements of equivalent proportionate size are represented by an equal distance on the graph. Thus the distance from 50p to 100p is the same as that from 100p to 200p, for both represent an increase of 100%. This is justified by the fact that an investor with a given quantity of money to invest would make the same profit in buying shares at 50p which rise to £1 as he would make if he bought them at £1 and they rose to £2.

The first chart reveals a basic upward trend up to the middle of the sixth week with minor downward reactions during the first, third and fifth weeks and a more serious reaction during the third and fourth weeks. A basic downward trend began in the middle of the sixth week and continued, with an upward reaction during the seventh week, until the middle of the eighth week. For the remainder of the eighth week there was no discernible trend.

The second chart covers a five-year period and it can be seen that the basic upward trend from the first chart is part of a rising primary trend extending into January 1969, while the basic downward trend

371

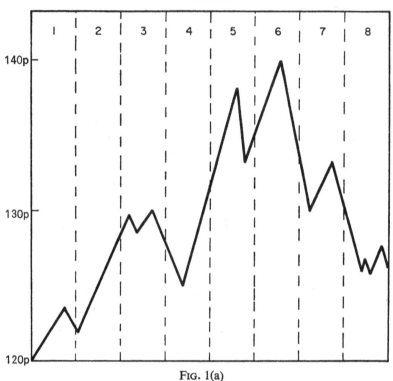

FIG. 1(a)

Chart showing the movement of the price of shares in XYZ Ltd for an
eight-week period, January-February 1967.

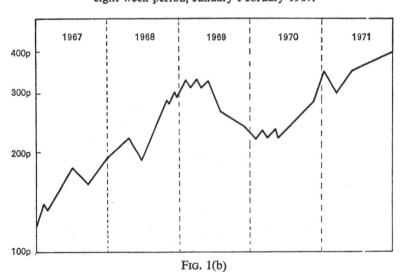

FIG. 1(b)

Chart showing the movement of the price of shares in XYZ Ltd for a
five-year period, January 1967-December 1971.

is revealed as an insignificant minor reaction in the context of the second chart. The entire price line might be regarded as a rising primary trend throughout the five-year period with minor secondary and tertiary reactions in each year and a more prolonged secondary reaction in 1969, bottoming off at the start of 1970.

The major problem of trend analysis is the discovery of secondary and tertiary trends in time to take advantage of them. An investor who decided that an upward primary trend had been established by April 1967, when the share price was 150p, would have made a profit of 250p per share by the end of 1971 when the price had reached 400p. However, if he had successfully predicted the secondary reactions he would have shown a much greater profit. If, for example, he had been able to predict the downward secondary trend in 1969 and had sold at above 300p and had bought back in 1970 at below 250p he would have shown a further profit of 50p per share. In fact a chartist would have successfully predicted the movement in question on the basis of the head and shoulder pattern in 1969 and the failure of the price to penetrate the resistance level of 220p in 1970.

Clearly it would be possible to increase profit further by a still more active trading policy. For instance, shares might have been sold at the end of June 1967 at 180p and repurchased at the end of September at 160p. Similarly, on the first chart, shares might have been sold short during the sixth week and bought during the seventh week at 130p. Where such dealings take place within the account the expenses are greatly reduced due to the fact that stamp duty is not payable, while brokers' commission may be reduced under certain circumstances. However, an active dealing policy is only successful where the trend is sufficiently steep to cover dealing expenses, including the jobber's turn. Consequently, where tertiary and minor secondary trends are acted upon they may be almost over before a clear signal is given by the charts so that they may be reversed before they have continued long enough to cover dealing expenses.

In addition to the time period of the trend it is necessary to have regard to its direction and steepness:

Flat trend. Where a share price moves within two flat parallel trend lines, investment policy will depend upon the width of the parallels. If, as in the example of Greenall, Whitley & Co. Ltd, the share price moves within two very narrow lines there is little scope for profit. If the price line moves upwards out of the parallels this is regarded as a buying signal while a downward breakthrough is regarded as a selling indicator. In fact, the share in question moved upwards out of the parallels during 1971 and rose to over 168p during that year.

GREENALL, WHITLEY AND CO. LTD

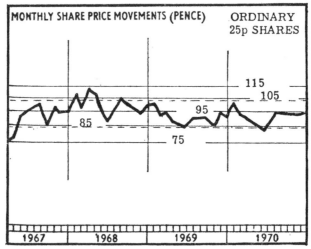

FIG. 2

Where the flat trend lines are fairly widely separated a profitable policy may be achieved by buying shares when they fail to penetrate the resistance level set by the lower line and selling them when they fail to penetrate the upper resistance level. If the price does pierce the higher line this is regarded as a bull indicator and the shares should be retained, while the penetration of the lower line is a bear signal and the shares should be avoided or sold short if it is wished to speculate.

An example of a fairly wide flat trend is provided by United Drapery Stores Ltd, whose shares moved between 75p and 115p between 1967 and 1970. They could have been bought towards the start of 1967 at 85p and sold during November 1967 at 98p. At the start of 1968 they touched the lower trend line and might have been bought at 80p, being sold in November 1968 at 115p when they failed to breach permanently the higher resistance level. In the middle of 1969 a further purchase might have been made at 75p, with a matching sale occurring at 98p later in the year, when the upper trend line was again unbroken. Finally, they should have been re-acquired in the summer of 1970 when they again touched 85p but failed to penetrate the lower resistance level. They should then have been held into 1971 when they finally pierced the upper trend line and reached 145p later that year.

374

UNITED DRAPERY STORES LTD

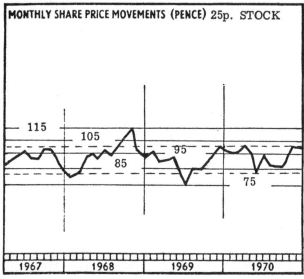

FIG. 3

Normal and steep upwards trends. If a price line moves upwards within two parallel trend lines the share should be held so long as the price remains above the lower trend line. If the price moves above the higher parallel this is regarded as a bull signal while a downwards penetration of the lower line is a bear signal, indicating that the share should be sold. The analysis of these trends may be illustrated by the charts of the Grand Metropolitan Hotels Ltd and Slater Walker Securities Ltd.

In the example of Grand Metropolitan Hotels Ltd, the share price moved within two normal upward trend lines until the middle of 1968 when the parallel lines became rather steeper. An attempt to break through the upper line in April 1969 was not maintained and the shares moved within less steep trend lines into 1971, during which year they moved up sharply to 196p. The message given by the chart throughout the period was that the shares should be retained, though an investor who was quick enough to discern and act upon the secondary downward trends in 1969 and 1970 might have further increased his profit.

The chart of Slater Walker Securities shows a much steeper trend than that of the Grand Metropolitan Hotels. When the shares moved

375

GRAND METROPOLITAN HOTELS

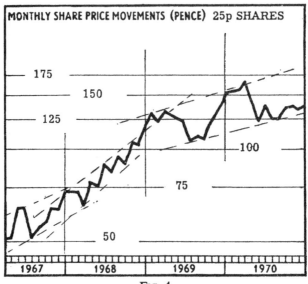

FIG. 4

SLATER WALKER SECURITIES

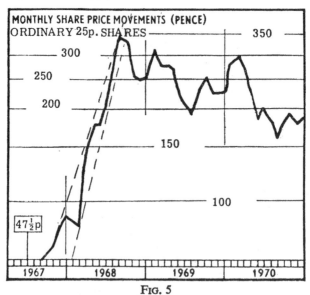

FIG. 5

outside the trend lines towards the end of 1968 in a downwards direction this signalled that the shares should be sold by investors. This advice was in fact justified for the shares moved in a primary downwards trend during the whole of 1969 and 1970 and fell to 160p, though during 1971 they recovered to 300p. More dynamic investors might have employed more sophisticated techniques to spot the upward secondary trends during the first quarters of 1969 and 1970. It should be stressed that these charts are intended purely as illustrations of simple trend analysis and that no attempt is made to discover optimal dealing activities within the trend lines.

Normal and steep downwards trends. The basic rule is that shares whose price is moving within parallel downward trend lines should not be purchased until the price line moves upwards and penetrates the upper trend line. An example of a normal downward trend is provided by the shares of Low & Bonar Group Ltd, which showed a downward trend throughout 1968, 1969 and 1970. During 1971, despite the general stock market recovery the share price did not rise substantially and stood at about 115p during the Autumn.

The share price curve of Lines Brothers Ltd exemplifies a steep downwards trend.

LOW AND BONAR GROUP LTD

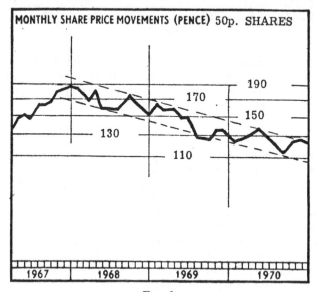

FIG. 6

The price moved within a steep downwards trend during 1969 and 1970, with the trend becoming steeper during 1970. The upper

LINES BROTHERS LTD

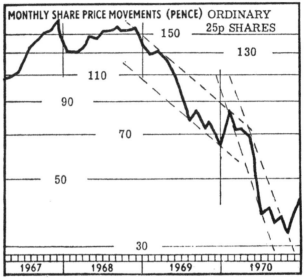

MONTHLY SHARE PRICE MOVEMENTS (PENCE) ORDINARY 25p SHARES

FIG. 7

parallel was pierced at the end of 1970 and during 1971 the share price rose to 90p. This recovery proved to be short-lived and by the Autumn of 1971 the share price had fallen to 5p on the rumour that the company might be liquidated.

(b) *Prophetic Patterns*

The two major patterns which are identified by chartists are the 'head and shoulders' formation and the triangle pattern.

The 'head and shoulders' pattern is well illustrated by the chart of Lister & Co. Ltd. In July 1968 the share price approached 85p, whereupon sellers entered the market and the price fell back to about 80p. A further advance to 92p was made towards the start of 1969, but this was again repulsed and the shares fell back to a level of about 78p. The question now was whether the next advance would be successful, thus establishing a normal upward trend, or whether it would be repulsed more easily, resulting in a 'head and shoulder' formation which indicates that the advance has finally

378

LISTER & CO. LTD

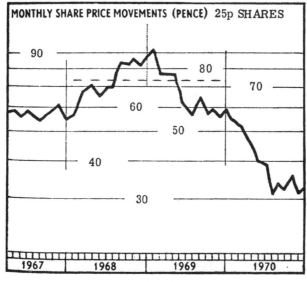

FIG. 8

been defeated. In this case the latter alternative occurred and the shares fell sharply after their final resistance had been decisively overcome.

The classic sequence of such a formation is thus a fairly strong surge forward in the share price which is forced back by selling. A still stronger advance, representing the head of the pattern, then follows. This too is repelled and a much weaker forward movement, indicating the shoulder of the pattern, takes place. The failure of this advance represents the final defeat of the bulls in the market for the share and it should be sold.

The second classic pattern is the triangle. This occurs where demand and supply are fluctuating in an indecisive fashion within a fairly broad range of prices. As the fluctuations become less sharp a triangular pattern becomes apparent. As the triangle closes the point of decision draws nearer and the chartist argues that where the price line moves upwards out of the area of the triangle, demand has predominated and the shares should be bought. If, as in the example of Greeff-Chemical Holdings Ltd, the price moves downwards out of the triangle, this is a bear signal and the share should be sold.

GREEFF-CHEMICAL HOLDINGS LTD

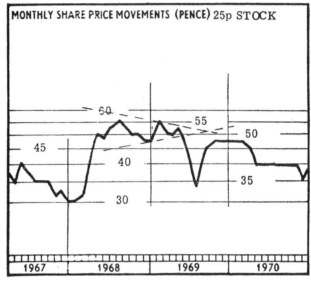

MONTHLY SHARE PRICE MOVEMENTS (PENCE) 25p STOCK

FIG. 9

In this example the share price fluctuated during the second half of 1968 between 47p and 56p. During the first few months of 1969 the fluctuations occur in the range 50p to 55p. It is clear that the point of decision has arrived and the fall below 47p in May 1970 suggested that the shares should be sold. Thereafter the shares fell sharply to 35p and did not recover to 50p until 1971.

(c) *Resistance Levels*

These occur where a considerable number of either buyers or sellers come into the market when a share attains or falls to a particular price. For example, where a broad flat trend is discerned resistance levels will be established at the price levels of the top line and the bottom line. When the price fails to penetrate the higher trend line investors who follow charts will enter the market as sellers, thus forcing the price down, while an upward movement from the lower trend line will be reinforced by chartist buyers. Chartist predictions may, therefore, have considerable influence and for this reason, whatever one's personal opinion regarding the worth of charts, it is necessary to understand them in order to predict the likely actions of their proponents.

Where the share price touches a resistance level twice in quick succession without succeeding in penetrating it this is known as a 'double top', where it is the upper resistance level which has been reached, and a 'double bottom' in the case of the lower resistance level. If the level is touched three times it is known as a 'triple top' or a 'triple bottom', as the case may be, and so on. The greater the number of times that the resistance level is contacted without penetration, the greater its strength. When it is finally breached this acts as a bear signal in the case of the lower resistance level for this indicates that the volume of buying which had previously entered the market and maintained the price at that level has now been swamped by an increased volume of selling. Here, as so often, chart theory is self-inducing, for technical analysts, who had previously supported the share at the lower level, would now withdraw from the market thus causing a further fall in the share price. Similarly, a rise through the upper resistance level would act as a bull signal, inducing chartists, who had previously sold when the share did not penetrate the upper level, to enter the market thus pushing up prices still further.

A good example of the analysis of resistance levels is provided by the chart of Lee, Arthur & Sons Ltd.

LEE, ARTHUR & SONS LTD

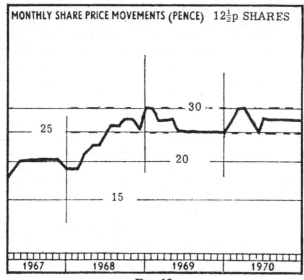

FIG. 10
381

Between the end of 1968 and the start of 1971 there were clearly identifiable resistance levels at about 30p and 20p. This situation continued during 1971 when during the first three-quarters of the year the share price moved within the range 20½–31¾p.

3. TECHNIQUES OF OVERALL MARKET ANALYSIS

The first significant attempt to formulate a theory for the prediction of future levels of share prices based upon charts and index numbers was the Dow Theory. This was based upon the work of Charles H. Dow, the first editor of the *Wall Street Journal*, who began the compilation of daily averages of stock prices in order to obtain a pattern of price movements. On January 1, 1897 he first published two averages—the index of industrial stocks and the index of rail stocks.

From his studies he pioneered chartist terminology, distinguishing between primary, secondary and tertiary trends. He also recognized the basic chartist tenet that an index of stock prices reflects all that is generally known about the overall prospects of business and expresses all the hopes and fears for the prospects of the individual companies of which it is comprised. Although he did not formally develop a theory based upon his indices his ideas were extended and formulated by W. P. Hamilton in the *Wall Street Journal* between 1903 and 1929 and in a book published in 1922.[1]

Movements of Dow's indices were analysed over a period of years and it was found that certain patterns tended to repeat themselves so that it was possible to predict future movements of the indices with some degree of success. The basic feature of the Dow Theory, which was based upon this analysis, was that a movement of one of the indices should not be acted upon unless it was confirmed by a movement in the same direction of the other index. Proponents of the theory argued that confirmed movements of this sort generally preceded a turn in the state of the economy by about six months and they claimed to have predicted successfully the market break of 1929 though their record at other times was inconsistent.

Since its formulation the theory has been adapted to include other confirmatory indices such as the breadth index, which is computed by dividing the figure of net advances or declines by the total number of issues which were dealt in, and the activity index. Despite the serious theoretical arguments against the theory, and, indeed, against all technical analysis, it has many adherents and as such constitutes an important factor on Wall Street.

[1] W. P. Hamilton, *The Stock Market Barometer* (New York: Barron's, 1922).

Although the pure form of the Dow Theory is not applicable to the London Stock Exchange due to the absence of an index of rail stocks, there are nevertheless many similar theories. Probably the most prominent exponent of technical analysis is A. G. Ellinger,[1] who advocates methods of analysis which are based upon the rule that trend changes in the index of ordinary shares should be confirmed by reference to other indices.

In *The Art of Investment* he argues that share prices are determined by three main factors:

(1) *The yield on fixed-interest securities.* Fixed-interest stocks are always in competition with variable dividend stocks for the funds of investors who are primarily concerned with income. As a result, a fall in the price of gilt-edged securities, indicating a rise in the rate of interest, would tend to exert a downward pressure upon the price of ordinary shares, thus causing a rise in dividend yields.

(2) *Dividends on ordinary shares.* These exert a great deal of influence. Even an investor who buys shares with the main object of obtaining capital gains is reliant upon future dividends, for the ultimate purchaser of the shares would not buy them unless dividends were anticipated. Dividends tend to be more influential upon prices than are earnings partly because they can be measured with greater accuracy than earnings, which are often very difficult to define, and partly because they determine the dividend yield which for many investors is the major determinant of investment policy.

(3) *The confidence factor.* This embraces all other factors which influence share prices, such as the state of business confidence and expectations regarding the future level of dividends. It is upon this factor that earnings exercise most influence, for future dividends obviously depend upon the current and anticipated level of earnings.

The confidence factor may be measured in the following way:

Take an average of share prices and call it P. Let the average of dividends on the shares be D and the average of fixed interest stock prices F. In order to eliminate the influence of the dividend and fixed-interest factors from the share price average, P should be divided by D and F, which will leave a residual R which may be regarded as the confidence factor, measuring the effect of all other influences.

[1] A. G. Ellinger, *The Art of Investment* (London: Bowes & Bowes, rev. ed., 1971).

The formula then appears as:

$$\frac{P}{F \times D} = R$$

$$\therefore \quad \frac{1}{F} \times \frac{P}{D} = R$$

However, $\frac{1}{F}$ must always vary proportionately with the yield on fixed-interest securities, which is given by the formula:

$$\frac{\text{Nominal Rate of Interest}}{\text{Price}} \times 100$$

This is due to the fact that, as the numerator (the nominal rate of interest) is constant, the yield is determined by the price alone. Thus the proportionate variation must always be the same as that of $\frac{1}{F}$.

Similarly, $\frac{D}{P}$ will always vary proportionately with the yield on ordinary shares, so that

$$\frac{P}{D} \text{ must always vary as } \frac{1}{\text{Yield on ordinary shares}}$$

Thus $\frac{1}{F} \times \frac{P}{D} = \dfrac{\text{Yield on fixed interest securities}}{\text{Yield on ordinary shares}} = \text{Confidence factor}$

Consequently, the higher the yield on fixed-interest securities compared with that on ordinary shares the higher the confidence factor.

There are two main indices of the confidence factor which are currently available:

(a) Moodies confidence index. This has been calculated since 1925, first monthly, then weekly, from the formula:

$$\frac{\text{Equity index} \times 100 \times 100}{\text{Consols index} \times \text{Dividend index}}$$

The equity index used is Moodies own, calculated up to 1950 from the prices of fifty leading industrial shares and, since then, of sixty shares selected to give fair representation to the various industries and different sizes of companies which comprise the market.

(*b*) Investment Research Confidence Indicator. This has been calculated on a weekly basis since 1944 from the formula:

$$\frac{100,000}{\text{F.T. Fixed Interest Stock Index} \times \text{F.T. Ordinary Yield Index}}$$

The numerator in this formula is unimportant, having been selected merely to provide an index which, like *The Financial Times* Ordinary Index, has three digits and one decimal place.

In addition, Ellinger suggests that an activity chart should be used in conjunction with the analysis of the three factors described above. *The Financial Times* publishes indices of the daily number of bargains marked, based upon the marks recorded between July and December 1942. The best of their indices is the five-day moving average index of activity in industrial shares which smooths out the exceptionally high bargains normally recorded on Mondays. If the activity chart, based on this index, shows a high level of transactions this suggests that demand for shares is paramount, while if activity is low, supply is predominant.

In his analysis of trends in share prices Ellinger therefore uses four charts:

(*A*) An activity chart based upon *The Financial Times* Five-day Moving Average Index.

(*B*) A dividend chart based upon the product of the F.T. Industrial Ordinary Share Index and the F.T. Index of Yields on Industrial Ordinary Shares.

(*C*) A chart depicting movements of the confidence factor.

(*D*) A graph plotting movements of the F.T. Fixed-interest Stock Index.

These four charts are compared with the F.T. Industrial Ordinary Index to explain past fluctuations in the index and to endeavour to predict its future trends. The confidence factor in particular is extremely important, for much business in the market is transacted by investors who have specialist knowledge of economic forecasting and their knowledge is reflected in this factor. Consequently, so long as the confidence chart reveals a rising trend, share prices will tend to rise.

Of the four charts described above, the index of fixed-interest stock prices is probably least important, for it is affected by long-run factors many of which have little influence upon current share prices. However, it has a fair record as a confirmatory indicator when used in connection with the Industrial Ordinary Index. Usually it moves down from the top or up from the bottom about six months before a similar change in the trend of share prices becomes apparent. Therefore where the trend of the ordinary index appears to be changing, the change should be confirmed by reference to the index of fixed-interest stocks.

The other three charts should normally rise during a bull market while the activity chart and the confidence factor should fall when bears predominate. It is argued that it is possible to predict the future course of the market by studying current movements of the ordinary index and confirming changes of trend by reference to the confirmatory charts. Investors will not be able to detect the very start of a bull market, for they must wait until the upward trend has been definitely confirmed; but they should receive the buying signal long before the top has been reached. In the same way charts will not give a selling signal until the downward trend has been well established, and this will certainly be some way past the top point of the preceding bull market.

In another publication Ellinger[1] analysed movements of the F.T. Industrial Ordinary Index by reference to fluctuations in the price of Consols $2\frac{1}{2}\%$ and the level of the F.T. Five-day Moving Average Activity Index, showing how changes of trend were often signalled in advance by a turn in the price of Consols and confirmed by simultaneous changes in the trend of activity.

Although Ellinger is the foremost chartist in the United Kingdom, his claims for the importance of technical analysis are remarkably modest. In *The Art of Investment* he argues that fundamental analysis[2] is still an extremely important element of investment appraisal. An investor must decide on the basis of such analysis whether the purchase of a particular share is justified. The use of charts indicates the appropriate time at which to buy. Overall market analysis will reveal whether the market is in a primary bull or a primary bear trend, while analysis of the chart of the share will show whether the price is likely to fall, in which case purchase should be delayed, or to rise, in which case an immediate purchase should be made.

Another well-known method of analysis based upon the use of indices is the Hatch System, which was formulated by Hargreaves Parkinson and expounded in two books, *The Hatch System* and *Advanced Hatch*. The system is based upon the argument that an investor cannot hope to detect when the market has reached the top of a peak or the bottom of a trough. However, if he could ensure that he sold at a level 10% after the top of the market and

[1] A. G. Ellinger, *The Post War History of the Stock Market* (Cambridge: Investment Research, 1966).

[2] *Op. cit.*, p. 157.

bought when the index was 10% above the bottom he would achieve as good an investment performance as he could possibly expect.

The index upon which the system is usually based is the F.T. Industrial Ordinary, though any index of ordinary shares is satisfactory so long as it is used consistently. The investor will average the daily index figure for each week, and each weekly figure for every month. If the market is rising he will not sell until he reaches a month whose average is 10% below the previous highest monthly average. Conversely, if it is falling he will start buying shares when the monthly average is 10% above its lowest level. By this method he would hope to leave a bull market at about 10% after its top point and to enter at about 10% above the bottom of a bear market.

The great advantage of the system is that investors are encouraged to hold on to shares in a bull market when they might otherwise have been tempted to sell. On the other hand, where the movement in the index is relatively narrow and only just exceeds the 10% margin investors may receive a selling signal too early or may enter the market and be forced to sell at a loss. As with all chart analysis the investor is faced with the choice of requiring an extremely positive signal, such as a 20% movement along a trend line backed by confirmatory signals from other indices, in which case the scope for profit is relatively low, or a relatively slight signal, such as a 5% upward or downward trend, with the result that there is a probability that he will be activated incorrectly by secondary and even tertiary trends. In fact, the research of Sidney S. Alexander[1] into the profitability of filter systems based on aggregate indices showed that for a wide range of filters such systems were not significantly more profitable than a straightforward 'buy and hold system'. The results of his research therefore cast serious doubts upon the efficiency of the Hatch System, which is based upon a variant of the filter technique.

A major drawback to analysis of the state of the market is that the major index, the F.T. Industrial Ordinary, covers only thirty shares so that it is not necessarily representative of the entire market. Similarly the activity indices which are available are based on the number of bargains marked, which probably only represents about half of the deals actually transacted and gives no indication of the turnover involved. In order to obtain a more representative indicator

[1] Sidney S. Alexander, 'Price Movements in Speculative Markets: Trends or Random Walks', *Industrial Management Review*, vol. 2, no. 2 (May 1961), pp. 7-26. 'Price Movements in Speculative Markets: Trends or Random Walks', no. 2 published in *The Random Character of Stock Market Prices*, ed. Paul H. Cootner (Cambridge: M.I.T. Press, 1964).

of the trend of the market the use of the Advance-Decline Line has become widespread in America. The use of this is explained by George K. Freeman[1], who argues that the A-D Line, which shows for each day the cumulative difference between the number of all stocks which rise and those which fall, normally reaches its peak before the industrial average. It therefore begins to fall at a time when the bull market, although still rising, is in its final stages and it therefore provides a selling signal at such times.

In the last section of this chapter the main arguments against technical analysis are stated. Even, however, if it is accepted that a correct analysis of overall market movements may be made on the basis of charts, the investor is still faced with the problem of determining which sector of the market, and which share within that sector, is most attractive. The importance of selection is shown by the following table, which is based upon movements of the F.T. Actuaries Share Indices between their commencement at 100 on April 10, 1962, and the end of September 1967.

	End of September 1967	1966	Percentage Change	Percentage Change since 10.4.1962
Capital Goods Group (187)	127·13	99·22	+28·13	+ 27·13
Aircraft (4)	220·29	187·92	+17·23	+120·29
Building materials (32)	128·57	94·95	+35·41	+ 28·57
Contracting and construction (15)	143·84	105·24	+36·68	+ 43·84
Electricals (13)	199·75	152·17	+31·27	+ 99·75
Engineering (79)	114·07	90·87	+25·53	+ 14·07
Machine tools (10)	120·07	104·23	+15·20	+ 20·07
Shipbuilding (5)	80·25	71·39	+12·41	− 19·75
Miscellaneous (29)	94·95	74·37	+27·67	− 5·05
Consumer Goods (Durable) Group (56)	119·88	88·29	+35·78	+ 19·88
Electricals (14)	119·48	78·39	+52·42	+ 19·48
Household goods (12)	118·85	94·93	+25·20	+ 18·85
Motors and distributors (14)	108·30	90·16	+20·12	+ 8·30
Rubber manufacturing (6)	127·29	105·80	+20·31	+ 27·29
Miscellaneous (10)	140·35	96·50	+45·44	+ 40·35
Consumer Goods (Non-Durable) Group (193)	111·11	88·72	+25·24	+ 11·11
Breweries (22)	111·95	84·28	+32·83	+ 11·95
Entertainment and catering (18)	131·35	90·43	+45·25	+ 31·35
Food manufacturing (36)	110·15	81·60	+34·99	+ 10·15

[1] 'Advance-Decline Line: A Clue to the Underlying Strength of the Market', Barron's *National Business and Financial Weekly*, January 21, 1963.

	End of September		Percentage Change	Percentage Change since 10.4.1962
	1967	1966		
Consumer Goods (Non-Durable)—continued				
Newspapers and publishing (15)	135·56	122·94	+10·27	+ 35·56
Paper and packaging (14)	108·28	104·75	+ 3·37	+ 8·28
Stores (34)	94·55	77·08	+22·66	− 5·45
Textiles (21)	144·14	121·83	+18·31	+ 44·14
Tobacco (3)	165·82	149·20	+11·14	+ 65·82
Miscellaneous (30)	107·74	82·96	+29·87	+ 7·74
Other Groups				
Chemicals (17)	119·35	97·99	+21·80	+ 19·35
Oil (3)	187·93	175·34	+ 7·18	+ 87·93
Shipping (11)	154·37	134·05	+15·16	+ 54·37
Miscellaneous (unclassified) (33)	109·65	81·95	+33·80	+ 9·65
500 Share Index	123·10	99·34	+23·92	+ 23·10
Financial Group (94)	88·49	73·83	+19·86	− 11·51
Banks (9)	96·91	84·14	+15·18	− 3·09
Discount Houses (6)	120·42	108·88	+10·60	+ 20·42
Hire Purchase (7)	118·25	83·14	+42·23	+ 18·25
Insurance (Life) (8)	90·89	72·88	+24·71	− 9·11
Insurance (Composite) (11)	68·49	60·30	+13·58	− 31·51
Investment Trusts (20)	124·84	97·21	+28·42	+ 24·84
Merchant Banks, Issuing Houses (7)	71·68	53·96	+32·84	− 28·32
Property (26)	74·13	62·61	+18·40	− 25·87
All Share Index (594 Shares)	114·67	93·11	+23·05	+ 14·67
Commodity Share Groups				
Rubbers (10)	110·98	109·60	+ 1·26	+ 10·98
Teas (10)	86·66	64·88	+33·57	− 13·33
Coppers (6)	117·21	116·80	+ 0·35	+ 17·21
Lead-Zincs (5)	452·95	252·72	+80·05	+352·95
Tins (11)	75·64	89·14	−15·14	− 24·36
20-year Government Stocks	92·91	89·50	+ 3·81	− 7·09
F.T. Industrial Ordinary Index	381·2	305·2	+ 24·9	+ 24·3 (306·6)

Between September 30, 1966 and 1967 the F.T. Actuaries 500 Share Index rose by 23·92%, from 99·34 to 123·10%. This overall rise was comprised of varying sectoral increases, ranging from 3·37% for paper and packaging and 7·18% for oil to 45·44% for miscellaneous consumer durables and 52·42% for electrical consumer durables. An even wider variety of movements is contained in the overall 23·10% increase in the index from its inception on April 10, 1962 to September 30, 1967. During that period aircraft shares rose by 120·29% and electrical capital goods by 99·75%, while shipbuilding shares fell by 19·75% and stores by 5·45%.

Even if the average price movement in a particular sector is correctly predicted the problem still remains of selecting the most favourable share within that sector. Of the sectors comprising the 500 Share Index, paper and packaging showed the worst performance between September 1966 and September 1967. The price movement of individual shares in that sector ranged from a fall of one-third to a rise of one-third. Within the electrical consumer durables sector, which had the best performance during the same period, the range of price movements was between a fall of $12\frac{1}{2}$% and an increase of 100%.

It is thus clear that the prediction of general market movements must be supplemented by the analysis of individual shares. The methods adopted by chartists to this end were described broadly earlier in this chapter. A more detailed analysis, based upon the price chart for International Computers and Tabulators Ltd for the years 1962 to 1967 is outlined below.

During the period illustrated by the chart the share price moved downwards from 600p to 130p and then partially recovered to 250p. With the advantage of hindsight the downward trend seems to have been fairly predictable. For example the resistance level indicated by the horizontal line AA was penetrated at the end of May 1962 and this should have acted as a selling signal for a chartist. Similar penetrations occurred through the horizontal lines BB, CC, DD, that through CC being reinforced by the failure of a subsequent rally to pierce the resistance level in an upwards direction.

The first stage of the price decline was bounded by the trend lines 1–2 and 4–5. In October 1964 the price line moved sideways out of these trend lines and, when the break through the resistance level at DD was effected, the new trend boundaries were seen to be 1–3 and 4–5. In April 1966 the shares bottomed out at 130p and in June broke upwards through the upper trend line 1–3. This proved to be too early a buying signal and the shares fell back again in September to 130p, thus creating a double bottom, indicated by the line EE. The upward movement from this resistance level and the failure to penetrate downwards the later resistance level at FF were both buying signals and the shares at the end of 1967 were still moving within the trend channels indicated by the lines 6–7 and 8–9. At the same time the upward trend was reinforced by the increased activity in the shares indicated by the vertical lines below the chart during 1966 and 1967.

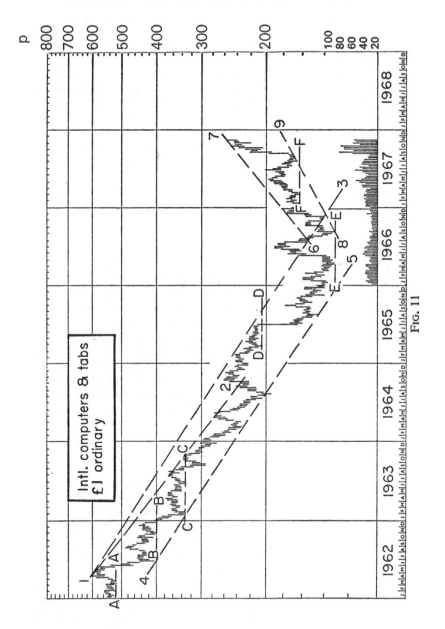

FIG. 11

4. A CRITICAL ASSESSMENT OF TECHNICAL ANALYSIS

Technical analysis is commonly subjected to four major criticisms. In the first place the so-called prophetic patterns are often dependent upon the scale of the chart. Trends and patterns which appear significant in charts which are based upon a scale measured in weeks, days or parts of days will often disappear in charts based upon months or years. Similarly the choice of scale on the vertical axis can affect the pattern. Consequently, because price lines are dependent upon the scales of the two axes it is possible for the same information to be presented and interpreted in very different ways.

Moreover, it is very difficult to determine whether a change in direction of a price line indicates a reversal of the primary trend or whether it is merely a secondary or tertiary trend. It is relatively easy, by waiting until the trend appears to have established itself or until it has been confirmed by other indices, to avoid being misled by a tertiary trend. However, it is very difficult to identify a secondary trend and an investor may easily act upon the assumption that a primary trend has been reversed when in fact the index has only entered a secondary phase, with the result that prices move against him as soon as he has acted in accordance with the signal. The chartist is thus faced with the dilemma that the more quickly he acts in response to signals the more likely he is to make the wrong decision. Moreover a very active dealing policy of this sort is extremely expensive due to the high incidence of dealing expenses. If, on the other hand, he waits until the trend has been firmly established he may have to bear a relatively large part of the loss in the case of a bear market or lose much of the potential profit in a bull market. Furthermore, there is no guarantee that the primary trend will not change as soon as he has made his decision.

Charts are also subject to the criticism that, although it is relatively easy to identify prophetic patterns on graphs of past price movements, it is often difficult to predict the ultimate pattern that the price line will delineate, and even when the pattern has been discerned, there is no guarantee that the signal will be correct. For instance, when shares fall out of a flat trend pattern thus providing a selling signal for chartists there is no reason why they should not immediately rise in response to unforeseen information.

The most powerful argument against technical analysis is provided by the random walk theory. This theory begins with the basic premise of chartism, namely that the share price at any given time reflects the collective opinion of the market regarding the worth of the share. However, whereas chartists go on to argue that changes of opinion can be detected from charts quickly enough to take appropriate action and that past graphical patterns have a tendency to repeat themselves, thus giving a signal to the investor who identified them, the adherents of the random walk theory postulate that the share price reacts only to new information. The availability and nature of new information is in no way influenced by the past performance of a share. Consequently as the information becomes available in a random fashion, share prices themselves move in a random and unpredictable fashion. In view of the fact that the theoretical arguments for the random walk theory are extremely cogent and have been reinforced by statistical testing, while the theory behind technical analysis has rarely been argued in an academic fashion and has never been successfully tested, there seems little reason to accept charts as an effective tool of investment.

On the other hand, it cannot be denied that charts are extremely useful in that they depict at a glance the past and current state of the market and of individual shares. As such they are an invaluable aid to fundamental analysts to whom the past performance of a company and its shares are an indicator, subject to adjustment for known and estimated variants, of its possible future progress.

Rather more important is the fact that, as charts are used by so many investors, they have become a material market influence. Signals given by charts, like purchases suggested by financial editors, tend to be self-realising, for if they are sufficiently positive and enough investors act upon them the share price will automatically move in the suggested direction. Thus if a head and shoulders formation is discerned and publicized and the share price moves downwards out of the pattern there will be an increase in selling orders which will reinforce the downward trend. Consequently fundamental analysts must be aware of the implications of charts and must appreciate that a large body of investors will act in accordance with their signals.

It should be stressed that the criticism which is levelled in this section at technical analysis is aimed at those who argue that charts alone are an adequate means of appraising investments. As Daniel Seligman[1] has pointed out in two excellent articles there is no logic behind or proof for their claims. On the other hand charts serve an undeniably useful purpose in the field of fundamental analysis and it is in this context that their use is warranted.

[1] 'Playing the Market with Charts', *Fortune Magazine*, Time Inc., February 1962 and 'The Mystique of Point-and-Figure', *Fortune Magazine*, Time Inc., March 1962.

CHAPTER 14

Recent Developments in the Field of
Investment Analysis

1. THE RANDOM WALK HYPOTHESIS AND OTHER
CONCEPTUAL ADVANCES

In recent years there have been considerable advances in the subject
of investment theory, almost all of which have been made in the
USA. One of the main reasons for the lack of interest in the United
Kingdom has been the inadequacy of basic material compared with
that available in the USA. Before 1948, company accounts were
extremely misleading and it was not until 1967 that companies were
required to reveal their sales. Moreover, although the Stock Exchange
has provided statistics of overall turnover since September 1964,
there is no information relating to the turnover in securities of
particular industries or companies. Research, therefore, is hampered
by vast gaps in the available information relating to share transactions
and to company performance. Moreover, such information as is
accessible is of comparatively recent vintage, so that there are no
long runs of consistent statistics which may be used for the formulation or proof of theories.

A further factor has been the neglect of investment theory by
schools, universities and professional bodies, which is appalling
considering the number of different investment decisions that have
to be made by individuals, companies and Government bodies.
Fortunately this omission is gradually being repaired at universities
and the business schools at both teaching and research levels.
However, the professional bodies, as so often, are lagging far behind
and are still concentrating on the mechanical rather than the inter-
pretative aspects of their subjects. Most of them include the subject
of investment in what is the equivalent of a general knowledge paper,

394

and only the actuarial bodies and the Institute of Bankers have a compulsory paper on the subject.

It seems certain that Britain will continue to lag behind in this field until more information is required of companies and until the Stock Exchange is prepared to reveal more details of what occurs behind its closed doors. This information is necessary for the free working of a competitive society, yet it is so often those who advocate competition and free enterprise who resist the pressure for greater disclosure.

American research covers a remarkably extensive range of topics. Particularly significant contributions have been made in the fields of risk analysis, portfolio analysis and price forecasting. An admirable selection of important papers on various aspects of investment theory may be found in *Frontiers of Investment Analysis*.[1] The material included therein is largely outside the scope of this book, partly because of its relatively advanced mathematical content and partly because many of the papers are highly theoretical and have not as yet been adapted for practical purposes. However, as will be shown later in this chapter, the development of the computer has facilitated the application of much theoretical material to practical investment appraisal.

The Random Walk Hypothesis

One theoretical development which has significant practical consequences for investment appraisal is the random walk hypothesis. This theory has led to the argument that highly developed stock exchanges, such as those in New York and London, are perfectly efficient markets, in that prices therein are determined by the interaction of intelligent investors who are all in possession of the entire corpus of current information. Thus at any given time the complex of stock prices will represent the interpretation by the market of the information currently available, including the expectations of investors concerning future information. As a result the current price of a security should approximate to its intrinsic value, the calculation of which is the main objective of fundamental analysis.

However, it is unlikely that the actual price of a security will correspond exactly to its intrinsic value, for the latter cannot be calculated precisely in an uncertain world. Consequently there will be differences of opinion between investors as to the true value of each share and this will cause the market value to fluctuate in a

[1] Edited by E. Bruce Fredrikson (Scranton, Pennsylvania: International Textbook Co., 1965).

random fashion around the intrinsic value. Competition between market participants will ensure that these fluctuations are not too violent, for if the market price were to move too far away from the intrinsic value, investors would buy or sell in order to reverse this movement.

The intrinsic value itself is in a constant state of flux, for it will be adjusted in respect of any relevant new information. Because this information is freely available to all investors market competition will ensure that the share price is immediately adjusted to take account of it. Neither the contents nor the timing of future information can be predicted with complete accuracy. Some factors such as budget proposals or dividend cuts may be predicted, while others, such as political crises and strikes, are often unpredictable. As a consequence the share price will always represent current market opinion concerning present information and predictable future information and will be adjusted immediately in response to the announcement of information which is unpredictable or has been incorrectly predicted. Information of a sort which will induce a change in price cannot by definition be correctly anticipated. Its arrival is random and entirely independent of previous price changes.

The basic conclusion of the theory is that share prices move in a random fashion in the very short run due to differences of opinion between investors. Thereafter their randomness is accentuated by the announcement of unpredictable information which is immediately assimilated by the stock price.

The evidence which has been accumulated in favour of the hypothesis is of two sorts. One approach has used statistical techniques to show that stock prices have in the past moved in a manner similar to a random walk. From this it is inferred that stock prices probably move in a random manner as a result of which current prices are entirely independent of past prices. The second method has analyzed the predictive ability of market experts, which has been tested by comparing their investment performance with that of portfolios selected by random methods.

The techniques which have been used for empirical research in this field are extremely advanced and quite outside the scope of this book. An elementary and very clear introduction to the subject can be found in an article by Eugene F. Fama.[1] A selection of the original papers, describing the research in detail, has been compiled

[1] Eugene F. Fama, 'Random Walks in Stock Market Prices', *Financial Analysts Journal* (September–October, 1965). Reproduced in *C.F.A. Readings in Financial Analysis*, The Institute of Chartered Financial Analysts (Homewood, Illinois: Irwin, 1966).

by Paul H. Cootner,[1] and the main points in these articles have been summarized by A. C. Rayner and I. M. D. Little.[2]

Proponents of the random walk hypothesis have argued that their thesis invalidates much of traditional or fundamental analysis and the entire basis of technical analysis. The theoretical case against traditional analysis is based upon the argument that in a perfectly efficient market, competition between market participators will cause the price of a security to approximate so closely to its intrinsic value that the differential will not be large enough to justify the costs of dealing. As all prices are thus determined by the consensus of opinion of a large number of intelligent traders who are all in possession of the same facts, fundamental analysis cannot provide an investor with an advantage over other investors. Moreover future prices will move in response to the announcement of future unpredictable information. This becomes available in a random fashion and is not susceptible to fundamental analysis, which is thus valueless for the analysis of either current or future prices.

The empirical case against traditional analysis is primarily based upon a comparison of the performance of shares selected by investment experts with that of shares chosen at random. Various surveys of this sort have shown that there is no significant advantage in accepting the advice of experts over choosing a portfolio by some random method. The pioneering work in this field was carried out by Alfred Cowles in two papers.[3] In the second of these he examined the success of four financial periodicals and seven financial services in forecasting the general trend of the New York stock market for periods between 1928 and 1943. His analysis shows that six of the eleven forecasters were relatively successful while five were unsuccessful, and that on average the forecasters performed only 0·2% per annum better than a random forecasting method.

Other criticisms of professional analysts have been contained in papers which show that the performance of mutual funds is on average no better than the performance of the general stock market price index, thus implying that they could obtain as good a result by investing in the index, thus saving the relatively high charges made by the funds. This was the conclusion of a study of mutual

[1] Paul H. Cootner (ed), *The Random Character of Stock Market Prices* (Cambridge: M.I.T. Press, 1964).

[2] A. C. Rayner & I. M. D. Little, *Higgledy Piggledy Growth Again* (Oxford: Blackwell, 1966).

[3] 'Can Stock Market Forecasters Forecast?' *Econometrica*, vol. 1 (July 1933), pp. 309–24. 'Stock Market Forecasting', *Econometrica*, vol. 12 (July–October, 1944), pp. 206–14.

funds which was sponsored by the Securities and Exchange Commission[1] and published in 1962 and it was confirmed by later research carried out by Irwin Friend and Douglas Vickers, both of whom participated in the original study. Their findings indicated that mutual funds on average provided neither a higher return for the same degree of risk nor a lower risk for the same return than that provided by a series of randomly selected portfolios.[2]

The case against technical analysis is even more forceful, for if the random walk hypothesis is correct and share prices are determined only by future information which becomes available in a random fashion, then they are not affected in any way by past price patterns. Consequently, technical analysis, which attempts to predict future prices on the basis of an analysis of past prices, is quite worthless. This, however, has already been argued in Chapter 13, where it was concluded that technical analysis of itself has no theoretical justification, though it may serve as a useful tool of fundamental analysis.

Technical analysis is therefore regarded purely as part of the integrated body of information which provides the material for fundamental analysis, and its displacement as an absolute method of investment appraisal is largely accepted. However, the arguments in favour of fundamental analysis against the random walk hypothesis are much more potent. The main aim of fundamental analysis is to examine all of the available information relating to a particular share, including factors relating to the state of the general economy and to the Stock Exchange as a whole. This analysis forms the basis for a prediction of future dividends and an estimate of the future share price. It has already been shown in Chapter 8 that this involves a great deal of guesswork, particularly in the assessment of the anticipated attitude of the market towards a given share. Nevertheless, it is an exercise which is justified in theory, given a state of imperfect knowledge, and which can and should be attempted in practice.

The main difference between traditional analysis and the random walk hypothesis concerns the efficiency of the market. Random walk adherents argue that the market is efficient and that its large number of intelligent participants, all in free possession of all

[1] *A Study of Mutual Funds*, prepared for the Securities and Exchange Commission by the Wharton School of Finance and Commerce, Report of the Committee on Interstate and Foreign Commerce, 87th Congress, 2nd Session, August 28, 1962.
[2] Irwin Friend and Douglas Vickers, 'Portfolio Selection and Investment Performance', *Journal of Finance*, September 1965.

available information, will tend to draw similar conclusions regarding the intrinsic value of shares, so that there is little scope for profits to be made by detecting differences between market and intrinsic values. Fundamental analysts, on the other hand, believe that the market is so imperfect and uncertain that analysts can draw such substantially different conclusions from the same information that successful analysis can provide a profit. This seems a far more satisfactory explanation of market behaviour than the concept of perfect efficiency. Moreover, the random walk theory cannot dispute the advantages to be gained by market manipulators, who can create and thus predict delusive information, and by insiders, who have foreknowledge of information and can use this to their benefit.

Despite the commonsense grounds for favouring fundamental analysis the random walk hypothesis enjoys considerable support at the academic level and is corroborated by an impressive accumulation of evidence. As has been shown, this evidence consists partly of a statistical study of share prices and partly of a comparison of the relative performance of experts and random selection methods.

The random walk theory is probably justified on mathematical grounds in that the statistical evidence suggests that share prices move *as if* they were determined by random factors. However, the determinants of share prices are so diverse and unquantifiable that it is impossible to move on to the argument that share prices *are indisputably* determined by random elements. To date the more forceful arguments against fundamental analysis have been those based on comparisons between portfolios chosen by experts and those selected at random, which have revealed no positive advantage in favour of the experts. This, however, is indicative of the lack of information available to analysts and the uncertain world in which they operate. It is, after all, unrealistic to expect analysts to forecast the future profits of a company, when the directors themselves are often unable to predict them with any substantial degree of accuracy.

The major defect of the random walk hypothesis is that it assumes an efficient market, while its empirical support has been amassed from statistics provided by an almost entirely imperfect market in which the quality of available information did not permit of meaningful analysis. Under conditions of almost complete uncertainty in which investment analysis is akin to guesswork practically all information is unpredictable and appears in a random fashion, with the result that movements in share prices are, by definition, random in manner. However, although randomness cannot be denied in an entirely imperfect market there seem to be arguments in favour of fundamental analysis when the quality and quantity of information improve and the tools of analysis become more highly developed. Such improvement has occurred in recent years and it seems reasonable to expect that fundamental analysis, which is completely justifiable under circumstances of relatively imperfect knowledge, will grow in stature. However, it is essential that the results of such analysis should remain secret, for the moment they are revealed to the market as a whole they will be incorporated into the corpus of information on the basis of which prices are determined. Thus information contained in stockbrokers' circulars or in the financial press cannot benefit its recipients, for it causes an immediate reaction in the relevant share prices. However, there is no reason why an individual investor or the research department of an institutional investor should not be able to make and benefit from more accurate forecasts of future information and share prices than those of the rest of the market.

Ironically, though, if the market were to become still more efficient with the result that there was a greater consensus of opinion between analysts, then the random walk theory would again be indisputable. It is unlikely, however, that in an uncertain world there would be a sufficient consensus of opinion to preclude the possibility of profits by superior analysis and predictions.

The random walk hypothesis is thus unassailable under conditions of complete uncertainty, which have in fact predominated up to the present time, and under conditions of relatively high efficiency, which are unlikely to occur. Fundamental analysis, however, is acceptable in the intermediate situation where the market is largely, though not entirely, imperfect. The quality of information necessary to provide such a market must be forthcoming if the market is to claim any sort of authority as an intelligent allocatory mechanism.

The Growing Importance of Computers

The increasing sophistication of computers and their easier availability due to the introduction of rental schemes has given them greater prominence in the field of investment since the mid-1950s in the USA and rather more recently in Great Britain. Initially they were used by stockbrokers primarily for mechanical administrative operations, such as the maintenance of clients' ledgers and the preparation of monthly statements. Similarly, the London Stock Exchange now uses a computer for the preparation of inter-broker accounts and for co-ordination of buying and selling deals in certain major stocks.

The main assets of the computer are its vast memory or information store and its ability to obey clear instructions with fantastic speed and complete accuracy. The extent of its speed of operation is shown by the fact that within twenty years of the initial development in 1946 of the computer, models had been evolved which were capable of performing one million elementary operations per second. So long as the operations required can be translated into arithmetic notations or a choice between alternatives on the basis of a definite criterion they can be performed at a speed far exceeding the potential of a human being. It must be stressed, however, that the computer, though it has a memory, does not have its own intelligence and decision mechanism. It can only operate in response to programmed instructions and if either these instructions or the information initially stored in the computer are incorrect the results will be erroneous.

Although the actual mechanism of a computer is enormously complex, the reasoning which underlies their operation is relatively straightforward. An electronic computer has five main functional elements:

(a) *Input devices*. The first essential is the translation of the relevant data and the instructions or programme in accordance with which the data is to be processed into a language which the computer can understand. The machine works by means of electrical impulses and in order to activate it the data and programme must be recorded on punched cards, paper tape or magnetic tape. The instructions must be of three basic types—quantitative instructions, data transfer instructions and conditional instructions. The first of these will regulate the arithmetical functions of the computer, such as addition, multiplication and comparison. Transfer instructions will govern the collection of information or directions from the input into the circuit, the transfer of data within the circuit and the output of the completed computation. Conditional instructions provide the flexibility of the system and require the machine to transfer from one stage to another subject to the fulfilment of certain conditions. For instance a programme for selecting securities which satisfy given criteria would tell the computer to continue to analyze a particular security if it had met the requirements examined to date, but to ignore it as soon as it failed. The input data will be either standard, representing information which is used repeatedly from one sequence of operations to another, or variable, being the information which is relevant only to the current programme. In the security selection programme mentioned above, the standard information might be the standard criteria which have been adopted for the appraisal, while the variable information would comprise details of the current performance of the securities which are being assessed. The programme itself would instruct the machine to compare the variable information relating to individual securities with the standard criteria and to print out a list of securities meeting the requirements together with details of their performance.

(b) *Storage units.* This is usually known as the memory of the computer and contains all the information which the machine has stored or remembered. In it will be assembled the data, the instructions and any processed data which is ready for further processing or for output. The speed and capacity of a computer will be determined by the speed with which it can transfer data between its storage units and the circuit (known as the access time) and by the total capacity of the storage unit.

(c) *Control unit.* The control unit motivates the computer in accordance with the instructions of the programme. It ensures that the required operations are performed and that the correct information is used.

(d) *Arithmetic unit.* This is by far the fastest part of the computer and performs all the calculations and logical operations required by the programme. The control unit ensures that it is provided with the correct information and instructions for this purpose.

(e) *Output devices.* The object of these devices is to translate the report of the computer on the completion of a programme from electrical impulses into a form readily intelligible by humans. This is achieved by so drafting the programme that it instructs the computer to transfer the required processed information to an output device, the most common of which are punched cards, paper tape and magnetic tape. From these the information may be converted into legible form by means of an electric typewriter or an electrostatic printer.

Probably the most common use of computers in industry is in the preparation of payrolls. Leo, the first computer to be brought into commercial use in England, was producing a weekly payroll for 15,000 employees for its owners, J. Lyons & Co., by 1957. The machine also prepared payslips and a detailed analysis of wages for accounting and costing applications and the entire operation took only six hours of computer time. The I.C.T. 1900 is capable of processing 1,000 sales invoices, each with an average of six items, where the total number of products handled by the firm is 500 and there are 5,000 customers' accounts, in less than two hours a day. In this time the computer will prepare sales invoices and delivery notes, up-date customers' accounts, prepare an analysis of sales by product and region, up-date stock inventory schedules and prepare a monthly statement of account for each customer with a separate list of overdue accounts.

Although the computer has primarily been used for routine recording operations it has been increasingly adapted to assist managerial planning in such matters as sales forecasting, production scheduling and operations research. In the same way stockbrokers and the research departments of institutional investors and universities have come to use them for forecasting and their applications to investment have increased rapidly. As a result there have been major developments both in the field of theory and in practice.

(i) *The Use of the Computer in Theoretical Investment Analysis*

The main advantage of the computer at this level has been its enormous speed of calculation which has permitted the processing of data to test hypotheses on a scale which would have been inconceivable if research workers alone had performed the necessary calculations. For example, nearly all of the work used to test the random walk hypothesis has been carried out by computers and it is reasonable to argue that this theory could not otherwise have evolved.

Another important development has been the growth of econometrics and the attempt to detect and quantify the variables which govern economic activity. This may be achieved partly by intuition and partly by a detailed computerized analysis of past economic activity. Once the variables have been identified and valued they can be applied to current economic data and adjusted for anticipated economic developments. In this way forecasts may be made of future trends in the economy and its component sectors. Clearly the greater the number of variables which have been incorporated into the model, the greater will be its accuracy. However, as the model is developed from the variables on the basis of a system of simultaneous equations, as their number increase, so does a computer become more essential. Probably the best-known American model is the Brookings Social Science Research Council Model, which is based upon several hundred equations.[1]

[1] J. Duesenberry, G. Fromm, L. Klein, and E. Kuh, *Brookings Quarterly Econometric Model of the United States* (Skokie, Illinois: Rand, McNally, 1965).

In England the most comprehensive research in this field is that which has been undertaken by a group of economists in the Department of Applied Economics at Cambridge under the direction of Richard Stone.[1] The object of this model is not to make specific forecasts of the future trend of the British economy, but to show what inter-sectoral adjustments must occur if given rates of growth are to be achieved. However, other universities and business schools are developing predictive models which will be used purely for economic forecasting.

(ii) *The Use of the Computer in Practical Investment Analysis*

The computer has become extremely important both in the selection of individual securities and the construction of investment portfolios. Several stockbrokers and investment agencies use computers to prepare data for a considerable number of shares much more quickly and comprehensively than was possible before their introduction. This type of information is very useful for screening purposes. An investor can decide exactly what investment characteristics he requires of a share, such as a given price-earnings ratio and dividend yield, or a given percentage increase in profits over the past three years, and the computer will immediately provide a list of shares which comply with those conditions.

Other firms of stockbrokers make their own assessments of the factors which determine the relative attractiveness of securities and prepare regular lists of appropriate securities for their clients. For example, in March 1967 Joseph Sebag and Co. prepared a circular, for private circulation to their clients, entitled *Investment Timing by Computer*. The system which they advocate is based upon the premise that over a period of time a share may be regarded as having a proper or intrinsic value. However, as argued by the random walk proponents, the market price will tend to wander randomly around this value. The system adopts exponential weighting techniques in order to determine the 'basic trend value' over a period of thirty-nine weeks, placing greater emphasis upon recent prices compared with those at the start of the period. The computer will show immediately the percentage variation between the current price and the basic trend price. The investor can determine what percentage variation constitutes an action signal and can immediately act upon it. Thus if a 10% variation is regarded as requiring action a share which has fallen below its basic trend value by that proportion is regarded

---

[1] See *A Programme for Growth* in a series published for the Department of Applied Economics, University of Cambridge, by Chapman and Hall Ltd London, from July 1962 onwards.

as cheap while one which is above it by the same proportion is dear.

This system provides extremely valuable information which could only be prepared by a computer. However, the action signals alone should not form the basis for investment decisions, for it is essential that all other information should be taken into account. For instance a share which appears to be dear might be so due to a permanent alteration in its market rating due to unexpected higher profits or a sudden takeover probability. Similarly a share which is shown as cheap might be in a state of precipitate decline due to an unanticipated dividend cut or profit decline. However, the information provided by the computer programme represents an invaluable tool of traditional analysis in that it enables an investor to measure the impact of recent events and information upon the price of a particular share, with the result that the market reaction may be compared with his own assessment of the relevance of the new factors.

The second major field of practical analysis in which the computer has proved invaluable is that of portfolio selection. A programme may be prepared to show how a portfolio might have performed under different investment strategies. For instance, a strategy which preferred extremely high diversification could be compared with one based on relatively few stocks. Similarly, one which concentrated on high-yielding stocks might be compared with one favouring low yields. In the light of this information and with adjustments for both known and predicted future circumstances a long-term portfolio strategy might be devised which optimized the requirements of the investor.

Another major development in this field has been the work of Dr. Harry Markowitz,[1] who developed the theory of risk aversion in portfolio management. He measures risk as the expected standard deviation of the actual return on a security from the expected average rate of return and assumes that for a given expected average rate of return the investor will prefer the stock with the lower risk. Thus an investor would prefer a stock with an expected average rate of return of 8% plus or minus 1% to one where the expected return is 8% plus or minus 2%. Most investors attempt to minimize these deviations from the average by diversifying their portfolio though they are still faced with the danger that there will be a preponderance of deviations within their portfolio in the same direction.

In order to obtain an optimum portfolio Markowitz devised a

[1] Viz. 'Portfolio Selection', *Journal of Finance*, March 1952. *Portfolio Selection* (New York: John Wiley & Sons, 1959).

mathematical programme capable of solution by computer which requires the following information:

(a) Predictions of the most likely rate of return and the probable degree of variance of all securities which are under consideration for inclusion in the portfolio.

(b) Estimates of the inter-relationships between the securities concerned. In this way the effect will be assessed of a variance of 5% from the most likely rate of return on one security on the extent of variance of the other securities under consideration.

(c) The extent of any limits within which the portfolio must be managed. For instance, there may be a provision that not more than 10% of the portfolio should be invested in a single company or that not more than 5% of the equity of a particular company should be held.

With the above information, a series of portfolios may be constructed, indicating the expected overall average rate of return and the anticipated degree of risk of each portfolio. The portfolio manager can then select the one which provides the highest rate of return compatible with his attitude towards risk.

Although this programme is subject to both conceptual difficulties (in that the definition of risk and the assumption of risk aversion are extremely arguable) and practical difficulties (mainly in the assessment of the inter-relationship of different securities), it has a major advantage in that it compels portfolio managers to formulate their objectives and to examine the predicted outcomes of a large number of alternative portfolios. In this way the degree of investment rationality is greatly increased, though the basic problems of appraising the individual securities still remains.

2. THE EMERGENCE OF NEW INFLUENCES ON THE LONDON STOCK EXCHANGE

(i) *The Rise of Institutional Investors*

The largest group of institutional investors during the post-war period has been the insurance companies. Between 1946 and 1970 their holdings of ordinary shares increased from a book value of less than £250 m. to over £3,500 m. The increase in their assets and their constant trend towards equities are shown by the following table, based upon information given in the *Annual Abstract of Statistics.*

	1946	1951	1956	1961	1966	1970
Total Assets (£m.)	2,526	3,590	5,207	7,854	11,788	15,452
Asset Structure (%)						
Mortgages	5·9	8·7	11·4	13·0	15·0	14·4
Loans	5·9	3·8	3·7	3·8	3·7	1·3
British Govern-						
ment securities	39·9	31·7	23·4	17·0	14·8	21·1
Debentures	10·3	10·4	12·9	13·9	17·0	15·4
Preference shares	7·9	7·4	6·7	4·7	3·7	2·1
Ordinary shares	9·6	11·5	15·9	21·9	21·5	23·6
Property	4·7	6·4	7·9	9·1	9·4	11·6
Other assets	15·8	20·1	18·1	16·6	14·9	10·5
	100·0%	100·0%	100·0%	100·0%	100·0%	100·0%

The above figures represent book values and will in the case of ordinary shares be materially less than the market value, so that the proportion of ordinary shares held is actually much higher. Nevertheless the table gives a rough indication of the switch to equities and shows that during the 1950s ordinary shares as a percentage of total assets in terms of book value almost doubled. During the 1960s this percentage levelled out due primarily to the income advantages of fixed-interest securities resulting from the reverse yield gap. Nevertheless insurance companies still had an important influence upon the equity market, partly because the market value of shares already held was increasing and partly because total assets, and thus equity investments, which were a stable proportion thereof, were increasing.

Thus while the insurance companies largely ceased the switching of assets from Government securities into equities during the 1960s they still had a strong impact on the market for ordinary shares. This impact was reinforced by the tremendous expansion of unit trusts during the same period, as a result of which their annual net investment in equities rose from one-quarter of that of insurance companies in 1963 to exceed that of insurance companies in 1968 and 1969. This indicates the strong competition which insurance companies faced from unit trusts and accounts for the rise in the total funds of unit trusts from £201 m. at the end of 1960 to £1,398 m. at the end of 1970.

The influence of institutional investors upon the London Stock Exchange may be demonstrated by the table on page 408.

This table is reproduced from *The Owners of Quoted Ordinary Shares: A Survey for 1963*,[1] which forms part of the Programme

[1] London: Chapman and Hall, 1966.

Beneficial owners of quoted shares in UK Companies, July 1, 1957
and December 31, 1963

	Market values £m.		Percentages	
Category of owner:	1957	1963	1957	1963
Persons, executors and trustees	7,631	14,848	65·8	54·0
Insurance	1,023	2,750	8·8	10·0
Pension funds	400	1,761	3·4	6·4
Investment trusts	600	2,037	5·2	7·4
Unit trusts (including investment clubs) (1)	60	344	0·5	1·3
Banks	100	344	0·9	1·3
Stock exchange firms	100	385	0·9	1·4
Other finance (2)	188	721	1·6	2·6
Charities and non-profit	220	584	1·9	2·1
Non-financial companies	312	1,403	2·7	5·1
Public sector (3)	457	400	3·9	1·5
Overseas (4)	509	1,921	4·4	7·0
	11,600	27,498	100·0	100·0

(1) In 1963, investment clubs accounted for £6 m. out of the total of £344 m. for this category.

(2) In 1963 the breakdown of the £721 m. total for this category was:

	£m.
Unquoted investment trusts	430
Property companies	118
Financial trusts	173
Total	721

(3) The bulk of the equity investment of the public sector consists of the British Government investment in British Petroleum Ltd.

(4) About one-half of all overseas holdings in 1963 were registered through the nominee companies of British banks, so that a detailed geographical distribution cannot be prepared. Of the remainder, £288 m. was held by personal investors (45% of this figure being held by residents of the Irish Republic) and £763 m. was held by overseas companies (429 m. of it by US companies).

for Growth, which is being prepared at the Department of Applied Economics at the University of Cambridge and which is described earlier in this chapter. Although the data in the table is estimated it is based upon sample entries in the register of members of a selection of companies and the final results are in broad accordance with official statistics relating to particular categories of investors.

The figures reveal that the proportion of all ordinary shares held by institutional investors (defined as insurance companies, pension funds, investment trusts, unit trusts and banks) has risen from 18·8% in 1957 to 26·4% in 1963. This tendency seems likely to continue, for institutional investors made net acquisitions of equities totalling more than £3,500 m. during the years 1964–70. At the present time institutional investors probably hold about one-third of all UK equities.

The effects of the increasing participation of institutional investors in the stock market are difficult to quantify. One obvious benefit has been the improved quality of investment research, for the institutions invest on such a large scale that they can either finance their own research department or can choose a stockbroker who provides an advisory service of the required quality.

In the same way the size of their holdings gives them the power to act as watchdogs over the interests of smaller shareholders. So far the institutions have hesitated to interfere with the management of companies where they feel that policies are being followed which are detrimental to the shareholders. They have generally preferred to sell their shares in such cases rather than run the risk of provoking charges that they are using their position of strength to dispute the experience of the management.

Furthermore it has been argued that intervention by institutional investors in the internal affairs of public companies might lead to greater interference by the Government into the affairs of the institutions themselves. At the present time they are relatively free from such interference, especially with regard to their investment policies. In this respect they enjoy a considerable advantage over their American and European counterparts.

Another argument in favour of non-intervention is that their investments represent the combined savings of a multitude of investors, who would probably have completely contradictory views over the correct course of action in different situations. It might be argued that the institutions were abusing their power if they used their votes to secure a major change in the affairs of a company. They will thus normally take a neutral view, refraining from interference in matters of general policy and supporting the existing board against small groups of dissatisfied shareholders.

The greater power of the institutions coupled with the increased freedom of criticism which financial editors now appear to enjoy should both operate to the benefit of the smaller investor. However, as is shown in the next section, the continuing flood of new money invested by the institutions has considerably worsened the basic shortage of stock in the market. Moreover, their tendency to hold stocks firm is a further influence in this direction. In this respect a vicious circle operates, for the market is so short of stock that an entirely fluid, switching policy on the part of the institutions would be far too expensive for transactions in large blocks of shares and would cause prices to move against them, while dealing costs, particularly the jobber's turn, would involve still further expense.

For this reason it has been argued that there is a tendency for the use of the 'third market', in which financial institutions exchange large blocks of shares between themselves without having recourse to stockbrokers or to the Stock Exchange. It is by no means certain that such a market exists at all, but the disproportionate influence which even medium-sized blocks of shares have upon market prices suggests that it would be a logical development as the influence of the institutions increases.

All in all, the development of the institutions is beneficial to the market in that it has caused more emphasis to be placed upon investment research and expertise. For such expertise to be adequately judged and rewarded, however, it is essential that full comparable information should be made available by all institutions and that investors should have regard to the record of each institution when making investment decisions. In the field of insurance in particular, this is not true at present, for full information concerning the investment performance of each company is not generally available, while the purchase of policies by the public is far too often based upon advertising and direct selling techniques rather than upon the investment record of the insurance company.

(ii) *The Phenomenon of Stock Shortage*

In the autumn of 1968 *The Financial Times* share index reached a new all-time high at a time when company profits were only moderate, unemployment was high and business confidence appeared to have disintegrated. At the time, it was argued that the rise in share prices was attributable to the chronic shortage of stock which had brought about a wide gap between the number of potential buyers and sellers. In order to equate supply and demand the inflation of share prices was inevitable.

The decreasing availability of ordinary shares can be accounted for by three major factors. In the first place, there is an increasing tendency for investors to hold shares for a relatively long period, thus refraining from switching operations. In the case of institutional investors this is due to the fact that it is extremely expensive to switch holdings of ordinary shares on account of the Capital Gains Tax and the expenses of dealing, of which the jobber's turn is becoming increasingly burdensome. Moreover, there is the constant fear that if equities are sold it might prove difficult to replace them due to the thinness of the market. Finally, the institutional investors are only infrequently forced to liquidate their holdings, for their current income is normally more than sufficient to meet their current outgoings. For instance, most insurance companies are able to meet claims out of current premium income without having to disturb their investment holdings.

Similarly, shareholders in the personal sector tend to avoid switching partly due to capital gains taxation, which up to 1971 was especially severe where a high-rate surtax payer sold shares at a profit within one year of acquisition, though this may well be counteracted by tax-loss selling. Often in the case of director-controlled companies, the shares confer a controlling interest and must be held if control is to be maintained. Finally, many public companies hold shares in other companies in order to exert influence over their policy decisions. Obviously these shares must be held permanently if it is desired to continue this influence.

In addition to the increasing tendency for shares to be held firm, there has been a gradual dissipation of quoted securities due to liquidations and takeovers, which was exacerbated by steel national-ization and the spate of takeovers in 1967 and 1968. Although this effect has to some extent been counter-balanced by the impact of new issues of equities, it remains a very relevant factor. At the same time the quantity of equity issues has decreased substantially during the 1960s, primarily due to the introduction in 1964 of the Corporation Tax which gives favourable treatment to debenture finance.

While the volume of equity issues has declined the amount of money invested each year in equities by the institutions has remained constantly high, as is shown by the table overleaf which is based on material published in *Financial Statistics*.

The impact of this money is all the more marked because much of it is raised from small investors whose savings would not other-wise be sufficiently large to justify the purchase of Stock Exchange securities. Moreover, most of this saving is contractual and is likely to persist at a level of about £600 m. per annum. If the current trend in equity issues continues the excess of new money over new shares will also be maintained, with the result that stock shortage will be intensified. At the moment the deficiency is met by net sales of securities by the personal sector, which has favoured increased liquidity in recent years. Between 1963 and 1970 net sales of company securities by the personal sector averaged about £650 m. per annum,

The Stock Exchange and Investment Analysis

Net acquisitions at cost of UK quoted ordinary shares by the major institutional investors 1963–70

	1963 £m.	1964 £m.	1965 £m.	1966 £m.	1967 £m.	1968 £m.	1969 £m.	1970 £m.
Unit trusts (1)	42·2	55·0	57·7	82·0	82·6	189·7	131·9	47·7
Investment trusts	65·3	9·4	−1·2	34·0	10·70	101·2	−29·0	−28·9
Insurance companies (2)	118·6	156·1	86·0	103·4	99·6	223·7	148·1	261·5
Superannuation funds— public (2)	40·2	41·3	37·1	34·0	36·5	61·7	83·1	155·3
Superannuation funds— local auth. (2)	34·3	34·0	36·0	33·7	38·1	52·3	52·6	70·8
Superannuation funds— private (2)	134·2	133·3	101·6	124·4	121·9	167·0	83·2	162·9
Total	434·8	429·1	317·2	411·5	485·7	795·6	469·9	669·3
Sales by private sector (£m.)2	572	660	737	538	661	686	560	916

(1) These figures relate only to those unit trusts which make a return to the Board of Trade, with the result that the totals are probably slightly understated.

(2) These figures include an unknown, but probably small, quantity of unquoted shares and shares quoted on stock exchanges other than London.

these sales being taken up primarily by financial institutions and industrial and commercial companies. However, the total of company securities held privately in 1965 has been estimated at £11,800 m.[1] so that if this tendency continues it must push share prices up, especially as subsequent sales will have the result that only the firmly held shares are retained.

One final factor is the permission given to executors and trustees under the Trustee Investments Act 1961 to invest up to half of their portfolios in equities. Prior to this Act, trust funds could only be invested in equities where express provision was made in the terms of the trust. Although no figures are available to measure the effect of this change on trustee holdings of ordinary shares the long-run impact must be to increase the demand for equities due to the creation of an entire new class of potential holders.

In the long run therefore, despite the low market of 1969 and 1970, stock shortage seems likely to persist and unless investors generally take an exceptionally bearish view of the future or the current high yields on fixed-interest stocks continue, the excess of potential buyers over sellers is likely to act as a long-term cushion for share prices.

[1] Report of H.M. Commissioners of Inland Revenue 1967; Command 3200, p. 220. See also E. Victor Morgan, 'Personal Saving and the Capital Market', *District Bank Review*, September 1967.

PART IV: TAXATION AND PORTFOLIO ANALYSIS

CHAPTER 15

The Effects of Taxation

1. THE TAXATION OF INDIVIDUALS[1]

The tax burden of an individual investor is a vital factor in the field of investment analysis because it determines the net return that will be received from an investment. The major rules relating to direct taxation may be described under four heads:

(a) *Income Tax*

The standard computation used to calculate the income tax liability of an individual is as follows:

	Earned income	
Deduct:	Expenses	
	Net earned income	
Add:	Unearned income	(including building society
	Gross income	interest received)
Deduct:	Charges	
	Statutory total income	
Deduct:	Reliefs and allowances	(including building society
	Taxable income	interest received)

All of the taxable income bears tax at the standard rate of 38·75%.

[1] The rules described in this chapter are those in force after the 1971 Budget. The changes so far proposed for 1972–73 and subsequent years are described in Chapter 17.

413

Notes:

(1) Earned income includes trading profits, professional fees, salaries and wages, most pensions (including state old age pensions) and family allowances.

(2) Expenses are extremely difficult to obtain as a deduction from earned income except where that income arises from trading profits or professional fees. The only items commonly deductible from income arising from employment are superannuation contributions and professional subscriptions.

(3) Unearned income is any taxable income which does not come within the definition of earned income.

(4) Charges cannot be defined in any simple fashion. The most common examples are payments under a deed of covenant and the interest element of building society mortgage repayments. Up to April 1969 loan interest was allowed as a charge but since 1969 relief has been given only in respect of interest on loans incurred in connection with a trade or with the purchase or improvement of property. Relief will continue until April 5, 1975 in respect of interest paid on loans (but not overdrafts) which existed on or before April 15, 1969.

(5) The major reliefs and allowances are as follows:

(A) Earned income relief. An allowance of two-ninths of the first £4,005 and 15% of any excess over £4,005 is granted against the lower of net earned income and statutory total income.

(B) Wife's earned income relief. A married man will receive a relief amounting to seven-ninths of his wife's net earned income with a maximum relief of £325.

(C) Personal allowance. This is granted in the sum of £465 for a married man who wholly maintains his wife and £325 for other persons.

(D) Child allowance. The amount of this allowance depends upon the age of the child at the start of the tax year:

Under 11	£155
Over 11 but under 16	£180
16 or over	£205

If an allowance is claimed in respect of a child of sixteen or over he must at the start of the tax year either be receiving full-time instruction at an educational establishment or undergoing full-time training for at least two years for a trade, profession or vocation. If the income to which the child is entitled as of right (excluding scholarship income) exceeds £115 the appropriate allowance is reduced by the amount of the excess over £115. Where the income of a child is assessed upon its parent it will not be taken into account for this purpose.

(E) Life assurance relief. Premiums paid on policies assuring the life of the taxpayer or his wife give rise to relief as follows:

If total premiums are less than £10	The amount of the premiums
If total premiums are above £10 and below £25	£10
If total premiums are £25 or above	Two-fifths of the premiums

The total allowable premiums are restricted to one-sixth of the statutory total income, while the allowable premium on an individual policy is limited to 7% of the capital sum assured. Generally speaking, relief is only given on policies with a term of life of at least ten years. Moreover premiums must be paid at least annually and no premiums may exceed twice the amount of the premiums payable in any other period.

(F) Age exemption. A single taxpayer who is aged 65 or over at the end of the tax year and whose statutory total income does not exceed £504 is totally exempt from income tax. For a married couple, one of whom is aged 65 or over, similar exemption is given where their total income does not exceed £786. If the income is slightly above these amounts the tax payable is limited to 47·5% of the excess of the actual total income over the exemption limit.

(G) Where a taxpayer or his wife is aged 65 or over at the end of the tax year and the statutory total income does not exceed £1,000, a deduction of two-ninths of the unearned income is granted. If the income is slightly above £1,000 the taxpayer may claim to pay tax on a notional income of £1,000 plus eleven-twentieths of the amount by which his actual income exceeds that sum.

(H) Small income relief. Where the income of the taxpayer is not greater than £450 a deduction of two-ninths of unearned income is allowed. If the income is slightly higher than £450 the tax payable is limited to the tax on a notional income of £450 plus 52·5% of the excess of the actual income over that sum.

(I) A woman who is divorced or separated from her husband, or is unmarried, and who has sole responsibility for a child may claim an allowance of £100. A man in similar circumstances may also claim the allowance as can a married man whose wife is totally incapacitated by physical or mental infirmity.

(J) Relief may also be given in certain circumstances in respect of the maintenance of dependent relatives, in respect of the employment of a housekeeper or the use of the household services of a daughter, and to blind persons.

(K) The total allowances are reduced by £42 in respect of each child for which the increased family allowances are received.

(6) Certain income is entirely exempt from tax. The most common examples are:

(A) Wound and disability pensions.

(B) Unemployment benefits, sickness benefits, maternity benefits and death grants under the National Insurance Acts.

(C) The first £21 of interest on deposit accounts with the National Savings Bank or the Trustee Savings Bank is exempt from tax. This exemption may be granted to both a husband and a wife where they have either separate accounts or a joint account.

(D) Interest on National Savings Certificates or Tax Reserve Certificates and prizes won on Premium Savings Bonds.

(E) Income from scholarship or educational endowments.

(F) Redundancy payments not exceeding £1,200 and compensation for loss of office not exceeding £5,000.

(G) Building society interest received is regarded as tax-free and societies pay a composite rate of tax to the Inland Revenue based on the average tax rate of all lenders. No further income tax is payable by lenders, but no repayments of tax may be claimed by a low rate taxpayer.

(7) Wherever possible the Inland Revenue attempts to ensure the deduction of tax at source. Thus any organizations which pay interest or dividends are required to deduct tax at standard rate on the amount paid and pay it over to the Inland Revenue. Another example is the P.A.Y.E. system, where the employer deducts tax at source and the Inland Revenue collects the tax in bulk rather than from each employee separately. The major exceptions to this principle are payments of interest to banks or building societies and

416

receipts of interest from banks, which are paid gross. Moreover, interest is paid gross on certain Government securities. The most common of these are $3\frac{1}{2}\%$ War Loan, all stocks registered on the Post Office Register and any holding on which the half-yearly interest does not exceed £2·50p.

A relatively simple example of an income tax computation will illustrate the major points made above:

A company director has the following sources of income for the tax year 1971–72:

	£
Director's remuneration	1600
National Insurance sickness benefit	30
Army disability pension	300
Sales commission	500
Rent received	80
$3\frac{1}{2}\%$ War Loan interest	100
Dividend income	400
Building society interest received	50
Post Office Savings Bank interest	20

It is further ascertained that his wife earned a salary of £550 and that he paid insurance premiums of £100 in respect of an eleven-year endowment policy on which the sum assured was £1,000. His superannuation payments for the year totalled £100. He also pays interest at 7% on a £10,000 private loan used to purchase his house. Moreover he has two children aged 18 and 20, both of whom are at university. The elder child has earned income of £114 plus trustee savings bank deposit account interest of £14.

The total tax payable will be calculated as follows:

				Tax charge (credit)
			£	£
Earned income:	Director's remuneration		1,600	
	Sales commission		500	
	Wife's salary		550	
			2,650	
Less: Expenses:	Superannuation		100	
	Net earned income		2,550	
Unearned income:	Rent received	80		
	$3\frac{1}{2}\%$ War Loan interest	100		
	Dividend income	490		(155·00)

o   417

			Tax charge (credit)
		£	£
Building society interest received	50		
Post Office Savings Bank interest	5		
	—	635	
		3,185	
Less: Charges: Loan interest		700	271·25
		—	
Statutory total income		2,485	
Less: Reliefs and allowances			
(including building society interest received)			
Building society interest received	50		
Earned income relief			
(2/9 × £2,485)	553		
Wife's earned income relief	325		
Child relief (2 × 205)	410		
Life assurance relief (2/5 × £70)	28		
Personal allowance	465		
	—	1,831	
		—	
Taxable income £654			
Tax on £654 @ 38·75%		253·43	
Add: Tax deducted at source from loan interest		271·25	
		—	
		524·68	
Less: Tax withheld at source from dividend income		155·00	
		—	
Net tax payable		£369·68	

The tax payable would normally be collected by the Inland Revenue as follows:

	£
Schedule A: Rent received £80 @ 38·75%	31·00
Schedule D Case III: Untaxed interest £105 @ 38·75%	40·69
Schedule E Deducted under P.A.Y.E. arrangements:	
Husband's salary	258·08
Wife's salary	39·91
	—
	£369·68

Notes:

(1) The national insurance sickness benefit and the army disability pension are totally exempt from income tax.

(2) All items from which tax was deducted at source must be shown gross in the computation. Any amount suffered at source will then be credited to the taxpayer while any amounts withheld by him must be accounted for to the Inland Revenue and will be added to the tax due on the taxable income.

(3) The allowable premiums for calculating life assurance relief are restricted to £70, being 7% of the sum assured under the policy.

(4) There is no restriction of child relief in respect of the elder child, for his exempt income is ignored, leaving income of £114.

(5) The wife's income is always added to that of the husband in tax computations. Thus if their joint earned income exceeds £4,005, their earned income relief on the excess is limited to 15%. Had they been single they could each earn £4,005 without any such limitation.

(6) Although building society interest is nominally tax-free it is included in the statutory total income and may counteract any restriction of earned income relief caused by an excess of charges over unearned income. The interest is then deducted under reliefs and allowances so that it does not give rise to any tax charge.

As far as an investor is concerned there are certain aspects of the computation which are especially important.

(*A*) The yield received from a security consists of interest and dividends plus any capital profit on redemption or sale or minus any capital loss. The full amount of interest and dividends (unless it comes under an exempt category) is regarded as unearned income. The treatment of the capital profit or loss will depend upon the period for which the security was held. If it was realized within one year from the date of purchase it will be a short-term transaction. Any gain will be included as unearned income of the year of sale, while a loss may be set off against a short-term gain realized in the same year or carried forward until it can be set off against future short-term gains. If the security was realized more than a year after purchase it will be governed by the rules of the long-term capital gains tax which are considered below.

(*B*) It has already been explained that the interest on some securities may be paid gross. This will in theory always be to the benefit of the investor. If he pays tax at less than standard rate he will be relieved of the effort of making a tax repayment claim, while if he pays tax at standard rate he will have the use of the tax payable for a period of up to a year. This represents an interest-free loan which could be used to earn further interest.

(C) An investor should compare investments on the basis of net yields, after deducting income tax and capital gains tax (where relevant), because the investments may have different tax characteristics.

The net yield should be calculated by computing the tax liability under each available investment, for there is no single formula which will cover all investments and all tax circumstances.

For example, a married investor may receive an annual salary of £2,100 out of which he pays building society interest of £400, representing 8% on a loan of £5,000. He also has a daughter who was born during the past year. His net disposable income would be calculated as follows:

		£
Earned income		2,100
Less: Charges		400
Statutory total income		1,700
Less: Reliefs and allowances:		
Earned income relief (2/9 × £1,700)	378	
Personal allowance	465	
Child allowance	155	
		998
Taxable income		£702
Tax payable	£702 @ 38·75% =	£272·03

Disposable income   £1,700−£272·03 = £1,427·97

The investor now inherits £4,000 and considers three competing opportunities of utilizing this fund:

(A) Repay part of the building society loan, thus reducing his charges and increasing his disposable income.

(B) Invest the sum in a building society deposit account at the rate of 5½% tax paid.

(C) Purchase gilt-edged securities which offer a gross yield of 9%.

The increase in disposable income accruing from each of these alternatives may be computed as follows:

	£	£	£	£	£	£
Earned income		2,100		2,100		2,100
Unearned income		—		220		360
		2,100		2,320		2,460
Less: Charges		80		400		400
Statutory total income		2,020		1,920		2,060
Less: Reliefs and allowances:						
Earned income relief (based on statutory total income)	449		423		458	
Personal allowance	465		465		465	
Building society interest received	—		220		—	
Child allowance	155		155		155	
	——	1,069	——	1,263	——	1,078
		951		657		982
Tax payable @ 38·75%		£368·52		£254·59		£380·53
New disposable income (statutory total income minus tax payable)		1,651·48		1,665·41		1,679·47
Old disposable income		1,427·97		1,427·97		1,427·97
		£223·51		£237·44		£251·50
Increase expressed as percentage of £4,000 indicating net personal yield on the investment		5·59%		5·94%		6·29%

Thus, although advertisements for deposits by building societies often gross up their interest rates at standard rate, which would increase the return from 5½% to nearly 9⅜%, this ignores the effect which the interest has on earned income relief. In terms of net yield the gilt-edged security is preferable under the circumstances above, but the building society might be preferred on the grounds of greater liquidity. Only an extreme aversion to debt would favour the first alternative. Whenever one has borrowed on fixed-interest terms which are not materially above the current market rates and the interest is deductible for tax purposes, it is better to continue the loan for as long as possible. Any capital sums which become available should be invested in growth securities whose yield should relatively quickly exceed the fixed interest on the loan. Moreover, part of the yield will be in the form of long-term capital gains which bear tax at a lower rate than the relief which is given in respect of the fixed interest.

However, where an investor is faced with the choice of paying cash for an asset, or acquiring the asset on hire purchase terms while investing his cash, it will usually be advantageous to buy the asset outright. This is partly because the effective rate of hire purchase interest is normally between 15% and 30% and partly because the interest is not deductible for tax purposes unless it can be charged against business profits or professional earnings.

(b) *Capital Gains Tax*

It is usual to distinguish between the income and capital components of yield, notwithstanding that there is in economic terms no essential difference between these types of return. Equity, therefore, demands that each should be taxed, otherwise taxpayers whose return is predominantly of a form regarded as capital would benefit substantially to the detriment of those whose return was primarily income.

It was not until 1962 that capital gains were taxed on a regular basis in the United Kingdom. In the budget of that year it was laid down that gains arising from the disposal of securities and chargeable property other than land within six months of their acquisition, provided that the acquisition was after April 9, 1962, should be taxed as unearned income of the year of disposal. In the case of land or an interest in land the period between acquisition and disposal was extended to three years.

This short-term capital gains tax was extremely complicated and did not prove very remunerative for the Inland Revenue. From April 6, 1965, the scope of capital gains taxation was drastically extended. Short-term gains were now defined as gains arising from the disposal of chargeable assets within one year from the date of acquisition, while disposals more than twelve months after acquisition were made subject to long-term capital gains tax. Finally, from 1971/72 onwards the short-term capital gains tax has been abolished and all such gains are now liable to the long-term capital gains tax.

The main rules of capital gains taxation as far as the investor is concerned are:

(i) *The Definition of Chargeable Assets*

This covers all forms of property with the following major exceptions:

(1) Private motor cars.
(2) An individual's principal private residence.
(3) Tangible movable property which is a wasting asset.
(4) Tangible movable property sold for £1,000 or less.
(5) Gifts made to a charity or to an approved scientific research association.
(6) Gifts not exceeding £100 in one year
(7) National Savings Certificates, National Development Bonds and Premium Savings Bonds.
(8) Life assurance policies and contracts for deferred annuities except where the person making the disposal is not the original beneficial owner and acquired the rights thereto for a consideration in money or money's worth.
(9) From April 15, 1969 disposals of British Government and Government-guaranteed securities more than twelve months after acquisition are entirely exempt.

(ii) *The Definition of a Disposal*

In economic terms an investor benefits when a gain accrues, whether or not it is actually realized. For instance, where a capital gain has accrued he can consume income up to that amount without being any worse off. However, the taxation of capital gains at the point of accrual presents serious conceptual and administrative problems and gains are thus taxed at the time of realization, despite the fact that this gives the taxpayer considerable discretion over the size and timing of his tax commitments.

A realization can take place in four ways:

Disposal in consideration of a capital sum. This includes a voluntary sale, a forced takeover on cash terms and capital sums received by way of compensation for loss, forfeiture or surrender of assets or rights.

Disposal at death. On the death of an individual the assets of which he was competent to dispose are deemed to be realized and to be acquired by the personal representatives or executor at the market value at the date of death. In the case of deaths after March 30, 1971, such a disposal will not give rise to capital gains tax, though it will of course attract estate duty.

Disposal by way of gift. Where a chargeable asset is transferred as a gift this is regarded as a disposal on which the market value at the date of transfer is regarded as the notional consideration.

Disposal by destruction or loss. Where the value of an asset has become negligible, as might be the case with shares in a company which is moribund or is in the course of a lengthy winding-up, the inspector may regard the asset as having been sold and immediately re-acquired at the negligible value concerned.

(iii) *Rules Relating to Assets held at April 6, 1965*

When the Capital Gains Tax has been in operation for some years the computation of liability will in most cases merely involve a comparison of the acquisition and disposal prices. If this basis had been adopted when the tax was first introduced the use of the acquisition price in the capital gains computation would have made the tax retrospective in respect of assets held at April 6, 1965. However, it was ruled that gains arising from assets held at that date would only bear tax on any gain which accrued after April 6, 1965. The rules for determining the market value at April 6, 1965 depend upon the type of asset involved:

Quoted securities. The market value on April 6, 1965 is to be based on the quotations in the *Stock Exchange Daily Official List* by taking the higher of (*a*) a figure half-way between the two prices in the quotation, and (*b*) a figure half-way between the highest and lowest prices of recorded bargains. Tables showing the officially agreed market values at April 6, 1965 may be obtained from the London Stock Exchange. The actual acquisition cost will be substituted for the April 6, 1965 valuation if this results in a lower gain or a lower loss. Where one method shows a gain while the other shows a loss the disposal will be ignored for tax purposes. These rules are illustrated below:

Acquisition Cost 6.4.60	Market Value 6.4.65	Sale Proceeds 6.4.70	Capital Gain/Loss for Tax Purposes
£	£	£	£
200	100	150	—
125	100	150	25+
50	100	150	50+
200	100	50	50−
75	100	50	25−
25	100	50	—

The Finance Act 1968 permits investors to elect once and for all to disregard the acquisition cost of quoted ordinary shares which they held on April 6, 1965 and to base the computation of their capital gains or losses on the market value as at April 6, 1965. The election must be made in respect of all ordinary shares which were held at that date and which were disposed of after March 19, 1968, whether before or after the date on which the election was made. An investor has the right to make a similar election in respect of all of his holdings of fixed-interest securities and preference shares.

Units in a unit trust. These are valued at a figure halfway between the published buying and selling prices. The same rules apply for quoted securities in relation to the substitution of actual cost, and the units may be included with quoted securities in a once and for all election of market value at April 6, 1965 for the computation of gains.

Land with development value. The actual market value at April 6, 1965 must be obtained. Actual cost may be substituted under similar circumstances to those already described for quoted securities.

Other assets. Any gain or loss is regarded as being spread evenly over the whole period for which the asset was held. Thus if an asset was acquired for £1,000 on April 6, 1963 and sold for £2,000 on April 6, 1973 the value at April 6, 1965 is deemed to be

$$£1,000 + \left(\frac{2}{10} \times £1,000 \right) = £1,200$$

The capital gain would thus be £800. The taxpayer may, however, elect to have the actual market value at April 6, 1965 substituted for the value estimated as above, unless this would result either in a tax loss higher than the actual loss suffered or in a tax loss where there was an actual gain over the whole period of ownership.

(iv) *Identification of Disposals out of a Pool of Identical Assets*

This problem arises primarily where an individual has a holding of securities of the same class which have been acquired at different dates and at different prices. The rules for identifying and valuing the shares comprised in a part-disposal of such a holding depend upon the dates at which the shares were acquired:

425

(A) *Whole holding acquired before April 6, 1965.* Here the 'first-in, first-out' rule applies, so that the first shares to be sold will be the earliest acquisitions making up the total of the sale. However, in respect of shares acquired after April 9, 1962 and disposed of before April 6, 1971 the short-term capital gains tax provisions may have been applied. These laid down that any sale within six months of acquisition of shares of the same class bought after April 9, 1962 should be deemed to include those shares. Within the six-month period the 'first-in, first-out' rule applied. For acquisitions after April 6, 1965 the six-month period was, of course, replaced by one year. For example, an investor makes the following sales and purchases in respect of a particular share:

		Number of Shares	*Cost/Proceeds* £
December 17, 1962	Buys	200	200
May 5, 1963	Buys	200	500
October 28, 1963	Buys	300	600
November 25, 1963	Buys	400	600
April 13, 1964	Sells	400	1,000
August 31, 1964	Buys	100	300
December 12, 1966	Sells	500	1,200
January 15, 1968	Sells	300	750

The gains in respect of each sale would be computed as follows:

(a) Sale of 400 shares on April 13, 1964. There were two purchases within the six months immediately preceding this sale and the proceeds will be compared with the cost of those purchases on a 'first-in, first-out' basis.

	£	£
Proceeds		1,000
Cost of relevant acquisitions:		
28.10.63 300 shares	600	
25.11.63 100 shares $\left(\dfrac{100}{400} \times £600\right)$	150	
	—	750
Short-term gain 1964–5		250

In this example and throughout this chapter the apportionment of original cost in the case of part-disposal of shares which have not altered in form since their acquisition is based on the proportion of shares which have been sold. This method has the advantage of simplicity and is accepted by the Inland Revenue. The strict basis of allocation should be to

426

multiply cost or the market value at April 6, 1965 by the fraction:

$$\frac{\text{Proceeds of shares sold}}{\text{Proceeds of shares sold and market value of remaining shares at date of sale}}$$

(b) Sale of 500 shares on December 12, 1966. This will be identified on the 'first-in, first-out' method as there were no purchases during the preceding year. The value with which the proceeds are to be compared will be either the acquisition price or the market value at April 6, 1965, whichever shows the lower gain or the lower loss:

Number of Shares	Date of Acquisition	Cost £	Market Value at 6.4.65 £	Proceeds £	Capital Gain £
200	17.12.62	200	400	480	80
200	5. 5.63	500	400	480	—
100	25.11.63	150	200	240	40
			Capital gains 1966–7		120

In the case of the second block of shares the use of acquisition cost yields a profit while the market value basis shows a loss. These shares thus have a neutral effect on the computation. With the other two blocks the use of market value yields a lower gain, so that this basis will be used, resulting in a gain of £120.

(c) Sale of 300 shares on January 15, 1968. This sale is related to the remaining 200 shares from the purchase on November 25, 1963, which cost £300 and had a market value of £400 on April 6, 1965. The apportioned proceeds of £500 are compared with the latter value, resulting in a capital gain of £100. The remainder of the sale comprises the 100 shares which were acquired on August 31, 1964 at a cost of £300. The value at April 6, 1965 was £200. The sale proceeds of £250 yield a profit when compared with the latter value and a loss when compared with the actual cost. There is, therefore, neither a gain nor a loss for tax purposes. The net gain on the transaction is thus £100.

(B) *Whole holding acquired after April 6, 1965.* First of all any sales must be compared with purchases during the preceding year on a 'first-in, first-out' basis. The remainder of the shares are pooled together and the proceeds of any sale are compared with the average cost of shares in the pool. The difference between this method and

427

that used for shares acquired before April 6, 1965 may be illustrated by moving forward each sale and purchase in the previous example by three years:

		Number of Shares	Cost/Proceeds £
December 17, 1965	Buys	200	200
May 5, 1966	Buys	200	500
October 28, 1966	Buys	300	600
November 25, 1966	Buys	400	600
April 13, 1967	Sells	400	1,000
August 31, 1967	Buys	100	300
December 12, 1969	Sells	500	1,200
January 15, 1971	Sells	300	750

The computation of capital gains in respect of each sale would now become:

(a) Sale of 400 shares on April 13, 1967. These would be identified on a 'first-in, first-out' basis against the three purchases which were made during the preceding twelve months:

	£	£
Proceeds		1,000
Cost of relevant acquisitions:		
5. 5.66 200 shares	500	
28.10.66 200 shares $\left(\dfrac{200}{300}\times£600\right)$	400	
	——	900
Short-term gain 1967–8		100

(b) Sale of 500 shares on December 12, 1969. As there are no acquisitions during the preceding twelve months the pool system will apply. The proceeds of the sale are compared with the average cost of the shares sold, based on the total holding at the date of sale. At December 12, 1969 the average cost of shares in the pool was £1·62½p:

	Number of Shares	Cost £
17.12.1965	200	200
28.10.1966	100	200
25.11.1966	400	600
31. 8.1967	100	300
	——	——
	800	£1,300

$$\frac{£1,300}{800} = £1·625 = £1·62\tfrac{1}{2}p$$

The cost of the 500 shares sold, as determined on this basis, is thus £812·50, producing a capital gain of £387·50.

(c) Sale of 300 shares on January 15, 1971. In view of the fact that there were no further acquisitions after the previous sale, the average pool cost remains the same. The cost of the shares sold is thus calculated as £487·50, resulting in a gain of £262·50.

(C) *Holding acquired partly before and partly after April 6, 1965.* Under these circumstances the computation becomes extremely complicated and three rules apply:

(a) The short-term capital gains tax rules on a 'first-in, first-out' basis will apply to shares acquired between April 10, 1962 and April 6, 1965 which were sold within six months of acquisition and to shares acquired after April 6, 1965, which were sold within twelve months of acquisition before April 6, 1971.

(b) Shares acquired before April 6, 1965 which have not already been identified above will be identified on a 'first-in, first-out' basis and the proceeds will be compared with both the acquisition cost and the market value at April 6, 1965 in the normal way, unless, of course, the investor has elected market value as the basis for all of his holdings of equities.

(c) Shares acquired after April 6, 1965 are pooled at acquisition cost in the normal way.

In order to illustrate these rules the original example used above has been further adapted:

		Number of Shares	Cost/Proceeds £
December 17, 1963	Buys	200	200
May 5, 1964	Buys	200	500
October 28, 1964	Buys	300	600
November 25, 1964	Buys	400	600
April 13, 1965	Sells	400	1,000
August 31, 1965	Buys	100	300
December 12, 1968	Sells	500	1,200
January 15, 1970	Sells	300	750

The computation of capital gains in respect of each sale would now be as follows:

(a) Sale of 400 shares on April 13, 1965. This would be related to acquisitions during the preceding six months as in the original example. The shares involved would thus be the

429

300 purchased on October 28, 1964 and 100 of those bought on November 25, 1964 giving rise to a short-term capital gain for 1965–66 of £250.

(b) Sale of 500 shares on December 12, 1968. This will be identified on the principle of 'first-in, first-out', whereby it will comprise the following shares:

Number of Shares	Date of Acquisition	Cost	Market Value at 6.4.65	Proceeds	Gain
		£	£	£	£
200	17.12.63	200	400	480	80
200	5. 5.64	500	400	480	—
100	25.11.64	150	200	240	40
			Assessment 1968–9		£120

(c) Sale of 300 shares on January 15, 1970. This sale consisted of 200 shares bought on November 11, 1964 at a cost of £300 and 100 shares bought on August 31, 1965 at a cost of £300. £500 of the sale proceeds would be matched with the 200 shares acquired on November, 11, 1964. These shares had a value of £400 on April 6, 1965 and the capital gain will be £100 regardless of whether the investor had elected to compute his gains on the market value basis. The remaining £250 sale proceeds will be matched against the August 1965 purchase giving a loss of £50 and a net gain for 1969–70 of £50.

The rules for the identification and valuation of shares are still more complicated where capitalization or rights issues are involved:

(1) *Basic rules for capitalization and rights issues.* The basic procedure is to add the new shares to the original holding to which they relate while increasing the cost by any amount payable for the shares (in the case of a rights issue). Thus if an investor bought 100 shares at 150p each in 1963 and a capitalization issue of one for two was made in 1967 the holding would become 150 shares with a cost of £150. If, instead, a rights issue of one share for two at a cost of £1 had been made the new holding would be 150 shares with a cost of £200. In each case the market value at April 6, 1965 must be similarly adjusted.

A rather fuller example will illustrate the application of this rule where there have been multiple purchases. An investor undertakes the following transactions:

430

1960 Purchases 200 shares at 200p at a cost of £400.
1963 Purchases 300 shares at 300p at a cost of £900.
1966 A capitalization issue of one for one is made.
1968 A rights issue of one share at £1 for every five held is made and the investor subscribes for his allotment.
1970 Sells 1,200 shares at 125p for a total of £1,500.
The market value of the shares at April 6, 1965 is 250p.

First of all, the new shares and their cost must be allocated to the original purchases to which they relate:

		First Acquisition		Second Acquisition	
		Shares	Cost £	Shares	Cost £
1960	Purchase 200 @ 200p	200	400		
1963	Purchase 300 @ 300p			300	900
1966	Capitalization issue 1 for 1	200		300	
1968	Rights issue, 1 for 5 @ 100p	80	80	120	120
		480	480	720	1,020

$$\text{Average cost} \quad \frac{£480}{480} = 100p \qquad \frac{£1,020}{720} = 141\tfrac{1}{2}p$$

Then the adjusted value at April 6, 1965 must be computed:

		Shares	Value £
6.4.65	500 shares @ 250p	500	1,250
1966	Capitalization issue, 1 for 1	500	—
1968	Rights issue, 1 for 5 @ 100p	200	200
		1,200	1,450

$$\text{Adjusted value at 6.4.65} \quad \frac{£1,450}{1,200} = 121p$$

The sale of the entire holding at 125p per share in 1970 will be allocated between the two holdings. The first of these will give rise to a gain of £19·20 (480 × (125p − 121p)), while the second will be ignored, for comparison with the revised value at April 6, 1965 gives a profit, while comparison with adjusted cost shows a loss.

(2) *Sale of new shares with 'nil paid'.* If new shares are sold in the form of an allotment letter these shares are separately identifiable, and the 'first-in, first-out' rule does not apply. Thus, if an investor

431

buys 400 shares in December 1964 and a further 200 in June 1967 and a capitalization issue of one for four is made in January 1968, he will receive 150 new shares, of which 100 will relate to the first purchase and 50 to the second. If the new shares are sold as allotment letters they will represent a separate disposal of which 100 shares will fall within the long-term tax, while the remaining 50 will be regarded as short-term. If the allotment letters are retained and later exchanged for share certificates, the new shares are consolidated with the old (assuming of course that they are of the same class), so that the subsequent disposal of 150 shares before June 1968 would be matched with 150 of the 250 shares held in respect of the June 1967 purchase. Thus the whole sale would now fall within the scope of the short-term tax.

The value of the shares sold is calculated from the formula:

$$\frac{A}{A+B} \times C$$

Where A = Proceeds from the sale of the new shares.

B = Market value of the balance of the holding at the date of the sale.

C = Original cost or market value at April 6, 1965, whichever is appropriate.

For example, an investor may have purchased 500 shares in X Ltd for £1,000 in August 1963. At April 6, 1965 the market value of each share is 150p. In December 1967 a rights issue is made of one new share at £2 for every five shares held. At that date the market price of the company's shares is £3. After the issue the market price of the old shares on an ex-rights basis would fall to 280p and the rights to the 125 new shares would be valued at 80p each. A sale of the entire rights would fetch £100 and the capital gains computation would be:

Value based on original cost $\frac{100}{100+1400} \times £1{,}000 = £67$

Value based on market value at 6.4.65 $\frac{100}{100+1400} \times £750 = £50$

When compared with the proceeds of £100 the use of original cost gives the lower gain, so the assessment will be in the sum of £33.

If the proceeds from the sale of the new shares represent less than 5% of the total market value of the holding at that date, the investor can elect to have them deducted from the original cost of the holding so that payment of any capital gains tax is deferred until the rest of the holding is sold. This relieves the Inland Revenue of the necessity of making large numbers of minute assessments where very small rights or capitalization issues are made.

Where rights are sold 'nil paid' and fall under the short-term gains rules the treatment is different from that for the long-term tax and is based on the computation used under the long-term tax for sales of new shares partly paid as described below.

(3) *Sale of new shares partly paid.* Where a rights issue is made on instalment terms and the new shares have been accepted by payment of the first instalment, these shares are regarded as costing the full amount of the instalments with the unpaid instalments being an outstanding liability. If, in these circumstances, the allotment letter is sold, the formula for determining the cost will still be $\dfrac{A}{A+B} \times C$, but A will now represent the proceeds of the new shares plus the amount outstanding thereon at the date of sale.

For example, an investor undertakes the following transactions in the shares of a company:

   1964 Buys 400 shares at £1.
April 6, 1965 Market value per share is £2.
   1968 The company makes a rights issue of one new share at 150p for every four shares already held. £1 is payable on acceptance and 50p at the end of four months. After paying the first call the investor sells his hundred new shares at 175p. At the date of sale the old shares are valued at 225p.

Value at original cost:

$$\frac{225^*}{225+900} \dagger \times £550\ddagger = £110$$

 * Proceeds of the new shares £175 (i.e. $100 \times 175\text{p}$) plus the amount outstanding, £50 (i.e. $100 \times 50\text{p}$).

 † Market value of the old shares at the date of sale (i.e $400 \times 225\text{p}$).

 ‡ Adjusted original cost, representing the original cost of £400 plus the total amount payable on the new shares of £150 (i.e. $100 \times 150\text{p}$).

Value based on market value at 6.4.65:

$$\frac{225}{225 \times 900} \times £950^* = £190$$

 * Represents the total market value at 6.4.65 (£800) plus the total cost of the new shares (£150).

Comparison of the market value at April 6, 1965 with the sale proceeds gives the lower gain, so the assessment will be in the sum of £35 (i.e. £225 − £190). In determining the capital gains on future sales of the old shares the new figure of original cost will be £440 (i.e. £550 − £110), while the adjusted market value at April 6, 1965 will become £760 (i.e. £950 − £190).

(4) *Fully paid shares.* So long as the shares are in the form of an allotment letter they are regarded as being of a separate class from the old shares and a sale of the allotment letter will constitute a sale of the new shares alone. However, once the new shares become fully paid (in the case of a rights issue) or after the last date for renunciation has passed (in the case of a capitalization issue) the new shares will be merged with the old shares to which they relate, provided, of course, that they are of the same class, and the basic rules of identification will apply.

(5) *Capitalization and rights issues of shares of a class different from the old shares.* Under these circumstances it is necessary to apportion the original cost between the different classes of shares. The apportionment is carried out by means of the usual formula

$$\frac{A}{A+B} \times C$$

except that in this case A and B represent the market value of the two different classes on the date on which dealings first started in shares of the new class. This contrasts with the case where new shares are sold in letter form, where market values at the date of sale are the basis of the apportionment.

For instance, an investor buys 300 ordinary shares at 200p in 1960. The market value on April 6, 1965 is 270p. In 1968 a rights issue is made of one preferred ordinary share at 100p for every three shares held. When dealings start in the new shares a premium of 50p is established. On the same day the ordinary shares are quoted at 300p. Once the new shares cease to be dealt in as allotment letters the apportioned value of the two classes of shares is determined as follows:

Original cost: Ordinary shares:

$$\frac{900}{150+900} \times £700 = £600$$

Preferred ordinary shares:

$$\frac{150}{150+900} \times £700 = £100$$

Market value at 6.4.65: Ordinary shares:

$$\frac{900}{150+900} \times £910 = £780$$

Preferred ordinary shares:

$$\frac{150}{150+900} \times £910 = £130$$

(6) *Takeover bids.* Yet another occasion when identification problems arise is in the event of takeover bids. Where the shares of the company are taken over for cash this is regarded as an outright disposal. If there is a straightforward exchange of shares in another company for those previously held, then the new shares will be substituted and will assume the cost of the earlier shares in any future computations. If the takeover was before April 6, 1965, the market value of the new shares will be used for the market valuation at that date, while if the takeover was after that date the market value of the old shares will be taken.

The main complications arise where the takeover consideration consists of more than one class of security or of a mixture of cash and shares. In the first of these cases the cost of each class of the new shares is derived by apportioning the original cost on the basis of the market value of the new shares on the day on which dealings therein commence. Where, however, the new shares are sold in letter form the rules are the same as for sales of capitalization and rights issues in the form of allotment letters.

Where the old shares are exchanged for both cash and shares the cash element gives rise to a part-disposal, while the stock element merely involves the substitution of one shareholding for another.

For example, an investor buys 500 shares in A Ltd at 240p in 1960, and a further 200 at 350p in 1963. The value of each share on April 6, 1965 is 300p. In 1968 Z Ltd makes a takeover bid for A Ltd offering three ordinary shares in Z Ltd plus 100p cash for each share in A Ltd. At the date when the offer is accepted the shares in Z Ltd are valued at 100p.

The cash element in the takeover will constitute a part-disposal, the capital gain on which will be calculated as follows:

1960 Purchase: This becomes £500 cash and 1,500 shares in Z Ltd valued at £1,500. The cost of the £500 disposal must now be calculated:

Original cost: $\dfrac{500}{500+1500} \times £1,200 = £300$

Market value at
6.4.65: $\dfrac{500}{500+1500} \times £1,500 = £375$

In this case, the use of market value at April 6, 1965 gives the lower gain, in the sum of £125 (i.e. £500 – £375). The new original cost of the 1,500 shares in Z Ltd is £900 (i.e. £1,200 – £300) and the adjusted market value at April 6, 1965 is £1,125 (i.e. £1,500 – £375)

1963 Purchase   This becomes £200 cash and 600 shares in Z Ltd valued at £600. The cost of the £200 disposal is:

Original cost: $\dfrac{200}{200+600} \times £700 = £175$

Market value at
6.4.65: $\dfrac{200}{200+600} \times £600 = £150$

Here the computation of the capital gain is based on original cost giving a gain of £25. The new original cost of the 600 shares becomes £525, while their adjusted market value at April 6, 1965 is £450.

(v) *Treatment of Insurance Companies, Investment Trusts and Unit Trusts*

Insurance companies are required to apportion their tax between the different funds which they hold. Gains applicable to policy holders' funds are taxed at the lowest of corporation tax rate, $37\frac{1}{2}\%$, or the top rate of capital gains tax for an individual (currently 30%). Moreover, the policy-holders are not normally liable to capital gains tax on any gains arising on the maturity of their policies. On the other hand, the shareholders' funds bear capital gains tax at the corporation tax rate in the same way as gains made by any company. In addition, the shareholders themselves will pay tax on any gains emanating from their holdings of shares in the company.

Capital gains tax paid by approved investment trusts and unit trusts may be passed on to their shareholders and unit-holders. Each year the tax paid (at the lower of corporation tax and basic capital gains tax rates) is apportioned between the members, who will each receive a certificate stating the amount of tax which has been paid during the year in respect of their holding. This amount is then added to the original cost of the investment in determining any future capital gains of the member himself. This procedure is very cumbersome, particularly for unit trusts whose membership is continually fluctuating or includes many investors who are purchasing units on a monthly instalment basis. In many ways it would seem more satisfactory to exempt trusts from the tax, leaving the members with a full charge in respect of their gains.

(vi) *The Rate of Capital Gains Tax*

The capital gains tax assessment for a tax year will be based upon the gains or losses resulting from disposals during that year. Allowance will be given for the normal expenses of purchase and sale and, in a moderate amount, for other expenses such as the cost of contacting one's broker.

The basic rate of tax is 30% though the taxpayer may, if his gains do not exceed £5,000, elect to have half of his gain included in his income tax assessment, while the other half is ignored. Thus an investor whose marginal rate of tax is 38·75% and who has a chargeable gain of £1,000 has the choice of paying £300 (i.e. 30% × £1,000) or £193·75 (£500 @ 38·75%), so that the effective rate of capital gains tax for a standard rate taxpayer is 19·375%. Election under this rule is advantageous for anyone whose marginal combined rate of income tax and surtax is less than 60%. Where the gain exceeds £5,000 a taxpayer making election must include £2,500 plus the excess of the gain over £5,000 in his income for income and surtax purposes. Any gains brought into a taxpayer's income tax assessment under this election are available for all reliefs and allowances, except life assurance relief and earned income relief, which have not already been granted against other income of the year. They are not available either for loss relief or for restoring any earned income relief restricted by an excess of charges over unearned income. For companies capital gains are taxed at the corporation tax rate.

For 1967–8 and subsequent years of assessment an individual is not chargeable to capital gains tax if his net taxable gains for the year do not exceed £50. If the gains exceed £50 the amount of tax payable is limited to the excess. Thus an investor who makes net gains of £60 for 1968-9 need pay tax of only £10 instead of £18 (i.e. 30% × £60). It may still, of course, prove more beneficial to elect to have half of the gain taxed as income.

For 1971/72 and subsequent years an individual is not chargeable to capital gains tax for a year of assessment if the aggregate consideration for all disposals of assets made by him during that year does not exceed £500. If the consideration slightly exceeds £500 the tax payable shall not exceed one-half of the excess over £500.

(vii) *Investment Implications of the Tax*

In most cases the rate of short-term tax is at least double that of the long-term tax so that investors are encouraged to hold on to shares showing a gain for at least a year, thus reducing the flexibility of their portfolio. On the other hand, there is every incentive to take a short-term loss, for this can be carried forward indefinitely if not used in the current year, but can be set off only against short-term gains. Similarly long-term losses can be carried forward and set off only against long-term gains. In this connection the identification rules further restrict flexibility, for if shares are bought in a company of a class already held, neither holding can be sold within a year without falling within the scope of the short-term rules.

The general effect of the long-term tax is that an investor receives only 70% of the gain from a security and bears only 70% of any losses (assuming that there are gains available for a set-off). There is thus a tendency to hold on to shares when prices are rising, thus delaying tax, and to sell them when prices are falling, thus establishing a tax loss. This, of course, increases fluctuations in what is already a very thin market. However, any tax on accrued gains must ultimately be paid and flexibility should not be altogether sacrificed in order to secure the deferment of tax payments. All in all, the tax effects should be included in the normal investment criteria, which should still be the basis of investment decisions. This may result in a pattern of tax-loss selling towards the end of the tax year of shares which have performed particularly badly during the year. This phenomenon is very common in America, but even in this case the investor should still attach more importance to the likely future performance of the share rather than to the establishment of a tax loss. It is, of course, possible to sell shares and buy them back, but certain tax rules relating to such transactions must be observed very carefully, and the expenses of the deals must be met.

A major complication occurs in the case of shares which were bought before April 6, 1965. These will have a neutral range representing the difference between the price on that date and the original cost. Within this range, which may be extremely wide, sales will give rise to neither a loss nor a gain for tax purposes. For example, a share may have been bought in 1960 for 150p and had risen to 300p on April 6, 1965 (the position would be the same if these prices were reversed). If the shares now stand at anything below 300p they could rise to that level without giving rise to a tax charge. Consequently, switching is discouraged, for if these shares were sold and another holding acquired, the second holding would have to perform sufficiently better to provide for the tax payable on the gain. In fact, its performance would have to be 43% better than that of the previous holding, so long as the latter remains within the neutral range.

If on the other hand the stock still stood at 300p in 1968 it could fall in value to 150p without giving rise to any tax relief. In this case the investor should switch to a share with similar prospects, for his risk is lessened by the possibility of loss relief if the value of the second holding falls.

In deciding whether to make an irrevocable election under the Finance Act 1968 to have all gains on quoted shares held at April 6, 1965 based on the market value at that date rather than on original cost an investor should determine the relationship for his shares between original cost and market value at April 6, 1965. Only if those market values are generally higher than original cost should the option be exercised.

Another important implication for investors is that they must now keep full records of all share transactions and should also appreciate the tax effect of their decisions, for this will be an important investment consideration. In this connection, this chapter presents only a selection of the rudimentary rules of the capital gains tax and any serious investor should possess one or more of the standard tax guides.

(c) *Surtax*

Surtax is chargeable on the excess over £2,000 of the taxable income of an individual as defined for income tax after the following adjustments:

(i) Building society interest received and the exempt portion of the Post Office Savings Bank or Trustee Savings Bank interest must be grossed up at the standard rate of income tax.

(ii) The Finance Act 1968 provided for the charge of surtax on the proceeds of insurance policies under certain circumstances:

(*a*) In the case of policies which do not qualify for life assurance relief, surtax is charged on the excess of the proceeds over the premiums paid in the event of the death of the life assured, the maturity of the policy, its surrender in whole or in part, or its assignment in whole or in part for money.

(*b*) In the case of policies which qualify for life assurance relief, surtax may be chargeable in the event of the surrender of the policy in whole or in part within ten years of the inception of the policy or, if sooner, before it has run for three-quarters of its term. Similarly surtax may be charged on the assignment of the policy for money or money's worth, or on its maturity if previously converted into a paid-up policy.

(iii) The reliefs and allowances for income tax are allowed except that the personal allowance is only granted to the extent by which it exceeds the single person's allowance of £325, while life assurance relief and wife's earned income relief are not granted.

(iv) Payments made under deed of covenant to charities are not deductible nor are such payments to any person where the covenant is dated after April 6, 1965.

(v) An earnings allowance is granted, comprising £2,000 or such smaller sum as would reduce earned income (after the deduction of earned income relief) to £2,000. The effect of this is to exempt earned income up to £5,000.

The following are the rates of surtax to be applied to the taxable income thus adjusted:

On the first £2,000	Nil
On the next £500	10·0%
On the next £500	12·5%
On the next £1,000	17·5%
On the next £1,000	22·5%
On the next £1,000	27·5%
On the next £2,000	32·5%
On the next £2,000	37·5%
On the next £2,000	42·5%
On the next £3,000	47·5%
On the remainder	50·0%

Persons with surtaxable income not exceeding £2,500 are exempt from surtax. Where such income is marginally above £2,500 there is a tapering relief under which the surtax charge will not exceed 40% of the income above £2,500.

The amount of surtax due is payable on the January 1st following the end of the tax year to which it relates. Thus surtax for the year 1970/71 is payable on January 1, 1972.

A brief illustration will illustrate the use of the above rules:
The taxable income of Mr Smith for 1971/72 is calculated as follows:

	£	£
Earned income: Salary		6,400
Unearned income: Dividends (gross amount, received net)	700	
Building society interest	100	
	——	800
		7,200
Less: Charges: Payments under deed of covenant dated May 30, 1965 (gross amount)		250
Statutory total income		6,950

Less: Reliefs and allowances:

Personal allowance	465	
Child relief	310	
Earned income relief (1970/71 level)		
$2/9 \times £4,005 = 890$		
$+ 15\% \times £2,395 = 359$		
	1,249	
Life assurance relief	60	
Building society interest	100	
		2,184
Taxable income		4,766

Surtax computation

Taxable income for income tax purposes		4,766
Adjustments: Add: Proportion of personal allowance not deductible		325
Life assurance relief		60
Payment under deed of covenant		250
Grossed-up building society interest		
$100 \times \dfrac{100}{100 - 38 \cdot 75}$		163
(using 1970/71 standard rate)		
		5,564

Deduct: Earnings allowance:

Earned income	6,400	
Less: Earned income relief (as above)	1,249	
	5,151	
Excess over £2,000 = £3,151		
Earnings allowance therefore restricted to		2,000
Taxable income for surtax purposes		3,564
Tax on first £2,000		Nil
Tax on next £500 @ 10%		50·00
Tax on next £1,000 @ 12·5%		125·00
Tax on next £64 @ 17·5%		11·20
Total surtax payable		£186·20

(1) It is assumed that the surtax rates for 1971–72, which are not announced until the 1972 budget, will be the same as for 1970/71.

The surtax payable is additional to the income tax liability, so that an individual who has a taxable income for surtax purposes of

441

above £15,000 will have a marginal tax rate on unearned income of 88·75% (50% surtax plus 38·75% income tax). Consequently the income element of the yield on a security is almost worthless to such a person and he much would prefer either a capital gain or a return which is entirely tax-free. Needless to say, there are very few cases where the return on an investment is either wholly or in part free of all tax. The most common examples are:

(a) Premium Savings Bond prizes.
(b) National Savings Certificates.
(c) The £2 bonus on National Development Bonds and British Savings Bonds which are held for a five-year period.
(d) Under certain circumstances sums received on the maturity or sale of life insurance policies.

Of these four investments, the first three are limited as to the amount that may be held, and in any case offer relatively low yields. Life assurance schemes, however, whether operated through insurance companies or unit trusts, still offer considerable advantages to surtax payers despite the restrictions of the Finance Act 1968.

The advantages of capital gains are demonstrated by the fact that a top-rate surtax payer would only receive a net amount of £11·25p for every £100 of marginal gross income. However, a capital gain of £100 would yield a net return of £70, which is the equivalent to the net return on an additional £622 of gross income.

It is thus clear that the tax position of an investor has an important influence on the nature of the return which he seeks so that at least an acquaintance with tax law is essential in the analysis of investments.

(d) *Double Taxation Relief for Individuals*

Under normal circumstances all income which arises in the UK is subject to UK tax. Similarly, all income received from overseas by a UK resident is liable to tax in this country. As many other countries have similar rules it is clear that instances of double taxation of the same income will frequently occur. With the present high rates of taxation in most industrialized countries this not only leads to considerable injustice but might also seriously affect international investment and mobility of capital. For these reasons the UK has negotiated a series of double taxation agreements with most Commonwealth countries and the major industrial countries. Although these agreements differ in detail, most of them provide for the exemption of certain classes of income in one of the two signatory countries, or for the provision of tax credits where income is taxed in both countries.

Currently, these agreements are in the course of re-negotiation, primarily in order to adjust the provisions relating to dividends. Previously, they generally provided for a tax credit in respect of overseas tax suffered by UK residents. The overseas tax would include, in the case of ordinary dividends, both the direct tax deducted at source from the dividend and the indirect tax, or underlying tax, which was paid by the company in respect of its profits. The amount of the credit was based on the lower of the total overseas tax rate and the effective (or average) rate of tax paid by the taxpayer. If, by virtue of the restriction of relief by reference to the effective rate of tax, part of the foreign tax was unrelieved, this amount could be deducted from the UK assessment.

In simple terms, where the effective UK rate exceeded the foreign tax rate the tax credit consisted of the gross foreign income multiplied by the foreign rate. If the effective UK rate was less than the foreign rate the UK assessment would consist of the net foreign income grossed up at the effective UK rate. The tax credit, which is deductible from the tax payable on the assessment, was calculated by multiplying the amount of the assessment by the effective UK rate.

For example, a UK investor received a net dividend of £300 from overseas. His effective rate of UK tax was 40p in the £, while the rate of overseas tax was 50%. His UK assessment and the tax credit would be computed as follows, having regard to the fact that the effective UK rate is lower than the foreign rate:

The *UK assessment* is $£300 \times \dfrac{20}{12} = £500$

The *UK tax credit* is £500 @ 40p $= £200$

The gross foreign assessment is $£300 \times \dfrac{20}{10} = £600$

The unrelieved foreign tax is:

Actual foreign tax	£300	
Less: tax credit	£200	
	——	£100
UK assessment		£500

At the time of writing the agreement with the United States has been re-negotiated, and it indicates the changes that are likely to be made in other agreements. The rate of direct tax, or withholding tax, on dividends paid between the two countries is to be 15%, while no relief is to be given in respect of indirect tax, except in the

443

case of companies which own more than 10% of the voting shares of a company in the other country.

At the same time the Government has introduced a general rule that, from 1966–7 onwards, the marginal rate of tax of the taxpayer will be used instead of the effective rate in the computation of the tax credit. This means that the likely future trend will be the calculation of the tax credit on the lower of the overseas direct rate of tax and the taxpayer's marginal rate of tax. The effect of this rule is to reduce the allowable rate of overseas tax (by excluding indirect taxation) and to increase the taxpayer's rate of tax against which this is measured, for in any progressive system of taxation the marginal rate will be higher than the effective rate.

As a result those low rate taxpayers whose tax credit was limited by their effective rate will tend to benefit while surtax payers whose credit was limited by the overseas rate of tax will lose to the extent of any indirect tax previously included in the overseas rate. Similarly, investment trusts which had previously received relief in respect of indirect overseas tax will receive much lower tax credits.

The effect of the new rules coupled with the level of the investment dollar premium and the requirement to liquidate part of one's investment dollar pool on a sale has greatly reduced the attraction of American securities. Their main advantages at the moment are that they have a better growth record than British securities and provide a better hedge against devaluation. However, the new rules have made British securities more attractive to overseas investors, for the rate of direct tax on dividends therefrom has fallen from 41·25% to 15%.

All in all, the position concerning tax credit relief is very much in a state of transition and an investor must examine the latest double tax agreements if he is interested in investing in an overseas country. Although the likely trend will be similar to that described above, the current rules depend upon whether or not a new agreement has yet been negotiated. Even when all the agreements have been re-negotiated there will still be differences of detail between them.

Where income is received from a country with which there is no reciprocal agreement, the Inland Revenue will give unilateral relief in respect of the overseas tax suffered. For 1968-9 and future years the relief is limited to the lower of the direct overseas tax and the effective rate of income tax of the taxpayer and is given in the form of a deduction from the assessable income. This contrasts with the position under reciprocal agreements whereby the amount of the tax credit is deducted not from the amount of the assessment, but from the tax payable thereon.

2. THE TAXATION OF COMPANIES

Prior to the introduction of the corporation tax on profits for financial years which ended after April 5, 1965, the earnings of British companies were taxed in two different ways. In the first place they were charged with profits tax, which was a direct levy on the company in its corporate capacity. It was identical to the corporation tax in everything but name and consequently the latter was by no means so dramatic an innovation as has been suggested.

In addition to profits tax, companies also paid income tax at standard rate on their profits. Although this was paid by the company it was theoretically deemed to have been borne by the shareholders. The company was thus regarded for income tax purposes as a body of shareholders trading together under a corporate name with each shareholder bearing tax on his share of the profits of the company. To the extent that profits were distributed as dividends this principle held good, for the company paid net of tax dividends out of its taxed profits, and the tax attributable to the dividend was adjusted to each shareholder's marginal rate. Thus those shareholders whose marginal rate of tax was less than standard rate received repayment, while those who were paying surtax were required to pay further tax. However, where profits were retained by a company this principle was not followed, and the tax that the company had paid on those profits at standard rate was not adjustable to the marginal rate of the individual shareholders. Therefore shareholders whose marginal rate was below standard rate could not make a tax repayment claim in respect of tax paid by the company on retained profits. Similarly surtax payers could not be required to pay any further tax. This had obvious advantages to surtax payers, particularly in the absence of a capital gains tax at that time.

With rates of profits tax of 15p in the £ (15%) and income tax of 41·25p in the £, the position was that retained profits were taxed at 56·25%, regardless of the marginal tax rate of the individual shareholders, while distributed profits were taxed at 15p plus the marginal rate of the respective shareholder. This is, of course, an oversimplification in that it ignores the effects of surtax directions, profits tax abatement, net UK rates and the fact that the basis of assessment for income tax and profits tax was different. Moreover, as is shown below, the effective rate of profits tax was well in excess of 15%. Nevertheless, it does demonstrate the differing and illogical treatment of retained and distributed earnings under the old system.

The corporation tax is much simpler in its operation. The basic innovation was that profits tax was increased in amount and became known as corporation tax. At the same time, income tax on the profits of companies was abolished, with the result that companies pay corporation tax on the full amount of their profits, while shareholders pay income tax on the dividends received by them The income tax payable by the shareholders is, in fact, deducted from the dividends at source and the company pays over the tax to the Inland Revenue.

The implications of the corporation tax may be discussed under five main headings:

(a) *Retention and Distribution Policies*

The effect of the corporation tax on retention and distribution policies may be explained by examples showing its impact on companies with different distribution policies. The rate of corporation tax is taken as 40%, though it has since been increased to 45%.

(1) *Distribution of full amount of profits*

	Old System			Current System
	£	£		£
Profit		100,000	*Profit*	100,000
Profits tax	15,000		Corporation tax	40,000
Income tax	41,250			
	———	56,250	Available for dividend	60,000
		———	Income tax @ 41·25%	24,750
		£43,750		———
			Net dividend	£35,250

This is the equivalent of:

Gross dividend	74,468
Income tax @ 41·25%	30,718
	———
Net dividend	£43,750

From these figures it can be seen that a company which paid the whole amount of its profits as dividends would have found it impossible to maintain its dividend out of profits unless profits were increased. Under the old system such a company would have to pay tax totalling £56,250. Of this amount the £15,000 profits tax was the responsibility of the company and the shareholders could not be credited with it in any way. Moreover, the cumulative effect of the disallowance of profits tax as a deduction from profits for income tax purposes meant that £10,532 income tax could not be passed on to the shareholders. Consequently the effective rate of profits tax was above 25·5%. The remaining income tax of £30,718 was deemed to have been borne by the shareholders and would have been adjusted in their hands to their marginal rate of tax, subject to any net UK rate restrictions.

Under the current system, which is clearly less complicated than that previously in force, the company bears the corporation tax of £40,000 while the shareholders bear income tax of £24,750. This is deducted by the company from the dividends and paid over to the Inland Revenue, who adjust the amount deducted to the marginal rate of each shareholder. The final result, where profits are only maintained, is a fall in the total net dividend from £43,750 to £35,250.

(2) *Distribution of one-half of profits*

	£	£		£
Profit		100,000	*Profit*	100,000
Profits tax	15,000		Corporation tax	40,000
Income tax	41,250			
		56,250		
Available for dividend		43,750	Available for dividend	60,000
Retention		21,875	Retention (as before)	21,875
Paid to shareholders		£21,875	Gross dividend	38,125
			Income tax @ 41·25%	15,726
			Net dividend	£22,399

This is the equivalent of: £
Gross dividend   37,234
Income tax @ 41·25%   15,359

Net dividend   £21,875

These figures indicate that companies which previously retained one-half of their profits are in a position to increase either their dividend or their retentions or both, now that corporation tax is in force, assuming that profits have been maintained. Moreover, the greater the proportion of profits that a company previously retained the stronger is its position now with regard to the increase of its dividends or retentions. As a result of this it has been argued that one effect of the corporation tax is to encourage firms to retain profits. However, the tax does nothing to influence the decisions of firms whether to retain or distribute their earnings. As can be seen from the examples above, both companies have £60,000 available

447

for dividend under the current system, and the corporation tax does nothing to influence their decision as to the distribution or retention of the £60,000.

The only way in which the present system can be said to encourage retentions is by giving companies greater discretion over the appropriation of their profits. However, the actual manner in which these profits are appropriated is decided entirely by the directors, and may or may not result in higher retentions. It is difficult to analyze the effect of corporation tax because of fluctuations in company earnings, differences in levels of franked investment income and differences in capital structures, but a survey of subsequent company results indicates that the vast majority of companies have maintained dividends where possible, regardless of the level of retentions.

(b) *The Effect on Investment Policies of Companies*

Not only does the corporation tax not positively encourage retentions, but it also reduces the incentives to the investment of retained funds. This is due to the fall in the value of capital allowances under the corporation tax. Under the old system the capital allowances given over the life of a new machine amounted to 130% of its cost. With the previous tax rates of 41·25% income tax and 15% profits tax a company received relief amounting to 56·25% of 130%, namely 73%, of the cost of the machine. The greater the acceleration of the depreciation allowances, the greater was the value of this relief when the time-discount factor is taken into account. Under the current system, however, the value of the relief, with an initial corporation tax rate of 40%, fell to 40% × 130%, namely 52% of the cost of the machine.

In 1966, the Government purported to answer criticisms of this devaluation of depreciation allowances by introducing a system of investment grants. This system attempted to meet two of the objections most often laid against investment allowances. In the first place, it provides immediate cash grants in respect of investment in certain classes of new assets, and it was claimed that such grants would be more comprehensible to businessmen and thus more likely to influence their investment plans. Moreover, they would provide an advantage over previous systems where time-discounting methods of appraisal were used.

The second major advantage claimed for the new system was its discretionary nature. Grants were limited with a few exceptions to new plant and machinery used in a qualifying manufacturing or extractive process. At the same time the existing development areas were drastically extended and higher rates of grants laid down in respect of investment there.

The system applied to assets acquired after January 16, 1966 and the major rates were initially as follows:

Old System	Investment Grant %	Investment Allowance %	Initial Allowance %
New plant and machinery	—	30	10
Second-hand machinery	—	—	30
New industrial buildings	—	15	5

New System			
New plant and machinery:			
Qualifying	20	—	—
Non-qualifying	—	—	30
All second-hand plant and machinery	—	—	30
New industrial buildings	—	—	15

Considerably higher grants and allowances were given in respect of investment in development areas, where the investment grant for qualifying expenditure on plant and machinery, for instance, was 40%. There was further discrimination in that some assets receive special treatment, with ships, computers and plant, machinery and buildings for scientific research receiving more favourable, and motor vehicles less favourable treatment.

The Government quickly showed that it intended to use the system as a flexible fiscal weapon, and it increased the rates of grants for new qualifying plant and machinery for 1967 onwards to 45% and 25% for development areas and other areas respectively.

However, the new system did not entirely live up to the claims which were made for it. In the first place it was by no means certain that indiscriminate support given to manufacturing and extractive industries at the expense of the services sector was in the best interests of the economy. Secondly, the simplicity of the system seems to have been undermined by excessive paperwork and problems of definition.

Finally, the grants resulted in a serious accounting problem,[1] for there were at least six different methods of accounting for cash grants. Two of these methods were recommended by the English Institute of Chartered Accountants while the Scottish Institute advocated a third. Consequently, there was no conformity between

[1] Viz. 'Accounting for Investment Grants', *Accountancy*, April 1967, pp. 260–62, vol. LXXVIII, no. 884.

companies in the method adopted, and, in any event, many companies did not even indicate which method they were using, so that inter-firm comparison became still more difficult.

In 1970 investment grants were abolished for all capital expenditure on or after October 27, 1970. From that date all expenditure on new or second-hand plant and machinery, except motor vehicles, gives rise to allowances of 60% of the expenditure in the first year and 25% of the written-down value in subsequent years. In the case of new plant and machinery (other than mobile equipment) bought for use for industrial purposes in a development area the entire expenditure may be deducted in the first year. In July 1971 the first-year allowance was increased to 80%, and it was further increased to 100% for expenditure incurred after March 21, 1972.

(c) Encouragement of Debentures

The corporation tax has made finance provided by ordinary or preference share capital much more expensive than loan or debenture finance:

X Ltd		Y Ltd	
Ordinary shares	500,000	Ordinary shares	500,000
7% Preference shares	500,000	7% Debenture stock	500,000
Capital employed	£1,000,000	Capital employed	£1,000,000
Profit	100,000	Profit	100,000
Corporation Tax @ 40%	40,000	Debenture interest (allowable deduction for tax purposes)	35,000
	60,000		65,000
Preference dividend (including tax deducted by company and paid to Inland Revenue)	35,000	Corporation tax @ 40%	26,000
Available for ordinary shareholders	£25,000	Available for ordinary shareholders	£39,000

The reason for the advantage of debenture finance is that debenture and loan interest is an allowable deduction from profits for tax purposes, while preference and ordinary dividends are not. The higher the rate of tax, and the higher the interest rate, the greater will be the advantage of debentures.

As a result of this, the new issue market has been largely dominated since 1965 by debenture issues, and there have been constant fears that the Government will cease to allow debenture interest as a deduction for tax purposes. So far their only action has been the increase in April 1967 of the capital duty payable on debenture issues to the same level as that payable on issues of ordinary and preference shares.

(d) *Effect on UK Companies with Substantial Overseas Earnings*

The corporation tax has had an extremely detrimental effect on companies which pay overseas taxation. Where such taxation is paid in a country with which the UK has a double taxation agreement its amount may be credited against the company's liability for UK tax. However, any excess of overseas taxation over the amount due in respect of UK tax will not rank for relief. With the reduction of the rate of tax on companies from 56·25% to 40% such excesses are more likely to occur, thus increasing the burden of taxation for such companies compared with those who pay only UK tax.

The effect of corporation tax may be illustrated by the example of a company which pays a 60% rate of overseas tax and which in the past retained one-half of its distributable profits.

	Old System		Current System
	£		£
Profit	100,000	Profit	100,000
Overseas tax	60,000	Overseas tax	60,000
Distributable profit	40,000	Distributable profit	40,000
Retentions	20,000	Retentions	20,000
Dividend (net)	20,000	Dividend (gross)	20,000
		Less: Tax at 41·25%	8,250
This is the equivalent of:			£11,750
Gross dividend:	34,043		
Less: Tax @ 41·25%	14,043		
Net dividend	£20,000		

It is thus clear that, due to the decrease in the credit given for overseas tax, overseas companies would be forced to curtail severely either or both of retentions or dividends. In order to reduce the immediate impact of the changeover the Government introduced a form of transitional relief known as overspill relief. In simple terms, the company selects as a base year out of the three tax years 1962–3, 1963–4 and 1964–5 the year in which the credit given for overseas tax exceeds by the greatest margin the amount of notional corporation tax at 40% on the gross overseas profits. Subject to certain limitations the company will receive a non-taxable cash grant in the amount of the margin for the base year for each of the three tax years 1966–7, 1967–8 and 1968–9. Thereafter the relief is reduced as follows:

1969–70	80% of the margin
1970–71	60% of the margin
1971–72	40% of the margin
1972–73	20% of the margin
Future years	Nil

If during this period the actual excess of overseas tax over UK tax is less than that for the base year, or if the company increases its dividend payments, then the amount of the relief will be restricted.

One advantage of corporation tax is that the problems raised by the net UK rate have now disappeared. Previously the company could pay a net dividend to its shareholders out of the distributable profits, although the Inland Revenue had not actually received tax at the standard rate either from the company or the shareholders. However, the Inland Revenue would not repay tax which it had not received, so that where an investor who was liable to tax at less than standard rate made a repayment claim the amount of the repayment was limited to the rate of UK tax which the Inland Revenue had actually received from the company. This rate was known as the net UK rate. For some companies this rate was nil, indicating that the company paid no UK tax and that no repayment claims could be made in respect of dividends paid by it.

Now that all companies deduct tax at standard rate from dividends paid and pay the full amount of this tax over to the Inland Revenue no such limitation of repayment claims exists.

It would appear that the Government hoped through the introduction of the corporation tax to encourage companies with substantial overseas earnings to bring those earnings within its charge, which is at a lower rate than that in many overseas markets. Certainly, the very low net UK rates of many UK companies indicated that they were bringing a very small proportion of their total profits into this country. However, the extent to which more profits will be transferred to the UK with accompanying benefits for the balance of payments will depend upon the laws and restrictions of overseas countries, many of which restrict the export of earnings.

It is impossible to predict the long-run effect of the corporation tax on overseas companies. Although many of them initially had to cut either dividends or retentions, their profits have grown and have been boosted further by devaluation. At the present time their advantages as a devaluation hedge more than outweigh the short-run impact of corporation tax.

(e) *Close Companies*

These are UK resident companies which are under the control of five or fewer participators. A participator is defined simply as a person who has an interest in the company either as a shareholder, option holder or loan creditor. However, it is provided that a company may be excluded where at least 35% of the voting shares are held by the public and are quoted and dealt in on a recognized stock exchange during the previous twelve months.

Where a company falls within the definition of a close company it will suffer the following drawbacks:

(1) Prior to the Corporation Tax Year 1969 the allowance for directors' remuneration (other than that of whole-time service directors) as a deduction from profits in computing corporation tax could be restricted.

(2) Certain payments to participators, such as excessive rates of interest and annuities, may be sometimes regarded as distributions and will not be deductible from profits in computing corporation tax.

(3) Loans to participators or their associates will be charged to income tax on the grossed-up amount of the loan. This tax will be credited to the company when the loan is repaid.

(4) The most important implication is that close companies may be required to distribute 60% of their net trading income and virtually the whole of their net investment income. This gives these companies an excuse to avoid dividend restrictions imposed by the Government. However, the company may claim that a higher than standard level of retentions is necessary for the maintenance or expansion of the business. The Inland Revenue has in the past interpreted such rules relatively generously and it is possible that examples of the compulsory increase of distributions will be relatively rare.

CHAPTER 16

The Principles of Portfolio Selection

The value of an ordinary share was defined earlier as the anticipated future dividends and capital gain or loss on realization discounted at a rate of interest which allows for the risk attached to that income stream. One argument frequently levelled against this theory is that it does not account for the observed popularity of diversification in investment portfolios, for it would have the result that an investor faced with competing investments would invest the whole of his capital in the security which offered the highest net discounted value.[1]

However, this argument can be countered by distinguishing between portfolio risk and the risk attached to an individual investment. It is commonly accepted that the risk attached to a portfolio of investments will tend to be less than that of an individual share, for an adverse variance in the return on one share will probably be balanced by a favourable variance on another. As a result the possibility of extremely high losses or gains is reduced with the result that the likely range of variances from the predicted returns will be considerably narrowed.

The net discounted value theory of investment has regard to the risk of an individual share by adjusting the rate of discount, but it tends to ignore the question of portfolio risk. However, portfolio risk can be incorporated into this theory by arguing that an investor ranks available securities in order of net discounted value and then selects those which give him the mix of return and portfolio risk

[1] See Harry Markowitz, 'Portfolio Selection', *Journal of Finance*, vol. VII, no. 1 (March 1952), pp. 77–91 and J. Fred Weston and William Beranek, 'Programming Investment Portfolio Construction', *Financial Analysts' Journal* (May 1955).

which he requires. An investor who has a predilection for risk might invest the whole of his capital in the one share which offers the highest return, or might undertake a complete gamble by buying options. On the other hand, an investor who was averse to risk might prefer a more moderate but more certain return from a portfolio of holdings in unit and investment trusts.

In order to define the attitude of an investor to the structure of his portfolio it is necessary to examine the personal and technical factors which would influence his choice:

(a) *Degree of Risk Aversion*

The extent of the risk inherent in a particular investment or in a portfolio and the attitude of investors to that risk is entirely subjective and is thus incapable of quantitative analysis. Admittedly a great deal of research is being carried out in the United States on the measurement of risk, primarily through the use of probability theory, but this research is still very theoretical in nature and is outside the scope of this volume. One major problem is that risk is not always defined clearly. Normally it is regarded as the degree of certainty of the predicted return and measures the extent to which the actual return is likely to vary from that predicted. However, certain other risks have to be taken into account. For example, there is the possibility that the rate of interest will alter, thus causing a change in the capital value of securities assuming that the interest or dividend thereon remains as predicted. At the same time there is an inflation risk which indicates the extent to which the anticipated return after adjustment for economic risk compensates for changes in the cost of living.

The investor's measurement of these risks and his attitude thereto are entirely subjective. At one extreme, an investor with an absolute risk preference would be attracted by the option market, where he can purchase the right to buy or to sell shares at a given price during the next three months. For example, he may predict that a particular share will rise in value in the short term. If that share currently stands at 100p and the investor has only £500 capital, he would only be able to buy 500 shares and his profit would be limited to the increase in value on those shares. At the same time his potential loss would not exceed the loss on 500 shares. If he was not averse to risk or if he was absolutely certain about the imminent rise he could purchase a call option at perhaps 5p per share which would entitle him to buy the shares at $102\frac{1}{2}$p (the higher price allows for the dealer's cost of financing the operation) within three months.

In this way he can take out an option on 10,000 shares and, if the shares rise, his gain would be increased twenty times over that provided by outright purchase, less, of course, the cost of the option. If the price rises by less than the cost of the option the difference will represent a loss. However, if the shares fall in value he would abandon the option and would lose the whole of his £500.

If the option is exercised it becomes subject to capital gains tax so that any gain over the cost of the option will be taxed, while relief will be given where a loss results. Even if it is not exercised the abandonment of the option on or after April 20, 1971 will constitute a disposal of an asset (namely the option) and relief will be given in respect of its cost.

Where an investor anticipates that the price of a share will drop he can purchase a put option which gives him the right to sell the shares within three months at a price slightly lower than the current price. The normal cost of an option is about 10% of the market price of the share, while the striking price will be slightly above the market price in the case of a call option and slightly below for a put, the difference representing the dealer's finance cost.

If he predicts that the price of a share will fluctuate considerably, but is not certain of the direction of the fluctuations, he can take a double option, which will cost double the price of a single option and will enable him either to buy or to sell the shares at a given price. One advantage of a double option is that a single striking price is given for both sides of the option. On the other hand only one side of the option can be exercised so that no tax relief is available in respect of the other side.

Although options are regarded as a speculation, they can often be used as a means of insurance. Thus if an investor holds tobacco shares and expects a fall in their price due to an increase in tobacco duty or the publication of a cancer report, he may purchase a put option, so that his potential loss is limited to a definite figure.

Furthermore, there are other types of speculative activity which are still more in the nature of gambling. For instance, a speculator might take up a bear position in a share and sell a large quantity, which he does not possess, hoping to be able either to buy them before delivery at a cheaper price or to delay delivery until the price falls. Similarly, he might behave as a bull and buy far more shares than he can afford in the hope that they will rise in value quickly enough for him to sell without having to take delivery.

Beneath this speculative extreme comes the investor who is not particularly averse to risk. His portfolio would probably consist entirely of equities, with a preponderance of speculative stocks.

456

An investor with a more marked degree of risk aversion would tend to have a more balanced portfolio, with a mixture of variable and fixed-interest securities and further diversification by industry and geographical area. The portfolio of an investor who is decidedly averse to risk would contain a slight equity element, possibly in the form of convertible debentures, in order to combat the risk of inflation, gilt-edged securities to avoid economic risk and variable-interest deposit accounts to avoid interest risk. Finally an investor who has a total aversion to risk is in an impossible situation for there is no portfolio which avoids all of the forms of risk mentioned above. Probably the most acceptable form of investment under these circumstances is a debenture with an interest rate tied to the cost of living index, or to some other inflation indicator. Even this bond, however, does not avoid the interest risk, while there is also an economic risk depending upon the quality of the borrowing company.

(b) *Objectives of the Investor*

In this connection it is usual to distinguish between the basic objectives of income and growth. It has already been stressed that the return on a share consists of the dividend income and the capital growth. Obviously some investors will have preference for immediate income in the form of dividends while others will be prepared to defer the realization of the bulk of their return by taking it in the form of an eventual capital gain. The time-preference of an investor will depend upon various factors:

(i) *Age.* Clearly, the greater the age of an investor, the greater his need for income, whether in the form of dividends or short-term capital gains.

(ii) *Income from other sources.* The higher the income that an investor receives from other sources, the less will be his dependence upon income from his portfolio. Thus an investor with high external income will be able to bias his portfolio in favour of capital growth and will be more amenable to speculative investments.

(iii) *Tax burden of the investor.* This would, for obvious reasons, have an effect similar to that of external income, for the higher the external income, the greater the tax burden of the investor. An investor who pays relatively little tax would clearly prefer immediate income, for this would have a time advantage over growth and would not result in a high level of marginal taxation. On the other hand, a high rate surtax payer would derive little net benefit from income and would prefer capital growth which is only taxed on realization and then at a maximum rate of 30%.

(iv) *Size of the capital of the investor.* The smaller the size of the funds available, the less will be the scope for risk taking, for the investor will be unable to minimize portfolio risk because his capital is too small to permit diversification. Under these circumstances he should place a large proportion of his funds in unit trusts or investment trusts. Because it is uneconomical to invest less than £100 in one shareholding an investor should have capital of at least £1,000 if he intends to buy shares of individual companies and wishes to achieve some degree of diversification.

(v) *Family responsibilities.* An investor who is married and has children will normally have a higher degree of risk aversion than a single person. Moreover, the timing of the return on the portfolio will be more important. For example, certain periods may be foreseen as requiring greater expenditure and the planning of the portfolio must provide for greater income for these periods. An obvious instance of this is the provision of school fees, which can be predicted well in advance and may be provided for by life assurance policies.

The distinction between growth and income is to some extent misleading for capital gains may be realized on a regular basis to provide income. A more important distinction is probably that between income (whether in the form of capital gains, interest or dividends) which is relatively certain and that which is less definite. Thus where it is argued that an investor needs income it is implied that he required relatively certain receipts while an investor seeking growth will accept an irregular income stream.

(c) *Legal Constraints*

Under certain circumstances the choice of a portfolio is restricted by legal constraints. For example, the trust deed establishing a unit trust may limit the choice of securities, while the Board of Trade regulations prevent a unit trust from investing more than 5% of its funds in one company. Similarly, the investment of money held in a trust fund may have been restricted by the individual who established the trust. Where such a fund is established without any guidance as to how it is to be invested the rules laid down by the

Trustee Investments Act 1961 will apply. Prior to this Act trust funds whose investment was not specifically directed by the trust deed could only be invested in trustee securities, which were primarily gilt-edged securities. The failure of these to maintain their monetary value, let alone their real value, resulted in the depreciation of many trust funds. Consequently there was a demand that trustees should be empowered to invest in equities and a committee was established to inquire into the powers of investment of trustees. Their report resulted in the Trustee Investments Act 1961, which greatly broadens the range of trustee securities.

The Act empowers a trustee to obtain a valuation of the trust fund, whereupon he may divide the portfolio into two equal parts, one of which will be invested in narrower-range investments, the other in wider-range investments. The narrower-range investments are divided into two groups:

Those not requiring advice. Defence Bonds, National Development Bonds, British Savings Bonds, National Savings Certificates and deposits with the Post Office Savings Bank or a trustee savings bank.

Those requiring advice. This category includes:

Securities issued and registered in the UK by the UK Government or by the Government of an overseas territory in the Commonwealth.

Local authority securities and loans.

Debentures or guaranteed and preference stocks of water companies which have paid a dividend of at least 5% for each of the previous ten years.

Debentures (including loan stock and notes) of a UK company whose total issued and paid-up share capital is not less than £1 m. and which has paid a dividend on all of its issued capital in each of the five preceding years.

Special investment accounts with trustee savings banks.

Deposits with approved building societies.

Mortgages on freehold or leasehold property with at least sixty years' unexpired lease.

Perpetual rent charges on land.

The major items within the wider range are:

Fully paid shares issued and registered in the UK by a company incorporated in the UK whose issued and paid-up share capital

totals at least one million pounds and which has paid a dividend
on all of its issued shares in each of the preceding five years.

Share accounts in an approved building society.

Units in an authorized unit trust.

Any of the narrower-range securities may also be included in
the wider range.

In order to safeguard investment under these rules the Act provides
that trustees should seek the advice 'of a person who is reasonably
believed by the trustees to be qualified by his ability and practical
experience of financial matters'. Such advice is required on the
initial valuation of the fund and on any investment in the wider range
or in the second group of the narrower range. The advice must
be given in writing and, although trustees are not legally required
to comply with it, they obviously ignore it at their own risk. As
they are legally liable for any loss which the fund suffers as a result
of their negligence there is every incentive for them to seek and accept
such advice.

In addition to the basic attitudes and objectives of the investor
there are several general factors which should be taken into account
in the management of a portfolio:

(1) *Planning.* The investor must clarify his objectives from the start
and should build up his portfolio in accordance therewith. His
objectives must be ranked and those with the highest ranking should
be satisfied first. Thus, if he attaches the utmost importance to
providing for the education of his children, an educational assurance
policy should be the first item in his portfolio. However, the plan
of action once made must not be blindly adhered to. *Flexibility*
is extremely important and the investor must always be aware of
changed circumstances. If his personal objectives change, the
structure of the portfolio must be adjusted accordingly. In the same
way, if one of the portfolio investments is no longer suitable to
meet his objectives, or if another investment seems able to attain
them more completely then he should discard the first investment,
always bearing in mind the expenses involved in switching.

Another aspect of planning is *timing.* The investor must endeavour
to look ahead and buy the securities which are appropriate to his
portfolio at the most advantageous time. For instance, it might
appear that a particular selection of ordinary shares might meet the
long-term requirements of an investor. If, however, he suspects
that share prices will fall during the next few months he would do
better to remain liquid and delay his purchase until he is able to
buy more cheaply.

(2) *Marketability*. It is important that the investments which comprise the portfolio should be readily marketable. This is not always possible. Insurance policies, for instance, which are a necessary component of most portfolios, tend to be extremely unmarketable. However, as far as securities are concerned, an individual investor should only buy those with a Stock Exchange quotation, otherwise he will find it extremely difficult to liquidate them in the event of an emergency. Even a Stock Exchange quotation does not entirely guarantee marketability, for there are some securities in which there are so few dealings that it is difficult to find a buyer at short notice, and a sale may have to be made on disadvantageous terms. Fortunately, however, for most such securities it is far less difficult to sell than to buy.

(3) *Liquidity*. An investor should maintain a proportion of his portfolio in cash or near-cash, whether held in deposit accounts or in securities which may be quickly realized without affecting the balance of the portfolio. This is because cash may be needed immediately due either to suddenly changed circumstances of the investor, due perhaps to an accident, or to unforeseen investment opportunities, such as rights issues on existing shares. The proportion that should be held in liquid form will depend upon the attitudes of the investor. A cautious investor might insure against every conceivable eventuality and still hold a large amount in cash. At the other extreme a more speculative investor might invest all of his cash and undertake still more investment with borrowed funds.

(4) *Advice*. Although an investor should become conversant with stock market procedure and techniques of investment analysis, he should always be prepared to seek professional advice. Both the quantity and quality of this advice have increased in recent years. General newspapers have devoted more space to financial affairs and have greatly improved the quality of their 'city pages', while the more specialized financial press continues to provide information from company reports together with features on particular companies. Both of these groups will normally answer the queries of investors. The quality of advice given by stockbrokers is somewhat variable, but many brokers have now built up large research teams whose work is of a very high standard and far exceeds work currently being done in many of the traditional universities, who seem to regard investment analysis as a non-academic subject.

In addition to the more traditional sources of advice, full-time research organizations and investment counsellors have become

461

popular in recent years. The first of these normally provides regular information and advice on a private basis in return for an annual subscription. An investment counsellor, on the other hand, takes control of the investor's portfolio and manages it in accordance with its stated objectives. This is by no means a new phenomenon, for merchant banks and joint-stock banks have provided this service for many years, though they have specialized primarily in the management of trust funds. The growth of a professional class of investment counsellors specializing in private portfolios has not yet developed very far in this country, unlike the United States, where there are several thousand firms providing this service. The basis of the charge for such management may be either an annual fee of about $\frac{1}{2}\%$ of the capital of the portfolio or a fee based on performance. In return for this the counsellor will establish a portfolio in the light of his client's requirements and will issue selling and buying orders to his brokers when he feels that changes are necessary. The client, however, retains his certificates and must transact all of the necessary paperwork.

The extent to which an investor requires such large-scale management will depend upon the size of the portfolio and the degree of confidence which he has in his own judgment. Most investors would probably feel that their stockbroker can provide quite adequate advisory services, particularly with the current emphasis on research and advice in the larger stockbroking firms.

(5) *Security.* An investor must ensure that the real value of his capital is maintained. Until the end of the Second World War it was thought that gilt-edged securities offered the greatest security and they tended to offer relatively low yields. The traditional view of yield structures was as follows:

Yield on gilt-edged	$x\%$
Yield on debentures	$x+\frac{1}{2}\%$
Yield on preference shares	$x+1\%$
Yield on ordinary shares	$x+2\%$

Since 1945, due to the influence of sharply rising prices, gilt-edged securities have been at a considerable disadvantage, because they only offer a fixed return, while the value of that return and of the underlying capital has been eroded by inflation. Ordinary shares, on the other hand, have risen in value by more than enough to cover rising prices and offer more security in real terms than gilt-edged stocks.

Consequently, the structure of yields has been reversed in recent years and ordinary shares have tended to offer lower yields than gilt-edged. However, although equities in general offer greater effective security than gilts, individual equities may be far less secure, for there is always the possibility that the company may perform badly or even fail altogether. Therefore an investor should not invest the whole of his capital in one company, but should spread his risk by buying shares in a number of companies.

(6) *Diversification and balance.* In accordance with the principles stated earlier an investor should ensure that all foreseeable financial eventualities are provided for or insured against before he constructs his portfolio. Thus disability and accident insurances are a prerequisite. Then the portfolio should include a certain proportion of life assurance policies together with some liquid resources to provide against unforeseen circumstances. The structure of the remainder will depend upon the attitudes of the investor. Normally, unless these attitudes represent extremes of risk aversion or of gambling, the portfolio should be based upon a policy of diversification and balance.

Diversification implies not only the choice of shares in different companies, but also the selection of different classes of securities. Thus a balanced portfolio would contain both equities and fixed-interest stocks, both gilt-edged and industrial securities. At the same time there should be diversification by industry and by geographical area. Obviously complete diversification is impossible in a portfolio of average size, nor is it necessary or desirable, for it would by definition result in only an average performance, for the greater the diversification the more difficult it is to vary the performance of the portfolio from the average level. Thus an investor seeking an above-average return will have to weigh this factor against the greater risk which he will have to carry by virtue of the poorer balance of his portfolio. All in all, diversification, like the other factors which affect the structure of a portfolio, is only one of the many matters which must be taken into account, and the emphasis which is to be placed thereon will differ according to the attitudes of the investor concerned.

The advantages of diversification can be illustrated by the following example:

An investor analyzes two companies and concludes that an investment of £1,000 in either company is equally likely to yield a net present value of −£400 or +£600. If he has £2,000 available capital and invests the entire amount in one of the companies there is equal probability that his return will have a net present value of −£800 or +£1,200. If the two companies are entirely independent and are not influenced by the same overall factors then an investment of £1,000 in each company will yield the following range of possible outcomes:

A	B	A + B	Probability
−400	−400	−800	0·25
−400	+600	+200⎫	
+600	−400	+200⎭	0·50
+600	+600	+1200	0·25

By investing in two securities rather than one the investor has increased his chance of obtaining a positive return from 0·50 to 0·75. More important, he has reduced the degree of variance in the expected return. Where only one investment was held the average expected return was £200 (i.e. $\frac{1}{2}$(£1,200 − £800)), but there was no chance that this return would actually be achieved. Instead there was equal probability of two extreme results. The two-security portfolio offers a 50% chance of achieving the average return, while the probability of a loss of £800 is reduced to 25%. Thus diversification increases the chance of attaining an average yield and reduces the degree of variance in the range of possible outcomes. In doing this, however, it decreases the probability of attaining the highest potential return so that a risk-taker, who is prepared to accept a highly variable series of outcomes in order to increase the probability of the most profitable result, would not wish to diversify to the same extent.

In the example above it was assumed that the investments were independent. If their outcomes had been interdependent so that both were either negative or positive there would be only two possible results for an investment of £2,000, namely − £800 or +£1,200. These are the same outcomes as were possible for an investment of £2,000 in just one company. Consequently, no effective diversification would have been achieved by investing in both companies. Most investments, of course, are neither completely independent from nor completely dependent on other investments. One of the major problems of portfolio analysis is the measurement of the degree of interdependence between investments. For instance, two companies in the same industry might be interdependent in that they might both be affected in the same way by a given economic stimulus, while at the same time being relatively independent in that one produces primarily for the home market, the other for overseas markets.

While an investor should ensure that he has achieved effective diversification by selecting a portfolio of investments whose outcomes are relatively independent, such a policy will require a larger capital than would a single investment. Consequently, an adequately diversified personal portfolio would be beyond the means of any small savers who were not prepared to accept the greater risks implied by a small number of holdings. This would have discouraged the investment of the overall large volume of small savings in Stock Exchange investments had it not been for the growth of institutional portfolios in which small investors could obtain a share. Thus unit trusts, investment trusts and, to a lesser extent, insurance companies and pension funds allow investors to have a share in a large diversified portfolio in return for a moderate immediate capital sum or a regular monthly contribution. Similarly, an investor might join an investment club in which the same result is achieved with greater personal involvement.

The principles outlined above indicate the main factors which should influence a portfolio manager. Many investors, however, have regard to other principles which can be extremely misleading. Two such influences are the policy of averaging and the idea, frequently encountered, that low-priced shares are cheap and high-priced shares are dear. The second of these can be quickly disposed of.

An investment decision is based primarily on the yield expected from a share and not on its price. If an investor with capital of £100 seeks a yield of $7\frac{1}{2}\%$ it should be immaterial whether he buys ten shares at £10 each offering a dividend of 75p per share or 100 shares at £1 each paying a dividend per share of $7\frac{1}{2}$p. The yield on the total invested is the same in each case. Nevertheless, the notion persists that shares with a high market value are dear, while those with a relatively low value are cheap and those with a very low value are suspiciously cheap. For this reason a majority of individual investors would prefer to buy the holding of shares at £1 rather than that at £10. Although this basic attitude is illogical there are reasons for preferring shares which are moderately priced. In the first place highly priced or 'heavy' shares tend to be less marketable partly because investors regard them as dear and partly because there are obviously less of them on the market. At the same time extremely low-valued shares are unpopular, partly because they are regarded as excessively cheap and partly because the jobber's turn tends to be a higher proportion of the price, for obviously a jobber's margin of, say, 2p represents a greater burden on a share valued at 10p than on one valued at 100p.

It is far more difficult to dispose of 'averaging' as an investment policy, for it is held in high regard by many investors and is constantly advocated by the financial Press. A typical example of averaging which illustrates the fallacy involved is as follows:

'An investor buys 400 shares in a large company, in whose long-term prospects he has complete confidence, at a price of 400p. Six months later the price of the share has fallen to 300p, but the faith of the investor in the company is unshaken. He therefore buys a further 400 shares at the new price. At this point he owns 800 shares which have a total cost of £2,800 and an average cost of 350p each. If the share price falls still further to 200p and a further 400 shares are bought the holding will consist of:

	Shares	Cost per Share	Total Cost £
First acquisition	400	400p	1,600
Second acquisition	400	300p	1,200
Third acquisition	400	200p	800
	1,200		£3,600

The investor now holds 1,200 shares at an average cost of 300p, and is in a good position if the shares begin to rise, for they will only have to rise by 50% from their current level of 200p for the whole of the investor's loss to be recovered. If, on the other hand, the entire holding had been acquired at 400p the price would need to rise by 100% for the loss to be recouped. By buying in a declining market in this way good quality stock is acquired at a lower cost, thus reducing the average cost of the holding. Thus the investor buys several times, averages his purchases and realizes a better price for the stock than would have been achieved by buying the stock at one price.'

The above paragraph which is based on a leading American textbook is typical of the opinions which are commonly held and expressed on the subject of averaging. The last sentence, in particular, is quite erroneous, for the price paid for a share has no effect on the price for which it may be sold. In fact the entire theory surrounding averaging is quite fallacious. The price paid for a share is quite irrelevant for current investment decisions except for calculating the capital gains tax position arising from transactions in that share. Apart from this proviso, the relevant factors are the anticipated future return on a share compared with those offered by other securities, its relative risk status, and its effect on the balance of the portfolio.

For instance, the investor in the example above should have

acquired the second batch of shares on the basis of their future prospects and not for the purposes of averaging. At the time of the purchase he held 400 shares in the company with a market value of 300p each. The decision to buy more of those shares should have been based on the conclusion that they offered a better return than any other available share, having regard to relative risk and to portfolio balance. If this were not the case then another share should have been bought.

It is obvious that, when an investor buys further shares of a type which he already holds, it is possible to calculate an average cost for each share. This, however, is merely self-evident and does not begin to justify the establishment of averaging as a fetish. The danger of the popular advocacy of averaging lies in the fact that it encourages investors to blindly add to existing holdings without regard to alternative investment opportunities in the vain hope that they can thereby cut a loss which has been irrevocably made on the earlier, more expensive, holdings.

Probably the main reason for the popularity of averaging is the reluctance of an investor to realize or even admit to a loss. If 400 shares are bought at 400p and fall to 300p the investor has made a loss of 100p per share, whether or not he chooses to sell his shares. Certainly the acquisition of 400 more shares at 300p will not reduce the amount of the existing loss. If it is argued that the average price per share is now 350p so that the loss on the first holding is only 50p per share, the obvious reply is that there would also be an immediate loss of 50p on each new share, so that their purchase would hardly seem to be justified purely on the grounds of averaging.

To demonstrate the problems of individual portfolio policy, a few illustrative portfolios are reproduced hereunder, with the reminder that there is no such thing as a model portfolio and that in each case different advisers might have different opinions as to both the requirements of the investor and the selection of individual shares.

(1) George Peterson, a retired company director, is aged 75 and has capital with a current value of £20,000 invested in 3½% War Loan. He has income of £600 from a pension and has no dependants, his wife being dead and his two children married and prosperous. He has a decided aversion to risk which caused him to invest in War Loan when he retired ten years ago. Since then the real value of both his income and capital has declined and he has realized that his undated gilt-edged securities have not overcome inflation risk. For these reasons he seeks investment advice.

467

The first priority of the portfolio must clearly be to maximize real income with the minimum of risk. One method of doing this would be to purchase an annuity with the full amount of his capital. This would have several drawbacks. He would be entirely dependent upon one company; he might live for a far longer time than he suspects so that in his later years the real value of his income has been seriously eroded, and his capital will have entirely disappeared.

At the same time it is necessary to determine the amount of capital which Peterson wishes to leave to his children. If he feels that they have no need of his capital he may decide to contract it gradually through the purchase of subsequent annuities as his anticipated death draws nearer and the fear of income erosion diminishes. If, however, he wishes to leave the bulk of his capital he should invest a sizeable proportion in equities in an attempt to maintain its real value.

In view of his stated risk aversion, part of the capital should remain in gilt-edged securities, though these should be redeemable, preferably at a near date, in order to preserve their money value. The remainder should be spread over a number of unit trusts, for these provide greater diversification, and thus less portfolio risk, than direct investment in equities.

The suggested portfolio, under broad classifications, and with the approximate return that would be expected at the time of writing would be:

Amount Invested	Type of Investment	Annual Anticipated Income
£10,000	Two annuities each of £5,000	£1,700*
£5,000	Medium-term Government securities	£250†
£5,000	Units in five or six unit trusts	£200‡
£20,000		£2,150

* Of this figure, £500 would be regarded as income for tax purposes, the remaining £1,200 being a return of capital which is not subject to tax.

† This figure represents the flat or running yield. In addition to this there would be a tax-free capital gain of £5,000 after six years.

‡ This represents the anticipated amount of the annual distribution. In addition capital growth of an unpredictable amount might be expected.

The total annual income would now be £2,750 (including the pension of £600), of which £1,550 would be subject to tax, giving rise to a tax liability of about £400 and leaving a disposable income of some £2,350. It might be claimed that the above portfolio is somewhat illiquid. However, liquidity is rather less important where the bulk of the income is quite certain. In any event, if he requires liquidity he can either set aside, say, £500 at the outset in a deposit account, or build up such an account from any surplus from his annual income.

(2) Robert Brown is a university lecturer aged 30 with a salary of £2,000 and no other source of income. He is married with three children, all under seven years of age. His mother has recently died, leaving him a capital sum of £10,000. His primary aim is to maintain at least the real value of the capital, with the supplementation of his income as a secondary aim. He is not substantially averse to risk but does not wish to take any more risk than is necessary in the maintenance of his capital. Friends whom he has consulted have offered different advice ranging from a suggestion that he should pay off the outstanding balance of £3,000 which is due to a building society in respect of his house, to offers of a directorship in a small private company should he invest his capital therein.

It is obvious that he should not accept such advice. A building society mortgage is a long-dated fixed-interest loan and in inflation-ary circumstances both of these characteristics are favourable to the borrower. The mortgage should thus be maintained, for he would expect to earn more over time from investment in equities than the amount which he would save through the repayment of the mortgage. The suggestion that he should invest his money in a small private company is, of course, out of the question, for it would represent a speculative and unmarketable investment.

It is felt that liquidity is rather more important in this case due to the likely demand for such assets as consumer durables, etc.— items which might reflect the more prosperous circumstances of the family. It is therefore proposed to put £500 in a bank deposit account whence it could be withdrawn on demand. In order to provide an element of guaranteed growth and income, £1,500 might be invested in a long-dated Government stock. For instance $3\frac{1}{2}\%$ Funding 1999/2004 is priced at 45 at the time of writing, offering a flat yield of 7·184% and a gross redemption yield of 8·531%. For £1,500 he could buy just under £3,500 nominal value of this stock, which would offer annual interest of £122 and a guaranteed capital gain of nearly £2,000 after 26 years. It should be possible, of course, to sell the stock at a capital profit as the redemption date draws nearer or when interest rates fall. The remaining £8,000 might be split between recovery stocks and growth stocks, with £3,000 invested in the former and £5,000 in the latter. The actual choice of the stocks would depend upon the advice of the stockbroker.

The recovery stocks should be shares in companies which have favourable long-term prospects but which are currently experiencing depressed trading conditions, with the result that the dividend yield on their shares is markedly higher than the average yield on equities. The stated dividend yield on such stocks might be 8%, though the amount actually received might only be 6%, due to cuts in dividend. In the long run these stocks offer just as much scope for capital appreciation as growth stocks, for the market tends to be over-pessimistic about such stocks while there is a tendency to be over-optimistic about growth stocks.

The growth stocks will offer a much lower immediate yield, probably about 4%, but this should rise over time. The stocks should be carefully chosen, avoiding stocks which are exceptionally popular. The danger with a growth stock is that the market is already antici-pating a good performance by the company concerned. If the performance is, in fact, good then it will have little effect on the price, while a poor performance will cause the price to fall sharply. Only an exceptionally good result will induce a rise in the share price. There are many examples of erstwhile market favourites which were priced over-optimistically and are now depressed in price, showing substantial capital losses.

The suggested portfolio would be as follows:

Amount Invested £	Type of Investment	Anticipated annual income £
500	Bank deposit a/c	20
1,500	Long-dated Government security	122
3,000	Ten to fifteen recovery stocks	180
5,000	Fifteen to twenty growth stocks	200
£10,000		£522

With a portfolio of this size constant watch should be kept on the individual stocks with a view both to taking profits or cutting losses where necessary and to switching into better stocks. The shares that are bought should, of course, be diversified both industrially and geographically.

Finally, Brown should consider whether he has sufficient insurance having regard to his new standard of living. In particular, he should consider the purchase of a disability policy and an endowment policy out of his increased income.

(3) John Cartwright is a company chairman aged 50 with an annual salary of £25,000. He is married with two children and has

capital of £100,000 available for investment. He pays a combined marginal rate of income tax and surtax of 88·75%, which means that only 11·25p out of every £ of income is available for consumption. On the other hand, a capital gain would only bear tax at 30%, so that there is every incentive to invest with a view to capital growth. He does not, however, wish to speculate overmuch.

One way in which he could make an absolutely certain capital gain would be an investment in short-dated gilt-edged securities which are standing at a discount below the redemption price. At the time of writing there are stocks standing at 90, which are redeemable at par within four years. If the full amount of his capital were invested in this stock a holding with a nominal value of about £110,700 could be acquired, thus providing a definite tax-free gain of £10,700.

If Cartwright felt that the above course was not sufficiently profitable he might prefer to build up a portfolio of growth stocks which offer a very low current income yield but excellent prospects of eventual capital gains. The size of his capital would enable a very well-balanced portfolio to be built up and his broker would advise him on the stocks to be selected. In view of the size of the portfolio there would be considerable scope for holding shares in smaller, more speculative companies or even in private companies, for it would not matter if part of the portfolio was not readily marketable. In addition to shares, property investment might be considered, while insurance policies offer many advantages, particularly as income tax relief is given against the premiums, while the maturity proceeds are not subject to tax.

So far in this chapter the emphasis has been on portfolio planning for individual investors. The principles applicable to institutional investors are much the same, though the primary objectives will differ from one institution to another:

Insurance companies. It is argued in the major book on insurance company investment[1] that the portfolio policies of both general and life offices are substantially similar, subject to the need of general offices to maintain cash reserves at branches to provide for the prompt payment of claims and to their preference for marketable securities for the same reasons. The importance of liquidity should not, however, be exaggerated, for it is estimated that for both funds current premiums are normally sufficient for the payment of claims

[1] George Clayton and W. T. Osborn, *Insurance Company Investment* (London: George Allen & Unwin, 1965).

as they fall due. For life funds a certain degree of unmarketability is acceptable, and they may be invested in property and unquoted securities, particularly debentures. In recent years equities have become more popular as a hedge against inflation for both types of fund. Due to the greater predictability of claims on their funds, life offices have a preference for redeemable securities with maturity dates which coincide with their outgoings. As far as flexibility is concerned, there is constant switching between gilt-edged stocks as the yields of particular stocks fall out of line with general rates. In equities, however, switching is a more cumbersome operation due to the general thinness of the market, as a consequence of which sales or purchases of large blocks of shares cause a price movement against the dealer. Neither type of fund has a complete aversion to risk, as is shown by the extent of equity investment, but the extent of diversification and balance will generally be calculated to minimize portfolio risk.

Banks. The commercial banks are far more conscious of liquidity than other financial institutions, primarily because so many of their borrowings are repayable on demand. Moreover, they cannot afford to take much risk as their depositors' money is at stake. Consequently their portfolios are liquid (the conventional requirement being $12\frac{1}{2}\%$ in the form of cash) with Treasury Bills, quoted Government stocks and, to a lesser extent, industrial debentures, forming the dominant elements.

Superannuation and Pension Funds. These are exempt from tax and are thus indifferent as between income and capital returns, except insofar as timing is concerned. Like life funds their outgoings are contractual and predictable on an actuarial basis. Thus part of the fund would be invested in gilt-edged securities to provide certainty of payment, and the remainder in equities to maintain the real value of the fund.

Unit Trusts and Investment Trusts. The basic objective of the portfolio will depend upon the stated objects of the fund. Thus high income trusts, growth trusts, commodity trusts, etc. must invest in the type of security which will comply with their objects. The main problem is that many of them are forced to invest in relatively unmarketable shares in order to maintain their portfolio with the result that they may force the price against them whenever they buy or sell. Risk is relatively unimportant for the funds have no contractual commitments. Normally, however, portfolio risk is lessened by diversifying the portfolio. Liquidity, too, is largely unimportant, unless it is indicated by the poor state of the market. However, liquidity involves foregoing the higher interest which could have been earned by investment in securities, so that it is an expensive luxury which should not be maintained for too long unless a really pessimistic view is taken of the market.

The approach in this chapter has been largely descriptive, consisting mainly of an outline of the subjective factors to which an investor must have regard in the construction of his portfolio. Although this approach is still used by all but the most sophisticated analysts it is rapidly being superseded at the theoretical level by more mathematical techniques in which attempts are made to quantify the various subjective factors. These techniques were pioneered by Markowitz,[1] who prepared a programme which would compute the number of possible portfolio combinations and the probable rate of return and degree of variance of each from a given list of securities. The programmer would need to know the expected rate of return and expected range of variance of each security, the extent of interdependence between the outcomes for the securities, and the extent of any constraints to which the portfolio manager was subject, such as a minimum number of securities for the portfolio. From the list of possible portfolios the manager could select that which best suited his portfolio objectives.

To date the empirical results of this technique have been disappointing. There are probably two major reasons for this. In the first place the technique itself has drawbacks. For instance variability of return is regarded as the sole measurement of risk. However there are other crucial types of risk, such as risk of inflation, illiquidity, tax changes etc., which should be taken into account. Admittedly these could be incorporated into the analysis, possibly by means of utility functions, but they would cause enormous complications. Moreover, the technique, complex though it is, is not capable of solving a problem whose variable factors are infinite in number. A portfolio comprised only of stocks quoted on the London Stock Exchange, thus ignoring many important American and European stocks, would be selected from about 10,000 stocks in any combination and with all possible proportions of each stock. Moreover, each possible portfolio would need to be considered for all possible time periods, and would need to be reconsidered as

[1] Harry M. Markowitz, *Portfolio Selection: Efficient Diversification of Investments*, Cowles Foundation Monograph no. 16 (New York: J. Wiley & Sons, 1959) and 'Portfolio Selection', *Journal of Finance*, March 1952.

new information became available to the market. Finally, the problems of assessing the interdependence of the outcomes for all possible constituent stock are quite insurmountable.

Some of these defects, it is true, are overcome by limiting the scope of the analysis. This may be achieved by undertaking a comprehensive analysis of only a limited number of stocks, the others being entirely omitted from the computation. Again the constraints imposed by the portfolio manager place a further limit upon the number of possible portfolios which are considered by the programme.

In addition to the drawbacks inherent in the technique there are further serious deficiencies in the quality of the information which is used in the assessment of the values placed upon the characteristics of each stock for the purpose of the programme. Little information is available concerning the future prospects of companies, their risks and their interdependence. Such information as is available is expensive to process and changes so quickly that it is often outdated before it is incorporated into the programme.

Although it is accepted that future theoretical developments in investment analysis will be based upon the definition of security analysis as the measurement of the variable factors which affect the price of a share and of portfolio analysis as the identification of the optimum portfolio subject to the criteria and constraints of the portfolio manager, the precepts of traditional analysis are by no means as antediluvian as some writers would suggest.[1] At the practical level it is similar to security analysis, for both involve the isolation of factors which determine share prices and the prediction of future prices. In the selection of the portfolio the traditional analyst would suggest that the investor should select from those stocks with the highest net present values a combination which satisfies his subjective portfolio requirements. Ultimately a fusion of techniques for the measurement of these subjective requirements with the Markowitz technique for selection will produce a practical method of optimization. But at the present time it is argued that deficient standards of corporate reporting, especially in the United Kingdom, coupled with the magnitude of the subjective element which is involved justifies the retention of traditional analysis.

[1] E.g. Eugene M. Lerner and Willard T. Carleton, *A Theory of Financial Analysis* (New York: Harcourt Brace & World, 1966).

APPENDIX

CHAPTER 17

Current Developments in the Fields of Taxation Policy and Disclosure in Company Accounts

Since the first edition of this text fundamental changes have occurred in the areas of taxation policy and corporate disclosure. At the time of writing (May 1972) these changes are still in progress and the ultimate developments in both fields are as yet unclear. The object of this chapter is to summarize those steps which have so far been taken and to explain their implications for investors.

1. CHANGES IN TAXATION POLICY

At the time of the 1971 Budget the Chancellor took the unprecedented step of outlining in considerable detail various basic reforms to the tax system which were currently under consideration. These reforms included the merging of income tax and surtax, the removal of discrimination against distributed profits, and the possible replacement of selective employment tax and purchase tax by a value-added tax.

(a) *The Reform of Personal Direct Taxation*

In his Budget speech the Chancellor argued that the existing system of personal direct taxation was too cumbersome, too complex and riddled with anomalies. There were two taxes on personal income (income tax and surtax), each of which was subject to separate and often different rules and was computed and collected separately and at different times. Another anomaly was the fact that the existing system was structured in terms of investment income, with a complicated pattern of allowances for earned income, despite the fact that earned income constituted almost 95% of the total income brought under charge. This caused considerable misunderstanding of the true value of allowances and of the true marginal rate of tax, many people thinking that their marginal rate of tax was higher than it actually was because they confused it with standard rate.

It was therefore proposed to replace the existing income tax and surtax with a single graduated personal tax with the following four principal features:

(i) The existing pattern of personal allowances would be substantially retained but the amounts would be adjusted to ensure that they maintained their current equivalent value. In the Finance Acts of 1971 and 1972 the new allowances were specified as follows:

	Existing Amount £	*New Amount* £
Earned income relief	7/9 × £4,005; 15% × excess	Abolished
Personal allowance—married	465 (£600 for 1972–73)	775
Personal allowance—single	325 (£460 for 1972–73)	595
Wife's earned income relief	325 (460 for 1972– 73), or, if less, seven-ninths of earned income	595 or, if less, seven- ninths of earned income
Child allowance—over 16	205	265
11–16	180	235
under 11	155	200
Housekeeper	75	100
Dependent relative	75	100
Dependent relative (if maintained by single woman)	110	145
Allowance for widows, etc. with children	100	130
Life assurance relief	Total premiums up to £10; £10 for premiums £10–£25. Above £25: two-fifths of premiums	Total premiums up to £10. £10 for premiums £10– £20. Above £20: one-half of premiums
Family allowance deduction	42	60

At the same time old age relief and small income relief, both of which depended upon earned income relief, would be abolished.

(ii) The new tax structure would be based upon a basic rate corresponding to the current standard rate less earned income relief. In the Finance Act 1971, this rate was established at 30%.

(iii) There would be higher rates above the basic rate applicable to higher incomes. These rates were stated as follows in the 1972 Budget:

Rates of tax on the excess of total income over £5,000:

First £1,000	40%
Next £1,000	45%
Next £1,000	50%
Next £2,000	55%
Next £2,000	60%
Next £3,000	65%
Next £5,000	70%
Remainder	75%

(iv) The distinction between earned and unearned income would be maintained by way of a surcharge on investment income in place of the present earned income relief. The amount of the surcharge was stated in the 1972 Budget as 15% and it will only apply on that part of investment income in excess of £2,000.

The new system is to come into operation for the tax year 1973–4, from which year deductions under P.A.Y.E. will extend to the full graduated scale of rates. Income tax will be deducted from dividends and interest at the basic rate and the higher rates of tax and any surcharge payable will be assessed separately. The replacement of surtax by higher rates of tax payable on a current year basis will mean that in 1973–4 some surtax payers will be paying tax on their current earnings plus surtax in respect of their earnings for the previous year. To assist such persons payment of part of any substantial sums of surtax for 1972–3 on earnings will be allowed to be deferred for one year. Further relief for surtax payers was given in the 1972 Budget which exempted from surtax for 1971–2 and 1972–3 those with total incomes (after reliefs) not exceeding £3,000.

By these measures the Government has greatly reduced the degree of discrimination against unearned income which previously existed. Consequently all but those very small investors who are already exempt from tax can expect an increase in the net yields which they receive from their investments. This increase will be further enhanced by the encouragement given to companies to distribute more of their profits under the new system of corporation tax outlined below.

A further stimulus to investors was given in the 1972 Budget by the proposal that relief should be given against taxable income in respect of all interest paid in excess of £35 (interest paid in respect of the purchase of or improvement to property continuing to be allowed in full). This provision will clearly encourage investors, especially surtax payers, to borrow money for the purchase of shares, though provisions are made to exclude from relief the purchase of large quantities of redeemable securities with borrowed money.

(b) *The Reform of Corporate Taxation*

The Chancellor also criticized the existing system of corporation tax on account of the substantial discrimination which it entailed in favour of retained as opposed to distributed profits. It was argued that this discrimination distorted the working of market forces and thus encouraged the misallocation of scarce investment resources. In particular, it made it difficult for companies that needed to raise equity capital from the market and lessened the pressure of the market and shareholders on the efficiency of a company and on the profitability of new investment. It was therefore proposed to replace the present system of corporation tax by one which would be neutral as between distributed and undistributed profits. This could be achieved in one of three ways:

(i) A return to the pre-1965 system, as described in Chapter 15. Company profits, whether distributed or not, would be subject to corporation tax at a single rate as at present, and dividends would as now be subject to income tax at the basic rate. The difference would be that companies would be allowed to retain this tax instead of paying it over to the Inland Revenue under Schedule F. Thus, assuming a corporation tax rate of 50% and a basic rate for income tax of 30%, a company with pre-tax profits of £100,000 which distributed all of its earnings would be in the following position:

	£
Profit	100,000
Corporation tax	50,000
After-tax profit	50,000
Gross dividend payable	71,429
Less: Income tax @ 30%	
(retained by company)	21,429
Net dividend payable	50,000

The net tax suffered by the company would be £28,571, representing a rate of about 28·6%. If no dividends were paid the company would suffer tax at 50%, so that the effective rate of corporation tax would depend upon the distribution policy of the company. The drawbacks to a system such as this have already been discussed in Chapter 15 and include principally the confusion of company tax and shareholder tax and the need to reintroduce the net UK rate in respect of companies with substantial overseas earnings.

(ii) The imputation system. This system is broadly similar to the pre-1965 system and all company profits would again be subject to corporation tax at the same rate, with a proportion of this tax being available as a credit against the income tax liability of the shareholders. It would differ, however, in that income tax would be deducted at basic rate from dividends by the company and paid over to the Inland Revenue. This payment would represent an advance payment of the company's eventual corporation tax liability. This would overcome the problem of the net UK rate, for the Inland Revenue would always have received the income tax in respect of which shareholders might make repayment claims, and would mean that companies with a potential rate of corporation tax lower than the basic rate of income tax due to relief for foreign tax would effectively have to pay a supplementary charge.

Given the same facts as in the previous illustration the tax payments of the company would be as follows:

	£	£	
Profit		100,000	
Corporation Tax	50,000		
Less: Payment on account	21,429	28,571	(28·6%)
		71,429	
Gross dividend payable		71,429	
Less: Income tax @ 30%			
(paid over to Inland Revenue)		21,429	
Net dividend payable		50,000	

The net position is thus exactly the same as under the pre-1965 system except that the net UK rate problem is averted. However, there is still no clear demarcation between company taxation and shareholder taxation.

(iii) The two-rate system. Under this system distributed profits would be liable to corporation tax at a lower rate than retained profits. In addition, distributed profits would suffer deduction of income tax at basic rate, this tax being paid over to the Inland Revenue as an advance payment of the shareholder's own eventual tax liability.

479

Given the same facts as in the illustrations above and a distribution relief of 30% the tax payments of the company would be:

	£	£	
Profit		100,000	
Corporation Tax	50,000		
Less: Distribution relief			
(£71,429 × 30%)	21,429	28,571	(28·6%)
		71,429	
Gross dividend payable		71,429	
Less: Income tax @ 30%			
(paid over to Inland Revenue)		21,429	
Net dividend payable		50,000	

This system is broadly similar to the imputation method and like that method avoids net UK rate complications. However, it has the additional advantage of maintaining a clear demarcation between the corporation tax liability of the company and the income tax liability of the company.

Although in a Green Paper published in March 1971, the Government stated that it favoured the two-rate system, the final decision in the 1972 Budget was in favour of the imputation system. From the point of view of investors it is clear that companies will be encouraged to distribute profits for the effective rate of corporation tax on distributed profits on the figures used above would be 28·6% compared with a rate of 50% retained profits. However, in the same way that the introduction of corporation tax did not induce an increase in retained profits it is doubtful whether the new proposals will bring about substantial dividend increases.

Possibly of more importance to investors is the possibility of another break in the index of earnings performance. Until the introduction of corporation tax the main indicator of earnings performance was the earnings yield, which was based on an artificial figure of earnings obtained by grossing-up at the standard rate the figure of net profit after income tax and profits tax. Since 1965 the main indicator has been the price-earnings ratio, which is based upon the figure of net profit after corporation tax. Both of these indices were based on figures which were comparable for all companies, which all suffered the same rates of tax, whether income tax and profits tax before 1965 or corporation tax thereafter. However, the imputation system involves an effective rate of corporation tax which is dependent upon the distribution policy of the company and which might vary within a very wide range. It is thus going to be virtually impossible to define earnings per share in a way which will provide meaningful, as opposed to artificial, comparability between companies. Of the solutions which have been suggested, five appear to have received most support.

(i) To base earnings per share on the profit before tax. This would ensure comparability by ignoring taxation altogether. However, it would ignore the impact of its investment policy and distribution policy upon the tax borne by a company. Thus an important component of managerial skill would be ignored.

(ii) To assume that all profits are distributed. This would induce comparability, but would be artificial and would ignore the actual tax borne by the company. There would also be serious difficulties in connection with overseas companies.

(iii) To assume that all profits are retained. Whereas the previous suggestion assumed the most optimistic situation, this method would imply the most pessimistic. Again it involves an artificial and unrealistic comparability.

(iv) To assume a retention policy based upon an average either of all companies or of the company's past policies. This is clearly more realistic than the previous two assumptions but is still artificial. In view of the fact that all three of these assumptions involve an arbitrary and artificial adjustment to the figure of profit before tax which is used in the first method, it could be argued that they are inferior to that method.

(v) To use net earnings per share on the basis of the actual tax suffered by the company. This would ensure comparability and would take account of the dividend policy of the company. On the other hand, the trend of earnings could be distorted by changes in dividend policy as opposed to changes in operating efficiency.

At the time of writing there is no uniformity of opinion as to the relative merits of these five definitions and it is far from certain which of them will be adopted by investment analysts.

(c) *The Introduction of Value-added Taxation*

From April 1973, both selective employment tax and purchase tax will be abolished and a value-added tax will become operative. The main criticism of selective employment tax was the arbitrary discrimination which it made between manufacturing and services, while purchase tax showed similar discrimination in that its burden was borne by a limited number of goods and not at all by services.

Value-added tax, on the other hand, is far more comprehensive and can be applied to all goods and services. In the 1972 Budget it was stated that the rate of tax would be 10% and that it would apply to all goods and services with the exception of certain terms detailed in Schedule 5 of the Finance Act 1972. At the present time it is difficult to predict the impact of the tax on investors. The immediate impact will clearly be in the selection of those companies which are likely to benefit from the introduction of the tax, such as those with a large volume of exports, for the Chancellor has implied that the tax may be rebated in respect of exports, and those who are in a strong enough position to pass the tax on to their customers.

2. DEVELOPMENTS IN DISCLOSURE IN COMPANY ACCOUNTS

Towards the end of the 1960s it became clear that an increasing number of companies were becoming aware of the extent to which the variety of accepted accounting principles could be exploited in order to manipulate their profit and loss account. The object of the exercise was to enhance the figure of earnings per share which was a prime factor in the price-earnings ratio and was thus crucial to the price of the shares of the company. Among the many techniques used to achieve this were the alteration of the basis of calculating depreciation, the inclusion or exclusion at will of the results of associated companies, the almost fraudulent extension of the definition of 'exceptional' and 'non-recurring' expenses and the write-off of losses and expenditure to reserves on every conceivable pretext. As a result the credibility of published accounts and the standing of the professional accounting bodies were seriously diminished.

On December 12, 1969 the Institute of Chartered Accountants, possibly prompted by the strong and well-publicized criticisms made by Professor Stamp,[1] produced a 'Statement of Intent on Accounting Standards in the 1970s':

'It is the Council's intention to advance accounting standards along the following lines:

(i) *Narrowing the Areas of Difference and Variety in Accounting Practice.*
The complexity and diversity of business activities give rise to a variety of accounting practices justifiably designed for and acceptable in particular circumstances. While recognizing the impracticability of rigid uniformity, the Council will intensify its efforts to narrow

[1] This controversy is summarized in *Accounting Principles and the City Code: The Case for Reform* by E. Stamp and C. Marley (London: Butterworths, 1970).

the areas of difference and variety in accounting practice by publishing authoritative statements on best accounting practice which will, wherever possible, be definitive.

(ii) *Disclosure of Accounting Bases.*

The Council intends to recommend that when accounts include significant items which depend substantially on judgments of value, or on the estimated outcome of future events or uncompleted transactions, rather than on ascertained amounts, the accounting bases adopted in arriving at their amount should be disclosed.

(iii) *Disclosure for Departure from Established Definitive Accounting Standards.*

The Council intends to recommend that departure from definitive standards should be disclosed in company accounts or in the notes thereto.

(iv) *Wider Exposure for Major New Proposals on Accounting Standards.*

In establishing major new accounting standards the Council will provide an opportunity for appropriate representative bodies to express their views by giving wide exposure to its draft proposals.

(v) *Continuing programme for encouraging improved Accounting Standards in Legal and Regulatory measures.*

The Council will continue its programme of suggesting appropriate improvements in accounting standards established by legislation, of which the proposals on 'Companies Legislation in the 1970s' submitted to the President of the Board of Trade in March this year are an example. The Council will also continue to support and encourage the improvement of accounting standards in relevant regulatory measures such as the City Code on Takeovers and Mergers and Stock Exchange requirements.

Auditing

In support of the proposals on accounting standards outlined above, the Council will, after appropriate notice, recommend that if disclosure of accounting bases or of departures from definitive accounting standards is not made in the accounts or in notes thereto, appropriate reference should be made in auditors' reports.

Support and Maintenance of Standards

The Council will do all in its power to assist and support members in the observance of established standards. To this end, it intends to strengthen its machinery for investigating and pointing the lessons of lapses from standards.

Restatement of the Underlying Nature of Company Accounts
Those who prepare, audit and use company accounts should keep in mind the following essential points, against the background of which this statement of intent is issued.

'Company accounts are presented by directors, not by auditors. The auditors' function is to express an independent opinion on the truth and fairness of the view presented by the accounts.

'The activities of a company are continuous, whereas the period covered by the accounts is no more than an arbitrary segment of time out of a company's continuing existence. The determination of amounts of income and expenditure properly attributable to an accounting period, particularly in respect of uncompleted trans- actions, and of the amounts at which related items are shown in the balance sheet, can be arrived at only by informed judgment exercised in accordance with accounting conventions.

Implementation.
'The Council will forthwith establish machinery for furthering these proposals and to this end will seek the advice and assistance of representatives of industry, finance and commerce.'

Within a week of the publication of the Statement of Intent the Accounting Standards Steering Committee was formed to co- ordinate and expedite the Council's programme. The work of this committee and its progress during its early months have been out- lined in an excellent paper by K. Sharp.[1]

At the end of 1971 the work of the committee had reached the following stage:

(a) *Completed accounting standards: (i) Accounting for the Results of Associated Companies*

The exposure draft of standard accounting practice for this subject was published in June 1970 and reproduced in *Accountancy*, July 1970, pp. 496–8. The formal agreed Statement of Standard Account- ing Practice was issued in January 1971 (see *Accountancy*, February 1971, pp. 61–5). The major features of the Statement were a formal definition of 'associated company' and a requirement that the invest- ing group's share of profits less losses of associated companies should be brought into the consolidated accounts of the group.

(ii) *Disclosure of accounting policies* (see *Accountancy,*February 1971, pp. 95–6 for the exposure draft and *Accountancy*, December 1971 for the standard). This standard defines the terms 'fundamental

[1] Ken Sharp. 'Accounting Standards after 12 Months', *Accountancy*, May 1971, pp. 239–45.

accounting concepts', 'accounting bases' and 'accounting policies'. It requires disclosure where fundamental concepts different from those defined have been used and requires the disclosure of the accounting policies which have been adopted for dealing with items which are judged material or critical in determining profit or loss for the year and in stating the financial position in the accounts. Where the accounting policies significantly depart from the established accounting standards the departure should be disclosed and explained.

(b) *Accounting standards issued as exposure drafts and still under consideration:* (i) Accounting for Acquisitions and Mergers, January 1971 (see *Accountancy*, February 1971, pp. 97–9). This is a very complicated and contentious draft which attempts to define 'acquisitions' and 'mergers' and which, to put it extremely simply, proposes that an acquisition should be recorded in the books of the acquiring company at cost, which in the case of a consideration in the form of shares will be based on the market value of the shares issued; while in the case of a merger the shares issued by the holding company will be recorded at nominal value.

(ii) Earnings per share, March 1971 (see *Accountancy*, April 1971, pp. 219–30). This draft proposes that the audited accounts of quoted companies should state the earnings per share for the year and for the previous year, earnings being defined as the profit of the period after tax, but before extraordinary items, and after deducting minority interests and preference dividends. The basis of calculating earnings should be stated as should the anticipated dilution of earnings which will result from such factors as the conversion of convertible debentures or the ranking for dividend of deferred shares. This draft will, of course, need considerable changes due to the proposed corporation tax changes described earlier in this chapter.

(iii) Treatment of extraordinary and prior year items, August 1971. This draft defines 'extraordinary items' as 'those material items which derive from events or transactions outside the ordinary activities of the business and which are not expected to recur frequently', and states that such items should be disclosed, net of tax, below the profit for the year after tax and minority interests. 'Exceptional items' are those arising from the ordinary activities of the business and should be included in the trading profit for the year, but identified if material. Prior year adjustments should be shown alongside retained profits brought forward from the previous year, but they are narrowly defined as specific and material adjustments which can be identified with a particular prior year or years. This draft, if accepted, will do a great deal to stem the growing practice of defining 'extraordinary and non-recurring' in a very broad sense and writing off such items direct to reserves.

(c) *Subjects under consideration or listed for action*

  (i) Form and content of profit and loss account and balance sheet.
  (ii) Fundamental principles of inventory valuation (exposure draft issued May 1972).
  (iii) Accounting for contract work in progress.
  (iv) Accounting for changes in the purchasing power of money.
  (v) Treatment of investments in the accounts of trading companies and industrial holding companies.
  (vi) Accounting for research and development.
  (vii) Fundamental objects and principles of periodic financial statements.
  (viii) Accounting for goodwill.
  (ix) Fundamental principles, form and content of group accounts.
  (x) Fundamental principles of depreciation.
  (xi) Treatment of deferred taxation.
  (xii) Accounting for diversified operations.
  (xiii) Source and application of funds statements.

At the same time, in a Statement on Auditing issued in February 1971, the Council of the Institute of Chartered Accountants have stressed that these accounting standards represent a definitive approach to the concept of what gives a true and fair view and that any significant departures made by the directors in preparing the accounts should be referred to in the auditors' report, whether or not they are disclosed in the notes to the accounts.

At this stage it is too early to predict the importance of these standards for investors. However, although standardization in itself will not automatically bring about comparability of financial data, it will at least stamp out the more flagrant abuses and restore to some extent the reliability of published accounts.

The importance of these moves towards standardization was emphasized in May 1972 when the Stock Exchange Council revised its listing requirements to require the accounts of listed companies to be drawn up in accordance with the standards approved by the accountancy bodies. Furthermore, any departure from these standards must be disclosed and explained. Finally the Council threatened to withdraw the listing of the securities of companies which delay issuing their annual report and accounts for more than six months without adequate explanation.

BIBLIOGRAPHY

ARTICLES

American. There is a vast number of worthwhile papers on the subject of investment which have been written by American authors. Fortunately there are several books of readings in which the best of these articles have been reprinted :

Stephen H. Archer & Charles A. D'Ambrosio, *The Theory of Business Finance: A Book of Readings* (New York: Macmillan, 1967). Richard E. Ball, *Readings in Investments* (Boston: Allyn & Bacon, 1965). Richard E. Ball & Z. Lew Melnyk, *Theory of Managerial Finance* (Boston: Allyn & Bacon, 1967). Paul H. Cootner (ed.), *The Random Character of Stock Market Prices* (Cambridge: M.I.T. Press, 1964). E. Bruce Fredrickson (ed.), *Frontiers of Investment Analysis* (Scranton, Pa.: International Textbook, 1965). Institute of Chartered Financial Analysts, *C.F.A. Readings in Financial Analysis* (Homewood, Ill.: Irwin, 1966). Eugene Lerner (ed.), *Readings in Financial Analysis and Investment Management* (Homewood, Ill.: Irwin, 1963). James Van Horne, *Foundations for Financial Analysis* (Homewood, Ill.: Irwin, 1966). Harold A. Wolf & Lee Richardson, *Readings in Finance* (New York: Appleton-Century-Crofts, 1966). H. K. Wu & A. Zakon (eds.), *Elements of Investments* (New York: Holt, Rinehart & Winston, 1964).

Other important papers, including those written too late for inclusion in the above books, may be found in the following journals:

Accounting Review. American Economic Review. Econometrica. Economic Review. Financial Analysts Journal. Fortune. Harvard Business Review. Indiana Business Review. Industrial Management Review. International Economic Review. International Monetary Fund Staff Papers. Journal of the American Statistical Association. Journal of Business. Journal of Finance. Journal of Financial and Quantitative Analysis. Journal of Political Economy. Journal of Risk and Insurance. Management Science. Marquette Business Review. Mississippi Valley Journal of Business and Economics. National Banking Review. Nebraska Journal of Economics and Business. New England Business Review. Oregon Business Review. Quarterly Journal of Economics. Quarterly Review of Economics and Business. The Review of Economics and Statistics. The Review of Economics Studies. The Southern Economic Journal. Survey of Current Business. University of Washington Business Review. Western Economic Journal. Yale Economic Essays. Journal of Business Finance.

British. Although there is at present no book of readings on investment which contains papers from British sources, the author hopes to compile such a volume in the near future. The only journal which is devoted to papers on investment is *The Investment Analyst,* which is the official journal of the Society of Investment Analysts. The proceedings of the Congresses of the European Federation of Financial Analysts Societies also contain many useful studies.

Other interesting articles and papers in this field may be found from time to time in the following journals:

Accountancy. Accountant. The Banker. Bulletin Oxford University Institute of Economics and Statistics. Economica. Economic Journal. The Economist. International Economic Papers. Investors Chronicle. Journal of the Chartered Insurance Institute. Journal of Economic Studies. Journal of Industrial Economics. Journal of Institute of Actuaries. Journal of the Royal Statistical Society. Manchester School of Economic and Social Studies. Management Today. Moorgate and Wall Street Journal. Oxford Economic Papers. Planned Savings. Quarterly Bulletin (Bank of England). Scottish Journal of Political Economy. Times Review of Industry and Technology. Transactions of the Faculty of Actuaries. Transactions of the Manchester Statistical Society. The Unitholder. Yorkshire Bulletin. Journal of Business Finance. The reviews published by the different British banks also contain useful material.

BOOKS

General Textbooks

Frederick Amling, *Investments: An Introduction to Analysis and Management* (Englewood Cliffs, N.J.: Prentice-Hall, 1965). Ralph E. Badger, Harold W. Torgerson & Harry G. Guthmann, *Investment Principles and Practices* (Englewood Cliffs, N.J.: Prentice-Hall, 5th ed., 1961). H. Barrada, *How to Succeed as an Investor* (London: Newnes, 1966). Douglas H. Bellemore, *Investments* (New York: Simmons-Boardman, 2nd ed., 1960). Douglas H. Bellemore, *The Strategic Investor* (New York: Simmons-Boardman, 1963). John C. Clendenin, *Introduction to Investments* (New York: McGraw-Hill, 4th ed., 1964). Jerome B. Cohen & Edward D. Zinbarg, *Investment Analysis and Portfolio Management* (Homewood, Ill.: Irwin, 1967). Benjamin Graham, David L. Dodd & Sidney Cottle, *Security Analysis* (New York: McGraw-Hill, 4th ed., 1962). Benjamin Graham, *The Intelligent Investor* (New York: Harper & Row, 3rd ed., 1965). Julius Grodinsky, *Investments* (New York: Ronald Press Co., 1953). Douglas A. Hayes, *Investments: Analysis and Management* (New York: Macmillan, 2nd ed., 1966). *Investors Chronicle, Beginners, Please* (London: Eyre & Spottiswoode, 3rd ed., 1967). Eugene M. Lerner & Willard T. Carleton, *A Theory of Financial Analysis* (New York: Harcourt Brace & World, 1966). John H. Prime, *Investment Analysis* (Englewood Cliffs, N.J.: Prentice-Hall, 4th ed., 1967). H. B. Rose, *The Economic Background to Investment* (Cambridge: Cambridge University Press for the Institute of Actuaries and the Faculty of Actuaries, 1960). James Rowlatt & David Davenport, *The Pan Guide to Saving and Investment*

(London: Pan Books, 2nd ed., 1966). Harry C. Sauvain, *Investment Management* (Englewood Cliffs, N.J.: Prentice-Hall, 3rd ed., 1967).

The Stock Exchange—History, Functions and Criticism

F. E. Armstrong, *The Book of the Stock Exchange* (London: Pitman, 6th ed., 1968). William J. Baumol, *The Stock Market and Economic Efficiency*, The Millar Lectures No. 6 (New York: Fordham University Press, 1965). H. D. Berman, *The Stock Exchange* (London: Pitman, 5th ed., 1966). P. G. M. Dickson, *The Financial Revolution in England* (London: Macmillan, 1967). Herbert E. Dougall, *Capital Markets and Institutions* (Englewood Cliffs, N.J.: Prentice-Hall, 1965). J. Dundas Hamilton, *Stockbroking Today* (London: Macmillan, 1968). *Economic Policies and Practices—Paper No. 3: A Description and Analysis of Certain European Capital Markets* (Joint Economic Committee, 88th Congress, 2nd Session: U.S. Government Printing Office, Washington, 1964). Wilford Eiteman, Charles A. Dice & David K. Eiteman, *The Stock Market* (New York: McGraw Hill, 4th ed., 1966). European Group for Financial Research, *The European Stock Exchanges* (2nd ed., 1965). Irwin Friend, *Investment Banking and the New Issues Market* (Philadelphia: Wharton School of Finance and Commerce, University of Pennsylvania, 1965). J. K. Galbraith, *The Great Crash* (Boston: Houghton Mifflin Co., 1955). John W. Hazard & Milton Christie, *The Investment Business— A Condensation of the S.E.C. Report* (New York: Harper & Row, 1964). R. F. Henderson, *The New Issue Market and the Finance of Industry* (Cambridge: Bowes & Bowes, 1951). Donald D. Hester & James Tobin (eds.), *Financial Markets and Economic Activity*, Cowles Foundation Monograph No. 21 (New York: J. Wiley & Sons, 1967). Sir Oscar Hobson, *How the City Works* (London: Dickens Press, 8th ed., 1966). George L. Leffler & Loring C. Farwell, *The Stock Market* (New York: Ronald Press, 3rd ed., 1963). Fritz Machlup, *The Stock Market, Credit and Capital Formation* (London: William Hodge & Co., 1940). Henry G. Manne, *Insider Trading and the Stock Market* (New York: The Free Press, 1966). Martin Mayer, *Wall Street: The Inside Story of American Finance* (London: Bodley Head, Rev. ed., 1959). A. J. Merrett, M. Howe & G. D. Newbould, *Equity Issues and the London Capital Market* (London: Longmans, 1967). E. Victor Morgan & W. A. Thomas, *The Stock Exchange, Its History and Functions* (London: Elek Books, 1962). Colin A. Perry, *Stock Exchange Transactions* (London: Pitman, 1960). *Report of Special Study of Securities Markets of the Securities and Exchange Commission, Parts I and II* (88th Congress, 1st session, House Document No. 95, Washington, D.C.: U.S. Government Printing Office, 1963). Sidney M. Robbins, *The Securities Markets: Operations and Issues* (New York: Free Press, 1966). Birl E. Shultz (ed. Albert P. Squiet), *The Securities Market* (New York: Harper & Row, Rev. ed., 1963). Robert Sobel, *The Big Board* (New York: Free Press, 1965). David E. Spray (ed.), *The Principal Stock Exchanges of the World: Their Operation, Structure and Development* (Washington, D.C.: International Economic Publishers, 1964).

THE STOCK EXCHANGE AND INVESTMENT ANALYSIS

Stock Exchange Securities and Other Investments

Louis Brand, *Investing for Profit in Convertible Bonds* (New York: Standard & Poor's, Rev. ed., 1964). Gordon Cummings, *The Complete Guide to Investment* (Harmondsworth: Penguin Books, 3rd ed., 1966). F. R. Jervis, *The Company, the Shareholder and Growth* (London: Institute of Economic Affairs, 1966). Kalb, Voorhis & Co., *A Guide to Convertible Bonds* (New York, 1965). *Life Assurance* (A *Which* Supplement, London, Consumer's Association, 1967). C. O. Merriman, *Mutual Funds and Unit Trusts: A Global View* (London: Pitman, 1965). Alex Rubner, *The Ensnared Shareholder* (London: Macmillan, 1965). *The Stock Exchange Year Book* (two vols. published annually by Thomas Skinner, London).

The Analysis of Investments

Leon B. Allen, *A Method for Stock Profits without Price Forecasting* (Garden City, N.Y.: Doubleday & Co., 1962). Frank Ayres, Jr., *Mathematics of Finance* (New York: Schaum Publishing Co., 1963). William Beranek, *The Effect of Leverage on the Market Value of Common Stock* (Wisconsin Commerce Reports, Vol. VII No. 2., Madison: University of Wisconsin, 1964). Harold Bierman, Jr., *Financial Accounting Theory* (New York: Macmillan, 1965). George W. Bishop, Jr., *Charles H. Dow and the Dow Theory* (New York: Appleton-Century-Crofts, 1960). John A. Brittain, *Corporate Dividend Policy* (Washington, D.C.: Brookings Institution, 1966). William F. Butler & Robert A. Kavesh (eds.), *How Business Economists Forecast* (Englewood Cliffs, N.J.: Prentice-Hall, 1966). Richard H. Chase *et al.*, *Computer Applications in Investment Analysis* (Hanover, N.H.: Amos Tuck School, Dartmouth College, 1966). Gordon Donaldson, *Corporate Debt Capacity* (Boston: Harvard Graduate School of Business Administration, 1961). Garfield A. Drew, *New Methods for Profit in the Stock Market* (Wells, Vt.: Fraser Publishing Co., 4th ed., 1966). Edgar O. Edwards & Philip W. Bell, *The Theory and Measurement of Business Income* (Berkeley: University of California, 1961). R. D. Edwards & John Magee Jr., *Technical Analysis of Stock Trends* (Springfield, Mass.: Stock Trend Service, 4th ed., 1958). A. G. Ellinger, *The Art of Investment* (London: Bowes & Bowes, Rev. ed., 1961). Roy A. Foulke, *Practical Financial Statement Analysis* (New York: McGraw Hill, 5th ed., 1961). Seymour Friedland, *The Economics of Corporate Finance* (Englewood Cliffs, N.J.: Prentice-Hall, 1966). Myron J. Gordon, *The Investment, Financing and Valuation of the Corporation* (Homewood, Ill.: Irwin, 1962). Robert A. Gordon, *Business Fluctuations* (New York: Harper & Row, 2nd ed., 1961). Paul Grady, *Inventory of Generally Accepted Accounting Principles for Business Enterprises* (New York: American Institute of Certified Public Accountants, 1965). Benjamin Graham & Charles McGolrick, *The Interpretation of Financial Statements* (New York: Harper & Row, 1964). Joseph E. Granville, *A Strategy of Daily Stock Market Timing for Maximum Profit* (Englewood Cliffs, N.J.: Prentice-Hall, 1960). Joseph E. Granville, *New Key to Stock Market Profits*

BIBLIOGRAPHY

(Englewood Cliffs, N.J.: Prentice-Hall, 1963). T. A. Hamilton Baynes, *Share Valuations* (London: Heinemann, 1966). Erich A. Helfert, *Techniques of Financial Analysis* (Homewood, Ill.: Irwin, 1967). Investment Research, *The Post-War History of the Stock Market* (Cambridge, 1966). H. Jones, *The Mathematics of Money* (London: Blackie & Son, 1965). Jackson Martindell, *The Appraisal of Management* (New York: Harper & Row, 1962). Gerhard G. Mueller, *International Accounting* (New York: Macmillan, 1967). A. C. Rayner, & I. M. D. Little, *Higgledy Piggledy Growth Again* (Oxford: Basil Blackwell, 1966). M. S. Rix, *Investment Arithmetic* (London: Pitman, 2nd ed., 1964). Alexander A. Robichek (ed.), *Financial Research and Management Decisions* (New York: Wiley, 1967). Beryl W. Sprinkel, *Money and Stock Prices* (Homewood, Ill.: Irwin, 1964). George J. Staubus, *A Theory of Accounting to Investors* (Berkeley: University of California Press, 1961). John B. Williams, *The Theory of Investment Value* (Cambridge, Mass.: Harvard University Press, 1938). Harry D. Wolfe, *Business Forecasting Methods* (New York: Holt, Rinehart & Winston, 1966).

Taxation and Portfolio Analysis

George E. Bates, *Investment Management: A Casebook* (New York: McGraw Hill, 1959). Hugh Bullock, *The Story of Investment Companies* (New York: Columbia, University Press, 1959). J. K. Butters, L. E. Thompson & L. L. Bollinger, *Effects of Taxation on Investment by Individuals* (Cambridge: Harvard University, Graduate School of Business Administration, 1953). K. S. Carmichael, *Income Tax and Profits Tax* (London: H.F.L. (Publishers) Ltd., 27th ed., 1966). K. S. Carmichael, *Corporation Tax* (London: H.F.L. (Publishers) Ltd., 1966). Geoffrey P. E. Clarkson, *Portfolio Selection: A Simulation of Trust Investment* (Ford Foundation Doctoral Dissertation Winner) (Englewood Cliffs, N.J.: Prentice-Hall, 1962). George Clayton & W. T. Osborn, *Insurance Company Investment: Principles and Policy* (London: George Allen & Unwin, 1965). Peter O. Dietz, *Pension Funds: Measuring Investment Performance* (New York: The Free Press, 1966). Elvin F. Donaldson & John K. Pfahl, *Personal Finance* (New York: Ronald Press, 4th ed., 1966). D. E. Farrar, *The Investment Decision Under Uncertainty* (Englewood Cliffs, N.J.: Prentice-Hall, 1962). Irwin Friend *et al.*, *A Study of Mutual Funds* (Prepared for the Securities and Exchange Commission by the Wharton School of Finance and Commerce. U.S. Government Printing Office, Washington, 1962). Donald D. Hester & James Tobin (eds.), *Risk Aversion and Portfolio Choice*, Cowles Foundation Monographs No. 19 (New York: J. Wiley & Sons, 1967). Donald D. Hester & James Tobin (eds.), *Studies of Portfolio Behaviour*, Cowles Foundation Monographs No. 20 (New York: J. Wiley & Sons, 1967). Daniel M. Holland, *Dividends under the Income Tax* (A Study by the National Bureau of Economic Research, published by Princeton University Press, 1962). Percy F. Hughes (ed.), *Daily Mail Income Tax Guide*. Annual. Percy F. Hughes & K. R. Tingley (eds.), *Key to Capital Gains Tax* and *Key to*

491

Corporation Tax (London: Taxation Publishing Co., 1967). *Key to Income Tax and Surtax* (London: Taxation Publishing Co., Annually). Roger A. Lyon, *Investment Portfolio Management in the Commercial Bank* (New Brunswick, N.J.: Rutgers University Press, 1960). Harry M. Markowitz, *Portfolio Selection: Efficient Diversification of Investments* (Cowles Foundation Monographs No. 16, New York: J. Wiley & Sons, 1959). Basil Moore, *An Introduction to the Theory of Finance: A Portfolio Approach to Asset Holding under Uncertainty* (New York: Free Press, 1967). Richard A. Musgrave & Carl S. Shoup (eds.), *Readings in the Economics of Taxation* (Homewood, Ill.: Irwin, 1959). *A Programme for Growth No. 7: The Owners of Quoted Ordinary Shares—A Survey for 1963* (Published for the Department of Applied Economics, University of Cambridge by Chapman & Hall, London, 1966). T. J. Sophian, *The Taxation of Capital Gains* (London: Butterworths, 2nd ed., 1967). Oliver Stanley, *A Guide to Taxation* (London: Methuen, 1967). James E. Walter, *The Investment Process: As Characterized by Leading Life Insurance Companies* (Boston: Graduate School of Business Administration, Harvard University, 1962). G. S. A. Wheatcroft & A. E. W. Park, *Capital Gains Taxes* (London: Sweet & Maxwell, 1967). R. Glynne Williams, *Comprehensive Aspects of Taxation* (London: Donnington Press, 27th ed., 1966).

Recent Publications

Richard A. Brealey, *An Introduction to Risk and Return from Common Stocks* (Cambridge, Mass.: M.I.T. Press, 1969). C.F.A., *Investment Company Portfolio Management* (Homewood, Ill.: Irwin, 1970. Geoffrey Cooper and Richard J. Cridlan, *Law and Procedure of the Stock Exchange*, (London: Butterworths, 1971). D. C. Corner and H. Burton, *Investment and Unit Trusts in Britain and America* (London: Elek Books, 1969). A. G. Ellinger, *The Art of Investment* (London: Bowes and Bowes, 1971). Irwin Friend, Marshall Blume and Jean Crockett, *Mutual Funds and other Institutional Investors* (New York: McGraw-Hill, 1970). T. G. Goff, *Theory and Practice of Investment* (London: Heinemann, 1971). William H. Jean, *The Analytical Theory of Finance* (New York: Holt, Rinehart and Winston, 1970). Harvey A. Krow, *Stock Market Behaviour* (New York, Random House, 1969). Burton G. Malkiel and Richard E. Quandt, *Strategies and Rational Decision in the Securities Options Market* (Cambridge, Mass.: M.I.T. Press, 1969). Henry G. Marne (ed.) *Economic Policy and the Regulation of Corporate Securities* (Washington, D.C.: American Enterprise Institute, 1969). Guy Naylor, *Guide to Shareholders Rights* (London: Allen and Unwin, 1969). Philip A. Shade, *Common Stocks—A Plan for Intelligent Investing* (Homewood, Ill.: Irwin, 1971). William F. Sharpe, *Portfolio Theory and Capital Markets* (New York, McGraw-Hill, 1970). William L. Silber, *Portfolio Behaviour of Financial Institutions* (New York: Holt, Rinehart and Winston, 1970). Keith V. Smith, *Portfolio Management* (New York: Holt, Rinehart and Winston, 1970). Paul F. Smith, *Economics of Financial Institutions and Markets*

BIBLIOGRAPHY

(Homewood, Ill.: Irwin, 1971). Basil Taylor (ed.) *Investment Analysis and Portfolio Selection* (London: Elek Books, 1970). J. C. Van Horne, *Function and Analysis of Capital Market Rates* (Englewood Cliffs, N.J.: Prentice-Hall, 1970). Donald E. Vaughn, *Survey of Investments* (New York: Holt, Rinehart and Winston, 1967). David A. West (ed.) *Readings in Investment Analysis* (Scranton, Penn.: International Textbook Co., 1969). Richard R. West and Seha M. Tiniç, *The Economics of the Stock Market* (New York: Praegar, 1971).

Tables

1. COMPOUND AMOUNT OF 1
$$(1+i)^n$$

n	0.25%	0.5%	1%	1.25%	1.5%	2%	2.5%	3%	3.5%	4%	5%	6%	7%	8%	n
1	1.00250	1.00500	1.01000	1.01250	1.01500	1.02000	1.02500	1.03000	1.03500	1.04000	1.05000	1.06000	1.07000	1.08000	1
2	1.00501	1.01003	1.02010	1.02516	1.03023	1.04040	1.05062	1.06090	1.07122	1.08160	1.10250	1.12360	1.14490	1.16640	2
3	1.00752	1.01508	1.03030	1.03797	1.04568	1.06121	1.07689	1.09273	1.10872	1.12486	1.15763	1.19102	1.22504	1.25971	3
4	1.01004	1.02015	1.04060	1.05095	1.06136	1.08243	1.10381	1.12551	1.14752	1.16986	1.21551	1.26248	1.31080	1.36049	4
5	1.01256	1.02525	1.05101	1.06408	1.07728	1.10408	1.13141	1.15927	1.18769	1.21665	1.27628	1.33823	1.40255	1.46933	5
6	1.01509	1.03038	1.06152	1.07738	1.09344	1.12616	1.15969	1.19405	1.22926	1.26532	1.34010	1.41852	1.50073	1.58687	6
7	1.01763	1.03553	1.07214	1.09085	1.10984	1.14869	1.18869	1.22987	1.27228	1.31593	1.40710	1.50363	1.60578	1.71382	7
8	1.02018	1.04071	1.08286	1.10449	1.12649	1.17166	1.21840	1.26677	1.31681	1.36857	1.47746	1.59385	1.71819	1.85093	8
9	1.02273	1.04591	1.09369	1.11829	1.14339	1.19509	1.24886	1.30477	1.36290	1.42331	1.55133	1.68948	1.83846	1.99900	9
10	1.02528	1.05114	1.10462	1.13227	1.16054	1.21899	1.28008	1.34392	1.41060	1.48024	1.62889	1.79085	1.96715	2.15892	10
11	1.02785	1.05640	1.11567	1.14642	1.17795	1.24337	1.31209	1.38423	1.45997	1.53945	1.71034	1.89830	2.10485	2.33164	11
12	1.03042	1.06168	1.12683	1.16075	1.19562	1.26824	1.34489	1.42576	1.51107	1.60103	1.79586	2.01220	2.25219	2.51817	12
13	1.03299	1.06699	1.13809	1.17526	1.21355	1.29361	1.37851	1.46853	1.56396	1.66507	1.88565	2.13293	2.40985	2.71962	13
14	1.03557	1.07232	1.14947	1.18995	1.23176	1.31948	1.41297	1.51259	1.61869	1.73168	1.97993	2.26090	2.57853	2.93719	14
15	1.03816	1.07768	1.16097	1.20483	1.25023	1.34587	1.44830	1.55797	1.67535	1.80094	2.07893	2.39656	2.75903	3.17217	15
16	1.04076	1.08307	1.17258	1.21989	1.26899	1.37279	1.48451	1.60471	1.73399	1.87298	2.18287	2.54035	2.95216	3.42594	16
17	1.04336	1.08849	1.18430	1.23514	1.28802	1.40024	1.52162	1.65285	1.79467	1.94790	2.29202	2.69277	3.15882	3.70002	17
18	1.04597	1.09393	1.19615	1.25058	1.30734	1.42825	1.55966	1.70243	1.85749	2.02582	2.40662	2.85434	3.37993	3.99602	18
19	1.04858	1.09940	1.20811	1.26621	1.32695	1.45681	1.59865	1.75351	1.92250	2.10685	2.52695	3.02560	3.61653	4.31570	19
20	1.05121	1.10490	1.22019	1.28204	1.34686	1.48595	1.63862	1.80611	1.98979	2.19112	2.65330	3.20714	3.86968	4.66096	20
21	1.05383	1.11042	1.23239	1.29806	1.36706	1.51567	1.67958	1.86029	2.05943	2.27877	2.78596	3.39956	4.14056	5.03383	21
22	1.05647	1.11597	1.24472	1.31429	1.38756	1.54598	1.72157	1.91610	2.13151	2.36992	2.92526	3.60354	4.43040	5.43654	22
23	1.05911	1.12155	1.25716	1.33072	1.40838	1.57690	1.76461	1.97359	2.20611	2.46472	3.07152	3.81975	4.74053	5.87146	23
24	1.06176	1.12716	1.26973	1.34735	1.42950	1.60844	1.80873	2.03279	2.28333	2.56330	3.22510	4.04893	5.07237	6.34118	24
25	1.06441	1.13280	1.28243	1.36419	1.45095	1.64061	1.85394	2.09378	2.36324	2.66584	3.38635	4.29187	5.42743	6.84848	25
26	1.06707	1.13846	1.29526	1.38125	1.47271	1.67342	1.90029	2.15659	2.44596	2.77247	3.55567	4.54938	5.80735	7.39635	26
27	1.06974	1.14415	1.30821	1.39851	1.49480	1.70689	1.94780	2.22129	2.53157	2.88337	3.73346	4.82235	6.21387	7.98806	27
28	1.07241	1.14987	1.32129	1.41599	1.51722	1.74102	1.99650	2.28793	2.62017	2.99870	3.92013	5.11169	6.64884	8.62711	28
29	1.07510	1.15562	1.33450	1.43369	1.53998	1.77584	2.04640	2.35657	2.71188	3.11865	4.11614	5.41839	7.11426	9.31727	29
30	1.07778	1.16140	1.34785	1.45161	1.56308	1.81136	2.09757	2.42726	2.80679	3.24340	4.32194	5.74349	7.61226	10.06266	30
31	1.08048	1.16721	1.36133	1.46976	1.58653	1.84759	2.15000	2.50008	2.90503	3.37313	4.53804	6.08141	8.14511	10.86767	31
32	1.08318	1.17304	1.37494	1.48813	1.61032	1.88454	2.20376	2.57508	3.00671	3.50806	4.76494	6.45339	8.71527	11.73708	32
33	1.08589	1.17891	1.38869	1.50673	1.63448	1.92223	2.25885	2.65234	3.11194	3.64838	5.00319	6.84059	9.32534	12.67605	33
34	1.08860	1.18480	1.40258	1.52557	1.65900	1.96068	2.31532	2.73191	3.22086	3.79432	5.25335	7.25103	9.97811	13.69013	34
35	1.09132	1.19073	1.41660	1.54464	1.68388	1.99989	2.37321	2.81386	3.33359	3.94609	5.51602	7.68609	10.67658	14.78534	35
36	1.09405	1.19668	1.43077	1.56394	1.70914	2.03989	2.43254	2.89828	3.45027	4.10393	5.79182	8.14725	11.42394	15.96817	36
37	1.09679	1.20266	1.44508	1.58349	1.73478	2.08068	2.49335	2.98523	3.57103	4.26809	6.08141	8.63609	12.22362	17.24563	37
38	1.09953	1.20868	1.45953	1.60329	1.76080	2.12230	2.55568	3.07478	3.69601	4.43881	6.38548	9.15425	13.07927	18.62528	38
39	1.10228	1.21472	1.47412	1.62333	1.78721	2.16474	2.61957	3.16803	3.82537	4.61637	6.70475	9.70351	13.99482	20.11530	39
40	1.10503	1.22079	1.48886	1.64362	1.81402	2.20804	2.68506	3.26204	3.95926	4.80102	7.03999	10.28572	14.97446	21.72452	40
41	1.10780	1.22690	1.50375	1.66416	1.84123	2.25220	2.75220	3.35990	4.09783	4.99306	7.39199	10.90286	16.02267	23.46248	41
42	1.11057	1.23303	1.51879	1.68497	1.86885	2.29724	2.82100	3.46070	4.24126	5.19278	7.76159	11.55703	17.14426	25.33948	42
43	1.11334	1.23920	1.53398	1.70603	1.89688	2.34319	2.89152	3.56452	4.38970	5.40050	8.14967	12.25045	18.34435	27.36664	43
44	1.11612	1.24539	1.54932	1.72735	1.92533	2.39005	2.96381	3.67145	4.54334	5.61652	8.55715	12.98548	19.62846	29.55597	44
45	1.11891	1.25162	1.56481	1.74895	1.95421	2.43785	3.03790	3.78160	4.70236	5.84118	8.98501	13.76461	21.00245	31.92045	45
46	1.12171	1.25788	1.58046	1.77081	1.98353	2.48661	3.11385	3.89504	4.86694	6.07482	9.43426	14.59049	22.47262	34.47409	46
47	1.12452	1.26417	1.59626	1.79294	2.01328	2.53634	3.19169	4.01190	5.03728	6.31782	9.90597	15.46592	24.04571	37.23201	47
48	1.12733	1.27049	1.61223	1.81535	2.04348	2.58707	3.27149	4.13225	5.21359	6.57053	10.40127	16.39387	25.72891	40.21057	48
49	1.13015	1.27684	1.62835	1.83805	2.07413	2.63881	3.35328	4.25622	5.39606	6.83335	10.92133	17.37750	27.52993	43.42742	49
50	1.13297	1.28323	1.64463	1.86102	2.10524	2.69159	3.43711	4.38391	5.58493	7.10668	11.46740	18.42015	29.45703	46.90161	50

2. PRESENT VALUE OF 1
V_{n_t}

Year	Percentage												
	1	2	3	4	5	6	7	8	9	10	15	20	25
1	0.990099	0.980392	0.970874	0.961538	0.952381	0.943396	0.934579	0.925926	0.917431	0.909091	0.869565	0.833333	0.800000
2	0.980296	0.961169	0.942596	0.924556	0.907029	0.889996	0.873439	0.857339	0.841680	0.826446	0.756144	0.694444	0.640000
3	0.970590	0.942322	0.915142	0.888996	0.863838	0.839619	0.816298	0.793832	0.772183	0.751315	0.657516	0.578704	0.512000
4	0.960980	0.923845	0.888487	0.854804	0.822702	0.792094	0.762895	0.735030	0.708425	0.683013	0.571753	0.482253	0.409600
5	0.951466	0.905731	0.862609	0.821927	0.783526	0.747258	0.712986	0.680583	0.649931	0.620921	0.497177	0.401878	0.327680
6	0.942045	0.887971	0.837484	0.790315	0.746215	0.704961	0.666342	0.630170	0.596267	0.564474	0.432328	0.334898	0.262144
7	0.932718	0.870560	0.813092	0.759918	0.710681	0.665057	0.622750	0.583490	0.547034	0.513158	0.375937	0.279082	0.209715
8	0.923483	0.853490	0.789409	0.730690	0.676839	0.627412	0.582009	0.540269	0.501866	0.466507	0.326902	0.232568	0.167772
9	0.914340	0.836755	0.766417	0.702587	0.644609	0.591898	0.543934	0.500249	0.460428	0.424098	0.284262	0.193807	0.134218
10	0.905287	0.820348	0.744094	0.675554	0.613913	0.558395	0.508349	0.463193	0.422411	0.385543	0.247185	0.161506	0.107374
11	0.896324	0.804263	0.722421	0.649581	0.584679	0.526788	0.475093	0.428883	0.387533	0.350494	0.214943	0.134588	0.085899
12	0.887449	0.788493	0.701380	0.624597	0.556837	0.496969	0.444012	0.397114	0.355535	0.318631	0.186907	0.112157	0.068719
13	0.878663	0.773033	0.680951	0.600574	0.530321	0.468839	0.414964	0.367698	0.326179	0.289664	0.162528	0.093464	0.054976
14	0.869963	0.757875	0.661118	0.577475	0.505068	0.442301	0.387817	0.340461	0.299246	0.263331	0.141329	0.077887	0.043980
15	0.861349	0.743015	0.641862	0.555265	0.481017	0.417265	0.362446	0.315242	0.274538	0.239392	0.122894	0.064905	0.035184
16	0.852821	0.728446	0.623167	0.533908	0.458112	0.393646	0.338735	0.291890	0.251870	0.217629	0.106865	0.054088	0.028147
17	0.844377	0.714163	0.605016	0.513373	0.436297	0.371364	0.316574	0.270269	0.231073	0.197845	0.092926	0.045073	0.022518
18	0.836017	0.700159	0.587395	0.493628	0.415521	0.350344	0.295864	0.250249	0.211994	0.179859	0.080805	0.037561	0.018014
19	0.827740	0.686431	0.570286	0.474642	0.395734	0.330513	0.276508	0.231712	0.194490	0.163508	0.070265	0.031301	0.014412
20	0.819544	0.672971	0.553676	0.456387	0.376889	0.311805	0.258419	0.214548	0.178431	0.148644	0.061100	0.026084	0.011529
21	0.811430	0.659776	0.537549	0.438834	0.358942	0.294155	0.241513	0.198656	0.163698	0.135131	0.053131	0.021737	0.009223
22	0.803396	0.646839	0.521893	0.421955	0.341850	0.277505	0.225713	0.183941	0.150182	0.122846	0.046201	0.018114	0.007379

23	0.795442	0.634156	0.506692	0.405726	0.325571	0.261797	0.210947	0.170315	0.137781	0.111678	0.040174	0.015095	0.005903
24	0.787566	0.621721	0.491934	0.390121	0.310068	0.246979	0.197147	0.157699	0.126405	0.101526	0.034934	0.012579	0.004722
25	0.779768	0.609531	0.477606	0.375117	0.295303	0.232999	0.184249	0.146018	0.115968	0.092296	0.030378	0.010483	0.003778
26	0.772048	0.597579	0.463695	0.360689	0.281241	0.219810	0.172195	0.135202	0.106393	0.083905	0.026415	0.008735	0.003022
27	0.764404	0.585862	0.450189	0.346817	0.267848	0.207368	0.160930	0.125187	0.097608	0.076278	0.022970	0.007280	0.002418
28	0.756836	0.574375	0.437077	0.333477	0.255094	0.195630	0.150402	0.115914	0.089548	0.069343	0.019974	0.006066	0.001934
29	0.749342	0.563112	0.424346	0.320651	0.242946	0.184557	0.140563	0.107328	0.082155	0.063039	0.017369	0.005055	0.001547
30	0.741923	0.552071	0.411987	0.308319	0.231377	0.174110	0.131367	0.099377	0.075371	0.057309	0.015103	0.004213	0.001238
31	0.734577	0.541246	0.399987	0.296460	0.220359	0.164255	0.122773	0.092016	0.069148	0.052099	0.013133	0.003511	0.000990
32	0.727304	0.530633	0.388337	0.285058	0.209866	0.154957	0.114741	0.085200	0.063438	0.047362	0.011420	0.002926	0.000792
33	0.720103	0.520229	0.377026	0.274094	0.199873	0.146186	0.107235	0.078889	0.058200	0.043057	0.009931	0.002438	0.000634
34	0.712973	0.510028	0.366045	0.263552	0.190355	0.137912	0.100219	0.073045	0.053395	0.039143	0.008635	0.002032	0.000507
35	0.705914	0.500028	0.355383	0.253415	0.181290	0.130105	0.093663	0.067635	0.048986	0.035584	0.007509	0.001693	0.000406
36	0.698925	0.490223	0.345032	0.243669	0.172657	0.122741	0.087535	0.062625	0.044941	0.032349	0.006529	0.001411	0.000325
37	0.692005	0.480611	0.334983	0.234297	0.164436	0.115793	0.081809	0.057986	0.041231	0.029408	0.005678	0.001176	0.000260
38	0.685153	0.471187	0.325226	0.225285	0.156605	0.109239	0.076457	0.053690	0.037826	0.026735	0.004937	0.000980	0.000208
39	0.678370	0.461948	0.315754	0.216621	0.149148	0.103056	0.071455	0.049713	0.034703	0.024304	0.004293	0.000816	0.000166
40	0.671653	0.452890	0.306557	0.208289	0.142046	0.097222	0.066780	0.046031	0.031838	0.022095	0.003733	0.000660	0.000133
41	0.665003	0.444010	0.297628	0.200278	0.135282	0.091719	0.062412	0.042621	0.029209	0.020086	0.003246	0.000576	0.000106
42	0.658419	0.435304	0.288959	0.192575	0.128840	0.086527	0.058329	0.039464	0.026797	0.018260	0.002823	0.000472	0.851 4*
43	0.651900	0.426769	0.280543	0.185168	0.122704	0.081630	0.054513	0.036541	0.024584	0.016600	0.002455	0.000394	0.681 4
44	0.645445	0.418401	0.272372	0.178046	0.116861	0.077009	0.050946	0.033834	0.022555	0.015091	0.002134	0.000328	0.544 4
45	0.639055	0.410197	0.264439	0.171198	0.111297	0.072650	0.047613	0.031328	0.020692	0.013719	0.001856	0.000273	0.436 4
46	0.632728	0.402154	0.256737	0.164614	0.105997	0.068538	0.044499	0.029007	0.018984	0.012472	0.001614	0.000228	0.348 4
47	0.626463	0.394268	0.249259	0.158283	0.100949	0.064658	0.041587	0.026859	0.017416	0.011338	0.001403	0.000190	0.279 4
48	0.620260	0.386538	0.241999	0.152195	0.096142	0.060998	0.038867	0.024869	0.015978	0.010307	0.001220	0.000158	0.223 4
49	0.614119	0.378958	0.234950	0.146341	0.091564	0.057546	0.036324	0.023027	0.014659	0.009370	0.001061	0.000132	0.178 4
50	0.608039	0.371528	0.228107	0.140713	0.087204	0.054288	0.033948	0.021321	0.013449	0.008519	0.000923	0.000110	0.143 4

3. PRESENT VALUE OF ANNUITY OF 1 PER PERIOD

A_{n_i}

Percentage

Year	1	2	3	4	5	6	7	8	9	10	15	20	25
1	0·990099	0·980392	0·970874	0·961538	0·952381	0·94396	0·934579	0·925926	0·917431	0·909091	0·869565	0·833333	0·800000
2	1·97040	1·94156	1·91347	1·88609	1·85941	1·83339	1·80802	1·78326	1·75911	1·73554	1·62571	1·52778	1·44000
3	2·94099	2·88388	2·82861	2·77509	2·72325	2·67301	2·62432	2·57710	2·53129	2·48685	2·28323	2·10648	1·95200
4	3·90197	3·80773	3·71710	3·62990	3·54595	3·46511	3·38721	3·31213	3·23972	3·16987	2·85498	2·58873	2·36160
5	4·85343	4·71346	4·57971	4·45182	4·32948	4·21236	4·10020	3·99271	3·88965	3·79079	3·35216	2·99061	2·68928
6	5·79548	5·60143	5·41719	5·24214	5·07569	4·91732	4·76654	4·62288	4·48592	4·35526	3·78448	3·32551	2·95142
7	6·72819	6·47199	6·23028	6·00205	5·78637	5·58238	5·38929	5·20637	5·03295	4·86842	4·16042	3·60459	3·16114
8	7·65168	7·32548	7·01969	6·73274	6·46321	6·20979	5·97130	5·74664	5·53482	5·33493	4·48732	3·83716	3·32891
9	8·56602	8·16224	7·78611	7·43533	7·10782	6·80169	6·51523	6·24689	5·99525	5·75902	4·77158	4·03097	3·46313
10	9·47130	8·98259	8·53020	8·11090	7·72173	7·36009	7·02358	6·71008	6·41766	6·14457	5·01877	4·19247	3·57050
11	10·3676	9·78685	9·25262	8·76048	8·30641	7·88687	7·49867	7·13896	6·80519	6·49506	5·23371	4·32706	3·65640
12	11·2551	10·5753	9·95400	9·38507	8·86325	8·38384	7·94269	7·53608	7·16073	6·81369	5·42062	4·43922	3·72512
13	12·1337	11·3484	10·6350	9·98565	9·39357	8·85268	8·35765	7·90378	7·48690	7·10336	5·58315	4·53268	3·78010
14	13·0037	12·1062	11·2961	10·5631	9·89864	9·29498	8·74547	8·24424	7·78615	7·36669	5·72448	4·61057	3·82408
15	13·8651	12·8493	11·9379	11·1184	10·3797	9·71225	9·10791	8·55948	8·06069	7·60608	5·84737	4·67547	3·85926
16	14·7179	13·5777	12·5611	11·6523	10·8378	10·1059	9·44665	8·85137	8·31256	7·82371	5·95423	4·72956	3·88741
17	15·5623	14·2919	13·1661	12·1657	11·2741	10·4773	9·76322	9·12164	8·54363	8·02155	6·04716	4·77463	3·90993
18	16·3983	14·9920	13·7535	12·6593	11·6896	10·8276	10·0591	9·37189	8·75563	8·20141	6·12797	4·81219	3·92794
19	17·2260	15·6785	14·3238	13·1339	12·0853	11·1581	10·3356	9·60360	8·95011	8·36492	6·19823	4·84350	3·94235
20	18·0456	16·3514	14·8775	13·5903	12·4622	11·4699	10·5940	9·81815	9·12855	8·51356	6·25933	4·86958	3·95388
21	18·8570	17·0112	15·4150	14·0292	12·8212	11·7641	10·8355	10·0168	9·29224	8·64869	6·31246	4·89132	3·96311
22	19·6604	17·6580	15·9369	14·4511	13·1630	12·0416	11·0612	10·2007	9·44243	8·77154	6·35866	4·90943	3·97049

23	20·4558	18·2922	16·4436	14·8568	13·4886	12·3034	11·2722	10·3711	9·58021	8·88322	6·39884	4·92453	3·97639
24	21·2434	18·9139	16·9355	15·2470	13·7986	12·5504	11·4693	10·5288	9·70661	8·98474	6·43377	4·93710	3·98111
25	22·0232	19·5235	17·4131	15·6221	14·0939	12·7834	11·6536	10·6748	9·82258	9·07704	6·46415	4·94759	3·98489
26	22·7952	20·1210	17·8768	15·9828	14·3752	13·0032	11·8258	10·8100	9·92897	9·16095	6·49056	4·95632	3·98791
27	23·5596	20·7069	18·3270	16·3296	14·6430	13·2105	11·9867	10·9352	10·0266	9·23722	6·51353	4·96360	3·99033
28	24·3164	21·2813	18·7641	16·6631	14·8981	13·4062	12·1371	11·0511	10·1161	9·30657	6·5351	4·96967	3·99226
29	25·0658	21·8444	19·1885	16·9837	15·1411	13·5907	12·2777	11·1584	10·1983	9·36961	6·55088	4·97472	3·99381
30	25·8077	22·3965	19·6004	17·2920	15·3725	13·7648	12·4090	11·2578	10·2737	9·42691	6·56598	4·97894	3·99505
31	26·5423	22·9377	20·0004	17·5885	15·5928	13·9291	12·5318	11·3498	10·3428	9·47901	6·57911	4·98245	3·99604
32	27·2696	23·4683	20·3888	17·8736	15·8027	14·0840	12·6466	11·4350	10·4062	9·52638	6·59053	4·98537	3·99683
33	27·9897	23·9886	20·7658	18·1476	16·0025	14·2302	12·7538	11·5139	10·4644	9·56943	6·60046	4·98781	3·99746
34	28·7027	24·4986	21·1318	18·4112	16·1929	14·3681	12·8540	11·5869	10·5178	9·60857	6·60910	4·98984	3·99797
35	29·4086	24·9986	21·4872	18·6646	16·3742	14·4982	12·9477	11·6546	10·5668	9·64416	6·61661	4·99154	3·99838
36	30·1075	25·4888	21·8323	18·9083	16·5469	14·6210	13·0352	11·7172	10·6118	9·67651	6·62314	4·99295	3·99870
37	30·7995	25·9695	22·1672	19·1426	16·7113	14·7368	13·1170	11·7752	10·6530	9·70592	6·62881	4·99412	3·99896
38	31·4847	26·4406	22·4925	19·3679	16·8679	14·8460	13·1935	11·8289	10·6908	9·73265	6·63375	4·99510	3·99917
39	32·1630	26·9026	22·8082	19·5845	17·0170	14·9491	13·2649	11·8786	10·7255	9·75696	6·63805	4·99592	3·99934
40	32·8347	27·3555	23·1148	19·7928	17·1591	15·0463	13·3317	11·9246	10·7574	9·77905	6·64178	4·99660	3·99947
41	33·4997	27·7995	23·4124	19·9931	17·2944	15·1380	13·3941	11·9672	10·7866	9·79914	6·64502	4·99717	3·99957
42	34·1581	28·2348	23·7014	20·1856	17·4232	15·2245	13·4524	12·0067	10·8134	9·81740	6·64785	4·99764	3·99966
43	34·8100	28·6616	23·9819	20·3708	17·5459	15·3062	13·5070	12·0432	10·8380	9·83400	6·65030	4·99803	3·99973
44	35·4555	29·0800	24·2543	20·5488	17·6628	15·3832	13·5579	12·0771	10·8605	9·84909	6·65244	4·99836	3·99978
45	36·0945	29·4902	24·5187	20·7200	17·7741	15·4558	13·6055	12·1084	10·8812	9·86281	6·65429	4·99863	3·99983
46	36·7272	29·8923	24·7754	20·8847	17·8801	15·5244	13·6500	12·1374	10·9002	9·87528	6·65591	4·99886	3·99986
47	37·3537	30·2866	25·0247	21·0429	17·9810	15·5890	13·6916	12·1643	10·9176	9·88662	6·65731	4·99905	3·99989
48	37·9740	30·6731	25·2667	21·1951	18·0772	15·6500	13·7305	12·1891	10·9336	9·89693	6·65853	4·99921	3·99991
49	38·5881	31·0521	25·5017	21·3415	18·1687	15·7076	13·7668	12·2122	10·9482	9·90630	6·65959	4·99934	3·99993
50	39·1961	31·4236	25·7298	21·4822	18·2559	15·7619	13·8007	12·2335	10·9617	9·91481	6·66051	4·99945	3·99994

4. AMOUNT OF ANNUITY OF 1 PER PERIOD

$$S_{n_i}$$

n	0.25%	0.5%	1%	1.25%	1.5%	2%	2.5%	3%	3.5%	4%	5%	6%	7%	8%	n
1	1·00000	1·00000	1·00000	1·00000	1·00000	1·00000	1·00000	1·00000	1·00000	1·00000	1·00000	1·00000	1·00000	1·00000	1
2	2·00250	2·00500	2·01000	2·01250	2·01500	2·02000	2·02500	2·03000	2·03500	2·04000	2·05000	2·06000	2·07000	2·08000	2
3	3·00751	3·01503	3·03010	3·03766	3·04523	3·06040	3·07562	3·09090	3·10623	3·12160	3·15250	3·18360	3·21490	3·24640	3
4	4·01503	4·03010	4·06040	4·07563	4·09090	4·12161	4·15252	4·18363	4·21494	4·24646	4·31013	4·37462	4·43994	4·50611	4
5	5·02506	5·05025	5·10101	5·12657	5·15227	5·20404	5·25633	5·30914	5·36247	5·41632	5·52563	5·63709	5·75074	5·86660	5
6	6·03763	6·07550	6·15202	6·19065	6·22955	6·30812	6·38774	6·46841	6·55015	6·63298	6·80191	6·97532	7·15329	7·33593	6
7	7·05272	7·10588	7·21354	7·26804	7·32299	7·43428	7·54743	7·66246	7·77941	7·89829	8·14201	8·39384	8·65402	8·92280	7
8	8·07035	8·14141	8·28567	8·35889	8·43284	8·58297	8·73612	8·89234	9·05169	9·21423	9·54911	9·89747	10·25980	10·63663	8
9	9·09053	9·18212	9·36853	9·46337	9·55933	9·75463	9·95452	10·15911	10·36850	10·58280	11·02656	11·49132	11·97799	12·48756	9
10	10·11325	10·22803	10·46221	10·58167	10·70272	10·94972	11·20338	11·46388	11·73139	12·00611	12·57789	13·18079	13·81645	14·48656	10
11	11·13854	11·27917	11·56683	11·71394	11·86326	12·16872	12·48347	12·80780	13·14199	13·48635	14·20679	14·97164	15·78360	16·64549	11
12	12·16638	12·33556	12·68250	12·86036	13·04121	13·41209	13·79555	14·19203	14·60196	15·02581	15·91713	16·86994	17·88845	18·97711	12
13	13·19680	13·39724	13·80933	14·02112	14·23683	14·68033	15·14044	15·61779	16·11303	16·62684	17·71298	18·88214	20·14064	21·49530	13
14	14·22979	14·46423	14·94742	15·19638	15·45038	15·97394	16·51895	17·08632	17·67699	18·29191	19·59863	21·01507	22·55049	24·21492	14
15	15·26537	15·53655	16·09690	16·38633	16·68214	17·29342	17·93193	18·59891	19·29568	20·02359	21·57856	23·27597	25·12902	27·15211	15
16	16·30353	16·61423	17·25786	17·59116	17·93237	18·63928	19·38022	20·15688	20·97103	21·82453	23·65749	25·67253	27·88805	30·32428	16
17	17·34429	17·69730	18·43044	18·81105	19·20136	20·01207	20·86473	21·76159	22·70501	23·69751	25·84037	28·21288	30·84022	33·75023	17
18	18·38765	18·78579	19·61475	20·04619	20·48938	21·41231	22·38635	23·41444	24·49969	25·64541	28·13238	30·90565	33·99903	37·45024	18
19	19·43362	19·87972	20·81089	21·29677	21·79672	22·84056	23·94601	25·11687	26·35718	27·67123	30·53900	33·75999	37·37896	41·44626	19
20	20·48220	20·97912	22·01900	22·56298	23·12367	24·29737	25·54466	26·87037	28·27968	29·77808	33·06595	36·78559	40·99549	45·76196	20
21	21·53341	22·08401	23·23919	23·84502	24·47032	25·78332	27·18327	28·67649	30·26947	31·96920	35·71925	39·99273	44·86518	50·42292	21
22	22·58724	23·19443	24·47159	25·14308	25·83758	27·29898	28·86286	30·53678	32·32890	34·24797	38·50521	43·39229	49·00574	55·45676	22
23	23·64371	24·31040	25·71630	26·45737	27·22515	28·84496	30·58443	32·45288	34·46041	36·61789	41·43048	46·99583	53·43614	60·89330	23
24	24·70282	25·43196	26·97346	27·78808	28·63352	30·42186	32·34904	34·42647	36·66653	39·08260	44·50200	50·81558	58·17667	66·76476	24
25	25·76457	26·55912	28·24320	29·13544	30·06302	32·03030	34·15776	36·45926	38·94986	41·64591	47·72710	54·86451	63·24904	73·10594	25
26	26·82899	27·69191	29·52563	30·49963	31·51397	33·67090	36·01171	38·55304	41·31310	44·31174	51·11345	59·15638	68·67647	79·95442	26
27	27·89606	28·83037	30·82089	31·88087	32·98668	35·34432	37·91200	40·70963	43·75906	47·08421	54·66913	63·70577	74·48382	87·35077	27
28	28·96580	29·97452	32·12910	33·27938	34·48148	37·05121	39·85980	42·93092	46·29063	49·96758	58·40258	68·52811	80·69769	95·33883	28
29	30·03821	31·12439	33·45039	34·69538	35·99870	38·79223	41·85630	45·21885	48·91080	52·96629	62·32271	73·63980	87·34653	103·96593	29
30	31·11331	32·28002	34·78489	36·12907	37·53868	40·56808	43·90270	47·57542	51·62267	56·08494	66·43885	79·05819	94·46079	113·28321	30
31	32·19109	33·44142	36·13274	37·58068	39·10176	42·37944	46·00027	50·00268	54·42947	59·32834	70·76079	84·80168	102·07304	123·34587	31
32	33·27157	34·60862	37·49407	39·05044	40·68829	44·22703	48·15028	52·50276	57·33450	62·70147	75·29883	90·88978	110·21815	134·21354	32
33	34·35404	35·78167	38·86901	40·53857	42·29862	46·11157	50·35403	55·07784	60·34121	66·20953	80·06377	97·34316	118·93343	145·95062	33
34	35·43924	36·96058	40·25770	42·04530	43·93309	48·03380	52·61289	57·73018	63·45315	69·85791	85·06696	104·18375	128·25876	158·62667	34
35	36·52924	38·14538	41·66028	43·57087	45·59209	49·99447	54·92821	60·46208	66·67401	73·65222	90·32031	111·43478	138·23688	172·31680	35
36	37·62056	39·33610	43·07688	45·11551	47·27597	51·99436	57·30141	63·27594	70·00760	77·59831	95·83632	119·12087	148·91346	187·10215	36
37	38·71461	40·53279	44·50765	46·67945	48·98511	54·03425	59·73395	66·17422	73·45787	81·70225	101·62814	127·26812	160·33740	203·07032	37
38	39·81140	41·73545	45·95272	48·26294	50·71989	56·11494	62·22730	69·15945	77·02889	85·97034	107·70955	135·90421	172·56102	220·31595	38
39	40·91093	42·94413	47·41225	49·88623	52·48068	58·23723	64·78298	72·23423	80·72490	90·40915	114·09502	145·05846	185·64029	238·94122	39
40	42·01320	44·15885	48·88637	51·48956	54·26789	60·40198	67·40256	75·40126	84·55028	95·02552	120·79977	154·76197	199·63511	259·05652	40
41	43·11823	45·37964	50·37524	53·13318	56·08191	62·61002	70·08762	78·66330	88·50953	99·82654	127·83976	165·04768	214·60957	280·78104	41
42	44·22603	46·60654	51·87899	54·79734	57·92314	64·86222	72·83981	82·02320	92·60737	104·81960	135·23175	175·95054	230·63224	304·24352	42
43	45·33660	47·83957	53·39778	56·48231	59·79199	67·15947	75·66081	85·48389	96·84863	110·01238	142·99334	187·50758	247·77650	329·58301	43
44	46·44994	49·07887	54·93316	58·18834	61·68887	69·50266	78·55232	89·04841	101·23833	115·41288	151·14301	199·75803	266·12085	356·94965	44
45	47·56606	50·32416	56·48107	59·91568	63·61420	71·89271	81·51613	92·71986	105·78167	121·02939	159·70016	212·74351	285·74931	386·50562	45
46	48·68498	51·57578	58·04589	61·66464	65·56841	74·33056	84·55403	96·50146	110·48403	126·87057	168·68516	226·50812	306·75176	418·42607	46
47	49·80669	52·83366	59·62634	63·43545	67·55194	76·81717	87·66788	100·39650	115·35097	132·94539	178·11942	241·09861	329·22439	452·90015	47
48	50·93121	54·09783	61·22261	65·23839	69·56522	79·35352	90·85958	104·40840	120·38826	139·26321	188·02539	256·56453	353·27009	490·13216	48
49	52·05854	55·36832	62·83483	67·04374	71·60107	81·94059	94·13107	108·54065	125·60184	145·83373	198·42666	272·95841	378·99900	530·34374	49
50	53·18868	56·64516	64·46318	68·88179	73·68283	84·57940	97·48435	112·79687	130·99791	152·66708	209·34800	290·33590	406·52893	573·77016	50

INDEX

For Product Safety Concerns and Information please contact our EU
representative GPSR@taylorandfrancis.com Taylor & Francis Verlag GmbH,
Kaufingerstraße 24, 80331 München, Germany

Printed and bound by CPI Group (UK) Ltd, Croydon, CR0 4YY
08/05/2025
01864327-0008